Comprehensive
Microsoft® Excel 5.0 for Windows™

Comprehensive
Microsoft® Excel 5.0 for Windows™

June Jamrich Parsons
University of the Virgin Islands

Dan Oja
GuildWare, Inc.

David Auer
Western Washington University

Course Technology, Inc. One Main Street, Cambridge, MA 02142
An International Thomson Publishing Company

Albany • Bonn • Boston • Cincinnati • London • Madrid • Melbourne • Mexico City
New York • Paris • San Francisco • Singapore • Tokyo • Toronto • Washington

Comprehensive Microsoft Excel 5.0 for Windows is published by Course Technology, Inc.

Managing Editors	Marjorie Schlaikjer, Mac Mendelsohn
Product Managers	Nicole Jones-Pinard, Barbara Clemens
Production Editor	Pale Moon Productions
Text Designer	Sally Steele
Cover Designer	John Gamache

© 1995 Course Technology, Inc.
A Division of International Thomson Publishing, Inc.

For more information contact:
Course Technology, Inc.
One Main Street
Cambridge, MA 02142

International Thomson Publishing Europe
Berkshire House 168-173
High Holborn
London WCIV 7AA
England

Thomas Nelson Australia
102 Dodds Street
South Melbourne, 3205
Victoria, Australia

Nelson Canada
1120 Birchmount Road
Scarborough, Ontario
Canada M1K 5G4

International Thomson Publishing GmbH
Königswinterer Strasse 418
53227 Bonn
Germany

International Thomson Publishing Asia
211 Henderson Road
#05-10 Henderson Building
Singapore 0315

International Thomson Publishing Japan
Hirakawacho Kyowa Building, 3F
2-2-1 Hirakawacho
Chiyoda-ku, Tokyo 102
Japan

International Thomson Editores
Campos Eliseos 385, Piso 7
Col. Polanco
11560 Mexico D.F. Mexico

All rights reserved. This publication is protected by federal copyright law. No part of this publication may be reproduced, stored in a retrieval system, or transmitted in any form or by any means, electronic, mechanical, photocopying, recording, or otherwise, or be used to make a derivative work (such as translation or adaptation), without prior permission in writing from Course Technology, Inc.

Trademarks

Course Technology and the open book logo are registered trademarks of Course Technology, Inc.

I(T)P The ITP logo is a trademark under license.

Microsoft and Visual Basic are registered trademarks of Microsoft Corporation and Windows and AutoSum are trademarks of Microsoft Corporation.

Some of the product names and company names used in this book have been used for identification purposes only and may be trademarks or registered trademarks of their respective manufacturers and sellers.

Disclaimer

Course Technology, Inc. reserves the right to revise this publication and make changes from time to time in its content without notice.

ISBN 1-56527-324-9 (text)

Printed in the United States of America

10 9 8 7 6 5 4 3 2 1

From the Publisher

At Course Technology, Inc., we believe that technology will transform the way that people teach and learn. We are very excited about bringing you, college professors and students, the most practical and affordable technology-related products available.

The Course Technology Development Process

Our development process is unparalleled in the higher education publishing industry. Every product we create goes through an exacting process of design, development, review, and testing.

Reviewers give us direction and insight that shape our manuscripts and bring them up to the latest standards. Every manuscript is quality tested. Students whose backgrounds match the intended audience work through every keystroke, carefully checking for clarity and pointing out errors in logic and sequence. Together with our own technical reviewers, these testers help us ensure that everything that carries our name is error free and easy to use.

Course Technology Products

We show both *how* and *why* technology is critical to solving problems in college and in whatever field you choose to teach or pursue. Our time-tested, step-by-step instructions provide unparalleled clarity. Examples and applications are chosen and crafted to motivate students.

The Course Technology Team

This book will suit your needs because it was delivered quickly, efficiently, and affordably. Every employee contributes to this process. The names of all of our employees are listed below:

Tim Ashe, David Backer, Stephen M. Bayle, Josh Bernoff, Michelle Brown, Ann Marie Buconjic, Jody Buttafoco, Kerry Cannell, Jim Chrysikos, Barbara Clemens, Susan Collins, John M. Connolly, Kim Crowly, Myrna D'Addario, Lisa D'Alessandro, Jodi Davis, Howard S. Diamond, Kathryn Dinovo, Joseph B. Dougherty, Lauri Duncan, MaryJane Dwyer, Kristin Dyer, Chris Elkhill, Don Fabricant, Viktor Frengut, Jeff Goding, Laurie Gomes, Eileen Gorham, Catherine Griffin, Tim Hale, Jamie Harper, Roslyn Hooley, John Hope, Marjorie Hunt, Nicole Jones-Pinard, Matt Kenslea, Susannah Lean, Kim Mai, Margaret Makowski, Tammy Marciano, Elizabeth Martinez, Debbie Masi, Don Maynard, Dan Mayo, Kathleen McCann, Jay McNamara, Mac Mendelsohn, Kim Munsell, Amy Oliver, Michael Ormsby, Kristine Otto, Debbie Parlee, Kristin Patrick, Charlie Patsios, Darren Perl, Kevin Phaneuf, George J. Pilla, Cathy Prindle, Nancy Ray, Laura Sacks, Deborah Shute, Jennifer Slivinski, Christine Spillett, Michelle Tucker, David Upton, Mark Valentine, Karen Wadsworth, Anne Marie Walker, Renee Walkup, Tracy Wells, Donna Whiting, Janet Wilson, Lisa Yameen.

Preface

Course Technology, Inc. is proud to present this new book in its Windows Series. *Comprehensive Microsoft Excel 5.0 for Windows* is designed for a full-term course on Microsoft Excel. This book capitalizes on the energy and enthusiasm students have for Windows-based applications and clearly teaches students how to take full advantage of Excel's power. It assumes no prerequisite knowledge of computers, the Windows environment, or Microsoft Excel 5.0.

Organization and Coverage

Comprehensive Microsoft Excel 5.0 for Windows contains eleven tutorials that provide hands-on instruction. In these tutorials, students learn to plan, build, test, and document Excel worksheets.

The text emphasizes the ease-of-use features included in the Excel software. Using this book, students will learn how to do more advanced tasks sooner than they would using other texts. By the end of the book, students will have learned all the important features of Microsoft Excel 5.0 from basic spreadsheet design and creation through formulas, charts, Solver, PivotTables, multiple worksheets, what-if analysis, and macros.

Approach

Comprehensive Microsoft Excel 5.0 for Windows distinguishes itself from other Windows books because of its unique two-pronged approach. First, it motivates students by demonstrating *why* they need to learn the concepts and skills. This book teaches Excel using a task-driven rather than a feature-driven approach. By working through the tutorials—each motivated by a realistic case—students learn how to use Excel in situations they are likely to encounter in the workplace, rather than learn a list of features one-by-one, out of context. Second, the content, organization, and pedagogy of this book make full use of the Windows environment. What content is presented, when it's presented, and how it's presented capitalize on Excel's power to perform complex modeling tasks earlier and more easily than was possible under DOS.

Features

Comprehensive Microsoft Excel 5.0 for Windows is an exceptional textbook also because it contains the following features:

- **"Read This Before You Begin" Page** This page is consistent with Course Technology's unequaled commitment to helping instructors introduce technology into the classroom. Technical considerations and assumptions about hardware, software, and default settings are listed in one place to help instructors save time and eliminate unnecessary aggravation.
- **Tutorial Case** Each tutorial begins with a spreadsheet-related problem that students could reasonably encounter in business. Thus, the process of solving the problem will be meaningful to students.

- **Step-by-Step Methodology** The unique Course Technology, Inc. methodology keeps students on track. They click or press keys always within the context of solving the problem posed in the Tutorial Case. The text constantly guides students, letting them know where they are in the process of solving the problem. The numerous screen shots include labels that direct students' attention to what they should look at on the screen.
- **Page Design** Each *full-color* page is designed to help students easily differentiate between what they are to *do* and what they are to *read*. The steps are easily identified by their color background and numbered bullets. Windows default colors are used in the screen shots so instructors can more easily assure that students' screens look like those in the book.
- **TROUBLE?** TROUBLE? paragraphs anticipate the mistakes that students are likely to make and help them recover from these mistakes. This feature facilitates independent learning and frees the instructor to focus on substantive conceptual issues rather than common procedural errors.
- **Reference Windows and Task Reference** Reference Windows provide short, generic summaries of frequently used procedures. The Task Reference appears at the end of the book and summarizes how to accomplish tasks using the mouse, the menus, and the keyboard. Both of these features are specially designed and written so students can use the book as a reference manual after completing the course.
- **Questions, Tutorial Assignments, and Case Problems** Each tutorial concludes with meaningful, conceptual Questions that test students' understanding of what they learned in the tutorial. The Questions are followed by Tutorial Assignments, which provide students additional hands-on practice of the skills they learned in the tutorial. Finally, each tutorial ends with three or more complete Case Problems that have approximately the same scope as the Tutorial Case.
- **Exploration Exercises** The Windows environment encourages students to learn by exploring and discovering what they can do. The Exploration Exercises are Questions, Tutorial Assignments, or Case Problems designated by an **E** that encourage students to explore the capabilities of the computing environment they are using and to extend their knowledge using the Windows on-line Help facility and other reference materials.
- **Reference Section** This section provides lists of Microsoft Excel commands, toolbar buttons, functions, and selected Visual Basic objects, statements, properties, and methods.
- **Additional Cases** Four interactive cases help students incorporate all their knowledge of Microsoft Excel in new, real-life settings.

The CTI WinApps Setup Disks

The CTI WinApps Setup Disks bundled with the instructor's copy of this book contain an innovative Student Disk generating program designed to save instructors time. Once this software is installed on a network or standalone workstation, students can double-click the "Make Excel 5 Comprehensive Student Disks" icon in the CTI WinApps group window. Double-clicking this icon transfers all the data files students need to complete the tutorials, Tutorial Assignments, and Case Problems to high-density disks in drive A or B. Tutorial 1 provides complete step-by-step instructions for making the Student Disks.

Adopters of this text are granted the right to install the CTI WinApps group window on any standalone computer or network used by students who have purchased this text.

For more information on the CTI WinApps Setup Disks, see the section in this book called "Read This Before You Begin."

The Supplements

- **Instructor's Manual** The Instructor's Manual is written by the authors and is quality assurance tested. It includes:
  - Answers and solutions to all the Questions, Tutorial Assignments, Case Problems, and Additional Cases. Suggested solutions are also included for the Exploration Exercises.
  - Disks (3.5-inch or 5.25-inch) containing solutions to all the Questions, Tutorial Assignments, Case Problems, and Additional Cases.
  - Tutorial Notes, which contain background information from the authors about the Tutorial Case and the instructional progression of the tutorial.
  - Technical Notes, which include troubleshooting tips as well as information on how to customize the students' screens to closely emulate the screen shots in the book.
  - Transparency Masters of key concepts.
- **Test Bank** The Test Bank contains 50 questions per tutorial in true/false, multiple choice, and fill-in-the-blank formats, plus two essay questions. Each question has been quality assurance tested by students to achieve clarity and accuracy.
- **Electronic Test Bank** The Electronic Test Bank allows instructors to edit individual test questions, select questions individually or at random, and print out scrambled versions of the same test to any supported printer.

Acknowledgments

Through their contributions, many people are responsible for the successful completion of this book, and the authors would like to express their gratitude to an excellent team.

Our thanks go to our Product Managers, Nicole Jones-Pinard and Barbara Clemens, our Developmental Editor, Ann Shaffer, and our Production Editor, Robin Geller, for their endless patience and good cheer. To the rest of the Course Technology production staff, thanks for working tirelessly under tight deadlines to produce a quality, professional product. Thanks also to Robert Gillette, Jeff Goding, and Student Testers Godfrey Degamo, Mark Vodnik, Larissa Mann, and Jeremy Parker. Thanks to Roger Hayen for the Additional Cases. Special thanks to Donna Auer for her patience. Finally, our thanks to our series editor Susan Solomon.

June Jamrich Parsons, Dan Oja, and David Auer

Brief Contents

From the Publisher	v
Preface	vi

Microsoft Windows 3.1 Tutorials — WIN 1

Read This Before You Begin		WIN 2
TUTORIAL 1	Essential Windows Skills	WIN 3
TUTORIAL 2	Effective File Management	WIN 37
Windows Tutorials Index		WIN 65
Windows Task Reference		WIN 71

Microsoft Excel 5.0 for Windows Tutorials — EX 1

Read This Before You Begin		EX 2
TUTORIAL 1	Using Worksheets to Make Business Decisions	EX 3
TUTORIAL 2	Planning, Building, Testing, and Documenting Worksheets	EX 42
TUTORIAL 3	Formatting and Printing	EX 86
TUTORIAL 4	Functions, Formulas, and Absolute References	EX 127
TUTORIAL 5	Charts and Graphing	EX 159
TUTORIAL 6	Using Solver for Complex Problems	EX 200
TUTORIAL 7	Managing Data with Excel	EX 232
TUTORIAL 8	Working with Multiple Worksheets	EX 273
TUTORIAL 9	Data Tables and Scenario Management	EX 314
TUTORIAL 10	Integrating Excel with Other Windows Applications	EX 337
TUTORIAL 11	Application Development with Macros and Visual Basic	EX 382
ADDITIONAL CASES		EX 427

References	EX 441
Index	EX 481
Task Reference	EX 501

Contents

From the Publisher   v
Preface   vi

Microsoft Windows 3.1 Tutorials

Read This Before You Begin   WIN 2

TUTORIAL 1
Essential Windows Skills

Using the Program Manager, the CTI Keyboard Tutorial, the CTI Mouse Practice, CTI WinApps and Windows Menus, Dialog Boxes, Toolbar and Help   WIN 3

- Using the Windows Tutorials Effectively   WIN 4
- Starting Your Computer and Launching Windows   WIN 4
- Basic Windows Controls and Concepts   WIN 5
- Organizing Application Windows on the Desktop   WIN 11
- Using Windows to Specify Tasks   WIN 19
- Using Paintbrush to Develop Your Windows Technique   WIN 26
- Questions   WIN 33
- Tutorial Assignments   WIN 35

TUTORIAL 2
Effective File Management

Using the File Manager   WIN 37

- Files and the File Manager   WIN 38
- Formatting a Disk   WIN 41
- Preparing Your Student Disk   WIN 43
- Finding Out What's On Your Disks   WIN 44
- Changing the Current Drive   WIN 45
- The File Manager Window   WIN 46
- The Directory Tree   WIN 47
- Organizing Your Files   WIN 48
- Expanding and Collapsing Directories   WIN 50
- The Contents List   WIN 50
- Filenames and Extensions   WIN 51
- Moving Files   WIN 52
- Renaming Files   WIN 55
- Deleting Files   WIN 56
- Data Backup   WIN 56
- The Copy Command   WIN 57
- Copying Files Using a Single Disk Drive   WIN 58
- Making a Disk Backup   WIN 60
- Questions   WIN 62
- Tutorial Assignments   WIN 63

WINDOWS TUTORIALS INDEX   WIN 65

WINDOWS TASK REFERENCE   WIN 71

Microsoft Excel 5.0 for Windows Tutorials

Read This Before You Begin   EX 2

TUTORIAL 1
Using Worksheets to Make Business Decisions

Evaluating Sites for a World-Class Golf Course   EX 3

- Using Tutorials Effectively   EX 4
- Making Your Excel Student Disks   EX 4

Launching Excel	EX 7
What Is Excel?	EX 9
The Excel Window	EX 9
The Title Bar EX 10	
The Menu Bar EX 10	
The Toolbars EX 10	
The Formula Bar EX 10	
The Worksheet Window EX 10	
The Pointer EX 11	
Scroll Bars and Sheet Tabs EX 11	
The Status Bar EX 11	
Opening a Workbook	EX 12
Scrolling the Worksheet	EX 14
Using a Decision-Support Worksheet	EX 15
Changing Values and Observing Results	EX 16
Correcting Mistakes	EX 17
The Undo Button	EX 18
Splitting the Worksheet Window	EX 19
Removing the Split Window	EX 20
Making and Documenting the Decision	EX 21
Saving the Workbook	EX 21
Printing the Worksheet and Chart	EX 23
Creating a Chart with the ChartWizard	EX 25
Printing a Specific Page	EX 28
Values, Text, Formulas, and Functions	EX 30
Values EX 30	
Text EX 31	
Formulas EX 31	
Functions EX 32	
Automatic Recalculation EX 33	
Excel Help	EX 34
Closing the Worksheet	EX 36
Exiting Excel	EX 36
Exiting Windows	EX 36
Questions	EX 37
Tutorial Assignments	EX 38
Case Problems	EX 39

TUTORIAL 2

Planning, Building, Testing, and Documenting Worksheets

Creating a Standardized Income and Expense Template for Branch Offices	EX 42
Developing Effective Worksheets	EX 43
Planning the Worksheet	EX 43
Building the Worksheet	EX 47
Entering Labels EX 47	
Changing Column Width EX 48	
Creating a Series with AutoFill	EX 50
Renaming the Sheet	EX 52
Saving the New Workbook	EX 53
Entering Formulas	EX 54
Using the Fill Handle to Copy a Formula	EX 56
Relative and Absolute References	EX 57
The SUM Function	EX 58
Using the Mouse to Select Cell References	EX 59
Testing the Worksheet	EX 61
Inserting a Row or Column	EX 63
Using AutoFormat	EX 65
The AutoSum Button	EX 68
Clearing Cells	EX 69
Number Sign (###) Replacement	EX 70
Testing the Worksheet with Realistic Data	EX 73
Clearing Test Values from the Worksheet	EX 74
Documenting the Worksheet	EX 74
Adding a Text Note	EX 75
Checking the Spelling of the Worksheet	EX 76
Protecting Cells in the Worksheet	EX 77
Saving the Worksheet as an Excel Template	EX 80
Questions	EX 81
Tutorial Assignments	EX 82
Case Problems	EX 83

TUTORIAL 3
Formatting and Printing
Producing a Projected Sales Impact
Report   EX 86
- Formatting Worksheet Data   EX 89
- Changing the Font, Font Style,
  and Font Size   EX 90
- Aligning Cell Contents   EX 92
- Centering Text Across Columns   EX 93
- Currency Formats   EX 94
- The Format Painter Button   EX 96
- Number Formats   EX 96
- Percentage Formats   EX 97
- Adding and Removing Borders   EX 98
- Using Patterns and Color for Emphasis   EX 101
- Activating a Toolbar   EX 103
- Adding Comments to the Worksheet   EX 105
- Print Preview   EX 110
- Portrait and Landscape Orientations   EX 111
- Headers and Footers   EX 111
- Centering the Printout and Removing Cell
  Gridlines and Row/Column Headings   EX 113
- Displaying Formulas   EX 116
- A Visual Basic Module to Print Formulas   EX 117
- Opening a Module   EX 117
- Running a Module   EX 118
- Tips for Using the Print
  Formulas Module   EX 121
- Questions   EX 122
- Tutorial Assignments   EX 122
- Case Problems   EX 123

TUTORIAL 4
Functions, Formulas, and Absolute References
Managing Loan Payments   EX 127
- Excel Functions   EX 130
- The MAX Function   EX 132
- The MIN Function   EX 134
- The AVERAGE Function   EX 134
- Calculating Loan Payments with the
  PMT Function   EX 137
- The IF Function   EX 141
- Displaying and Formatting the Date
  with the TODAY Function   EX 145
- Absolute References   EX 148
- Questions   EX 154
- Tutorial Assignments   EX 155
- Case Problems   EX 156

TUTORIAL 5
Charts and Graphing
Charting Sales Information   EX 159
- Excel Charts   EX 161
- Creating a 3-D Pie Chart   EX 164
- Selecting Non-adjacent Ranges   EX 165
- Selecting and Activating the Chart   EX 168
- Moving and Changing the Size
  of a Chart   EX 169
- Pulling Out a Wedge of a Pie Chart   EX 170
- Changing Chart Patterns   EX 171
- Creating a Line Chart   EX 173
- Revising the Chart Data Series   EX 177
- Adding and Editing Chart Text   EX 178
- Using Boldface for the Legend
  and Axis Labels   EX 180

Adding Horizontal Gridlines to a Chart	EX 180
Formatting Chart Lines	EX 181
Creating a Column Chart	EX 182
Using Pictures in a Column Chart	EX 184
Stretching and Stacking Pictures	EX 186
Displaying the Title in a Colored Box with a Shadow	EX 187
Creating a 3-D Column Chart	EX 188
Rotating a 3-D Column Chart	EX 192
Applying a Border Around a Chart	EX 193
Previewing and Printing the Worksheet and Charts	EX 194
Tips for Creating Charts	EX 196
Questions	EX 196
Tutorial Assignments	EX 197
Case Problems	EX 198

TUTORIAL 6
Using Solver for Complex Problems

Determining the Most Profitable Product Mix	EX 200
Creating the Worksheet	EX 202
Performing What-If Analysis	EX 206
Seeking a Solution by Trial and Error	EX 207
Using Goal Seek	EX 208
Solving More Complex Problems	EX 212
Formulating the Problem	EX 214
Solving Complex Problems by Trial and Error	EX 215
Using Solver	EX 216
The Integer Constraint	EX 222
Generating an Answer Report	EX 224
Questions	EX 228
Tutorial Assignments	EX 229
Case Problems	EX 229

TUTORIAL 7
Managing Data with Excel

Analyzing Personnel Data	EX 232
Sorting Data	EX 235
Sorting Data by One Column	EX 236
Sorting by Two Columns	EX 238
Maintaining a List with Excel's Data Form	EX 239
Manual Search EX 240	
Criteria Search EX 241	
Using Wildcards EX 243	
Maintaining Data in a List	EX 244
Deleting Records EX 244	
Adding New Records EX 245	
Filtering a List	EX 247
Using AutoFilter EX 248	
Using PivotTables	EX 253
Adding Row and Column Labels EX 255	
Selecting a Data Field for a PivotTable EX 256	
Selecting a Calculation Method for a PivotTable EX 256	
Completing a PivotTable EX 258	
Internal and External Databases	EX 262
Creating a PivotTable from an External Database	EX 262
Activating the MS Query Add-In EX 262	
Using Microsoft Query EX 263	
Questions	EX 269
Tutorial Assignments	EX 269
Case Problems	EX 270

TUTORIAL 8
Working with Multiple Worksheets

Creating a Consolidated Cash Flow Statement	EX 273
Effective Workbook Organization	EX 274
Using a Documentation Worksheet in a Workbook EX 275	
Referencing Cells and Ranges in Other Worksheets	EX 282
LOOKUP Functions	EX 283
Modifying the Documentation Worksheet	EX 287
Inserting, Deleting, Moving, and Copying Workbook Sheets	EX 288
Inserting a Chart Sheet EX 290	
Moving a Sheet EX 291	
Copying a Sheet EX 292	
Defining and Using Names	EX 293
Using the Go To Command	EX 295
Using the Exchange Rates	EX 296
Checking for Possible Errors	EX 298
Apparent Errors Caused by Rounding	EX 299
The ROUND Functions and Nesting Functions	EX 300
Creating the Consolidation Worksheet	EX 303
Entering the Consolidation Formulas	EX 304
Working with a Group of Worksheets	EX 306
Questions	EX 309
Tutorial Assignments	EX 309
Case Problems	EX 311

TUTORIAL 9
Data Tables and Scenario Management

Analyzing a Consolidated Cash Flow Statement with a What-If Analysis	EX 314
Data Tables	EX 316
One-Input Data Tables	EX 317
Two-Input Data Tables	EX 321
Controlling the Recalculation of a Worksheet with Tables	EX 325
Using Scenario Manager in What-If Analysis	EX 326
Scenario Summary Reports	EX 330
Questions	EX 331
Tutorial Assignments	EX 331
Case Problems	EX 332

TUTORIAL 10
Integrating Excel with Other Windows Applications

Data Analysis Using MS Query	EX 337
Each Application Has Its Purpose	EX 338
Transferring and Sharing Data Among Windows Applications	EX 338
Pasting Data EX 338	
Embedding Data EX 339	
Linking Data EX 340	
Editing an Embedded Object EX 344	
How Relational Databases Work	EX 347
The J. J. Svensen Database	EX 348
Using Microsoft Query	EX 350
MS Query Cue Cards	EX 350
The Microsoft Query Toolbar	EX 352
Selecting a Data Source	EX 353
Querying Only One Table	EX 356
Using the Criteria Pane	EX 358
How Dynamic Data Exchange (DDE) Works	EX 360
Querying More Than One Table	EX 361
Grouping PivotTable Data	EX 366
Using Object Linking and Embedding (OLE) to Link Files	EX 369
Using Excel as an OLE Client and Paintbrush as an OLE Server EX 372	
Keeping Linked Files Together	EX 377
Questions	EX 377
Tutorial Assignments	EX 378
Case Problems	EX 379

TUTORIAL 11

Application Development with Macros and Visual Basic

Building a Quality Control System
Using Statistical Process Control **EX 382**

- **Statistical Process Control (SPC)** **EX 384**
- **Control Charts** **EX 386**
- **Macros vs. Procedures vs. Modules** **EX 390**
- **Recording a Macro** **EX 391**
- **The Visual Basic Toolbar** **EX 394**
- **Using Visual Basic** **EX 394**
  - Visual Basic Comments EX 394
  - Visual Basic Sub Procedures EX 395
  - Visual Basic Objects, Properties, and Methods EX 396
- **Running a Macro** **EX 400**
- **Calculating the Control Chart Center Line** **EX 401**
- **User-Defined Functions** **EX 402**
- **Calculating the Control Chart Control Limits** **EX 405**
- **Writing Visual Basic Procedures** **EX 411**
  - Variable Types in Visual Basic EX 412
  - Selecting a Worksheet and an Active Cell EX 413
  - Prompting for User Input EX 413
  - Visual Basic Control Structures EX 415
  - Entering Values into Worksheet Cells EX 417
  - Formatting Worksheet Cells EX 418
  - Copying Worksheet Cells EX 418
- **Adding a Command to the Tools Menu to Run the Macro** **EX 419**
- **Questions** **EX 422**
- **Tutorial Assignments** **EX 422**
- **Case Problems** **EX 424**

ADDITIONAL CASES

Additional Case 1: Sales Invoicing for Island Dreamz Shoppe **EX 427**

Additional Case 2: Performance Reporting for Boston Scientific **EX 432**

Additional Case 3: Negotiating Salaries for the National Basketball Association **EX 435**

Additional Case 4: Managing Tours for Executive Travel Services **EX 438**

REFERENCES **EX 441**

Reference 1: Commands **EX 442**

Reference 2: Buttons **EX 450**

Reference 3: Functions **EX 456**

Reference 4: Visual Basic **EX 467**

INDEX **EX 481**

TASK REFERENCE **EX 501**

REFERENCE WINDOWS

Opening a Workbook EX 12

Correcting Mistakes Using Edit Mode EX 17

Saving a Workbook with a New Filename EX 22

Printing a Worksheet EX 24

Creating a Chart with ChartWizard EX 26

Using the Help Button EX 34

Changing Column Width EX 49

Entering a Formula EX 56

Copying Cell Contents with the Fill Handle EX 57

Entering the SUM Function EX 58

Inserting a Row or Column EX 64

Using AutoFormat EX 65

Clearing Cells EX 69
Adding a Text Note EX 75
Using the Spelling Button EX 76
Protecting Cells EX 78
Adding a Border EX 99
Removing a Border EX 100
Applying Patterns and Color EX 102
Activating and Removing Toolbars EX 103
Adding a Text Box and Comment EX 105
Using the Function Wizard EX 132
Typing Functions Directly in a Cell EX 132
Using MAX to Display the Largest Number in a Range of Cells EX 133
Using MIN to Display the Smallest Number in a Range of Cells EX 134
Using AVERAGE to Calculate the Average of the Numbers in a Range of Cells EX 135
Using PMT to Calculate a Monthly Payment EX 138
Using the IF Function to Specify the Conditions EX 142
Editing Cell Reference Types EX 148
Selecting Non-adjacent Ranges EX 165
Selecting a Pattern for a Data Marker EX 172
Revising the Chart Data Series Using the ChartWizard EX 177
Creating a Picture Chart EX 184
Using Goal Seek EX 209
Using Solver EX 217
Sorting Rows in a Data List EX 236
Searching for a Record Using the Data Form EX 241

Deleting a Record Using the Data Form EX 245
Adding a Record Using the Data Form EX 246
Filtering a List with AutoFilter EX 248
Generating a PivotTable EX 253
Activating the MS Query Add-In EX 262
Referencing Cells and Ranges in Other Worksheets EX 282
Using VLOOKUP to Display Values Found in a Lookup Table EX 284
Inserting a Worksheet EX 288
Deleting a Sheet EX 289
Inserting a Chart Sheet EX 290
Defining a Name EX 294
Using the Go To Command EX 295
Using ROUND to Round the Stored Results of a Formula to the Desired Number of Decimals EX 301
Grouping and Ungrouping Worksheets EX 306
Editing an Embedded Object Using OLE EX 345
Opening and Closing MS Query Cue Cards EX 351
Selecting a Data Source EX 353
Creating a Query that Uses Only One Table EX 356
Updating a Result Set in Excel EX 360
Creating a Query that Uses Two or More Tables EX 362
Grouping Data in a PivotTable EX 367
Using Excel as an OLE Server for a Write Document EX 370
Using Excel as an OLE Client for a Windows Paintbrush Graphic Image EX 373
Recording an Excel Macro EX 391
Running an Excel Macro EX 400
Adding a Command to the Tools Menu to Run an Excel Macro EX 419

Microsoft Windows™ 3.1 Tutorials

1. **Essential Windows Skills**
2. **Effective File Management**

Read This Before You Begin

To the Student

To use this book, you must have a Student Disk. Your instructor will either provide you with a Student Disk or ask you to make your own by following the instructions in the section called "Preparing Your Student Disk" in Windows Tutorial 2. See your instructor or lab manager for further information.

Using Your Own Computer If you are going to work through this book using your own computer, you need:

- The Student Disk. ***You will not be able to complete the tutorials and exercises in this book using your own computer until you have the Student Disk.*** Ask your instructor or lab manager for details on how to get it.

- A computer system running Microsoft Windows 3.1 and DOS.

To the Instructor

Making the Student Disk To complete the tutorials in this book, your students must have a copy of the Student Disk. To relieve you of having to make multiple Student Disks from a single master copy, we provide you with the CTI WinApps Setup Disk, which contains an automatic Student Disk generating program. Once you install the Setup Disk on a network or standalone workstation, students can easily make their own Student Disks by double clicking on the "Make Win 3.1 Student Disk" icon in the CTI WinApps icon group. Double clicking this icon transfers all the data files students will need to complete the tutorials and Tutorial Assignments to a high-density disk in drive A or B. If some of your students will use their own computers to complete the tutorials and exercises in this book, they must first get the Student Disk. The section called "Preparing Your Student Disk" in Windows Tutorial 2 provides complete instructions on how to make the Student Disk.

If you have disk copying resources available, you might choose to use them for making quantities of the Student Disk. The "Make Win 3.1 Student Disk" provides an easy and fast way to make multiple Student Disks.

Installing the CTI WinApps Setup Disk: To install the CTI WinApps icon group from the Setup Disk, follow the instructions inside the disk envelope that was bundled with your book. By adopting this book, you are granted a license to install this software on any computer or computer network used by you or your students.

Readme File: A Readme.txt file located on the Setup Disk provides additional technical notes, troubleshooting advice, and tips for using the CTI WinApps software in your school's computer lab. You can view the Readme file using any word processor you choose.

System Requirements for installing the CTI WinApps Disk The minimum software and hardware requirements your computer system needs to install the CTI WinApps icon group are as follows:

- Microsoft Windows version 3.1 on a local hard drive or on a network drive
- A 286 (or higher) processor with a minimum of 2 MB RAM (4 MB RAM or more is strongly recommended).
- A mouse supported by Windows
- A printer that is supported by Windows 3.1
- A VGA 640 x 480 16-color display is recommended; an 800 x 600 or 1024 x 768 SVGA, VGA monochrome, or EGA display is also acceptable
- 1.5 MB of free hard disk space
- Student workstations with at least 1 high-density disk drive. If you need a 5.25 inch CTI WinApps Setup Disk, contact your CTI sales rep or call customer service at 1-800-648-7450. In Canada call Times Mirror Professional Publishing/Iwin Dorsey at 1-800-268-4178.
- If you wish to install the CTI WinApps Setup Disk on a network drive, your network must support Microsoft Windows.

TUTORIAL 1

Essential Windows Skills

Using the Program Manager, CTI WinApps, and Help

OBJECTIVES

In this tutorial you will:
- Start your computer
- Launch and exit Windows
- Use the mouse and the keyboard
- Identify the components of the Windows desktop
- Launch and exit applications
- Organize your screen-based desktop
- Switch tasks in a multi-tasking environment.
- Use Windows menus
- Explore Windows toolbars

CASE

A New Computer, Anywhere, Inc. You're a busy employee without a minute of spare time. But now, to top it all off, a computer technician appears at your office door, introduces himself as Steve Laslow, and begins unpacking your new computer!

You wonder out loud, "How long is it going to take me to learn this?"

Steve explains that your new computer uses Microsoft Windows 3.1 software and that the **interface**—the way you interact with the computer and give it instructions—is very easy to use. He describes the Windows software as a "gooey," a **graphical user interface (GUI)**, which uses pictures of familiar objects such as file folders and documents to represent a desktop on your screen.

Steve unpacks your new computer and begins to connect the components. He talks as he works, commenting on three things he really likes about Microsoft Windows. First, Windows applications have a standard interface, which means that once you learn how to use one Windows application, you are well on your way to understanding how to use others. Second, Windows lets you use more than one application at a time, a capability called **multitasking**, so you can easily switch between applications such as your word processor and your calendar. Third, Windows lets you do more than one task at a time, such as printing a document while you create a pie chart. All in all, Windows makes your computer an effective and easy-to-use productivity tool.

Using the Windows Tutorials Effectively

This tutorial will help you learn about Windows 3.1. Begin by reading the text that explains the concepts. Then when you come to numbered steps on a colored background, follow those steps as you work at your computer. Read each step carefully and completely *before* you try it.

Don't worry if parts of your screen display are different from the figures in the tutorials. The important parts of the screen display are labeled in each figure. Just be sure these parts are on your screen.

Don't worry about making mistakes—that's part of the learning process. **TROUBLE?** paragraphs identify common problems and explain how to get back on track. Do the steps in the **TROUBLE?** paragraph *only* if you are having the problem described.

Starting Your Computer and Launching Windows

The process of starting Windows is sometimes referred to as **launching**. If your computer system requires procedures different from those in the steps below, your instructor or technical support person will provide you with step-by-step instructions for turning on your monitor, starting or resetting your computer, logging into a network if you have one, and launching Windows.

To start your computer and launch Windows:
1. Make sure your disk drives are empty.
2. Find the power switch for your monitor and turn it on.
3. Locate the power switch for your computer and turn it on. After a few seconds you should see C:\> or C> on the screen.

    TROUBLE? If your computer displays a "non-system disk" error message, a floppy disk was left in a disk drive at startup. To continue, remove the disk and press [Enter].

4. Type **win** to launch Windows. See Figure 1-1.

Figure 1-1
Launching Windows

⑤ Press the key labeled [Enter]. Soon the Windows 3.1 title screen appears. Next you might notice an hourglass on the screen. This symbol means your computer is busy with a task and you must wait until it has finished.

After a brief wait, the title screen is replaced by one similar to Figure 1-2. Don't worry if your screen is not exactly the same as Figure 1-2. You are ready to continue the Tutorial when you see the Program Manager title at the top of the screen. If you do not see this title, ask your technical support person for assistance.

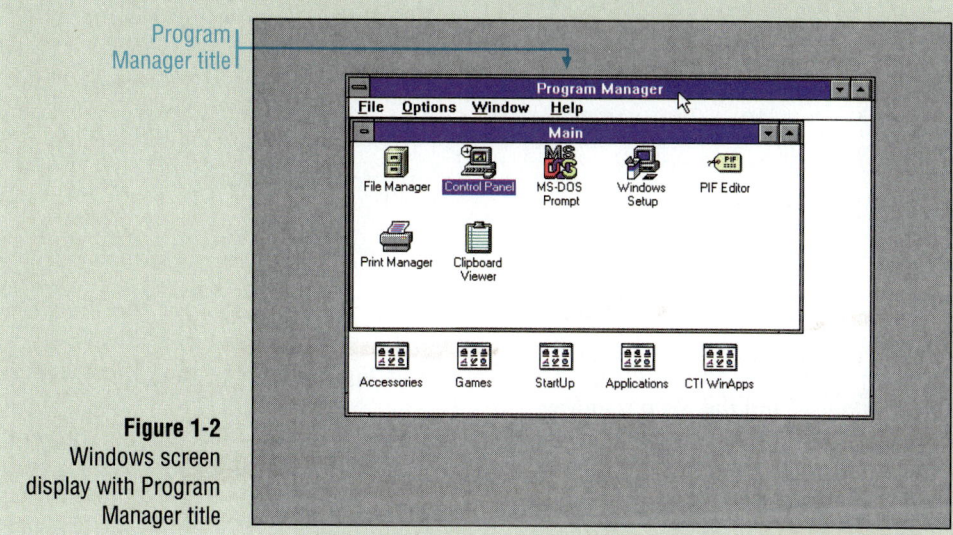

Figure 1-2
Windows screen display with Program Manager title

Basic Windows Controls and Concepts

Windows has a variety of **controls** that enable you to communicate with the computer. In this section you'll learn how to use the basic Windows controls.

The Windows Desktop

Look at your screen display and compare it to Figure 1-3 on the following page. Your screen may not be exactly the same as the illustration. You should, however, be able to locate components on your screen similar to those in Figure 1-3 on the following page.

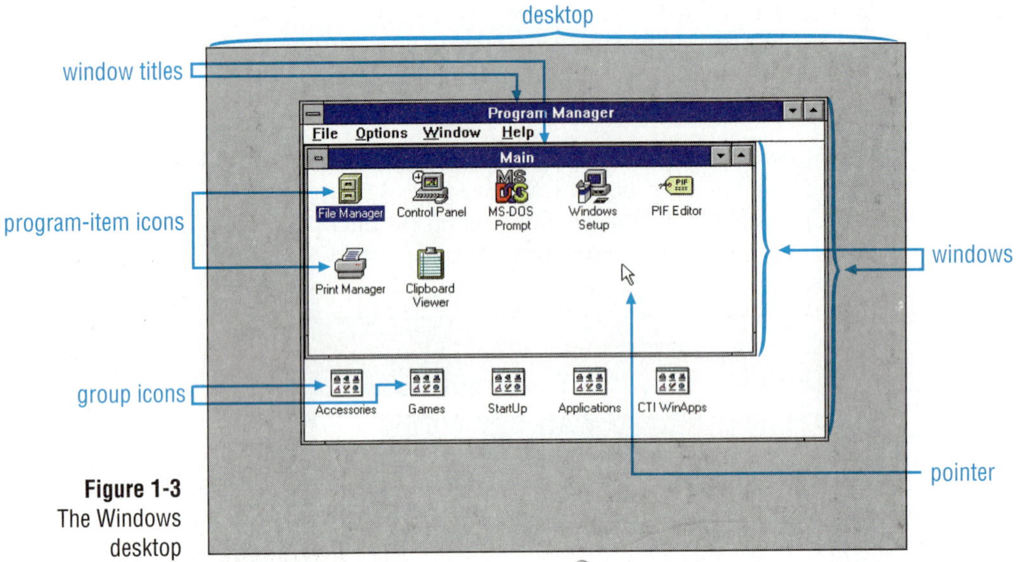

Figure 1-3
The Windows desktop

(Labels on figure: desktop, window titles, program-item icons, group icons, windows, pointer)

The screen represents a **desktop**, a workspace for projects and for the tools that are needed to manipulate those projects. Rectangular **windows** (with a lowercase *w*) define work areas on the desktop. The desktop in Figure 1-3 contains the Program Manager window and the Main window.

Icons are small pictures that represent real objects, such as disk drives, software, and documents. Each icon in the Main window represents an **application**, that is, a computer program. These icons are called **program-item icons**.

Each **group icon** at the bottom of the Program Manager window represents a collection of applications. For example, the CTI WinApps icon represents a collection of tutorial and practice applications, which you can use to learn more about Windows. A group icon expands into a group window that contains program-item icons.

The **pointer** helps you manipulate objects on the Windows desktop. The pointer can assume different shapes, depending on what is happening on the desktop. In Figure 1-3 the pointer is shaped like an arrow.

The Program Manager

When you launch Windows, the Program Manager application starts automatically and continues to run as long as you are working with Windows. Think of the Program Manager as a launching pad for other applications. The **Program Manager** displays icons for the applications on your system. To launch an application, you would select its icon.

Using the Mouse

The **mouse** is a pointing device that helps you interact with the screen-based objects in the Windows environment. As you move the mouse on a flat surface, the pointer on the screen moves in the direction corresponding to the movement of the mouse. You can also control the Windows environment from the keyboard; however, the mouse is much more efficient for most operations, so the tutorials in this book assume you are using one.

Basic Windows Controls and Concepts **WIN 7**

Find the arrow-shaped pointer on your screen. If you do not see the pointer, move your mouse until the pointer comes into view. You will begin most Windows-based operations by **pointing**.

To position the pointer:

❶ Position your right index finger over the left mouse button, as shown in Figure 1-4.

TROUBLE? If you want to use your mouse with your left hand, ask your technical support person to help you. Be sure you find out how to change back to the right-handed mouse setting, so you can reset the mouse each time you are finished in the lab.

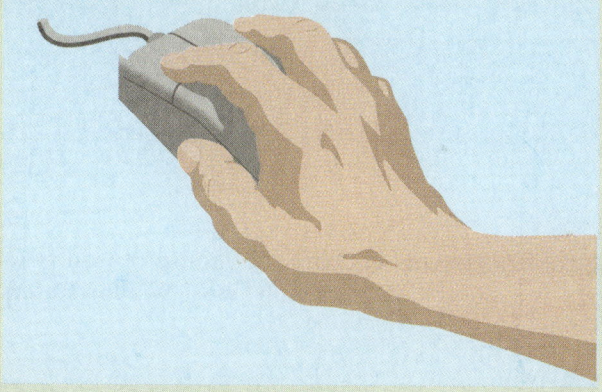

Figure 1-4
How to hold the mouse

❷ Locate the arrow-shaped pointer on the screen.

❸ Move the mouse and watch the movement of the pointer.

❹ Next, move the mouse to each of the four corners of the screen.

TROUBLE? If your mouse runs out of room, lift it, move it into the middle of a clear area on your desk, and then place it back on the table. The pointer does not move when the mouse is not in contact with the tabletop.

❺ Continue experimenting with mouse pointing until you feel comfortable with your "eye-mouse coordination."

Pointing is usually followed by clicking, double-clicking, or dragging. **Clicking** means pressing a mouse button (usually the left button) and then quickly releasing it. Clicking is used to select an object on the desktop. Windows shows you which object is selected by highlighting it.

To click an icon:

❶ Locate the Print Manager icon in the Main window. If you cannot see the Print Manager icon, use any other icon for this activity.

❷ Position the pointer on the icon.

❸ Once the pointer is on the icon, *do not move the mouse*.

❹ Press the left mouse button and then quickly release it. Your icon should have a highlighted title like the one in Figure 1-5 on the following page.

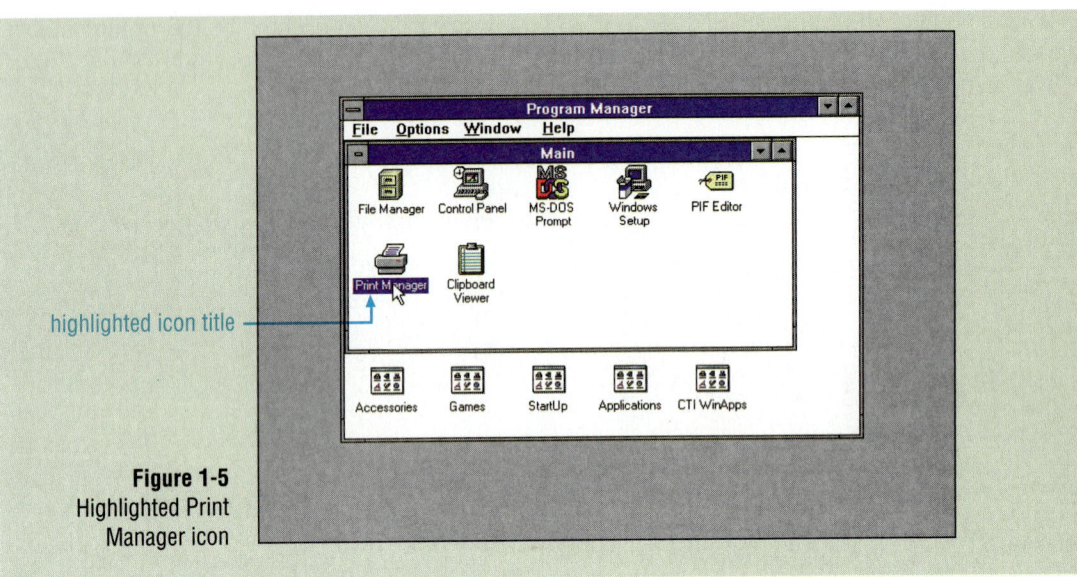

Figure 1-5
Highlighted Print Manager icon

Double-clicking means clicking the mouse button twice in rapid succession. Double-clicking is a shortcut. For example, most Windows users double-click to launch and exit applications.

To double click:
1. Position the pointer on the Program Manager Control-menu box, as shown in Figure 1-6.

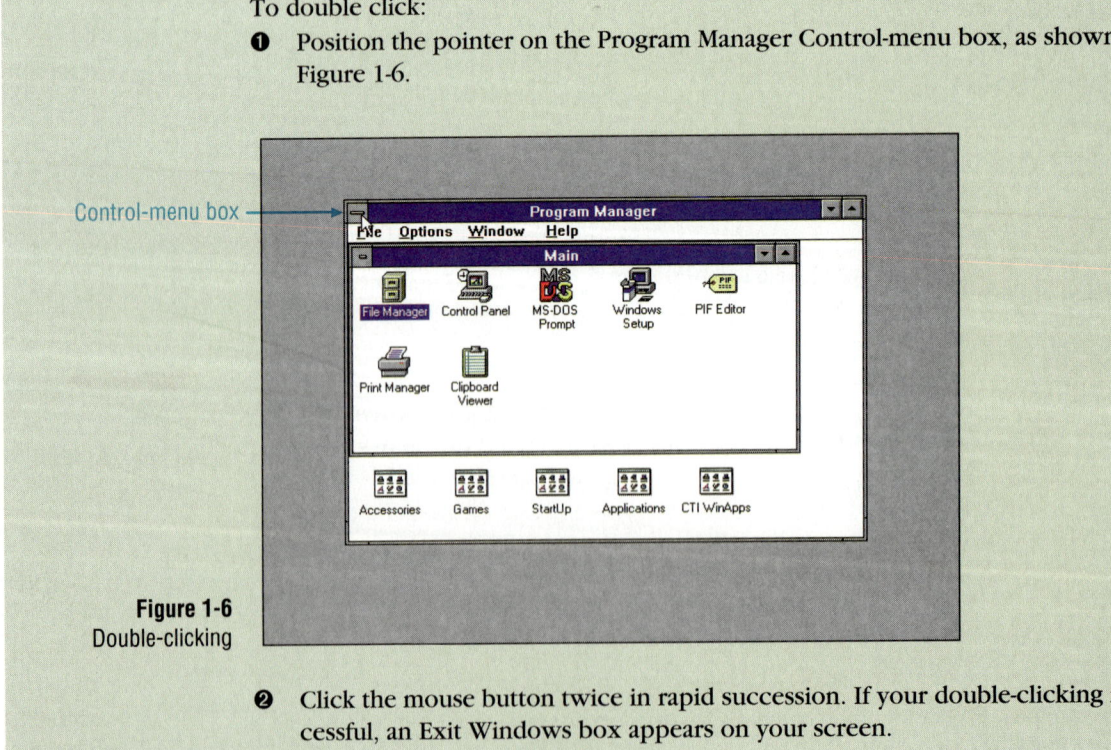

Figure 1-6
Double-clicking

2. Click the mouse button twice in rapid succession. If your double-clicking is successful, an Exit Windows box appears on your screen.
3. Now, single-click the **Cancel button**.

Dragging means moving an object to a new location on the desktop. To drag an object, you would position the pointer on the object, then hold the left mouse button down while you move the mouse. Let's drag one of the icons to a new location.

To drag an icon:

❶ Position the pointer on any icon on the screen, such as on the Clipboard Viewer icon. Figure 1-7 shows you where to put the pointer and what happens on your screen as you carry out the next step.

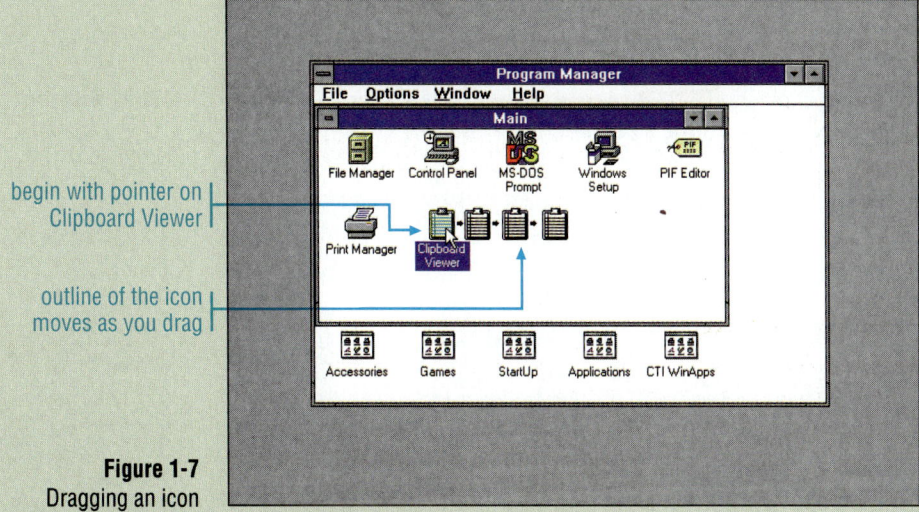

Figure 1-7
Dragging an icon

❷ Hold the left mouse button down while you move the mouse to the right. Notice that an outline of the icon moves as you move the mouse.

❸ Release the mouse button. Now the icon is in a new location.

TROUBLE? If the icon snaps back to its original position, don't worry. Your technical support person probably has instructed Windows to do this. If your icon automatically snapped back to its original position, skip Step 4.

❹ Drag the icon back to its original location.

Using the Keyboard

You use the keyboard to type documents, enter numbers, and activate some commands. You can use the on-screen CTI Keyboard Tutorial to learn the special features of your computer keyboard. To do this, you need to learn how to launch the Keyboard Tutorial and other applications.

Launching Applications

Earlier in this tutorial you launched Windows. Once you have launched Windows, you can launch other Windows applications such as Microsoft Works. When you launch an application, an application window opens. Later, when you have finished using the application, you close the window to exit.

Launching the CTI Keyboard Tutorial

To launch the **CTI Keyboard Tutorial,** you need to have the **CTI WinApps** software installed on your computer. If you are working in a computer lab, these applications should already be installed on your computer system. Look on your screen for a group icon or a window labeled "CTI WinApps."

If you don't have anything labeled "CTI WinApps" on your screen's desktop, ask your technical support person for help. If you are using your own computer, you will need to install the CTI WinApps applications yourself. See your technical support person or your instructor for a copy of the Setup Disk and the Installation Instructions that come with it.

To open the CTI Win Apps group window:
1. Double-click the **CTI WinApps group icon.** Your screen displays a CTI WinApps group window similar to the one in Figure 1-8.

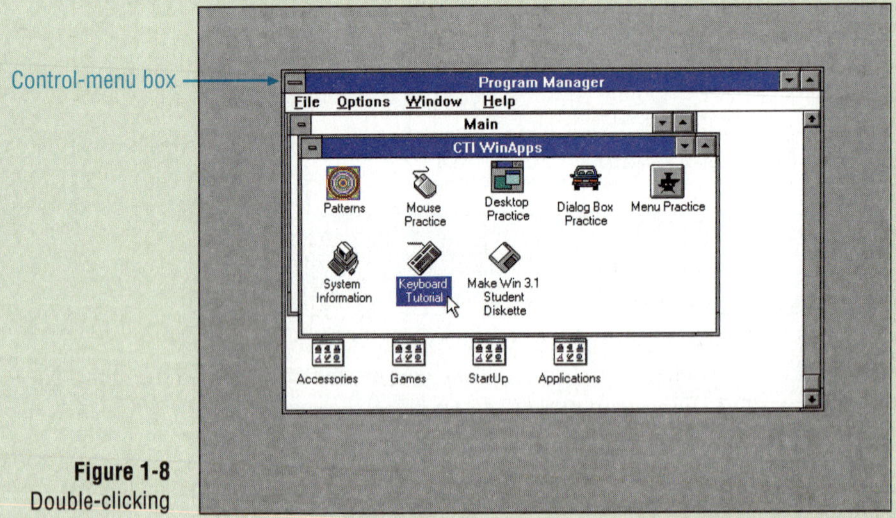

Figure 1-8
Double-clicking

The CTI WinApps group window contains an icon for each application provided with these tutorials. Right now we want to use the Keyboard Tutorial application.

To launch the Keyboard Tutorial:
1. Double-click the **Keyboard Tutorial icon.** Within a few seconds, the tutorial begins.
2. Read the opening screen, then click the **Continue button.** The CTI Keyboard Tutorial window appears. Follow the instructions on your screen to complete the tutorial. See Figure 1-9.

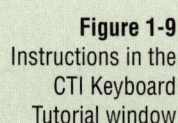

Figure 1-9
Instructions in the CTI Keyboard Tutorial window

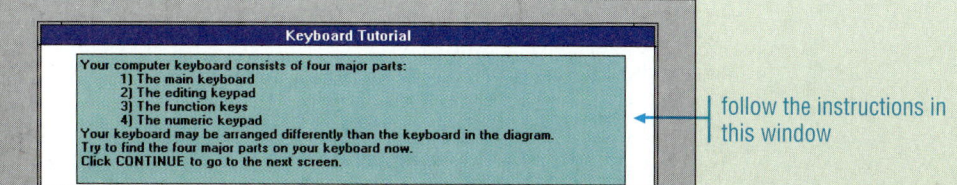

follow the instructions in this window

> **TROUBLE?** Click the Quit button at any time if you want to exit the Tutorial.

❸ When you have completed the Keyboard Tutorial, click the **Quit button**. This takes you back to the Program Manager and CTI WinApps group window.

> **TROUBLE?** *If you did not have trouble in Step 3, skip this entire paragraph!* If the Program Manager window is not open, look for its icon at the bottom of your screen. Double-click this icon to open the Program Manager window. To prevent this problem from happening again, click the word Options on the Program Manager menu bar, then click Minimize on Use.

Launching the CTI Mouse Practice

To discover how to use the mouse to manipulate Windows controls, you should launch the Mouse Practice.

To launch the Mouse Practice:

❶ Make sure the Program Manager and the CTI WinApps windows are open. It is not a problem if you have additional windows open.

> **TROUBLE?** If the Program Manager window is not open, look for its icon at the bottom of your screen. Double-click this icon to open the Program Manager window. To prevent this problem from happening again, click the word Options that appears near the top of the Program Manager window, then click Minimize.

❷ Double-click the **Mouse Practice icon**. The Mouse Practice window opens.

> **TROUBLE?** If you don't see the Mouse Practice icon, try clicking the scroll bar arrow button or see your technical support person.

❸ Click, drag, or double-click the objects on the screen to see what happens. Don't hesitate to experiment.

❹ When you have finished using the Mouse Practice, click the **Exit button** to go back to the Program Manager and continue the tutorial steps.

Organizing Application Windows on the Desktop

The Windows desktop provides you with capabilities similar to your desk; it lets you stack many different items on your screen-based desktop and activate the one you want to use.

There is a problem, though. Like your real desk, your screen-based desktop can become cluttered. That's why you need to learn how to organize the applications on your Windows desktop.

Launching the CTI Desktop Practice

The Desktop Practice application will help you learn the controls for organizing your screen-based desktop.

To Launch the Desktop Practice:

❶ Double-click the **Desktop Practice icon** to open the Desktop Practice window, shown in Figure 1-10. Your windows might be a different size or in a slightly different position. Don't worry. What's important is that you see a window with the title "Desktop Practice."

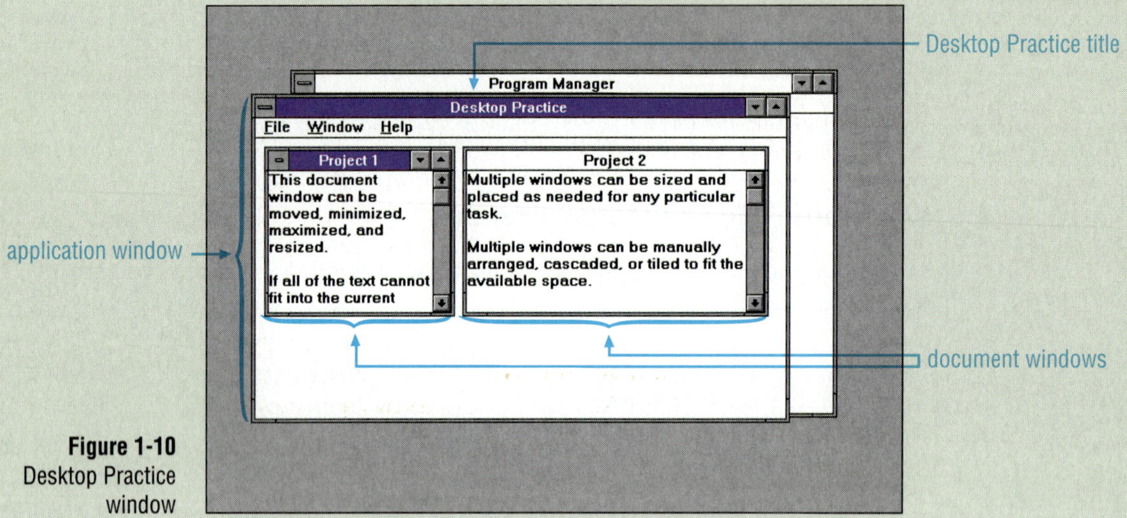

Figure 1-10
Desktop Practice window

Launching the Desktop Practice application opens three new windows on the desktop: Desktop Practice, Project 1, and Project 2. You might be able to see the edges of the Program Manager window "under" the Desktop Practice window. Essentially, you have stacked one project on top of another on your desktop.

The Desktop Practice window is an **application window**, a window that opens when you launch an application. The Project 1 and Project 2 windows are referred to as **document windows**, because they contain the documents, graphs, and lists you create using the application. Document windows are also referred to as **child windows**, because they belong to and are controlled by a "parent" application window.

The ability to have more than one document window open is one of many useful features of the Windows operating environment. Without this capability, you would have to print the documents that aren't being displayed so you could refer to them.

The Anatomy of a Window

Application windows and document windows are similar in many respects. Take a moment to study the Desktop Practice window on your screen and in Figure 1-11 on the following page to familiarize yourself with the terminology. Notice the location of each component but *don't* activate the controls.

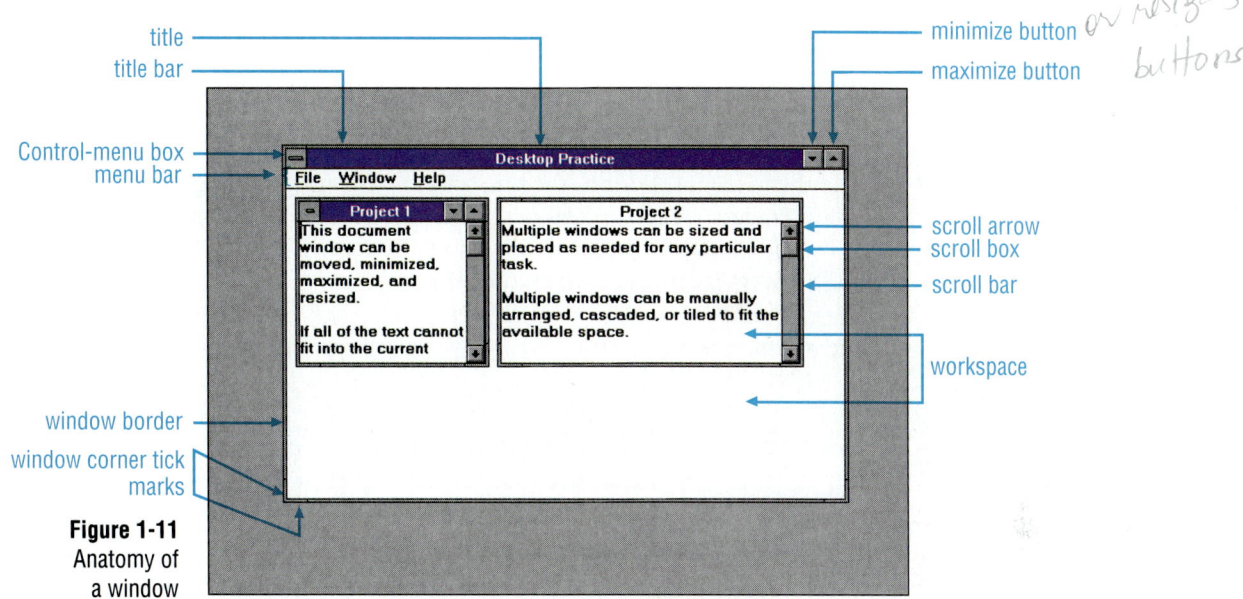

Figure 1-11
Anatomy of a window

At the top of each window is a **title bar**, which contains the window title. A darkened or highlighted title bar indicates that the application window is active. In Figure 1-11, the Desktop Practice application and the Project 1 document windows are active.

In the upper-right of the application window are two buttons used to change the size of a window. The **minimize button**—a square containing a triangle with the point down—is used to shrink the window. The **maximize button**, with the triangle pointing up, is used to enlarge the window so it fills the screen. When a window is maximized, a **restore button** with two triangles replaces the maximize button. Clicking the restore button reduces a maximized window to its previous size.

The **Control-menu box**, located in the upper-left of the Desktop Practice application window, is used to open the **Control menu**, which allows you to switch between application windows.

The **menu bar** is located just below the title bar on application windows. Notice that child windows do not contain menu bars.

The thin line running around the entire perimeter of the window is called the **window border**. The **window corners** are indicated by tick marks on the border.

The gray bar on the right side of each document window is a **scroll bar**, which you use to view window contents that don't initially fit in the window. Both application windows and document windows can contain scroll bars. Scroll bars can appear on the bottom of a window as well as on the side.

The space inside a window where you type text, design graphics, and so forth is called the **workspace**.

Maximizing and Minimizing Windows

The buttons on the right of the title bar are sometimes referred to as **resizing buttons**. You can use the resizing buttons to **minimize** the window so it shrinks down to an icon, **maximize** the window so it fills the screen, or **restore** the window to its previous size.

Because a minimized program is still running, you have quick access to the materials you're using for the project without taking up space on the desktop. You don't need to launch the program when you want to use it again because it continues to run.

A maximized window is useful when you want to focus your attention on the project in that window without being distracted by other windows and projects.

To maximize, restore, and minimize the Desktop Practice window:

❶ Locate the maximize button (the one with the triangle pointing up) for the Desktop Practice window. You might see a portion of the Program Manager window behind the Desktop Practice window. Be sure you have found the Desktop Practice maximize button. See Figure 1-12.

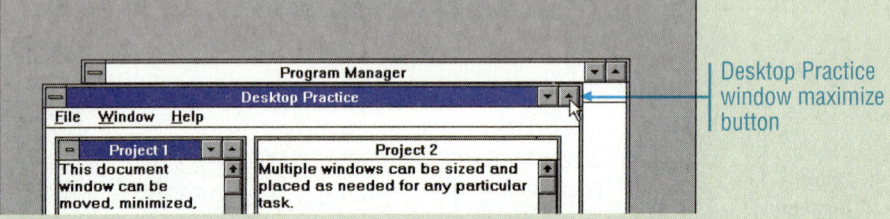

Figure 1-12
Maximizing a window

❷ Click the **maximize button** to expand the window to fill the screen. Notice that in place of the maximize button there is now a restore button that contains double triangles.

❸ Click the **restore button**. The Desktop Practice window returns to its original size.

❹ Next, click the **minimize button** (the one with the triangle pointing down) to shrink the window to an icon.

❺ Locate the minimized Desktop Practice icon at the bottom of your screen. See Figure 1-13.

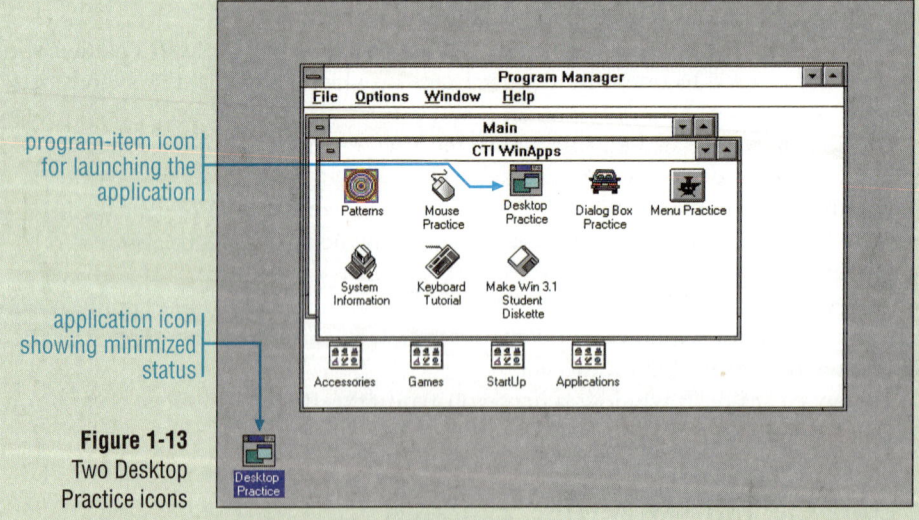

Figure 1-13
Two Desktop Practice icons

TROUBLE? If you cannot locate the Desktop Practice icon at the bottom of your screen, the Program Manager is probably maximized. To remedy this situation, click the restore button on the Program Manager Window.

When you *close an* application window, you exit the application and it stops running. But when you *minimize an* application, it is still running even though it has been shrunk to an icon. It is important to remember that minimizing a window is not the same as closing it.

The icon for a minimized application is called an **application icon.** As Figure 1-13 illustrates, your screen shows two icons for the Desktop Practice application. The icon at the bottom of your screen is the application icon and represents a program that is currently running even though it is minimized. The other Desktop Practice icon is inside the CTI WinApps window. If you were to double-click this icon, you would launch a second version of the Desktop Practice application. *Don't launch two versions of the same application.* You should restore the Desktop Practice window by double-clicking the minimized icon at the bottom of your screen. Let's do that now.

To restore the Desktop Practice window:
❶ Double-click the minimized **Desktop Practice icon** at the bottom of your screen. The Desktop Practice window opens.

Changing the Dimensions of a Window

Changing the dimensions of a window is useful when you want to arrange more than one project on your desktop. Suppose you want to work with the Desktop Practice application and at the same time view the contents of the Program Manager window. To do this, you will need to change the dimensions of both windows so they don't overlap each other.

To change the dimensions of the Desktop Practice window:
❶ Move the pointer slowly over the top border of the Desktop Practice window until the pointer changes shape to a double-ended arrow. See Figure 1-14.

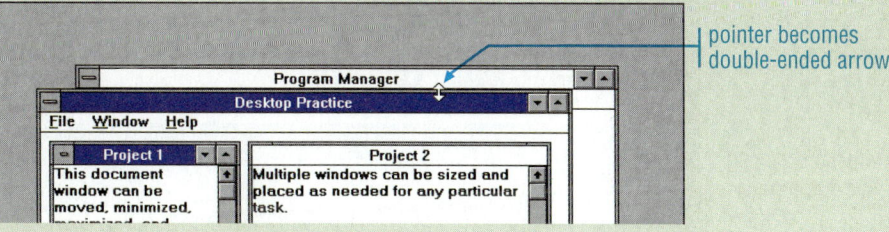

Figure 1-14
Preparing to change the window dimensions

❷ Press the left mouse button and hold it down while you drag the border to the top of the screen. Notice how an outline of the border follows your mouse movement.
❸ Release the mouse button. As a result the window adjusts to the new border.
❹ Drag the left border of the Desktop Practice window to the left edge of the screen.
❺ Move the pointer slowly over the lower-right corner of the Desktop Practice window until the pointer changes shape to a double-ended diagonal arrow. Figure 1-15 on the following page shows you how to do this step and the next one.

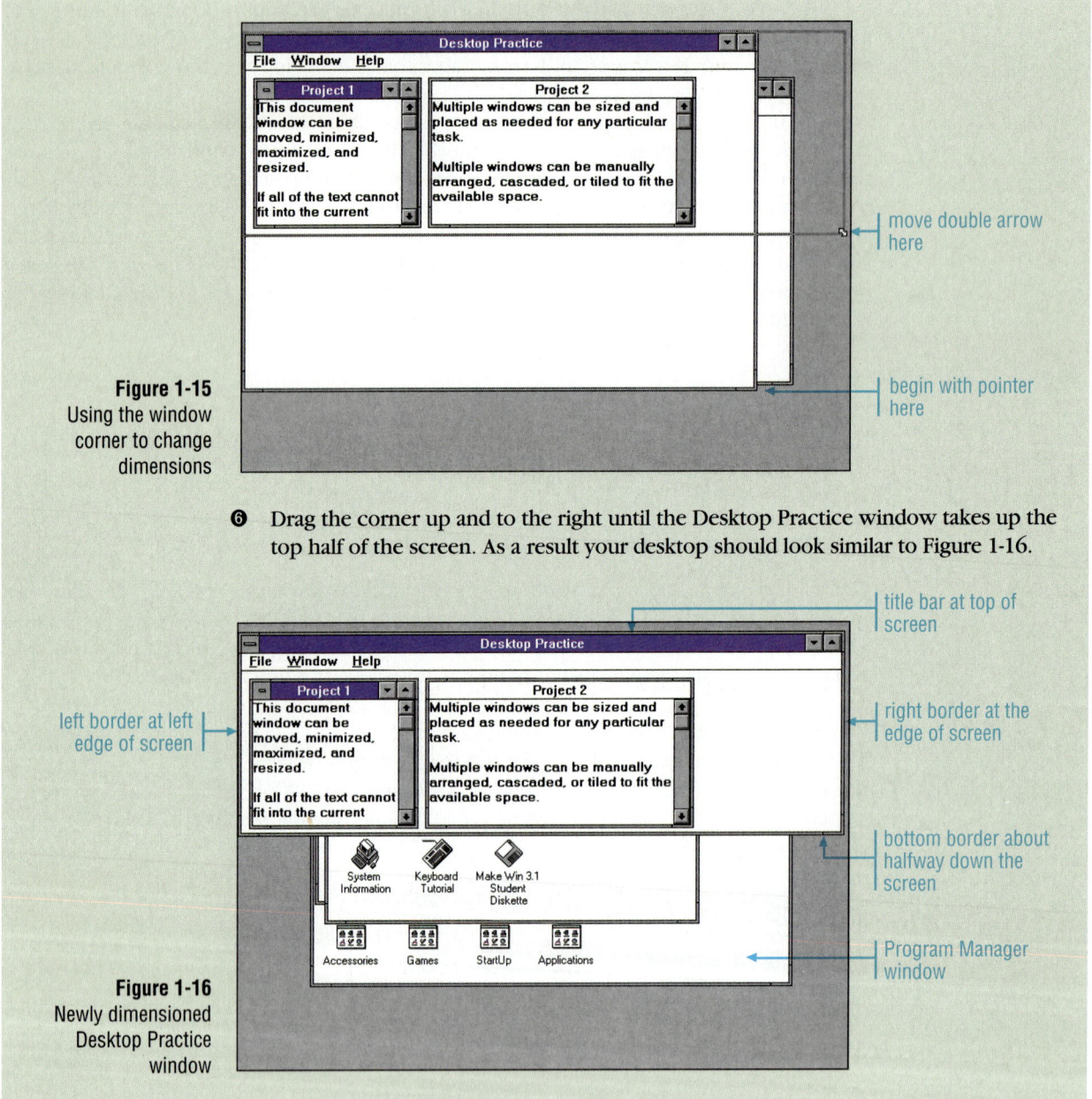

Figure 1-15
Using the window corner to change dimensions

Figure 1-16
Newly dimensioned Desktop Practice window

6 Drag the corner up and to the right until the Desktop Practice window takes up the top half of the screen. As a result your desktop should look similar to Figure 1-16.

Switching Applications

In the preceding steps you arranged the application windows so they were both visible at the same time. A different approach to organizing windows is to maximize the windows and then switch between them using the **Task List**, which contains a list of all open applications.

Let's maximize the Desktop Practice window. Then, using the Task List, let's switch to the Program Manager window, which will be hidden behind it.

To maximize the Desktop Practice window and then switch to the Program Manager:

❶ Click the **maximize button** on the Desktop Practice title bar. As a result the maximized Desktop Practice window hides the Program Manager window.

❷ Click the **Control-menu box** on the left side of the Desktop Practice title bar. Figure 1-17 shows you the location of the Control-menu box and also the Control menu, which appears after you click.

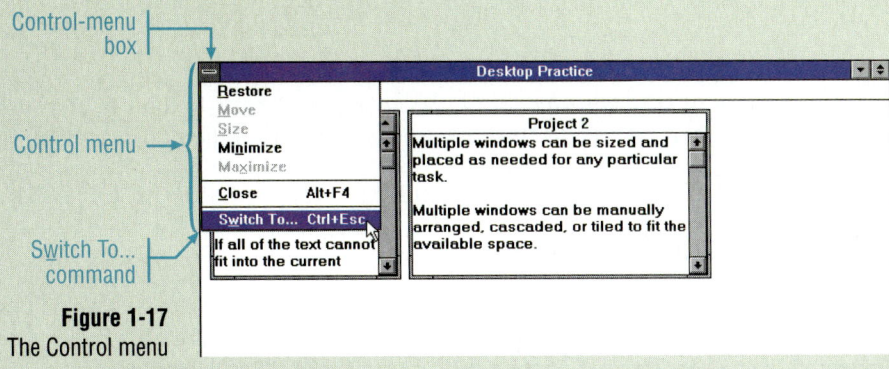

Figure 1-17
The Control menu

❸ Click **Switch To...** The Task List box appears, as shown in Figure 1-18.

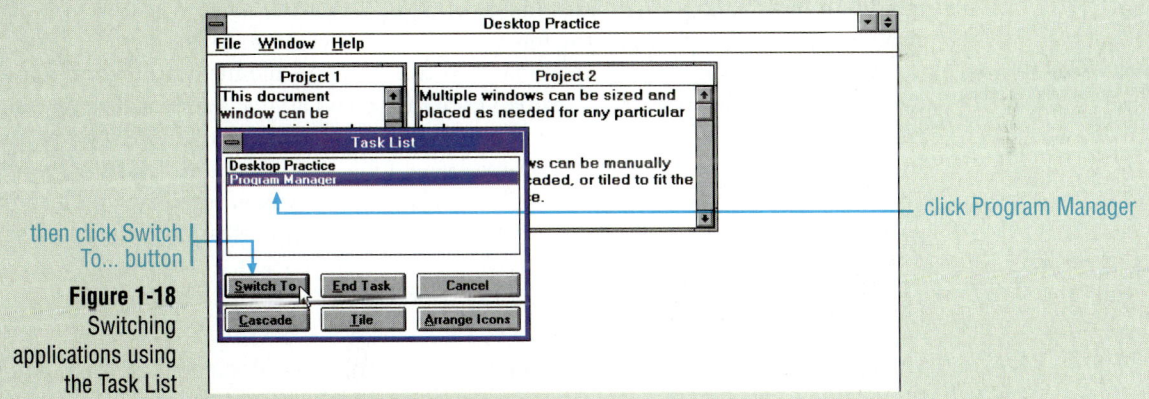

Figure 1-18
Switching applications using the Task List

❹ Click the **Program Manager option** from the list, then click the **Switch To button** to select the Program Manager. As a result the Program Manager reappears on the bottom half of your screen.

❺ If it is not already maximized, click the **maximize button** on the Program Manager window so both applications (Program Manager and Desktop Practice) are maximized.

The Program Manager window is active and "on top" of the Desktop Practice window. To view the Desktop Practice window, you will need to switch application windows again. You could switch tasks using the mouse, as we did in the last set of steps, or you can use the keyboard to quickly cycle through the tasks and activate the one you want. Let's use the keyboard method for switching windows this time, instead of using the Task List.

To switch to the Desktop Practice window using the keyboard:

❶ Hold down **[Alt]** and continue holding it down while you press **[Tab]**. Don't release the Alt key yet! On the screen you should see a small rectangle that says "Desktop Practice."

TROUBLE? Don't worry if you accidentally let go of the Alt key too soon. Try again. Press [Alt][Tab] until the "Desktop Practice" rectangle reappears.

❷ Release the Alt key. Now the maximized Desktop Practice window is open.

When a window is maximized, it is easy to forget what's behind it. If you forget what's on the desktop, call up the Task List using the Control menu or use [Alt][Tab] to cycle through the tasks.

Organizing Document Windows

Think of document windows as subwindows within an application window. Because document windows do not have menu bars, the commands relating to these windows are selected from the menu bar of the application window. For example, you can use the Tile command in the Window menu to arrange windows so they are as large as possible without any overlap. The advantage of tiled windows is that one window won't cover up important information. The disadvantage of tiling is that the more windows you tile, the smaller each tile becomes and the more scrolling you will have to do.

You can use the Cascade command in the Window menu to arrange windows so they are all a standard size, they overlap each other, and all title bars are visible. Cascaded windows are often larger than tiled windows and at least one corner is always accessible so you can activate the window. Try experimenting with tiled and cascading windows. The desktop organizational skills you will learn will help you arrange the applications on your desktop so you can work effectively in the Windows multi-tasking environment.

Closing a Window

You close a window when you have finished working with a document or when you want to exit an application program. The steps you follow to close a document window are the same as those to close an application window. Let's close the Desktop Practice window.

To close the Desktop Practice application window:

❶ Click the **Control-menu box** on the Desktop Practice window.

❷ Click **Close** as shown in Figure 1-19 on the following page. The Desktop Practice window closes and you see the Program Manager window on the desktop.

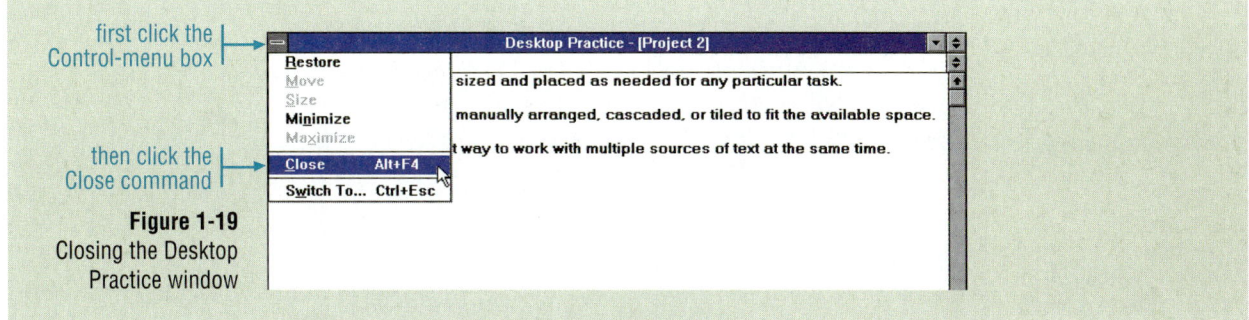

Figure 1-19
Closing the Desktop Practice window

Using Windows to Specify Tasks

In Windows, you issue instructions called **commands** to tell the computer what you want it to do. Windows applications provide you with lists of commands called **menus**. Many applications also have a ribbon of icons called a **toolbar**, which provides you with command shortcuts. Let's launch the Menu Practice application to find out how menus and toolbars work.

To launch the Menu Practice application:

❶ If the CTI WinApps window is not open, double-click its group icon at the bottom of the Program Manager window.

❷ Double-click the **Menu Practice** icon to open the Menu Practice window. See Figure 1-20.

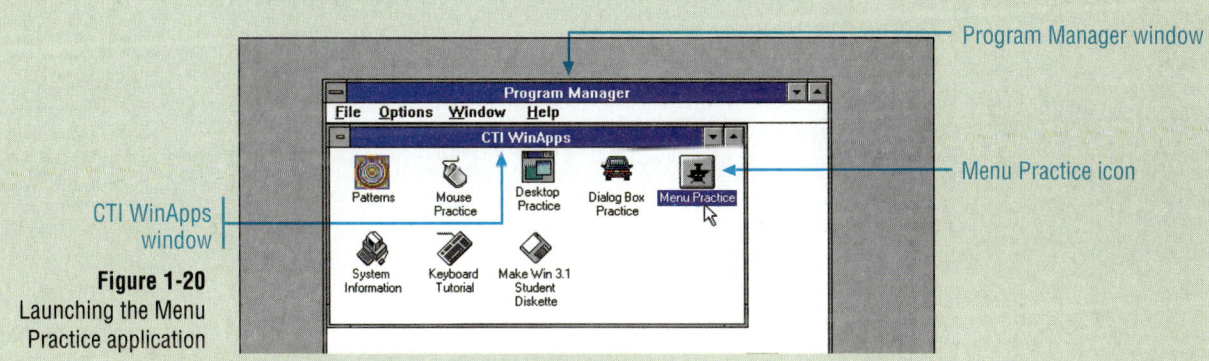

Figure 1-20
Launching the Menu Practice application

❸ Click the **maximize button** (the one with the triangle point up) for the Menu Practice window. The maximized Menu Practice window is shown in Figure 1-21 on the following page.

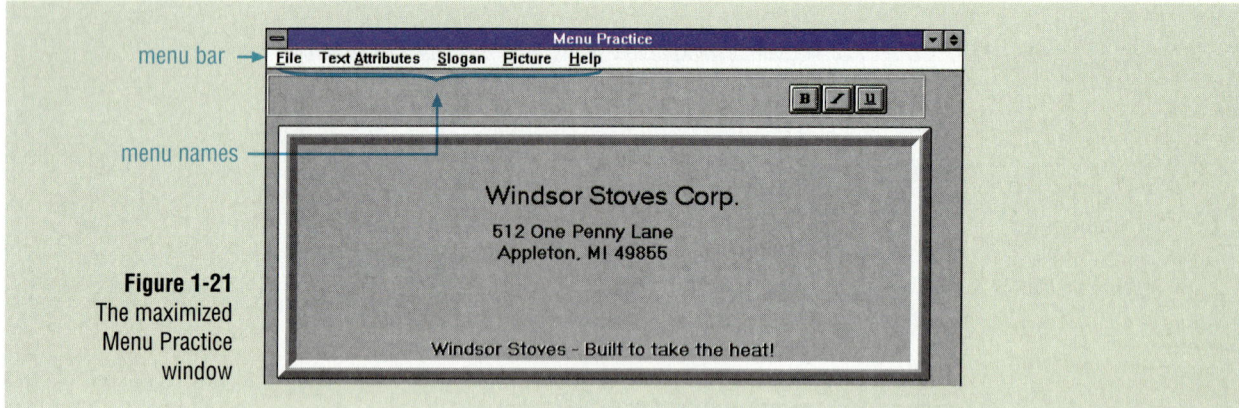

Figure 1-21
The maximized Menu Practice window

Opening and Closing Menus

Application windows, but not document windows, have menu bars such as the one shown in Figure 1-21. The menu bar contains menu names such as File, Text Attributes, Slogan, Picture, and Help. Let's practice opening and closing menus.

To open a menu:
❶ Click **File**. Figure 1-22 shows you where to click and the menu that appears.

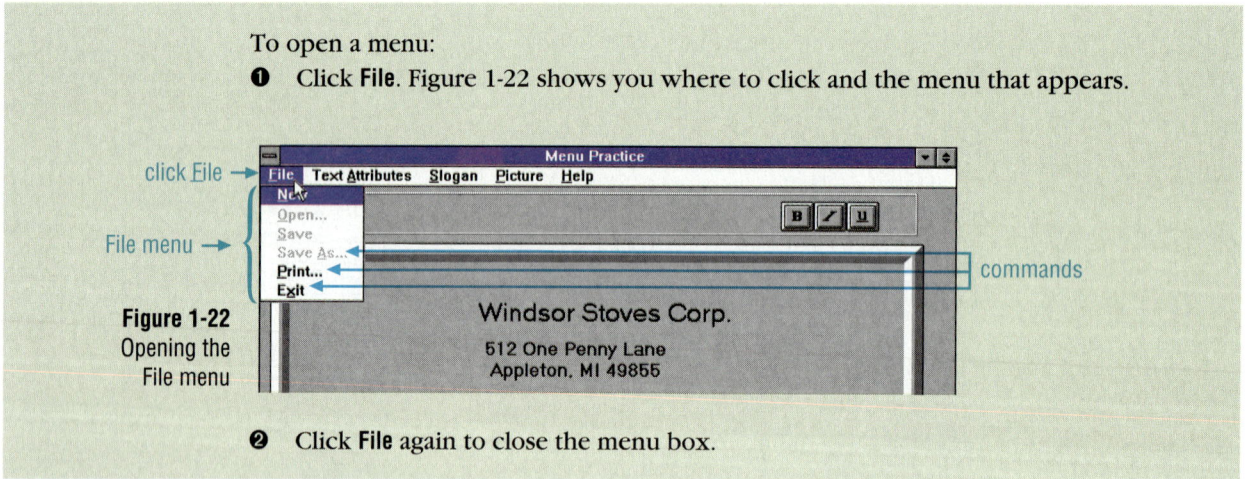

Figure 1-22
Opening the File menu

❷ Click **File** again to close the menu box.

When you click a menu name, the full menu drops down to display a list of commands. The commands on a menu are sometimes referred to as **menu items**.

Menu Conventions

The commands displayed on the Windows menus often include one or more **menu conventions**, such as check marks, ellipses, shortcut keys, and underlined letters. These menu conventions provide you with additional information about each menu command.

A check mark in front of a menu command indicates that the command is in effect. Clicking a checked command will remove the check mark and deactivate the command. For example, the Windsor Stoves logo currently has no graphic because the Show Picture command is not active. Let's add a picture to the logo by activating the Show Picture command.

To add or remove a check mark from the Show Picture command:
1. Click **Picture**. Notice that no check mark appears next to the Show Picture command.
2. Click **Show Picture**. The Picture menu closes, and a picture of a stove appears.
3. Click **Picture** to open the Picture menu again. Notice that a check mark appears next to the Show Picture command because you activated this command in Step 2.
4. Click **Show Picture**. This time clicking Show Picture removes the check mark and removes the picture.

Another menu convention is the use of gray, rather than black, type for commands. Commands displayed in gray type are sometimes referred to as **grayed-out commands**. Gray type indicates that a command is not currently available. The command might become available later, when it can be applied to the task. For example, a command that positions a picture on the right or left side of the logo would not apply to a logo without a picture. Therefore, the command for positioning the picture would be grayed out until a picture was included with the logo. Let's explore how this works.

To explore grayed-out commands:
1. Click **Picture**. Figure 1-23 shows the Picture menu with two grayed-out choices.

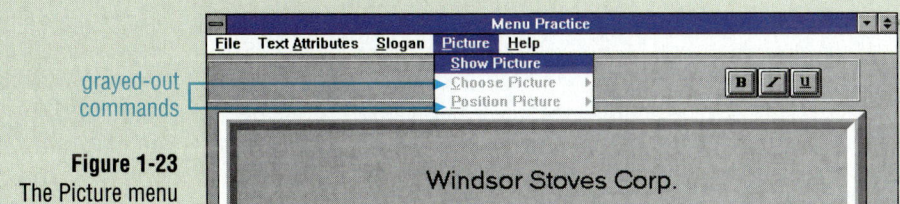

Figure 1-23
The Picture menu

2. Click the grayed-out command **Position Picture**. Although the highlight moves to this command, nothing else happens because the command is not currently available. You cannot position the picture until a picture is displayed.
3. Now click **Show Picture**. The Picture menu closes, and a picture is added to the logo.
4. Click **Picture**. Now that you have opened the Picture menu again, notice that the Choose Picture and Position Picture commands are no longer grayed out.

A **submenu** provides an additional set of command choices. On your screen the Choose Picture and Position Picture commands each have triangles next to them. A triangle is a menu convention that indicates a menu has a submenu. Let's use the submenu of the Position Picture command to move the stove picture to the right of the company name.

To use the position Picture submenu:
1. Click **Position Picture**. A submenu appears with options for left or right. In Figure 1-24 on the following page, the picture is to the left of the company name.

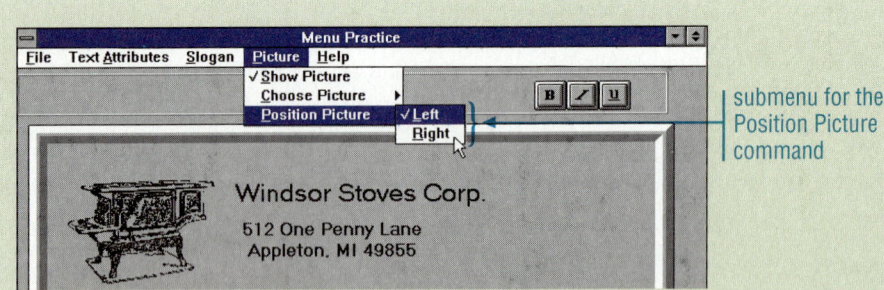

Figure 1-24
Viewing a submenu

submenu for the Position Picture command

❷ Click **Right**. Selecting this submenu command moves the picture to the right of the company name.

Some menu conventions allow you to use the menus without a mouse. It is useful to know how to use these conventions because, even if you have a mouse, in some situations it might be faster to use the keyboard.

One keyboard-related menu convention is the underlined letter in each menu name. If you wanted to open a menu using the keyboard, you would hold down the Alt key and then press the underlined letter. Let's open the Text Attributes menu using the keyboard.

To open the Text Attributes menu this way:

❶ Look at the menu name for the Text Attributes menu. Notice that the A is underlined.
❷ Press **[Alt][A]**. The Text Attributes menu opens.

TROUBLE? Remember from the Keyboard Tutorial that the [Alt][A] notation means to hold down the Alt key and press A. Don't type the brackets and don't use the Shift key to capitalize the A.

You can also use the keyboard to highlight and activate commands. On your screen the Bold command is highlighted. You use the arrow keys on the keyboard to move the highlight. You activate highlighted commands by pressing [Enter]. Let's use the keyboard to activate the Underline command.

To choose the Underline command using the keyboard:

❶ Press [↓] two times to highlight the Underline command.
❷ Press **[Enter]** to activate the highlighted command and underline the company name. Now look at the ■, *I*, and U buttons near the upper-right corner of the screen. The U button has been "pressed" or activated. This button is another control for underlining. You'll find out how to use these buttons later.

Previously you used the Alt key in combination with the underlined letter in the menu title to open a menu. You might have noticed that each menu command also has an underlined letter. Once a menu is open, you can activate a command by pressing the underlined letter—there is no need to press the Alt key.

To activate the Italic command using the underlined letter:

❶ Press **[Alt][A]**. This key combination opens the Text Attributes menu. Next, notice which letter is underlined in the Italic command.

❷ Press **[I]** to activate the Italic command. Now the company name is italicized as well as underlined.

Look at the menu in Figure 1-25. Notice the Ctrl+B to the right of the Bold command. This is the key combination, often called a **shortcut key**, that can be used to activate the Bold command even if the menu is not open. The Windows Ctrl+B notation means the same thing as [Ctrl][B] in these tutorials: hold down the Control key and, while holding it down, press the letter B. When you use shortcut keys, don't type the + sign and don't use the Shift key to capitalize. Let's use a shortcut key to boldface the company name.

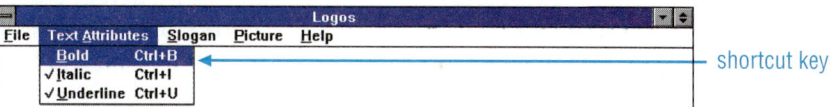

Figure 1-25
The Text Attributes menu

To Boldface the company name using a shortcut key:

❶ Press **[Ctrl][B]** and watch the company name appear in boldface type.

The **ellipsis (...)** menu convention means that when you select a command with three dots next to it, a dialog box will appear. A **dialog box** requests additional details about how you want the command carried out. We'll use the dialog box for the Choose Slogan command to change the company slogan.

To use the Choose Slogan dialog box:

❶ Click **Slogan**. Notice that the Choose Slogan command is followed by an ellipsis.

❷ Click **Choose Slogan...** and study the dialog box that appears. See Figure 1-26. Notice that this dialog box contains four sets of controls: the "Use Slogan" text box, the "Slogan in Bold Letters" check box, the "Slogan 3-D Effects" control buttons, and the OK and Cancel buttons. The "Use Slogan" text box displays the current slogan.

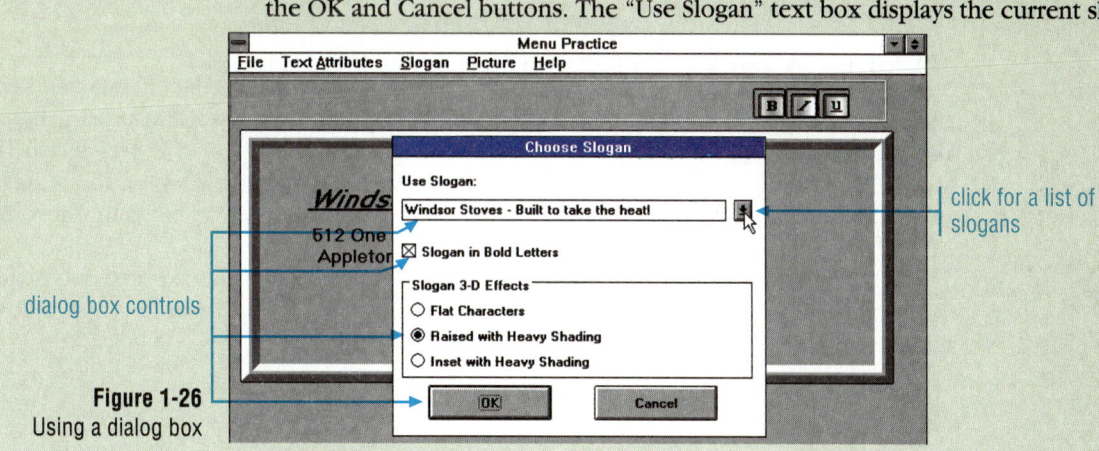

Figure 1-26
Using a dialog box

> ❸ Click the **down arrow button** on the right of the slogan box to display a list of alternative slogans.
>
> ❹ Click the slogan **Windsor Stoves - Built to last for generations!**
>
> ❺ Click the **OK button** and watch the new slogan replace the old.

You have used the Menu Practice application to learn how to use Windows menus, and you have learned the meaning of the Windows menu conventions. Next we'll look at dialog box controls.

Dialog Box Controls

Figure 1-27 shows a dialog box with a number of different controls that could be used to specify the requirements for a rental car. **Command buttons** initiate an immediate action. A **text box** is a space for you to type in a command detail. A **list box** displays a list of choices. A drop-down list box appears initially with only one choice; clicking the list box arrow displays additional choices. **Option buttons**, sometimes called radio buttons, allow you to select one option. **Check boxes** allow you to select one or more options. A **spin bar** changes a numeric setting.

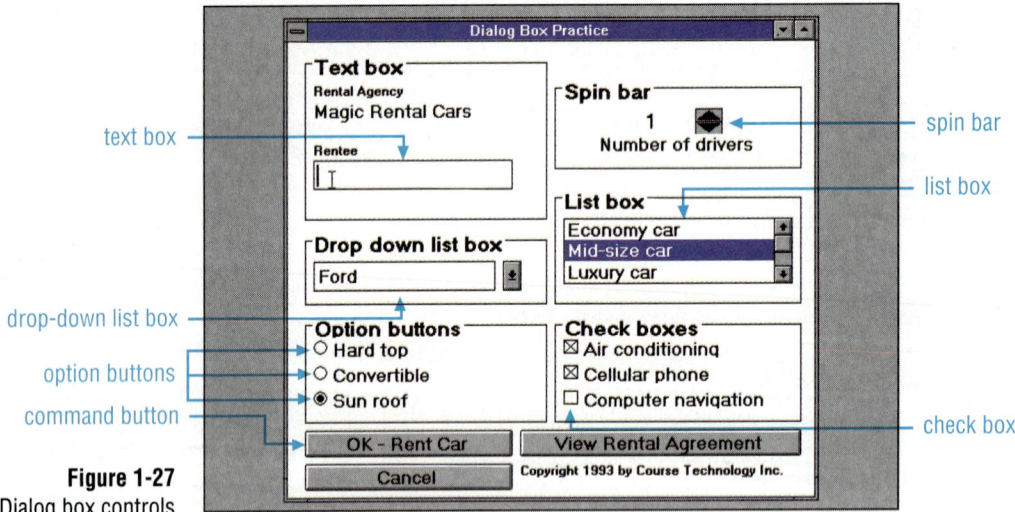

Figure 1-27
Dialog box controls

Windows uses standard dialog boxes for tasks such as printing documents and saving files. Most Windows applications use the standard dialog boxes, so if you learn how to use the Print dialog box for your word processing application, you will be well on your way to knowing how to print in any application. As you may have guessed, the rental car dialog box is not a standard Windows dialog box. It was designed to illustrate the variety of dialog box controls.

Let's see how the dialog box controls work. First, we will use a text box to type text. The Choose Slogan dialog box for the Menu Practice application has a text box that will let us change the slogan on the Windsor Stoves Corp. logo.

To activate the Use Slogan text box:

❶ Click **Slogan** to open the Slogan menu.

❷ Click **Choose Slogan...** and the Choose Slogan dialog box appears.

❸ Move the pointer to the text box and notice that it changes to an **I-bar** shape for text entry. See Figure 1-28.

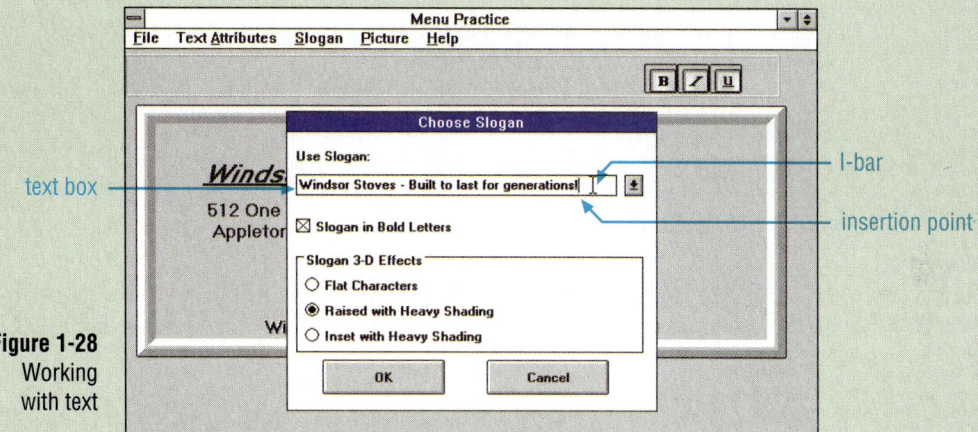

Figure 1-28
Working with text

❹ Click the **left mouse button** to activate the text box. A blinking bar called an **Insertion point** indicates that you can type text into the box. Also notice that all the text is highlighted.

❺ Press **[Del]** to erase the highlighted text of the old slogan.

When you work with a dialog box, be sure to set all the components the way you want them *before* you press the Enter key or click the OK button. Why? Because the Enter key, like the OK button, tells Windows that you are finished with the entire dialog box. Now let's type a new slogan in the text box and change the slogan 3-D effect.

To type a new slogan in a text box:

❶ Type **Quality is our Trademark!** but don't press [Enter], because while this dialog box is open, you are also going to change the slogan 3-D effect.

TROUBLE? If you make a typing mistake, press [Backspace] to delete the error, then type the correction.

❷ Look at the Slogan 3-D Effects list. Notice that the current selection is Raised with Heavy Shading.

❸ Click **Inset with Heavy Shading**.

❹ Click the **OK button** and then verify that the slogan and the 3-D effect have changed.

TROUBLE? If you are working on a monochrome system without the ability to display shade of gray, you may not be able to see the 3-D effect.

Using the Toolbar

A **toolbar** is a collection of icons that provides command shortcuts for mouse users. The icons on the toolbar are sometimes referred to as buttons. Generally the options on the toolbar duplicate menu options, but they are more convenient because they can be activated by a single mouse click. The toolbar for the Menu Practice application shown in Figure 1-29 has three buttons that are shortcuts for the Bold, Italic, and Underline commands. In a previous exercise you underlined, boldfaced, and italicized the company name using the menus. As a result the B, U, and I buttons are activated. Let's see what they look like when we deactivate them.

Figure 1-29
The Menu Practice toolbar

To change the type style using the toolbar:
1. Click **B** to remove the boldface.
2. Click **I** to turn off italics.
3. Click **U** to turn off underlining.
4. Click **B** to turn on boldface again.

You might want to spend a few minutes experimenting with the Menu Practice program to find the best logo design for Windsor Stoves Corp. When you are finished, close the Menu Practice window.

To close the Menu Practice window:
1. Click the **Control-menu box**.
2. Click **Close**. The Menu Practice program closes and returns you to Windows Program Manager.

You have now learned about Windows menus, dialog boxes and toolbars. In the next section, you will survey the Paintbrush application, experiment with tools, and access on-line help.

Using Paintbrush to Develop Your Windows Technique

After you have learned the basic Windows controls, you will find that most Windows *applications* contain similar controls. Let's launch the Paintbrush application and discover how to use it.

To launch the Paintbrush application:

1. Be sure the Program Manager window is open. If it is not open, use the skills you have learned to open it.

2. You should have an Accessories icon or an Accessories window on the desktop. If you have an Accessories group icon on the desktop, double-click it to open the Accessories group window.

   TROUBLE? If you don't see the Accessories icon or window, click the Window menu on the Program Manager menu bar. Look for Accessories in the list. If you find Accessories in this list, click it. If you do not find Accessories, ask your technical support person for help.

3. Double-click the **Paintbrush icon** to launch the Paintbrush application. Your screen will look similar to the one in Figure 1-30.

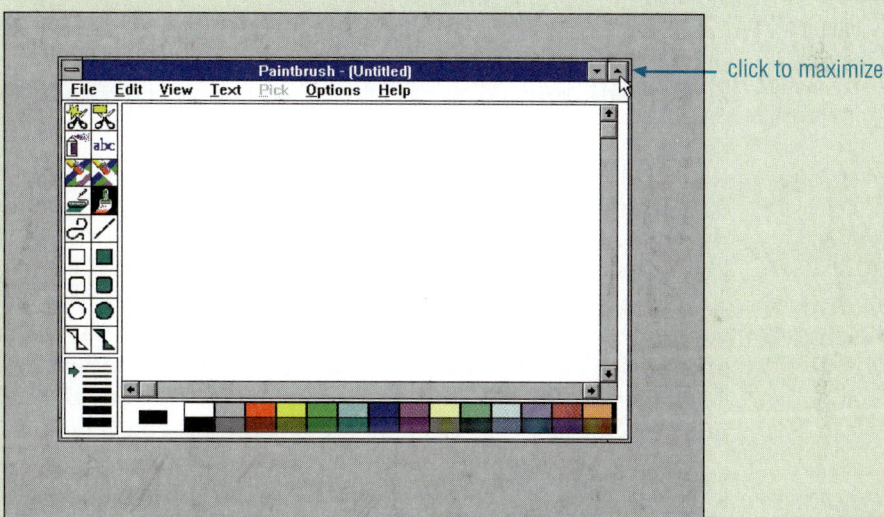

Figure 1-30
The Paintbrush window

4. Click the Paintbrush window **maximize button** so you will have a large drawing area.

Surveying the Paintbrush Application Window

Whether you are using a reference manual or experimenting on your own, your first step in learning a new application is to survey the window and familiarize yourself with its components.

Look at the Paintbrush window on your screen and make a list of the components you can identify. If you have not encountered a particular component before, try to guess what it might be.

Now refer to Figure 1-31 on the following page, which labels the Paintbrush window components.

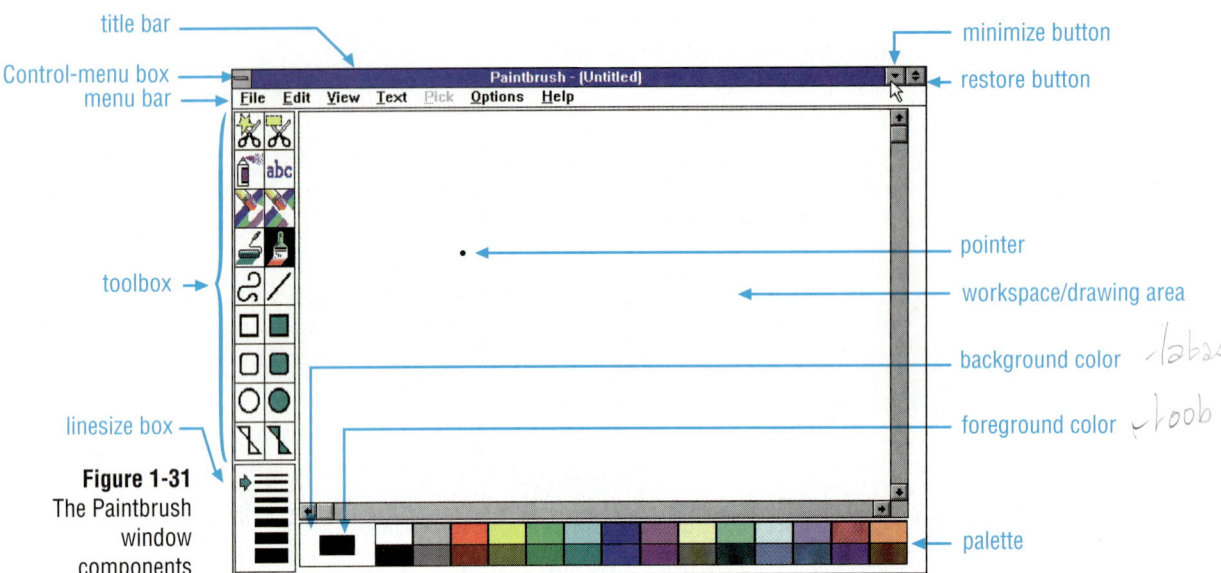

Figure 1-31
The Paintbrush window components

The darkened title bar shows that the Paintbrush window is activated. The resizing buttons are in the upper-right corner, as usual. Because there is a restore button and because the window takes up the entire screen, you know that the window is maximized. The Control-menu box is in the upper-left corner, and a menu bar lists seven menus.

On the left side of the window are a variety of icons. This looks similar to the toolbar you used when you created the logo, only it has more icons, which are arranged vertically. The Windows manual refers to this set of icons as the **toolbox**.

Under the toolbox is a box containing lines of various widths. This is the **linesize box**, which you use to select the width of the line you draw.

At the bottom of the screen is a color **palette**, which you use to select the foreground and background colors. The currently selected colors for the foreground and background are indicated in the box to the left of the palette.

The rectangular space in the middle of the window is the drawing area. When the pointer is in the drawing area, it will assume a variety of shapes, depending on the tool you are using.

Experimenting with Tools

The icons on toolbars might be some of the easiest Windows controls, but many people are a little mystified by the symbols used for some of the tools. Look at the icons in the Paintbrush toolbox and try to guess their use.

You can often make good guesses, when you know what the application does. For example, you probably guessed that the brush tool shown in Figure 1-32 is used for drawing a picture. However, you might not be able to guess how the brush and the roller tools differ.

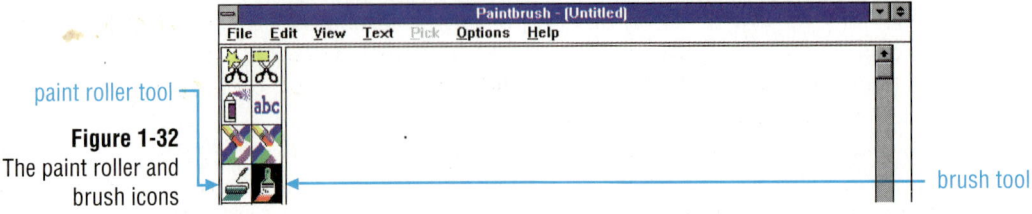

Figure 1-32
The paint roller and brush icons

If you can make some reasonable guess about how a tool works, it's not a bad idea to try it out. Can you write your name using the paintbrush tool? Let's try it.

To use the brush tool:

❶ Locate and click the **brush tool** in the toolbox. The brush tool becomes highlighted, indicating that it is now the selected tool.

❷ Move the pointer to the drawing area. Notice that it changes to a small dot.

❸ Move the pointer to the place where you want to begin writing your name.

When the left mouse button is down, the brush will paint. When you release the mouse button, you can move the pointer without painting.

❹ Use the mouse to control the brush as you write your name. Don't worry if it looks a little rough. Your "John Hancock" might look like the one in Figure 1-33.

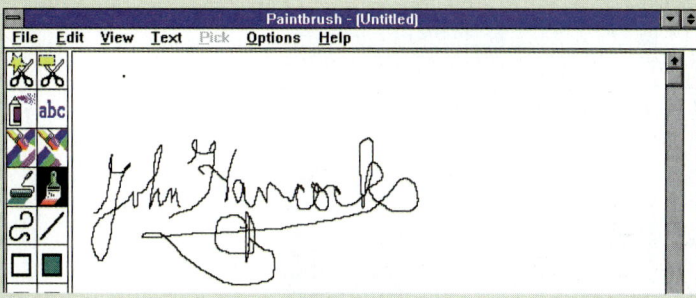

Figure 1-33
Your "John Hancock"

You will recall that we were curious about the difference between the brush and the paint roller. Let's experiment with the paint roller next.

To try the paint roller:

❶ Click the **paint roller** tool.

❷ Position the pointer in the upper-left corner of the drawing area and click. What happened?!

Did you get a strange result? Don't panic. This sort of thing happens when you experiment. Still, we probably should find out a little more about how to control the roller. To do this, we'll use the Paintbrush Help facility.

Using Help

Most Windows applications have an extensive on-line Help facility. A **Help facility** is an electronic reference manual that contains information about an application's menus, tools, and procedures. Some Help facilities also include **tutorials,** which you can use to learn the application.

There are a variety of ways to access Help, so people usually develop their own technique for finding information in it. We'll show you one way that seems to work for many Windows users. Later you can explore on your own and develop your own techniques.

When you use Help, a Help window opens. Usually the Help window overlays your application. If you want to view the problem spot and the Help information at the same time, it is a good idea to organize your desktop so the Help and application windows are side by side.

To access Help and organize the desktop:

❶ Click **Help**. A Help menu lists the Help commands.

❷ Click **Contents** to display a Paintbrush Help window similar to the one in Figure 1-34.

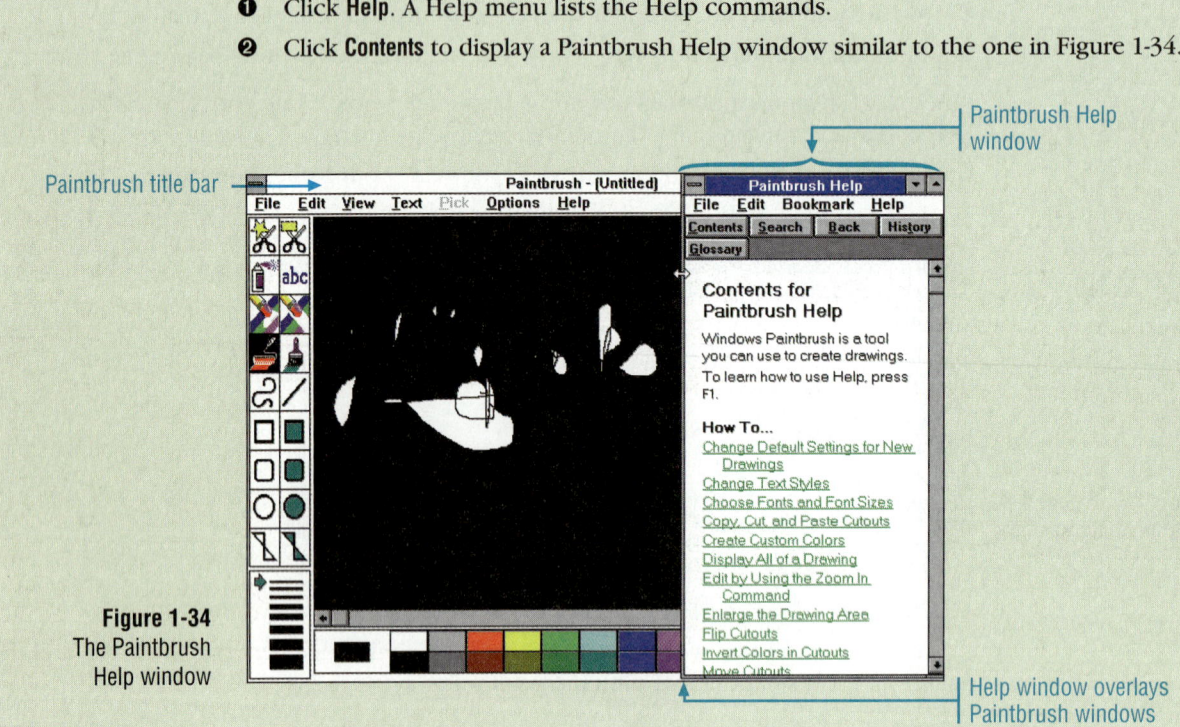

Figure 1-34
The Paintbrush Help window

❸ If the Paintbrush Help window is not the same size and shape as the one in Figure 1-34, drag the corners of the Help window until it looks like the one in the figure.

The Paintbrush application window is partially covered by the Help window. We need to fix that.

❹ Click the **Paintbrush title bar** to activate the Paintbrush window.

❺ Click the **restore button** to display the window borders and corners.

❻ Drag the corners of the Paintbrush application until your screen resembles the one in Figure 1-35 on the following page.

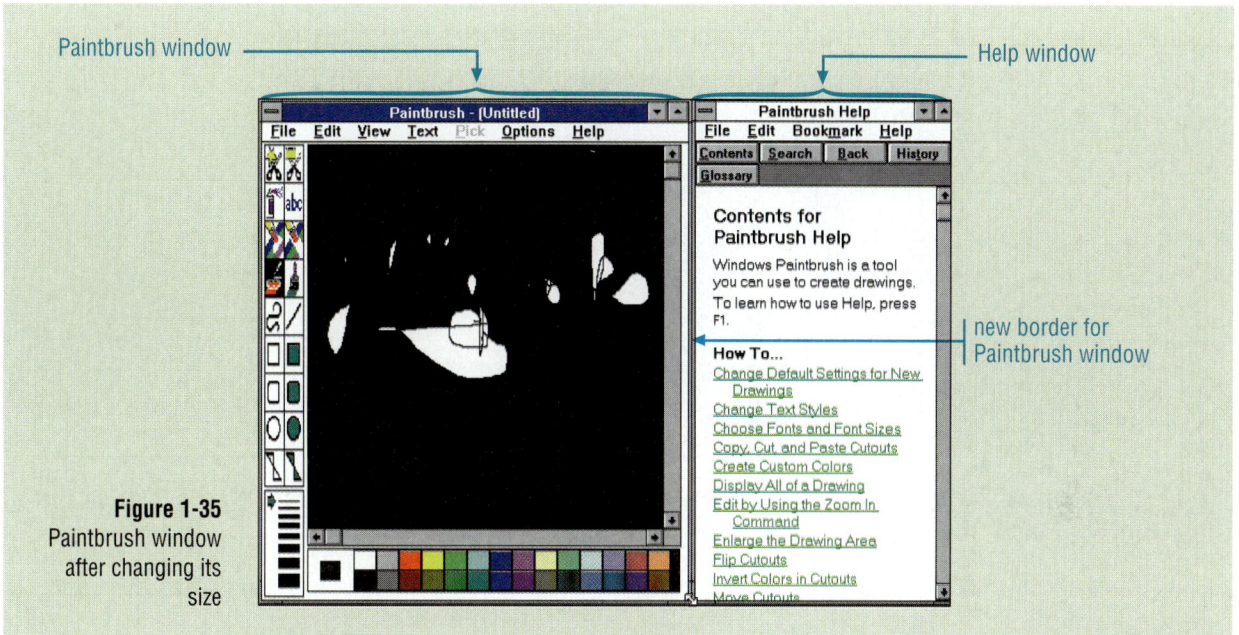

Figure 1-35
Paintbrush window after changing its size

Now that the windows are organized, let's find out about the roller tool. The Paintbrush Help window contains a Table of Contents, which is divided into three sections: How To, Tools, and Commands.

The **How To** section is a list of procedures that are explained in the Help facility. Use this section when you want to find out how to do something. The **Tools** section identifies the toolbar icons and explains how to use them. The **Commands** section provides an explanation of the commands that can be accessed from the menu bar.

To find information about the paint roller tool on the Help facility:

❶ Use the scroll box to scroll down the text in the Help window until you see the Tools section heading.

❷ Continue scrolling until the Paint Roller option comes into view.

❸ Position the pointer on the Paint Roller Option. Notice that the pointer changes to a pointing hand, indicating that Paint Roller is a clickable option.

❹ Click the **left mouse button**. The Help window now contains information about the paint roller, as shown in Figure 1-36 on the following page.

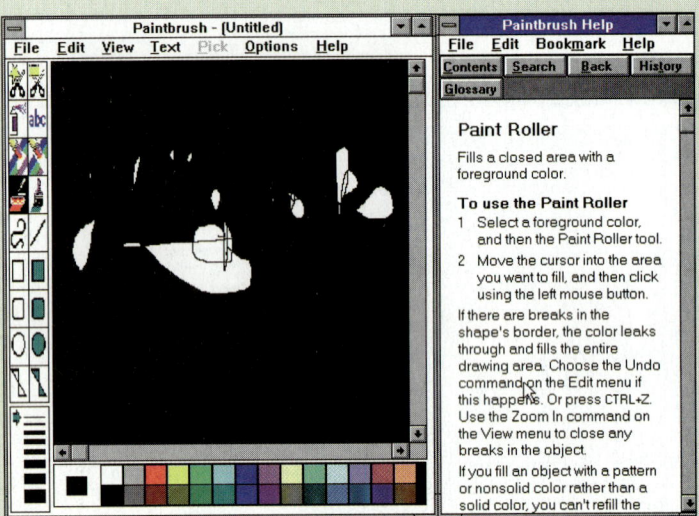

Figure 1-36
Paint Roller Help

⑤ Read the information about the Paint Roller, using the scroll bar to view the entire text.

What did you learn about the paint roller? The first item you likely discovered is that the paint roller is used to fill an area. Well, it certainly did that in our experiment. It filled the entire drawing area with the foreground color, black. Next you might have noted that the first step in the procedure for using the paint roller is to select a foreground color. In our experiment, it would have been better if we selected some color other than black for the fill. Let's erase our old experiment so we can try again.

To start a new painting:

① Click **File** on the Paintbrush menu bar (not on the Help menu bar) to open the File menu.

② Click **New**, because you want to start a new drawing. A dialog box asks, "Do you want to save current changes?"

③ Click the **No button** to clear the drawing area, because you don't want to save your first experiment.

Now you can paint your name and then use the roller to artistically fill areas. When you have finished experimenting, exit the Paintbrush application.

To exit Paintbrush:

① Click the **Control-menu box** and then click **Close**.

② In response to the prompt "Do you want to save current changes?" click the **No button**. The Paintbrush window closes, which also automatically closes the Help window.

You've covered a lot of ground. Next, it's time to learn how to exit Windows.

Exiting Windows

You might want to continue directly to the Questions and Tutorial Assignments. If so, stay in Windows until you have completed your work, then follow these instructions for exiting Windows.

To exit Windows:
1. Click the **Control-menu box** in the upper-left of the Program Manager window.
2. Click **Close**.
3. When you see the message "This will end your Windows session," click the **OK button**.

■　　　■　　　■

Steve congratulates you on your Windows progress. You have learned the terminology associated with the desktop environment and the names of the controls and how to use them. You have developed an understanding about desktop organization and how to arrange the application and document windows so you will use them most effectively. You have also learned to use menus, dialog boxes, toolbars and Help.

Questions

1. GUI is an acronym for _____.
2. A group window contains which of the following?
   a. application icons
   b. document icons
   c. program-item icons
   d. group icons
3. What is one of the main purposes of the Program Manager?
   a. to organize your diskette
   b. to launch applications
   c. to create documents
   d. to provide the Help facility for applications
4. Which mouse function is used as a shortcut for more lengthy mouse or keyboard procedures?
   a. pointing
   b. clicking
   c. dragging
   d. double-clicking
5. To change the focus to an icon, you _____ it.
   a. close
   b. select
   c. drag
   d. launch

6. What is another name for document windows?
   a. child windows
   b. parent windows
   c. application windows
   d. group windows
7. In Figure 1-37 each window component is numbered. Write the name of the component that corresponds to the number.

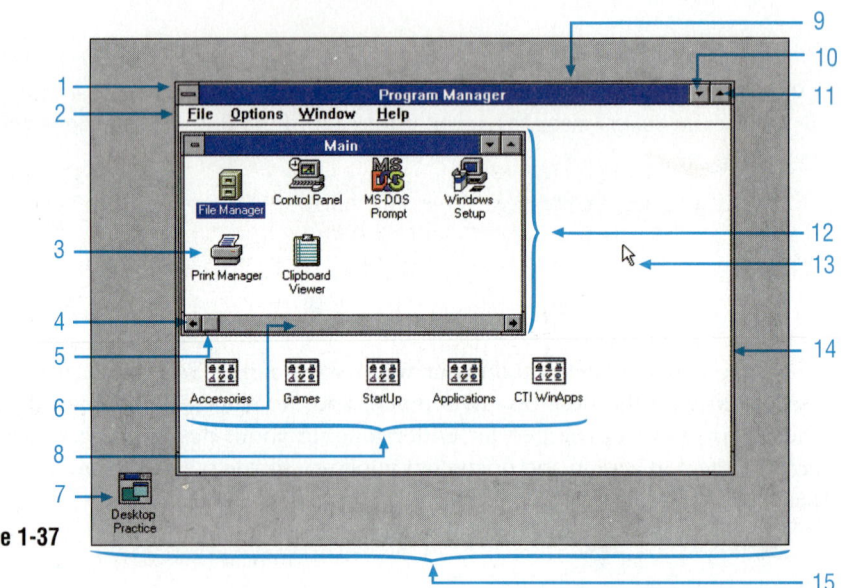

Figure 1-37

8. In Windows terminology you _____ a window when you want to get it out of the way temporarily but leave the application running.
9. You _____ a window when you no longer need to have the application running.
10. The _____ provides you with a way to switch between application windows.
    a. Task List
    b. program-item icon
    c. Window menu
    d. maximize button
11. How would you find out if you had more than one application running on your desktop?
12. _____ refers to the capability of a computer to run more than one application at the same time.
13. Which menu provides the means to switch from one document to another?
    a. the File menu
    b. the Help menu
    c. the Window menu
    d. the Control menu
14. Describe three menu conventions used in Windows menus.
E 15. The flashing vertical bar that marks the place your typing will appear is _____.
E 16. If you have access to a Windows reference manual such as the *Microsoft Windows User's Guide*, look for an explanation of the difference between group icons, program-item icons, and application icons. For your instructor's

information, write down the name of the reference, the publisher, and the page(s) on which you found this information. If you were writing a textbook for first-time Windows users, how would you describe the difference between these icons?

 17. Copy the definition of "metaphor" from any standard dictionary. For your instructor's information, write down the dictionary name, the edition, and the page number. After considering the definition, explain why Windows is said to be a "desktop metaphor."

Tutorial Assignments

If you exited Windows at the end of the tutorial, launch Windows and do Assignments 1 through 15. Write your answers to the questions in Assignments 1, 2, 3, 4, 5, 9, 10, 11, 12, 13, and 15. Also fill out the table in Assignment 7.

1. Close all applications except the Program Manager and shrink all the group windows to icons. What are the names of the group icons on the desktop?
2. Open the Main window. How many program-item icons are in this window?
3. Open the Accessories window. How many program-item icons are in this window?
4. Open, close, and change the dimensions of the windows so your screen looks like Figure 1-38.
   a. How many applications are now on the desktop?
   b. How did you find out how many applications are on the desktop?

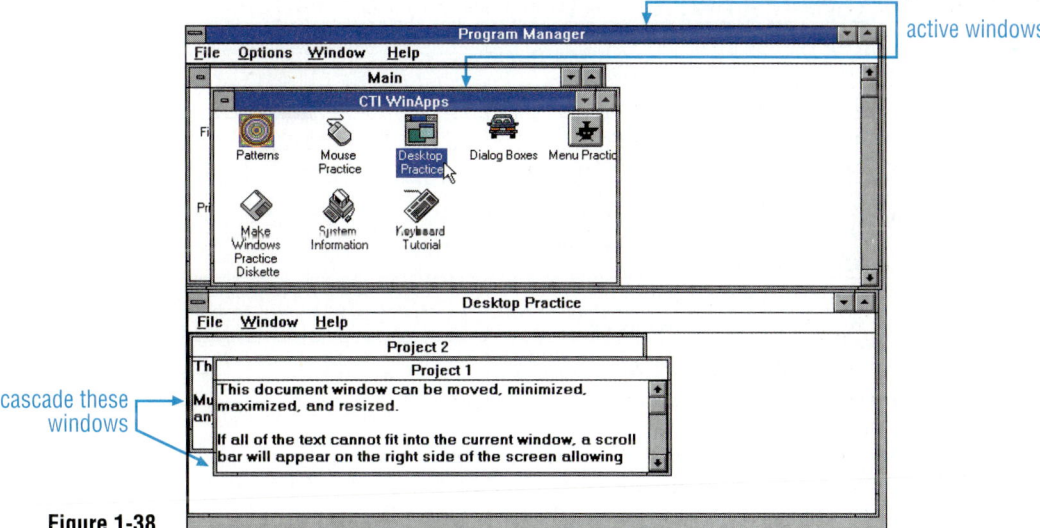

Figure 1-38

5. Open, close, and change the dimensions of the windows so your screen looks like Figure 1-39 on the following page. After you're done, close the Desktop Practice window using the fewest mouse clicks. How did you close the Desktop Practice window?

Open the CTI WinApps window and do Assignments 6 through 8.

Figure 1-39

6. Double-click the System Information icon.
7. Using the information displayed on your screen, fill out the following table:

CPU Type:	
Available Memory:	
Number of Diskette Drives:	
Capacity of Drive A:	
Capacity of Drive B:	
Horizontal Video Resolution:	
Vertical Video Resolution:	
Screen Colors or Shades:	
Network Type:	
DOS Version:	
Windows Version:	
Windows Mode:	
Windows Directory:	
Windows Free Resources:	
Available Drive Letters:	
Hard Drive Capacities:	

8. Click the Exit button to return to the Program Manager.

Launch the Mouse Practice application and do Assignments 9 through 14.

9. What happens when you drag the letter to the file cabinet?
10. What happens when you double-click the mouse icon located in the lower-left corner of the desktop?
11. What happens when you click an empty check box? What happens when you click a check box that contains an "X"?
12. Can you select both option buttons at the same time?
13. What happens when you click "Item Fourteen" from the list?
14. Exit the Mouse Practice.

Launch the Desktop Practice and do Assignments 15 through 17.

15. What is the last sentence of the document in the Project 2 window?
16. Close the Desktop Practice window.
17. Exit Windows.

TUTORIAL 2

Effective File Management

Using the File Manager

OBJECTIVES

In this tutorial you will:

- Open and close the File Manager
- Format and make your student disk containing practice files
- Change the current drive
- Identify the components of the File Manager window
- Create directories
- Change the current directory
- Move, rename, delete, and copy files
- Make a disk backup
- Learn how to protect your data from hardware failures

CASE

A Professional Approach to Computing at Narraganset Shipyard Ruth Sanchez works at the Narraganset Shipyard, a major government defense contractor. On a recent business trip to Washington, DC, Ruth read a magazine article that convinced her she should do a better job of organizing the files on her computer system. The article pointed out that a professional approach to computing includes a plan for maintaining an organized set of disk-based files that can be easily accessed, updated, and secured.

Ruth learns that the Windows File Manager can help to organize her files. Ruth has not used the File Manager very much, so before she begins to make organizational changes to the valuable files on her hard disk, she decides to practice with some sample files on a disk in drive A.

In this Tutorial, you will follow the progress of Ruth's File Manager practice and learn how to use Windows to manage effectively the data stored in your computer.

Files and the File Manager

A **file** is a named collection of data organized for a specific purpose and stored on a floppy disk or a hard disk. The typical computer user has hundreds of files.

The Windows File Manager provides some handy tools for organizing files. Ruth's first step is to launch the File Manager. Let's do the same.

To launch the File Manager:
- ❶ Launch Windows.
- ❷ Compare your screen to Figure 2-1. Use the skills you learned in Tutorial 1 to organize your desktop so only the Program Manager window and the Main window are open.

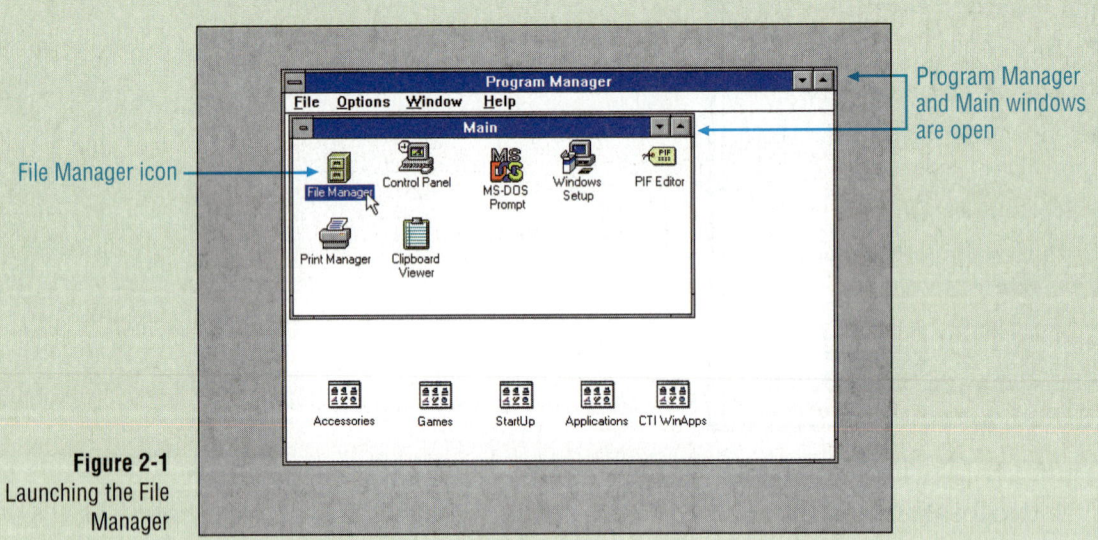

Figure 2-1
Launching the File Manager

- ❸ Double-click the **File Manager icon** to launch the File Manager program and open the File Manager window.
- ❹ If the File Manager window is not maximized, click the **maximize button**.
- ❺ Click **Window**, then click **Tile**. You should now have one child window on the desktop. See Figure 2-2a on the following page. Don't worry if the title of your child window is not the same as the one in the figure.

Files and File Manager   WIN 39

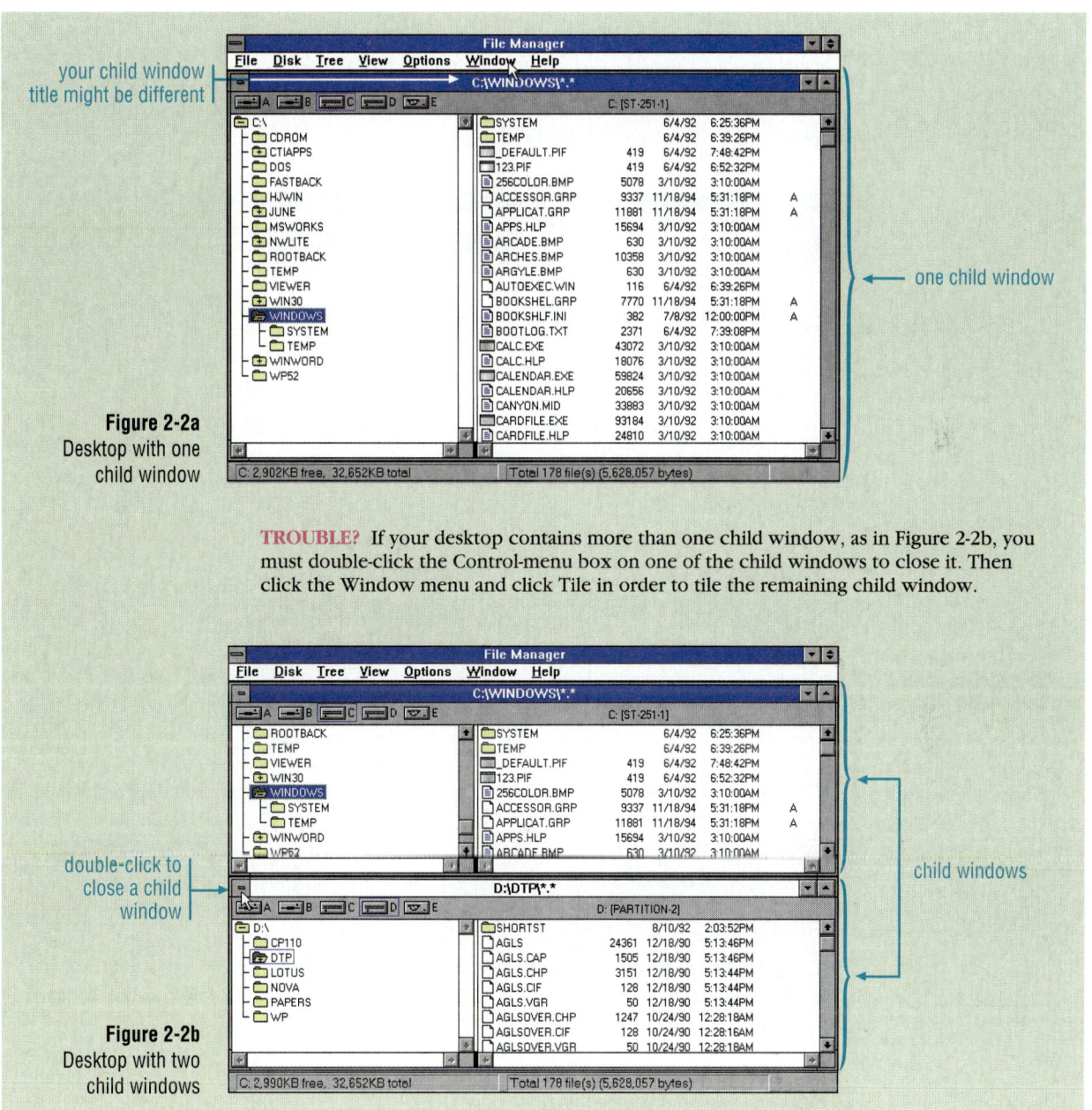

Figure 2-2a Desktop with one child window

Figure 2-2b Desktop with two child windows

TROUBLE? If your desktop contains more than one child window, as in Figure 2-2b, you must double-click the Control-menu box on one of the child windows to close it. Then click the Window menu and click Tile in order to tile the remaining child window.

Ruth decides to check her File Manager settings, which affect the way information is displayed. By adjusting your File Manager settings to match Ruth's, your computer will display screens and prompts similar to those in the Tutorial. *If you do not finish this tutorial in one session, remember to adjust the settings again when you begin your next session.*

To adjust your File Manager settings:

1. Click **Tree**. Look at the command "Indicate Expandable Branches." See Figure 2-3. If no check mark appears next to this command, position the pointer on the command and click. If you see the check mark, go to Step 2.

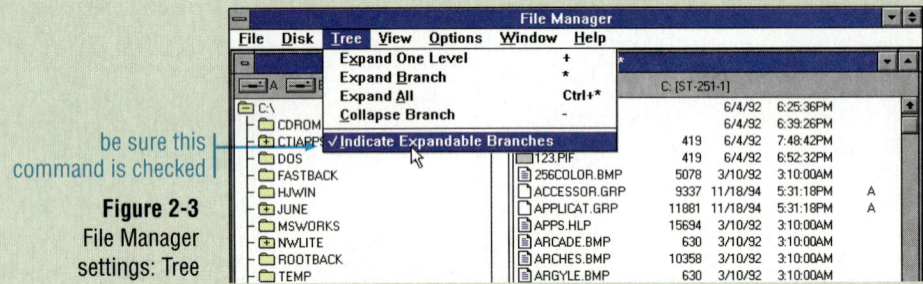

Figure 2-3
File Manager settings: Tree

2. Click **View**. Make any adjustments necessary so that the settings are the same as those in Figure 2-4.

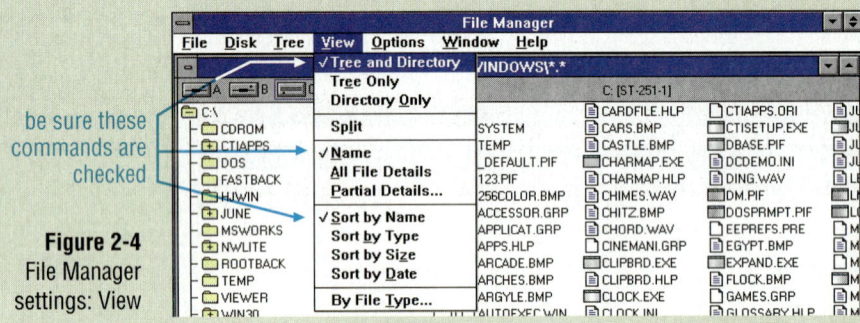

Figure 2-4
File Manager settings: View

TROUBLE? When you click a command to change the check mark, the menu closes. To change another command in the menu or to confirm your changes, you need to click the View menu again.

3. Click **Options** and then click **Confirmation...**. Referring to Figure 2-5, make any adjustments necessary so that all the check boxes contain an X, then click the **OK button**.

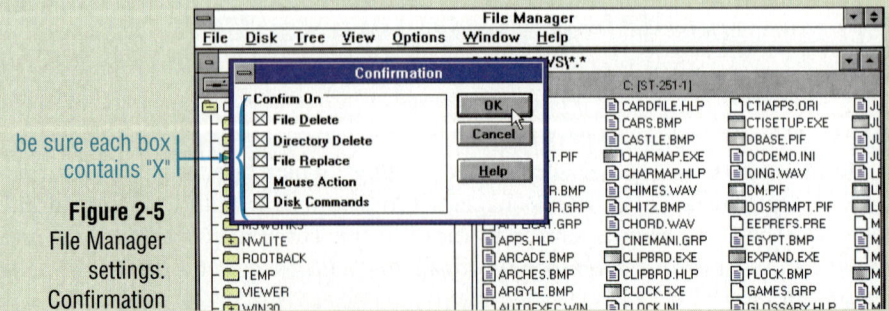

Figure 2-5
File Manager settings: Confirmation

4. Click **Options** again and then click **Font**. Make any adjustments necessary so your font settings match those in Figure 2-6 on the following page. Click the **OK button** whether or not you changed anything in this dialog box.

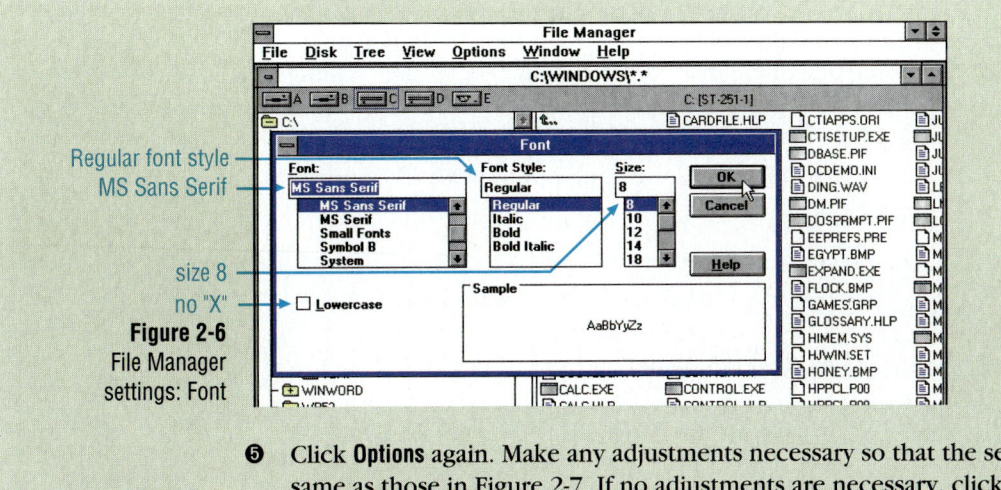

Figure 2-6
File Manager settings: Font

(Labels: Regular font style MS Sans Serif; size 8; no "X")

⑤ Click **Options** again. Make any adjustments necessary so that the settings are the same as those in Figure 2-7. If no adjustments are necessary, click **Options** again to close the menu.

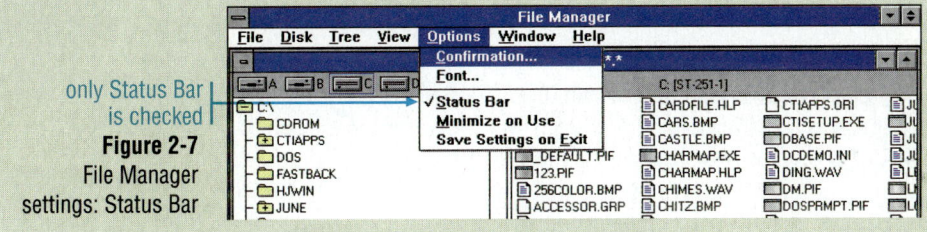

Figure 2-7
File Manager settings: Status Bar

(Label: only Status Bar is checked)

Formatting a Disk

Next, Ruth needs to format the disks she will use for her File Manager practice. Disks must be formatted before they can be used to store data. Formatting arranges the magnetic particles on the disks in preparation for storing data. You need to format a disk when:

- you purchase a new disk
- you want to recycle an old disk that you used on a non-IBM-compatible computer
- you want to erase all the old files from a disk

Pay attention when you are formatting disks. *The formatting process erases all the data on the disk*. If you format a disk that already contains data, you will lose all the data. Fortunately, Windows will not let you format the hard disk or network drives using the Format Disk command.

To complete the steps in this Tutorial you need two disks of the same size and density. You may use blank, unformatted disks or disks that contain data you no longer need. *The following steps assume that you will format the disks in drive A. If you want to use drive B for the formatting process, substitute drive B for drive A* in Steps 3, 4, and 6.

To format the first disk:

❶ Make sure your disk is *not* write-protected. On a 5.25-inch disk the write-protect notch should *not* be covered. On a 3.5-inch disk the hole on the left side of the disk should be *closed*.

❷ Write your name, course title, and course meeting time on an adhesive disk label. For the title of the disk, write Student Disk (Source Disk). Apply this label to one of the disks you are going to format. If you are using a 3.5-inch disk, do not stick the label on any of the metal parts.

❸ Put this disk into drive A. If your disk drive has a door or a latch, secure it. See Figure 2-8.

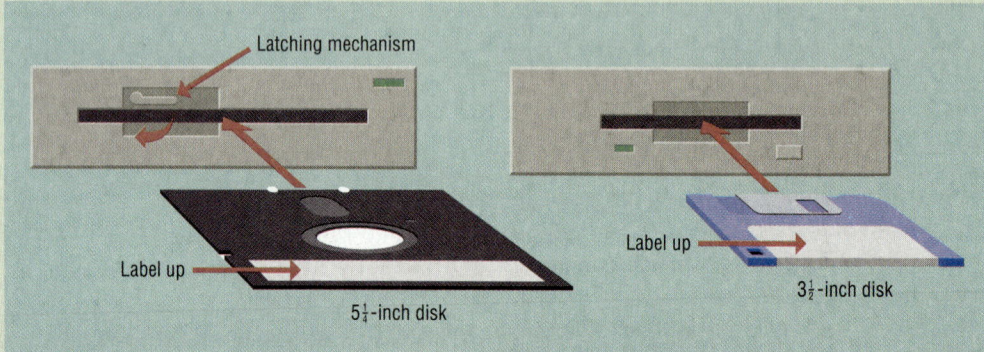

Figure 2-8
Inserting your disk

❹ Click **Disk** and then click **Format Disk....** A Format Disk dialog box appears. See Figure 2-9. If the Disk In box does not indicate Drive A, click the [↓] (down-arrow) button on this box, then click the Drive A option.

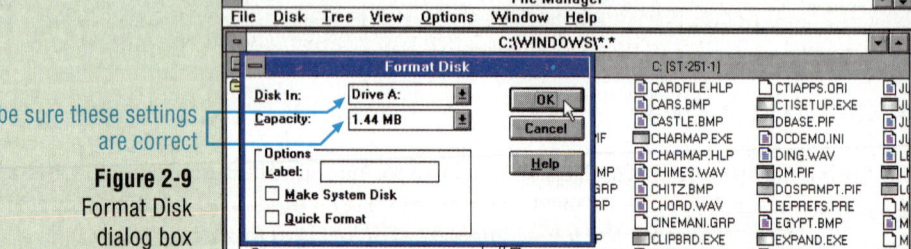

Figure 2-9
Format Disk dialog box

❺ Look at the number displayed in the Capacity box. If you are formatting a disk that cannot store the displayed amount of data, click the [↓] (down-arrow) button at the right side of the Capacity box and then click the correct capacity from the list of options provided.

TROUBLE? How can you determine the capacity of your disk? The chart in Figure 2-10 (on the next page) will help you. If you still are not sure after looking at the figure, ask your technical support person.

Diskette size	Diskette density	Diskette capacity
5 1/4-inch	DD	360K
5 1/4-inch	HD	1.2MB
3 1/2-inch	DD	720K
3 1/2-inch	HD	1.44MB

Figure 2-10
Disk capacities

❻ Click the **OK button**. The Confirm Format Disk dialog box appears with a warning. Read it. Look at the drive that is going to carry out the format operation (drive A). Be sure this is the correct drive. Double-check the disk that's in this drive to be sure it is the one you want to format.

❼ Click the **Yes button**. The Formatting Disk dialog box keeps you updated on the progress of the format.

❽ When the format is complete, the Format Complete dialog box reports the results of the format and asks if you'd like to format another disk. See Figure 2-11.

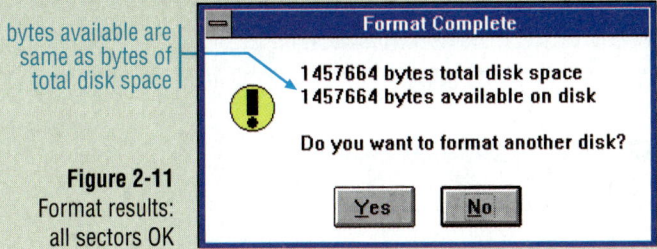

bytes available are same as bytes of total disk space

Figure 2-11
Format results: all sectors OK

Let's format your second floppy disk:

❶ Click the **Yes button** after you review the formatting results.

❷ Remove your Student disk from drive A.

❸ Write your name, course title, and course meeting time on the label for the second disk. For the title of this disk write Backup (Destination Disk). Apply this label to your second disk and place this disk in drive A.

❹ Be sure the **Disk In box** is set to drive A and the capacity is set to the capacity of your disk. (Remember to substitute B here if you are formatting your disk in drive B.)

❺ Click the **OK button** to accept the settings. When you see the Confirm Format Disk dialog box, check to be sure you have the correct disk in the correct drive.

❻ Click the **Yes button** to confirm that you want to format the disk. When the format is complete, review the format results.

❼ You do not want to format another disk, so click the **No button** when the computer asks if you wish to format another disk.

❽ *Remove the backup disk from drive A.* You will not need this backup disk until later.

Preparing Your Student Disk

Now that Ruth has formatted her disks, she is going to put some files on one of them to use for her file management exploration. To follow Ruth's progress, you must have copies of her files. A collection of files has been prepared for this purpose. You need to transfer them to one of your formatted disks.

To transfer files to your Student Disk:

❶ Place the disk you labeled Student Disk (Source Disk) in drive A.

WIN 44   TUTORIAL 2   Effective File Management

The File Manager window is open, but you need to go to the Program Manager window to launch the application that will transfer the files.

❷ Hold down [Alt] and continue to press [Tab] until Program Manager appears in the box, then release both keys. Program Manager becomes the active window.

❸ If the CTI WinApps window is not open, double-click the **CTI WinApps group icon**. If the CTI WinApps window is open but is not the active window, click it. Your screen should look similar to Figure 2-12.

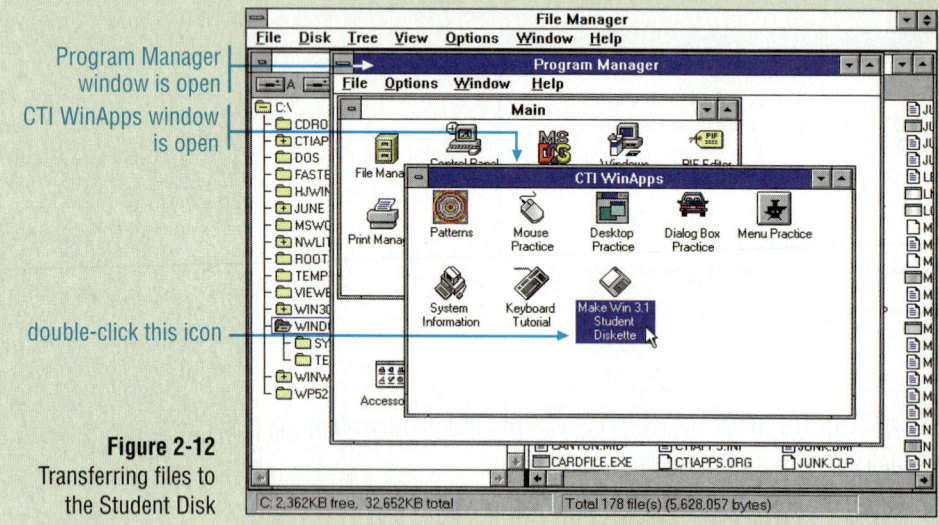

Program Manager window is open
CTI WinApps window is open
double-click this icon

Figure 2-12
Transferring files to the Student Disk

❹ Double-click the **Make Win 3.1 Student Disk icon**. A dialog box appears.
❺ Make sure the drive that is selected in the dialog box corresponds to the drive that contains your disk (drive A or drive B), then click the **OK button**. It will take 30 seconds or so to transfer the files to your disk.
❻ Click the **OK button** when you see the message "24 files copied successfully!"
❼ Double-click on the **CTI WinWorks Apps Control-menu box** to close the window.

Now the data files you need should be on your Student Disk. To continue the Tutorial, you must switch back to the File Manager.

To switch back to the File Manager:
❶ Hold down [Alt] and press [Tab] until a box with File Manager appears. Then release both keys.

Finding Out What's on Your Disks

Ruth learned from the article that the first step toward effective data management is to find out what's stored on her disks. To see what's on your Student Disk, you will need to be sure your computer is referencing the correct disk drive.

Changing the Current Drive

Each drive on your computer system is represented by a **drive icon** that tells you the drive letter and the drive type. Figure 2-13 shows the drive types represented by these icons.

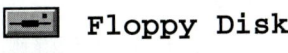 Floppy Disk

Hard Disk

Network Drive

Figure 2-13
Drive icons

CD-ROM Drive

Near the top of the File Manager window, a **drive icon ribbon** indicates the drives on your computer system. See Figure 2-14. Your screen may be different because the drive icon ribbon on your screen reflects your particular hardware configuration.

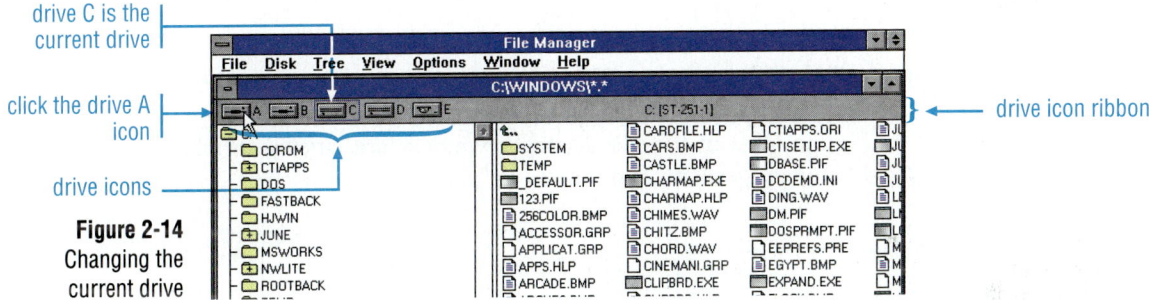

Figure 2-14
Changing the current drive

Your computer is connected to a number of storage drives or devices, but it can work with only one drive at a time. This drive is referred to as the **current drive** or **default drive**. You must change the current drive whenever you want to use files or programs that are stored on a different drive. The drive icon for the current drive is outlined with a rectangle. In Figure 2-14, the current drive is C.

To work with Ruth's files, you must be sure that the current drive is the one in which you have your Student Disk. *For this Tutorial we'll assume that your Student Disk is in drive A. If it is in drive B, substitute "drive B" for "drive A" in the rest of the steps for this Tutorial.*

Follow the next set of steps to change the current drive, if your current drive is not the one containing your Student Disk.

To change the current drive to A:

❶ Be sure your Student Disk is in drive A.

❷ Click the **drive A icon**. Drive A becomes the current drive. See Figure 2-15 on the following page.

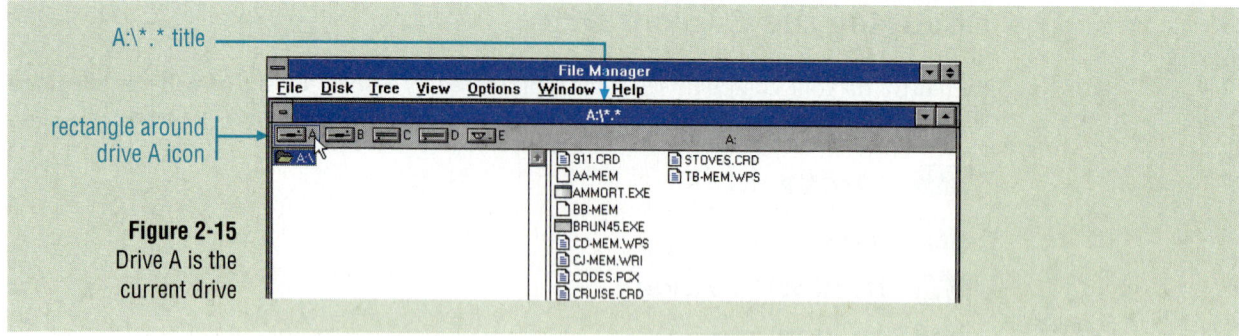

Figure 2-15 Drive A is the current drive

After you make drive A the current drive, your screen should look similar to Figure 2-15. Don't worry if everything is not exactly the same as the figure. Just be sure you see the A:*.* window title and that there is a rectangle around the drive A icon (or the drive B icon if drive B contains your floppy disk).

The File Manager Window

The components of the File Manager window are labeled in Figure 2-16. Your screen should contain similar components.

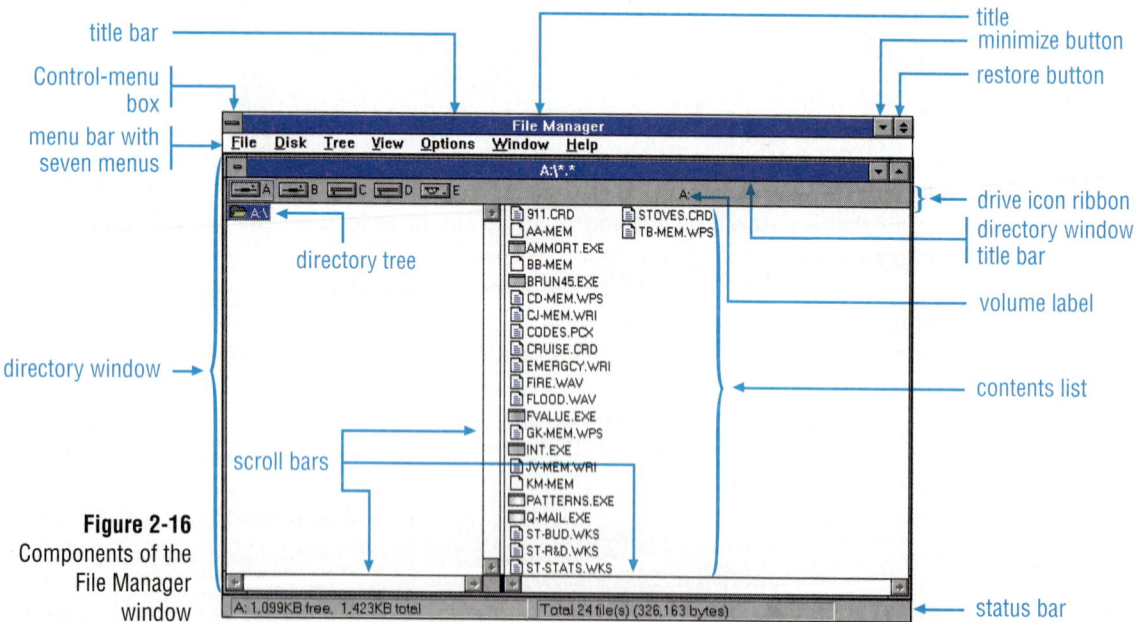

Figure 2-16 Components of the File Manager window

The top line of the File Manager window contains the Control-menu box, the title bar, the title, and the resizing buttons. The File Manager menu bar contains seven menus.

Inside the File Manager window is the **directory window**, which contains information about the current drive. The title bar for this window displays the current drive, in this case, A:*.*. This window has its own Control-menu box and resizing buttons.

Below the directory window title bar is the drive icon ribbon. On this line, the drive letter is followed by a volume label, if there is one. A **volume label** is a name you can assign to your disk during the format process to help you identify the contents of the disk. We did not assign a volume label, so the area after the A: is blank. Why is there a colon after the drive letter? Even though the colon is not displayed on the drive icons, when you type in a drive letter, you must always type a colon after it. The colon is a requirement of the DOS operating system that Windows uses behind the scenes to perform its file management tasks.

At the bottom of the screen, a status bar displays information about disk space. Remember that a byte is one character of data.

Notice that the directory window is split. The left half of the directory window displays the **directory tree**, which illustrates the organization of files on the current drive. The right half of the directory window displays the **contents list**, which lists the files on the current drive. Scroll bars on these windows let you view material that doesn't fit in the current window.

The Directory Tree

A list of files is called a **directory**. Because long lists of files are awkward to work with, directories can be subdivided into smaller lists called **subdirectories**. The organization of these directories and subdirectories is depicted in the directory tree.

Suppose you were using your computer for a small retail business. What information might you have on your disk, and how would it be organized? Figure 2-17 shows the directory tree for a hard disk (drive C) of a typical small business computer system.

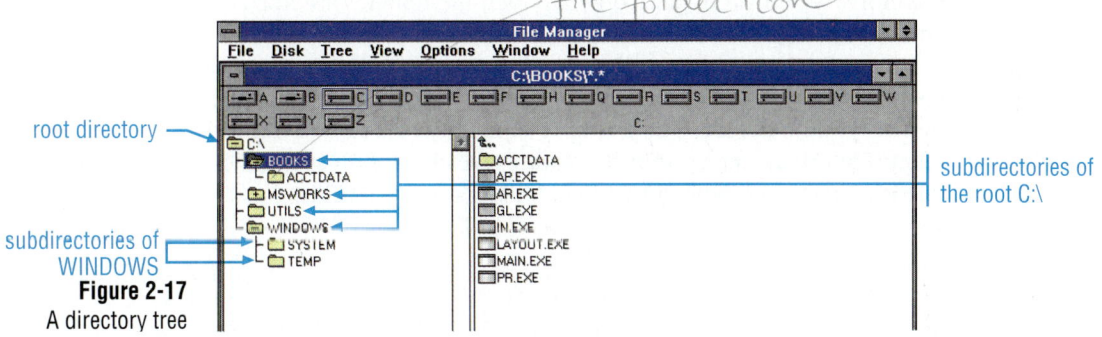

Figure 2-17
A directory tree

At the top of the directory tree is the **root directory**, called C:\ . The root directory is created when you format a disk and is indicated by a backslash after the drive letter and colon. Arranged under the root directory are the subdirectories BOOKS, MSWORKS, UTILS, and WINDOWS.

Directories other than the root directory can have subdirectories. In Figure 2-17 you can see that the BOOKS directory has a subdirectory called ACCTDATA. The WINDOWS directory contains two subdirectories, SYSTEM and TEMP. MSWORKS also has some subdirectories, but they are not listed. You'll find out how to expand the directory tree to display subdirectories later in the this tutorial.

Windows uses directory names to construct a path through the directory tree. For example, the path to ACCTDATA would be C:\BOOKS\ACCTDATA. To trace this path on Figure 2-17, begin at the root directory C:\, follow the line leading to the BOOKS directory, then follow the line leading to the ACCTDATA directory.

Each directory in the directory tree has a **file folder icon**, which can be either open or closed. An open file folder icon indicates the **active** or **current directory**. In Figure 2-17 the current directory is BOOKS. Only one directory can be current on a disk at a time.

Now look at the directory tree on your screen. The root directory of your Student Disk is called A:\. The file folder icon for this directory is open, indicating that this is the current directory. Are there any subdirectories on your disk?

The answer is no. A:\ has no subdirectories because its file folder icon does not contain a plus sign or a minus sign. A plus sign on a folder indicates that the directory can be expanded to show its subdirectories. A minus sign indicates that the subdirectories are currently being displayed. A file folder icon without a plus or a minus sign has no subdirectories.

Organizing Your Files

Ruth's disk, like your Student Disk, contains only one directory, and all her files are in that directory. As is typical of a poorly organized disk, files from different projects and programs are jumbled together. As Ruth's disk accumulates more files, she will have an increasingly difficult time finding the files she wants to use.

Ruth needs to organize her disk. First, she needs to make some new directories so she has a good basic structure for her files.

Creating Directories

When you create a directory, you indicate its location on the directory tree and specify the new directory name. The directory you create becomes a subdirectory of the current directory, which is designated by an open file folder. Directory names can be up to eight characters long.

Your Student Disk contains a collection of memos and spreadsheets that Ruth has created for a project code named "Stealth." Right now, all of these files are in the root directory. Ruth decides that to improve the organization of her disk, she should place her memos in one directory and the Stealth spreadsheets in another directory. To do this, she needs to make two new directories, MEMOS and STEALTH.

To make a new directory called MEMOS:

❶ Click the **file folder icon** representing the root directory of drive A. Figure 2-18 shows you where to click. This highlights the root directory A:\, making it the current directory.

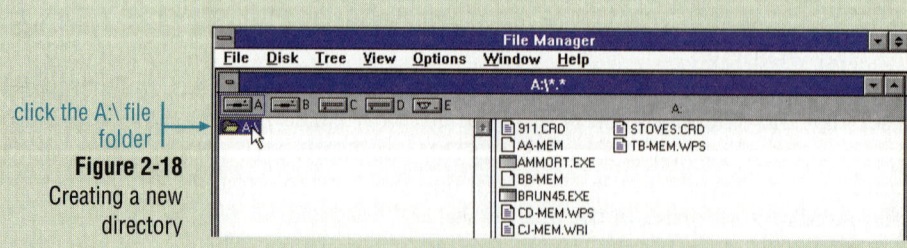

click the A:\ file folder

Figure 2-18
Creating a new directory

❷ Click **File**, then click **Create Directory...**. The Create Directory dialog box indicates that the current directory is A:\ and displays a text box for the name of the new directory.

❸ In the text box, type **MEMOS**, then click the **OK button**. It doesn't matter whether you type the directory name in uppercase or lowercase letters.

As a result, your screen should look like Figure 2-19. A new directory folder labeled MEMOS is now a subdirectory of A:\. The A:\ file folder now displays a minus sign to indicate that it has a subdirectory and that the subdirectory is displayed.

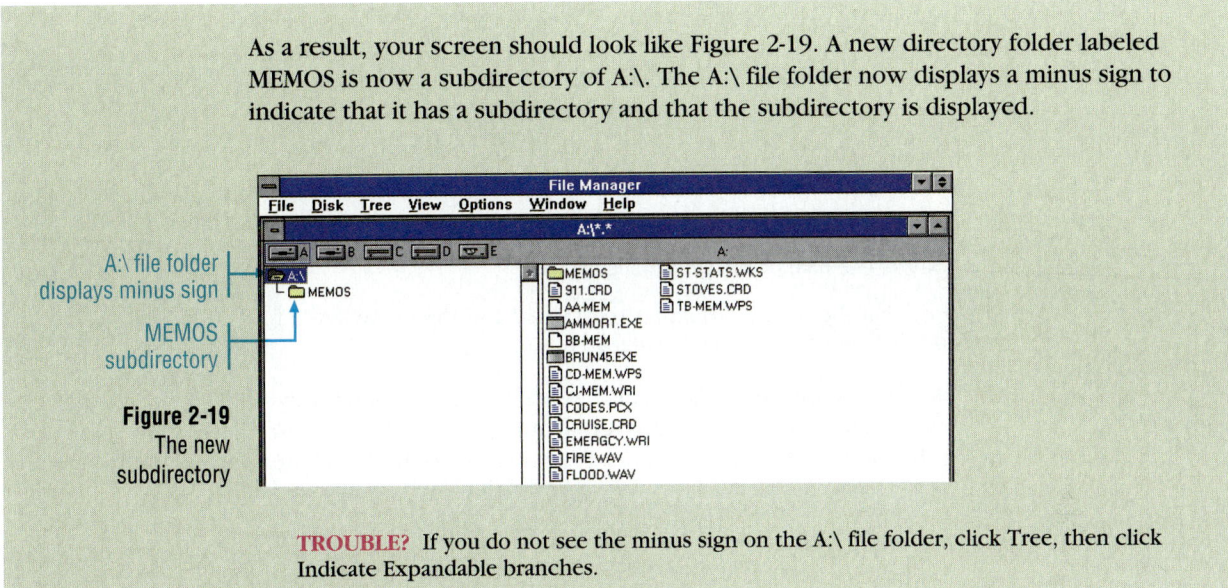

A:\ file folder displays minus sign

MEMOS subdirectory

Figure 2-19
The new subdirectory

TROUBLE? If you do not see the minus sign on the A:\ file folder, click Tree, then click Indicate Expandable branches.

Next Ruth will make a directory for the spreadsheets. She wants her directory tree to look like the one in Figure 2-20a, not the one in Figure 2-20b.

Figure 2-20a
SHEETS is a subdirectory of A:\

Figure 2-20b
SHEETS is a subdirectory of MEMOS

The spreadsheet directory should be a subdirectory of the root, *not* of MEMOS.

To make a directory for spreadsheets:

❶ Click the **directory folder icon for A:**.

❷ Click **File**, then click **Create Directory...**.

❸ In the text box type **SHEETS**, then click the **OK button**.

❹ Make sure that your newly updated directory tree resembles the one in Figure 2-20a. There should be two directories under A:\ — MEMOS and SHEETS.

TROUBLE? If your directory tree is structured like the one in Figure 2-20b, use your mouse to drag the SHEETS directory icon to the A:\ file folder icon.

Now Ruth's disk has a structure she can use to organize her files. It contains three directories: the root A:\, MEMOS, and SHEETS. Each directory can contain a list of files. Ruth is happy with this new structure, but she is not sure what the directories contain. She decides to look in one of the new directories to see what's there.

Changing Directories

When you change directories, you open a different directory folder. If the directory contains files, they will be displayed in the contents list.

First, Ruth wants to look in the MEMOS directory.

To change to the MEMOS directory:
❶ Click the **MEMOS directory file folder icon**.

Notice that the A:\ file folder icon is closed and the MEMOS file folder icon is open, indicating that the MEMOS directory is now current.

Look at the status line at the bottom of your screen. The left side of the status line shows you how much space is left on your disk. The right side of the status line tells you that no files are in the current directory, that is, in the MEMOS directory. This makes sense. You just created the directory, and haven't put anything in it.

❷ Click the **A:\ file folder icon** to change back to the root directory.

Expanding and Collapsing Directories

Notice on your screen that the A:\ file folder icon has a minus sign on it. As you know, the minus sign indicates that A:\ has one or more subdirectories and that those subdirectories are displayed. To look at a simplified directory tree, you would **collapse** the A:\ directory. You would **expand** a directory to redisplay its subdirectories. Ruth wants to practice expanding and collapsing directories.

To expand and then collapse a directory:
❶ Double-click the **A:\ file folder icon** to collapse the directory. As a result the MEMOS and SHEETS branches of the directory tree are removed and a plus sign appears on the A:\ file folder icon.
❷ Double-click the **A:\ file folder icon** again. This time the directory expands, displaying the MEMOS and SHEETS branches. Notice the minus sign on the A:\ file folder icon.

The Contents List

The **contents list** on the right side of the desktop contains the list of files and subdirectories for the current directory. On your screen the directory tree shows that A:\ is the current directory. The status bar shows that this directory contains 26 files and subdirectories. These files are listed in the contents list. Ruth recalls that she had to follow a set of rules when she created the names for these files. Let's find out more about these rules, since you will soon need to create names for your own files.

Filenames and Extensions

A **filename** is a unique set of letters and numbers that identifies a program, document file, directory, or miscellaneous data file. A filename may be followed by an **extension**, which is separated from the filename by a period.

The rules for creating valid filenames are as follows:
- The filename can contain a maximum of eight characters.
- The extension cannot contain more than three characters.
- Use a period only between the filename and the extension.
- Neither the filename nor extension can include any spaces.
- Do not use the following characters: / [ ] ; = " \ : | ,
- Do not use the following names: AUX, COM1, COM2, COM3, COM4, CON, LPT1, LPT2, LPT3, PRN, or NUL.

Ruth used the letters ST at the beginning of her spreadsheet filenames so she could remember that these files contain information on project Stealth. Ruth used the rest of each filename to describe more about the file contents. For example, ST-BUD is the budget for project Stealth, ST-R&D is the research and development cost worksheet for the project, and ST-STATS contains the descriptive statistics for the project. Ruth's memos, on the other hand, begin with the initials of the person who received the memo. She used MEM as part of the filename for all her memos. For example, the file CJMEM.WRI contains a memo to Charles Jackson.

The file extension usually indicates the category of information a file contains. We can divide files into two broad categories, program files and data files. **Program files** contain the programming code for applications and systems software. For example, the computer program that makes your computer run the WordPerfect word processor would be classified as a program file. Program files are sometimes referred to as **executable files** because the computer executes, or performs, the instructions contained in the files. A common filename extension for this type of file is .EXE. Other extensions for program files include .BAT, .SYS, .PIF, and .COM. In the contents list, program files are shown with a **program file icon**, like the one you see next to the file PATTERNS.EXE on your screen and in Figure 2-21.

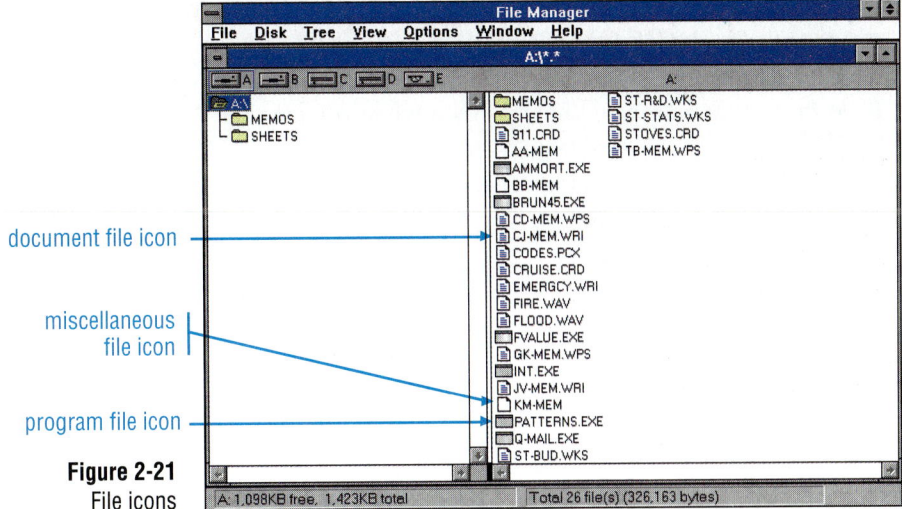

Figure 2-21
File icons

The second file category is data files. **Data files** contain the information with which you work: the memos, spreadsheets, reports, and graphs you create using applications such as word processors and spreadsheets. The filename extension for a data file usually indicates which application was used to create the file. For example, the file CD-MEM.WPS was created using the Microsoft Works word processor, which automatically puts the extension .WPS on any file you create with it. The use of .WPS as the standard extension for Works word processing documents creates an association between the application and the documents you create with it. Later, when you want to make modifications to your documents, Works can find them easily by looking for the .WPS extension.

Data files you create using a Windows application installed on your computer are shown in the contents list with a **document file icon** like the one you see next to CD-MEM.WPS on your screen. Data files you create using a non-Windows application or a Windows application that is not installed on your computer are shown in the contents list with a **miscellaneous file icon** like the one you see next to AA-MEM on your screen. AA-MEM was created using a non-Windows word processor.

Now that you have an idea of the contents for each of Ruth's files, you will be able to help her move them into the appropriate directory.

Moving Files

You can move files from one disk to another. You can also move files from one directory to another. When you move a file, the computer copies the file to its new location, then erases it from the original location. The File Manager lets you move files by dragging them on the screen or by using the File Manager menus.

Now that Ruth has created the MEMOS and SHEETS directories, the next step in organizing her disk is to put files in these directories. She begins by moving one of her memo files from the root directory A:\ to the MEMOS subdirectory. She decides to move JV-MEM.WRI first.

To move the file JV-MEM.WRI from A:\ to the MEMOS subdirectory:

❶ Position the pointer on the filename JV-MEM.WRI and click the mouse button to select it. On the left side of the status bar, the message "Selected 1 file(s) (1,408 bytes)" appears.

❷ Press the mouse button and hold it down while you drag the file icon to the MEMOS file folder in the directory tree.

❸ When the icon arrives at its target location, a box appears around the MEMOS file icon. Release the mouse button. Figure 2-22 on the following page illustrates this procedure.

Moving Files **WIN 53**

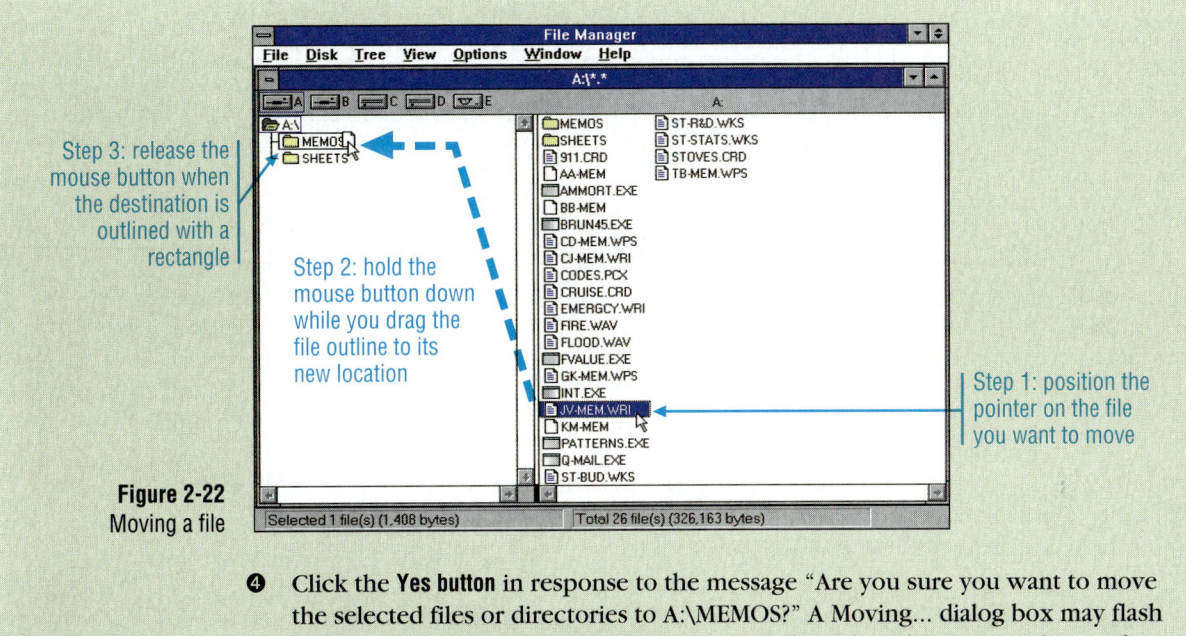

Figure 2-22
Moving a file

❹ Click the **Yes button** in response to the message "Are you sure you want to move the selected files or directories to A:\MEMOS?" A Moving... dialog box may flash briefly on your screen before the file is moved. Look at the contents list on the right side of the screen. The file JV-MEM.WRI is no longer there.

Ruth wants to confirm that the file was moved.

❺ Single click the **MEMOS file folder icon** in the directory tree on the left side of the screen. The file JV-MEM.WRI should be listed in the contents list on the right side of the screen.

TROUBLE? If JV-MEM.WRI is not in the MEMOS subdirectory, you might have moved it inadvertently to the SHEETS directory. You can check this by clicking the SHEETS directory folder. If the file is in SHEETS, drag it to the MEMOS directory folder.

❻ Click the **A:\file folder icon** to display the files in the root directory again.

Ruth sees that several memos are still in the root directory. She could move these memos one at a time to the MEMOS subdirectory, but she knows that it would be more efficient to move them as a group. To do this, she'll first select the files she wants to move. Then, she will drag them to the MEMOS directory.

To select a group of files:

❶ The directory A:\ should be selected on your screen and the files in this directory should be displayed in the right directory window. If this is not the case, click the directory icon for A:\.

❷ Click the filename **CD-MEM.WPS** to select it.

❸ Hold down **[Ctrl]** while you click the next filename you want to add to the group, **CJMEM.WRI**. Now two files should be selected. Ruth wants to select two more files.

❹ Hold down **[Ctrl]** while you click **GK-MEM.WPS**.

❺ Hold down **[Ctrl]** while you click **TB-MEM.WPS**. Release **[Ctrl]**. When you have finished selecting the files, your screen should look similar to Figure 2-23 on the following page. Notice the status bar message, "Selected 4 file(s) (4,590 bytes)."

WIN 54   TUTORIAL 2   Effective File Management

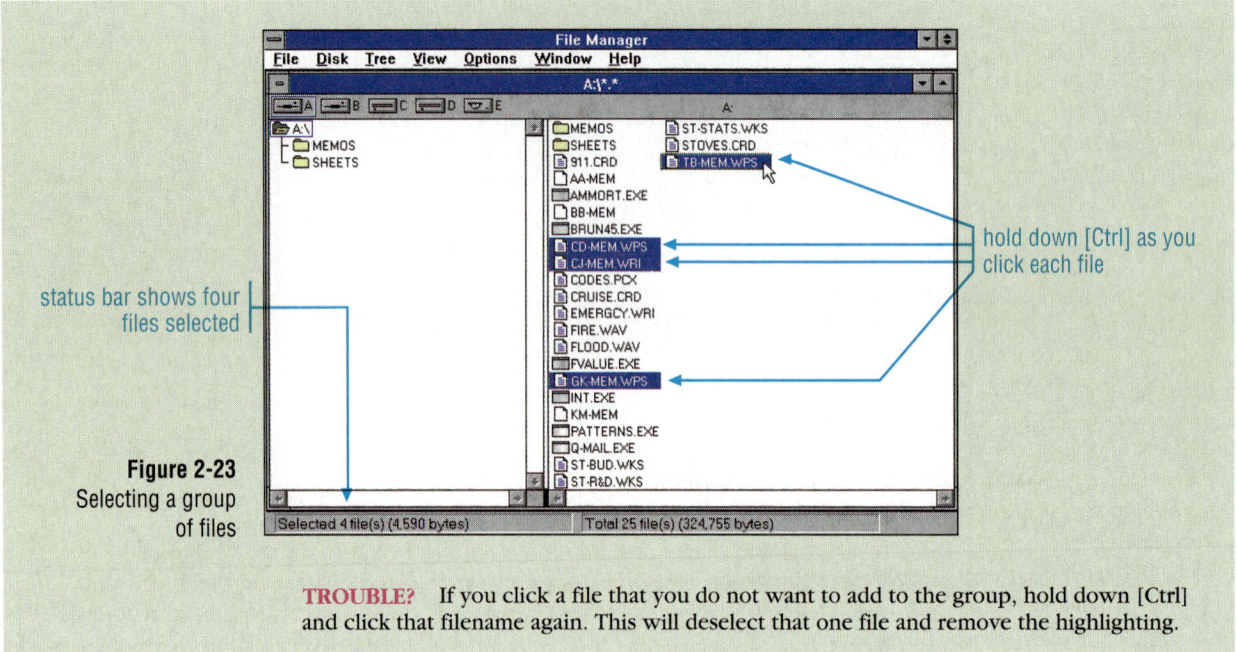

Figure 2-23
Selecting a group of files

> **TROUBLE?** If you click a file that you do not want to add to the group, hold down [Ctrl] and click that filename again. This will deselect that one file and remove the highlighting.

Now that Ruth has selected the files she wants to move, she can drag them to their new location.

To move a group of files:

❶ Position the pointer on any one of the highlighted filenames.

❷ Press the mouse button and drag the pointer, which now is attached to a multiple file icon, to the MEMOS directory icon. See Figure 2-24.

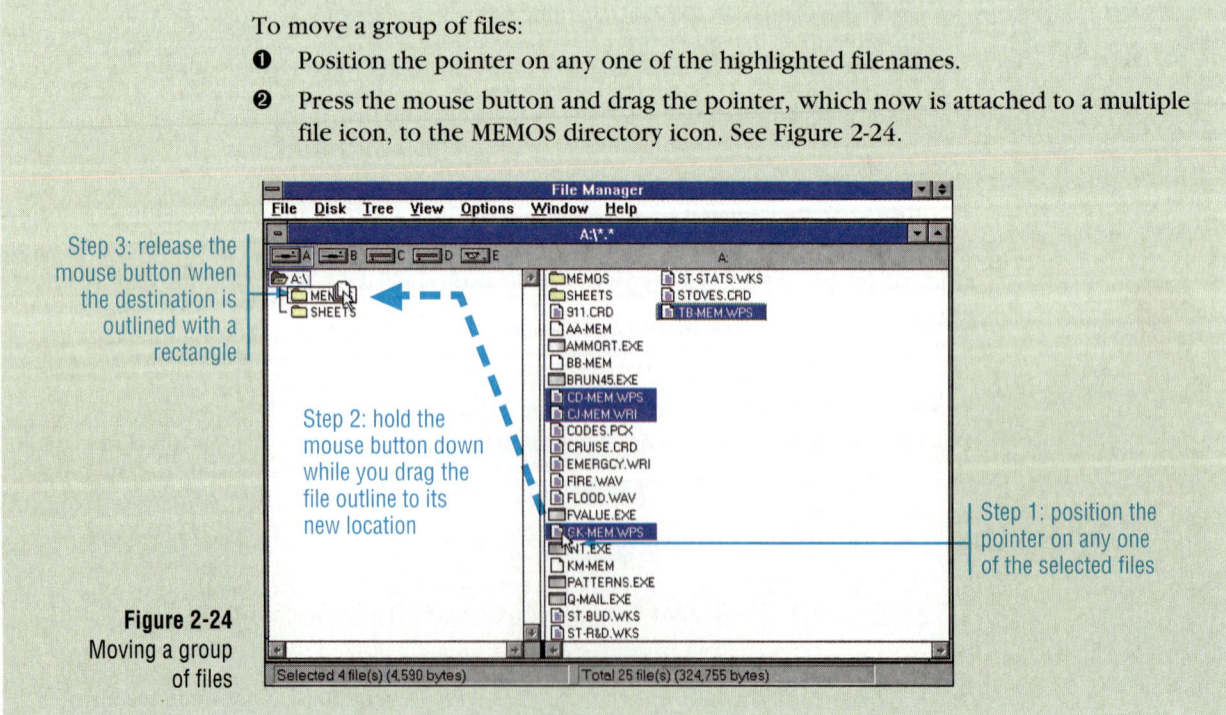

Figure 2-24
Moving a group of files

❸ When the you move the file icon onto the MEMOS directory, a box will outline the directory icon. Release the mouse button. The Confirm Mouse Operation dialog box appears.

❹ Click the **Yes button** to confirm that you want to move the files. After a brief period of activity on your disk drive, the contents list for the A:\ directory is updated and should no longer include the files you moved.

❺ Click the **MEMOS directory icon** to verify that the group of files arrived in the MEMOS directory.

❻ Click the **A:\ directory icon** to once again display the contents of the root directory.

Renaming Files

You may find it useful to change the name of a file to make it more descriptive of the file contents. Remember that Windows uses file extensions to associate document files with applications and to identify executable programs, so when you rename a file you should not change the extension.

Ruth looks down the list of files and notices ST-BUD.WKS, which contains the 1994 budget for project Stealth. Ruth knows that next week she will begin work on the 1995 budget. She decides that while she is organizing her files, she will change the name of ST-BUD.WKS to ST-BUD94.WKS. When she creates the budget for 1995, she will call it ST-BUD95.WKS so it will be easy to distinguish between the two budget files.

To change the name of ST-BUD.WKS to ST-BUD94.WKS:

❶ Click the filename **ST-BUD.WKS**.

❷ Click **File**, then click **Rename**. See Figure 2-25. The Rename dialog box shows you the current directory and the name of the file you are going to rename. Verify that the dialog box on your screen indicates that the current directory is A:\ and that the file you are going to rename is ST-BUD.WKS.

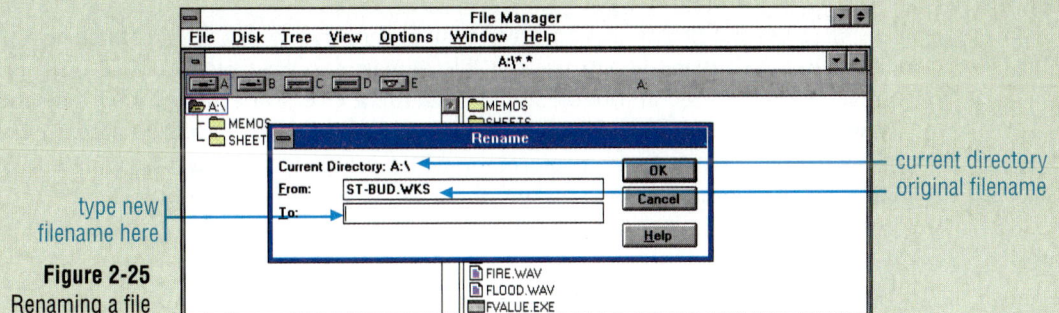

Figure 2-25
Renaming a file

TROUBLE? If the filename is not ST-BUD.WKS, click the Cancel button and go back to Step 1.

❸ In the To text box type **ST-BUD94.WKS** (using either uppercase or lowercase letters).

❹ Click the **OK button**.

❺ Check the file listing for ST-BUD94.WKS to verify that the rename procedure was successful.

Deleting Files

When you no longer need a file, it is good practice to delete it. Deleting a file frees up space on your disk and reduces the size of the directory listing you need to scroll through to find a file. A well-organized disk does not contain files you no longer need.

Ruth decides to delete the ST-STATS.WKS file. Although this file contains some statistics about the Stealth project, Ruth knows by looking at the file's date that those statistics are no longer current. She'll receive a new file from the Statistics department next week.

To delete the file ST-STATS.WKS:

❶ Click the filename **ST-STATS.WKS**.

❷ Click **File**, then click **Delete**. The Delete dialog box shows you that the file scheduled for deletion is in the A:\ directory and is called ST-STATS.WKS. See Figure 2-26.

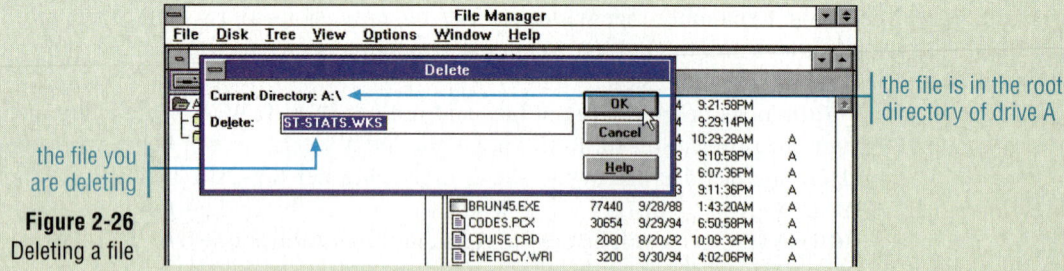

Figure 2-26
Deleting a file

TROUBLE? If the filename ST-STATS.WKS is not displayed in the Delete dialog box, click the Cancel button and go back to Step 1.

❸ Click the **OK button**. The Confirm File Delete dialog box appears. This is your last chance to change your mind before the file is deleted.

❹ Click the **Yes button** to delete the file. Look at the contents list to verify that the file ST-STATS.WKS has been deleted.

After using a floppy disk in drive A to experiment with the File Manager, Ruth feels more confident that she can use the File Manager to organize her hard disk. However, she feels slightly uncomfortable about something else. Ruth just learned that one of her co-workers lost several days worth of work when his computer had a hardware failure.

Ruth resolves to find out more about the problems that can cause data loss so she can take appropriate steps to protect the data files on her computer.

Data Backup

Ruth's initial research on data loss reveals that there is no totally fail-safe method to protect data from hardware failures, human error, and natural disasters. She does discover, however, some ways to reduce the risk of losing data. Every article Ruth reads emphasizes the importance of regular backups.

A **backup** is a copy of one or more files, made in case the original files are destroyed or become unusable. Ruth learns that Windows provides a Copy command and a Copy Disk command that she can use for data backup. Ruth decides to find out how these commands work, so she refers to the *Microsoft Windows User's Guide* which came with the Microsoft Windows 3.1 software. She quickly discovers that the Copy and Copy Disk commands are in the Windows File Manager.

To prepare the File Manager for data backup:

❶ If you are returning from a break, launch Windows if it is not currently running. Be sure you see the Program Manager window.

❷ Relaunch the File Manager if necessary. Make sure your Student Disk is in drive A.

TROUBLE? If you want to use drive B instead of drive A, substitute "B" for "A" in any steps when drive A is specified.

❸ Click the File Manager **maximize button** if the File Manager is not already maximized.

❹ If necessary, click the **drive A icon** on the drive ribbon to make drive A the default drive.

❺ Click **View** and be sure that a check mark appears next to All File Details.

❻ Click **Window**, then click **Tile**. As a result, your desktop should look similar to Figure 2-27. Don't worry if your list of directories and files is different from the one shown in the figures.

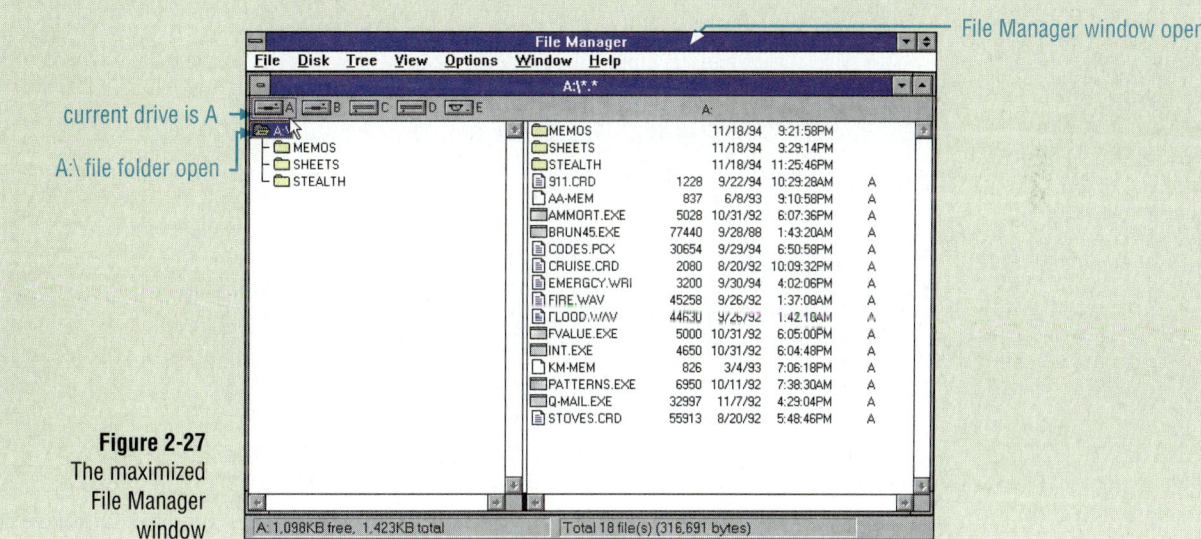

Figure 2-27
The maximized File Manager window

Now that Ruth has the File Manager window set-up, she decides to practice with the Copy command first.

The Copy Command

The Copy command duplicates a file in a new location. When the procedure has been completed, you have two files, your original and the copy. The additional copy of the file is useful for backup in case your original file develops a problem and becomes unusable.

The Copy command is different from the Move command, which you used earlier. The Move command deletes the file from its old location after moving it. When the move is completed, you have only one file.

If you understand the terminology associated with copying files, you will be able to achieve the results you want. The original location of a file is referred to as the **source**. The new location of the file is referred to as the **destination** or **target**.

You can copy one file or you can copy a group of files. In this Tutorial you will practice moving one file at a time. You can also copy files from one directory to another or from one disk to another. The disks you copy to and from do not need to be the same size. For backup purposes you would typically copy files from a hard disk to a disk.

Copying Files Using a Single Disk Drive

Ruth has been working on a spreadsheet called ST-BUD94.WKS for an entire week, and the data on this spreadsheet are critical for a presentation she is making tomorrow. The file is currently on a disk in drive A. Ruth will sleep much better tonight if she has an extra copy of this file. But Ruth has only one floppy disk drive. To make a copy of a file from one floppy disk to another, she must use her hard disk as a temporary storage location.

First, she will copy the file ST-BUD94.WKS to her hard disk. Then she will move the file to another floppy disk. Let's see how this procedure works.

To copy the file ST-BUD94.WKS from the source disk to the hard disk:

❶ Make sure your Student Disk is in drive A. Be sure you also have the backup disk you formatted earlier in the tutorial.

❷ Find the file ST-BUD94.WKS. It is in the root directory.

❸ Click the filename **ST-BUD94.WKS**.

❹ Click **File**, then click **Copy**.

TROUBLE? If you see a message that indicates you cannot copy a file to drive C, click the OK button. Your drive C has been write-protected, and you will not be able to copy ST-BUD94.WKS. Read through the copying procedure and resume doing the steps in the section entitled "Making a Disk Backup."

❺ Look at the ribbon of drive icons at the top of your screen. If you have an icon for drive C, type **C:** in the text box of the Copy dialog box. If you do not have an icon for drive C, ask your technical support person which drive you can use for a temporary destination in the file copy process, then type the drive letter.

❻ Confirm that the Copy dialog box settings are similar to those in Figure 2-28, then click the **OK button**. The file is copied to the root directory of drive C (or to the directory your technical support person told you to use).

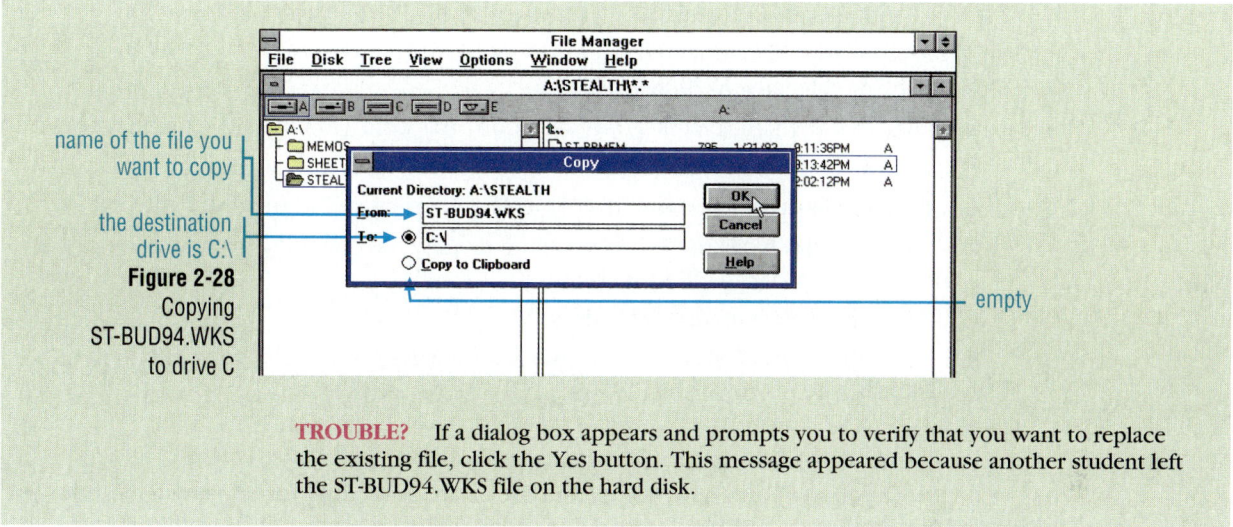

Figure 2-28
Copying ST-BUD94.WKS to drive C

TROUBLE? If a dialog box appears and prompts you to verify that you want to replace the existing file, click the Yes button. This message appeared because another student left the ST-BUD94.WKS file on the hard disk.

After the file has been copied to the hard disk, Ruth needs to switch disks. She will take her original disk out of drive A and replace it with the disk that will receive the copy of the ST-BUD94.WKS file. After Ruth switches disks, she must tell the File Manager to **refresh** the directory tree and the contents list so they show the files and directories for the disk that is now in the drive.

To switch disks and refresh the contents list:
1. Remove your Student Disk from drive A.
2. Put your Backup Disk in drive A.
3. Click the **drive A icon** on the drive ribbon to refresh the contents list. The directory tree will contain only the A:\ folder, because your backup disk does not have the directories you created for your original Student Disk.

Now let's look for the copy of ST-BUD94.WKS that is on drive C.

To locate the new copy of ST-BUD94.WKS:
1. Click the **drive C icon** (or the drive your technical support person told you to use).
2. Click the **C:\ file folder icon** (or the directory your technical support person told you to use).
3. If necessary, use the scroll bar on the side of the content list to find the file ST-BUD94.WKS in the contents list.

Now you need to move the file from the hard disk to the backup disk in drive A. You must use Move instead of Copy so you don't leave the file on your hard disk.

> To move the new file copy to drive A:
> ❶ Click the filename **ST-BUD94.WKS**.
> ❷ Click **File**, then click **Move**. (Don't use Copy this time.) A Move dialog box appears.
> ❸ Type **A:** in the text box.
> ❹ Click the **OK button**. As a result, ST-BUD94.WKS is moved to the disk in drive A.
> ❺ Click the **drive A icon** on the drive ribbon to view the contents list for the Backup disk. Verify that the file ST-BUD94.WKS is listed.
> ❻ Remove the Backup disk from drive A.
> ❼ Insert the **Student Disk** in drive A and click the **drive A icon** in the drive ribbon to refresh the contents listing.

Now you and Ruth have completed the entire procedure for copying a file from one disk to another on a single floppy disk system. In her research, Ruth also has discovered a Windows command for copying an entire disk. She wants to practice this command next.

Making a Disk Backup

The Windows Copy Disk command makes an exact duplicate of an entire disk. All the files and all the blank sectors of the disk are copied. If you have files on your destination disk, the Copy Disk command will erase them as it makes the copy so that the destination disk will be an exact duplicate of the original disk.

When you use the Copy Disk command, both disks must have the same storage capacity. For example, if your original disk is a 3.5-inch high-density disk, your destination disk also must be 3.5-inch high-density disk. For this reason, you cannot use the Copy Disk command to copy an entire hard disk to a floppy disk. If your computer does not have two disk drives that are the same size and capacity, the Copy Disk command will work with only one disk drive. When you back up the contents of one disk to another disk using only one disk drive, files are copied from the source disk into the random access memory (RAM) of the computer.

RAM is a temporary storage area on your computer's mother board which usually holds data and instructions for the operating system, application programs, and documents you are using. After the files are copied into RAM, you remove the source disk and replace it with the destination disk. The files in RAM are then copied onto the destination disk. If you don't have enough RAM available to hold the entire contents of the disk, only a portion of the source disk contents are copied during the first stage of the process, and the computer must repeat the process for the remaining contents of the disk.

Ruth wants to practice using the Copy Disk command to make a backup of a disk. She is going to make the copy using only one disk drive because she can use this procedure on both her computer at home, which has one disk drive, and her computer at work, which has two different-sized disk drives.

While Ruth makes a copy of her disk, let's make a backup of your Student Disk. After you learn the procedure, you'll be responsible for making regular backups of the work you do for this course. You should back up your disks at least once a week. If you are working on a particularly critical project, such as a term paper or a thesis, you might want to make backups more often.

Making a Disk Backup

To make a backup copy of your Student disk:

❶ Be sure your Student Disk is in drive A and that you have the disk you labeled Backup handy. If you want to be very safe, write-protect your source disk before continuing with this procedure. Remember, to write-protect a 5.25-inch disk, you place a tab over the write-protect notch. On a 3.5-inch disk you open the write-protect hole.

❷ Click **Disk**, then click **Copy Disk....** Confirm that the Copy Disk dialog box on your screen looks like the one in Figure 2-29. The dialog box should indicate that "Source In" is A: and "Destination In" is A:. If this is not the case, click the appropriate down-arrow button and select A: from the list. When the dialog box display is correct, click the **OK button**.

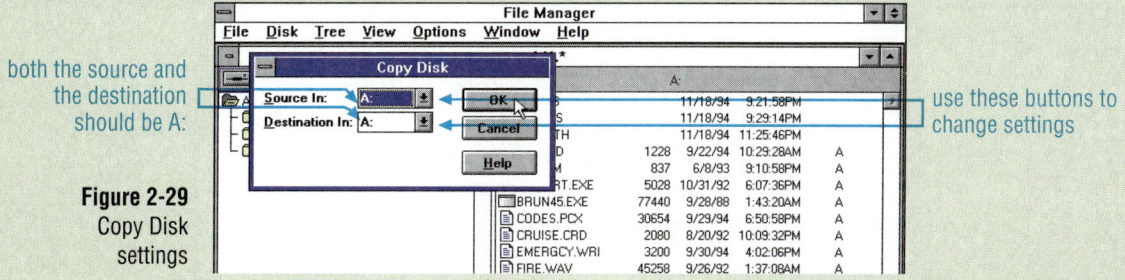

Figure 2-29
Copy Disk settings

both the source and the destination should be A:

use these buttons to change settings

❸ The Confirm Copy Disk dialog box reminds you that this operation will erase all data from the destination disk. It asks, "Are you sure you want to continue?"

❹ Click the **Yes button**. The next dialog box instructs you to "Insert source disk." Your source disk is the Student Disk and it is already in drive A.

❺ Click the **OK button**.

After a flurry of activity, the computer begins to copy the data from drive A into RAM. The Copying Disk dialog box keeps you posted on its progress.

❻ Eventually another message appears, telling you to "Insert destination disk." Take your Student Disk out of drive A and replace it with the disk you labeled Backup.

❼ Click the **OK button**. The computer copies the files from RAM to the destination disk.

Depending on how much internal memory your computer has, you might be prompted to switch disks twice more. Carefully follow the dialog box prompts, remembering that the *source* disk is your Student Disk and the *destination* disk is your Backup disk.

❽ When the Copy Disk operation is complete, the Copying Disk dialog box closes. If you write-protected your Student Disk in Step 1, you should unprotect it now; otherwise you won't be able to save data to the disk later.

As a result of the Copy Disk command, your Backup disk should be an exact duplicate of your Student Disk.

Ruth has completed her exploration of file management. Now, Ruth decides to finish for the day. If you are not going to proceed directly to the Tutorial Assignments, you should exit the File Manager.

To exit the File Manager:
❶ Click the File Manager **Control-menu box**.
❷ Click **Close**.
❸ If you want to exit Windows, click the **Program Manager Control-menu box**, then click **Close**, and finally click the **OK button**.

Questions

1. Which one of the following is not a characteristic of a file?
   a. It has a name.
   b. It is a collection of data.
   c. It is the smallest unit of data.
   d. It is stored on a device such as a floppy disk or a hard disk.
2. What process arranges the magnetic particles on a disk in preparation for data storage?
3. In which one of the following situations would formatting your disk be the least desirable procedure?
   a. You have purchased a new disk.
   b. You have difficulty doing a spreadsheet assignment, and you want to start over again.
   c. You want to erase all the old files from a disk.
   d. You want to recycle an old disk that was used on a non-IBM-compatible computer.
4. If the label on your 3.5 inch diskette says HD, what is its capacity?
   a. 360K
   b. 720K
   c. 1.2MB
   d. 1.44MB
5. The disk drive that is indicated by a rectangle on the drive ribbon is called the _____ drive or the _____ drive.
6. Refer to the File Manager window in Figure 2-30 on the following page. What is the name of each numbered window component?

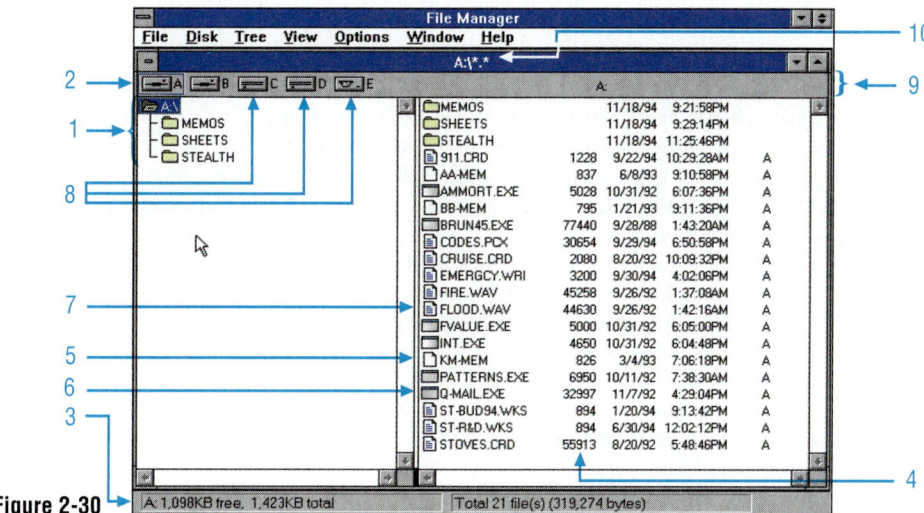

Figure 2-30

7. What is the directory that is automatically created when a disk is formatted?
8. What does a plus sign on a directory file folder icon indicate?
   a. The subdirectories are currently being displayed.
   b. The directory can be expanded.
   c. There are files in the directory.
   d. There are no subdirectories for this directory.
9. Indicate whether each of the following filenames is a valid or not valid Windows filename. If a filename is not valid, explain what is wrong.
   a. EOQ.WKS
   b. STATISTICS.WKS
   c. NUL.DOC
   d. VB-LET.DOC
   e. M
   f. M.M
   g. 92.BUD
   h. LET03/94
   i. CON.BMP
   d. Escape key

Tutorial Assignments

Launch Windows if necessary. Write your answers to Assignments 5, 6, 7, 8, 9, 11, 12, 13, and 14.
1. Move the two Microsoft Works spreadsheet files (.WKS extension) from the root directory to the SHEETS directory of your Student Disk.
2. You have a memo called BB-MEM that is about project Stealth. Now you need to change the filename to reflect the contents of the memo.
   a. Change the name to ST-BBMEM.
   b. Move ST-BBMEM into the MEMOS directory.
3. Create a directory called STEALTH under the root directory of your Student Disk. After you do this, your directory tree should look like Figure 2-30.
4. Now consolidate all the Stealth files.
   a. Move the file ST-BBMEM from the MEMOS directory to the STEALTH directory.

b. Move the files ST-BUD94.WKS and ST-R&D.WKS from the SHEETS directory to the STEALTH directory.
5. After doing Assignment 4, draw a diagram of your directory tree.
6. Make a list of the files that you now have in the MEMOS directory.
7. Make a list of the files that are in the SHEETS directory.
8. Make a list of the files that are in the STEALTH directory.
9. Describe what happens if you double-click the A:\ file folder icon.
10. Click to open the View menu and make sure the All File Details command has a check mark next to it.
11. Use the View menu to sort the files by date. What is the oldest file on your disk? (Be sure to look at all directories!)
12. Use the View menu to sort the files by type. Using this view, name the last file in your root directory contents list.
13. Use the View menu to sort the files by size. What is the name of the largest file on your Student Disk?
14. Change the current drive to C:, or, if you are on a network, to one of the network drives.
    a. Draw a diagram of the directory tree for this disk.
    b. List the filename of any files with .SYS, .COM, or .BAT extensions in the root directory of this disk.
    c. Look at the file icons in the contents list of the root directory. How many of the files are program files? Document files? Miscellaneous data files?
    d. Review the file organization tips that were in the article Ruth read. Write a short paragraph evaluating the organizational structure of your hard disk or network drive.

Windows Tutorials Index

A

Accessories icon, WIN 27
active directory, WIN 47
Alt key, WIN 22
application icon, WIN 15
applications
    filenames, WIN 52
    listing open, WIN 16
    switching, WIN 16-18
application window, WIN 12
    closing, WIN 14-15
    switching between, WIN 13

B

backup, WIN 56
Bold command, WIN 22, WIN 26
brush tool, WIN 28-29
buttons. *See* icons
byte, WIN 47

C

C:\, WIN 47
Cascade command, WIN 18
check box, WIN 24
check mark, WIN 20-21
child window, WIN 12. *See also* document window and window bar, WIN 13
Choose Picture command, WIN 21
Choose Slogan command, WIN 23-24
clicking, WIN 7
colon, WIN 47
colors, WIN 28
command buttons, WIN 24

commands, WIN 19
    availability, WIN 21
    grayed-out, WIN 21
computer, starting, WIN 4
contents list, WIN 47, WIN 50, WIN 59
Control menu, WIN 13
Copy command, WIN 56-60
Copy Disk command, WIN 56-57, WIN 60-61
copying files, WIN 56-60
Create Directory, WIN 48-49
CTI Win APPS, WIN 10-12
    system requirements, WIN 2
current directory, WIN 47

D

data files, WIN 52
    backup, WIN 56-57
Delete, WIN 56
desktop, WIN 3, WIN 5-6
destination, WIN 58, WIN 61
dialog box
    controls, WIN 24-26
directory, WIN 47-50
    changing, WIN 50
    collapsing, WIN 50
    creating, WIN 48-49
    expanding, WIN 50
    names, WIN 48
    tree, WIN 47-48, WIN 59
    window, WIN 46
disks
    backup, WIN 60-61
    capacities, WIN 42
    formatting, WIN 41-43
    naming, WIN 46-47

document window, WIN 12-13. *See also* child window
   organizing, WIN 18
double-clicking, WIN 8
dragging, WIN 9, WIN 52
drive icon, WIN 45
   ribbon, WIN 45
drives, WIN 45-46
   changing current, WIN 45-46

E

ellipsis (in menus), WIN 23-24
Enter key, WIN 25
.EXE, WIN 51. *See also* extensions
executable files, WIN 51
extensions, WIN 51-52, WIN 55

F

file folder icon, WIN 47
File Manager, WIN 37-41, WIN 57
   exiting, WIN 61-62
   moving files with, WIN 52-55
   settings, WIN 39-41
   window, WIN 46-47
filenames
   extensions, WIN 51-52
   invalid characters, WIN 51
files, WIN 38
   copying, WIN 56-60
   data, WIN 52
   deleting, WIN 56
   executable files, WIN 51
   listing, WIN 50
   moving, WIN 52-55
   moving a group, WIN 54-55
   naming, WIN 51
   organizing, WIN 48-50
   program, WIN 51

   renaming, WIN 55
   selecting a group, WIN 53-54
   transferring, WIN 43-44
Font, WIN 40-41
formatting, WIN 41-43

G

graphical user interface (GUI), WIN 3
group icons, WIN 6
GUI, see graphical user interface

H

Help facility, WIN 29-32
   Commands, WIN 31
   How To, WIN 31
   Tools, WIN 31
   tutorials, WIN 29

I

icons, WIN 6
   application, WIN 15
   group, WIN 6
insertion point, WIN 25
interface, WIN 3-4
Italic command, WIN 23, WIN 26

K

keyboard, WIN 9-11
   launching, WIN 9-12
   switching windows, WIN 17-18
   Tutorial, WIN 10
launching, WIN 4-5
linesize box, WIN 28
list box, WIN 24

M

maximizing windows, WIN 13-14
menu bar, WIN 13
Menu Practice program, WIN 19-26
menus, WIN 19-24
    and keyboard, WIN 22-23
    conventions, WIN 20-24
    opening and closing, WIN 20
minimizing windows, WIN 13, WIN 15
minus sign, WIN 48-49, WIN 50
mouse, WIN 6-9
    clicking, WIN 7
    double-clicking, WIN 8
    dragging, WIN 9
Move command, WIN 52-55, WIN 57
multi-tasking, WIN 4, WIN 12, WIN 18

O

OK button, WIN 25
option button, WIN 24
Options, WIN 40

P

Paintbrush, WIN 26-32
    help, 29-31
    launching, WIN 27
    tools, WIN 28-29
    window components, WIN 27-28
paint roller tool, WIN 29-32
palette, WIN 28
plus sign, WIN 48
pointer, WIN 6
    moving, WIN 7
    shapes, WIN 7, WIN 25, WIN 28
Position Picture command, WIN 21
program files, WIN 51
Program Manager, WIN 5-6

R

radio button. *See* option button
RAM (random access memory), WIN 60
Readme file, WIN 2
refresh, WIN 59
Rename, WIN 55
restore, WIN 13
root directory, WIN 47

S

selecting, WIN 7
shortcut keys, WIN 23
Show Picture command, WIN 20-21
source, WIN 58, WIN 61
spin bar, WIN 24
Student Disk
    preparing, WIN 2, WIN 43-44
subdirectory, WIN 47-48
    listing, WIN 50
    viewing, WIN 50
submenu, WIN 21

T

target, WIN 58
Task List, WIN 16
Text Attributes menu, WIN 22
text box, WIN 24
3-D effects, WIN 25
Tile command, WIN 18
title bar, WIN 13
toolbar, WIN 19
    description, WIN 26
toolbox, WIN 28
Tree, WIN 40

U

Underline command, WIN 22, WIN 26
underlined letter, WIN 22
Use Slogan, WIN 25

V

View, WIN 40
volume label, WIN 46-47

W

windows, WIN 6,
   active, WIN 13
   anatomy, WIN 12-13
   application, WIN 12
   child, WIN 12
   closing, WIN 18-19
   group, WIN 10
   resizing, WIN 13-16
Windows (Microsoft program)
   advantages, WIN 4
   basic controls, WIN 5-9
   exiting, WIN 33
   launching, WIN 4-5
   Users Guide, WIN 57
workspace, WIN 13
write protection, WIN 41

TASK REFERENCE
BRIEF MICROSOFT WINDOWS 3.1
Italicized page numbers indicate the first discussion of each task.

TASK	MOUSE	MENU	KEYBOARD
GENERAL / PROGRAM MANAGER			
Change dimensions of a window *WIN 15*	Drag border or corner	Click ▬, Size	Alt spacebar, S
Click *WIN 7*	Press mouse button, then release it		
Close a window *WIN 18*	Double-click ▬	Click ▬, Close	Alt spacebar, C or Alt F4
Double-click *WIN 8*	Click left mouse button twice		
Drag *WIN 9*	Hold left mouse button down while moving mouse		
Exit Windows *WIN 33*	Double-click Program Manager ▬, click OK	Click Program Manager ▬, Close, OK	Alt spacebar, C, Enter, or Alt F4, Enter
Help *WIN 30*		Click Help	F1 or Alt H
Launch Windows *WIN 4*			Type win and press Enter
Maximize a window *WIN 14*	Click ▲	Click ▬, Maximize	Alt spacebar, X
Minimize a window *WIN 14*	Click ▼	Click ▬, Minimize	Alt spacebar, N
Open a group window *WIN 10*	Double-click group icon	Click icon, click Restore	Ctrl F6 to group icon, Enter
Restore a window *WIN 14*	Click ⇕	Click ▬, Restore	Alt spacebar, R
Switch applications *WIN 16*		Click ▬, Switch To...	Alt Tab or Ctrl Esc
Switch documents *WIN 28*	Click the document	Click Window, click name of document	Alt W, press number of document
FILE MANAGER			
Change current/default drive *WIN 45*	Click 💾 on drive icon ribbon	Click Disk, Select Drive...	Alt D, S or Ctrl [drive letter]
Change current/default directory *WIN 50*	Click 📁		Press arrow key to directory
Collapse a directory *WIN 50*	Double-click 📁	Click Tree, Collapse Branch	-
Copy a file *WIN 58*	Hold Ctrl down as you drag the file	Click the filename, click File, Copy	F8
Create a directory *WIN 48*		Click File, Create Directory	Alt F, E
Delete a file *WIN 56*		Click the filename, click File, Delete	Click the filename, press Del, Enter
Diskette copy/backup *WIN 61*		Click Disk, Copy Disk...	Alt D, C

TASK REFERENCE
BRIEF MICROSOFT WINDOWS 3.1
Italicized page numbers indicate the first discussion of each task.

TASK	MOUSE	MENU	KEYBOARD
FILE MANAGER *(continued)*			
Exit File Manager WIN 62	Double-click File Manager	Click [—], Close	Alt F4
Expand a directory WIN 50	Double-click 📁	Click Tree, Expand Branch	[*]
Format a diskette WIN 41		Click Disk, Format Disk...	Alt D, F
Launch File Manager WIN 38	Double-click File Manager	Press arrow key to File Manager, click File, Open	Press arrow key to File Manager, Enter
Make Student Diskette WIN 43	Double-click Make Win 3.1 Student Diskette	Press arrow key to Make Win 3.1 Student Diskette, click File, Open	Press arrow key to Make Win 3.1 Student Diskette, Enter
Move a file WIN 52	Drag file to new directory	Click File, Move	F7
Rename a file WIN 55		Click File, Rename	Alt F, N
Select multiple files WIN 53	Hold Ctrl down and click filenames	Click File, Select Files...	Alt F, S
APPLICATIONS			
Exit application WIN 33	Double-click application	Click [—], Close	Alt F4
Launch application WIN 10	Double-click application icon	Press arrow key to icon, click File, Open	Press arrow key to icon, Enter

Microsoft Excel 5.0 for Windows™ Tutorials

1. **Using Worksheets to Make Business Decisions**
2. **Planning, Building, Testing, and Documenting Worksheets**
3. **Formatting and Printing**
4. **Functions, Formulas, and Absolute References**
5. **Charts and Graphing**
6. **Using Solver for Complex Problems**
7. **Managing Data with Excel**
8. **Working with Multiple Worksheets**
9. **Data Tables and Scenario Management**
10. **Integrating Excel with Other Windows Applications**
11. **Application Development with Macros and Visual Basic**

Additional Cases

Read This Before You Begin

To the Student

To use this book, you must have Student Disks. Your instructor will either provide you with them or ask you to make your own by following the instructions in the section "Making Your Excel Student Disks" in Tutorial 1. See your instructor or technical support person for further information. If you are going to work through this book using your own computer, you need a computer system running Microsoft Windows 3.1, Microsoft Excel 5.0 for Windows, and Student Disks. *You cannot complete the tutorials and exercises in this book using your own computer until you have the Student Disks.* You will need five blank, formatted disks. Label each with the appropriate tutorial number(s) based on the following table, which summarizes how the WinApps program will place files on your disks.

Student Disk	Tutorial(s)
1	1–7
2	8
3	9
4	10
5	11 and Additional Cases

To the Instructor

Making the Student Disks To complete the tutorials in this book, your students must have a copy of the Student Disks. To relieve you from making multiple Student Disks from master copies, we provide you with the CTI WinApps Setup Disks, which contain an automatic Student Disk generating program. Once you install the Setup Disks on a network or stand-alone workstation, students can easily make their own Student Disks by double-clicking the "Make Excel 5 Comprehensive Student Disks" icon in the CTI WinApps icon group. Double-clicking this icon transfers all the data files students will need to complete the tutorials, Tutorial Assignments, Case Problems, and Additional Cases to high-density disks in drive A or B. If some of your students will use their own computers to complete the tutorials and exercises in this book, they must first get the Student Disks. The section called "Making Your Excel Student Disks" in Tutorial 1 provides complete instructions on how to make the Student Disks.

Installing the CTI WinApps Setup Disks To install the CTI WinApps icon group from the Setup Disks, follow the instructions inside the disk envelope that was bundled with your book. By adopting this book, you are granted a license to install this software on any computer or computer network used by you or your students.

README File A README.TXT file located on one of the Setup Disks provides additional technical notes, troubleshooting advice, and tips for using the CTI WinApps software in your school's computer lab. You can view the README.TXT file using any word processor you choose.

Microsoft Excel Installation

Make sure the Microsoft Excel software has been installed on your computer using the complete setup option, rather than the laptop or typical installation. Tutorial 6 requires access to Excel's Solver. Tutorials 7 and 10 require the MS Query add-in and the PivotTable Wizard. Make sure the video driver is set to 16-color to avoid VRAM problems when using ChartWizard.

System Requirements

The minimum software and hardware requirements for your computer system are as follows:
- Microsoft Windows Version 3.1 or later on a local hard drive or a network drive.
- A 286 or higher processor with at least 4 MB RAM.
- A mouse supported by Windows 3.1.
- A printer supported by Windows 3.1.
- A VGA 64 × 480 16-color display is recommended; an 800 × 600 or 1024 × 768 SVGA, VGA monochrome, or EGA display is acceptable.
- At least 9 MB free hard disk space for a laptop (minimum) installation. A complete setup requires 24 MB free hard disk space.
- Student workstations with at least 1 high-density disk drive.
- If you want to install the CTI WinApps Setup Disks on a network drive, your network must support Microsoft Windows.

T U T O R I A L   1

OBJECTIVES

In this tutorial you will:
- Make Excel Student Disks
- Launch and exit Excel
- Discover how Excel is used in business
- Identify the major components of the Excel window
- Open, save, print, and close a worksheet
- Correct mistakes and use the Undo button
- Use an Excel decision-support worksheet
- Scroll a worksheet
- Split a worksheet window
- Create, save, and print a chart
- Learn how Excel uses values, text, formulas, and functions

Using Worksheets to Make Business Decisions

Evaluating Sites for a World-Class Golf Course

CASE

InWood Design Group In Japan, golf is big business. Spurred by the Japanese passion for the sport, golf is enjoying unprecedented popularity. But in that small mountainous country of 12 million golfers, there are fewer than 2,000 courses, the average fee for 18 holes on a public course is between $200 and $300, and golf club memberships are bought and sold like stock shares. The market potential is phenomenal, but building a golf course in Japan is expensive because of inflated property values, difficult terrain, and strict environmental regulations.

InWood Design Group is planning to build a world-class golf course, and one of the four sites under consideration for the course is in Chiba Prefecture, Japan. The other possible sites are Kauai, Hawaii; Edmonton, Canada; and Scottsdale, Arizona. Mike Mazzuchi and Pamela Kopenski are members of the InWood Design Group site selection team. The team is responsible for collecting information on the sites, evaluating that information, and recommending the best site for the new golf course.

The team identified five factors that are likely to determine the success of a golf course: climate, competition, market size, topography, and transportation. The team collected information on these factors for each of the four potential golf course sites. The next step is to analyze the information and make a site recommendation to management.

Using Microsoft Excel 5.0 for Windows, Mike created a worksheet that the team can use to evaluate the four sites. He will bring the worksheet to the next meeting to help the team evaluate the sites and reach a decision.

In this tutorial you will learn how to use Excel as you work along with the InWood team to select the best site for the golf course.

Using the Tutorials Effectively

The tutorials will help you learn about Microsoft Excel 5.0. They are designed to be used at your computer. Begin by reading the text that explains the concepts. Then when you come to the numbered steps, follow the steps on your computer. Read each step carefully and completely before you try it.

As you work, compare your screen with the figures to verify your results. Don't worry if your screen display differs slightly from the figures. The important parts of the screen display are labeled in each figure. Just make sure you have these parts on your screen.

Don't worry about making mistakes; that's part of the learning process. **TROUBLE?** paragraphs identify common problems and explain how to get back on track. You should complete the steps in the **TROUBLE?** paragraph *only* if you are having the problem described.

After you read the conceptual information and complete the steps, you can do the exercises found at the end of each tutorial in the sections entitled "Questions," "Tutorial Assignments," and "Case Problems." The exercises are carefully structured to help you review what you learned in the tutorials and apply your knowledge to new situations.

When you are doing the exercises, refer back to the Reference Window boxes. These boxes, which are found throughout the tutorials, provide you with short summaries of frequently used procedures. You can also use the Task Reference at the end of the tutorials; it summarizes how to accomplish tasks using the mouse, the menus, and the keyboard.

Before you begin the tutorials, you should know how to use the menus, dialog boxes, Help facility, Program Manager, and File Manager in Microsoft Windows. Course Technology, Inc. publishes two excellent texts for learning Windows: *A Guide to Microsoft Windows 3.1* and *An Introduction to Microsoft Windows 3.1*.

Making Your Excel Student Disks

Before you can work along with the InWood design team, you need to make Student Disks that contain all the practice files you need for the tutorials, the Tutorial Assignments, the Case Problems, and the Additional Cases. If your instructor or technical support person provides you with your Student Disks, you can skip this section and go to the section entitled "Launching Excel." If your instructor asks you to make your own Student Disks, you need to follow the steps in this section.

To make your Student Disks you need:
- Five blank, formatted, high-density 3.5-inch or 5.25-inch disks
- A computer with Microsoft Windows 3.1, Microsoft Excel 5.0, and the CTI WinApps group icon installed on it

If you are using your own computer, the CTI WinApps group icon will not be installed on it. Before you proceed, you must go to your school's computer lab and use a computer with the CTI WinApps group icon installed on it to make your Student Disks. Once you have made your own Student Disks, you can use them to complete all the tutorials and exercises in this book on any computer you choose.

To make your Excel Student Disks:

❶ Launch Windows and make sure the Program Manager window is open.

TROUBLE? The exact steps you follow to launch Microsoft Windows 3.1 might vary depending on how your computer is set up. On many computer systems, type WIN then press [Enter] to launch Windows. If you don't know how to launch Windows, ask your technical support person.

❷ Place your formatted disk for Tutorials 1–7 in drive A.

TROUBLE? If your computer has more than one disk drive, drive A is usually on top. If your Student Disk does not fit into drive A, then place it in drive B and substitute "drive B" anywhere you see "drive A" in the tutorial steps.

❸ Look for an icon labeled "CTI WinApps" like the one in Figure 1-1 or a window labeled "CTI WinApps" like the one in Figure 1-2.

TROUBLE? If you cannot find anything labeled "CTI WinApps," the CTI software might not be installed on the computer you are using. See your technical support person for assistance.

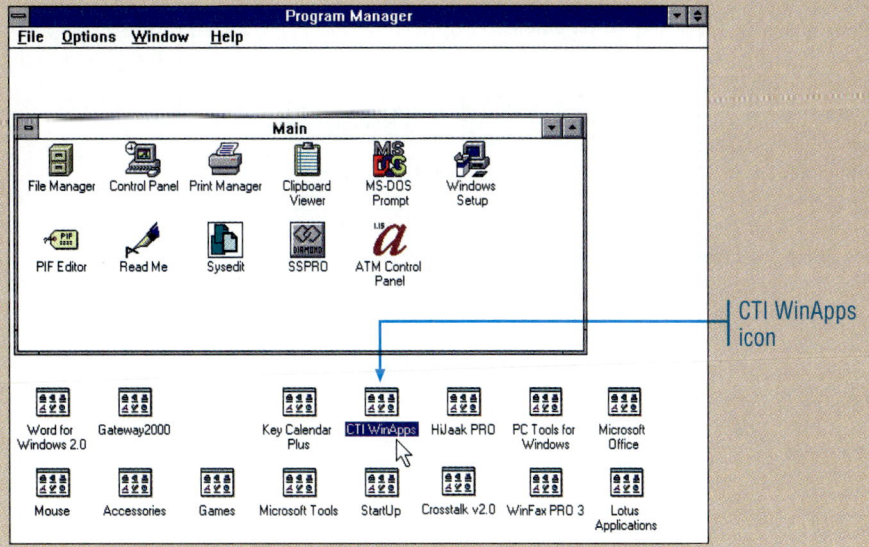

Figure 1-1 The CTI WinApps icon

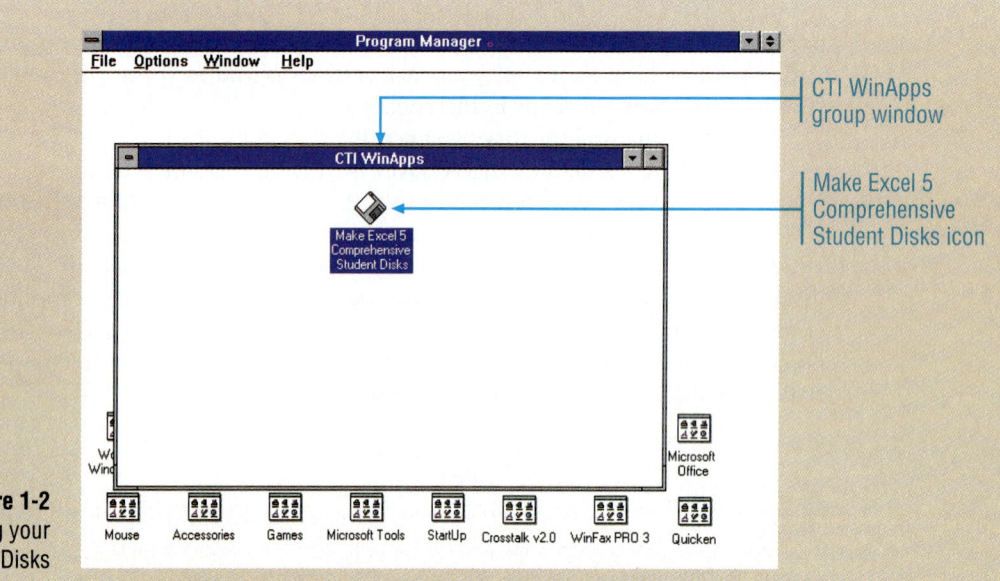

Figure 1-2
Making your Excel Student Disks

4. If you see an icon labeled "CTI WinApps," double-click the **CTI WinApps icon** to open the CTI WinApps group window. If the CTI WinApps window is already open, go to Step 5.

5. Double-click the **Make Excel 5 Comprehensive Student Disks icon**. The Make Excel 5 Comprehensive Student Disks window opens. See Figure 1-3.

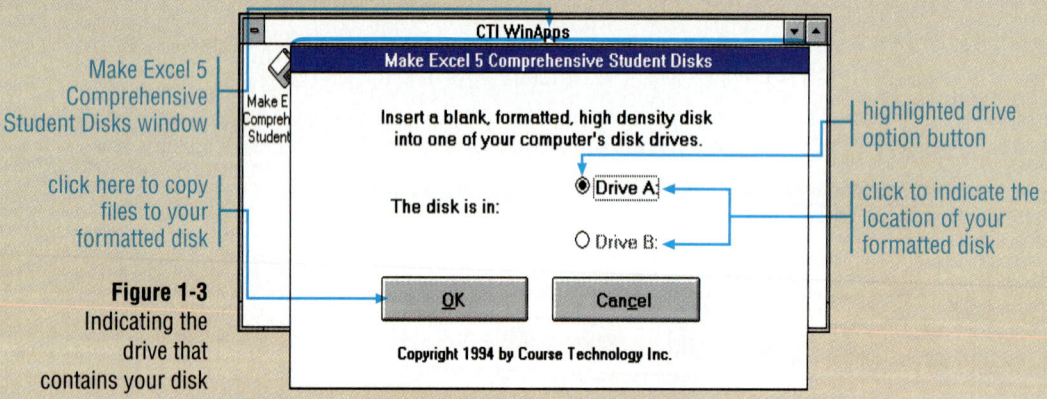

Figure 1-3
Indicating the drive that contains your disk

6. Make sure the drive that contains your disk corresponds to the drive option button that is highlighted in the dialog box on your screen. Click the **OK button**.

   Follow the directions on the screen to create your Student Disks. Refer to the table in the section "Read This Before You Begin" for more information about the number of disks you'll need and how to label them.

7. When the copying is complete, a message indicates the number of files copied to your disk. Click the **OK button**.

8. When you are finished copying disks, double-click the **Control menu box** on the CTI WinApps window to close it.

The files you need to complete the Excel tutorials and exercises are on your Student Disks. From now on, you will be instructed to open files on your Student Disk. Make sure you use the correct Student Disk for the tutorial you are completing. Refer to the table in the "Read This Before You Begin" section if you are not sure which disk to use.

Launching Excel

Mike arrives at the meeting a few minutes early so he can open his laptop computer and connect it to the large screen monitor in the company conference room. In a few moments Windows is up and running, Mike launches Excel, and the meeting is ready to begin.

Let's launch Excel to follow along with Mike as he works with the design team to make a decision about the golf course site.

To launch Excel:

❶ Look for an icon or window titled "Microsoft Office." See Figure 1-4.

TROUBLE? If you don't see anything called "Microsoft Office," click Window on the menu bar and, if you find "Microsoft Excel 5.0" in the list, click it. If you still can't find anything called "Microsoft Excel 5.0," ask your technical support person for help on how to launch Excel. If you are using your own computer, make sure the Excel software has been installed.

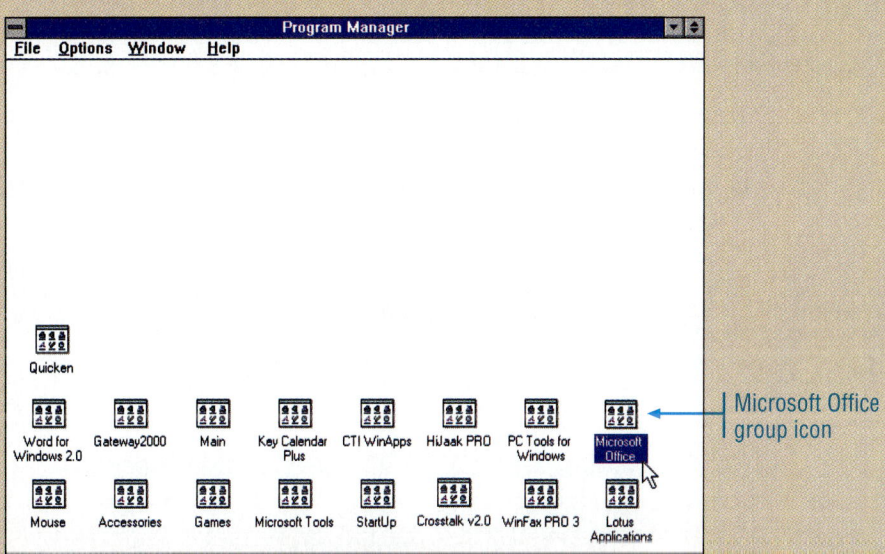

Figure 1-4
Launching Excel

❷ If you see the Microsoft Office group icon, double-click the **Microsoft Office group icon** to open the group window. If you see the Microsoft Office *group window* instead of the *group icon*, go to Step 3.

❸ Double-click the **Microsoft Excel program-item icon**. After a short pause, the Excel copyright information appears in a box and remains on the screen until Excel is ready for use. Excel is ready when your screen looks similar to Figure 1-5. Don't worry if your screen doesn't look *exactly* the same as Figure 1-5. You are ready to continue when you see the Excel menu bar.

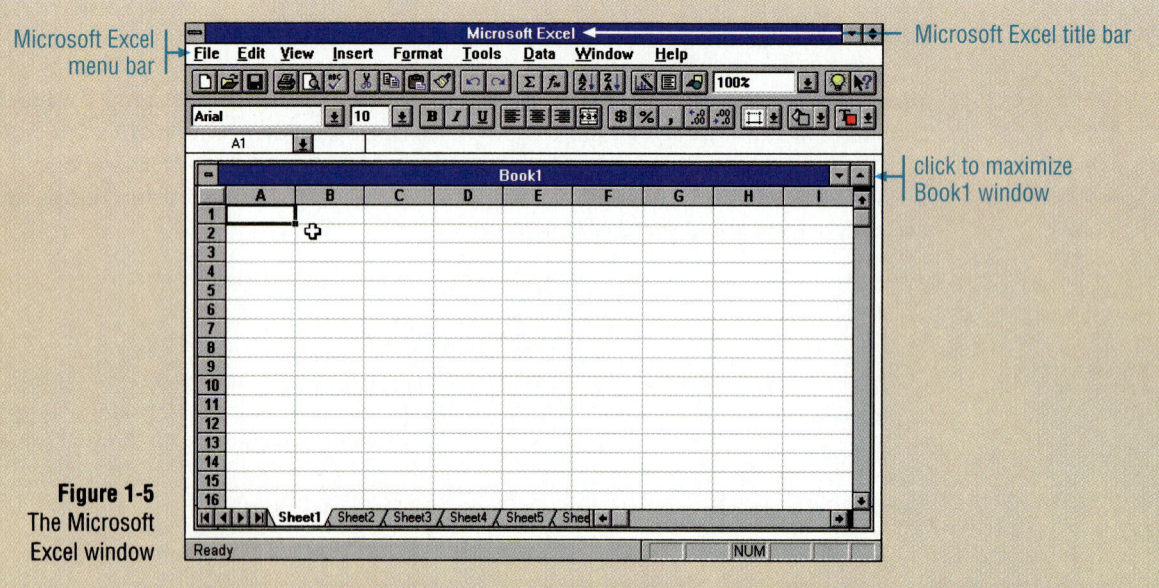

Figure 1-5
The Microsoft Excel window

4. Click the **application window Maximize button** if your Microsoft Excel application window is not maximized.

5. Click the **document window Maximize button** to maximize the Book1 window. Figure 1-6 shows the maximized Microsoft Excel and Book1 windows.

   TROUBLE? Your screen might display a little more or a little less of the grid shown in Figure 1-6 if you are using a display type that is different from the one used to produce the figures in the tutorials. This should not be a problem as you continue with the tutorial.

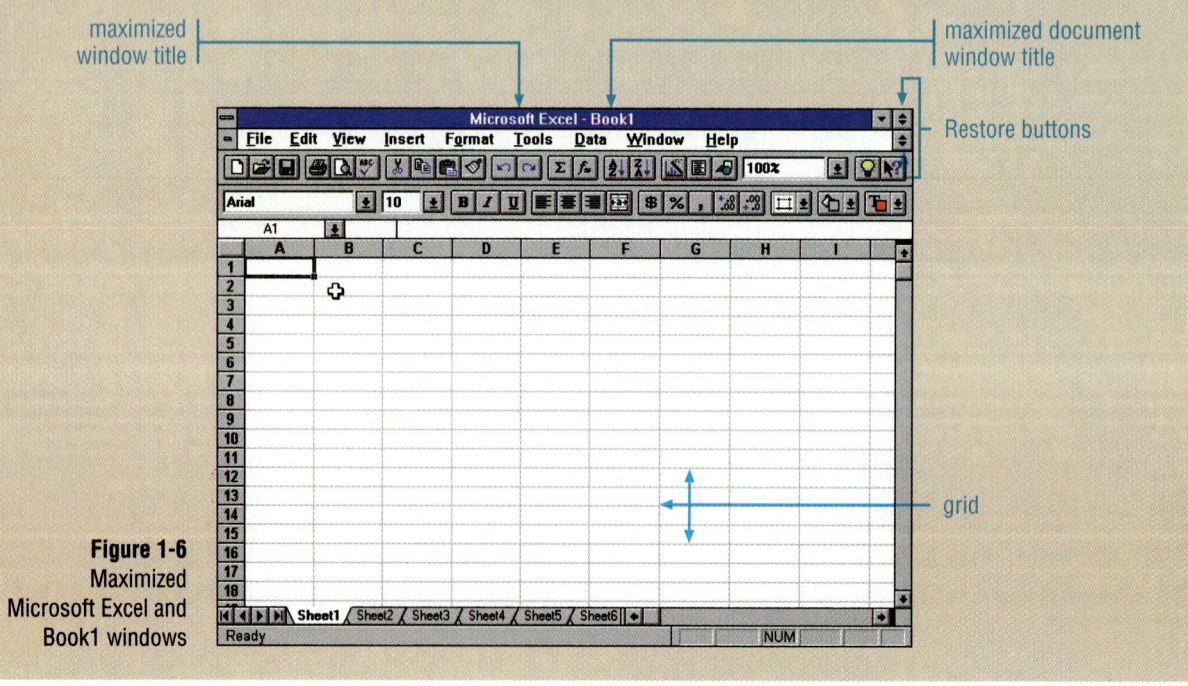

Figure 1-6
Maximized Microsoft Excel and Book1 windows

What Is Excel?

Excel is a computerized spreadsheet. A **spreadsheet** is an important business tool that helps you analyze and evaluate information. Spreadsheets are often used for cash flow analysis, budgeting, decision making, cost estimating, inventory management, and financial reporting. For example, an accountant might use a spreadsheet for a budget like the one in Figure 1-7.

Cash Budget Forecast

	January Estimated	January Actual
Cash in Bank (Start of Month)	$1,400.00	$1,400.00
Cash in Register (Start of Month)	100.00	100.00
Total Cash	$1,500.00	$1,500.00
Expected Cash Sales	$1,200.00	$1,420.00
Expected Collections	400.00	380.00
Other Money Expected	100.00	52.00
Total Income	$1,700.00	$1,852.00
Total Cash and Income	$3,200.00	$3,352.00
All Expenses (for Month)	$1,200.00	$1,192.00
Cash Balance at End of Month	$2,000.00	$2,160.00

Figure 1-7
A budget spreadsheet

To produce the spreadsheet in Figure 1-7, you could manually calculate the totals and then type your results, or you could use a computer and spreadsheet program to perform the calculations and print the results. Spreadsheet programs are also referred to as spreadsheet applications, electronic spreadsheets, computerized spreadsheets, or just spreadsheets.

In Excel 5.0, the document you create is called a **workbook.** You'll notice that the document currently on your screen is titled Book1, which is short for Workbook #1. Each workbook is made up of individual worksheets, or **sheets,** just as a spiral notebook is made up of sheets of paper. You'll learn more about using multiple sheets in later tutorials. For now, just keep in mind that the terms "worksheet" and "sheet" are often used interchangeably.

The Excel Window

Excel operates like most other Windows programs. If you have used other Windows programs, many of the Excel window controls will be familiar. Figure 1-8 shows the main components of the Excel window. Let's take a look at these components so you are familiar with their location.

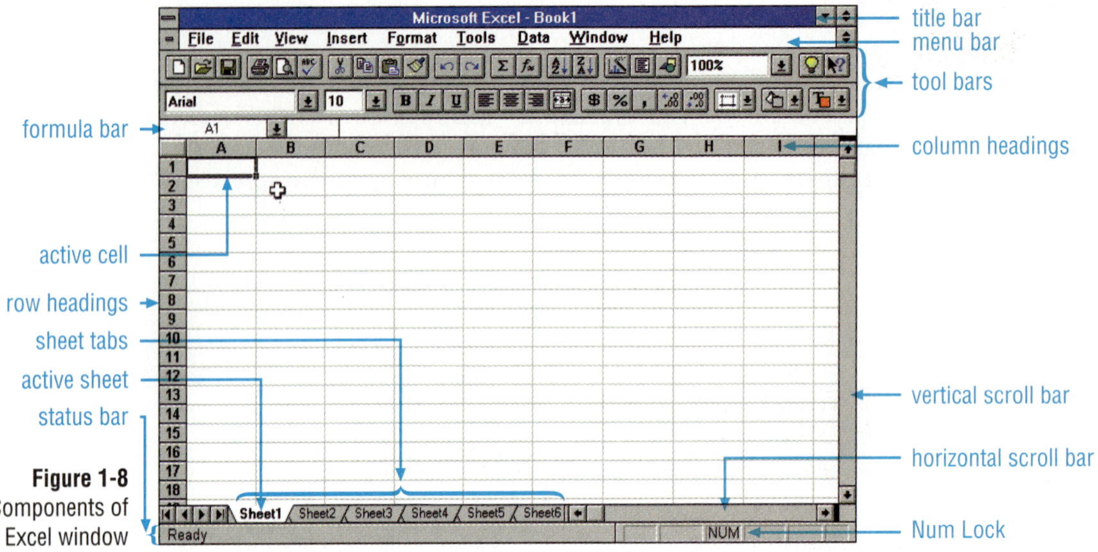

Figure 1-8 Components of the Excel window

Labels: title bar, menu bar, tool bars, column headings, vertical scroll bar, horizontal scroll bar, Num Lock, formula bar, active cell, row headings, sheet tabs, active sheet, status bar

The Title Bar

The **title bar** at the top of a window identifies the window. On your screen and in Figure 1-8 the title bar displays "Microsoft Excel - Book1." The title of the application window is "Microsoft Excel." Because the document window is maximized, the title of the document window, "Book1," is also displayed on the title bar.

The Menu Bar

The **menu bar** is located directly below the title bar. Each word in the menu bar is the title of a menu you can open to display a list of commands and options. The menu bar provides easy access to all the features of the Excel spreadsheet program.

The Toolbars

Two row of square buttons (or tools) and drop-down list boxes, located below the menu bar, make up the **toolbars**. These buttons and boxes provide shortcuts for accessing the most commonly used features of Excel.

The Formula Bar

The **formula bar**, located immediately below the toolbars, displays the data you enter or edit.

The Worksheet Window

The document window, usually referred to as the **worksheet window**, contains the sheet you are creating, editing, or using. The worksheet window includes a series of vertical columns indicated by lettered **column headings** and a series of horizontal rows indicated by numbered **row headings**.

A **cell** is the rectangular area at the intersection of a column and row. Each cell is identified by a **cell reference**, which is its column and row location. For example, the cell reference B6 indicates the cell at the intersection of column B and row 6. The column letter is always specified first in the cell reference. B6 is a correct cell reference, but 6B is not.

In Figure 1-8 the active cell is A1. The **active cell**, indicated by a black border, is the cell you have selected to work with. You can change the active cell when you want to work in a different location on the worksheet.

The Pointer

The **pointer** is the indicator that moves on your screen as you move your mouse. The pointer changes shape to indicate the type of task you can perform at a particular location. When you click a mouse button, something happens at the location of the pointer. In Figure 1-8 the pointer, which is located in cell B3, looks like a white plus sign. Let's see what other shapes the pointer can assume.

To explore pointer shapes:
❶ Move the pointer slowly down the row numbers on the far left of the workbook window. Then move it slowly, from left to right, across the formula bar. Notice how the pointer changes shape as you move it over different parts of the window. Do *not* click the mouse button yet. You will have a chance to do so later in the tutorial. You can also use the pointer to display the name of each button in the tool bar. This is helpful when you can't remember the function of a button.
❷ Move the pointer to the Cut button. After a short pause, the name of the button—"Cut"—appears just below the pointer. The message "Cuts selection and places it onto Clipboard" appears in the status bar.

Scroll Bars and Sheet Tabs

The **vertical scroll bar** (on the far right side of the workbook window) and the **horizontal scroll bar** (in the lower-right corner of the workbook window) allow you to move quickly around the worksheet. The **sheet tabs** allow you to move quickly between sheets by simply clicking on the sheet tab. Again, you'll learn how to use the sheet tabs in later tutorials.

The Status Bar

The **status bar** is located at the bottom of the Excel window. The left side of the status bar provides a brief description of the current command or task in progress. The right side of the status bar shows the status of important keys such as Caps Lock and Num Lock. In Figure 1-8 the status bar shows that the Num Lock mode is in effect, which means you can use your numeric keypad to enter numbers.

Opening a Workbook

When you want to use a workbook you have previously created, you must first open it. When you **open a workbook**, a copy of the workbook file is transferred into the random access memory (RAM) of your computer and displayed on your screen. Figure 1-9 shows that when you open a workbook called "GOLF.XLS," Excel copies the file from the hard drive or disk into RAM. When the workbook is open, GOLF.XLS is both in RAM and on the disk.

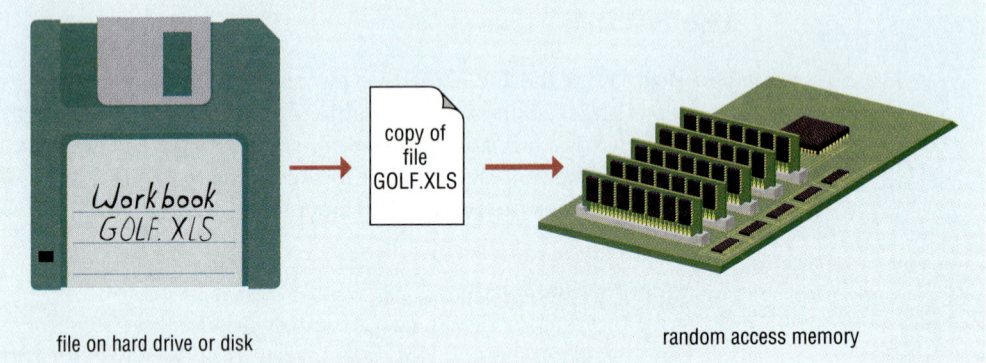

Figure 1-9
Opening a workbook

After you open a workbook, you can view, edit, print, or save it again on your disk.

REFERENCE WINDOW

Opening a Workbook

- Click the Open button on the Excel toolbar.

  or

  Click File, then click Open....

- Make sure the Drives box displays the icon for the drive that contains the workbook you want to open.

- Make sure the Directories box shows an open file folder for the directory that contains the workbook you want to open.

- Double-click the filename that contains the workbook you want to open.

Mike created a worksheet to help the site selection team evaluate the four potential locations for the golf course. The workbook, GOLF.XLS, is stored on your Student Disk. Let's open this file to display Mike's worksheet.

To open the GOLF.XLS workbook:

1. Make sure your Excel Student Disk is in drive A.

   TROUBLE? If you don't have a Student Disk, then you need to get one. Your instructor will either give you one or ask you to make your own by following the steps described earlier in this tutorial in "Making Your Excel Student Disk." See your instructor or technical support person for information.

Opening a Workbook **EX 13**

> **TROUBLE?** If your Student Disk won't fit in drive A, then try drive B. If drive B is the correct drive, then substitute "drive B" for "drive A" throughout these tutorials.

❷ Click the **Open button** to display the Open dialog box. Figure 1-10 shows the location of the Open button and the correct dialog box settings for opening the GOLF.XLS workbook.

> **TROUBLE?** If the a: drive icon is not displayed in the Drives box, click the down arrow button on the Drives box; then from the list of drives, click the a: drive icon.

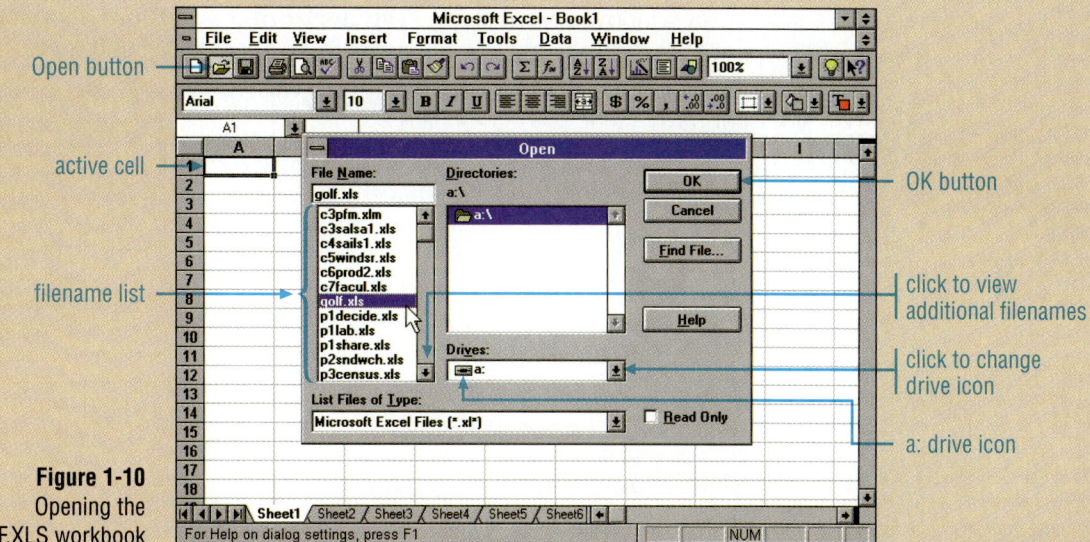

Figure 1-10
Opening the GOLF.XLS workbook

❸ Double-click the filename **GOLF.XLS** in the File Name list. The GOLF.XLS workbook appears. See Figure 1-11.

> **TROUBLE?** If you do not see GOLF.XLS in the File Name list, use the scroll bar to view additional filenames.

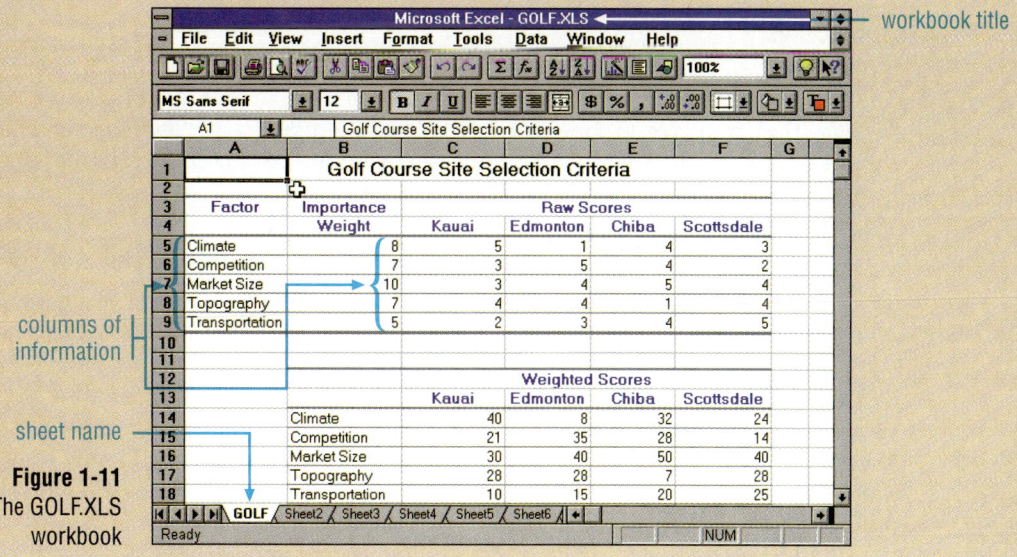

Figure 1-11
The GOLF.XLS workbook

Mike's worksheet contains columns of information and a chart. To see the chart you must scroll the worksheet.

Scrolling the Worksheet

The worksheet window has a horizontal scroll bar and a vertical scroll bar, as shown in Figure 1-12. The **vertical scroll bar**, located at the right edge of the worksheet window, moves the worksheet window up and down. The **horizontal scroll bar**, located at the lower-right corner of the worksheet window, moves the worksheet left and right.

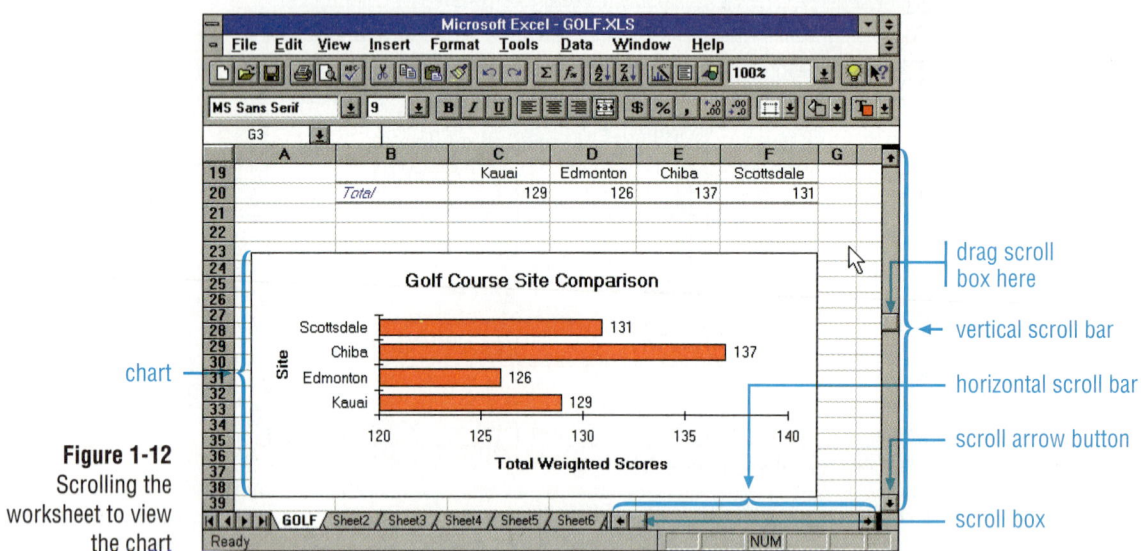

Figure 1-12
Scrolling the worksheet to view the chart

You click the scroll arrow buttons on the scroll bar to move the window one row or column at a time. You drag the **scroll box** to move the window more than one row or column at a time. Let's scroll the worksheet to view the chart.

To scroll the worksheet to view the chart:

❶ Drag the scroll box on the vertical scroll bar about half way down the screen. Release the mouse button. The worksheet window displays the section of the worksheet that contains the chart. See Figure 1-12.

   TROUBLE? If you drag the scroll box too far, or if the chart is not positioned like the one in Figure 1-12, use the scroll arrow buttons or scroll box until your screen matches Figure 1-12.

❷ After you view the chart, scroll the worksheet until you can see rows 3 through 20.

The number of rows and columns you see in your worksheet window depends on your computer's display type. If your computer has an EGA display, your screen displays fewer rows than the screens shown in the figures, but now that you know how to scroll the worksheet, you can scroll whenever you need to view an area of the worksheet that is not in the worksheet window.

Using a Decision-Support Worksheet

Mike explains the general layout of the decision-support worksheet to the rest of the team (Figure 1-13). Cells A5 through A9 contain the five factors on which the team is basing its decision: climate, competition, market size, topography, and transportation. The team assigned an *importance weight* to each factor to show its relative importance to the success of the golf course. The team assigned importance weights using a scale from 1 to 10; Mike entered the weights in cells B5 through B9. Market size, with an importance weight of 10, is the most important factor. The least important factor is transportation.

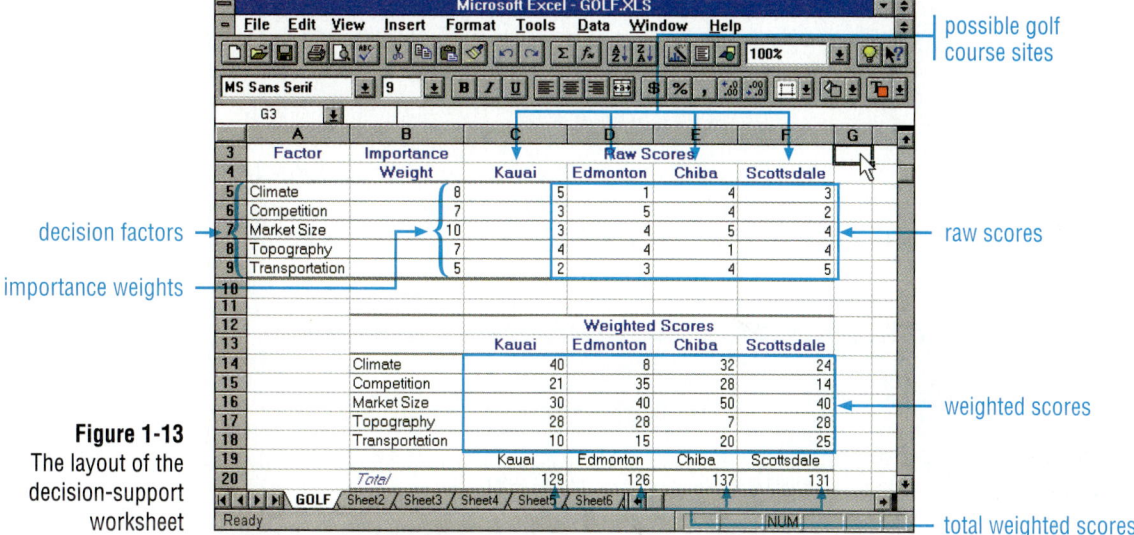

Figure 1-13
The layout of the decision-support worksheet

The four sites under consideration are listed in cells C4 through F4. The team used a scale of 1 to 5 to assign a *raw score* to each location for climate, competition, market size, topography, and transportation. Larger raw scores indicate the site is very strong in that factor. Smaller raw scores indicate the site is weak in that factor. For example, the raw score for Kauai's climate is 5. The other locations have scores of 1, 4, and 3 so it appears that Kauai, with warm, sunny days for 12 months of the year, has the best climate for the golf course. Edmonton, on the other hand, has cold weather and only received a climate raw score of 1.

The raw scores do not take into account the importance of each factor. Climate is important, but the team considers market size to be the most important factor. Therefore, the raw scores are not used for the final decision. Instead, the raw scores are multiplied by the importance weight to produce *weighted scores*. Which site has the highest weighted score for any factor? If you look at the scores in cells C14 through F18, you will see that Chiba's score of 50 for market size is the highest weighted score for any factor.

Cells C20 through F20 contain the total weighted scores for each location. With the current weighting and raw scores, it appears that Chiba is the most promising site, with a total score of 137.

As the team examines the worksheet, Pamela asks if the raw scores take into account the recent news that a competing design group has announced plans to build a $325 million golf resort just 10 miles away from InWood's Chiba site. Mike admits that he assigned the values before the announcement, so they do not reflect the increased competition in the Chiba market. Pamela suggests that they revise Chiba's raw score for competition to reflect this market change.

Changing Values and Observing Results

When you change a value in a worksheet, Excel recalculates the worksheet to display updated results. This feature makes Excel an extremely useful decision-making tool because it allows you to factor in changing conditions quickly and easily.

Another development group has announced plans to construct a new golf course in the Chiba area, so the team decides to lower the competition raw score for the Chiba site from 4 to 2.

To change the competition raw score for Chiba from 4 to 2:

❶ Click cell **E6**. A black border appears around cell E6 indicating it is the active cell. The formula bar shows E6 is the active cell and shows that the current value of cell E6 is 4.

❷ Type **2**. Notice that 2 appears in the cell and in the formula bar, along with three new buttons. These buttons—the Cancel box, the Enter box, and the Function Wizard button—provide shortcuts for entering data and formulas. You will learn how to use some of these in later tutorials. For now, you can simply ignore them. See Figure 1-14.

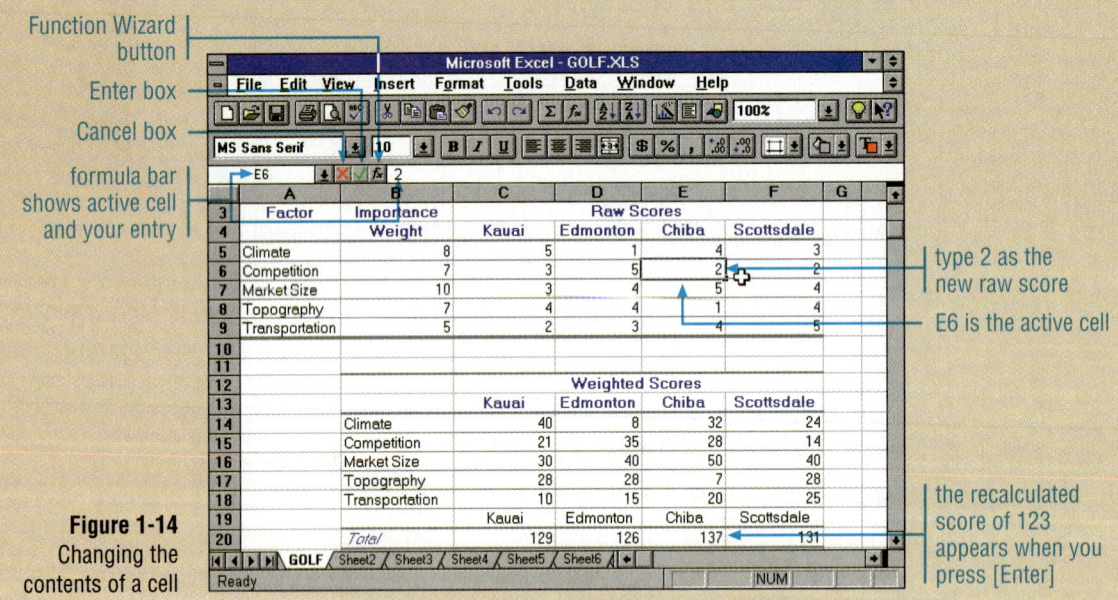

Figure 1-14
Changing the contents of a cell

❸ Press **[Enter]**. The worksheet recalculates the total weighted score for Chiba and displays it in cell E20. Cell E7 is now the active cell.

The team takes another look at the total weighted scores in row 20. Scottsdale just became the top ranking site, with a total weighted score of 131.

As the team continues to discuss the worksheet, several members express their concern over the importance weight used for transportation. On the current worksheet, transportation has an importance weight of 5. Pamela thinks they had agreed to use an importance weight of 2 at their last meeting. She asks Mike to change the importance weight for transportation.

To change the importance weight for transportation:

❶ Click cell **B9** to make it the active cell.

❷ Type **2** and press **[Enter]**. Cell B9 now contains the value 2 instead of 5. Cell B10 becomes the active cell.

With the change in the transportation importance weight, it appears that Kauai has pulled ahead as the most favorable site, with a total weighted score of 123.

Pamela, who has never used a spreadsheet program, asks Mike about mistakes. Mike explains that the most common mistake to make on a worksheet is a typing error. Typing mistakes are easy to correct, so Mike asks the group if he can take just a minute to demonstrate.

Correcting Mistakes

It is easy to correct a mistake as you are typing information in a cell, before you press the Enter key. If you need to correct a mistake as you are typing information in a cell, press the Backspace key to back up and delete one or more characters. When you are typing information in a cell, don't use the cursor arrow keys to edit because they move the cell pointer to another cell. Mike demonstrates how to correct a typing mistake by starting to type the word "Faktors" instead of "Factors."

To correct a mistake as you are typing:

❶ Click cell **B12** to make it the active cell.

❷ Type **Fak** to make an intentional error, *but don't press [Enter]*.

❸ Press **[Backspace]** to delete the "k."

❹ Type **ctors** and press **[Enter]**.

Now the word "Factors" is in cell B12, but Mike really wants the word "Factor" in the cell. He explains that after you press the Enter key, you use a different method to change the contents of a cell. The F2 key puts Excel into **Edit mode**, which lets you use the Backspace key, Left Arrow key, Right Arrow key, and the mouse to make changes to the text displayed in the formula bar.

REFERENCE WINDOW

Correcting Mistakes Using Edit Mode

- Click the cell you want to edit to make it the active cell.
- Press [F2] to begin Edit mode and display the contents of the cell in the formula bar.
- Use [Backspace], [Delete], [→], [←], or the mouse to edit the cell contents in the formula bar.
- Press [Enter] when the edit is complete.

Mike uses Edit mode to demonstrate how to change "Factors" to "Factor" in cell B12.

To change the word "Factors" to "Factor" in cell B12:
1. Click cell **B12** if it is not already the active cell.
2. Press **[F2]** to begin Edit mode. Note that "Edit" appears in the status bar, reminding you that Excel is currently in Edit mode.
3. Press **[Backspace]** to delete the "s."
4. Press **[Enter]** to complete the edit.

Mike points out that sometimes you might inadvertently enter the wrong value in a cell. To cancel that type of error, you can use the Undo button.

The Undo Button

Excel's **Undo button** lets you cancel the last change—and only the last change—you made to the worksheet. You can use Undo not only to correct typing mistakes, but to correct almost anything you did to the worksheet that you wish you hadn't. For example, Undo cancels formatting changes, deletions, and cell entries. If you make a mistake, use Undo to put things back the way they were. But keep in mind that Excel can't reverse an entire series of actions. It can only reverse the most recent change you made to the worksheet.

Mike changes the font size (in other words, the size of the characters) for the label in cell B12. Then he uses the Undo button to cancel the font size change.

To change the font size and then cancel this change using the Undo feature:
1. Click cell **B12** if it is not already the active cell.
2. Click the **Font Size drop-down list-box arrow**. A list of font sizes appears. See Figure 1-15.

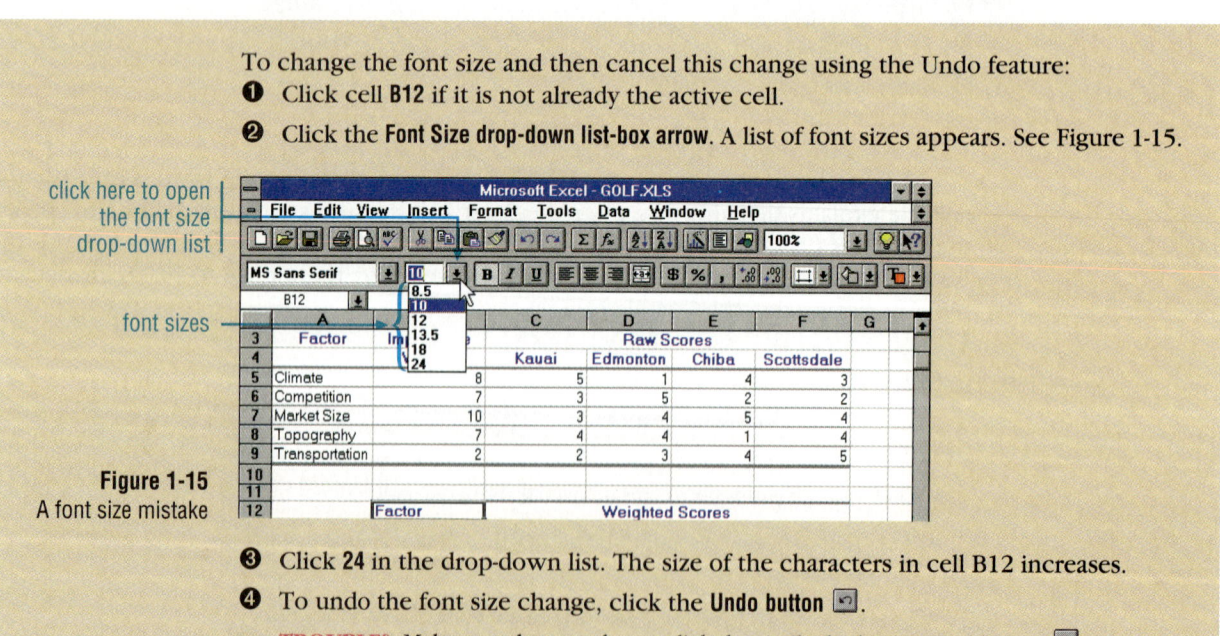

Figure 1-15
A font size mistake

3. Click **24** in the drop-down list. The size of the characters in cell B12 increases.
4. To undo the font size change, click the **Undo button** .

TROUBLE? Make sure that you do not click the similar-looking Repeat button.

Now that you know how to correct typing mistakes and use the Undo button to cancel your last entry or command, you can apply these skills as you need them.

Mike says that the team must continue working on the golf course site selection. The team wants to see the chart and the scores at the same time. Mike says he can do that by splitting the worksheet window.

Splitting the Worksheet Window

The worksheet window displays only a section of the entire worksheet. Although you can scroll to any section of the worksheet, you might want to view two different parts of the worksheet at the same time. To do this, you can split the window into two or more separate window panes using the split bar, shown in Figure 1-16.

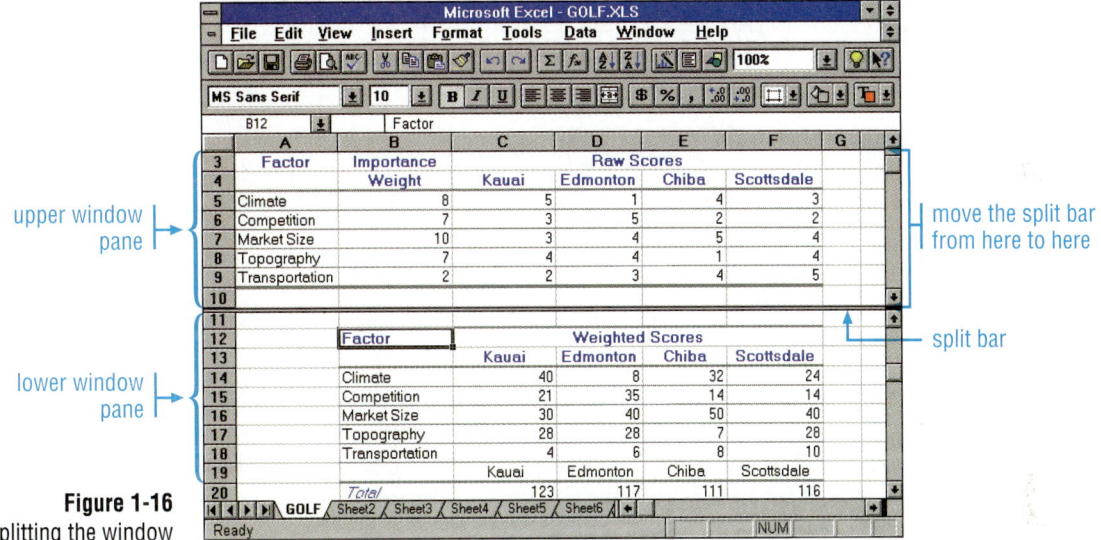

Figure 1-16
Splitting the window

A **window pane** is a subdivision of the worksheet window that can be scrolled separately to display a section of the worksheet. This is handy when you want to change some worksheet values and immediately see how these changes affect such things as totals or, as in this case, a chart.

Mike decides to split the worksheet window into two window panes. When he does this the top pane will display rows 3 through 9 of the worksheet. Then Mike needs to scroll the lower pane to display the chart.

To split the screen into two horizontal windows:

❶ Move ▷ over the horizontal split bar until it changes to ✢. Drag the split bar just below the bottom of row 10, then release the mouse button. Figure 1-16 shows the screen split into two horizontal windows.

Now you need to display the chart by using the scroll bar on the lower window pane.

❷ Drag the scroll box on the lower window pane about half way down the vertical scroll bar, then release the left mouse button. The lower window pane displays the chart. See Figure 1-17. Don't worry if your worksheet displays fewer rows than in the figure. Just make sure you can see row 9 in the upper window pane and the four bars of the chart in the lower window pane.

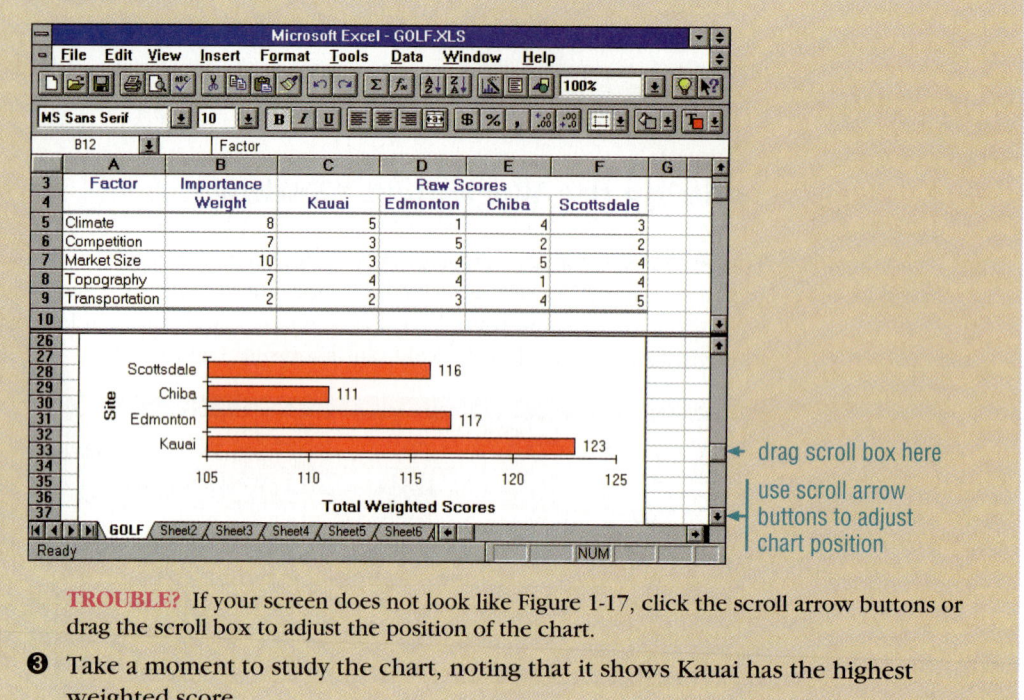

Figure 1-17
Chart displayed in lower window pane

→ drag scroll box here

| use scroll arrow buttons to adjust chart position

TROUBLE? If your screen does not look like Figure 1-17, click the scroll arrow buttons or drag the scroll box to adjust the position of the chart.

❸ Take a moment to study the chart, noting that it shows Kauai has the highest weighted score.

Pamela reviews her notes from the previous meetings and finds that the team had a long discussion about the importance of transportation, but eventually agreed to use 5 (instead of 2) as the importance weight. Now Mike needs to restore the original importance weight for transportation. The team will see its effect on the chart immediately.

To see the chart change when you change the importance weight in the worksheet:

❶ Click cell **B9** to make it the active cell.

❷ Type **5** and, as you press **[Enter]**, watch the chart change to reflect the new scores for all four sites.

Scottsdale once again ranks highest with a weighted score total of 131. Kauai ranks second with a total score of 129. Edmonton ranks third with a total score of 126. Chiba ranks last with a total score of 123.

Mike asks if everyone is satisfied with the current weightings and scores. The team agrees that the current worksheet is a reasonable representation of the factors that need to be considered for each site. Mike decides to remove the split screen so everyone can see all the scores and results on the worksheet.

Removing the Split Window

There are two ways to remove a split from your worksheet window. You can drag the split bar back to the top of the scroll bar, or you can use the Split command on the Window menu. You can use whichever method you prefer. If you are using a mouse, it is probably easier to use the split bar.

Mike drags the split bar to remove the split window.

> To remove the split window:
> ❶ Move the pointer over the split bar until it changes to ≑.
> ❷ Drag the split bar to the top of the scroll bar, then release the mouse button.
> ❸ If necessary, scroll the worksheet so you can see rows 3 through 20.

Making and Documenting the Decision

Pamela asks if the team is ready to recommend a final site. Mike wants to recommend Scottsdale as the primary site and Kauai as an alternative location. Pamela asks for a vote, and the team unanimously agrees with Mike's recommendation.

Mike suggests they save the modified worksheet under a different name. This will help document the decision process because it will preserve the original sheet showing Chiba with the highest score and it will save the current sheet, which shows Scottsdale with the highest score.

Saving the Workbook

When you save a workbook, it is copied from RAM onto your disk. Any charts that appear in the workbook are also saved.

Excel has more than one save command on the File menu. The two you'll use most often are the Save and Save As commands. The Save command copies the workbook onto a disk using the current filename. If an old version of the file exists, the new version will replace the old one. The Save As command asks for a filename before copying the workbook onto a disk. When you enter a new filename, the current file is saved under that new name. The previous version of the file remains on the disk under its original name. The flowchart in Figure 1-18 helps you decide whether to use the Save or the Save As command.

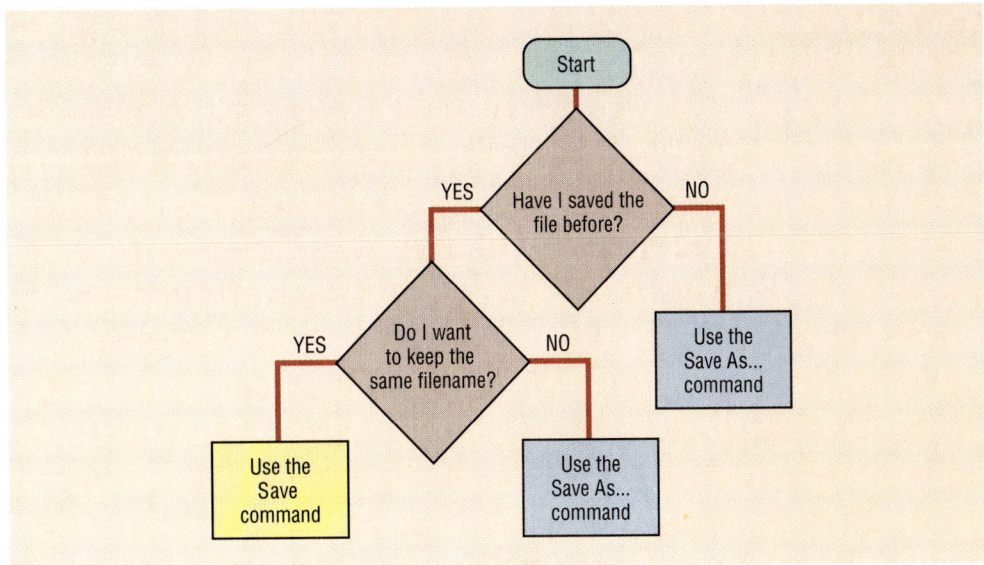

Figure 1-18
Deciding whether to use Save or Save As

When you type a filename, you can use either uppercase or lowercase letters. You do not need to type the .XLS extension. Excel automatically adds the extension when it saves the file.

> **REFERENCE WINDOW**
>
> **Saving a Workbook with a New Filename**
>
> - Click File, then Save As....
> - Type the filename for the modified workbook.
> - Make sure the Drives box displays the drive in which you want to save your workbook.
> - Make sure the Directories box shows an open file folder for the directory in which you want to store your workbook.
> - Click the OK button.

As a general rule, use the Save As command the first time you save a file or whenever you have modified a file and want to save both the old and new versions. Use the Save command when you have modified a file and want to save only the current version.

It is a good idea to use the Save As command to save and name your file soon after you start a new workbook. Then, as you continue to work, periodically use the Save command to save the workbook. That way, if the power goes out or the computer stops working, you're less likely to lose your work. Because you use the Save command frequently, the toolbar has a Save button, which provides you with a single mouse-click shortcut for saving your workbook.

Mike's workbook is named GOLF.XLS. On the screen, Mike and the team are viewing a version of GOLF.XLS that they have modified during this work session. The original version of this workbook—the one that shows Chiba with the highest score—is still on Mike's disk. Mike decides to save the modified workbook as GOLF2.XLS on the disk in drive A. Then he will have two versions of the workbook on the disk—the original version named GOLF.XLS and the revised version named GOLF2.XLS.

To save the modified workbook as GOLF2.XLS:

❶ Click **File**, then click **Save As...** to display the Save As dialog box.

❷ Type **GOLF2** in the File Name box, *but don't press [Enter]*. You can use lowercase or uppercase to type the filename.

Before you proceed, check the rest of the dialog box specifications to ensure that you save the workbook on your Student Disk.

❸ Make sure the a: drive icon is displayed in the Drives box. If it is not, click the **down arrow button** on the Drives box, then click the **a: icon** in the list. See Figure 1-19.

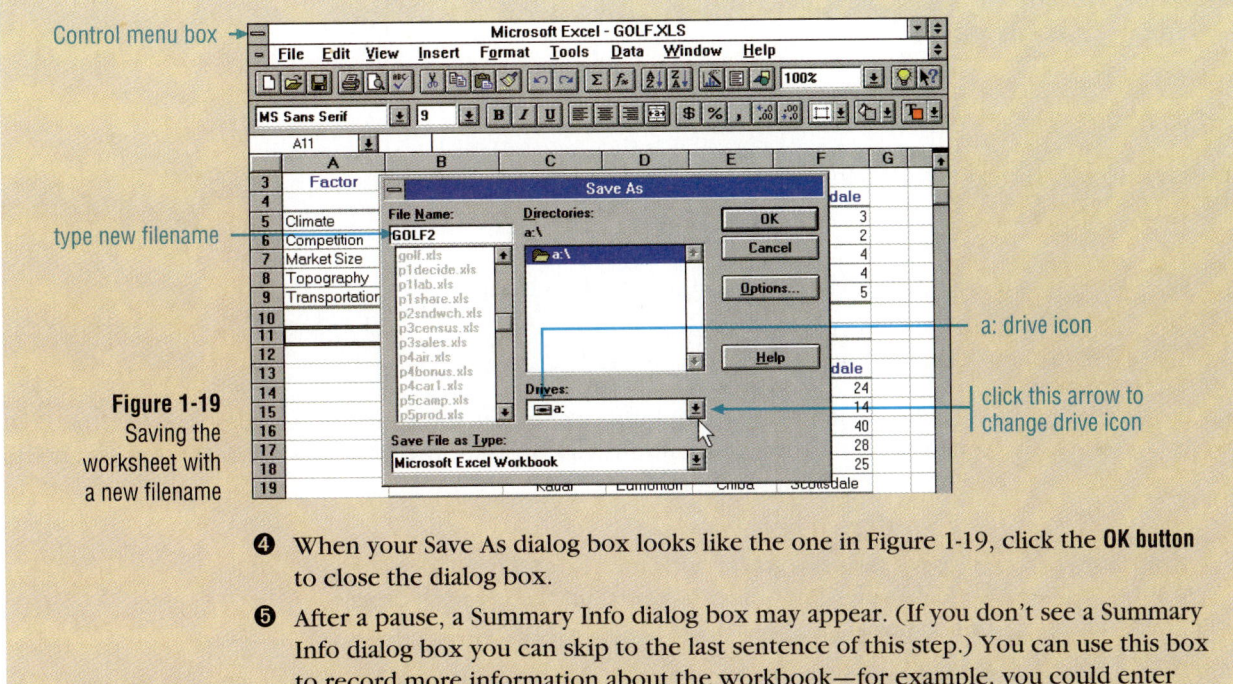

Figure 1-19
Saving the worksheet with a new filename

❹ When your Save As dialog box looks like the one in Figure 1-19, click the **OK button** to close the dialog box.

❺ After a pause, a Summary Info dialog box may appear. (If you don't see a Summary Info dialog box you can skip to the last sentence of this step.) You can use this box to record more information about the workbook—for example, you could enter your name in the Author box. When you are finished, click the **OK button** to return to the worksheet. The new workbook title, GOLF2.XLS, is displayed in the title bar.

If you want to take a break and resume the tutorial at a later time, you can exit Excel by double-clicking the Control menu box in the upper-left corner of the screen (shown in Figure 1-19). When you resume the tutorial, launch Excel, maximize the Microsoft Excel and Book1 windows, and place your Student Disk in the disk drive. Open the file GOLF2.XLS, then continue with the tutorial.

Printing the Worksheet and Chart

Pamela wants to have complete documentation for the team's written recommendation to management, so she asks Mike to print the worksheet and chart.

You can initiate the Print command using the File menu or the Print button. If you initiate printing with the Print command on the File menu, a dialog box lets you specify which pages of the worksheet you want to print, the number of copies you want to print, and the print quality. If you use the Print button, you will not have these options; Excel prints one copy of the entire worksheet at the default resolution, which is usually the highest resolution your printer can produce.

REFERENCE WINDOW

Printing a Worksheet

- Click the Print button.

or

- Click File, then click Print....
- Adjust any settings you want in the Print dialog box.
- Click the OK button.

Mike wants to print the entire worksheet and chart. He decides to select the Print command from the File menu instead of using the Print button because he wants to check the settings in the Print dialog box.

To check the print settings and then print the worksheet and chart:

1. Make sure your printer is turned on and contains paper.
2. Click **File**, then click **Print...** to display the Print dialog box.
3. Make sure your Print dialog box settings for Print What, Copies, and Page Range are the same as those in Figure 1-20.

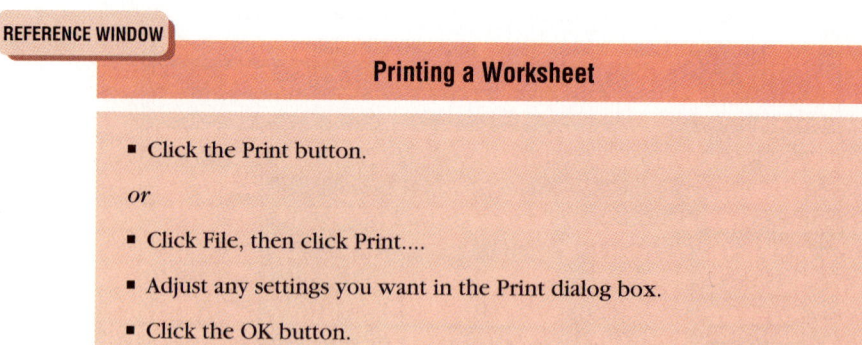

Figure 1-20
Printing the worksheet

4. Click the **OK button** to print the worksheet and chart. See Figure 1-21.

    TROUBLE? If the worksheet and chart do not print, see your technical support person for assistance.

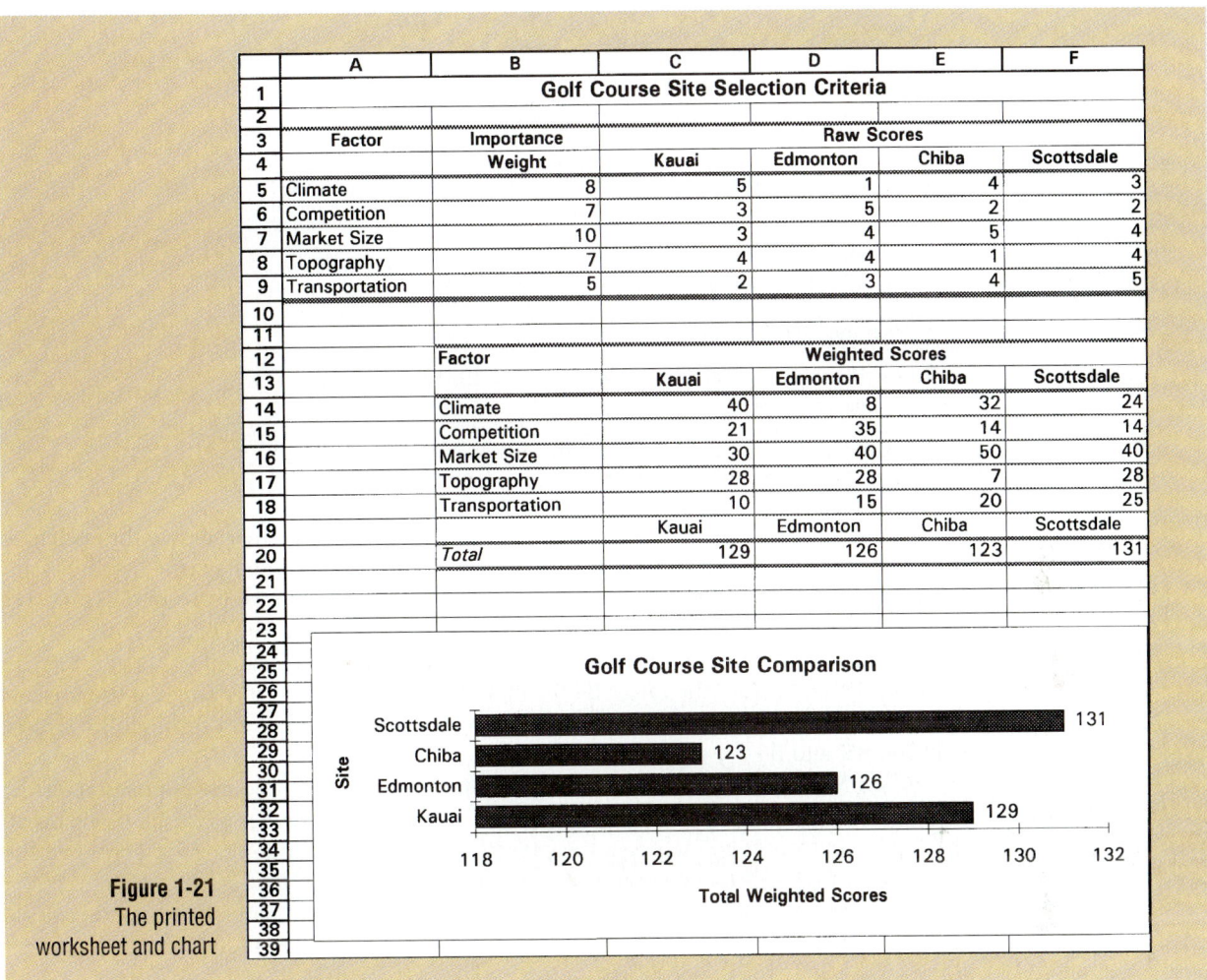

Figure 1-21
The printed worksheet and chart

Pamela asks Mike if they can create a chart that illustrates the weighted scores for every factor for each site. Mike says he can easily do that with the Excel ChartWizard.

Creating a Chart with the ChartWizard

The **ChartWizard** guides you through five steps to create a chart. You can select from a variety of chart types, including bar charts, column charts, line charts, and pie charts. Tutorial 5 describes the chart types in detail. After you create a chart using the ChartWizard, you can change it, move it to a new location, or save it.

REFERENCE WINDOW

Creating a Chart with ChartWizard

- Position the pointer in the upper-left corner of the area you want to chart.
- Drag the pointer to highlight all the cells you want to chart. Make sure to include row and column titles.
- Click the ChartWizard button.
- Drag the pointer to outline the area in the worksheet where you want the chart to appear.
- Follow the ChartWizard instructions to complete the chart.

Mike is ready to use the ChartWizard to create a bar chart that shows the weighted scores for each of the four sites. First he highlights the cells that contain the data he wants to chart. Then he activates the ChartWizard and follows the five steps to outline the area where he wants the chart to appear and to specify how he wants his chart to look.

A rectangular block of cells is referred to as **a range**. For example, you can refer to cells B4, B5, and B6 as "the range B4 through B6." Excel displays this range in the formula bar as B4:B6. The colon in the notation B4:B6 indicates the range B4 through B6, that is, cells B4, B5, and B6.

When Mike highlights the range of cells for the chart, he begins by positioning the pointer on the cell that will be the upper-left corner of the range. Next, he holds down the mouse button while he drags the pointer to the cell in the lower-right corner of the range. This **highlights**, or **selects**, all the cells in the range; that is, they change color, usually becoming black. The cell in the upper-left corner of the range is the active cell, so it does not appear highlighted, but it is included in the range. Let's see how this works.

To highlight the data in the range B13:F18 for the chart:

1. Position the pointer on cell B13, the upper-left corner of the range you want to highlight.
2. Hold down the mouse button while you drag the pointer to cell F18.
3. Release the mouse button. The range of cells from B13 to F18 is highlighted, except for cell B13. Cell B13 does not appear to be highlighted because it is the active cell, but it is still included in the highlighted range. See Figure 1-22.

   TROUBLE? If your highlight does not correspond to Figure 1-22, repeat Steps 1-3.

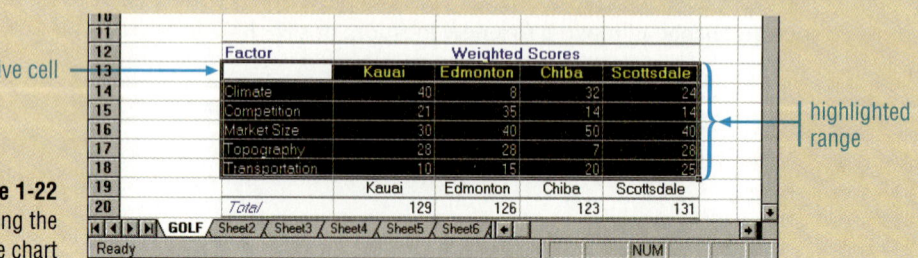

Figure 1-22
Highlighting the data for the chart

Next, Mike clicks the ChartWizard button and specifies the location of the chart. He wants to position the new chart between rows 45 and 64 on the worksheet, so he outlines the location for the new chart by dragging the pointer from cell A45 to cell F64.

To activate the ChartWizard and specify the location for the chart:

❶ Click the **ChartWizard button**. The prompt "Drag in document to create a chart" appears in the status bar and the pointer changes to ⁺⌊ᵢ.

❷ Use the vertical scroll bar to scroll the worksheet so you can view rows 45 through 64. (Note that the pointer becomes ⌘ when positioned over the scroll bar.)

❸ Drag ⁺⌊ᵢ from cell A45 to cell F64 to outline the location of the chart. See Figure 1-23.

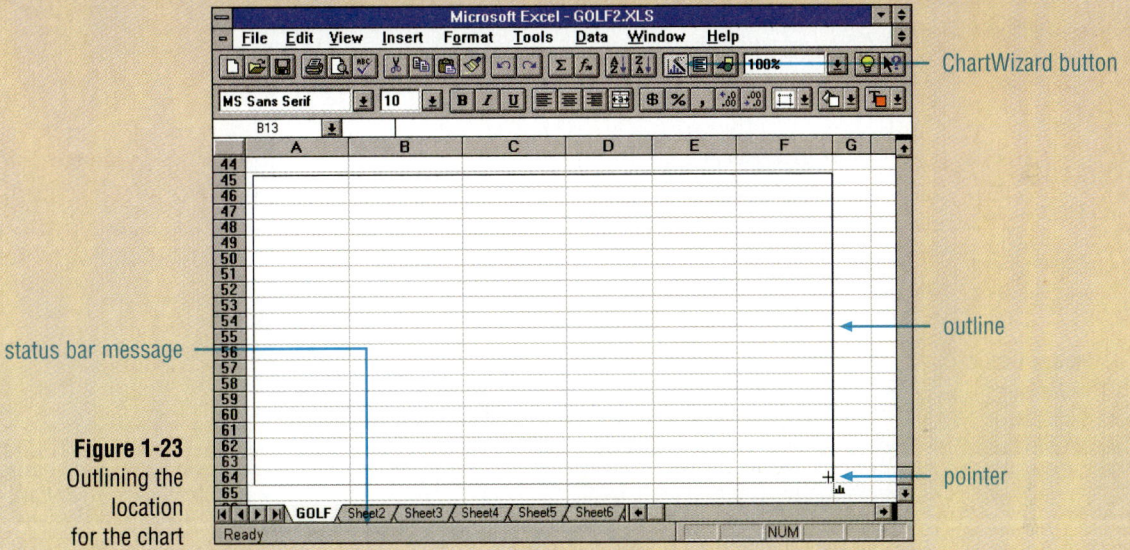

Figure 1-23
Outlining the location for the chart

❹ Release the mouse button.

❺ When the ChartWizard - Step 1 of 5 dialog box appears, make sure the Range box shows =$B$13:$F$18. See Figure 1-24. Don't be concerned about the dollar signs ($) in the cell references; you will learn about the dollar signs in Tutorial 4.

TROUBLE? If the Range box does not display $B$13:$F$18, you have highlighted the wrong cells to use for the chart. Drag the pointer from B13 to F18 and then release the mouse button.

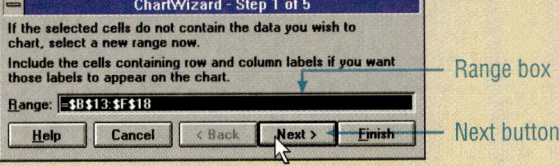

Figure 1-24
The ChartWizard - Step 1 of 5 dialog box

❻ Click the **Next > button** to display the ChartWizard - Step 2 of 5 dialog box.

❼ Double-click the chart type labeled **Bar**. The ChartWizard - Step 3 of 5 dialog box appears.

EX 28 TUTORIAL 1   Using Worksheets to Make Business Decisions

8. Double-click the box for format **6** to select a horizontal chart with gridlines. The ChartWizard - Step 4 of 5 dialog box appears, showing you a preview of your chart. Don't worry if the titles are not formatted correctly.

9. You will not make any additional changes to your chart at this point, so click the **Next > button** to display the ChartWizard - Step 5 of 5 dialog box.

10. Click the **Chart Title box**, then type **Weighted Scores** and click the **Finish button**. The chart appears in the worksheet. See Figure 1-25.

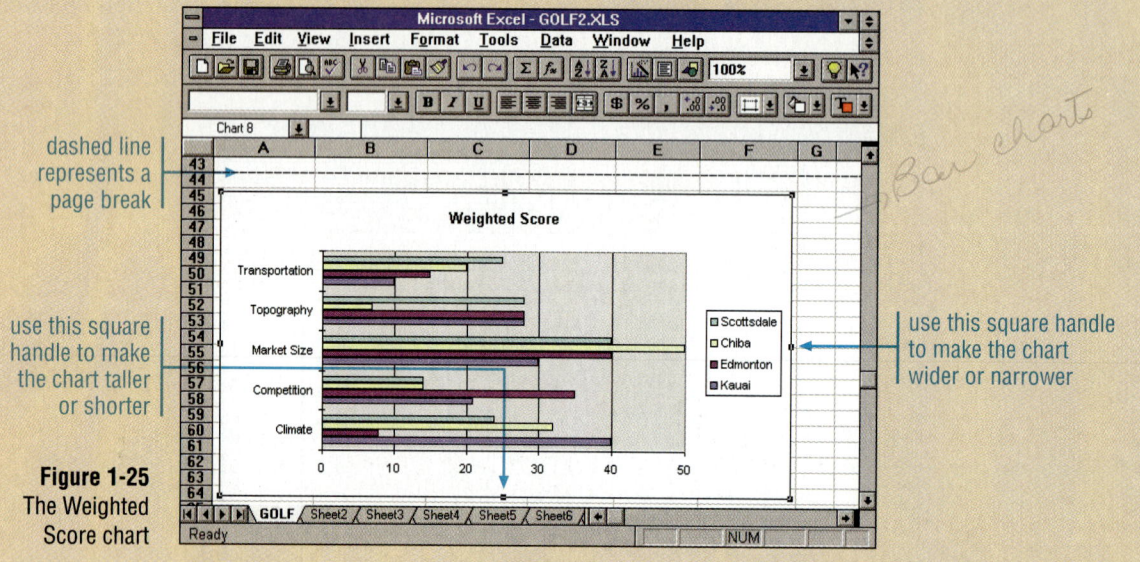

Figure 1-25 The Weighted Score chart

- dashed line represents a page break
- use this square handle to make the chart taller or shorter
- use this square handle to make the chart wider or narrower

Bar chart

TROUBLE? You may see an extra toolbar appear somewhere in the worksheet, along with the chart. This is the Chart Toolbar, which you can use to make quick changes to the chart. Because you will not be making any changes to the chart, you can close the Chart Toolbar by double-clicking the Control menu box.

The entire team is impressed with the Weighted Scores chart. Pamela asks Mike to print it.

Printing a Specific Page

The Weighted Scores chart is on page 2 of the worksheet. On your screen and on Figure 1-25, the dashed line between row 43 and row 44 represents a page break. To print the Weighted Scores chart, Mike must print page 2 of the worksheet. The Print dialog box setting for "Page(s) From:__ To:__" lets you specify which page you want to start *from* and which page you want to print *to*. To print only page 2, Mike prints from page 2 to page 2.

To print page 2 of the worksheet containing the Weighted Scores chart:

1. Click **File**, then click **Print...** to display the Print dialog box. Figure 1-26 shows the Print dialog box settings you will have when you complete Steps 2 through 4.

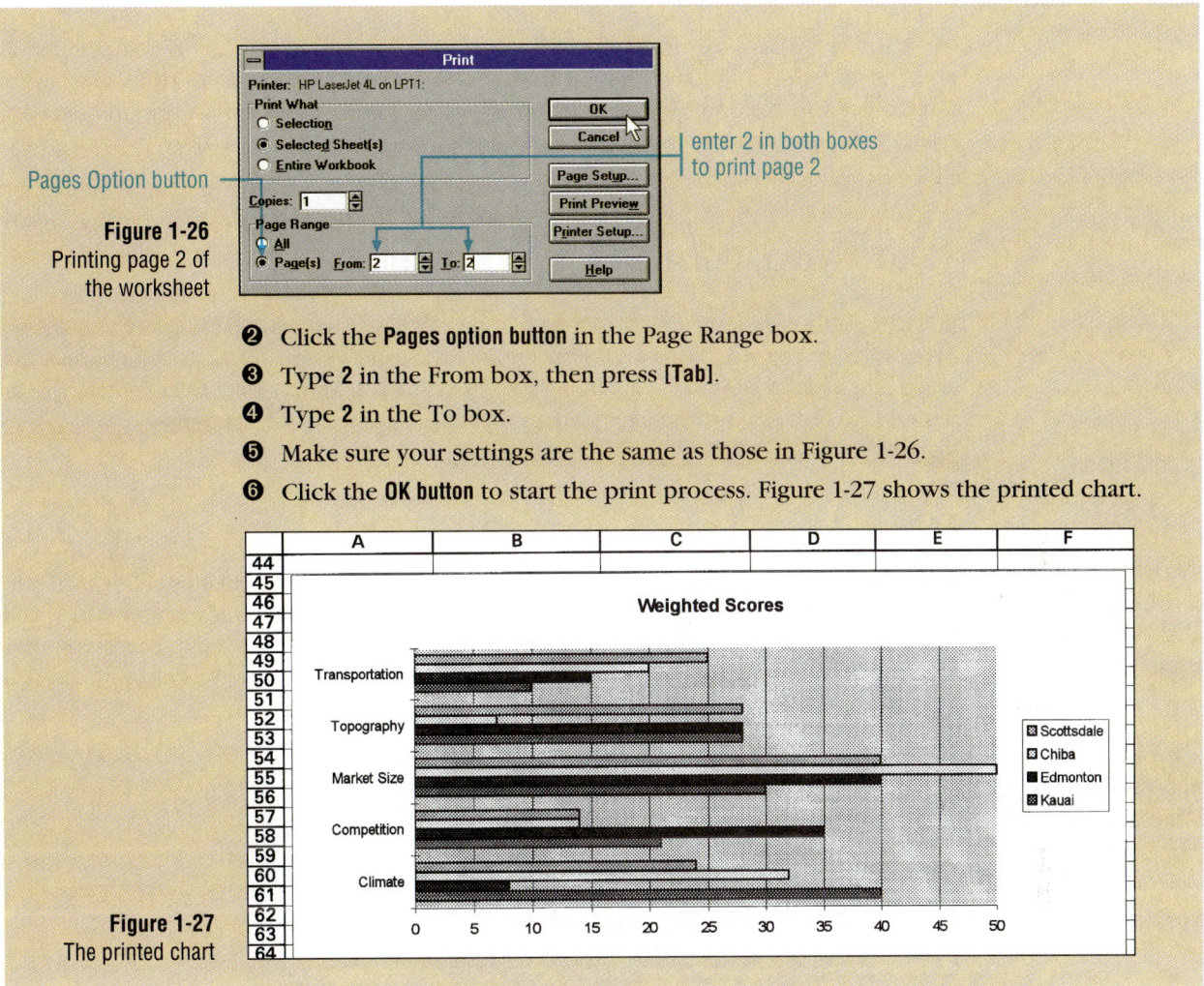

Figure 1-26
Printing page 2 of the worksheet

Figure 1-27
The printed chart

❷ Click the **Pages option button** in the Page Range box.

❸ Type **2** in the From box, then press **[Tab]**.

❹ Type **2** in the To box.

❺ Make sure your settings are the same as those in Figure 1-26.

❻ Click the **OK button** to start the print process. Figure 1-27 shows the printed chart.

Pamela suggests they save the worksheet and the Weighted Scores chart. They decide to save the workbook under the current name, GOLF2.XLS. This replaces the old version of GOLF2.XLS with the new version, which includes the Weighted Scores chart.

To save the workbook with the same filename:

❶ Click the **Save button** to replace the old version of the workbook with the new version.

If you want to take a break and resume the tutorial at a later time, you can exit Excel by double-clicking the Control menu box in the upper-left corner of the screen. When you resume the tutorial, launch Excel, maximize the Microsoft Excel and Book1 windows, and place your Student Disk in the disk drive. Open the file GOLF2.XLS, then continue with the tutorial.

Mike volunteers to put together the report with the team's final recommendation, and the meeting adjourns. After the meeting Pamela mentions to Mike that she is impressed with the way the spreadsheet program helped the team analyze the data and make a decision, but she admits that she doesn't really understand how it works. Mike offers to explain the basic concepts.

Values, Text, Formulas, and Functions

Mike explains that an Excel worksheet is a grid consisting of 256 columns and 16,384 rows. As noted earlier, the rectangular areas at the intersections of each column and row are called cells. A cell can contain a value, text, or a formula. Mike tells Pamela that to understand how the spreadsheet program works, she must understand how Excel manipulates values, text, formulas, and functions.

Values

Values are numbers, dates, and times that Excel can use for calculations. For example, 378, 11/29/94, and 4:40:31 are examples of values. As you type information into a cell, Excel determines if the characters you're typing can be used as a value. For example, if you type 456 Excel recognizes it as a value and displays it on the right side of the cell. Mike shows Pamela that cells B5 through B9 contain values.

To examine the contents of cells B5 through B9:

1. Use the vertical scroll bar to scroll up the worksheet until you can see rows 3 through 20.

2. Click cell **B5** to make it the active cell. The formula bar at the top of the screen displays B5 and its contents. See Figure 1-28.

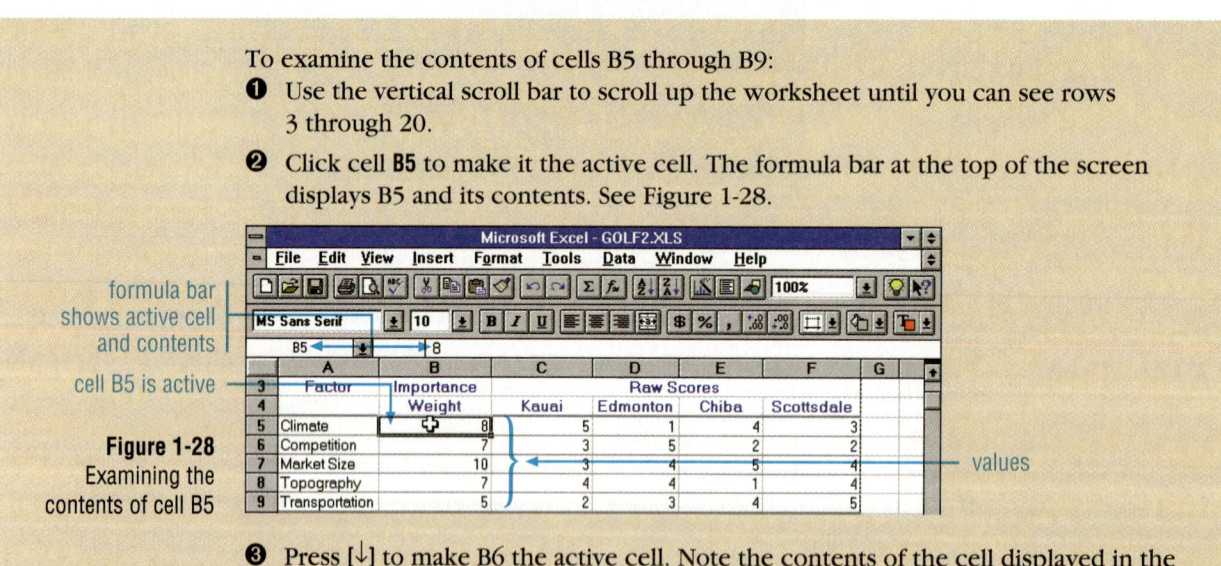

Figure 1-28 Examining the contents of cell B5

3. Press [↓] to make B6 the active cell. Note the contents of the cell displayed in the formula bar.

4. Press [↓] to look at the contents of cells B7, B8, and B9.

Text

Text is any set of characters that Excel does not interpret as a value. Text is often used to label the columns and rows in the worksheet. Examples of text are Total Sales, Acme Co., and Eastern Division.

Text entries cannot be used for calculations. Some data commonly referred to as "numbers" are treated as text by Excel. For example, a telephone number such as 227-1240 or a social security number such as 372-70-9654 is treated as text and cannot be used for calculations. Mike shows Pamela that cells A5 through A9 contain text.

To examine the contents of cells A5 through A9:

❶ Click cell **A5** to make it the active cell. The formula bar displays the cell reference A5 and the cell contents, "Climate." See Figure 1-29.

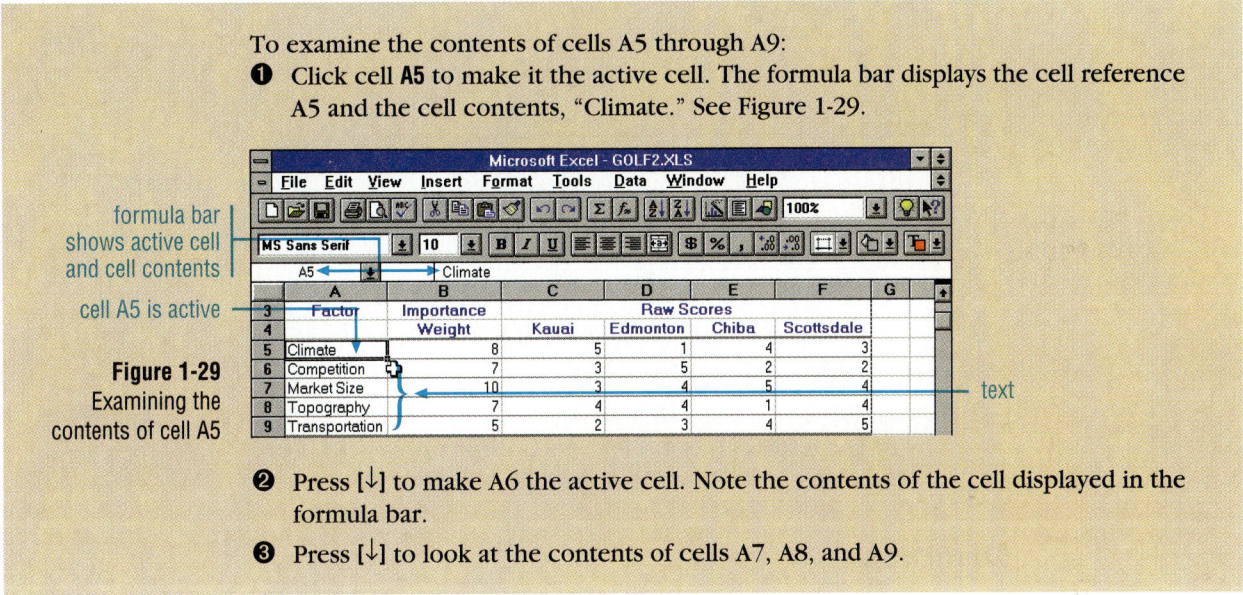

Figure 1-29 Examining the contents of cell A5

❷ Press [↓] to make A6 the active cell. Note the contents of the cell displayed in the formula bar.

❸ Press [↓] to look at the contents of cells A7, A8, and A9.

Formulas

Formulas specify the calculations you want Excel to perform. Formulas always begin with an equal sign (=). Most formulas contain **mathematical operators** such as +, -, *, / that specify how Excel should manipulate the numbers in the calculation. When you type a formula, use the asterisk (*) for multiplication and the slash (/) for division.

Formulas can contain numbers or cell references. Some examples of formulas are =20+10, =G9/2, and =C5*B5. The formula =C5*B5 instructs Excel to multiply the contents of cell C5 by the contents of cell B5.

The *result* of the formula is displayed in the cell in which you have entered the formula. To view the formula in a cell, you must first make that cell active, then look at the formula bar. Mike shows Pamela how to view formulas and their results.

To view the formula in cell C14:

❶ Click cell **C14** to make it the active cell. The formula bar shows =C5*B5 as the formula for cell C14. This formula multiplies the contents of cell C5 by the contents of cell B5. See Figure 1-30.

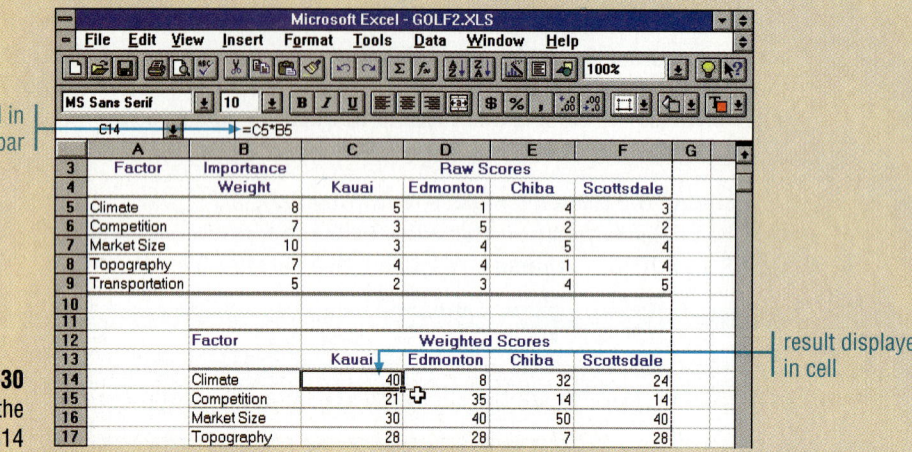

Figure 1-30
Viewing the formula in cell C14

❷ Look at cell C5. The number in this cell is 5.

❸ Look at cell B5. The number in this cell is 8.

❹ Look at the formula bar. Multiplying the contents of C5 by B5 means to multiply 5 by 8. The result of this formula, 40, is displayed in cell C14.

Functions

A **function** is a special prewritten formula that provides a shortcut for commonly used calculations. For example, you can use the SUM function to create the formula =SUM(D14:D18) instead of typing the longer formula =D14+D15+D16+D17+D18. The SUM function in this example sums the range D14:D18. (Recall that D14:D18 refers to the rectangular block of cells beginning at D14 and ending at D18.) Other functions include AVERAGE, which calculates the average value; MIN, which finds the smallest value; and MAX, which finds the largest value.

To view the function in the formula in cell C20:

❶ Click cell **C20** to make it the active cell. See Figure 1-31.

Values, Text, Formulas, and Functions   **EX 33**

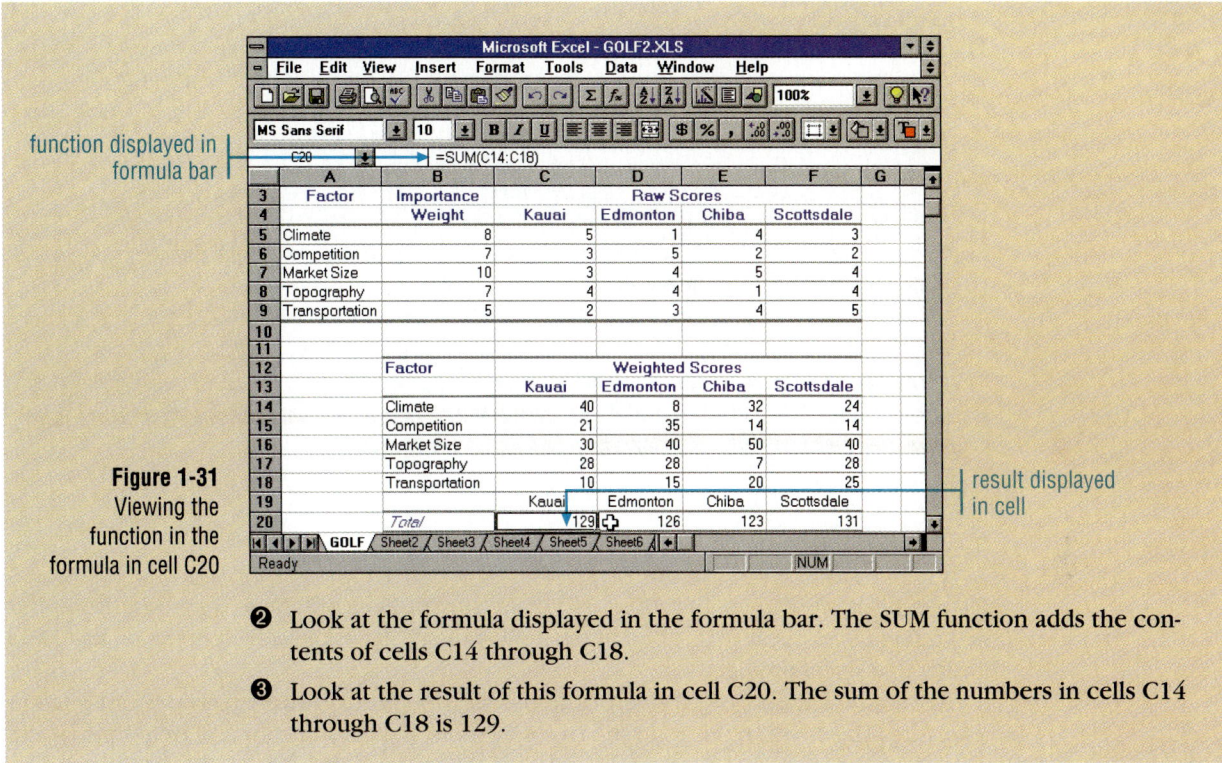

Figure 1-31
Viewing the function in the formula in cell C20

❷ Look at the formula displayed in the formula bar. The SUM function adds the contents of cells C14 through C18.

❸ Look at the result of this formula in cell C20. The sum of the numbers in cells C14 through C18 is 129.

Remember that the formula bar shows the *contents* of the cell, the formula =SUM(C14:C18). The worksheet cell shows the *result* of the formula. *To determine the actual contents of a cell, you must make that cell the active cell and view the contents in the formula bar.*

Automatic Recalculation

Mike explains that any time a value in a worksheet cell is changed, Excel automatically recalculates all the formulas. Changing a number in only one cell might result in many changes throughout the worksheet. Mike demonstrates by changing the importance weight for climate from 8 to 2.

To change the importance weight for climate:

❶ Note the current importance weight for climate (8), the weighted scores for climate in each location (Kauai 40, Edmonton 8, Chiba 32, and Scottsdale 24), and the total weighted scores for each location (Kauai 129, Edmonton 126, Chiba 123, and Scottsdale 131).

❷ Click cell **B5** to make it the active cell.

❸ Type **2** and press **[Enter]**. Watch the worksheet update the results of the formulas in cells C14 through F14 and cells C20 through F20.

Note the updated results for the climate weighted scores (10, 2, 8, and 6) and the weighted totals (99, 120, 99, and 113). *Remember, when a value is changed in a worksheet, every cell that depends on that value is recalculated.*

Excel Help

Mike explains to Pamela that there are many spreadsheet programs to choose from, but he prefers Excel because it is one of the easiest to use. He especially likes the on-line Help facility that Excel provides.

Located on the far right side of the toolbar, the **Help button** provides information about any object you point to in the Excel window. When you click the Help button, the pointer changes to ▸?. This pointer indicates that you are in Help mode. In Help mode, you can move the Help pointer to a screen object to view a one-line description of the object in the status bar, or you can click the object to open the Microsoft Excel Help window and view a more complete explanation of the object and its function. The Help button is especially handy if you want to find out the function of menu options.

REFERENCE WINDOW

Using the Help Button

- Click the Help button to begin Help mode and display the Help pointer ▸?.
- Position ▸? on the screen object or menu item you want to know more about.
- If the Help message in the status bar is not sufficient, click the mouse button to open the Microsoft Excel Help window.
- When you are finished viewing the Microsoft Excel Help window, double-click the Control menu box for the window.
- If the Help pointer is still displayed and you want to exit Help mode, click the Help button again.

Mike shows Pamela how to use the Help button to learn the function of the Cells command on the Format menu.

To use the Help button to learn the function of the Cells command on the Format menu:

❶ Click the **Help button** . The pointer changes to .

❷ Click the word **Format** in the menu bar. The Format menu opens. In the status bar at the bottom of the screen, Excel displays the message "Changes cell font, border, alignment, and other formats."

❸ To get detailed information on the Cells command, double-click **Cells...**. The Microsoft Excel Help window appears. See Figure 1-32. Note that the pointer changes shape to when you place it over the list of Help topics.

TROUBLE? If your Microsoft Excel Help window is not the same size as the one in Figure 1-32, drag the borders to make it the same size.

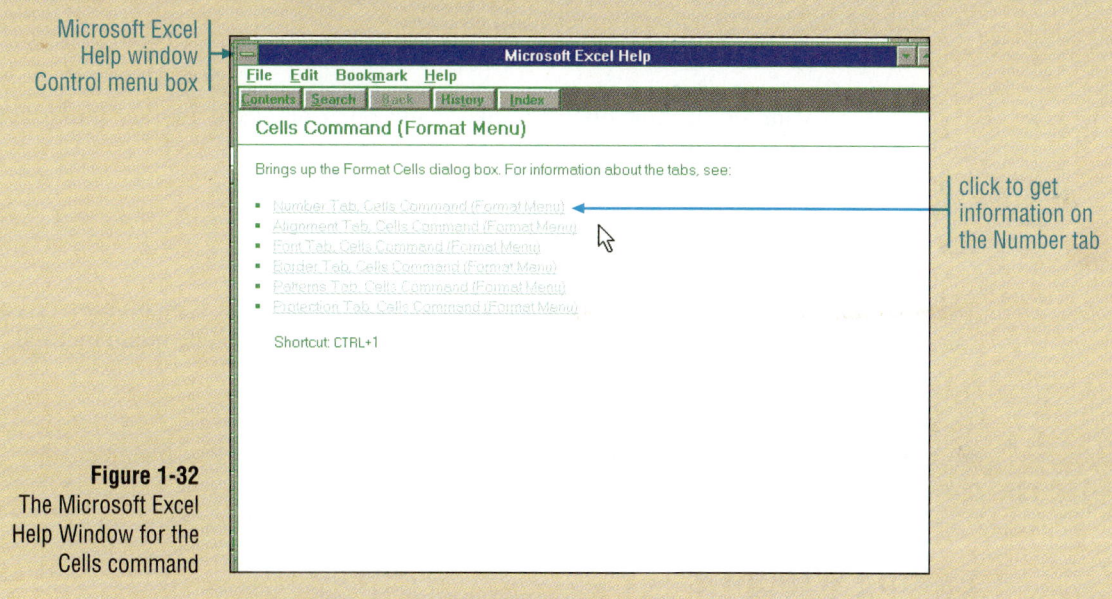

Figure 1-32
The Microsoft Excel Help Window for the Cells command

❹ To get information on the first topic, click **Number Tab, Cells Command (Format Menu)**. Another Help window appears.

❺ Read through the information in the Help window.

❻ Double-click the **Microsoft Excel Help window Control menu box** to close the window and return to the worksheet.

Mike explains that when you close the Microsoft Excel Help window, you automatically exit Help mode and your pointer returns to the arrow or white plus shape.

Mike tells Pamela that the Help menu on the menu bar also gives you access to on-line Help. The Help menu works like the Help menu provided in most Windows programs. In addition, you can click the TipWizard button to display the TipWizard box. (The TipWizard button is the button with the lightbulb on it, next to the Help button.) This TipWizard box tells you about quicker, more efficient ways of performing actions you've just performed. Mike doesn't have time to show Pamela how to use these features, but he assures her that she can easily explore the options on her own.

Closing the Worksheet

Mike closes the worksheet window. He does not want to save the changes that he made while demonstrating the worksheet to Pamela, so he does not use the Save command or the Save As command. When he tries to close the worksheet window, a message asks if he wants to save the changes he has made. Mike responds by clicking the No button.

To close the GOLF2.XLS workbook without saving changes:
1. Click **File**, then click **Close**. A dialog box displays the message "Save changes in 'GOLF2.XLS?'"
2. Click the **No button** to exit without saving changes.

The Excel window remains open so Mike could open or create another workbook. He does not want to do this, so his next step is to exit Excel.

Exiting Excel

There are several ways to exit Excel. You can double-click the Control menu box, or you can use the Exit command on the File menu. Mike generally uses the File menu method.

To exit Excel using the File menu:
1. Click **File**, then click **Exit** to exit Excel and return to the Windows Program Manager.

Exiting Windows

Before Mike turns off his computer, he exits Windows. Mike knows that it is a good idea to exit Windows before he turns off his computer so all files are properly closed.

To exit Windows:
1. Click **File** on the Program Manager menu bar to display the File menu.
2. Click **Exit Windows....** A dialog box displays the message "This will end your Windows session."
3. Click the **OK button** to exit Windows and return to the DOS prompt.

The InWood site selection team has completed its work. Mike's decision-support worksheet helped the team analyze the data and recommend Scottsdale as the best site for InWood's next golf course. Although the Japanese market was a strong factor in favor of locating the course in Japan's Chiba Prefecture, the mountainous terrain and competition from nearby courses reduced the desirability of this location.

Questions

1. List three uses of spreadsheets in business. p. EX 9
2. In your own words describe what a spreadsheet program does.
3. Identify each of the numbered components of the Excel window shown in Figure 1-33.

study!

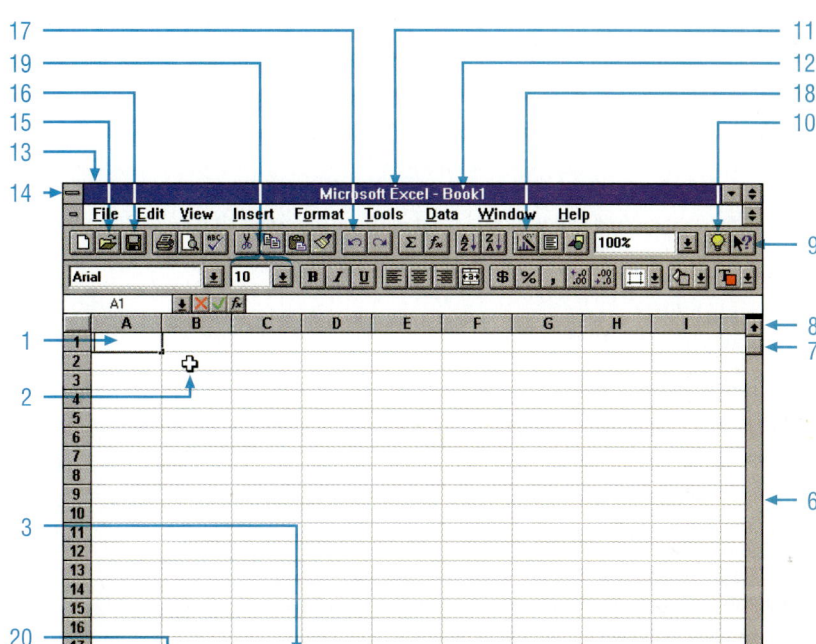

Figure 1-33

4. Identify each of the following buttons.
   a.
   b.
   c.
   d.
   e.
5. Draw four shapes the pointer can assume in the Excel window and describe the task you are performing when each pointer shape appears.
6. A(n) _____ is the rectangular area at the intersection of a column and row.
7. When you _____ a workbook, the computer copies it from your disk into RAM.
8. The cell with a black border around it is called the _____.
9. To view more than one window pane, use the _____ bar.
10. Use the _____ command the first time you want to save a file.
11. The _____ command is useful if you enter a number by mistake and want to restore the original value.
12. Any set of characters that Excel does not use for calculations is called _____.
13. The _____ guides you through five steps to create a chart.

14. If you want to save the new version of a file in place of the old version, use the _____ command.
15. Numbers, dates, and times that Excel uses for calculations are called _____.
16. How can you tell exactly what a cell contains?
17. The colon in the notation B4:B6 indicates a(n) _____.
18. A(n) _____ is a special prewritten formula that provides a shortcut for commonly used calculations.
19. A(n) _____ specifies the calculations you want Excel to make.
20. In the formula =B5*125, B5 is a(n) _____.
21. Identify each of the following mathematical operators:
    a. *
    b. −
    c. +
    d. /
22. Indicate whether Excel would treat each of the following cell entries as a value, text, or a formula:
    a. Profit
    b. 11/09/95
    c. February 10, 1996
    d. =AVERAGE(B5:B20)
    e. 11:01:25
    f. =B9*225
    g. =A6*D8
    h. 227−1240
    i. =SUM(C1:C10)
    j. 372-80-2367
    k. 123 N. First St.
23. How do you write the function that is the equivalent of the formula =A1+A2+A3+A4?
E 24. Use the resources in your library to find information on decision-support systems. Write a one- or two-page paper that describes what a decision-support system is and how one might be used in a business. Also include your ideas on the relationship between spreadsheets and decision-support systems.

Tutorial Assignments

The other company that had planned a golf course in Chiba, Japan has run into financial difficulties. There are rumors that the project may be canceled. A copy of the final InWood Design team workbook is stored on your Student Disk in the file T1GOLF2.XLS. Do the Tutorial Assignments below to modify this worksheet to show the effect that the cancellation of the other project would have on your site selection. Print your results for Tutorial Assignment 13. Write your answers to Tutorial Assignments 14 through 16.

1. Launch Windows and Excel. Make sure your Student Disk is in the disk drive.
2. Open the file T1GOLF2.XLS.
3. Use the Save As command to save the workbook as S1GOLF2.XLS so you do not modify the original workbook for this set of Tutorial Assignments.
4. Click the TipWizard button to display the TipWizard box. As you complete the following Tutorial Assignments notice that the information in the TipWizard box changes.
5. In the S1GOLF2.XLS worksheet change the competition raw score for Chiba from 2 to 3.
6. Use the vertical scroll bar to view the effect on the chart showing Weighted Scores.

7. Enter the text "Scores if the Competing Project in Chiba, Japan is Canceled" in cell B2.

The importance weight assigned to each factor is a critical component in the site selection worksheet. Create a bar chart that shows the importance weights assigned to each factor.

8. Highlight cells A4 through B9.
9. Activate the ChartWizard.
10. Locate the chart in cells A66 through F85.
11. Use the ChartWizard - Steps 1 through 4 to select a bar chart using format 6.
12. For the ChartWizard - Step 5 of 5, enter "Importance Weights" as the chart title and indicate that you do not want to use a legend for the chart.
13. Save the worksheet and chart as S1GOLF2.XLS.
14. Print the entire worksheet, including the charts.

E 15. Use the Help button to learn the function of the four buttons shown in Figure 1-34.

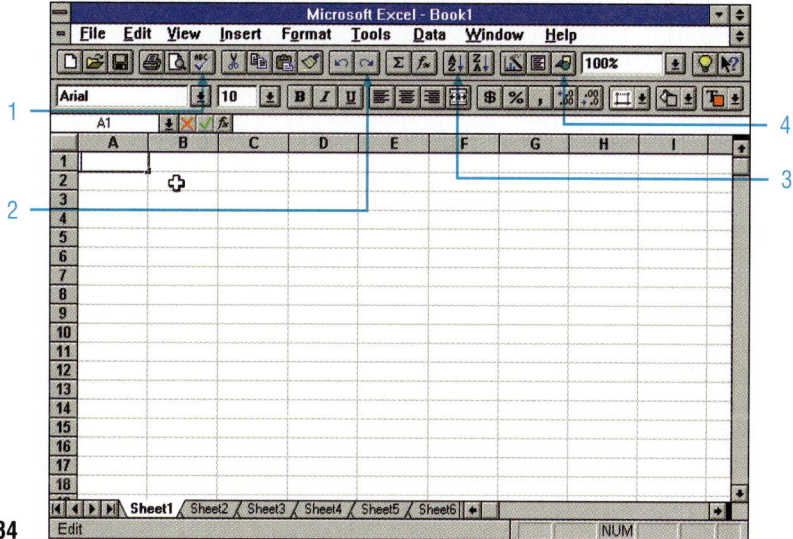

Figure 1-34

E 16. Use the Help button to learn more about the Print command on the File menu. How can you print a chart without printing the entire worksheet?

E 17. Use the scroll arrows to scroll through the tips in the TipWizard box. What new information did you learn? Click the TipWizard button in the toolbar to close the TipWizard box.

18. Exit Excel.

Case Problems

1. Selecting a Hospital Laboratory Computer System for Bridgeport Medical Center

David Choi is on the Laboratory Computer Selection Committee for the Bridgeport Medical Center. After an extensive search, the committee identified three vendors with products that appear to meet its needs. The Selection Committee prepared an Excel worksheet to help evaluate the strengths and weaknesses of the three potential vendors. The raw scores for two of the vendors, LabStar and Health Systems, have already been entered. Now the raw scores must be entered for the third vendor, MedTech. Which vendor's system is best for the Bridgeport Medical Center? Complete the following steps to find out:

1. If necessary, launch Windows and Excel. Make sure your Student Disk is in the disk drive.
2. Open the workbook P1LAB.XLS.
3. Use the Save As command to save the workbook as S1LAB.XLS so you don't modify the original workbook for this case.
4. Enter the following raw scores for MedTech:
   Cost = 6, Compatibility = 5, Vendor Reliability = 5, Size of Installed Base = 4, User Satisfaction = 5, Critical Functionality = 9, Additional Functionality = 8
5. Use the ChartWizard to create a column chart showing the total weighted scores for the three vendors. *Hint:* The chart will include cells C24 to E25. Position the chart below the worksheet in cells A28 to E46. Use a column chart with format 2. Enter "Total Weighted Scores" as the chart title.
6. Use the Save command to save the modified worksheet and chart.
7. Print the worksheet and chart.

2. Market Share Analysis at Aldon Industries

Helen Shalala is the Assistant to the Regional Director for Aldon Industries, a manufacturer of corporate voice mail systems. Helen prepared an analysis of the market share of the top vendors with installations in the region. Helen is on her way to a meeting with the marketing staff where she will use her worksheet to plan a new marketing campaign. Help Helen and her team evaluate the options and plan the best advertising campaign for Aldon Industries. Write your responses to questions 4 through 10, then create the chart and print it.

1. If necessary, launch Windows and Excel. Make sure your Student Disk is in the disk drive.
2. Open the workbook P1SHARE.XLS.
3. Use the Save As command to save the workbook as S1SHARE.XLS so you don't modify the original workbook for this case.
4. Examine the worksheet. Do the following ranges contain text, values, or formulas?
   a. B13:F13
   b. C3:C10
   c. A3:A10
   d. G3:G10
5. What is Aldon Industries' overall share of the market?
6. Examine the worksheet to determine in which state Aldon Industries currently has the highest market share.
7. Aldon Industries currently runs localized marketing campaigns in each state.
   a. In which state does Aldon Industries appear to have the most successful marketing campaign?
   b. In which state does Aldon Industries appear to have the least successful marketing campaign?
8. Which company is the overall market leader?
9. What is Aldon Industries' overall ranking in total market share (1st, 2nd, 3rd, etc.)?
10. Which companies rank ahead of Aldon Industries in total market share?
11. Michigan is the state in which Aldon Industries has its lowest market share. Use the ChartWizard to create a column chart showing the number of installations in Michigan for each company. *Hint:* The chart will include the range A2 through B10. Place the chart in cells A15 through F50. Select format 2 for the column chart. Enter "Installations in Michigan" as the chart title.
12. Save the worksheet and chart on your Student Disk.
13. Print the worksheet and chart.

3. Completing Your Own Decision Analysis

Think of a decision that you are trying to make. It might be choosing a new car, selecting a major, deciding where to go for vacation, or accepting a job offer. Use the workbook P1DECIDE.XLS to evaluate up to three options on the basis of up to five factors. Write your responses to questions 10 through 13 and print the worksheet and chart.

1. If necessary, launch Windows and Excel. Make sure your Student Disk is in the disk drive.
2. Open the workbook P1DECIDE.XLS.
3. Use the Save As command to save the workbook as S1DECIDE.XLS.
4. Click cell A1 and type the worksheet title.
5. Type the titles for up to three choices in cells C4, D4, and E4.
6. Type the titles for up to five factors in cells A6 to A10.
7. Type the importance weights for each of the five factors in cells B6 to B10.
8. Type the raw scores for each of your choices in columns C, D, and E.
9. Use the ChartWizard to create a column chart showing the total weighted scores for each choice.
10. Write a paragraph explaining your choice of factors and assignment of importance weights.
11. On the basis of the current importance weights and raw scores, which option appears most desirable?
12. How confident are you that the worksheet shows the most desirable choice?
13. Write a paragraph explaining your reaction to the results of the worksheet.
14. Save the worksheet and chart on your Student Disk.
15. Print the worksheet and chart.

TUTORIAL 2

Planning, Building, Testing, and Documenting Worksheets

OBJECTIVES

In this tutorial you will:
- Plan, build, test, and document a worksheet
- Enter labels, values, and formulas
- Change column width
- Create a series with AutoFill
- Use the fill handle to copy data and formulas
- Learn about relative and absolute references
- Use the SUM function and the AutoSum button
- Insert a row
- Format cells with the AutoFormat command
- Add a text note to a worksheet
- Check the spelling of a worksheet
- Lock and unlock cells
- Create an Excel template

Creating a Standardized Income and Expense Template for Branch Offices

CASE

SGL Business Training and Consulting

SGL Business Training and Consulting, headquartered in Springfield, Massachusetts, provides consulting services and management training for small businesses. SGL has 12 regional branch offices throughout the United States. The managers of these branch offices prepare a quarterly report called an "Income and Expense Summary" and send it to Otis Nunley, a staff accountant who works at SGL headquarters.

Each quarter Otis must compile the income and expense information from the 12 reports. This task has not been easy because the branch managers do not use the same categories for income and expenses. For example, some of the managers have money they can use for advertising, and so they list advertising as an expense; other managers do not have money for advertising, and therefore advertising is not an expense on their reports.

Otis knows that he can simplify the task of consolidating the branch office information if he can convince the branch managers to use a standardized form for their reports. He gets approval from management to create an Excel template as the standardized form that branch managers will use to report income and expenses.

A **template** is a preformatted worksheet that contains labels and formulas, but does not contain any values. Otis will send the template to the branch managers. Each manager will fill in the template with income and expense information, then send it back to Otis. With all the information in a standard format, Otis will be able to consolidate it easily into a company-wide report.

Otis studies the branch managers' reports and then plans how to create a standardized worksheet template for reporting income and expenses. In this tutorial, you will work with Otis as he plans, builds, tests, and documents the worksheet template for the SGL branch managers.

Developing Effective Worksheets

An effective worksheet is well planned, carefully built, thoroughly tested, and comprehensively documented. When you develop a worksheet, therefore, you should do each of the following activities:

- *Plan* the worksheet by identifying the overall goal of the project; listing the requirements for input, output, and calculations; and sketching the layout of the worksheet.
- *Build* the worksheet by entering labels, values, and formulas, then format the worksheet so it has a professional appearance.
- *Test* the worksheet to make sure that it provides correct results.
- *Document* the worksheet by recording the information others will need to understand, use, and revise the worksheet.

Although planning is generally the first activity of the worksheet development process, the four development activities are not necessarily sequential. After you begin to enter labels, values, and formulas for the worksheet, you might need to return to the planning activity and revise your original plan. You are also likely to return to the building activity to change some values or formulas after you have tested the worksheet. And, it is important to note that documentation activities can and should take place throughout the process of worksheet development. For example, you might jot down some documentation notes as you are planning the worksheet, or you might enter documentation on the worksheet itself as you are building it.

Planning the Worksheet

To create a plan for the SGL worksheet template, Otis first studies the content and format of the reports from the branch managers. He notices that although there are 12 branches, there are only three different report formats.

The reports from four of the branch managers look similar to the sample report in Figure 2-1. On these reports the labels for each quarter are arranged on the left side of the report. The column titles, arranged across the top of the report, are Income, Expenses, and Profit. The profit for each quarter is calculated by subtracting the expenses from the income. Annual totals are displayed at the bottom of the report.

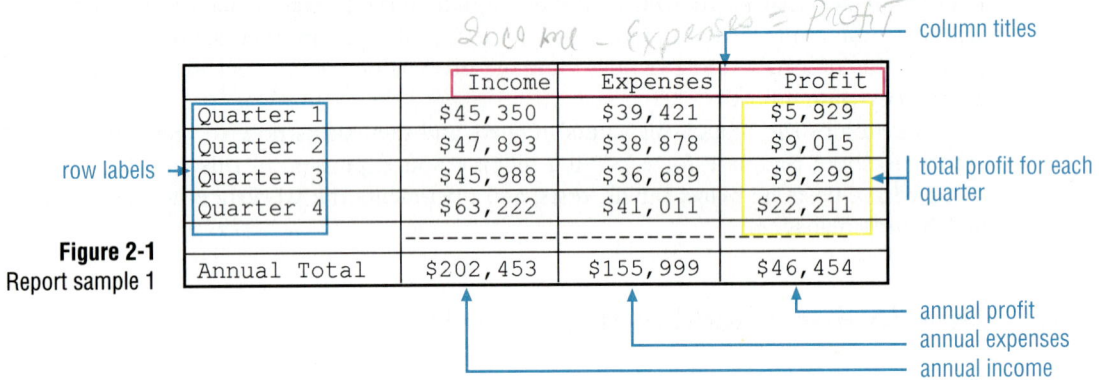

Figure 2-1
Report sample 1

The reports from five of the branch managers look similar to the sample report in Figure 2-2. The format of report sample 2 is very different from that of report sample 1. On report sample 2 the quarters are listed across the top as Q1, Q2, Q3, and Q4, rather than down the side. The income and expense categories are referred to as *revenue* and *expenses* and are listed down the left side of the report. This report has one revenue category and six expense categories. For each revenue or expense category, the sum of the amounts for each quarter produces the year-to-date totals shown on the right side of the report. The profit, shown at the bottom of the worksheet, is calculated by subtracting the total expenses from the total revenue.

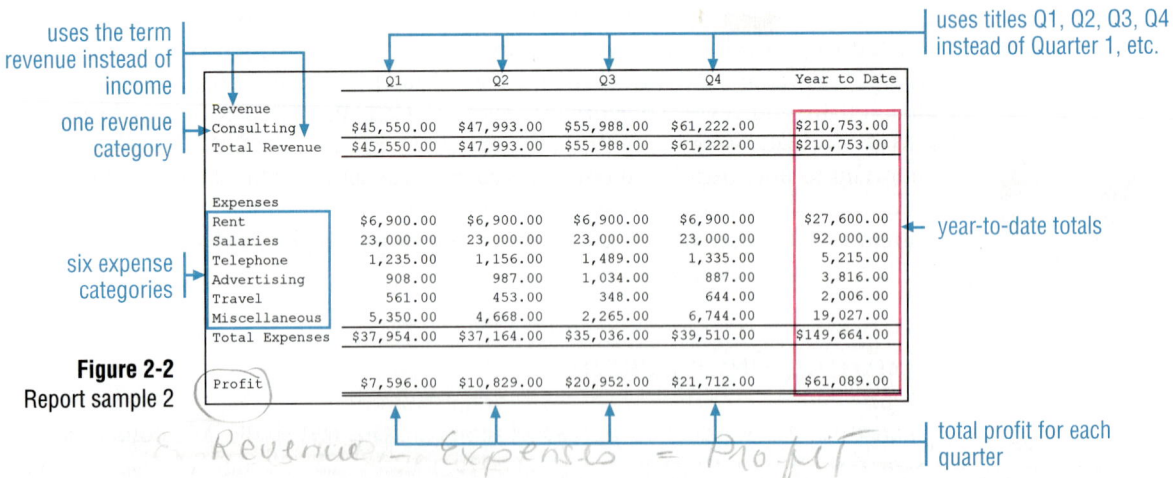

Figure 2-2
Report sample 2

The reports from the remaining branch managers look similar to the sample report in Figure 2-3. Notice the two income categories and eight expense categories. The titles for each quarter are listed across the top of the report. For each income or expense category, the sum of the amounts for each quarter produces the year-to-date totals shown on the right side of the report. The total profit for each quarter is shown in the last row of the report.

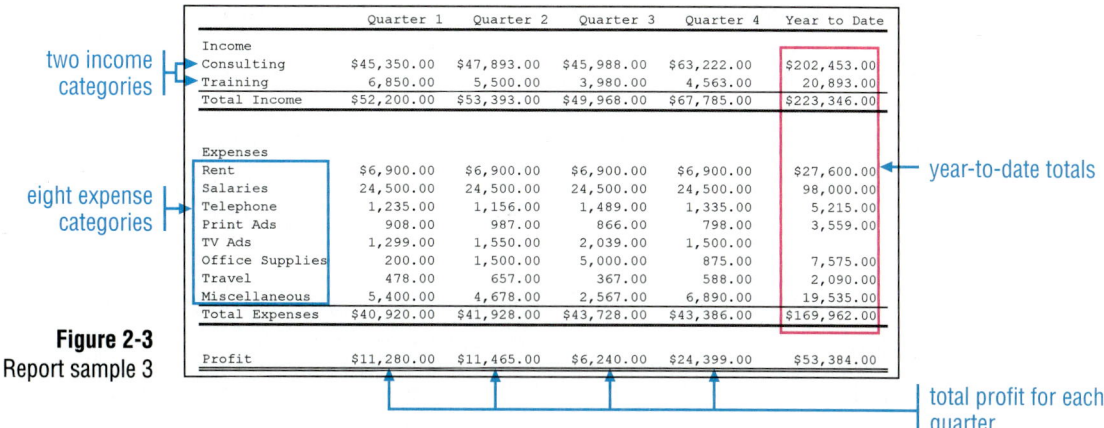

Figure 2-3
Report sample 3

After he studies the reports, Otis writes out a worksheet plan that:
- lists the goal(s) for the worksheet development project
- identifies the results, or *output*, that the worksheet must produce
- lists the information, or *input*, that is required to construct the worksheet
- specifies the calculations that use the input to produce the required output

The worksheet plan will guide Otis as he builds and tests the worksheet. Figure 2-4 shows the worksheet plan that Otis created.

Worksheet Plan for Loan Management Worksheet

My Goal:
To develop an Excel template that all branch managers can use to submit income and expense reports.

What results do I want to see?
Income categories for consulting and training.
Expense categories for rent, salaries, telephone, advertising, office supplies, travel, and miscellaneous.
Income and expenses for each quarter.
Total income for each quarter.
Total expenses for each quarter.
Total profit for each quarter.

What information do I need?
The amount for each income and expense category.

What calculations will I perform?
Total income = consulting income + training income
Total expenses = rent+salaries+telephone+advertising+office supplies+travel+miscellaneous
Profit = total income − total expenses

Figure 2-4
Otis's worksheet plan

TUTORIAL 2 Planning, Building, Testing, and Documenting Worksheets

After he completes the worksheet plan, Otis draws a sketch of the worksheet template, showing the worksheet titles, row labels, column titles, and formulas (Figure 2-5). He decides to list the income and expense categories down the left side of the worksheet and list the quarters across the top.

[Handwritten note: "just drag horizontally will automatically appear Qtr 1 – Qtr 4"]

Income and Expense Summary				
	Quarter 1	Quarter 2	Quarter 3	Quarter 4
Income				
Consulting	$9,999,999.99	$9,999,999.99	$9,999,999.99	$9,999,999.99
Training	:	:	:	:
Total Income	${total income formula}	${total income formula}	${total income formula}	${total income formula}
Expenses				
Rent	$9,999,999.99	$9,999,999.99	$9,999,999.99	$9,999,999.99
Salaries	:	:	:	:
Telephone	:	:	:	:
Advertising	:	:	:	:
Office Supplies	:	:	:	:
Travel	:	:	:	:
Miscellaneous	:	:	:	:
Total Expenses	${total expenses formula}	${total expenses formula}	${total expenses formula}	${total expenses formula}
Profit	${profit formula}	${profit formula}	${profit formula}	${profit formula}

Figure 2-5
Otis's sketch of his planned worksheet

The dollar signs indicate that Otis will format these cells for currency. The number 9,999,999.99 indicates the largest number these cells can hold and specifies how wide these columns must be on the final version of the worksheet.

Otis indicates which cells will contain formulas by using "curly brackets," {}. The formulas are described in the calculation section of the worksheet plan in Figure 2-4. For example, the {total income formula} shown on the sketch is described in the worksheet plan as:

total income = consulting income + training income

Look in the calculation section of the worksheet plan in Figure 2-4 to find the descriptions for the rest of the formulas on Otis's worksheet sketch.

Now that Otis has completed the worksheet plan and the worksheet sketch, he is ready to start building the worksheet. Let's launch Excel now and work with Otis as he builds the worksheet.

To launch Excel and maximize the worksheet:
1. Launch Windows and Excel following your usual procedure.
2. Make sure your Student Disk is in the disk drive.
3. Make sure the Microsoft Excel and Book1 windows are maximized.

Building the Worksheet

As you learned in Tutorial 1, a worksheet generally contains values, labels that describe the values, and formulas that perform calculations. When you build a worksheet, you usually enter the labels first. What you enter next depends on how you intend to use the worksheet. If you intend to use the worksheet as a template, you will enter formulas, then enter values. If you are not creating a template, you would generally enter the values before you enter the formulas.

In addition to entering labels, formulas, and perhaps, values, when you build a worksheet you should format it so the information is displayed in a way that is clear and understandable.

Otis intends to create a template to send to the branch managers, so he will enter the labels, enter the formulas, then format the worksheet. The branch managers will enter the values later.

Entering Labels

When you build a worksheet, the first step is to enter the labels you defined in the planning stage. When you type a label in a cell, Excel aligns the label at the left side of the cell. Labels that are too long to fit in a cell spill over into the cell or cells to the right, if those cells are empty. If the cell to the right is not empty, Excel displays only as much of the label as fits in the cell. Otis begins by entering the worksheet title.

To enter the worksheet title:
1. Click cell **A1** to make it the active cell.
2. Type **Income and Expense Summary** and press **[Enter]**. The title appears in cell A1 and spills over into cells B1 and C1. Cell A2 is now the active cell.

Otis continues working in column A to enter the labels for the income and expense categories he defined on his worksheet sketch in Figure 2-5.

To enter the labels for the income categories:
1. Click cell **A3** to make it the active cell.

    TROUBLE? If you make a mistake while typing, remember that you can use the Backspace key to correct errors.

2. Type **Income** and press **[Enter]** to complete the entry and move to cell A4.
3. In cell A4 type **Consulting** and press **[Enter]**.
4. In cell A5 type **Training** and press **[Enter]**.
5. In cell A6 type **Total Income** and press **[Enter]**.

Next, Otis enters the labels for the expense categories.

To enter the labels for the expense categories:

1. Click cell **A8** to make it the active cell.
2. Type **Expenses** and press **[Enter]** to complete the entry and move to cell A9.
3. Refer to Figure 2-6 and type the labels for cells A9 through A16: **Rent, Salaries, Telephone, Advertising, Office Supplies, Travel, Miscellaneous,** and **Total Expenses**.

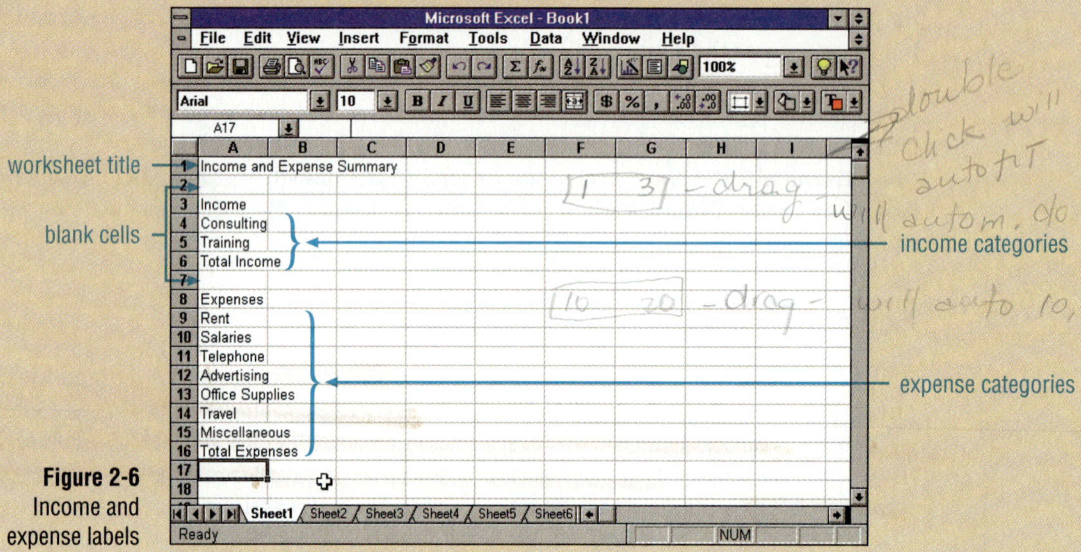

Figure 2-6
Income and expense labels

Otis wants to leave a blank row after the "Total Expenses" label and put the label "Profit" in cell A18.

To enter the label "Profit" in cell A18:

1. Press [↓] until the active cell is A18.
2. Type **Profit** and press **[Enter]**.

Otis notices that the text in some of the cells spills over into column B, so he decides to increase the width of column A.

Changing Column Width

The number of letters or numbers that Excel displays in a cell depends on the size and style of the lettering, or font, you are using and the width of the column. If you do not change the width of the columns on your worksheet, Excel automatically uses a column width that displays about eight and a half digits. To display the exact column width in the formula bar, simply press and hold the mouse button while the pointer is over the dividing line.

As shown in Figure 2-7, Excel provides several methods for changing column width. For example, you can click a column heading or drag the pointer to highlight a series of column headings and then use the Format menu. You can also use the dividing line between column headings. When you move the pointer over the dividing line between two column headings, the pointer changes to ✢. You can use the pointer to drag the dividing line to a new location. You can also double-click the dividing line to make the column as wide as the longest text label or number in the column.

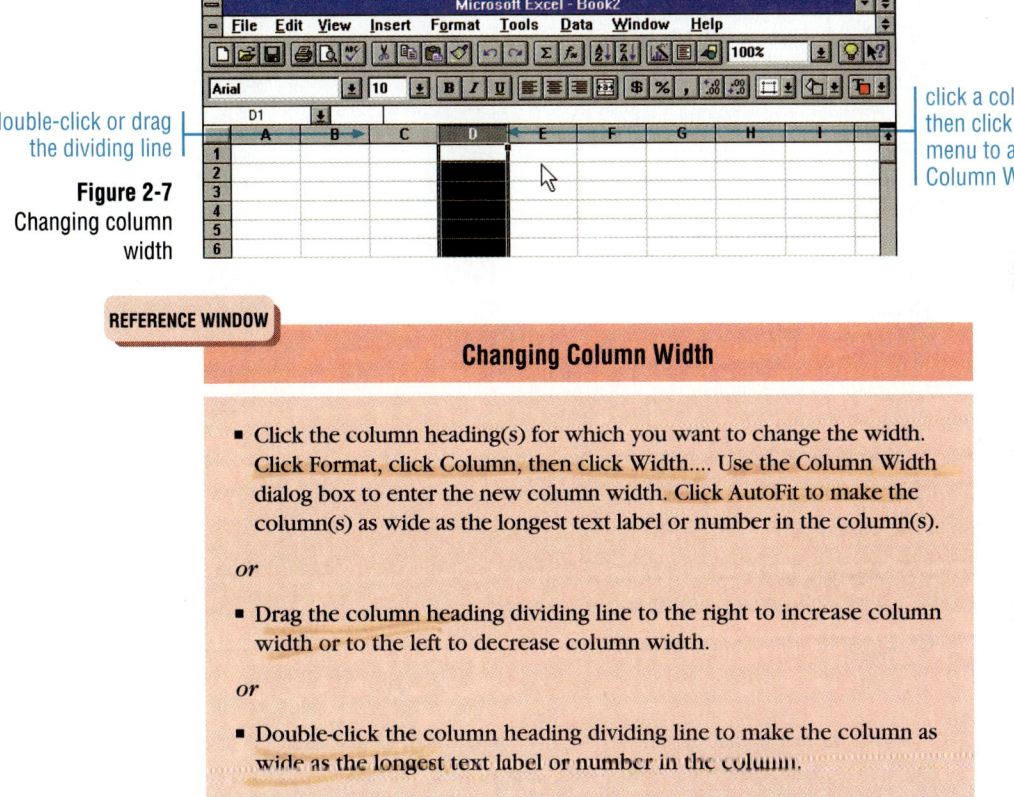

double-click or drag the dividing line

Figure 2-7
Changing column width

click a column heading, then click the Format menu to access the Column Width dialog box

REFERENCE WINDOW

Changing Column Width

- Click the column heading(s) for which you want to change the width. Click Format, click Column, then click Width.... Use the Column Width dialog box to enter the new column width. Click AutoFit to make the column(s) as wide as the longest text label or number in the column(s).

or

- Drag the column heading dividing line to the right to increase column width or to the left to decrease column width.

or

- Double-click the column heading dividing line to make the column as wide as the longest text label or number in the column.

Otis wants to change the width of column A so that all the labels fit within the boundary of column A. He decides to double-click the column heading dividing line.

To change the width of column A:

❶ Position the pointer on the box that contains the column heading for column A.

❷ Move the pointer slowly to the right until it is positioned over the dividing line between column A and column B. Notice how the pointer changes to ✢.

❸ Double-click the dividing line. Column A automatically adjusts to the appropriate width and the worksheet title fits completely in cell A1. See Figure 2-8.

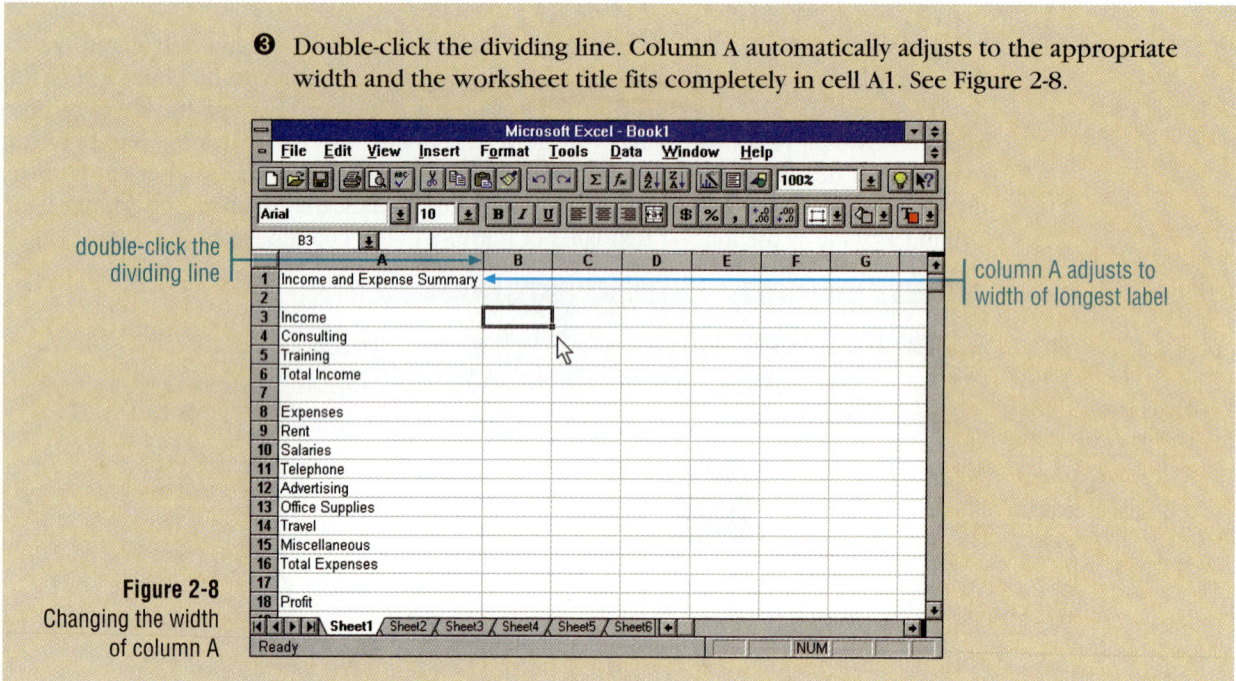

Figure 2-8
Changing the width of column A

Next, Otis begins to enter the column titles for each quarter. He starts by entering the label "Quarter 1" in cell B2.

To enter the label "Quarter 1" in cell B2:
❶ Click cell **B2** to make it the active cell.
❷ Type **Quarter 1** and press **[Enter]**.

Otis is not a fast typist. He wonders if there is any way to avoid typing the name of the next three quarters across the top of the worksheet. Then he remembers a feature called AutoFill.

Creating a Series with AutoFill

AutoFill is an Excel feature that automatically fills areas of the worksheet with a series of values or text. To use this feature you type one or two initial values or text entries, then AutoFill does the rest. AutoFill evaluates the initial entry or entries, determines the most likely sequence to follow, and completes the remaining entries in the range of cells you specify.

AutoFill recognizes series of numbers, dates, times, and certain labels. Figure 2-9 shows a selection of series that AutoFill recognizes and completes.

Initial Entry	Completed With
Monday	Tuesday, Wednesday, etc.
Mon	Tue, Wed, etc.
January	February, March, etc.
Jan	Feb, Mar, etc.
Quarter 1	Quarter 2, Quarter 3, etc.
Qtr1	Qtr2, Qtr3, etc.
11:00 AM	12:00 PM, 1:00 PM, etc.
Product 1	Product 2, Product 3, etc.
1992, 1993	1994, 1995, etc.
1, 2, 3, 4	5, 6, 7, etc.
1, 3, 5	7, 9, 11, etc.

Figure 2-9
Series completed by AutoFill

If you use a repeating series such as months or days of the week, you can begin anywhere in the series. If there are cells that need to be filled after the series ends, AutoFill repeats the series again from the beginning. For example, if you enter "October," AutoFill completes the series by entering "November" and "December," then it continues the series with "January," "February," and so on.

When you use AutoFill, you drag the fill handle to outline your initial entry and the cells you want to fill. The **fill handle**, shown in Figure 2-10, is the small black square in the lower-right corner of the active cell's border.

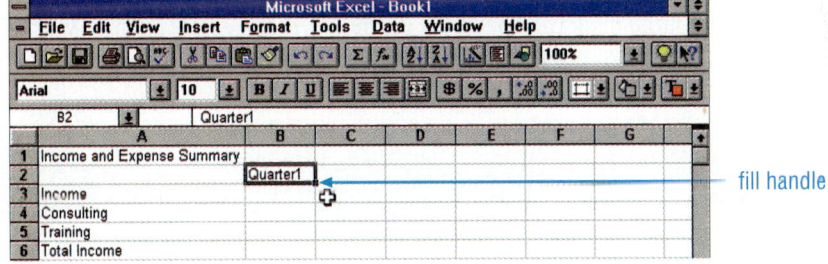

Figure 2-10
The fill handle

Otis uses AutoFill to enter the labels for the remaining quarters.

To fill in the labels for the rest of the quarters using AutoFill:

❶ Click cell **B2** to make it the active cell. Look closely at the black border that appears around the cell. Notice the fill handle, the small black square in the lower-right corner of the border.

❷ Move the pointer over the fill handle until the pointer changes to +.

❸ Click and drag the pointer across the worksheet to outline cells B2 through E2. See Figure 2-11.

Figure 2-11
Using AutoFill to fill in labels for cells B2 through E2

4. Release the mouse button. The label for each quarter appears in row 2 at the top of each column.
5. Click any cell to remove the highlighting from cells B2 through E2.

Renaming the Sheet

In the lower-left corner of the worksheet window, Otis notices that the sheet is currently named "Sheet1"—the name Excel uses automatically when it opens a new workbook. But now that the worksheet is taking shape, Otis decides to give it a more specific name: "Income and Expense." This way, if, in the future he uses other sheets in the workbook he'll be able to find the Income and Expense Summary quickly and easily.

To rename Sheet1:
1. Double-click the **Sheet1 tab** in the lower-left corner of the worksheet to open the Rename Sheet dialog box. See Figure 2-12.

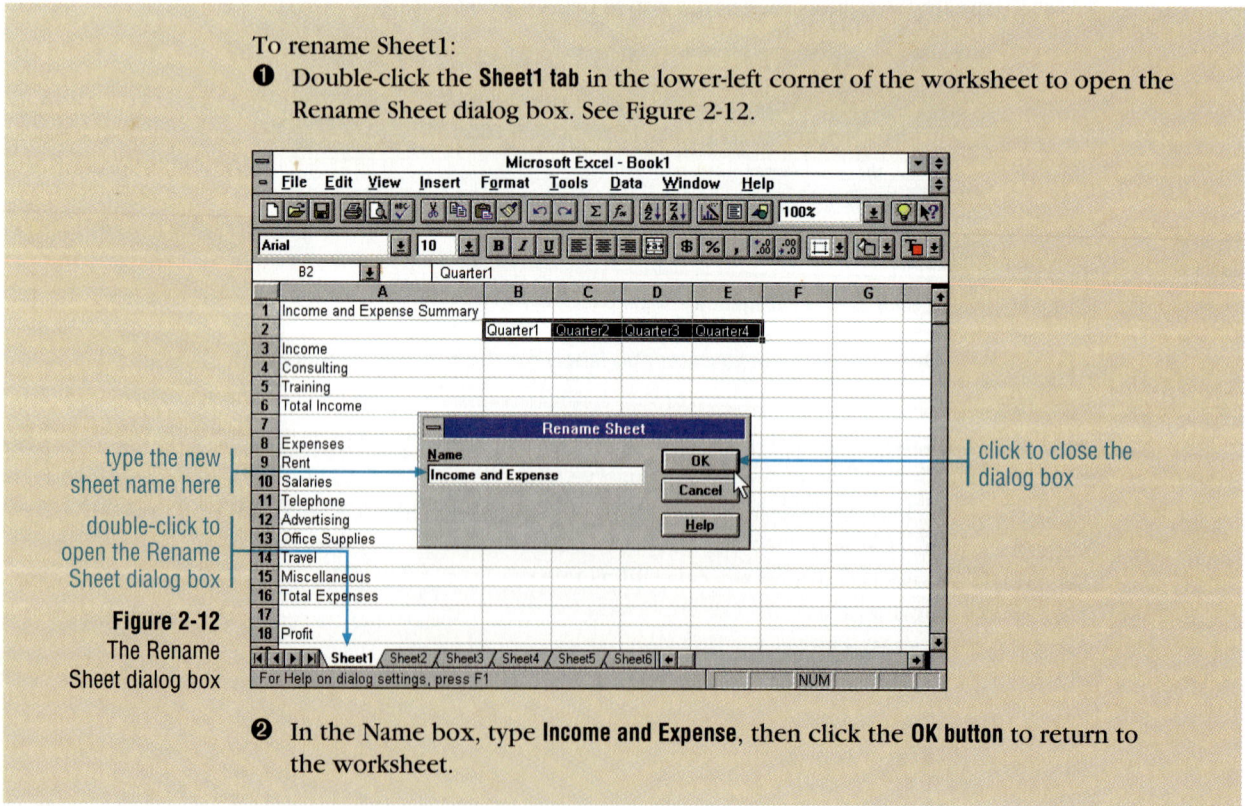

Figure 2-12
The Rename Sheet dialog box

2. In the Name box, type **Income and Expense**, then click the **OK button** to return to the worksheet.

Saving the New Workbook

Otis decides to save the workbook so he won't lose his work if the power goes out. Since this is the first time he has saved since renaming this sheet, Otis uses the Save As command to save the workbook and name it S2INC.XLS.

Excel filenames can contain up to eight characters. These characters can be letters, numbers, or any symbols except for spaces, commas, or the following: []"∧:,*?. Excel automatically adds the .XLS extension to the filename.

It is not always easy to create a descriptive filename using only eight characters, but it is possible to design a file naming scheme that provides meaningful abbreviations. For example, the files on your Student Disk are named and categorized using the first letter of the filename, as shown in Figure 2-13.

Figure 2-13
Categories of files

First Character of Filename	File Category	Description of File Category
C	Tutorial Case	The files you use to work through each tutorial
T	Tutorial Assignments	The files that contain the worksheets you need to complete the Tutorial Assignments at the end of each tutorial
P	Case Problems	The files that contain the worksheets you need to complete the Case Problems at the end of each tutorial
S	Saved Workbook	Any workbook that you save

The second character in the filenames on your Student Disk indicates the tutorial in which the file is created or used. For example, a filename that begins with C1 is a workbook you open in Tutorial 1; a filename that begins with S2 is a workbook you save in Tutorial 2. The remaining three to six characters of the filename are related to the content of the workbook. For example, in the next set of steps you will save your workbook as S2INC.XLS. The "S" signifies a file that you saved; the "2" means that you used the file in Tutorial 2; and "INC" refers to "income," to remind you that the file contains an income and expense summary worksheet. Let's save the file now.

To save the workbook as S2INC.XLS:

❶ Click **File**, then click **Save As...** to display the Save As dialog box.

❷ Type **S2INC** but don't press **[Enter]** because you need to check some additional settings. When you type the filename S2INC, you can use either uppercase or lowercase.

EX 54 TUTORIAL 2 Planning, Building, Testing, and Documenting Worksheets

3. Make sure the Drives box displays the icon for the drive that contains your Student Disk. If the correct drive icon is not shown, click the **Drives box down arrow button** to display a list of drives, then click the correct drive. Your Save As dialog box should look like the dialog box in Figure 2-14.

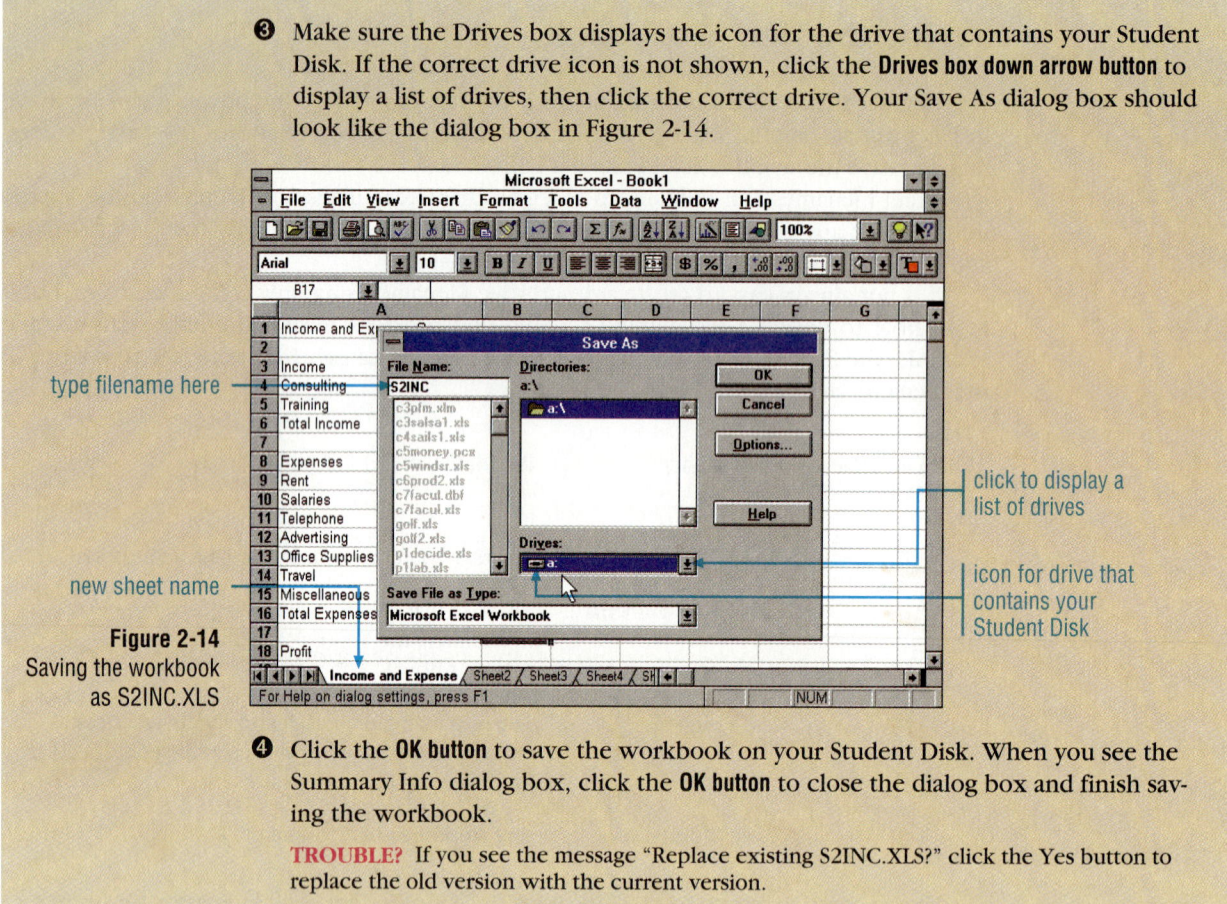

Figure 2-14
Saving the workbook as S2INC.XLS

4. Click the **OK button** to save the workbook on your Student Disk. When you see the Summary Info dialog box, click the **OK button** to close the dialog box and finish saving the workbook.

TROUBLE? If you see the message "Replace existing S2INC.XLS?" click the Yes button to replace the old version with the current version.

Now that Otis has entered the labels for the worksheet template, his next step is to enter the formulas.

Entering Formulas

You will recall from Tutorial 1 that formulas tell Excel what to calculate. When you enter a formula in a cell, begin the formula by typing an equal sign (=). The equal sign tells Excel that the numbers or symbols that follow it constitute a formula, not just data. Formulas can contain cell references such as A1 and G14, operators such as * and +, and numbers such as 30 or 247. Figure 2-15 shows some examples of the numbers, operators, and references you can include in a formula.

Example	Description	Example	Description
30	a number	<	less than sign
+	addition operator	>=	greater than or equal to sign
-	subtraction operator	<=	less than or equal to sign
/	division operator	<>	not equal to sign
*	multiplication operator	A1	reference to cell
%	percentage operator	(A1:A5)	reference to a range of cells
^	exponentiation operator	(A:A)	reference to entire column A
&	connects two text labels	(1:1)	reference to entire row 1
=	equal sign	(1:3)	reference to entire rows 1-3
>	greater than sign		

Figure 2-15 Examples of numbers, operators, and references used in formulas

Figure 2-16 shows that Excel displays the results of a formula in the cell in which you typed the formula. To view the formula itself, you must look at the formula bar.

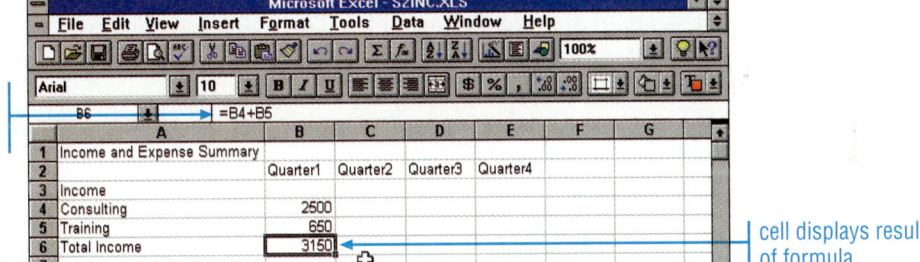

Figure 2-16 Viewing a formula and its result

formula bar shows the formula that is in cell B6

cell displays result of formula

When Excel calculates the results of a formula that contains more than one operator, it follows the standard order of operations shown in Figure 2-17.

Order	Operator	Description
1.	( )	parentheses
2.	^	exponentiation
3.	* /	multiplication or division
4.	+ -	addition or subtraction
5.	= <> > < >= <=	comparison

Figure 2-17 Order of operations

In accordance with the order of operations, Excel performs calculations by first doing any operations contained in parentheses, then any exponentiation, then any multiplication or division, and so on. For example, the result of the formula 3+4*5 is 23 because Excel completes the multiplication before the addition. The result of the formula (3+4)*5 is 35 because Excel calculates the operation in the parentheses first.

> **REFERENCE WINDOW**
>
> ### Entering a Formula
>
> - Click the cell where you want the result to appear.
> - Type = and then type the rest of the formula.
> - For formulas that include cell references, such as B2 or D78, you can type the cell reference or you can use the mouse or arrow keys to select each cell.
> - When the formula is complete, press [Enter].

Otis decides to enter the formula to calculate total income:

total income = consulting income + training income

The worksheet does not contain any values yet because Otis is building a template that will be filled in by the branch managers. Otis knows that when the consulting income is entered, it will be in cell B4. The training income will be in cell B5. Therefore, the formula for total income must add the contents of cells B4 and B5. Otis enters this formula as =B4+B5.

Otis wants the total income displayed in cell B6, so this is the cell in which he enters the formula.

To enter the formula for total income:

❶ Click cell **B6** because this is where you want the total income displayed.

❷ Type **=B4+B5** and press **[Enter]**. (You can use either uppercase or lowercase.) The result 0 appears in cell B6.

The result of the formula =B4+B5 is zero because cells B4 and B5 do not contain values.

Otis wants to enter the total income formulas for Quarters 2, 3, and 4. He could type the formula =C4+C5 in cell C6, then type the formula =D4+D5 in cell D6, and finally type the formula =E4+E5 in cell E6; but he can use a shortcut to copy the formula he entered for Quarter 1.

Using the Fill Handle to Copy a Formula

Earlier in this tutorial you used the fill handle in the lower-right corner of the active cell to fill the series that began with Quarter 1. You can also use the fill handle to copy the contents of a cell to other cells. Using the fill handle, you can copy formulas, values, and labels from one cell or from a group of cells.

> **REFERENCE WINDOW**
>
> **Copying Cell Contents with the Fill Handle**
>
> - Click the cell that contains the label, value, or formula you want to copy. If you want to copy the contents of more than one cell, highlight the cells you want to copy.
> - Drag the fill handle to outline the cells where you want the copy or copies to appear.
> - Release the mouse button.

Otis wants to copy the formula from cell B6 to cells C6, D6, and E6.

To copy the formula from cell B6 to cells C6, D6, and E6:
1. Click cell **B6** to make it the active cell.
2. Position the pointer over the fill handle (in the lower-right corner of cell B6) until the pointer changes to +.
3. Drag the pointer across the worksheet to outline cells B6 through E6.
4. Release the mouse button. Zeros now appear in cells B6 through E6.
5. Click any cell to remove the highlighting.

Otis thinks he might have made a mistake. The formula in B6 is =B4+B5. Because he copied this formula to cells C6, D6, and E6, Otis is concerned that Quarters 2, 3, and 4 will show the same total income as Quarter 1 when the branch managers enter their data. Otis decides to look at the formulas in cells C6, D6, and E6.

To examine the formulas in cells C6, D6, and E6:
1. Click cell **C6**. The formula =C4+C5 appears in the formula bar.
   It appears that when the formula from cell B6 was copied to cell C6, the cell references changed. The formula =B4+B5 became =C4+C5 when Excel copied it to column C.
2. Click cell **D6**. The formula =D4+D5 appears in the formula bar. When Excel copied the formula to column D, the cell references changed from B to D.
3. Click cell **E6**. The formula =E4+E5 appears in the formula bar.

When Otis copied the formula from cell B6, Excel automatically changed the cell references in the formulas to reflect the new position of the formulas in the worksheet.

Relative and Absolute References

Otis just learned how Excel uses relative references. A **relative reference** tells Excel which cell to use based on its location *relative* to the cell containing the formula. When you copy or move a formula that contains a relative reference, Excel changes the cell references so they refer to cells located in the same position relative to the cell that contains the new copy of the formula. Figure 2-18 shows how this works.

EX 58 TUTORIAL 2 Planning, Building, Testing, and Documenting Worksheets

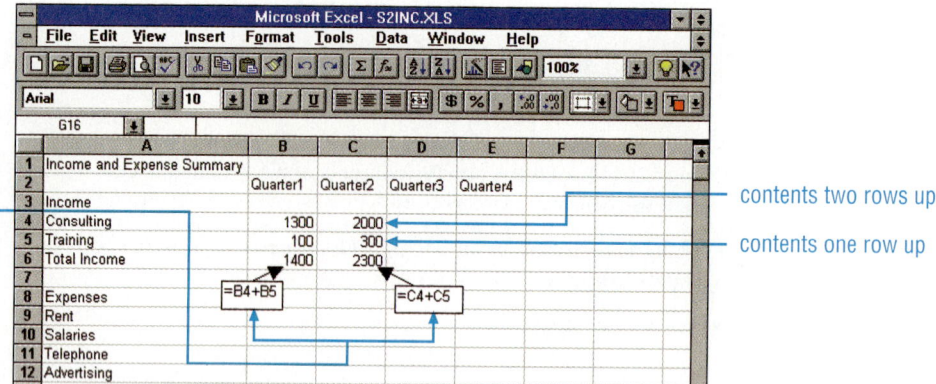

Figure 2-18
Relative references

Otis's original formula =B4+B5 contains relative references. Excel interpreted this formula to mean add the value from the cell two rows up (B4) to the cell one row up (B5) and display the result in the current cell (B6).

When Otis copied this formula to cell C6, Excel created the new formula to perform the same calculation, but starting at cell C6 instead of B6. The new formula means to add the value from the cell two rows up (C4) to the cell one row up (C5) and display the result in the current cell (C6).

All references in formulas are relative references unless you specify otherwise. Most of the time, you will want to use relative references because you can then copy and move formulas easily to different cells on the worksheet.

From time to time, you might need to create a formula that refers to a cell in a fixed location on the worksheet. A reference that always points to the same cell is an **absolute reference**. Absolute references contain a dollar sign before the column letter, the row number, or both. Examples of absolute references include $A$4, $C$27, $A17, and D$32. You will learn more about absolute references in Tutorial 4.

Otis continues to enter the other formulas he planned to put in the worksheet template, starting with the formula to calculate total expenses.

The SUM Function

The **SUM function** provides you with a shortcut for entering formulas that total the values in rows or columns. You can use the SUM function to replace a lengthy formula such as =B9+B10+B11+B12+B13+B14+B15 with the more compact formula =SUM(B9:B15).

REFERENCE WINDOW

Entering the SUM Function

- Type = to begin the function.

- Type SUM in either uppercase or lowercase, followed by (—an opening parenthesis. Do not put a space between SUM and the parenthesis.

- Type the range of cells you want to sum, separating the first and last cells in the range with a colon, as in B9:B15, or drag the pointer to outline the cells you want to sum.

Otis wants to enter a formula in cell B16 to calculate the total expenses by summing the expenses such as rent, salaries, and so forth. He uses the SUM function to do this.

To calculate the total expenses using the SUM function:
❶ Click cell **B16** because this is where you want to display the result of the formula.
❷ Type **=SUM(** to begin the formula. Don't forget to include the open parenthesis.
❸ Type **B9:B15)** and press **[Enter]**. Don't forget to include the closing parenthesis. The result, 0, appears in cell B16.

Normally, when typing a formula, you don't need to type the final parenthesis. Excel will automatically add it for you when you press [Enter]. You entered it yourself this time just for practice.

Now Otis can copy the formula in B16 to cells C16, D16, and E16.

To copy the formula from cell B16 to cells C16, D16, and E16:
❶ Make sure that cell B16 is the active cell.
❷ Drag the fill handle (in the lower-right corner of cell B16) to outline cells B16 through E16, then release the mouse button. Zeros appear in cells B16 through E16.
❸ Click any cell to remove the highlighting.

Otis reviews his worksheet plan and sketch to see what he should do next. He sees that he needs to enter the profit formula and considers how to do this.

Using the Mouse to Select Cell References

Excel provides several ways for you to enter cell references in a formula. One way is to type the cell references directly, as Otis did when he created the formula =B4+B5. Recall that he typed the equal sign, then typed B4, a plus sign, and finally B5. Another way to put a cell reference in a formula is to select the cell using the mouse or arrow keys. To use this method to enter the formula =B4+B5, Otis would type the equal sign, then click cell B4, type the plus sign, then click cell B5. Using the mouse to select cell references is often the preferred method because it minimizes typing errors.

Otis wants to calculate the profit for the first quarter:

profit = total income – total expenses

Otis looks at the worksheet to locate the cell references for the profit formula. Cell B6 contains the total income and cell B16 contains the total expenses, so Otis knows that the formula should be =B6–B16. Let's see how Otis creates the formula to calculate profit by selecting the cell references with the mouse.

To create the formula to calculate profit by selecting cell references:
❶ Click cell **B18** because this is where you want the result of the formula displayed.
❷ Type **=** to begin the formula.

❸ Click cell **B6**. Notice that a dashed box appears around cell B6. Also notice that B6 is added to the formula in the formula bar and in cell B18. See Figure 2-19.

TROUBLE? If you happen to click the wrong cell simply click again on the correct cell, B6.

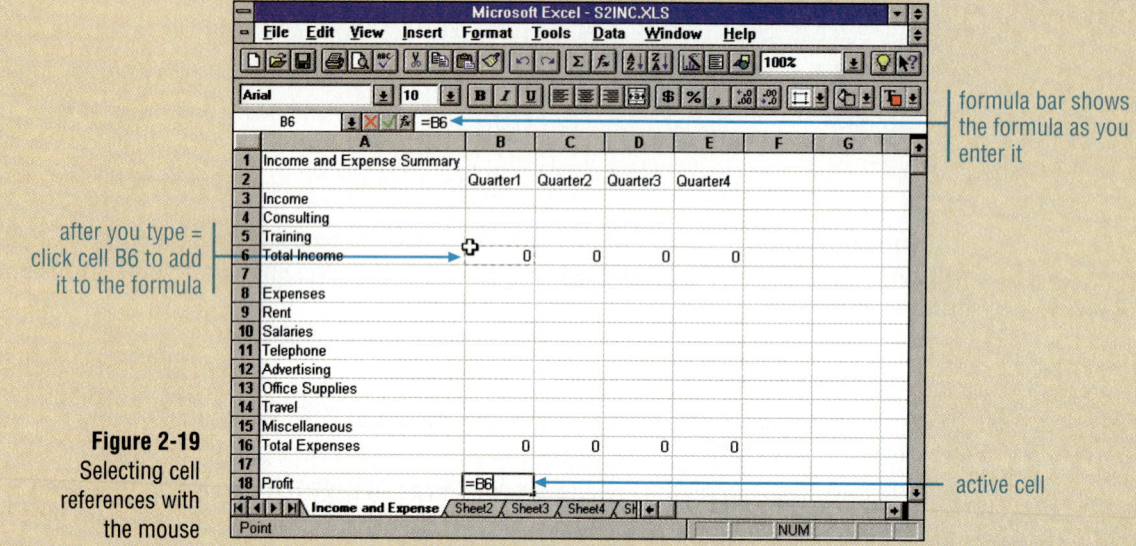

Figure 2-19
Selecting cell references with the mouse

❹ Type **–** (a minus sign). Notice that the dashed box disappears from cell B6. The formula bar and cell B18 now display =B6–.

❺ Click cell **B16**. A dashed box appears around cell B16, and the formula bar displays the entire formula =B6–B16.

❻ Press **[Enter]** to complete the formula. The result 0 appears in cell B18.

Now Otis copies the formula in B18 to cells C18, D18, and E18.

To copy the formula from B18 to cells C18, D18, and E18:
❶ Make cell B18 the active cell because it contains the formula you want to copy.
❷ Drag the fill handle to outline cells B18 through E18. Release the mouse button. Zeros appear in cells B18 through E18.
❸ Click any cell to remove the highlighting.

Now that all the formulas are entered, Otis decides to save the workbook.

❹ Click the **Save button** 🖫.

If you want to take a break and resume the tutorial at a later time, you can exit Excel by double-clicking the Control menu box in the upper-left corner of the screen. When you resume the tutorial, launch Excel, maximize the Microsoft Excel and Book1 windows, and place your Student Disk in the disk drive. Open the file S2INC.XLS, then continue with the tutorial.

■   ■   ■

Otis has entered labels and formulas and functions for each quarter. Before he proceeds, he decides to test the worksheet by entering test values.

Testing the Worksheet

Test values are numbers that generate a known result. You enter the test values in your worksheet to determine if your formulas are accurate. After you enter the test values, you compare the results on your worksheet with the known results. If the results on your worksheet don't match the known results, you have probably made an error.

Test values can be numbers from a real sample or simple numbers that make it easy to determine if the worksheet is calculating correctly. As an example of test values from a real sample, Otis could use numbers from an income and expense report that he knows has been calculated correctly. As an example of simple numbers, Otis could enter the value 1 in all the cells. Then it would be easy to do the calculations "in his head" to verify that the formulas are accurate.

Otis decides to use the number 100 as a test value because he can easily check the accuracy of the formulas he entered in the worksheet.

To enter the test value 100 in cells B4 and B5:

❶ Click cell **B4** to make it the active cell.

❷ Type **100** and press **[Enter]** to move to cell B5.

❸ Type **100** and press **[Enter]**. The value 200 appears in cell B6 and in cell B18.

Otis knows that 100 plus 100 equals 200. Since this is the result displayed in cell B6 for total income, it appears that the formula in this cell is correct. Otis decides to copy the test values from cells B4 and B5 to columns C, D, and E.

To copy the test values to cells C4 through E5:

❶ Drag the pointer to highlight cells B4 and B5, then release the mouse button.

❷ Drag the fill handle to outline cells B4 through E5. See Figure 2-20.

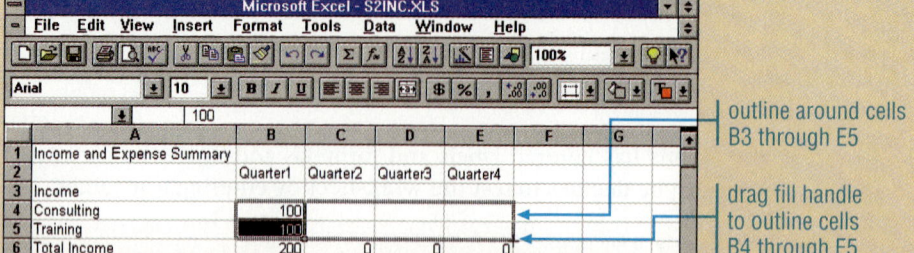

Figure 2-20
Copying test values

❸ Release the mouse button. The test value 100 appears in cells B4 through E5.

❹ Click any cell to remove the highlighting.

Otis notices that the formulas in cells B6, C6, D6, and E6 display 200 as the result of the formula that calculates total income. In addition, the formulas that calculate profit in cells B18, C18, D18, and E18 also display the value 200. This makes sense. The formula for profit is *total income – total expenses*. On the worksheet the total income is 200 and the total expenses are 0.

Otis decides to enter the test value 100 for each of the expense categories. He types the test value in cell B9, then copies it to cells B10 through B15. Then he copies the test values from column B to columns C, D, and E.

To enter a test value in cell B9, then copy it to cells B10 through B15:

❶ Click cell **B9** to make it the active cell.

❷ Type **100** and press **[Enter]**.

❸ Press [↑] to make cell B9 the active cell again.

❹ Drag the fill handle to outline cells B9 through B15, then release the mouse button. Do not remove the highlighting from the fill area. As a result the test value 100 appears in cells B9 through B15.

❺ Drag the fill handle again to outline cells B9 through E15, then release the mouse button. The test value 100 appears in cells B9 through E15.

❻ Click any cell to remove the highlighting. See Figure 2-21.

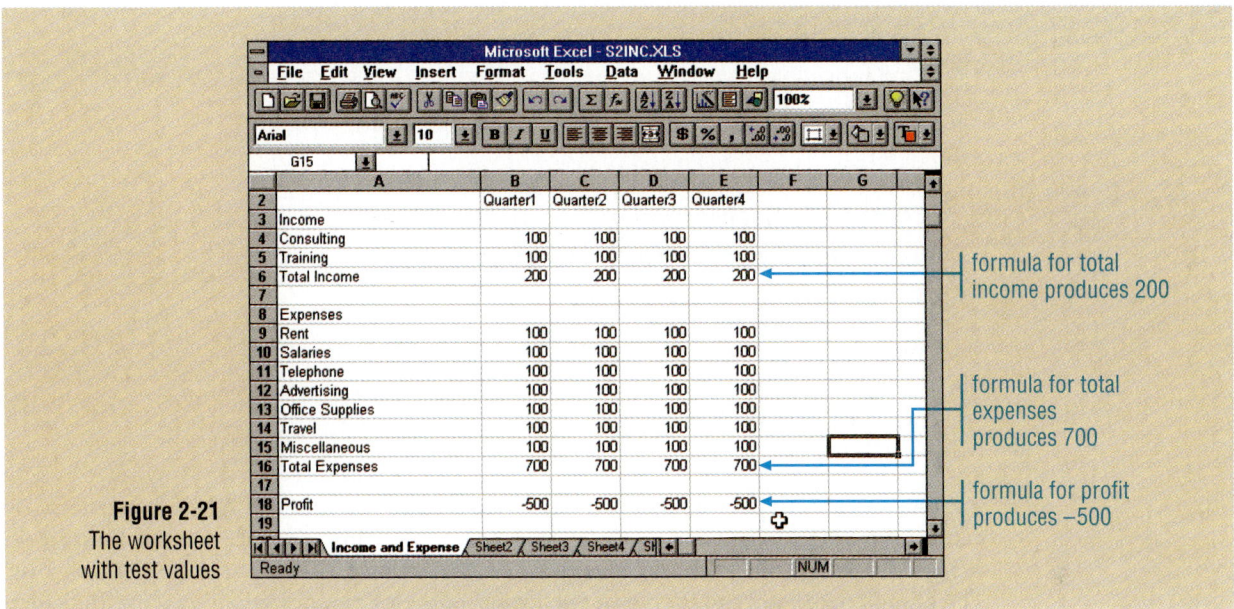

Figure 2-21
The worksheet with test values

Otis takes a moment to make sure that the formulas have produced the results he expected. The formulas for total expenses in cells B16, C16, D16, and E16 display 700. This looks correct because there are seven expense categories, each containing the test value 100.

The formulas for profit in cells B18, C18, D18, and E18 display -500. This also looks correct. Total income is 200, total expenses are 700, and 200 minus 700 equals -500.

Now Otis compares this worksheet to his worksheet sketch (Figure 2-5). He notices that on the worksheet sketch he left row 1 blank for the branch managers to type in their branch office names. He forgot to leave row 1 blank when he entered the labels on the worksheet, and now there isn't any space for the branch office name. Does Otis need to start over? No, Otis can use the Insert command to insert a blank row.

Inserting a Row or Column

You can insert a row or column in a worksheet to make room for new data or to make the worksheet easier to read. When you insert rows or columns, Excel repositions the other rows and columns in the worksheet and automatically adjusts the cell references in formulas to reflect the new location of values used in calculations. Using the **Insert command** you can insert an entire row or multiple rows. You can insert an entire column or multiple columns.

> **REFERENCE WINDOW**
>
> ## Inserting a Row or Column
>
> Use these instructions to insert a column by substituting "column" for "row."
>
> - Click any cell in the row where you want to insert the new row.
>
>   *or*
>
>   Highlight a range of rows where you want to insert new rows.
>
> - Click Insert and then click Rows. Excel inserts one row for every row in the highlighted range.

Otis decides to use the Insert menu to insert a row at the top of the worksheet. He cannot type a branch name in the new row because this template will be used by 12 branch offices. Instead, Otis decides to enter "SGL Branch Office Name" in the new row. The branch managers can then type the names of their branches when they use the worksheet. Let's see how Otis inserts a row for the branch office name.

To insert a row at the top of the worksheet:

1. Click cell **A1** because you want one new row to be inserted at the location of the current row.

2. Click **Insert** and then click **Rows**. Excel inserts a blank row at the top of the worksheet. All other rows shift down one row.

3. Make sure cell A1 is still active, then type **SGL Branch Office Name** and press **[Enter]**.

Adding a row changed the location of the data in the worksheet. For example, the consulting income that was originally in cell B4 is now in cell B5. Otis hopes that Excel adjusted the formulas to compensate for the new row.

Otis originally entered the formula =B4+B5 in cell B6 to calculate total income. Now the value for consulting income is in cell B5, and the value for training income is in cell B6. Let's take a look at the formula for total income, which is now located in cell B7.

To examine the contents of cell B7:

1. Click cell **B7**. The formula =B5+B6 appears in the formula bar.

Excel adjusted the formula to compensate for the new location of the data. Otis checks a few more formulas, just to be sure that they also have been adjusted.

To check the formulas in B17 and B19:

1. Click cell **B17**. The formula =SUM(B10:B16) appears in the formula bar. The original formula was =SUM(B9:B15). Excel adjusted this formula to compensate for the new location of the data.

2. Click cell **B19**. The formula =B7-B17 appears in the formula bar. This formula used to be =B6-B16.

After he examines the formulas in his worksheet, Otis concludes that Excel automatically adjusted all the formulas when he inserted the new row.

Now, Otis wants to use Excel's AutoFormat feature to improve the appearance of the worksheet by emphasizing the titles and displaying dollar signs in the cells that contain currency data.

Using AutoFormat

AutoFormat is a command that lets you change the appearance of your worksheet by selecting from a collection of predesigned worksheet formats. Each of the worksheet formats in the AutoFormat collection gives your worksheet a more professional appearance by using attractive fonts, borders, colors, and shading. AutoFormat also manipulates column widths, row heights, and the alignment of text in cells.

REFERENCE WINDOW

Using AutoFormat

- Highlight the cells you want to format.
- Click Format, then click AutoFormat....
- Select a format style from the Table Format list.
- Click the OK button to apply the format.

Otis decides to use AutoFormat's Financial 3 format to improve the appearance of the worksheet.

To apply AutoFormat's Financial 3 format:

❶ Highlight cells A1 through E19, then release the mouse button.

❷ Click **Format**, then click **AutoFormat....** The AutoFormat dialog box appears. See Figure 2-22.

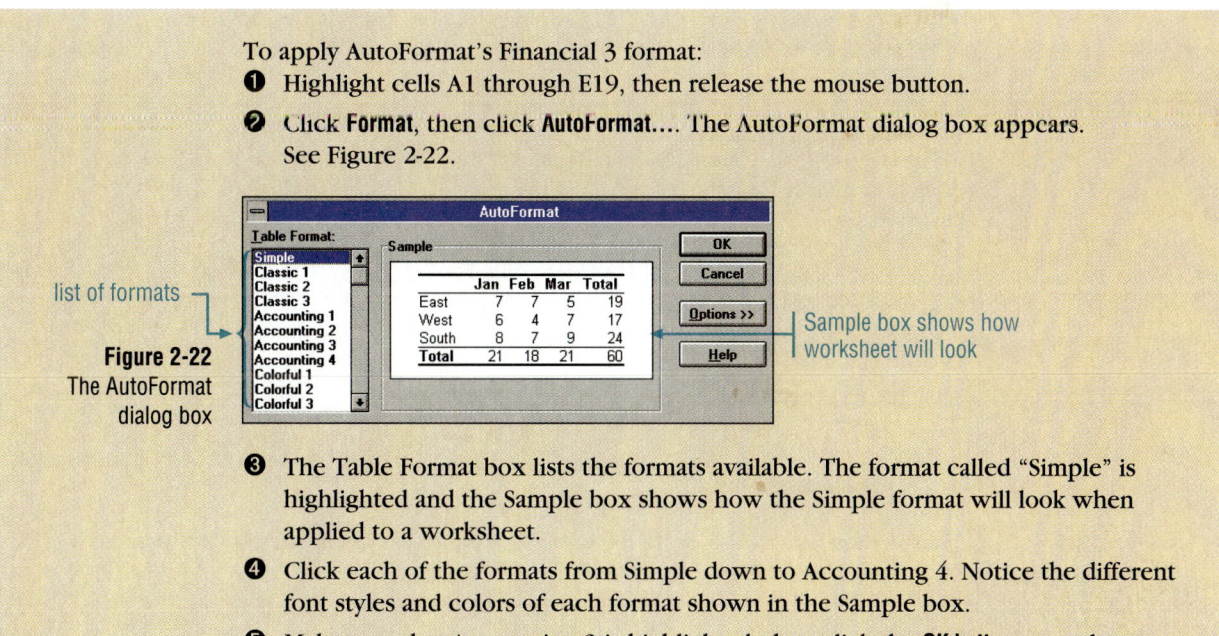

Figure 2-22
The AutoFormat dialog box

list of formats

Sample box shows how worksheet will look

❸ The Table Format box lists the formats available. The format called "Simple" is highlighted and the Sample box shows how the Simple format will look when applied to a worksheet.

❹ Click each of the formats from Simple down to Accounting 4. Notice the different font styles and colors of each format shown in the Sample box.

❺ Make sure that Accounting 3 is highlighted, then click the **OK button** to apply this format.

❻ Click any cell to remove the highlighting. The newly formatted worksheet is shown in Figure 2-23.

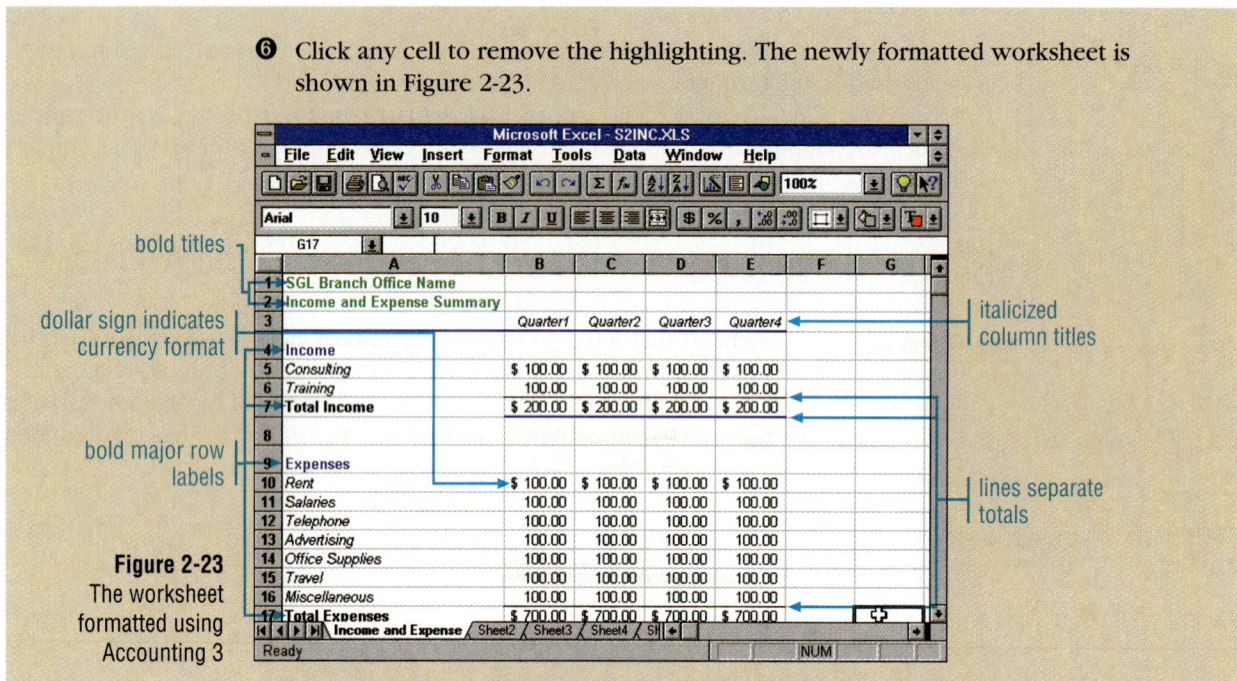

Figure 2-23
The worksheet formatted using Accounting 3

Otis is pleased with the appearance of his worksheet, but he realizes that he forgot to include a column to display year-to-date totals. He revises his worksheet plan, as shown in Figure 2-24.

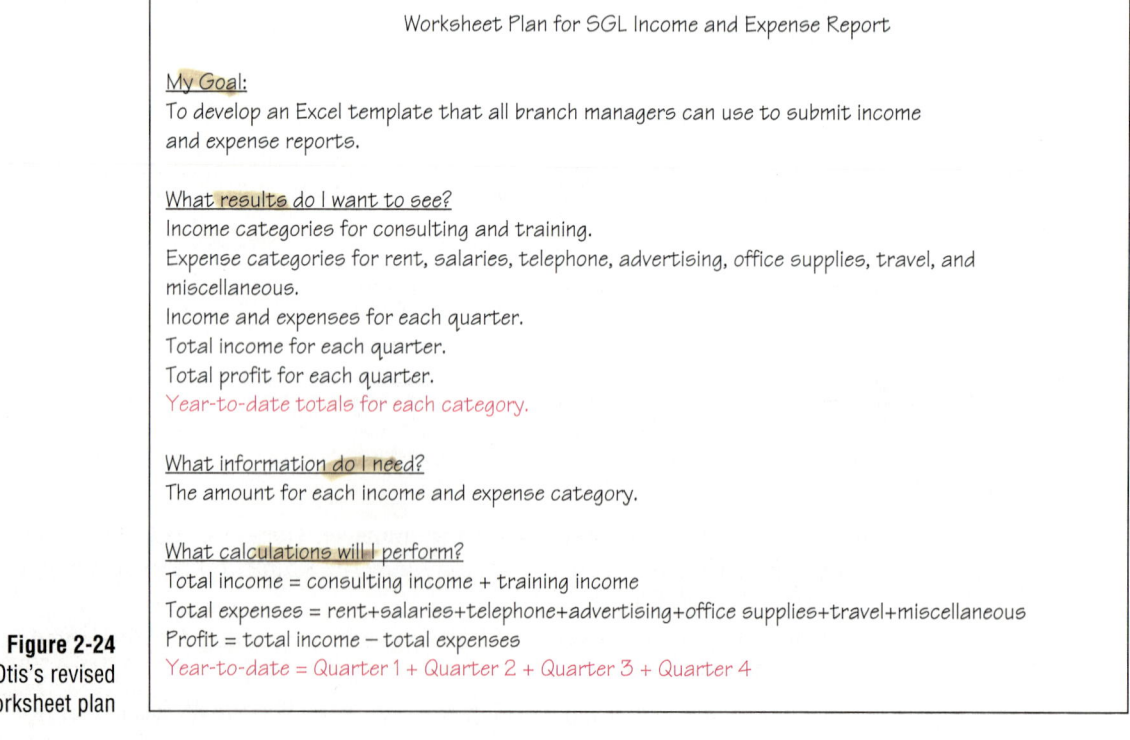

Figure 2-24
Otis's revised worksheet plan

Otis also revises his worksheet sketch (Figure 2-25) to show the column titles, formulas, and formats for the Year to Date column.

Income and Expenses Summary					
	Quarter 1	Quarter 2	Quarter 3	Quarter 4	Year to Date
Income					
Consulting	$9,999,999.99	$9,999,999.99	$9,999,999.99	$9,999,999.99	${year-to-date formula}
Training	:	:	:	:	:
Total Income	${total income formula}	${total income formula}	${total income formula}	${total income formula}	${year-to-date formula}
Expenses					
Rent	$9,999,999.99	$9,999,999.99	$9,999,999.99	$9,999,999.99	${year-to-date formula}
Salaries	:	:	:	:	:
Telephone	:	:	:	:	:
Advertising	:	:	:	:	:
Office Supplies	:	:	:	:	:
Travel	:	:	:	:	:
Miscellaneous	:	:	:	:	:
Total Expenses	${total expenses formula}	${total expenses formula}	${total expenses formula}	${total expenses formula}	${year-to-date formula}
Profit	${profit formula}	${profit formula}	${profit formula}	${profit formula}	${year-to-date formula}

Figure 2-25
Otis's revised worksheet sketch

Otis begins by entering the title for the Year to Date column in cell F3.

To enter the title for column F:
1. Click cell **F3** to make it the active cell.
2. Type **Year to Date** and press **[Enter]**.

Next, Otis needs to enter a formula in cell F5 to calculate the year-to-date consulting income. He could type the formula =SUM(B5:E5), but he decides to use the AutoSum button to eliminate some extra typing.

The AutoSum Button

The **AutoSum button**, the Σ button on the toolbar, automatically creates formulas that contain the SUM function. To do this, Excel looks at the cells adjacent to the active cell, guesses which cells you want to sum, and displays a formula that contains a "best guess" about the range you want to sum. You can press the Enter key to accept the formula or you can drag the mouse over a different range of cells to change the range in the formula. Let's use the AutoSum button to enter the formula for year-to-date consulting income in cell F5.

To enter the formula in cell F5 using the AutoSum button:

1. Click cell **F5** because this is where you want to put the formula.
2. Click the **AutoSum button** Σ. See Figure 2-26. Excel determines that you probably want to sum the contents of the range B5 through E5, which is exactly what you want to do.

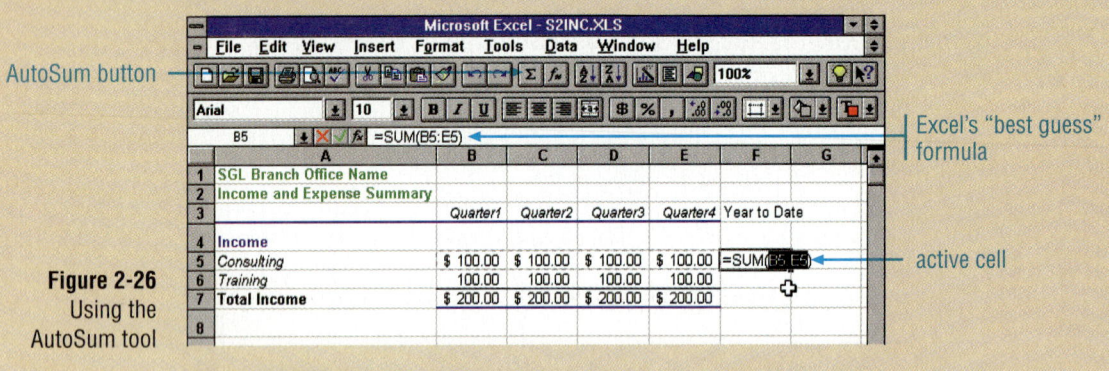

Figure 2-26
Using the AutoSum tool

3. Press [Enter] to complete the formula. The result $400.00 appears in cell F5.

Note that AutoSum assumed that you wanted to use the same format in cell F5 as you used in the cells containing the values for the sum. Therefore, cell F5 is formatted for currency with two decimal places.

Otis would like to use the same formula to calculate the year-to-date totals for all income and expense categories as well as the totals. He decides to use the fill handle to copy the formula from cell F5 to cells F6 through F19.

To copy the formula from cell F5 to cells F6 through F19:

1. Scroll the worksheet so you can see rows 5 through 19.
2. Click cell **F5** because this cell contains the formula you want to copy.
3. Drag the fill handle to outline cells F5 through F19, then release the mouse button.
4. Click any cell to remove the highlighting and view the results of the copy.
   See Figure 2-27.

Clearing Cells   EX 69

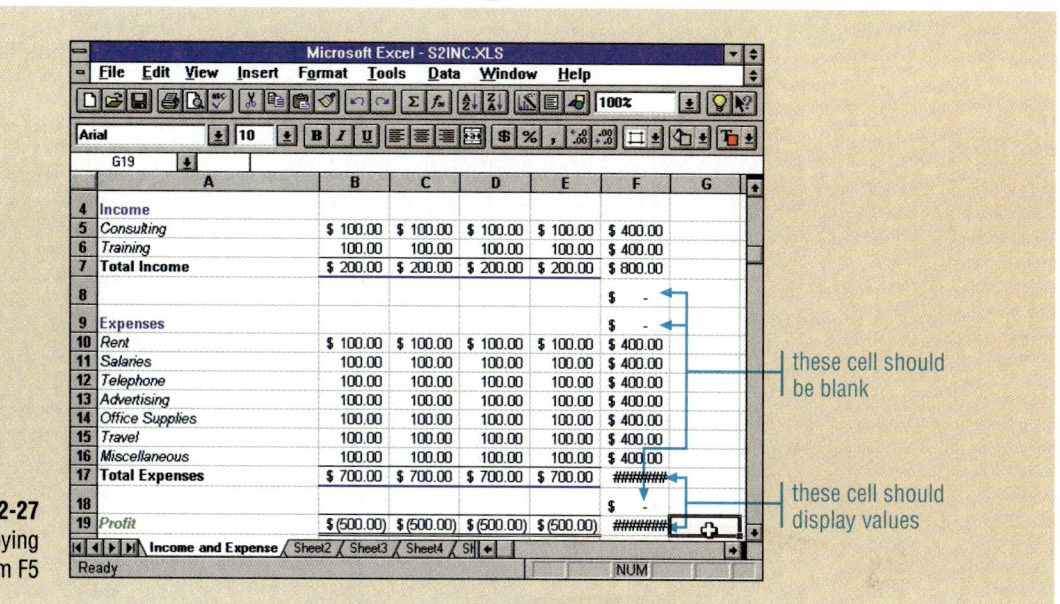

Figure 2-27
Result of copying formula from F5

Otis copied the formula from cell F5 to the range F6 through F19, but there are a few problems, as shown in Figure 2-26. Cells F8, F9, and F18 should be blank. Instead they contain a dollar sign and a hyphen. This is a result of the SUM function now located in those cells. Another problem is that number signs (###) appear in cells F17 and F19 instead of a value for the year-to-date total expenses and year-to-date profit.

Otis decides to clear the formulas from the cells in column F that should be blank.

Clearing Cells

If you want to erase the contents or the formats of a cell, you use either the Delete key or the Clear dialog box. Erasing the *contents* of a cell is known as *clearing a cell*. Keep in mind that clearing a cell is different from deleting the entire cell. When you *delete* a cell, the entire cell is removed from the worksheet and adjacent cells move to fill in the space left by the deleted cell.

When clearing a cell you have three choices. You can clear only the cell contents (i.e., the values or text entered in the cell), you can clear the formats in a cell, or you can clear both the cell contents and the formats. To do this, you can use the Delete key or the Clear dialog box on the Edit menu.

REFERENCE WINDOW

Clearing Cells

- Click the cell you want to clear or highlight a range of cells you want to clear.

- To delete the cell contents only, press [Del].

- To delete the formatting but not the contents, click Edit, click Clear, then click Formats.

Otis decides to clear the formula from cell F18 first. Then he highlights cells F8 and F9 and clears both formulas with one command.

To clear the formula from cells F18, F8, and F9:
1. Click cell **F18** because this is the first cell you want to clear.
2. Press [Del].
3. Highlight cells F8 through F9, then release the mouse button.
4. Press [Del].

Now that Otis has cleared the unwanted formulas from the cells, he turns his attention to the number signs in cells F17 and F19.

Number Sign (###) Replacement

If a value is too long to fit within the boundaries of a cell, Excel displays a series of number signs (###) in the cell. Excel displays the number signs as a signal that the number of digits in the value exceeds the width of the cell. It would be misleading to display only some of the digits of the value. For example, suppose you enter the value 5129 in a cell that is wide enough to display only two digits. Should Excel display the first two digits or the last two digits? You can see that either choice would be misleading, so Excel displays the number signs (###) instead. The values, formats, and formulas have *not* been erased from the cell. To display the value, you just need to increase the column width.

For example, on your worksheet cell F19 displays a maximum of eight entire digits. Because Excel formatted this cell for currency as a result of the AutoSum operation, Excel must have space in the column to display the dollar sign, the comma to indicate thousands, the decimal, two numbers after the decimal, and the parentheses for negative numbers. The value in this cell, ($2,000.00), requires a cell width of 11 digits.

Otis needs to make cells F17 and F19 wider. He also wants to have a double underline in cell F19, a thick single underline in cell F7, and single underlines in cells F3 and F17 so column F will look like the other columns in the worksheet. Rather than applying these formats separately, Otis decides to use AutoFormat again to reapply the Accounting 3 format to the entire worksheet. Reapplying the format will also widen column F because AutoFormat determines column width based on the numbers that are in the cells at the time you apply the format.

To reapply the Accounting 3 format to the entire worksheet:
1. Scroll the worksheet to display row 1.
2. Highlight cells A1 through F19, then release the mouse button.

    TROUBLE? If you don't see row 19 on the screen when you are highlighting the worksheet, move the pointer down past the bottom of the window and the worksheet will scroll.

3. Click **Format**, then click **AutoFormat...**. The AutoFormat dialog box appears.
4. Click the **Accounting 3** format, then click the **OK button** to apply the format.
5. Click any cell to remove the highlighting.

The entire worksheet is reformatted. Column F contains the same format as columns A through E. Otis wants to be sure that the width of column F was increased enough to display the value for year-to-date total expenses in cell F17 and year-to-date profit in cell F19.

To verify that cells F17 and F19 display values rather than number signs:
❶ If necessary, scroll the worksheet until rows 17 and 19 are visible. Cell F17 displays $2,800.00 instead of number signs.
❷ Cell F19 displays $(2,000.00) instead of number signs.

Otis still isn't satisfied with the format. He's not certain that the columns are wide enough. For example, what if a branch manager reports consulting income of $1 million for the first quarter? Will that value fit in cell B5? Let's try it.

To enter $1 million in cell B5:
❶ Click cell **B5** to make it the active cell.
❷ Type **1000000** and press **[Enter]**. Number signs appear in cells B5, B7, B19, F5, F7, and F19, as shown in Figure 2-28.

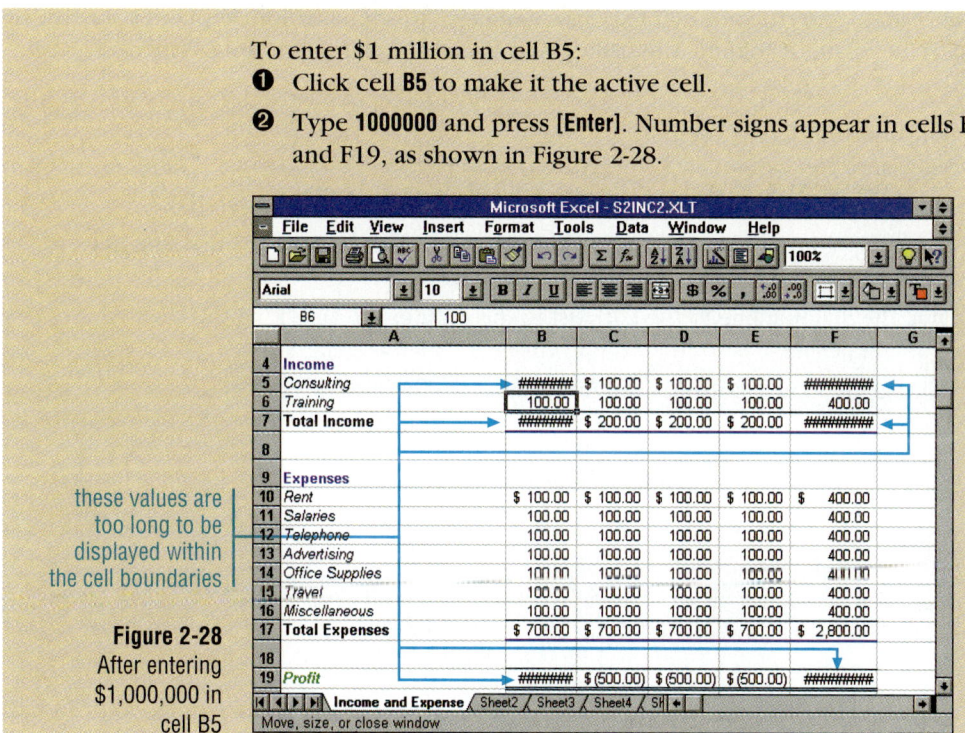

these values are too long to be displayed within the cell boundaries

Figure 2-28
After entering $1,000,000 in cell B5

Otis realizes that columns B through F need to display at least 13 digits. Because Otis used small test values, AutoFormat did not make the cells as wide as they will need to be when the branch managers enter their data. Otis decides to change the column width using the Column Width command.

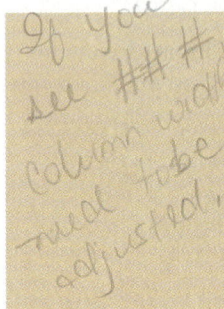

If you see ### column width need to be adjusted.

To change the width of columns B through F using the Column Width command:

1. Click the **column heading box** at the top of column B. This highlights column B.
2. Drag the pointer to column F, then release the mouse button. Columns B through F are highlighted.
3. Click **Format**.
4. Click **Column**, then click **Width...** to display the Column Width dialog box. The insertion point is flashing in the Column Width box.
5. Type **13** in the Column Width box, then click the **OK button**.
6. Click any cell to remove the highlighting and view the new column widths.

Otis thinks column A is too wide because the longest income or expense category label, "Total Expenses," is only 14 characters. He decides to allow the titles "SGL Branch Office Name" and "Income and Expense Summary" to spill over into adjacent columns. He adjusts the width of column A to make it just wide enough for the "Total Expenses" label.

To adjust the width of column A:

1. Make sure you can see cell A17, which contains the "Total Expenses" label.
2. Position the pointer on the column heading box at the top of column A.
3. Move the pointer slowly to the right until it is positioned over the dividing line between column A and column B and changes to ↔.
4. Drag the dividing line to the left, just to the right of the last "s" in the label "Total Expenses."
5. Release the mouse button. Column A adjusts to the new width.

Otis thinks this is a good time to save the workbook.

To save the workbook:

1. Click the **Save button** 🖫 to save the workbook on your Student Disk.

If you want to take a break and resume the tutorial at a later time, you can exit Excel by double-clicking the Control menu box in the upper-left corner of the screen. When you resume the tutorial, launch Excel, maximize the Microsoft Excel and Book1 windows, and place your Student Disk in the disk drive. Open the file S2INC.XLS, then continue with the tutorial.

■   ■   ■

Otis next wants to test his worksheet using realistic data.

Testing the Worksheet with Realistic Data

Before you trust a worksheet and its results, you should test it to make sure you have entered the correct formulas and have specified appropriate formats. You want the worksheet to produce accurate results, and you want the results to be displayed clearly.

Earlier Otis used the test value 100 because it enabled him to make the worksheet calculations in his head and verify that the formulas were correct. So far, the formulas appear to be correct, but Otis is still not satisfied.

Otis knows that this is an extremely important worksheet. Branch managers will enter values into the worksheet, and they will assume the worksheet calculates the correct results. Otis's reputation, the reputations of the branch managers, and the success of the corporation could depend on the worksheet's providing correct results. Otis is determined to test the worksheet thoroughly before he distributes it to any branch offices.

Otis wants to test the worksheet using realistic data, so he decides to enter last year's values from the Littleton, North Carolina branch office report, which is shown in Figure 2-29.

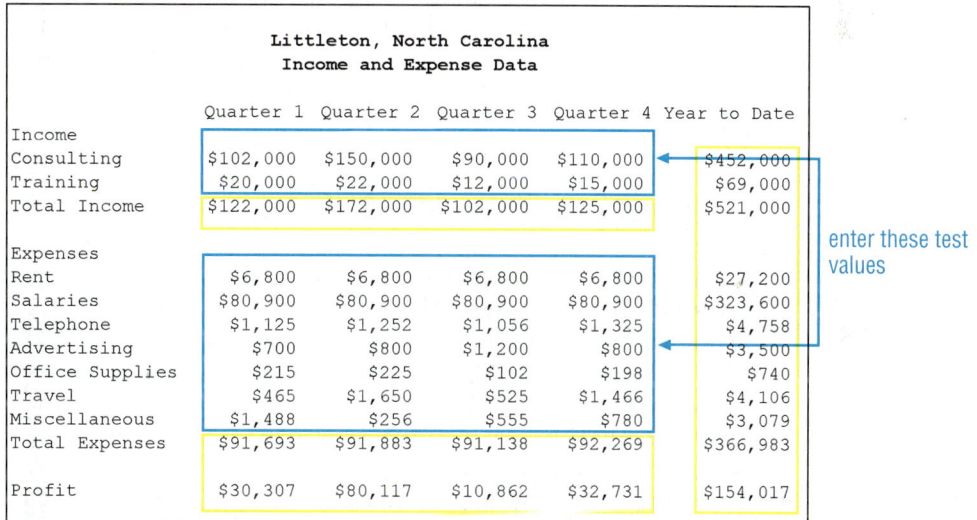

Figure 2-29
Littleton, North Carolina branch office data

To enter the Littleton test values:

1. Enter the test values shown in the blue-boxed area of Figure 2-29. Do not enter values in any cells that contain formulas. Because you have already formatted your worksheet, you should enter the test values without dollar signs or decimal places. Excel will automatically add the dollar signs and decimal places where appropriate.

   TROUBLE? If you enter a number in a cell that contains a formula and you notice it right away, click Edit, then click Undo Entry. If you don't notice the problem until after you have made other entries, retype the formula in the appropriate cell.

Next, Otis compares the results displayed on his worksheet with the results for the North Carolina branch values shown in the yellow-boxed area of Figure 2-29. The values produced by the formulas in his worksheet match the Littleton results. Now, Otis is more confident that the worksheet will provide the correct results.

Clearing Test Values from the Worksheet

The current worksheet contains test values that must not be included in the final worksheet template, so Otis needs to clear the test values from the worksheet.

To clear the test values from the worksheet:

❶ Highlight cells B5 through E6, then release the mouse button. ***Do not drag to column F.*** Column F contains formulas and you don't want to clear them.

   TROUBLE? If you highlight column F, drag the pointer from B5 to E6 again.

❷ Press [Del].

❸ Highlight cells B10 through E16, then release the mouse button. ***Do not drag to column F.***

❹ Press [Del].

❺ Click any cell to remove the highlighting.

Otis knows that it is important to document his worksheet so the branch managers will know how it is set up.

Documenting the Worksheet

The purpose of documenting a worksheet is to provide the information necessary to use and modify the worksheet. The documentation for your worksheet can take many forms; if you work for a company that does not have documentation standards or requirements, you must decide what type of documentation is most effective for your worksheets.

Your worksheet plan and worksheet sketch provide one type of worksheet documentation. As you know, the worksheet plan and sketch give you a "blueprint" to follow as you build and test the worksheet. This can be useful information for someone who needs to modify your worksheet because it states your goals, specifies the required input, describes the output, and indicates the calculations you used to produce the output.

Excel also provides a way to print all the formulas you entered in the worksheet. This is a very useful form of documentation, which you will learn about in Tutorial 3.

The worksheet plan, the worksheet sketch, and the formula printout are not, however, part of the worksheet and might not be readily available to the person using the worksheet.

You can include documentation as part of your worksheet. This documentation might be as simple as a header with your name and the date you created the worksheet. More complete documentation might include the information from your worksheet plan typed on a page of the worksheet. You can also include documentation by adding a text note to your worksheet.

Adding a Text Note

A **text note** is text that is attached to a cell. The note does not appear on the worksheet unless you double-click the cell to which it is attached. Cells that contain text notes display a small square in the upper-right corner. On a color monitor this square is red. You can attach text notes to a cell even if it contains data.

Text notes are suitable for documentation that not every user needs to see. Because some users might not know that cells with squares in the upper-right corner contain notes, you cannot be certain that everyone will read your text notes. A text note, then, is appropriate for documentation that an experienced Excel user might want to see.

> **REFERENCE WINDOW**
>
> **Adding a Text Note**
>
> - Click the cell to which you want to attach a text note.
> - Click Insert, then click Note....
> - Type the text of your note in the Text Note box. The insertion point will automatically move down when you reach the end of a line. If you need to type a short line and then move down, press [Enter].
> - When you finish typing the note, click the OK button.

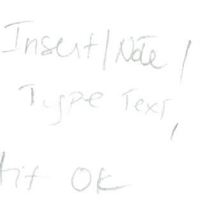

At SGL, management recommends that anyone who creates a worksheet should attach a text note to cell A1 with the following information:
- who created the worksheet
- the date the worksheet was created or revised
- a brief description of the worksheet

Otis adds a text note to his worksheet to provide the required documentation.

To add a text note to cell A1:

1. Click cell **A1** because this is the cell to which you want to attach the text note.
2. Click **Insert**, then click **Note...** to display the Cell Note dialog box.
3. Click in the **Text Note box** to make sure the insertion point is active, then type **Income and Expense Summary**.
4. Press **[Enter]** to move the insertion point to the next line.
5. Type **Created by Otis Nunley** and press **[Enter]**.
6. Type today's date and press **[Enter]**.
7. Type the rest of the note you see in Figure 2-30 without pressing [Enter]. Because the rest of the note is a paragraph, you do not need to press [Enter]; the words automatically wrap to the next line.

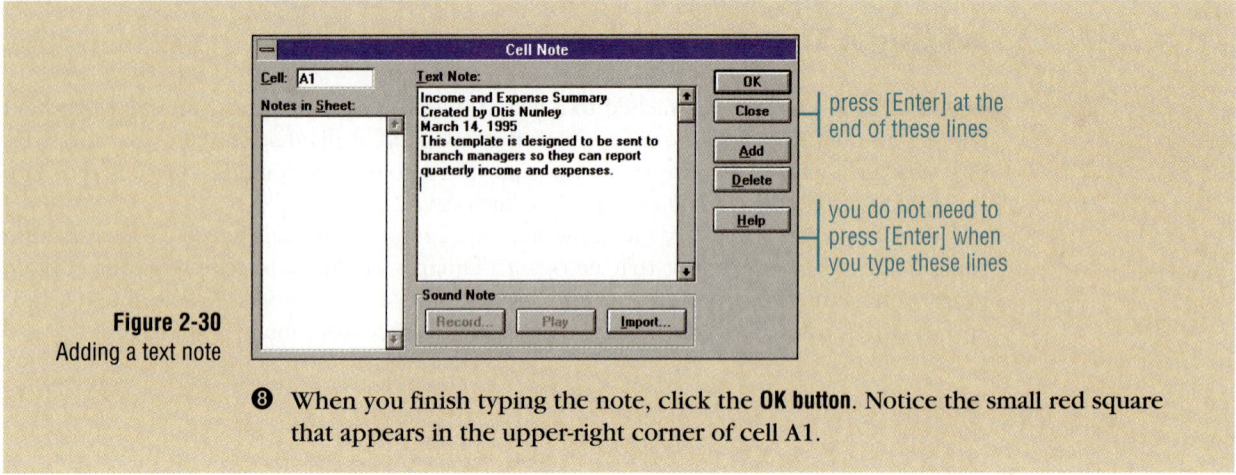

Figure 2-30
Adding a text note

8. When you finish typing the note, click the **OK button**. Notice the small red square that appears in the upper-right corner of cell A1.

Now that the worksheet is almost done, Otis wants to make sure that he hasn't misspelled any words.

Checking the Spelling of the Worksheet

Excel's **Spelling command** helps you find misspelled words in your worksheets. When you choose this command, Excel compares the words in your worksheet to the words in its dictionary. When it finds a word in your worksheet that is not in its dictionary, it shows you the word and provides options for correcting it or leaving it as is.

REFERENCE WINDOW

Using the Spelling Button

- Click cell A1 so you begin spell checking from the top of the worksheet.
- Click the Spelling button.
- Excel shows you any word that is in your worksheet, but not in its dictionary. Your options are:
  - If the word is correct and you do not want to change this one occurrence, click the Ignore button.
  - If the word is correct and you want Excel to ignore all future occurrences of the word, click the Ignore All button.
  - If you want Excel to suggest a correct spelling, click the Suggest button.
  - If you want to change the word to one of the suggestions listed in the Suggestions box, click the correct word, then click the Change button.
- If Excel does not provide an acceptable alternative, you can edit the word in the Change To box, then click the Change button.

Otis is ready to check the spelling of his worksheet.

To check the spelling of the entire worksheet:

❶ Click cell **A1** so Excel begins spell checking at the first cell in the worksheet.

❷ Click the **Spelling button** to check the spelling of the entire worksheet. Excel finds the word SGL. See Figure 2-31. SGL is the name of the company Otis works for. This word is not misspelled, but it is not in Excel's dictionary.

TROUBLE? Don't worry if your list of suggested alternatives is different, simply continue with Step 3.

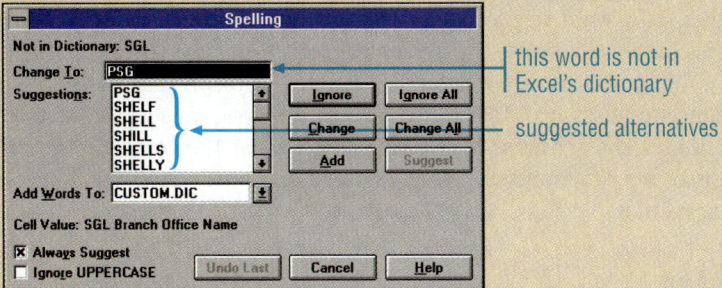

Figure 2-31
Checking the spelling in the worksheet

❸ Click the **Ignore All button** because you do not want to change SGL here or anywhere else it appears on the worksheet.

❹ When Excel finds the word "Otis" (in the text note) click the **Ignore All button** because you do not want to change this word here or anywhere else. Do the same for the word "Nunley."

❺ If Excel finds any other misspelled words in your worksheet, use the Spelling dialog box buttons to make the appropriate changes.

❻ When you see the message "Finished spell checking entire sheet" click the **OK button**.

Otis looks at the completed worksheet and thinks about the way it will be used. Branch managers will receive his template—a version of the worksheet with the titles and formulas, but with no values. At the start of each year, the branch managers will open a copy of the template and save it under a name that indicates the branch office name.

At the end of each quarter, the branch managers will retrieve the worksheet, enter the values for that quarter, then save and print the worksheet. The branch managers will send a printed copy to Otis, along with a disk containing a copy of the worksheet.

Otis foresees one problem with the template. What if a branch manager types a value over a cell containing a formula? The formula would be erased, the cell would not recalculate to reflect changes, and the worksheet would be unreliable. Otis needs some way to protect the worksheet.

Protecting Cells in the Worksheet

Excel lets you protect cells from changes while still allowing users to enter or change values in unprotected cells. Cells that are protected so that their contents cannot be changed are referred to as **locked cells**.

There are two commands you use to protect or unprotect cells: the Cell Protection command and the Protect Document command. The **Cell Protection command** lets you specify the protection status for any cell in the worksheet. In the worksheet you are currently building, the protection status of all cells is locked. How, then, can you change the contents of the cells in the worksheet when you build it? Here's where the Protect Document command comes into play. The protection status does not go into effect until you use the **Protect Document command** to put the worksheet into protected mode.

When you want to protect some cells in the worksheet, you first *unlock* the cells in which you want users to make entries. Then you use the Protection command on the Tools menu to activate the protection on those cells you left locked.

When you use the Protection command to protect the worksheet, Excel allows you to enter a password. If you use a password, you must make sure to remember it in order to unlock the worksheet in the future. Unless the material you are working on is confidential, it's probably easier not to use a password at all. You'll use one in this tutorial just for practice.

REFERENCE WINDOW

Protecting Cells

- Select the cells you want to *un*lock.
- Click Format, then click Cells....
- In the Format Cells dialog box, click the Protection tab.
- Remove the × from the Locked option box.
- Use the Tools, Protection, Protect Sheet... command to activate protection for the entire worksheet. All cells that were not set to unlocked will be protected.
- Save the modified worksheet.

Otis starts by unlocking the range of cells into which the managers *can* enter data. Then, he activates document protection for the rest of the worksheet.

To unlock the cells for data entry:

❶ Highlight cells B5 through E6, then release the mouse button.

❷ Click **Format**, then click **Cells....** The Format Cells dialog box appears.

❸ Click the **Protection tab**. Notice that the Locked box contains an ×. See Figure 2-32.

Protecting Cells in the Worksheet **EX 79**

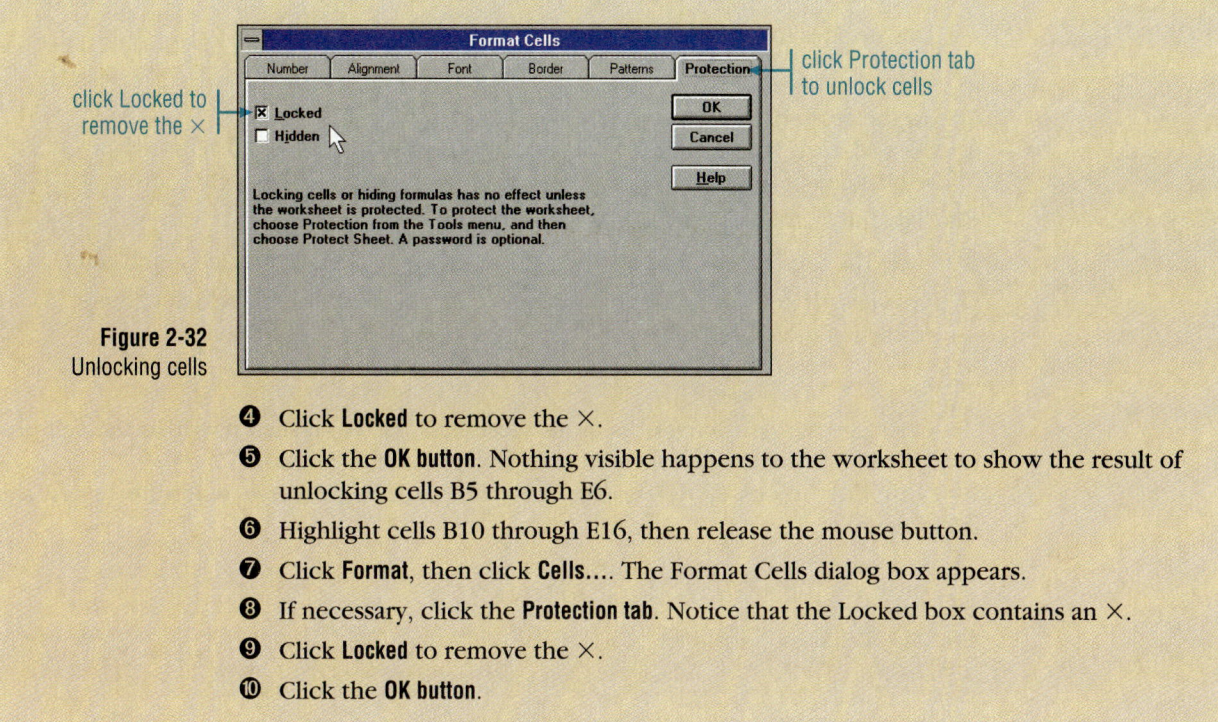

Figure 2-32
Unlocking cells

❹ Click **Locked** to remove the ×.
❺ Click the **OK button**. Nothing visible happens to the worksheet to show the result of unlocking cells B5 through E6.
❻ Highlight cells B10 through E16, then release the mouse button.
❼ Click **Format**, then click **Cells...**. The Format Cells dialog box appears.
❽ If necessary, click the **Protection tab**. Notice that the Locked box contains an ×.
❾ Click **Locked** to remove the ×.
❿ Click the **OK button**.

In addition to entering data in the cells, the branch managers need to type the appropriate branch office name in row 1. Otis unlocks cell A1 to allow the managers to enter the branch office name.

To unlock cell A1:
❶ Click **A1** to make it the active cell.
❷ Click **Format**, then click **Cells...**. The Format Cells dialog box appears.
❸ If necessary, click the **Protection tab**, then click **Locked** to remove the ×.
❹ Click the **OK button**.

Now that Otis has unlocked the cells for data entry, he turns protection on for the entire worksheet. This protects every cell that he didn't unlock.

To turn protection on:
❶ Click **Tools**, click **Protection**, then click **Protect Sheet...**. The Protect Sheet dialog box appears.
❷ Type **bluesky** as the password. The letters appear as x's or *'s in the text box.
❸ Click the **OK button**. You will be prompted to enter the password again to make sure that you remember it and that you entered it correctly the first time.
❹ Type **bluesky** again, then click the **OK button**. Nothing visible happens to show that you protected the worksheet.

Otis decides to test the worksheet protection.

To test the worksheet protection:
1. Click **A8**, then type **5**. A dialog box displays the message, "Locked cells cannot be changed."
2. Click the **OK button** to continue.
3. Click **B10**, then type **3**. The number 3 appears in the formula bar and in the cell.
4. Press **[Enter]**. You can make an entry in cell B10 because you unlocked it before protecting the worksheet.

Otis tests the remaining cells in his worksheet. He is satisfied now that the cell protection will prevent the managers from overwriting the formulas.

Now Otis needs to delete the entry he made in cell B10 when he tested the cell protection.

To clear cell B10:
1. Click **B10**, then press **[Del]**.

Now the worksheet is complete and Otis is ready to save it as a template.

Saving the Worksheet as an Excel Template

Excel templates are stored with an .XLT extension rather than the .XLS extension used for workbooks.

Figure 2-33 shows that when you open a template, Excel copies it from the disk to RAM and displays the template on your screen (1). You fill in the template with values, as you would with any worksheet (2). When you save this workbook, Excel prompts you for a new filename so you do not overwrite the template. Excel then saves the completed workbook under the new filename (3).

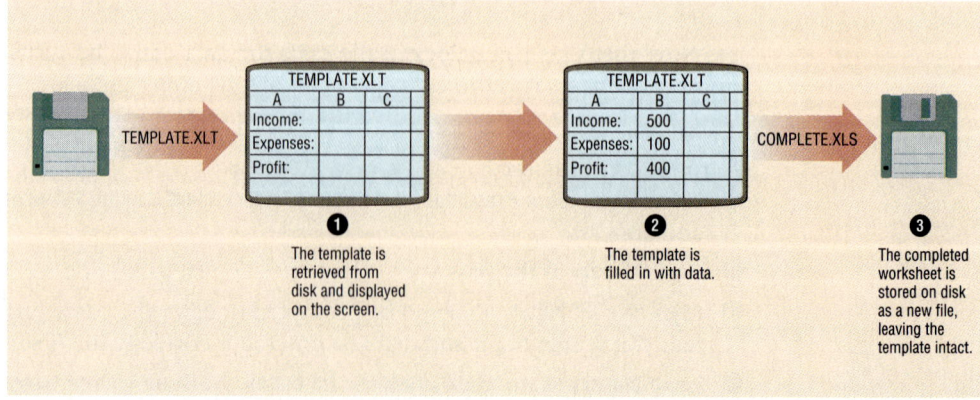

Figure 2-33
How a template works

Otis uses the Save As command to save the Income and Expense Summary worksheet as a template.

To save the worksheet as a template:

❶ Click **File**, then click **Save As...** to display the Save As dialog box.

❷ Click the **Save File as Type box down arrow button** to display a list of file types.

❸ Click **Template**. S2INC.XLT appears in the File Name box.

❹ Make sure the Drives box displays the icon for the disk drive that contains your Student Disk. See Figure 2-34.

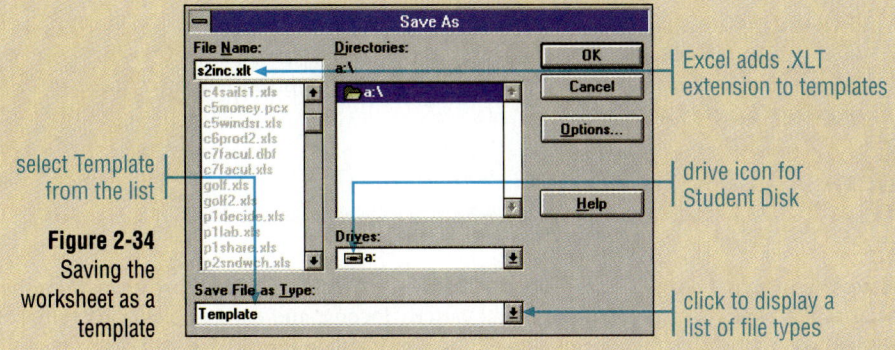

Figure 2-34
Saving the worksheet as a template

❺ Click the **OK button** to save the template. If you see the Summary Info dialog box, press **[Enter]** to close the dialog box and finish saving the template.

❻ Click **File**, then click **Close** to close the worksheet. Exit Excel if you are not going to proceed to the Tutorial Assignments.

Otis has finished his template and is ready to send it to the branch managers. He exits Excel and Windows before turning off his computer.

■ ■ ■

Questions

1. What command do you use to name a worksheet and save it?
2. The small black square in the lower-right corner of the active cell is called the _____.
3. What are the four activities required to create an effective worksheet?
4. Why would you use 1 as a test value?
5. Using the correct order of operations, calculate the results of the following formulas:
   a. 2+3*6
   b. (4/2)*5
   c. 2^2+5 = or $2^2 + 5 = 9$; in Excel $= 2^2+5$ + Enter $= 9$
   d. 10+10/2   Enter in Excel $= 10 + 10/2 = 15$
6. Describe the methods you can use to enter cell references in a formula.
7. All references in formulas are _____ unless you specify otherwise.
8. When you copy a formula, what happens to the relative references?
9. To clear the contents of a cell (but not the formatting) click the cell and then click _____.
10. Why does Excel display number signs (###) in a cell?
11. To protect a worksheet, you must first unlock those cells that the user will be allowed to change and then activate _____.

12. _____ references contain a dollar sign before the column letter, row number, or both.
13. What is the difference between clearing a cell and deleting a cell?
14. Explain the function of the following toolbar buttons:
    a. Σ
    b. ✓...
    c. 🖫
    d. 📂
15. How is a template different from a worksheet?
16. Which button will automatically complete a series such as Jan, Feb, Mar?
17. What are your options when you're using the Spelling command and Excel finds a word that is not in its dictionary?

Tutorial Assignments

You are the Branch Manager for the Duluth, Minnesota branch of SGL. Otis Nunley from the home office has just sent you a copy of the new quarterly income and expense summary template. Otis has asked you to test the template by filling in the information for the first two quarters of this year and sending a printed copy of the worksheet back to him. Open the template T2INC.XLT and do the following: STINC.XLS

1. Enter your name in cell A1 in place of the branch office name.
2. Enter the values for Quarter 1 and Quarter 2 as shown in Figure 2-35.
3. Compare your results with those in Figure 2-35 to verify that the formulas are correct.
4. Save the workbook as S2DLTH.XLS.
5. Print the worksheet.

Figure 2-35

Duluth Branch Office					
Income and Expense Summary					
	Quarter 1	Quarter 2	Quarter 3	Quarter 4	Year to Date
Income					
Consulting	$27,930.00	$33,550.00			$61,480.00
Training	11,560.00	13,520.00			25,080.00
Total Income	$39,490.00	$47,070.00	$0.00	$0.00	$86,560.00
Expenses					
Rent	$2,300.00	$2,300.00			$4,600.00
Salaries	7,200.00	7,200.00			14,400.00
Telephone	547.00	615.00			1,162.00
Advertising	1,215.00	692.00			1,907.00
Office Supplies	315.00	297.00			612.00
Travel	1,257.00	1,408.00			2,665.00
Miscellaneous	928.00	802.00			1,730.00
Total Expenses	$13,762.00	$13,314.00	$0.00	$0.00	$27,076.00
Profit	$25,728.00	$33,756.00	$0.00	$0.00	$59,484.00

Otis shows the Quarterly Income and Expense Summary template to his boss, Joan LeValle. She suggests several additions to the template. Joan mentions that some of the branch offices have started long-term education programs for their employees, so she wants you to add a separate expense category for education.

6. Open the workbook S2INC2.XLT.
7. Deactivate document protection by clicking Tools, clicking Protection, then selecting Unprotect Sheet.... Type "bluesky" as the password, then click the OK button.

8. Insert a row where row 14 is currently located.
9. Enter the row label "Education" in cell A14.
10. Use the fill handle to copy the formula from cell F13 to cell F14.
11. Use the Protection command to reactivate document protection, using bluesky as the password.
12. Save the workbook as the template S2INC3.XLT and then close the workbook.
13. Open the template S2INC3.XLT and test it by entering 1 as the test value for each of the income and expense categories for each quarter. Make any revisions necessary to formulas, formats, or cell protection so it works according to Otis's plan.
14. Save the workbook with the test values as S2TEST.XLS, then print it.

Professor ONLY wants the final one.

Case Problems

1. Tracking Ticket Sales for the Brookstone Dance Group

Robin Yeh is the ticket sales coordinator for the Brookstone Dance Group, a community dance company. Brookstone sells five types of tickets: season tickets, reserved seating, general admission, student tickets, and senior citizen tickets.

Robin needs a way to track the sales of each of the five ticket types. She has done the initial planning for an Excel worksheet that will track ticket sales and has asked you to create the worksheet.

Study Robin's worksheet plan in Figure 2-36 and her worksheet sketch in Figure 2-37, then build, test, and document a template into which Robin can enter ticket sales data.

Worksheet Plan for Brookstone Dance Group

Goal:
To create a worksheet to track monthly ticket sales.

What results do I want to see?
Total ticket sales for each month.
Total annual sales for each of the five ticket types.
Total annual sales for all ticket types.

What information do I need?
The monthly sales for each type of ticket

What calculations will I perform?
Total ticket sales = season tickets + reserved seating + general admission + student tickets + senior citizen tickets

Season ticket annual sales = sum of each month's sales of season tickets
Reserved seating annual sales = sum of each month's sales of reserved seating
General admission annual sales = sum of each month's sales of general admission
Student ticket annual sales = sum of each month's sales of student tickets
Senior citizen ticket annual sales = sum of each month's sales of senior citizen tickets

Figure 2-36

Figure 2-37

	Brookstone Dance Group Ticket Sales				
	April	May	June	July	YTD
Season tickets	:	:	:	:	{season ticket annual sales formula}
Reserved seating	:	:	:	:	{reserved seating annual sales formula}
General admission	:	:	:	:	{general admission annual sales formula}
Student tickets	:	:	:	:	{student ticket annual sales formula}
Senior citizen tickets	:	:	:	:	{senior citizen ticket annual sales formula}
Total ticket sales	{total ticket sales formula}	{total ticket sales formula}	{total ticket sales formula}	{total ticket sales formula}	{total ticket sales formula}

1. Launch Excel and make sure you have a blank worksheet on your screen. If the Excel window is open and you do not have a blank worksheet, click the New Workbook button.
2. Enter the labels for the first column as shown in Figure 2-37.
3. Use AutoFill to automatically fill in the month names.
4. Enter YTD in the cell to the right of the cell containing the label July.
5. Create the formulas to calculate total ticket sales and year-to-date sales for each ticket type.
6. Use the AutoFormat Classic 3 style as the format for the worksheet. Adjust column widths as necessary.
7. Add a text note to cell A1 that includes your name, the date, and a short description of the template.
8. Rename Sheet1 "Ticket Sales."
9. Test the template using 1000 as the test value, then make any changes necessary for the template to work correctly.
10. Clear the test values from the cells.
11. Unprotect the cells in which Robin will enter data; then, protect the document using bluesky as the password.
12. Save the workbook as a template named S2TCKTS.XLT.
13. Print the template and close it.
14. Open the template S2TCKTS.XLT and enter some realistic data for April, May, and June. You can make up this data, keeping in mind that Brookstone typically has total ticket sales of about 500 per month.
15. Print the worksheet with the realistic test data, then close the workbook without saving it.

2. Tracking Customer Activity at Brownie's Sandwich Shop

Sherri McWilliams is the assistant manager at Brownie's Sandwich Shop. She is responsible for scheduling waitresses and cooks. To plan an effective schedule, Sherri wants to know the busiest days of the week and the busiest hours of the day. She started to create a worksheet to help track the customer activity in the shop, and she has asked if you could help her complete the worksheet. Open the workbook P2SNDWCH.XLS and do the following:

1. Save the workbook as S2SNDWCH.XLS so you will not modify the original file if you want to do this case again.
2. Use AutoFill to complete the column titles for the days of the week.
3. Use AutoFill to complete the labels showing open hours from 11:00AM to 10:00PM.
4. Use the AutoSum button to create a formula to calculate the total number of customers in cell B15.

5. Copy the formula in cell B15 to cells C15 through H15.
6. Enter the column title "Hourly" in cell I1, and the title "Average" in cell I2. Sherri plans to use column I to display the average number of customers for each one-hour time period.

 E

7. Enter the formula =AVERAGE(B3:H3) in cell I3, then copy it to cells I4 through I15.
8. Enter "Sandwich Shop Activity" in cell A1 as the worksheet title.
9. Add a text note to cell A1 that includes your name, the date, and a brief description of the worksheet.
10. Rename Sheet1 "Customer Activity."
11. Save the workbook as S2SNDWCH.XLS.
12. Print the worksheet. *(Case 2 #12)*
13. On your printout, circle the busiest day of the week and the hour of the day with the highest average customer traffic.

3. Activity Reports for Magazines Unlimited

Norm McGruder was just hired as a fulfillment driver for Magazines Unlimited. He is responsible for stocking magazines in supermarkets and bookstores in his territory. Each week Norm goes to each store in his territory, removes the outdated magazines, and delivers the current issues.

Plan, build, test, and document a template that Norm can use to keep track of the number of magazines he removes and replaces from the Safeway supermarket during one week. Although Norm typically handles 100 to 150 different magazine titles at the Safeway store, for this Case Problem, create the template for only 12 of them: *Entertainment Weekly*, *Auto News*, *Fortune*, *Harpers*, *Time*, *The Atlantic*, *Newsweek*, *Ebony*, *PC Week*, *The New Republic*, *Forbes*, and *Vogue*.

Your worksheet should contain:
- a column that lists the magazine names
- a column that contains the number of magazines delivered
- a column that contains the number of magazines removed
- a column that contains a formula to calculate the number of magazines sold by subtracting the number of magazines removed from the number of magazines delivered
- a cell that displays the total number of magazines delivered
- a cell that displays the total number of magazines removed
- a cell that shows the total number of magazines sold during the week

To complete this Case Problem, do the following:
1. Create a worksheet plan similar to the one in Figure 2-4 at the beginning of the tutorial. Include a description of the worksheet goal, list the results you want to see, list the input information needed, and describe the calculations that must be performed.
2. Draw a worksheet sketch showing the layout for the template.
3. Build the worksheet by entering the title, the row labels, the column titles, and the formulas.
4. Format the worksheet using your choice of format from the AutoFormat list.
5. Test the worksheet using 1 as the test value. Make any changes necessary for the worksheet to function according to your plan.
6. Add a text note to cell A1 to document the worksheet.
7. Rename Sheet1 with an appropriate name.
8. Clear the test values from the worksheet.
9. Unprotect the cells in which you will enter the number of magazines delivered and removed; then, protect the entire document using bluesky as the password.
10. Save the workbook as a template called S2MAG.XLT.
11. Print the template, then enter some realistic test data and print it again.
12. Submit your worksheet plan, your worksheet sketch, the printout of the template, and the printout with the realistic test data.

TUTORIAL 3

Formatting and Printing

OBJECTIVES

In this tutorial you will:
- Change the font style, font size, and font
- Align cell contents
- Center text across columns
- Use the number, currency, and percentage formats
- Use borders, color, and patterns for emphasis
- Activate the Drawing toolbar
- Add comments to a worksheet
- Preview printouts
- Print in portrait and landscape orientations
- Center printouts on a page
- Remove cell gridlines from printouts
- Display formulas
- Use a module to print formulas

Producing a Projected Sales Impact Report

CASE **Pronto Authentic Recipe Salsa Company**

Anne Castelar is the owner of the Pronto Authentic Recipe Salsa Company, a successful business located in the heart of Tex-Mex country. She is working on a plan to add a new product, Salsa de Chile Guero Medium, to Pronto's line of gourmet salsas.

Anne wants to take out a bank loan to purchase additional food processing equipment to handle the increase in production required for the new salsa. She has an appointment with her bank loan officer at 2:00 this afternoon. In preparation for the meeting, Anne is creating a worksheet to show the projected sales of the new salsa and the expected effect on profitability.

Although the numbers and formulas are in place on the worksheet, Anne has not had time to format the worksheet for the best impact. She was planning to do that now, but an unexpected problem with today's produce shipment requires her to leave the office for a few hours. Anne asks her office manager, Maria Stevens, to complete the worksheet. Anne shows Maria a printout of the unformatted worksheet and explains that she wants the finished worksheet to look very professional—like the examples you see in business magazines. She also asks Maria to make sure that the worksheet emphasizes the profits expected from sales of the new salsa.

After Anne leaves, Maria develops the worksheet plan in Figure 3-1 and the worksheet format plan in Figure 3-2.

```
Worksheet Plan for Projected Sales Report

My Goal:
To format the worksheet so it produces a professional-looking printout.

What results do I want to see?
The profits that are expected from sales of the new salsa product.

What information do I need?
The unformatted worksheet.

What calculations will I perform?
None. Formulas have already been entered.
```

Figure 3-1
Maria's worksheet plan

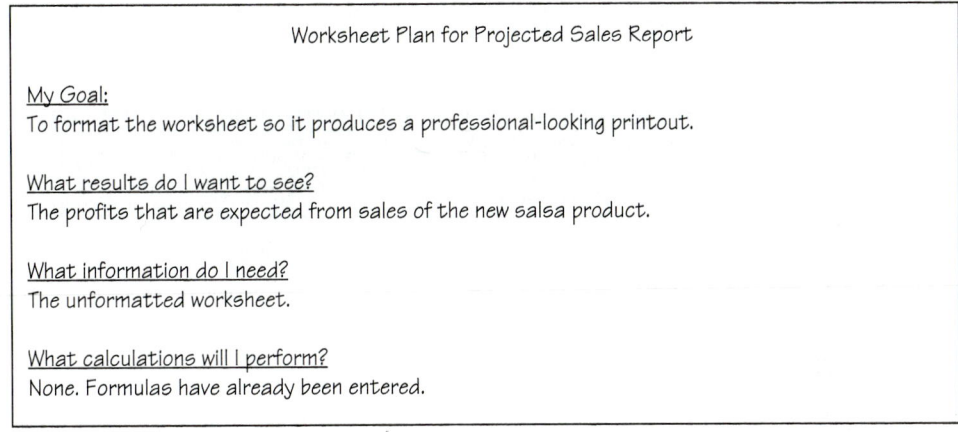

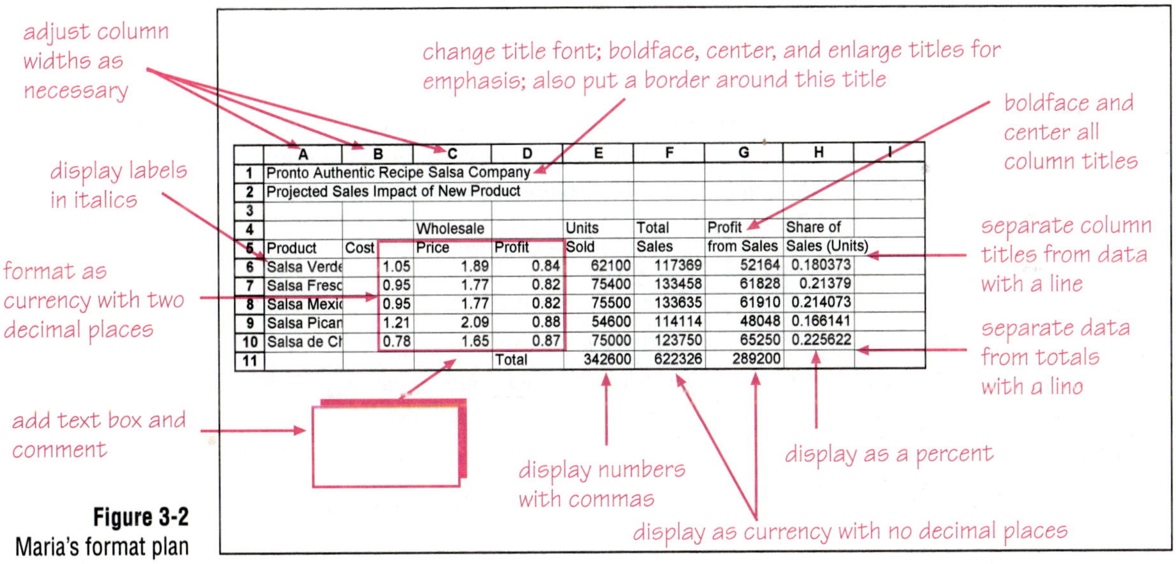

Figure 3-2
Maria's format plan

Now Maria is ready to launch Excel and open the worksheet. To begin, you need to launch Excel and maximize the application and document windows to organize your desktop.

To launch Excel and organize your desktop:

❶ Launch Excel following your usual procedure.

❷ Make sure your Student Disk is in the disk drive.

❸ Make sure the Microsoft Excel and Book1 windows are maximized.

Anne stored the workbook as C3SALSA1.XLS. Now Maria needs to open this file.

To open the C3SALSA1.XLS workbook:
1. Click the **Open button** to display the Open dialog box.
2. Double-click **C3SALSA1.XLS** in the File Name box to display the workbook shown in Figure 3-3.

   TROUBLE? Make sure the Drives list box displays the drive your Student Disk is in.

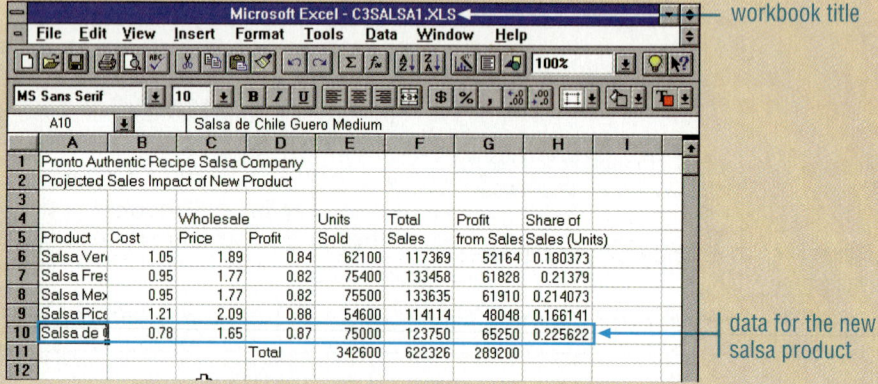

Figure 3-3
The C3SALSA1.XLS workbook

Before you begin to make changes to the workbook, let's save it using the filename S3SALSA1.XLS so you can work on a copy of the workbook. The original workbook, C3SALSA1.XLS, will be left in its original state in case you want to do this tutorial again.

To save the workbook as S3SALSA1.XLS:
1. Click **File**, then click **Save As...** to display the Save As dialog box.
2. Type **S3SALSA1** using either uppercase or lowercase.
3. Click the **OK button** to save the workbook under the new filename. When the save is complete, you should see the new filename, S3SALSA1.XLS, displayed in the title bar.

   TROUBLE? If you see the message "Replace existing C3SALSA1.XLS?" click the Cancel button and go back to Step 1. If you see the message "Replace existing S3SALSA1.XLS?" click the OK button to replace the old version of S3SALSA1.XLS with your new version.

Maria studies the worksheet and notices that the salsa names do not fit in column A. It would be easy to make column A wider, but Maria knows that if she widens this column some of the worksheet will scroll off the screen. It will be easier to do the other formatting tasks if she can see the entire worksheet, so she decides to make other formatting changes first.

Formatting Worksheet Data

Formatting is the process of changing the appearance of the data in the cells of the worksheet. Formatting can make your worksheets easier to understand and draw attention to important points.

Formatting changes only the appearance of the data; it does not change the text or numbers stored in the cells. For example, if you format the number .123653 using a percentage format that displays only one decimal place, the number will appear on the worksheet as 12.4%; however, the original number .123653 remains stored in the cell.

When you enter data in cells, Excel applies an automatic format, referred to as the General format. The **General format** aligns numbers at the right side of the cell and displays them without trailing zeros to the right of the decimal point. You can change the General format by using AutoFormat, the Format menu, the Shortcut menu, or toolbar buttons.

In Tutorial 2 you used AutoFormat to apply a predefined format to your entire workbook. AutoFormat is easy to use, but the predefined formats might not be suitable for every worksheet. If you decide to customize the format of a workbook, you can use Excel's extensive array of formatting options. When you select your own formats, you can format an individual cell or a range of cells.

There are multiple ways to access Excel's formatting options. The Format menu provides access to all the formatting commands (Figure 3-4).

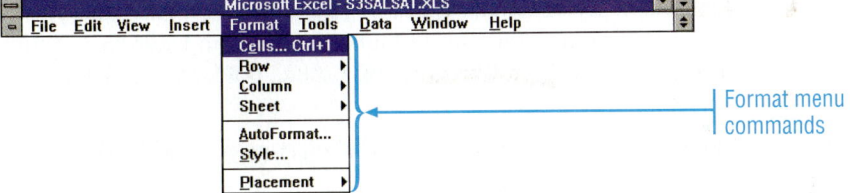

Figure 3-4
The Format menu

The Shortcut menu provides quick access to the Format dialog box (Figure 3-5). To display the Shortcut menu, make sure the pointer is on one of the cells in the range you have highlighted to format, then click the *right* mouse button.

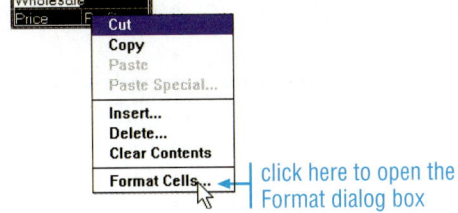

Figure 3-5
The Shortcut menu

The formatting toolbar contains formatting buttons, including the style buttons, font style box, font size box, and alignment buttons (Figure 3-6).

Figure 3-6
The formatting toolbar buttons

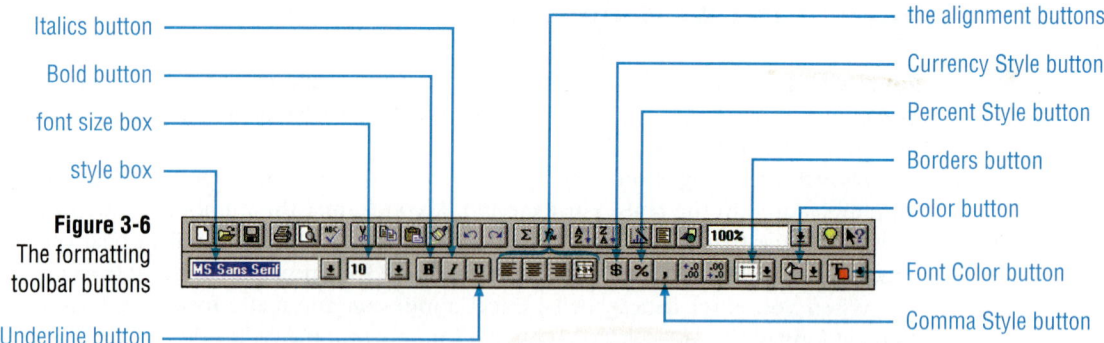

Labels: Italics button, Bold button, font size box, style box, Underline button, the alignment buttons, Currency Style button, Percent Style button, Borders button, Color button, Font Color button, Comma Style button

Most experienced Excel users develop a preference for which menu or buttons they use to access Excel's formatting options; however, most beginners find it easy to remember that all the formatting options are available from the Format menu.

Maria decides to use the Bold button to change the font style to boldface for some of the titles on the worksheet.

Changing the Font, Font Style, and Font Size

A **font** is a set of letters, numbers, punctuation marks, and symbols with a specific size and design. Some examples of fonts are shown in Figure 3-7. A font can have one or more of the following **font styles**: regular, italic, bold, and bold italic.

Font	Regular Style	Italic Style	Bold Style	Bold Italic Style
Times	AaBbCc	*AaBbCc*	**AaBbCc**	***AaBbCc***
Courier	AaBbCc	*AaBbCc*	**AaBbCc**	***AaBbCc***
Garamond	AaBbCc	*AaBbCc*	**AaBbCc**	***AaBbCc***
Helvetica Condensed	AaBbCc	*AaBbCc*	**AaBbCc**	***AaBbCc***

Figure 3-7
A selection of fonts

Most fonts are available in many sizes, and you can also select font effects, such as strikeout, underline, and color. The toolbar provides tools for boldface, italics, underline, changing font style, and increasing or decreasing font size. To access other font effects, you can open the Cells... dialog box from the Format menu.

Maria begins by formatting the word "Total" in cell D11 in boldface letters.

To change the font style for cell D11 to boldface:

❶ Click cell **D11**.

❷ Click the **Bold button** [B] to set the font style to boldface. See Figure 3-6 for the location of the Bold tool.

Maria also wants to display the worksheet titles and the column titles in boldface letters. To do this she first highlights the range she wants to format, then she clicks the Bold button to apply the format.

To display the worksheet titles and column titles in boldface:
1. Highlight cells A1 through H5.
2. Click the **Bold button** to apply the bold font style.
3. Click any cell to remove the highlighting.

Next, Maria decides to display the names of the salsa products in italics.

To italicize the row labels:
1. Highlight cells A6 through A10.
2. Click the **Italics button** to apply the italic font style. See Figure 3-6 for the location of the Italics tool.
3. Click any cell to remove the highlighting and view the formatting you have done so far. For now, don't worry that the labels aren't fully displayed. You'll widen the column later. See Figure 3-8.

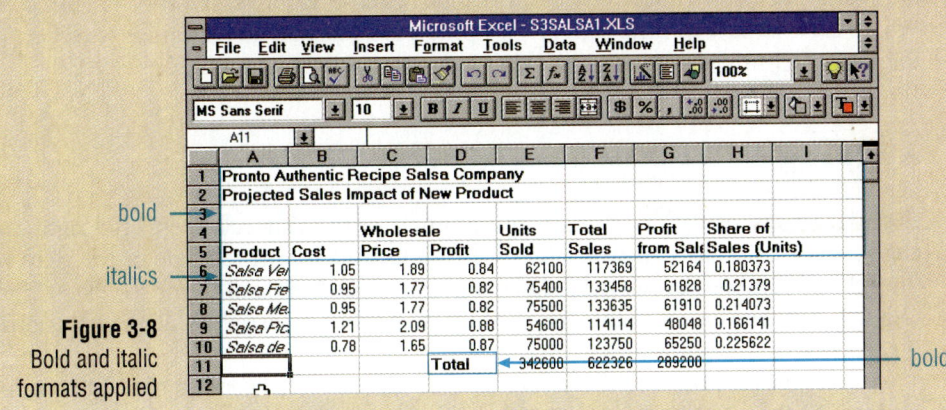

Figure 3-8
Bold and italic formats applied

Maria wants to increase the size of the worksheet titles for emphasis. She also wants to use a different font for the titles of this worksheet. Maria decides to use the Font dialog box (instead of the toolbar) so she can preview her changes. Remember, even though the worksheet titles appear to be in columns A through E, they are just spilling over from column A. To format the titles, Maria needs to highlight only cells A1 and A2—the cells in which the titles are entered.

To change the font and font size of the worksheet titles:
1. Highlight cells A1 through A2.
2. Click **Format**, then click **Cells...** to display the Format Cells dialog box.
3. Click the **Font tab**.
4. Use the Font box scroll bar to find the Times New Roman font. Click the **Times New Roman** font to select it.
5. Make sure the Font Style box is set to "Bold."
6. Click **14** in the Size box. A sample of the font Maria has chosen appears in the Preview box. See Figure 3-9.

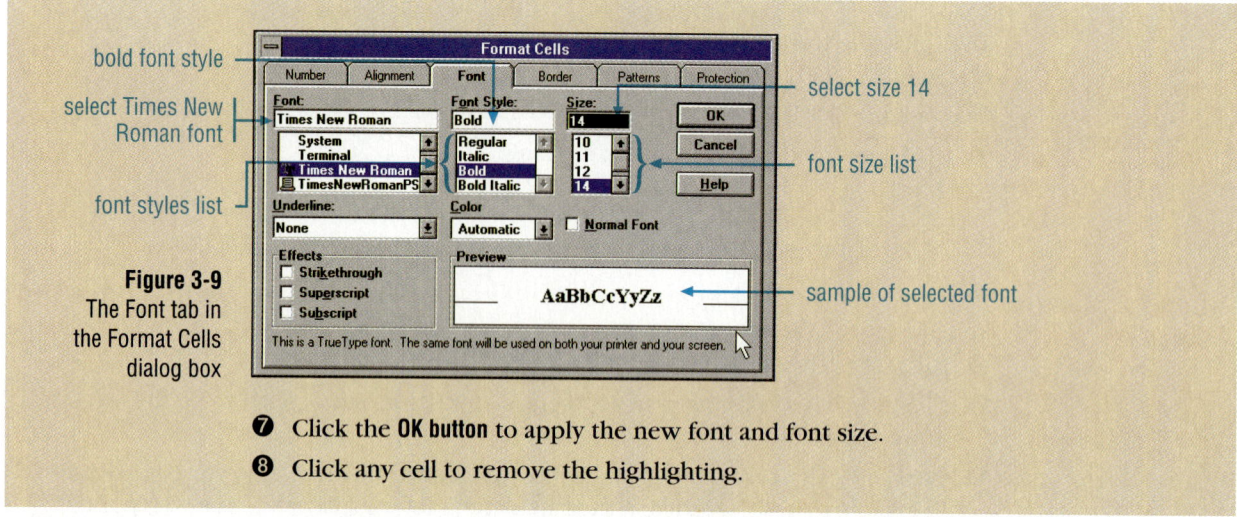

Figure 3-9
The Font tab in the Format Cells dialog box

❼ Click the **OK button** to apply the new font and font size.

❽ Click any cell to remove the highlighting.

Maria likes the Times New Roman font because it looks like the font used on the Pronto salsa jar labels. Pleased with her progress so far, Maria continues with her formatting plan. Her next step is to adjust the alignment of the column titles.

Aligning Cell Contents

The **alignment** of data in a cell is the position of the data relative to the right and left edges of the cell. The contents of cells can be aligned on the left side or the right side of the cell, or centered in the cell. When you enter numbers and formulas, Excel automatically aligns them on the right side of the cell. Excel automatically aligns text entries on the left side of the cell.

Excel's automatic alignment does not always create the most readable worksheet. Figure 3-10 shows a worksheet with the column titles left-aligned and the numbers in the columns right-aligned.

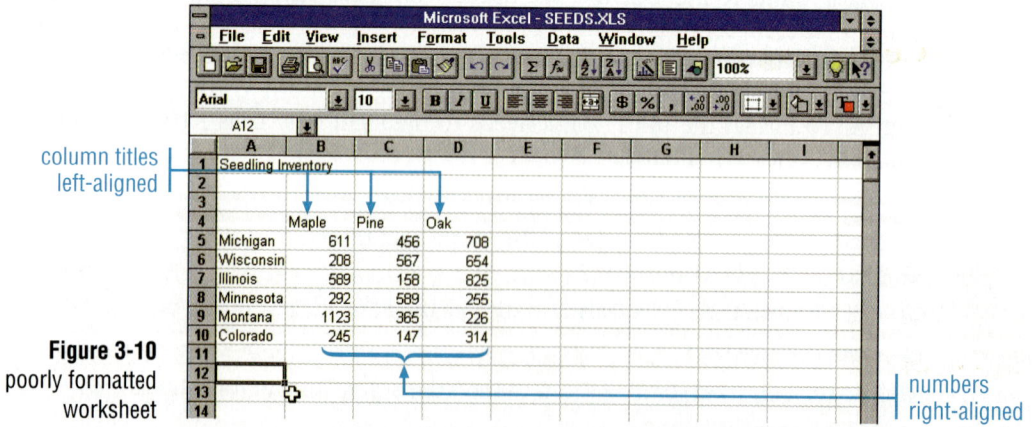

Figure 3-10
A poorly formatted worksheet

Notice how difficult it is to sort out which numbers go with each column title. The readability of the worksheet in Figure 3-10 would be improved by centering the column titles or aligning them on the right. As a general rule, you should center column titles, format columns of numbers so the decimal places are in line, and leave columns of text aligned on the left.

The Excel toolbar provides four alignment tools, as shown in Figure 3-11. You can access additional alignment options by selecting Alignment from the Format menu.

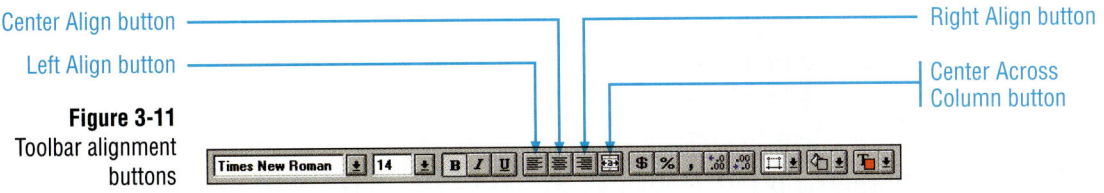

Figure 3-11
Toolbar alignment buttons

Maria decides to center the column titles.

To center the column titles:
1. Highlight cells A4 through H5.
2. Click the **Center button** on the toolbar to center the cell contents.
3. Click any cell to remove the highlighting and view the centered titles. See Figure 3-12.

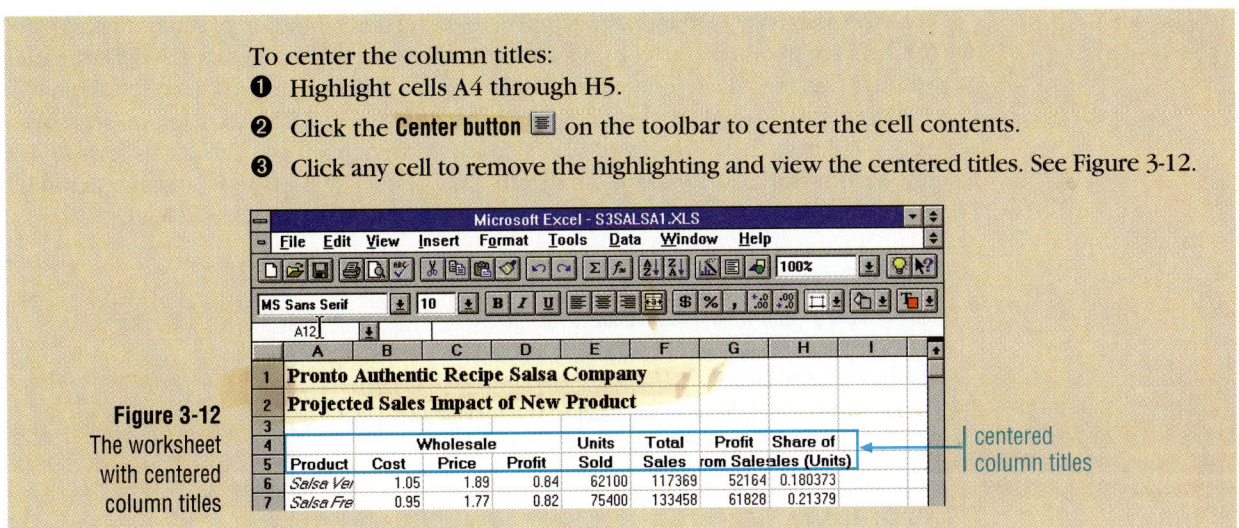

Figure 3-12
The worksheet with centered column titles

Maria notices that eventually she will need to change the width of columns G and H to display the entire column title, but for now she decides to center the main worksheet titles.

Centering Text Across Columns

Sometimes you might want to center the contents of a cell across more than one column. This is particularly useful for centering the titles at the top of a worksheet.

Maria uses the Center Across Columns button to center the worksheet titles in cells A1 and A2 across columns A through H.

To center the worksheet titles across columns A through H:
1. Highlight cells A1 through H2.
2. Click the **Center Across Columns button** to center the titles across columns A through H.
3. Click any cell to remove the highlighting.

Maria looks at her plan and sees that she needs to display the cost, price, profit, and total sales figures as currency.

Currency Formats

Excel provides four currency formats, as shown in Figure 3-13.

Currency Format	Positive	Negative
$#,##0_);($#,##0)	$214	($214)
$#,##0_);[Red]($#,##0)	$214	($214)
$#,##0.00_);($#,##0.00)	$213.52	($213.52)
$#,##0.00_);[Red]($#,##0.00)	$213.52	($213.52)

Figure 3-13
Examples of Excel's currency formats

For each currency format Excel supplies two versions, one for positive numbers and one for negative numbers. Excel uses a special set of symbols, or notation, to describe each of the currency formats. For example, in Figure 3-13 the first currency format is $#,##0_);($#,##0). How do you decipher what this means? The first set of symbols—$#,##0_)—indicates how Excel will display positive amounts if you select this format. The second set of symbols—($#,##0)—indicates how Excel will display negative amounts. The meaning of the $#,0_ symbols in the currency notation is explained in Figure 3-14.

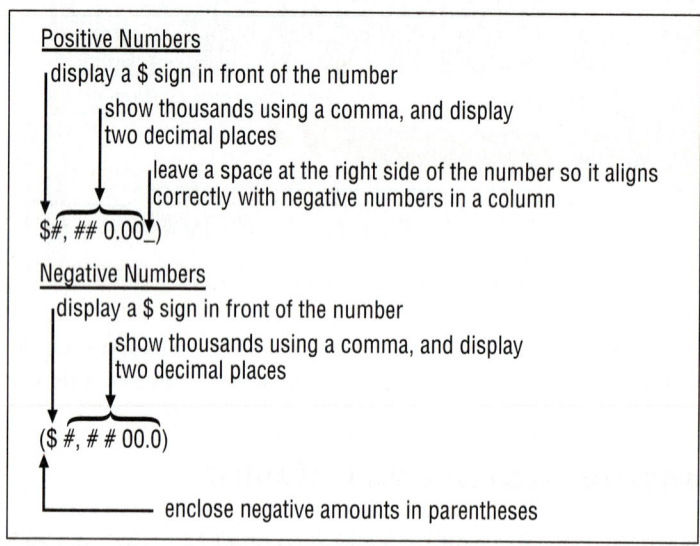

Figure 3-14
Notation for currency formats

Maria wants to format the amounts in columns B, C, and D as currency with two decimal places.

To format columns B, C, and D as currency with two decimal places:

❶ Highlight cells B6 through D10.

❷ Click **Format**, then click **Cells...** to display the Format Cells dialog box.

❸ Click the **Number tab**.

❹ Click **Currency** in the Category box.

❺ Click the third option down, **$#,##0.00_);($#,##0.00)** in the Format Codes box. A sample of this format appears at the bottom of the dialog box. See Figure 3-15.

Currency Formats **EX 95**

Format Codes or Defaults

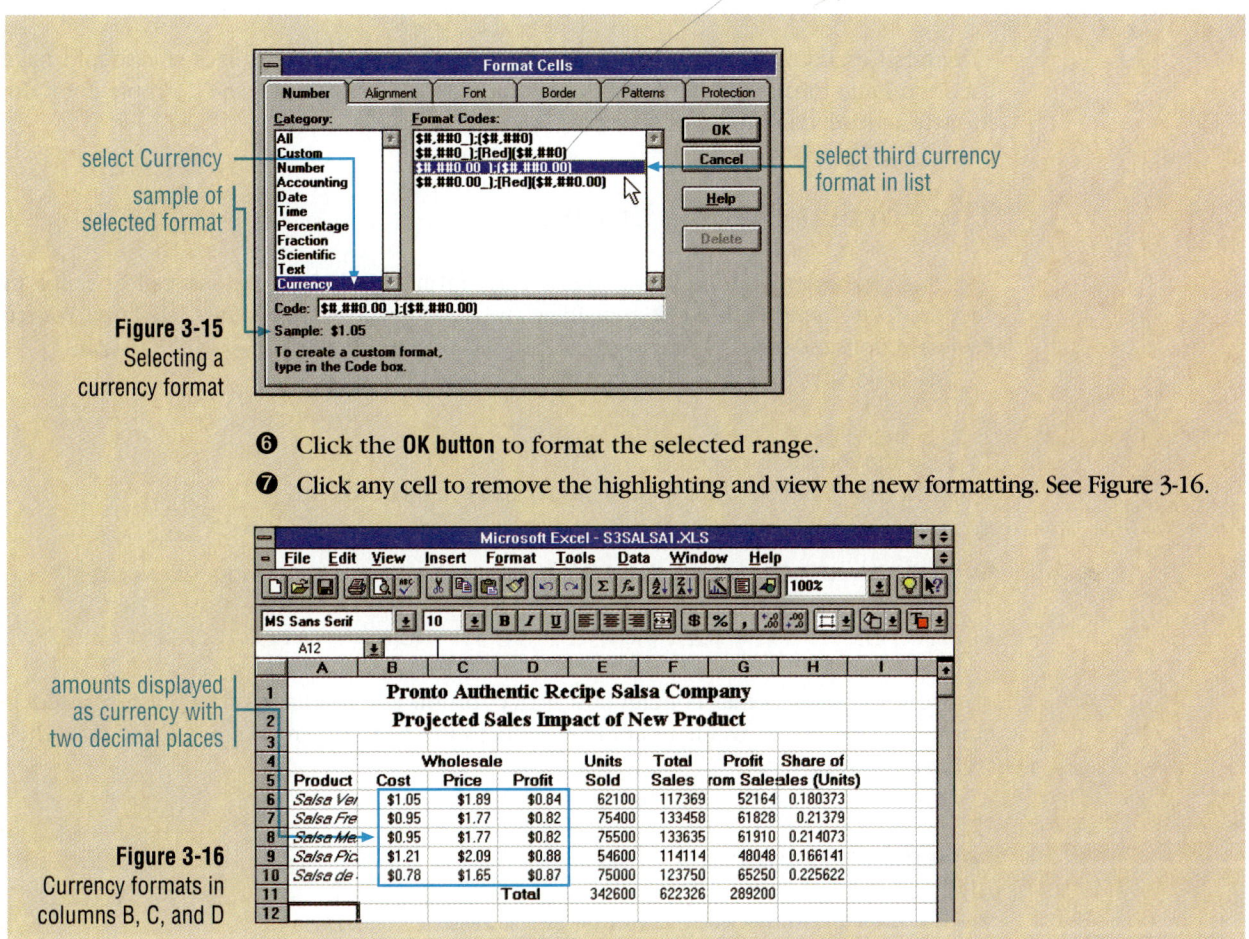

Figure 3-15 Selecting a currency format

Figure 3-16 Currency formats in columns B, C, and D

❻ Click the **OK button** to format the selected range.

❼ Click any cell to remove the highlighting and view the new formatting. See Figure 3-16.

When you have large dollar amounts in your worksheet, you might want to use a currency format that does not display any decimal places. To do this you can use the first or second currency format listed in the Cell Format dialog box. These formats round the amount to the nearest dollar; $15,612.56 becomes $15,613; $16,507.49 becomes $16,507; and so on.

Maria decides to format the Total Sales column as currency rounded to the nearest dollar.

To format cells F6 through F11 as currency rounded to the nearest dollar:
❶ Highlight cells F6 through F11.
❷ Click **Format**, then click **Cells...** to display the Format Cells dialog box.
❸ If necessary, click the **Number tab**.
❹ Click **Currency** in the Category box.
❺ Click the first option, **$#,##0_);($#,##0)**, in the Format Codes box and notice the sample format.
❻ Click the **OK button** to apply the format.
❼ Click any cell to remove the highlighting.

After formatting the Total Sales figures in column F, Maria realizes she should have used the same format for the numbers in column G. To save time, she'll simply copy the formatting from column F to column G.

The Format Painter Button

The Format Painter button allows you to copy formats quickly from one cell or range to another. You simply click a cell containing the formats you want to copy, click the Format Painter button, and then drag through the range to which you want to apply the formats.

Maria decides to use the Format Painter button now.

To copy the format from cell F6:

1. Click cell **F6** because it contains the format you want to copy.
2. Click the **Format Painter button**. The pointer turns into ⊕.
3. Highlight cells G6 through G11. When you release the mouse button, the cells appear in the proper format.

Now all the cells that contain cost, price, profit, and total sales data are formatted as currency. Next, Maria wants to apply formats to the numbers in columns E and H so they are easier to read.

Number Formats

You can select number formats to specify:
- the number of decimal places displayed
- whether to display a comma to delimit thousands, millions, and billions
- whether to display negative numbers with a minus sign, parentheses, or red numerals

Figure 3-17 shows Excel's number formats and examples of each. To access the Excel number formats, you would use the Number tab in the Format Cells dialog box.

Number Format	Positive	Negative
0	1556	-1556
0.00	1556.33	-1556.33
#,##0	1,556	-1,556
#,##0.00	1,556.33	-1,556.33
#,##0_);(#,##0)	1,556	(1,556)
#,##0_);[Red](#,##0)	1,556	(1,556)
#,##0.00_);(#,##0.00)	1,556.33	(1,556.33)
#,##0.00_);[Red](#,##0.00)	1,556.33	(1,556.33)

Figure 3-17
Examples of Excel's number formats

Maria wants to include a comma in the number format for column E, and she does not want to display any decimal places.

To format the contents in column E with a comma:
1. Highlight cells E6 through E11.
2. Click **Format**, then click **Cells...** to display the Format Cells dialog box.
3. If necessary, click the **Number tab**.
4. Click **Number** in the Category box.
5. Click the fourth option, **#,##0**, in the Format Codes box.
6. Click the **OK button** to apply the format.
7. Click any cell to remove the highlighting and view the format results. See Figure 3-18.

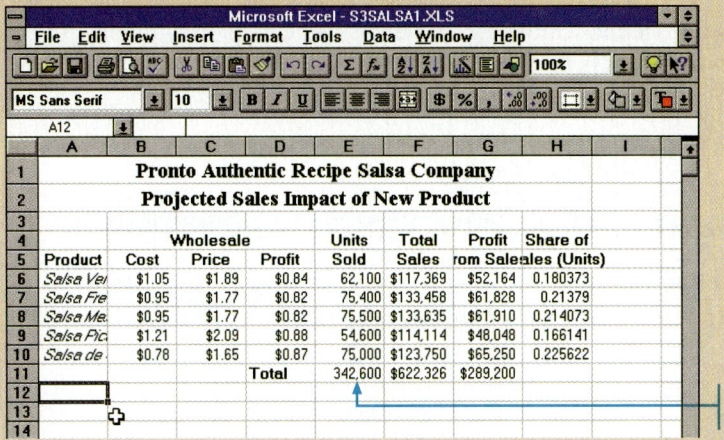

Figure 3-18
Comma format

commas separate thousands

Maria thinks the numbers in column H are difficult to interpret and decides that it is not necessary to display so many decimal places. What are her options for displaying percentages?

Percentage Formats

Excel provides two percentage formats: the 0% format and the 0.00% format. If you have the number 0.18037 in a cell, the 0% format would display this number as 18%, without any decimal places. The 0.00% format would display the number as 18.04%, with two decimal places.

Maria's format plan specifies a percentage format with no decimal places for the values in column H. She could use the Number tab to choose this format. But it's faster to use the Percent Style button. (Note that if Maria wanted to use the 0.00% style, she would have to select it using the Number tab in the Format Cells dialog box.)

To format the values in column H as a percentage with no decimal places:
1. Highlight cells H6 through H10.
2. Click the **Percent Style button**.
3. Click any cell to remove the highlighting and view the percentage format.

Maria checks her plan once again and confirms that she selected formats for all the cells on the worksheet. She delayed making any change to the width of column A because she knew that it would cause some of the columns to scroll off the screen and force her to scroll around the worksheet to format all the labels and values. Now that she has finished formatting the labels and values, she can change all the columns to the appropriate width to best display the information in them.

To do this, Maria could double-click the right column heading border for each column she wants to widen. But since she needs to widen several columns, it's easier to use the Format menu.

To change the width of the columns using the Format menu:

❶ Highlight cells A4 through H11.

❷ Click **Format**, click **Column**, then click **AutoFit Selection**.

❸ Click any cell to remove the highlighting and view the results of the change in column width. See Figure 3-19.

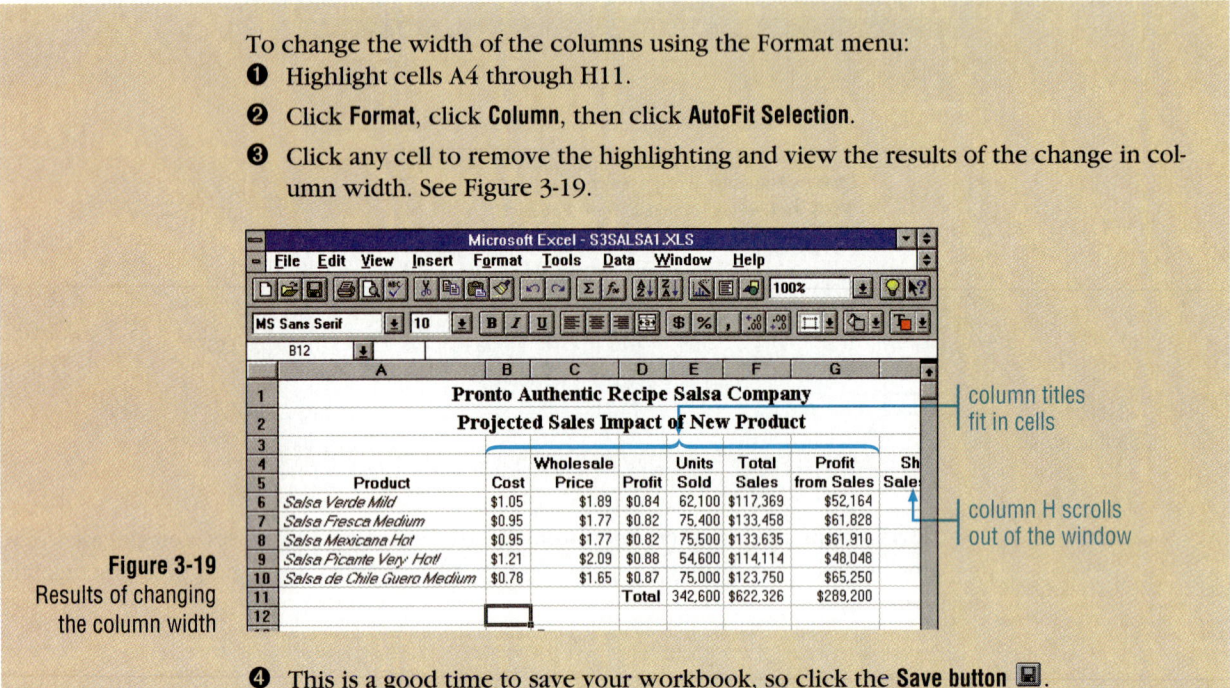

Figure 3-19
Results of changing the column width

❹ This is a good time to save your workbook, so click the **Save button** 🖫.

As Maria expected, the worksheet is now too wide to fit on the screen. She might need to scroll from side to side to complete some additional formatting tasks. Remember from the previous tutorials that when you want to see a part of the worksheet that is not displayed, you can use the scroll bars. If you are highlighting a range, but some of the range is not displayed, you can drag the pointer to the edge of the screen and the worksheet will scroll. You'll see how this works when you add some borders in the next set of steps.

Adding and Removing Borders

A well-constructed worksheet is clearly divided into **zones** that visually group related information. Figure 3-20 shows the zones on Maria's worksheet. Lines, called **borders**, can help to distinguish between different zones of the worksheet and add visual interest.

Adding and Removing Borders   EX 99

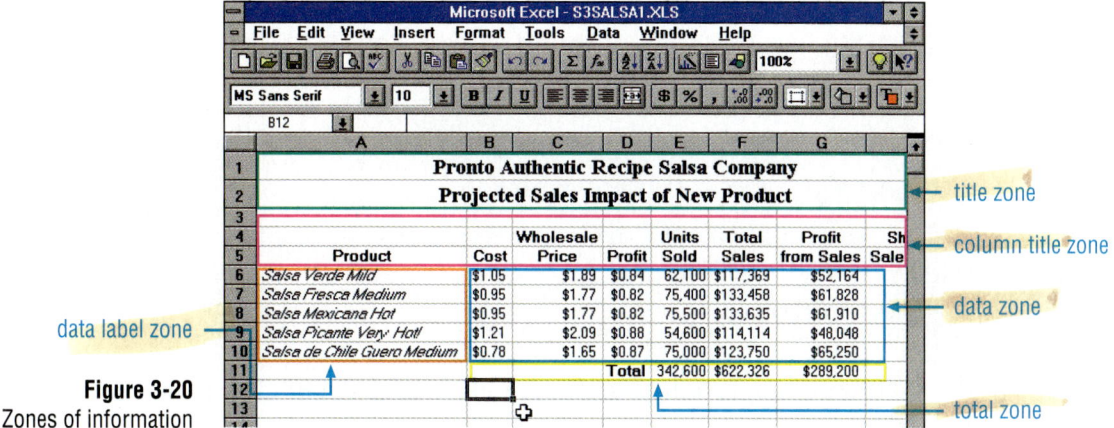

Figure 3-20
Zones of information

You can create lines and borders using either the Borders button or the Border tab in the Format Cells dialog box. You can put a border around a single cell or a group of cells using the Outline option. To create a horizontal line, you create a border at the top or bottom of a cell. To create a vertical line, you create a border on the right or left of a cell.

The border tab allows you to choose from numerous border styles, including different line thicknesses, double lines, dashed lines, and different line colors. With the Border Styles button, your choice of border styles is limited.

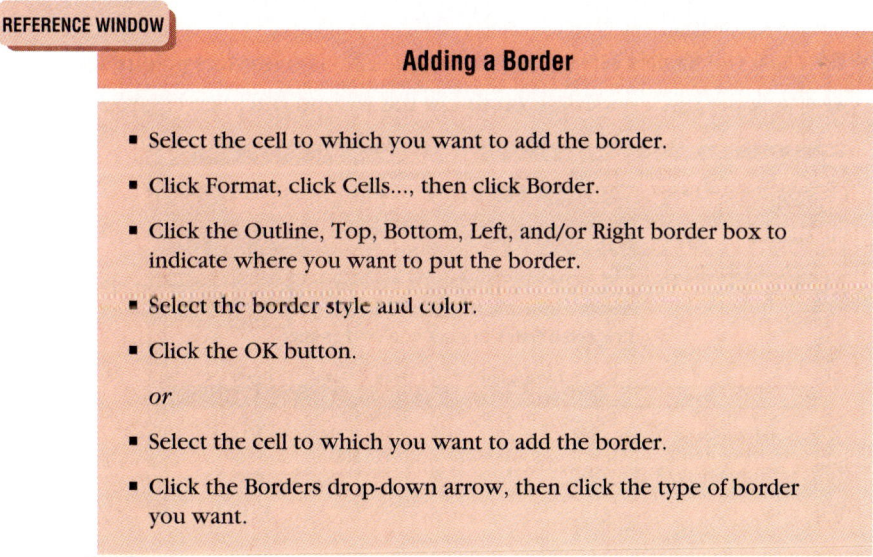

REFERENCE WINDOW

Adding a Border

- Select the cell to which you want to add the border.
- Click Format, click Cells..., then click Border.
- Click the Outline, Top, Bottom, Left, and/or Right border box to indicate where you want to put the border.
- Select the border style and color.
- Click the OK button.

  or

- Select the cell to which you want to add the border.
- Click the Borders drop-down arrow, then click the type of border you want.

If you want to remove a border from a cell or group of cells, you can use the Border dialog box. To remove all borders from a selected range of cells, make sure the Outline, Top, Bottom, Left, and Right border boxes are blank. Excel shades in a border box to show that some cells in the selected range contain a border but others do not. If a border box is gray and you want to remove the border, click the box to remove the gray shading.

REFERENCE WINDOW

Removing a Border

- Select the cell or cells that contain the border you want to remove.
- Click Format, click Cells..., then click Border.
- Look for the border box that contains a border or shading, then click this box until it is empty.
- Click the OK button.

Maria wants to put a thick line under all the column titles. To do this, she'll use the Borders button.

To put a line under the column titles:

1. Highlight cells A5 through H5.

   TROUBLE? If cell H5 is not displayed on your screen, drag the pointer from cell A5 to G5 then, without releasing the mouse button, continue moving the pointer to the right. The worksheet window will scroll so you can include cell H5 in the highlighted range. If the worksheet scrolls too fast and you highlight I, J, K, L, and M, move the mouse to the left—without releasing the mouse button—until H5 is the right-most cell in the highlighted range. If you released the mouse button too soon, use the scroll bars to scroll column A back on the screen, then go back to Step 1.

2. Click the **Borders button drop-down arrow**. The Borders palette appears.

3. Click the thick underline button in the second row. See Figure 3-21.

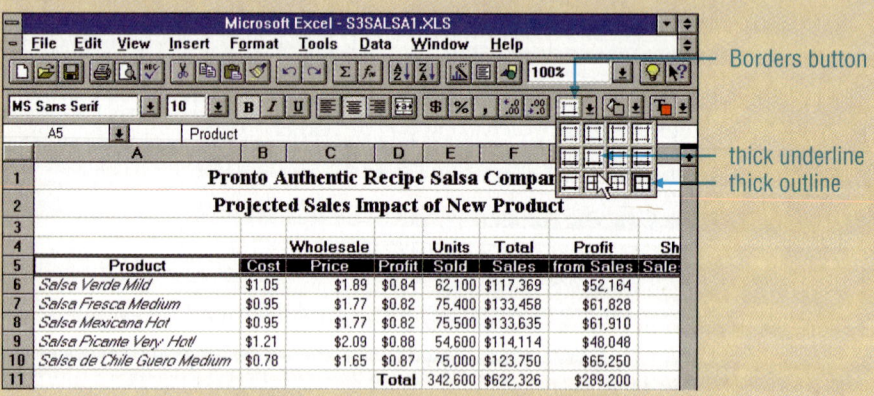

Figure 3-21
The new border

4. Click any cell to remove the highlighting and view the border.

Maria also wants to use a line to separate the data from the totals in row 11. This time she will use the Border tab in the Format Cells dialog box. First Maria highlights cells A11 through H11, then she selects a thick top border from the Border tab. Why would she use a top border here, when she used a bottom border for the column titles? It is good practice not to attach borders to the cells in the data zone because when you copy cells, the cell formats are also copied. Maria knows from experience that if she attaches borders to the wrong cells, she can end up with borders in every cell, or she can end up erasing borders she wanted when she copies cell contents down a column.

To add a line separating the data and the totals:
❶ Highlight cells A11 through H11.
❷ Click **Format**, click **Cells...**, then click the **Border tab**.
❸ Click **Top** to select a top border.
❹ Click the thickest line in the Style box.
❺ Click the **OK button** to apply the border.
❻ Click any cell to remove the highlighting and view the border.

Maria consults her format sketch and sees that she planned to put a border around the title zone to add a professional touch. Let's add this border now.

To place an outline border around the title zone:
❶ Highlight cells A1 through H2.
❷ Click the **Borders button drop-down arrow** .
❸ Click the thick outline button. See Figure 3-21.
❹ Click any cell to remove the highlighting and view the border. See Figure 3-22.

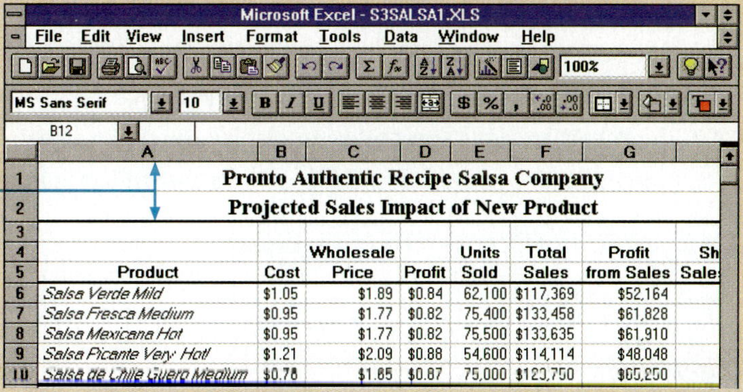

Figure 3-22
A border around the title zone

In addition to a border around the title zone, Maria wants to add color and a shaded pattern in the title zone.

Using Patterns and Color for Emphasis

Patterns and colors can provide visual interest, emphasize zones of the worksheet, or indicate data-entry areas. The use of patterns or colors should be based on the way you intend to use the worksheet. If you print the worksheet on a color printer and distribute it in hardcopy format, or if you are going to use a color projection device to display a screen image of your worksheet, you might want to take advantage of Excel's color formatting options. On the other hand, a printout you produce on a printer without color capability might look better if you use patterns, because it is difficult to predict how the colors you see on your screen will be translated into shades of gray on your printout.

EX 102 TUTORIAL 3   Formatting and Printing

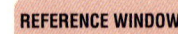

> **REFERENCE WINDOW**
>
> **Applying Patterns and Color**
>
> - Highlight the cells you want to fill with a pattern or color.
> - Click Format, click Cells..., then click the Patterns tab.
> - Select a pattern from the Pattern box. If you want the pattern to appear in a color, select a color from the Pattern box, too.
> - If you want to select a background color, select it from the Cell Shading box. You can also select colors by clicking the Color button on the toolbar and then clicking the desired color.

Maria wants her worksheet to look good when it is printed in black and white on the office laser printer, but she also wants it to look good on the screen when she shows it to her boss. Maria decides to use a yellow background with a light dot pattern, since it matches the color on the Pronto Salsa labels and looks fairly good on the screen and the printer. She decides to apply this format to the title zone using the Patterns tab.

To apply a pattern and color to the title zone:
1. Highlight cells A1 through H2.
2. Click **Format**, click **Cells...**, then click the **Patterns tab**.
3. Click the **Pattern box down arrow button** to display the patterns palette.
4. Select the polka-dot pattern in the top row, as shown in Figure 3-23.

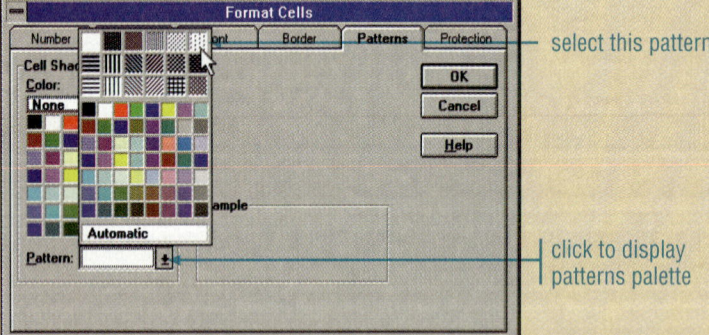

Figure 3-23
Selecting a pattern from the patterns palette

5. Click the yellow square in the top row of the Cell Shading box. A sample of the color and pattern you selected appears in the Sample box.

   TROUBLE? If you are using a monochrome monitor, skip Step 5.

6. Click the **OK button** to apply the pattern and the color.
7. Click any cell to remove the highlighting and view the pattern and color in the title zone. See Figure 3-24.

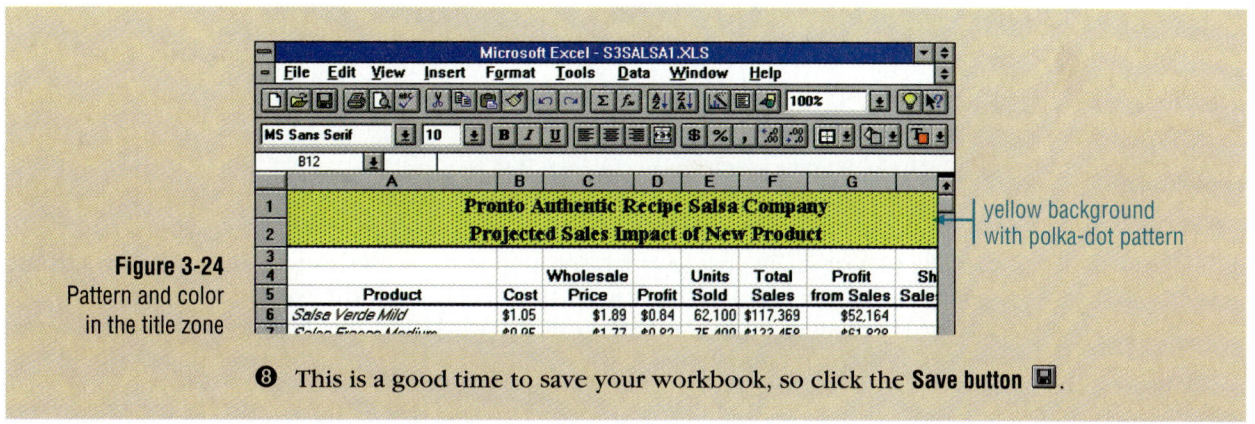

Figure 3-24
Pattern and color in the title zone

❽ This is a good time to save your workbook, so click the **Save button** 🔳.

If you want to take a break and resume the tutorial at a later time, you can exit Excel by double-clicking the Control menu box in the upper-left corner of the screen. When you resume the tutorial, launch Excel, maximize the Microsoft Excel and Book1 windows, and place your Student Disk in the disk drive. Open the file S3SALSA1.XLS, then continue with the tutorial.

■   ■   ■

Maria's next formatting task is to add a comment to the worksheet to emphasize the high profits expected from the new salsa product. She wants to put the comment in a box. To do this, she must use the Drawing toolbar.

Activating a Toolbar

Excel contains more than one toolbar. The two toolbars you have been using are called the Standard toolbar and the Formatting toolbar. (The Standard toolbar is the one on top.) Excel also has a number of other toolbars, including a Chart toolbar, a Drawing toolbar, and a Formatting toolbar. To activate a toolbar, it's usually easiest to use the toolbar shortcut menu, but to active the Drawing toolbar you can simply click the Drawing button on the Standard toolbar. When you are finished using a toolbar, you can easily remove it from the worksheet.

> **REFERENCE WINDOW**
>
> ### Activating and Removing Toolbars
>
> - To activate a toolbar, click on any toolbar with the right mouse button to display the toolbar shortcut menu. Then click the name of the toolbar you want to use.
>
> - To remove a toolbar, click on any toolbar with the right mouse button to display the toolbar shortcut menu. Then click the name of the toolbar you want to remove.

Maria needs the Drawing toolbar to accomplish her next formatting task.

To add the Drawing toolbar:
❶ Click the **Drawing button** on the Standard toolbar.

The toolbar might appear in any location in the worksheet window. Maria wants the toolbar out of the way, so she drags it to the bottom of the worksheet window. If your toolbar is not attached to the bottom of the worksheet window, follow the next set of steps to position it there.

To attach the Drawing toolbar to the bottom of the worksheet window:
❶ Position the pointer on the title bar of the Drawing toolbar.
❷ Drag the toolbar to the bottom of the screen. The outline of the toolbar changes to a long, narrow rectangle, as shown in Figure 3-25.

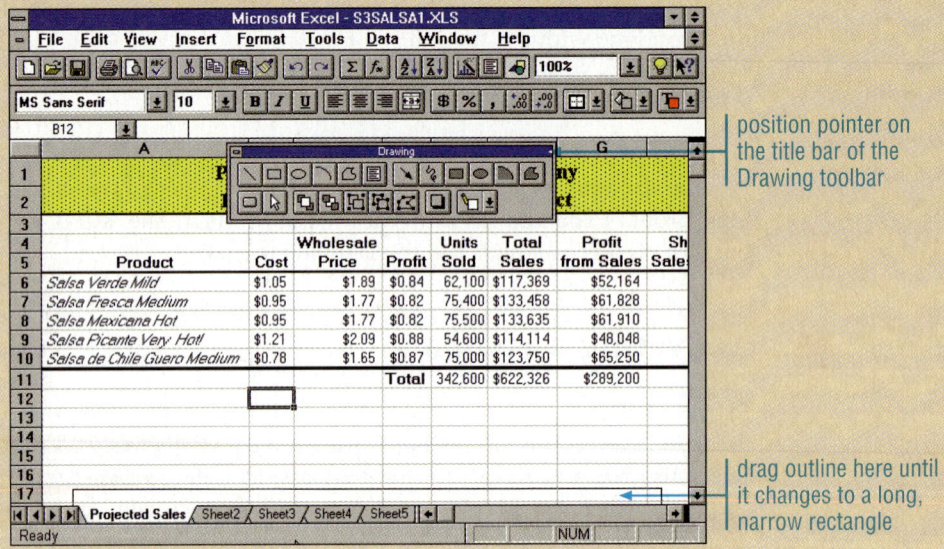

Figure 3-25
Positioning the Drawing toolbar

❸ Release the mouse button to attach the Drawing toolbar to the bottom of the worksheet window. See Figure 3-26.

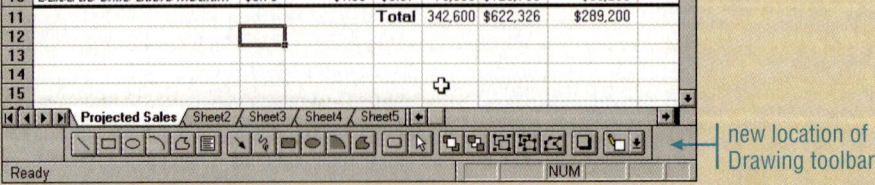

Figure 3-26
The Drawing toolbar attached to the bottom of the window

Now that the Drawing toolbar is where she wants it, Maria is ready to proceed with her plan to add a comment to the worksheet.

Adding Comments to the Worksheet

Excel's text box feature enables you to display a comment on a worksheet. Unlike the text note you attached to a cell in Tutorial 2, a **comment** is like an electronic "post-it" note that you paste on the worksheet inside a rectangular text box. You do not need to double-click a cell to display a comment as you do to display a text note.

To add a comment to your worksheet, you create a text box using the Text Box tool. Then you simply enter the text in the box. (Note that there are two Text Box tools, one on the Drawing toolbar and one on the Standard toolbar. You can use whichever one is more convenient.)

REFERENCE WINDOW

Adding a Text Box and Comment

- Click the Text Box button either in the Drawing toolbar or in the Standard toolbar.
- Position + where you want the text box to appear on the worksheet.
- Drag + to outline the size and shape of the text box you want.
- Type the text of the comment you want to display in the text box.
- Click any cell outside the text box when the comment is complete.

A text box is one example of an Excel object. Excel objects include shapes, arrows, and text boxes. If you need to move, modify, or delete an object, you must select it first. To select an object, you move the pointer over the object until the pointer changes to ↖, then click. When the object is selected, small square handles appear. You use the handles to adjust the size of an object, change the location of an object, or delete an object.

Maria wants to draw attention to the low price and high profit margin of the new salsa product. To do this, she plans to add a text box that contains a comment about expected profits. Refer to Maria's format plan in Figure 3-2 to see where she wants to locate the text box.

To add a comment in a text box:

❶ Click the **Text Box button** 🗔 on the Drawing toolbar. The pointer changes to +.

❷ Position the pointer in cell A13 to mark the upper-left corner of the text box.

❸ Drag + to cell C17, then release the mouse button to mark the lower-right corner of the text box. See Figure 3-27.

EX 106   TUTORIAL 3   Formatting and Printing

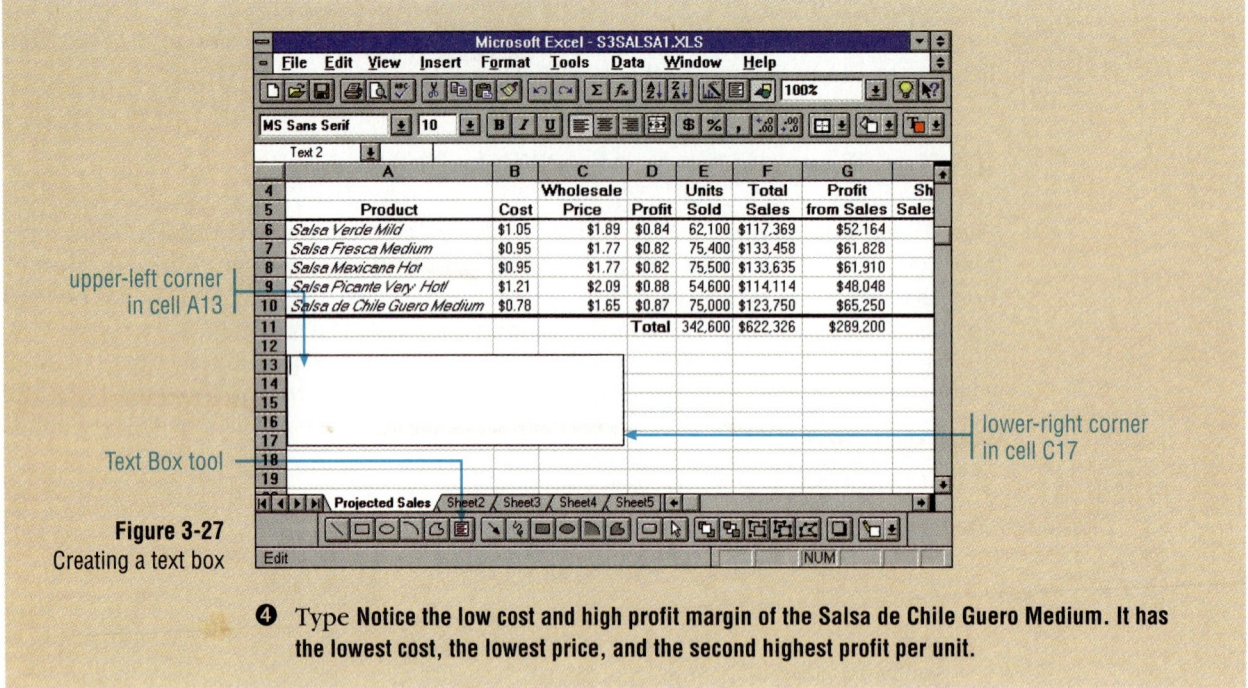

Figure 3-27
Creating a text box

❹ Type **Notice the low cost and high profit margin of the Salsa de Chile Guero Medium. It has the lowest cost, the lowest price, and the second highest profit per unit.**

Maria wants to use a different font style to emphasize the name of the new salsa product in the text box.

To italicize the name of the new salsa product:

❶ Position I in the text box just before the word "Salsa."

TROUBLE? If the size of your text box is slightly different from the one in the figure, the lines of text might break between different words. Don't worry if the text in your text box is not arranged exactly like the text in the figure.

❷ Drag I to the end of the word "Medium," then release the mouse button. See Figure 3-28.

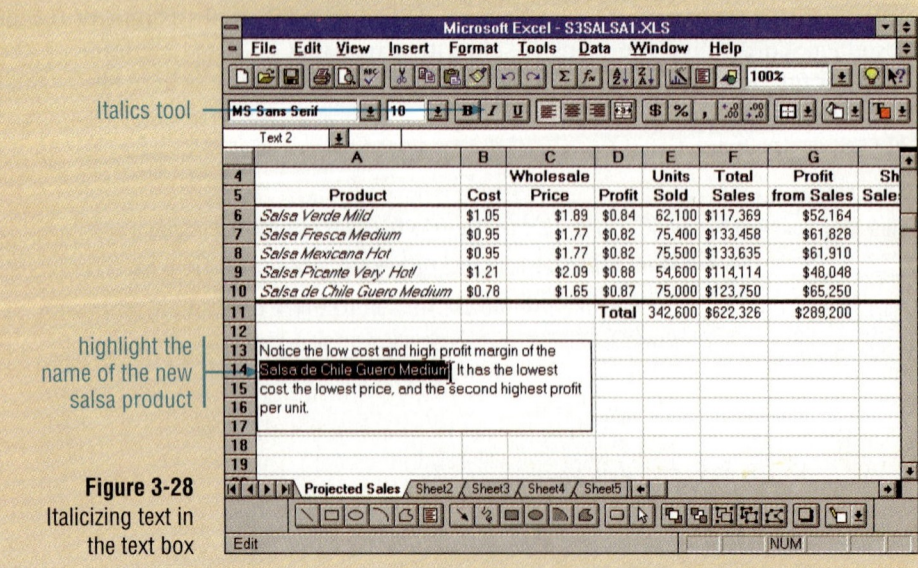

Figure 3-28
Italicizing text in the text box

❸ Click the **Italics button** .

❹ Click any cell to remove the highlighting. Now the new product name is italicized.

Maria decides to change the size of the text box so there is no empty space at the bottom of it.

To change the size of the text box:
❶ Click anywhere within the borders of the **text box** to select it and display the thick border with handles.
❷ Position the pointer on the center handle at the bottom of the box. The pointer changes to ↕. See Figure 3-29.

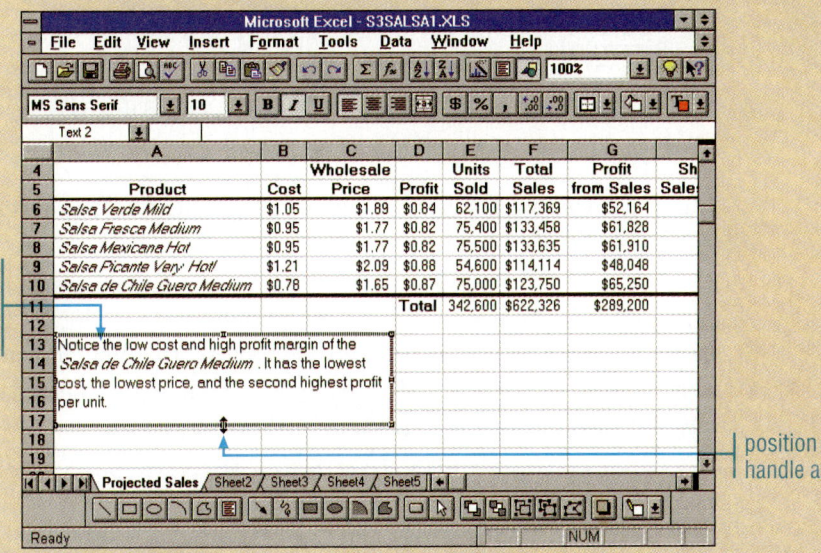

when text box is selected, a thick border with handles appears

position pointer on handle and drag up

Figure 3-29
Changing the size of the text box

❸ Click and drag ↕ up to shorten the box, then release the mouse button.

Maria wants to make a few more modifications to the text box. First she wants to add a 3-D drop shadow.

To add a drop shadow:
❶ Make sure the text box is still selected, as indicated by the thick border and handles.
❷ Click the **Drop Shadow button** in the Drawing toolbar.

Now Maria wants to make the text border thicker.

To modify the border of the text box:
❶ Make sure the text box is still selected.
❷ Click **Format**, click **Object...** to display the Format Object dialog box, then click the **Patterns tab**.

EX 108   TUTORIAL 3   Formatting and Printing

❸ Click the **Weight box down arrow button** to display the border thicknesses.

❹ Click the third border weight in the list, as shown in Figure 3-30. Notice that the Shadow box contains an ×. That's because you already added a shadow using the Drop Shadow button.

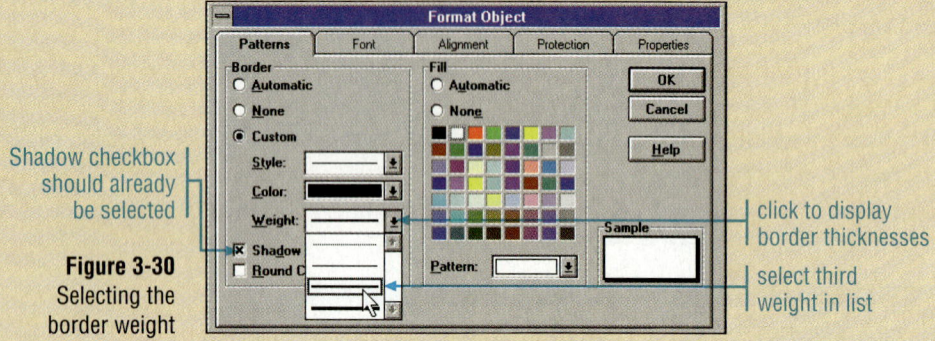

Shadow checkbox should already be selected

Figure 3-30
Selecting the border weight

click to display border thicknesses

select third weight in list

❺ Click the **OK button**, then click any cell to deselect the text box.

Maria decides to add an arrow pointing from the text box to the row that contains information on the new salsa.

To add an arrow:

❶ Click the **Arrow button** on the Drawing toolbar. The pointer changes to +.

❷ Position the pointer on the top edge of the text box in cell B12. Drag the pointer to cell B10, then release the mouse button. See Figure 3-31.

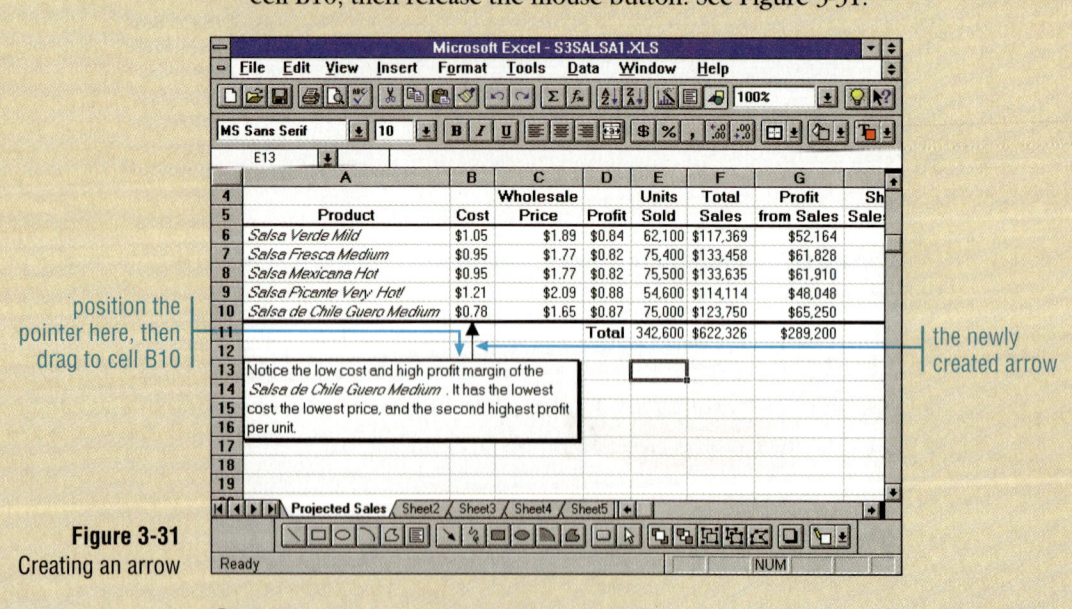

position the pointer here, then drag to cell B10

the newly created arrow

Figure 3-31
Creating an arrow

❸ Click any cell to deselect the arrow.

Like a text box, an arrow is an Excel object. To modify the arrow object, you must select it. When you select an arrow object, two small square handles appear on it. You can reposition either end of the arrow by dragging one of the handles to a new position.

Maria wants the arrow to point to cell D10 instead of B10. Let's see how you can reposition the arrow.

To reposition the arrow:

1. Move the pointer over the arrow object. The pointer changes to ↖.
2. Click the mouse button to select the arrow. Handles appear at each end of the arrow.
3. Move the pointer to the top handle on the arrowhead until the pointer changes to +.
4. Drag + to cell D10, then release the mouse button.
5. Click any cell to deselect the arrow object. See Figure 3-32.

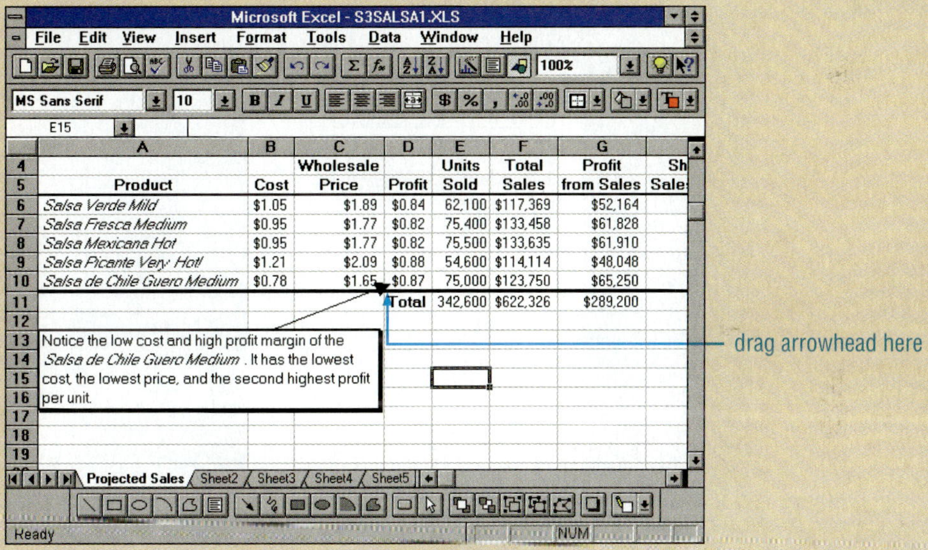

	A	B	C	D	E	F	G	Sh
4			Wholesale		Units	Total	Profit	Sh
5	Product	Cost	Price	Profit	Sold	Sales	from Sales	Sale
6	*Salsa Verde Mild*	$1.05	$1.89	$0.84	62,100	$117,369	$52,164	
7	*Salsa Fresca Medium*	$0.95	$1.77	$0.82	75,400	$133,458	$61,828	
8	*Salsa Mexicana Hot*	$0.95	$1.77	$0.82	75,500	$133,635	$61,910	
9	*Salsa Picante Very Hot!*	$1.21	$2.09	$0.88	54,600	$114,114	$48,048	
10	*Salsa de Chile Guero Medium*	$0.78	$1.65	$0.87	75,000	$123,750	$65,250	
11				Total	342,600	$622,326	$289,200	

Figure 3-32
Moving the arrow

Now that the text box is finished, you can remove the Drawing toolbar from the worksheet.

To remove the Drawing toolbar:

1. Click the **Drawing button** on the Standard toolbar.
2. This is a good time to save your workbook, so click the **Save button**.

If you want to take a break and resume the tutorial at a later time, you can exit Excel by double-clicking the Control menu box in the upper-left corner of the screen. When you resume the tutorial, launch Excel, maximize the Microsoft Excel and Book1 windows, and place your Student Disk in the disk drive. Open the file S3SALSA1.XLS, then continue with the tutorial.

The text box and arrow effectively call attention to the profits expected from the new salsa product. Now Maria is ready to print the worksheet.

Print Preview

Before you print a worksheet, you can see how the worksheet will look when it is printed by using Excel's print preview feature. When you request a print preview, you can see the margins, page breaks, headers, and footers that are not always visible on the screen.

To preview the worksheet before you print it:
❶ Click the **Print Preview button**. After a moment Excel displays the first page of the worksheet in the Print Preview window. See Figure 3-33.

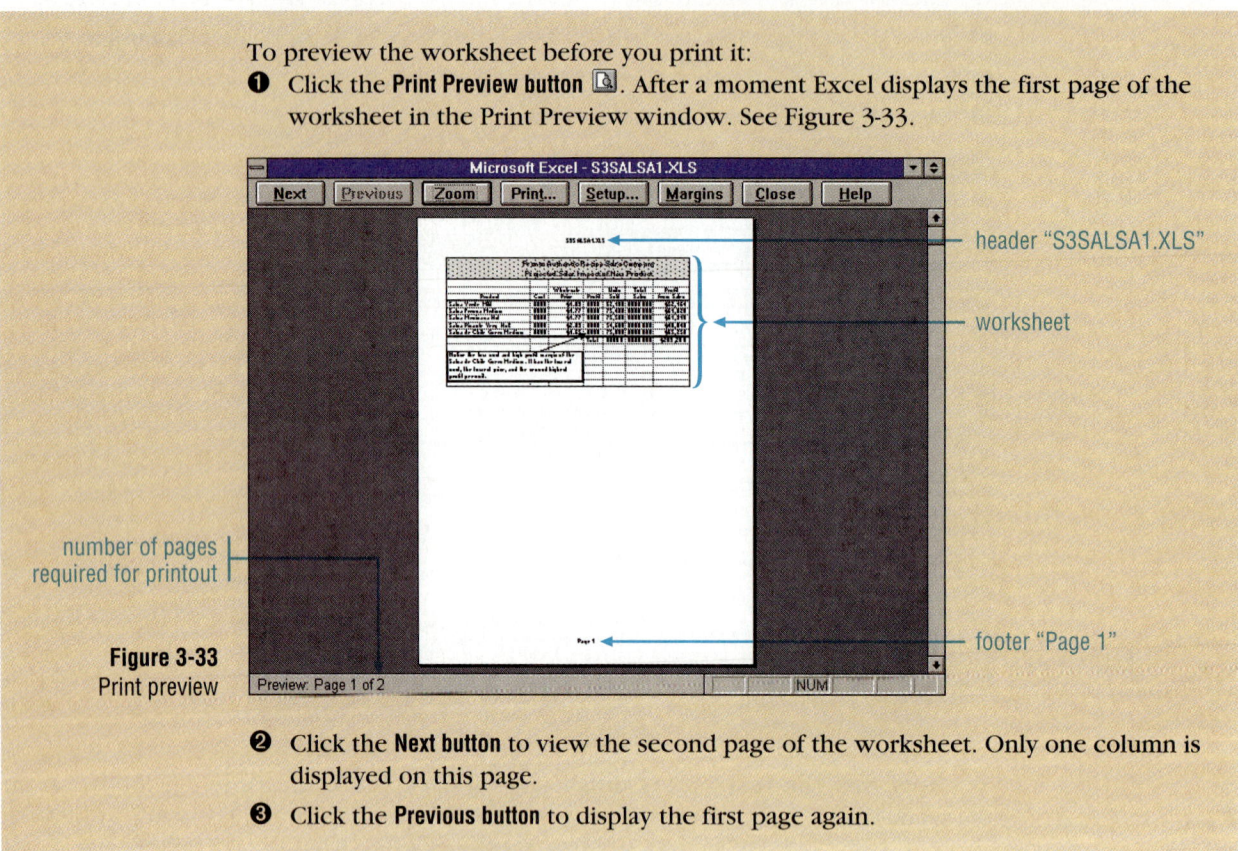

Figure 3-33
Print preview

❷ Click the **Next button** to view the second page of the worksheet. Only one column is displayed on this page.

❸ Click the **Previous button** to display the first page again.

When Excel displays a full page on the print preview screen, it is usually difficult to see the text of the worksheet because it is so small. If you want to read the text, you can use the Zoom button.

To display an enlarged section of the print preview:
❶ Click the **Zoom button** to display an enlarged section of the print preview.
❷ Click the **Zoom button** again to return to the full page view.

The print preview screen contains several other buttons. The Print button lets you access the Print dialog box directly from the preview screen. The Setup button lets you change the way the page is set up by adjusting the margins, creating headers and footers, adding page numbers, changing the paper size, or centering the worksheet on the page. The Margins button allows you to adjust the margins and immediately view the result of that change. The Close button returns you to the worksheet window.

By looking at the print preview, Maria sees that the worksheet is too wide to fit on a single page. She decides to print the worksheet sideways so it will fit on a single sheet of paper.

Portrait and Landscape Orientations

Excel provides two print orientations, portrait and landscape. The **portrait** orientation prints the worksheet with the paper positioned so it is taller than it is wide. The **landscape** orientation prints the worksheet with the paper positioned so it is wider than it is tall. Because many worksheets are wider than they are tall, landscape orientation is used frequently.

You can specify the print orientation using the Page Setup command on the File menu or by using the Setup button on the print preview screen. Let's use the landscape orientation for Maria's worksheet.

To change the print orientation to landscape:

❶ Click the **Setup... button** to display the Page Setup dialog box. If necessary, click the **Page tab**.

❷ Click **Landscape** in the Orientation box. The sample diagram—the sheet of paper with the large "A" on it—shows that the page will be oriented so it is wider than it is tall. See Figure 3-34.

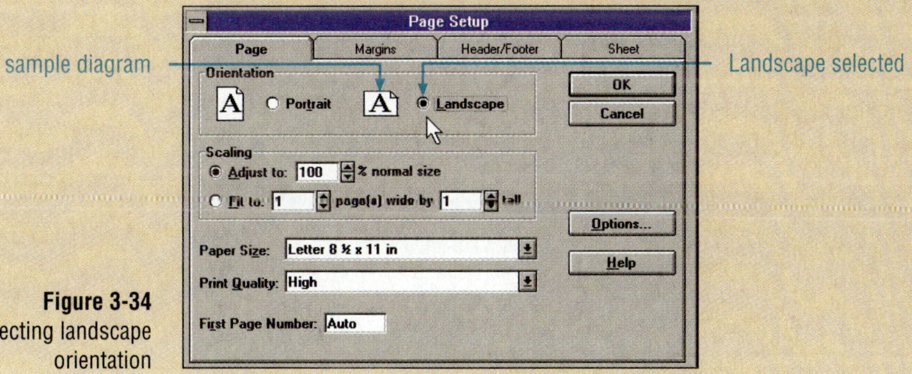

Figure 3-34
Selecting landscape orientation

While the Page Setup dialog box is open, let's use the Header/Footer tab to document the worksheet.

Headers and Footers

A **header** is text that is printed in the top margin of every page of a worksheet. A **footer** is text that is printed in the bottom margin of every page of a worksheet. Headers and footers are not displayed as part of the worksheet window. To see them, you must look at a print preview or a worksheet printout.

You can use a header or footer to provide basic documentation about your worksheet. A worksheet header could contain the name of the person who created the worksheet, the date the worksheet was created, and the filename of the worksheet. Excel automatically attaches a centered header containing the worksheet filename and a centered footer containing the page number, unless you specify otherwise. Refer back to Figure 3-33 to see the headers and footers displayed in the print preview.

Excel uses formatting codes in headers and footers. **Formatting codes** produce dates, times, and filenames that you might want to include in a header or footer. You can type these codes, or you can click a formatting code button to insert the code. Figure 3-35 shows the formatting codes and the tools you can use to insert them.

Tool	Tool Name	Formatting Code	Action
A	Font tool	none	set font size
#	Page Number tool	&[Page]	print page number
	Total Pages tool	&[Pages]	print total number of pages
	Date tool	&[Date]	print date
	Time tool	&[Time]	print time
	Filename tool	&[File]	print filename
	Tabname tool	&[Tab]	print tabname

Figure 3-35
The header and footer formatting

Maria wants to change the header and footer that Excel added automatically.

To change the worksheet header:

❶ Make sure the Page Setup dialog box is still open, then click the **Header/Footer tab**.

❷ Click the **Custom Header... button** to display the Header dialog box.

❸ Drag the pointer over &[File] in the Center Section box to highlight it. See Figure 3-36.

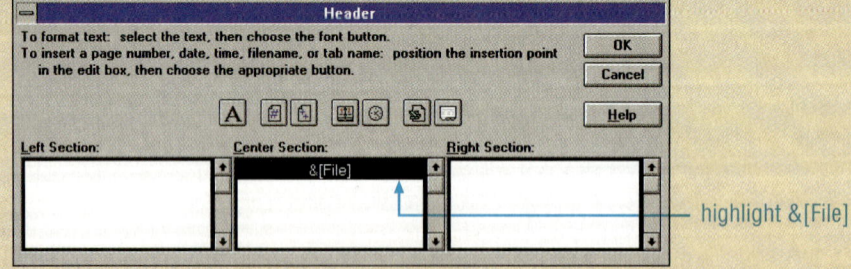

Figure 3-36
Deleting a header

highlight &[File]

❹ Press **[Del]** to delete &[File].

❺ Click the **Right Section box** to move the insertion point there. You should be able to see the insertion point blinking on the far right border of the box.

❻ Type **Pronto Salsa Company** and then press **[Spacebar]** so the company name doesn't run into the next item in the header.

❼ Click the **Date button** to add &[Date] to the header, then press **[Spacebar]**.

❽ Click the **Filename button** to add &[File] to the header. See Figure 3-37.

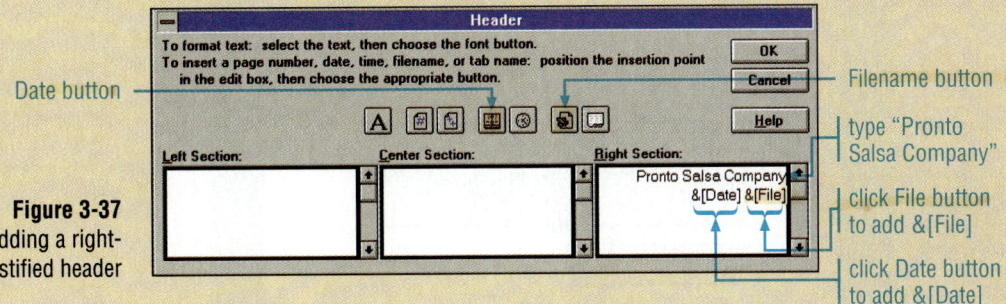

Figure 3-37
Adding a right-justified header

TROUBLE? Don't worry if &[Date] and &[File] are in different lines from "Pronto Salsa Company."

❾ Click the **OK button** to complete the header and return to the Page Setup dialog box.

Centering the Printout and Removing Cell Gridlines and Row/Column Headings

Maria thinks that worksheet printouts look more professional without gridlines and row/column headings. In her opinion, the row/column headings—the letters A, B, C, and so forth that identify the columns—are useful when you design and create the worksheet but are distracting on the printout. Maria also likes her worksheets to be centered on the printed page. Let's make those changes now.

To center the printout and remove the row/column headings and gridlines:

❶ Make sure the Page Setup dialog box is still open.

❷ Click the **Margins tab**.

❸ If the Horizontally box does not contain an ×, click the **Horizontally box** to place an × in it.

❹ If the Vertically box does not contain an ×, click the **Vertically box** to place an × in it.

❺ Click the **Sheet tab**.

❻ If the Gridlines box contains an ×, click the **Gridlines box** to remove the × from it.

❼ Make sure the Row & Column Headings box is empty.

EX 114 TUTORIAL 3 Formatting and Printing

● Click the **OK button** to complete the Page Setup changes and display a print preview that shows the effect of the changes you made. See Figure 3-38.

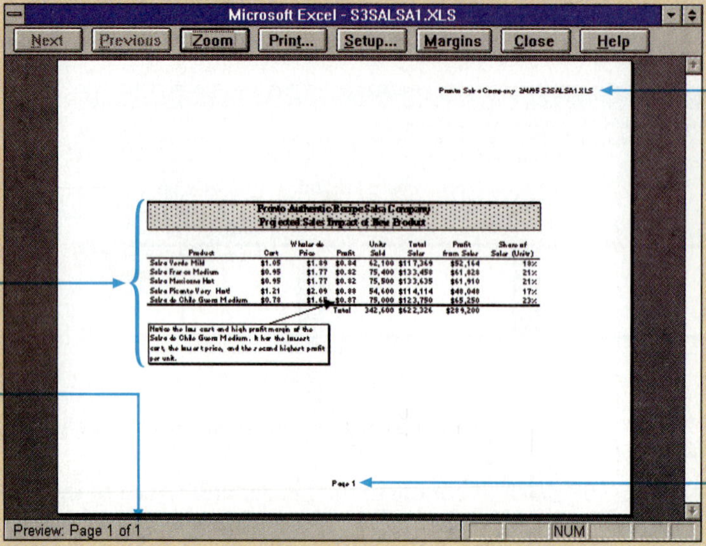

Figure 3-38
Previewing the printed worksheet

Callouts on figure:
- company name, date, and filename right-justified in header
- worksheet is centered and fits on one page
- number of pages required for printout
- page number footer

● If your screen doesn't match the figure, make any necessary adjustments using the Page Setup dialog box. When you're ready, click the **Close button** to close the print preview window.

The worksheet is ready to print, but Maria always saves her work before printing.

To save and print the worksheet:

● Click the **Save button**.

● Click the **Print button**.

TROUBLE? If you see a message that indicates you have a printer problem, click the Cancel button to cancel the printout. Check your printer to make sure it is turned on and is on-line; also make sure it has paper. Then go back and try Step 2 again. If you do not have a printer available, click the Cancel button.

Figure 3-39 shows Maria's printout. Maria is pleased with her work.

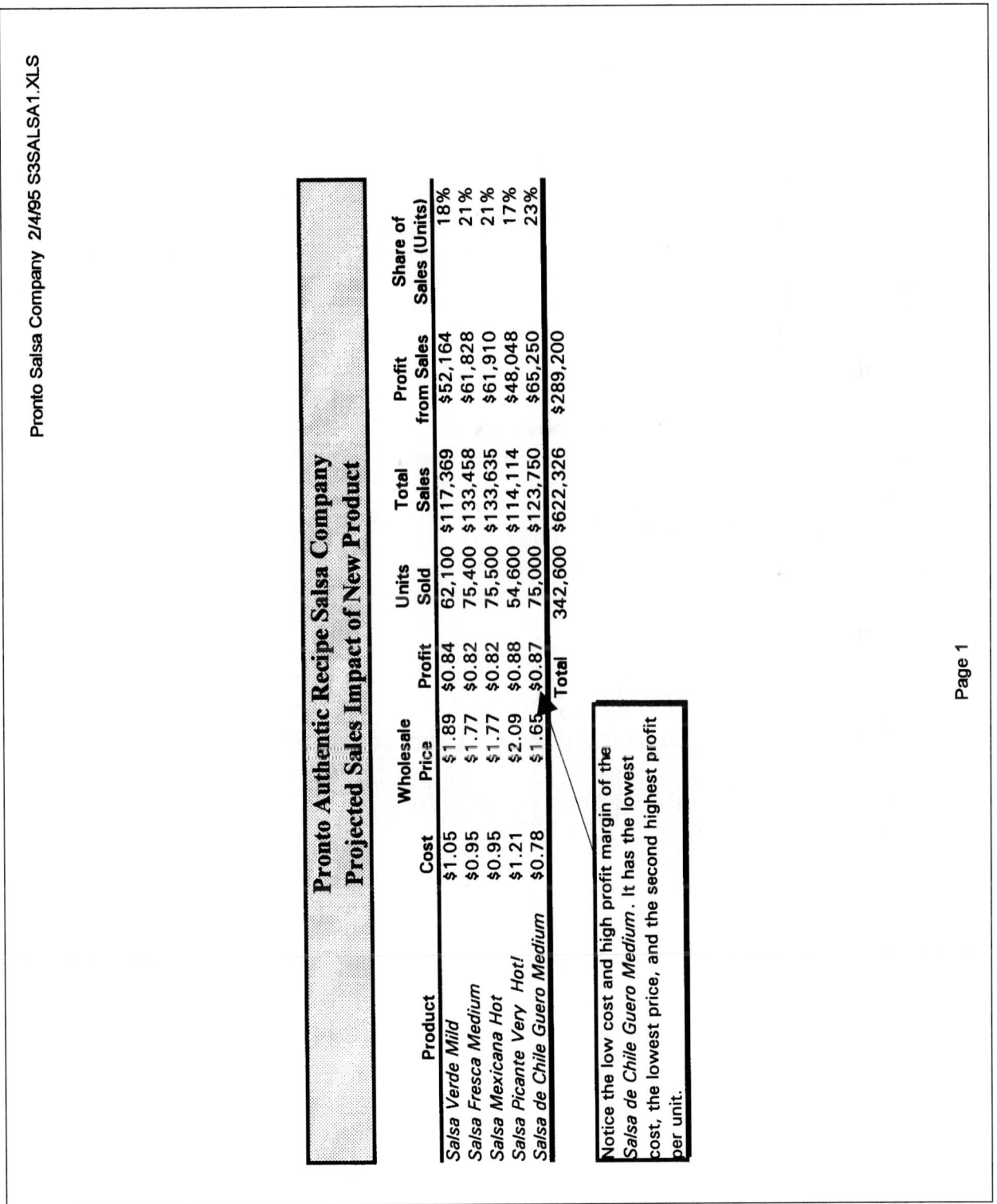

Figure 3-39
Maria's printed worksheet

Since she has a few minutes before her boss returns, Maria decides to produce some additional documentation for the worksheet.

Displaying Formulas

In Tutorial 2 you learned that you can add a text note to incorporate documentation into your worksheet, and you learned that the worksheet plan and sketch are valuable paper-based worksheet documentation. In this tutorial, you will learn how to document the formulas you used to create the worksheet.

You can document the formulas you entered on a worksheet by displaying the formulas and printing them. When you display formulas, Excel shows the formulas you entered in each cell instead of showing the results of the calculations. Maria wants a printout of the formulas in her worksheet for documentation. To see how she does this, let's first display the formulas she entered.

To display formulas:

❶ Click **Tools**, then click **Options**, to open the Options dialog box.

❷ Click the **View tab**, then click **Formulas** in the Windows Option box to place an × in the Formulas box.

❸ Click the **OK button** to return to the worksheet.

The worksheet columns have widened excessively, but Maria isn't concerned about worksheet format right now. She simply wants to make sure the formulas are displayed properly in the worksheet. (If Maria wanted to readjust the column width, she would have to repeat the AutoFit Selection command she used earlier.)

❹ Scroll the worksheet to look at columns D, E, F, G, and H—the columns that contain formulas. See Figure 3-40. (Don't be concerned if the columns on your screen are wider than those in the figure.)

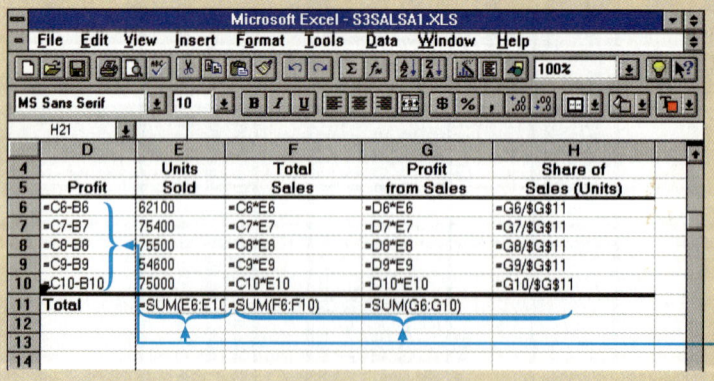

Figure 3-40
Displaying formulas

Maria could manually make the settings to print the worksheet with the formulas displayed, but to do so would be time consuming because she would have to change the column widths and make the appropriate settings in the Page Setup dialog box to show the gridlines and the row/column headings, center the worksheet on the page, and fit the printout on a single page. To avoid doing all this work every time she wants to print formulas, Maria created a Visual Basic module to automate this printing task.

Before you look at Maria's module, let's turn off the formulas display.

To turn off the formulas display:
1. Click **Tools**, then click **Options**, to open the Options dialog box.
2. Click the **View tab** if necessary, then click **Formulas** to remove the ×.
3. Click the **OK button** to return to the worksheet. The formulas are no longer displayed.
4. Scroll the worksheet so you can see column A.

A Visual Basic Module to Print Formulas

A Visual Basic **module**, also called a macro, automatically performs a sequence of tasks or commands such as menu selections, dialog box selections, or keystrokes. You create modules to automate the Excel tasks that you perform frequently and that require a series of steps. To create a module you can record the series of steps as you perform them, or you can enter a series of commands (in the Visual Basic programming language) that tell Excel how to do the task.

In this section of the tutorial, you will have the opportunity to use a prewritten module that prints formulas. You will learn how to run the module, and you will look at the commands that constitute the module. As you will discover, the print formulas module is very useful for documenting the worksheets you complete as course assignments.

Opening a Module

Your Student Disk contains a copy of Maria's module, which displays and prints worksheet formulas automatically. Maria created her print formulas module to do the following:
- Make a copy of the worksheet in a separate sheet
- Display formulas
- Adjust column width for best fit
- Turn on cell gridlines and row/column headings
- Fit the printout on a single page in landscape orientation
- Print the worksheet
- Erase the copy of the worksheet and return to the original worksheet

The module that prints worksheet formulas is stored in a workbook called PRINT1.XLM. The .XLM extension tells you that this workbook contains only a Visual Basic module. Let's open the workbook and look at the commands.

To open the PRINT1.XLM module:

1. Click the **Open button** to display the Open dialog box.

2. Double-click **PRINT1.XLM** to open the workbook. The print module appears, along with the Visual Basic toolbar. See Figure 3-41.

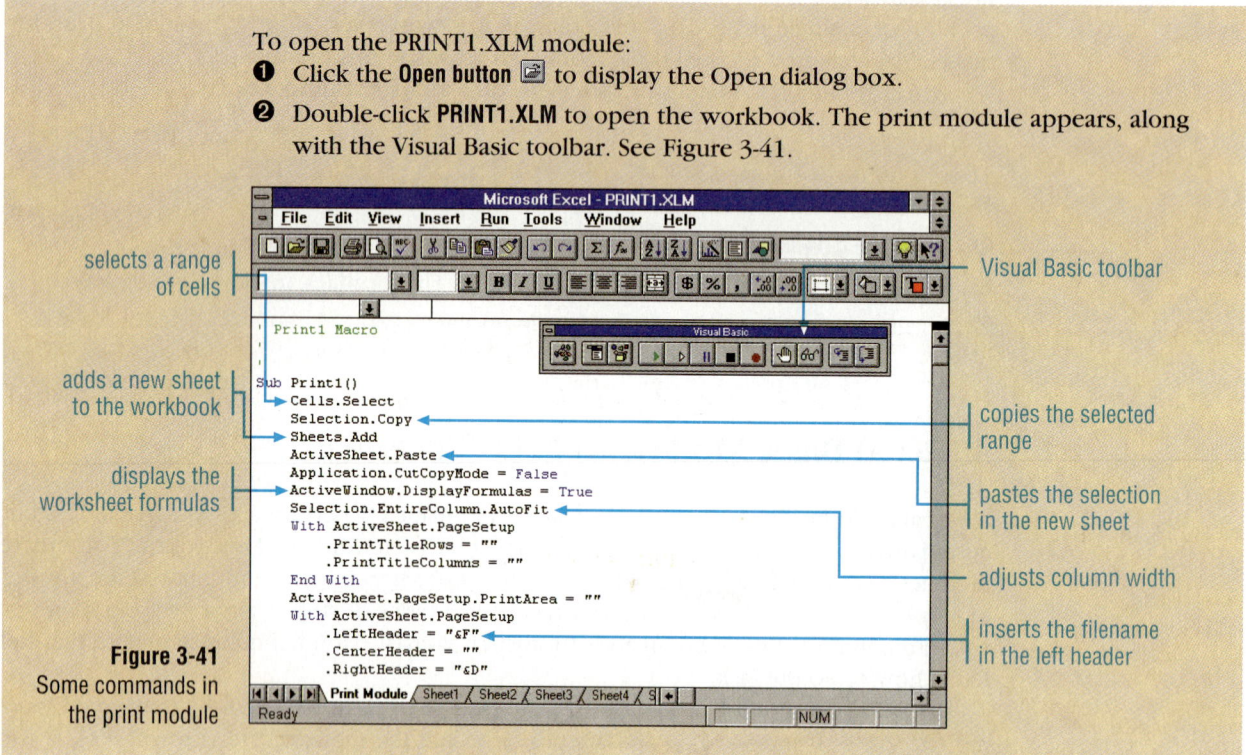

Figure 3-41
Some commands in the print module

Maria created this module by performing the steps for the formula printout while Excel recorded what she did. When Maria completed the steps, Excel translated her actions into the commands you see on the screen. Each row of the module displays one command. The Visual Basic toolbar allows you to run the module or make adjustments to it simply by clicking the proper toolbar button.

While the commands may seem difficult to understand at first, you can probably decipher a few just by taking a close look. For example, Sheets.Add tells Excel to add a new sheet to the workbook. Then, as you might expect, the next command, ActiveSheet.Paste tells Excel to paste something into the active sheet. Other commands are explained in Figure 3-41.

Running a Module

To use a module, you first insert a copy of the module in the workbook you're working on. Then you use the Macro command on the Tools menu to run the module. When you're finished, you should save the workbook, along with the newly added module sheet, so you can use the module whenever you open that workbook.

Maria begins by copying the module to the S3SALSA1.XLS workbook.

Running a Module   EX 119

To copy the module:

1. Click **Edit**, then click **Move or Copy Sheet...** to open the Move or Copy dialog box.
2. Click the **To Book down arrow button** and select **S3SALSA1.XLS**. Then click the **Create a Copy checkbox** to insert an ×.
3. In the Before Sheet box, click **Sheet2**. This tells Excel to place the module sheet, before Sheet2, directly after the Projected Sales sheet.
4. Check that the dialog box on your screen matches Figure 3-42. Then click the **OK button** to make the copy.

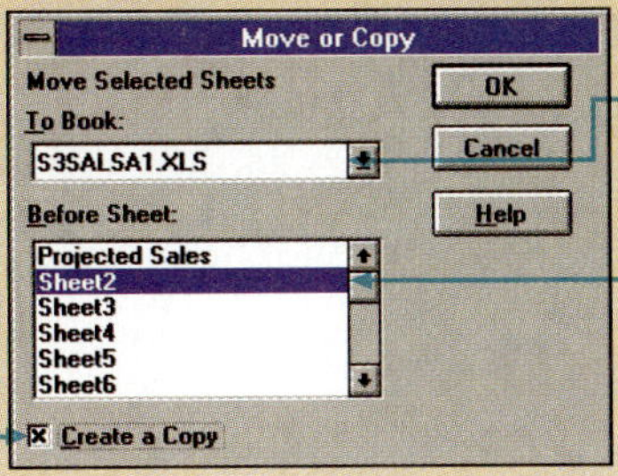

Figure 3-42
The Move or Copy dialog box

click to make a copy of the module

click to select S3SALSA1.XLS

select to insert the module after the "Projected Sales" sheet

Excel adds a module sheet to Maria's workbook. The module appears in the sheet exactly as it appeared in the PRINT1.XLM workbook.

Now, you're ready to run the macro and print the formulas.

To run the module:

1. Click the **Projected Sales tab** to display the Projected Sales sheet.
2. Click **Tools**, then click **Macro...** to display the Macro dialog box.
3. Click **Print1** to display Print1 in the Macro Name/Reference box.
4. Click the **Run button**.
5. After a moment, you'll see the message "Selected sheets will be permanently deleted. Continue?" Click the **OK button** because you do not want to save the copy of the worksheet that the module created. As a result, you will return to your Projected Sales worksheet. Excel prints the worksheet formulas. Notice that the formatting is slightly different on the printed worksheet due to the AutoFit command in the module.

Normally you would save the workbook with the new module sheet. But since you will be improving on the print module in the Tutorial Assignments, you don't want to save this version of the module.

6. Use the File menu to close the workbook. When you see the message "Save changes in 'S3SALSA1.XLS'?" click the **No button**.
7. Close the PRINT1.XLM workbook.

    TROUBLE? If you accidentally made some changes to the module, you will see the message "Save changes in 'PRINT1.XLM'?" Click the No button to save the module in its original form.

8. Exit Excel if you are not going to do the Tutorial Assignments right away.

Now Maria has a printout of the formulas in her worksheet (Figure 3-43), in addition to the printout showing the results of the formula calculations.

S3SALSA1.XLS 2/4/95

Pronto Authentic Recipe Salsa Company
Projected Sales Impact of New Product

Product	Cost	Wholesale Price	Profit	Units Sold	Total Sales	Profit from Sales	Share of Sales (Units)
Salsa Verde Mild	1.05	1.89	=C6-B6	62100	=C6*E6	=D6*E6	=G6/$G$11
Salsa Fresca Medium	0.95	1.77	=C7-B7	75400	=C7*E7	=D7*E7	=G7/$G$11
Salsa Mexicana Hot	0.95	1.77	=C8-B8	75500	=C8*E8	=D8*E8	=G8/$G$11
Salsa Picante Very Hot!	1.21	2.09	=C9-B9	54600	=C9*E9	=D9*E9	=G9/$G$11
Salsa de Chile Guero Medium	0.78	1.65	=C10-B1	75000	=C10*E10	=D10*E10	=G10/$G$11
			Total	=SUM(E6:E10)	=SUM(F6:F10)	=SUM(G6:G10)	

Notice the low cost and high profit margin of the *Salsa de Chile Guero Medium*. It has the lowest cost, the lowest price, and the second highest profit per unit.

Page 1

Figure 3-43

Tips for Using the Print Formulas Module

The print formulas module you used in this tutorial helped Maria print the formulas for her worksheet. In the Tutorial Assignments you will modify this module to create your own customized print formulas module called S3MYMOD.XLM. Your customized module will automatically print your name in the header of the formulas printout. You can use your customized module to print out the formulas for any worksheet you create.

Many of the Tutorial Assignments and Case Problems require you to produce a printout of your worksheet formulas, in addition to a printout of the results of the formula calculations. When you are completing worksheets for the Tutorial Assignments and Case Problems, you should follow these general steps:

1. Create the worksheet and format it as required.
2. When you are ready to print the worksheet, use the Print Preview command to see how the worksheet fits on the printed page. Make adjustments to the column widths on the worksheet if necessary.
3. Use the Page Setup dialog box to center the printout on the page and turn off the cell gridlines and row/column headings. Add your name to the header, and include the date and filename.
4. Print the worksheet.
5. Save the workbook at this point to save your print specifications.
6. Open your customized workbook, S3MYMOD.XLM
7. Use the Move or Copy Sheet command on the Edit menu to move a copy of the module worksheet to the workbook containing the sheet you want to print. Make sure you click the Create a Copy box.
8. Display the sheet containing the formulas you want to print.
9. Use the Macro... command on the Tools menu to open the Macro dialog box and select the print module. Then click the Run button.
10. When the module asks if you want to continue, click the OK button.
11. When you are sure the module is working properly, save the workbook with the new module worksheet.
12. If you are not going to print any other worksheets during your computing session, use the Window menu to activate the module workbook, then close it.

As Maria looks over the printed worksheet and formula printout, Anne returns and asks to see the formatted worksheet. Anne examines the printouts and briefly checks the accuracy of the formulas shown on the formulas printout. She praises Maria for her excellent work before rushing off to her appointment with the loan officer.

Questions

1. If the number .128912 is in a cell, what will Excel display if you:
   a. format the number using the 0% percentage format
   b. format the number using the $#,##0_) currency format
   c. format the number using the $#,##0.00_) currency format
2. Define the following terms using your own words:
   a. column titles
   b. font style
   c. Visual Basic module
   d. formatting
   e. formatting codes
   f. font effects
   g. headers
   h. footers
   i. column headings
3. Explain the advantages and disadvantages of using the AutoFormat command to apply a predefined format to your worksheet.
4. List three ways you can access formatting commands, options, and tools.
5. Explain why Excel might display 3,045.39 in a cell, but when you look at the contents of the cell in the formula bar, it displays 3045.38672.
6. List the formatting buttons that are available on the formatting toolbar.
7. Explain the options Excel provides for aligning data.
8. What is the general rule you should follow for aligning column headings, numbers, and text labels?
9. List four ways you can change column widths.
10. What is a potential problem with the way Excel automatically aligns data?
11. Why is it useful to include a comma to separate thousands, millions, and billions?
12. List the Excel formatting features you can use to draw attention to data or to provide visual interest.
13. List the toolbars that you can activate in Excel. Which of these toolbars have you used in Tutorials 1 through 3?

 14. Use the *Excel On-line Help*, the *Microsoft Excel User's Guide*, the *Microsoft-Windows 3.1 User's Guide*, or other similar documentation to learn more about objects. Write a short paragraph describing what you learned and how you might use objects when you design your own worksheets.
15. Explain how you should position borders so they are not disrupted when you copy cell contents.
16. Make a list of things you should look for when you do a print preview to ensure that your printed worksheets look professional.

Tutorial Assignments

Launch Windows and Excel, if necessary. Insert your Student Disk in the disk drive. Make sure the Excel and Book1 windows are maximized. Complete the following steps to customize the print formulas module so it automatically places your name in the header.

1. Open the module workbook PRINT1.XLM.
2. Move I to the line that reads .RightHeader = "&D".
3. Position I after the first quotation mark and click.

4. Type your own name, and make sure there is a space between your name and the &D formatting code.
5. Scroll back up to the fourth line of the module. Replace "Print1" with "MyMod" in the fourth line. The modified line should now read: Sub MyMod ( ).
6. Edit the first line so that it reads: ' MyMod Macro. Then click at the very beginning of the line to insert the insertion pointer before the apostrophe.
7. Save the revised module as S3MYMOD.XLM.
8. Test the module. Open the S3SALSA1.XLS workbook, then use the Window menu to activate the S3MYMOD.XLM workbook again.
9. Use the Move or Copy Sheet command on the Edit menu to insert a copy of the module in the S3SALSA1.XLS workbook. Then select the sheet containing the formulas you want to print.
10. Use the Macro… command on the Tools menu to open the Macro dialog box and select MYMOD. Your name, the date, and the filename S3SALSA1.XLS should appear in the header of the printed worksheet.

Next, revise the S3SALSA1.XLS workbook by doing the following:

11. Make the text box higher and narrower so it fits in columns A and B.
12. Move the tail-end of the arrow that goes from the top of the text box to cell D10, so that it comes from the right side of the text box.
13. Center the percentages displayed in column H.
14. Make the contents of cells A10 through H10 bold to emphasize the new product. Make any necessary column width adjustments.
15. Add shading to cells A10 through H10 using the same dot pattern and color you used for the titles.
16. Put your name in the header so it appears on the printout of the worksheet. Make sure the header also prints the date and worksheet filename.
17. Make sure the Page Setup menu settings are for landscape orientation, centered horizontally and vertically, no row/column headings, and no cell gridlines.
18. Preview the printout to make sure it fits on one page.
19. Print the worksheet.
20. Save your workbook.

Case Problems

1. Fresh Air Sales Incentive Program

Carl Stambaugh is the assistant sales manager at Fresh Air Inc., a manufacturer of outdoor and expedition clothing. Fresh Air sales representatives contact retail chains and individual retail outlets to sell the Fresh Air line of outdoor clothing products.

This year, to spur sales Carl has decided to run a sales incentive program for the sales representatives. Each sales representative has been assigned a sales goal 15% higher than his or her total sales for last year. All sales representatives who reach this new goal will be awarded an all-expense paid trip for two to Cozumel, Mexico.

Carl has been tracking the results of the sales incentive program with an Excel worksheet. He has asked you to format the worksheet so it will look professional. He also wants a printout before he presents the worksheet at the next sales meeting. Complete the following steps to format and print the worksheet:

1. Launch Windows and Excel as usual.
2. Open the workbook P3SALES.XLS, maximize the worksheet window, then save the workbook as S3SALES.XLS.

3. Make the formatting changes shown in Figure 3-44.

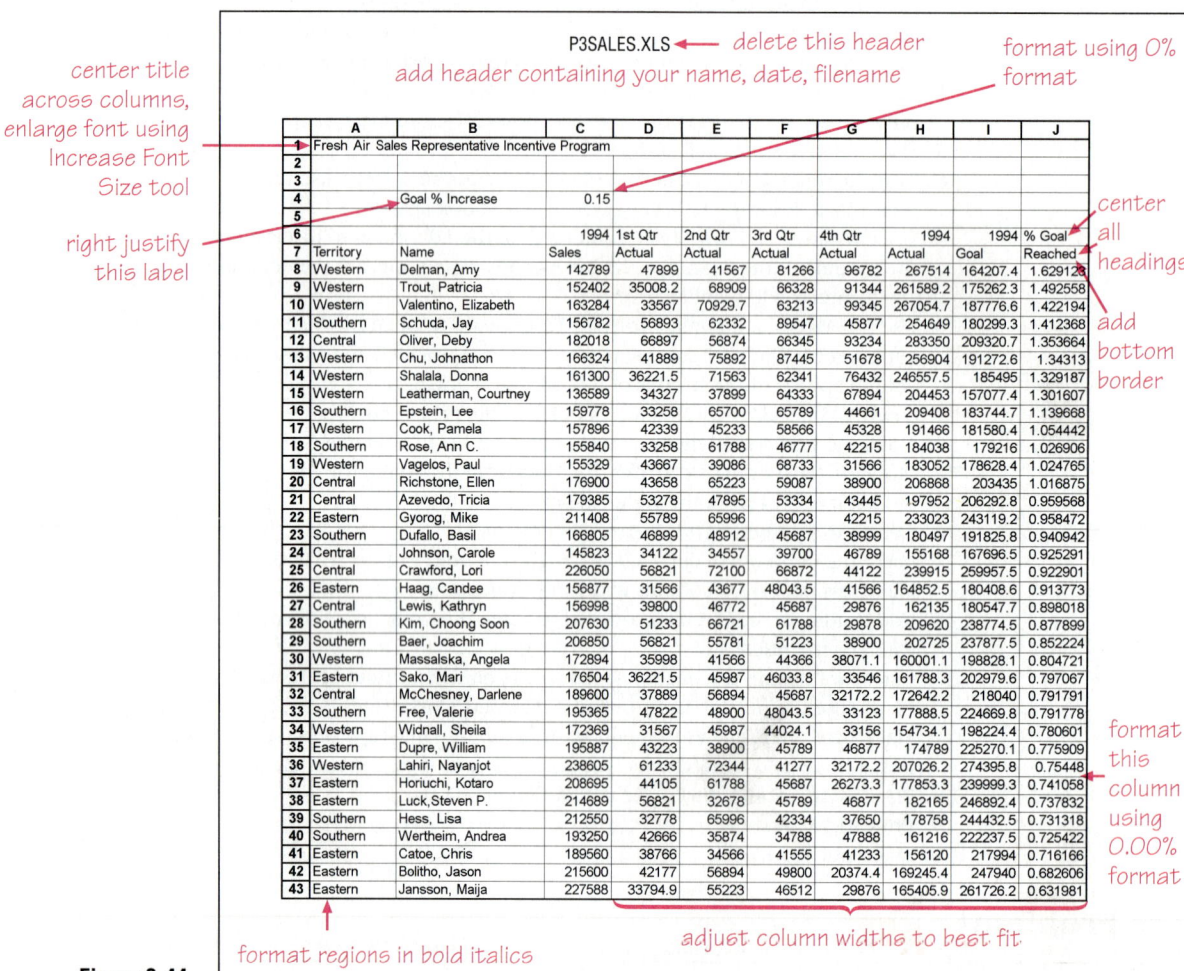

Figure 3-44

4. Use the Page Setup dialog box to scale the worksheet to fit on one page printed in landscape mode.
5. Center the worksheet horizontally and vertically.
6. Add a header, shown in Figure 3-44, and delete the formatting code &[File] from the Center Section of the header.
7. Save the workbook.
8. Preview the worksheet and make any page setup adjustments necessary to obtain the printed results you want.
9. Print the worksheet.
10. Use S3MYMOD.XLM, which you created in the Tutorial Assignments, to print the formulas for your worksheet.

2. Age Group Changes in the U.S. Population

Rick Stephanopolous is preparing a report on changes in the U.S. population. Part of the report focuses on age group changes in the population from 1970 through 1980. Rick has created a worksheet that contains information from the U.S. Census reports, and he is ready to format the worksheet. Complete the following steps to format the worksheet:

1. Launch Windows and Excel as usual.
2. Open the workbook P3CENSUS.XLS, maximize the worksheet window, then save the workbook as S3CENSUS.XLS.
3. Make the formatting changes shown in Figure 3-45, adjusting column widths as necessary.

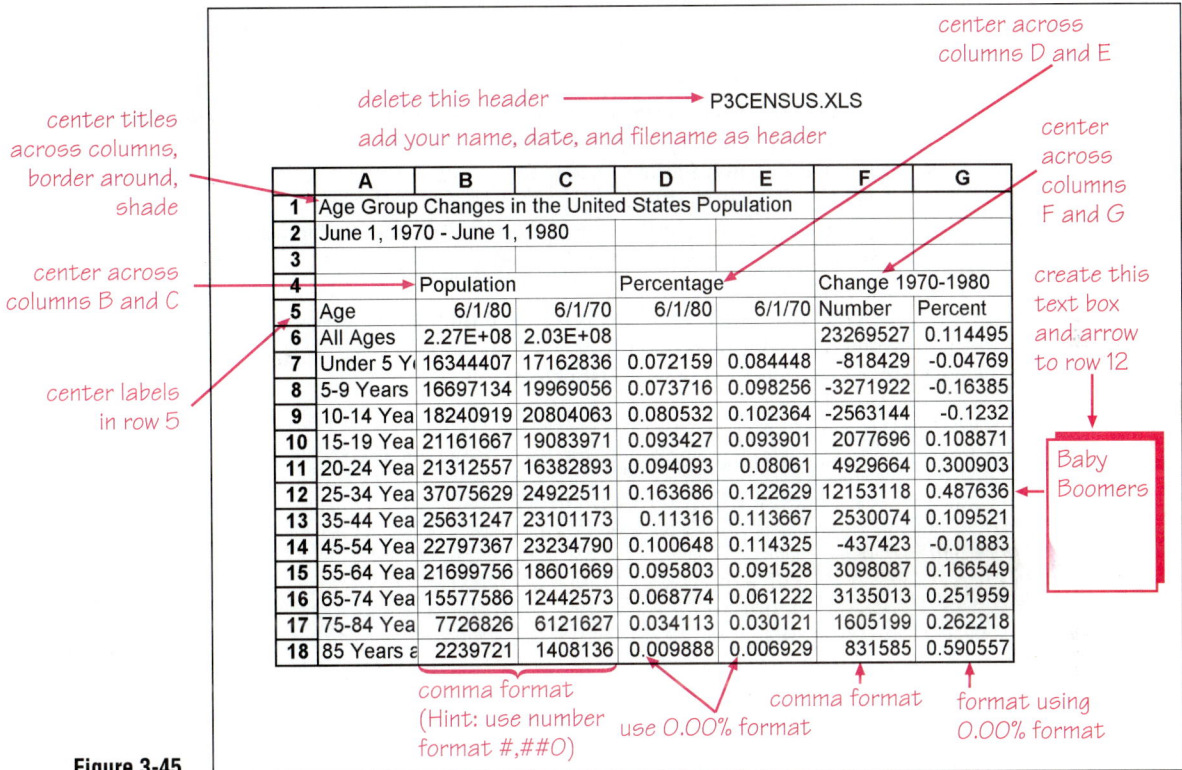

Figure 3-45

4. Use the Page Setup dialog box to modify the header so the Right Section consists of your name, a space, the current date, and the name of the file. Delete the formatting code &[File] from the Center Section of the header.
5. Save the workbook again.
6. Preview and print the worksheet.
7. Use S3MYMOD.XLM, which you created in the Tutorial Assignments, to print the formulas for your worksheet.

3. Creating and Formatting Your Own Worksheet

Design a worksheet for a problem with which you are familiar. The problem might be a business problem from one of your other business courses, or it could be a numeric problem from a biology, education, or sociology course. Follow the steps below to plan your worksheet, prepare your planning documents, and complete the worksheet.

1. Decide what problem you would like to solve.
2. Refer to Maria's worksheet plan in Figure 3-1 and Otis's worksheet plan in Figure 2-4. Write a similar document for the problem you would like to solve. Write a statement of your goal, list the results you want to see, list the information you need for the worksheet cells, and describe the formulas you will need for the worksheet calculations.

3. Sketch a plan for your worksheet showing the worksheet title(s), the data labels, column headings, and totals. Indicate the formats you will use for titles, headings, labels, data, and totals.
4. Build the worksheet by entering the titles and labels first, then entering the data and formulas.
5. Test the formulas using simple test data such as 1s or 10s.
6. After you are sure the formulas are correct, format the worksheet according to your plan.
7. Save the workbook periodically as you work.
8. When the worksheet is formatted, use Excel's print preview feature to determine the Page Setup settings you need to make.
9. Make the Page Setup settings needed to:
    a. center the worksheet
    b. print a header containing your name, the date, and the filename
    c. turn off row/column headings and cell gridlines
10. Print your worksheet.
11. Use S3MYMOD.XLM, which you created in the Tutorial Assignments, to print the formulas for your worksheet.
12. Submit the following to your instructor:
    a. your planning sheet
    b. your planning sketch
    c. a printout of the regular worksheet
    d. a printout of the worksheet formulas

TUTORIAL 4

Functions, Formulas, and Absolute References

OBJECTIVES

In this tutorial you will:

- Use the MAX function to find the largest number in a range of cells
- Use the MIN function to find the smallest number in a range of cells
- Use the AVERAGE function to calculate the average of a column of numbers
- Calculate monthly loan payments using the PMT function
- Create a formula using the IF function
- Use the TODAY function to display today's date
- Learn when to use absolute references in formulas

Managing Loan Payments

Superior Sails Charter Company The Superior Sails Charter Company is based in Sault Ste. Marie, Michigan, on the shores of Lake Superior and close to the North Channel, one of the most pristine boating areas in the Northern Hemisphere. The company owns a large fleet of boats purchased with bank loans. Shabir Ahmad works part time for the charter company to help pay for his college education. As of this month, the company finally has a computer. James LaSalle, the company owner, has asked Shabir to create some Excel worksheets so he will have better information with which to manage the business.

James asks Shabir to create a worksheet that contains the following information about each Superior Sails boat loan:

- original amount of the loan
- payments left to repay the loan
- interest rate of the loan
- payment amount per month

James also wants to see the total monthly amount that Superior Sails needs to pay for all of the loans, and he encourages Shabir to include any other information that might be useful for managing the boat loans.

Shabir thinks about the project, then develops the worksheet plan shown in Figure 4-1 and the sketch shown in Figure 4-2.

```
Worksheet Plan for Loan Management Worksheet

My Goal:
To develop a worksheet to help management keep track of loan
payments for boats in the Superior Sails fleet.

What results do I want to see?
Total payments due this month.
The amounts of the largest and smallest loans.
The average loan amount.

What information do I need?
A list of all boats in the Superior Sails fleet.
The amount, interest rate, and number of monthly payments for each loan.
The loan status (paid or due) for each boat.

What calculations will I perform?
largest loan = MAX (all loans)
smallest loans = MIN (all loans)
average loans = AVERAGE (all loans)
monthly payment amount = PMT (interest rate, number of payments, loan amount)
payments due this month = IF (loan is not paid, display the loan payment)
total payments due = SUM (all payments for loans not paid off)
percent of total payment = loan payment/total payments due
```

Figure 4-1
Shabir's worksheet plan

Superior Sails Charter Company - Loan Management Worksheet

Boat Type and Length	Loan Amount	Annual Interest Rate	Number of Monthly Payments	Monthly Payment Amount	Current Loan Status	Payments Due this Month	Percent of Total Payment
O'Day 34	$37,700	11.00%	60	${monthly payment amount formula}	xxxx	${payments due this month formula}	{percent of total payment formula}%
:	:	:	:	:	:	:	:
:	:	:	:	:	:	:	:
:	:	:	:	:	:	:	:
:	:	:	:	:	:	:	:
:	:	:	:	:	:	:	:
:	:	:	:	:	:	:	:
:	:	:	:	:	:	:	:
Largest loan:	${largest loan formula}		Total Payments Due			${total payments due formula}	
Smallest loan:	${smallest loan formula}						
Average loan:	${average loan formula}						

Figure 4-2
Shabir's worksheet sketch

Managing Loan Payments   EX 129

He decides that the worksheet should show the largest loan, the smallest loan, and the average amount of the loans, in addition to the information James specified. Shabir also decides to add a column that shows what percent each loan payment is of the total payment. This information might be useful if James decides to sell or replace any of his boats.

James approves Shabir's plan, then shows him where to find the information on the boat loans. Shabir begins to develop the worksheet according to his plan.

In this tutorial you will work with Shabir to create a worksheet to help James manage his boat loans. You will use several Excel functions to simplify the formulas you enter, and you will learn when to use absolute references in formulas. Let's get started by launching Excel and organizing the desktop.

To launch Excel and organize the desktop:
❶ Launch Windows and Excel following your usual procedure.
❷ Make sure your Student Disk is in the disk drive.
❸ Make sure the Microsoft Excel and Book1 windows are maximized.

Shabir already entered the labels for the worksheet and the loan data provided by James. Let's open Shabir's worksheet and look at what he has done so far.

To open the C4SAILS1.XLS workbook:
❶ Click the **Open button** to display the Open dialog box.
❷ Double-click **C4SAILS1.XLS** in the File Name box to display the workbook shown in Figure 4-3.

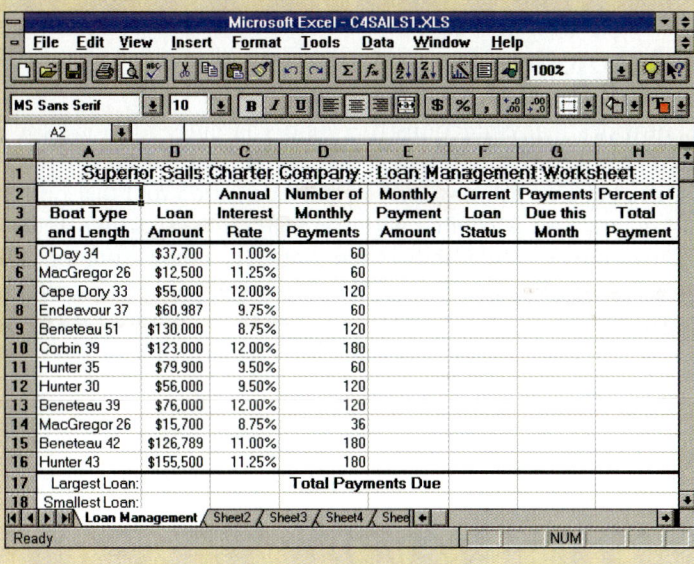

Figure 4-3
The C4SAILS1.XLS workbook

EX 130 TUTORIAL 4 Functions, Formulas, and Absolute References

Shabir listed the boats in column A and the loan amounts in column B; for example, the Beneteau 51-foot sailboat was purchased with a $130,000 loan. Shabir entered the annual interest rate for each loan in column C and formatted this column to display percents. Column D contains the number of monthly payments required to pay off the loan. The loans are payable in 3 years (36 months), 5 years (60 months), 10 years (120 months), or 15 years (180 months). Although columns E through H do not contain data yet, Shabir typed the titles for these columns and selected appropriate formats.

Now that you have had an opportunity to study what Shabir has done so far, let's save the workbook under a different name, so your changes will not alter the original file.

To save the workbook under a different filename:

❶ Click **File**, then click **Save As...** to display the Save As dialog box.

❷ Type **S4SAILS1** in either uppercase or lowercase.

❸ Click the **OK button** to save the workbook under the new filename on your Student Disk. Notice that the new workbook filename, S4SAILS1.XLS, appears in the title bar.

TROUBLE? If you see the message "Replace existing C4SAILS1.XLS?" click the Cancel button and make sure you entered S4SAILS1 as the filename. If you see the message "Replace existing S4SAILS1.XLS?" click the OK button to replace the old version of S4SAILS1.XLS with your current version.

Shabir plans to use several Excel functions to simplify the formulas for the loan management worksheet. He researches the functions in the *Microsoft Excel On-line Help* and the *Microsoft Excel Users Guide*. The next section includes information summarized from this reference manual.

Excel Functions

Excel provides many functions that help you enter formulas for calculations and other specialized tasks, even if you don't know the mathematical details of the calculation. As you learned in Tutorial 1, a function is a calculation tool that performs a predefined operation. You are already familiar with the SUM function, which adds the values in a range of cells. Excel provides hundreds of functions, including a function to calculate the average of a list of numbers, a function to find the square root of a number, a function to calculate loan payments, and a function to calculate the number of days between two dates. The functions are organized into the categories shown in Figure 4-4.

Figure 4-4
Excel function categories

Function Category	Examples of Functions in this Category
Financial	Calculate loan payments, depreciation, interest rate, internal rate of return
Date & Time	Display today's date and/or time; calculate the number of days between two dates
Math & Trig	Round off numbers; calculate sums, logs, and least common multiple; generate random numbers
Statistical	Calculate average, standard deviation, and frequencies; find minimum, maximum; count how many numbers are in a list
Lookup & Reference	Look for a value in a range of cells; find the row or column location of a reference
Database	Perform crosstabs, averages, counts, and standard deviation for an Excel database
Text	Convert numbers to text; compare two text entries; find the length of a text entry
Logical	Perform conditional calculations
Engineering	Convert binary to hexadecimal and binary to decimal; calculate Bessel function

Each function has a **syntax**, which tells you the order in which you must type the parts of the function, and where to put commas, parentheses, and other punctuation. The general syntax of an Excel function is:

NAME*(argument1, argument2,...)*

The syntax of most functions requires you to type the function name followed by one or more arguments in parentheses. Function arguments specify the values that Excel must use in the calculation, or the cell references that Excel must include in the calculation. For example, in the function SUM(A1:A20) the function name is SUM and the argument is A1:A20.

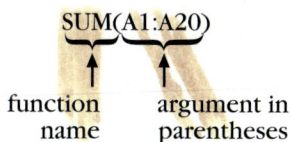

You can use a function in a simple formula such as =SUM(A1:A20), or a more complex formula such as =SUM(A1:A20)*26. As with all formulas, you enter the formula that contains a function in the cell where you want to display the results. The easiest way to enter functions in a cell is to use the Function Wizard, which asks you for the arguments and then enters the function for you.

> **REFERENCE WINDOW**
>
> ## Using the Function Wizard
>
> - Click the cell where you want to display the results of the function. Then click the Function Wizard button to open the Function Wizard - Step 1 of 2 dialog box.
> - Click the type of function you want in the Function Category box. (This will narrow the possibilities in the Function Name box.)
> - Click the function you want in the Function Name box.
> - Click the Next button to move on to the Step 2 of 2 box.
> - Enter values for each argument in the function either by typing in the appropriate cell addresses or by using the mouse to click the appropriate cells.
> - Press [Enter] (or click the Finish button) to close the dialog box and display the results of the function in the cell.

If you prefer, you can type the function directly in the cell. Although the function name is always shown in uppercase, you can type it in either uppercase or lowercase. Also, even though the arguments are enclosed in parentheses, you do not have to type the closing parenthesis if the function is at the end of the formula. Excel automatically adds the closing parenthesis when you press the Enter key to complete the formula.

> **REFERENCE WINDOW**
>
> ## Typing Functions Directly in a Cell
>
> - Click the cell where you want to display the result of the formula.
> - Type = to begin the formula.
> - Type the function name in either uppercase or lowercase.
> - Type (, an opening parenthesis.
> - Enter the appropriate arguments using the keyboard or mouse.
> - When the arguments are complete, press [Enter]. Excel enters the closing parenthesis and displays the results of the function in the cell.

Shabir consults his plan and decides that he wants to enter a formula to find the largest loan amount. To do this, he uses the MAX function.

The MAX Function

MAX is a statistical function that finds the largest number. The syntax of the MAX function is:

MAX(*number1,number2,...*)

In the MAX function, *number* can be a constant number such as 345, a cell reference such as B6, or a range of cells such as B5:B16. You can use the MAX function to simply display the largest number or to use the largest number in a calculation.

REFERENCE WINDOW

Using MAX to Display the Largest Number in a Range of Cells

- Click the cell where you want to display the result of the function.
- Click the Function Wizard button, then select the statistical function MAX.

or

Type =MAX(to begin the formula.

- Drag the pointer to outline the range of cells in which you want to find the largest number.
- Press [Enter] to complete the function.

Shabir wants to find the largest loan amount in the range of cells from B5 through B16. He wants to display the largest amount in cell B17 next to the label "Largest Loan:."

To use the MAX function to find the largest loan amount:

❶ Click cell **B17** to move to the cell where you want to type the formula that uses the MAX function.

❷ Type **=MAX(** to begin the formula. *or use the fx (function wizard)*

❸ Drag the pointer to outline cells B5 through B16, then release the mouse button. See Figure 4-5.

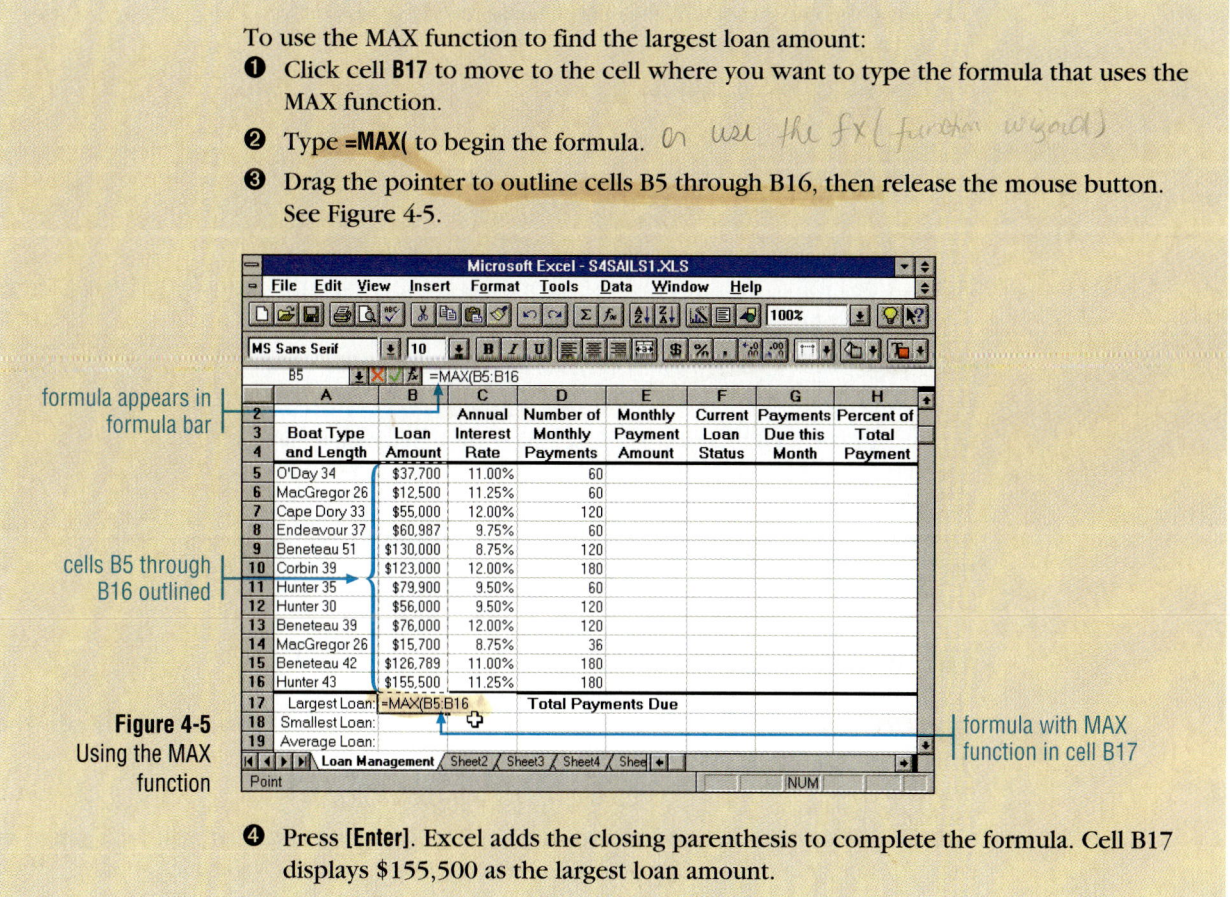

Figure 4-5
Using the MAX function

❹ Press **[Enter]**. Excel adds the closing parenthesis to complete the formula. Cell B17 displays $155,500 as the largest loan amount.

Next, Shabir wants to find the smallest loan amount.

The MIN Function

 MIN is a statistical function that finds the smallest number. The syntax of the MIN function is:

MIN(*number1,number2,...*)

You can use the MIN function to simply display the smallest number or to use the smallest number in a calculation.

> **REFERENCE WINDOW**
>
> **Using MIN to Display the Smallest Number in a Range of Cells**
>
> - Click the cell where you want to display the result of the formula.
> - Click the Function Wizard button, then select the statistical function MIN.
>
>   *or*
>
>   Type =MIN(to begin the function.
> - Drag the pointer to outline the range of cells in which you want to find the smallest number.
> - Press [Enter] to complete the function.

Shabir wants to find the smallest loan amount and display it in cell B18.

To use the MIN function to find the smallest loan amount:

1. Click cell **B18** to move to the cell where you want to type the formula that uses the MIN function.
2. Type **=MIN(** to begin the formula.
3. Drag the pointer to outline cells B5 through B16. Release the mouse button.
4. Press **[Enter]**. Cell B18 displays $12,500 as the smallest loan amount.

Shabir consults his plan again and decides that his next step is to calculate the average loan amount.

The AVERAGE Function

 AVERAGE is a statistical function that calculates the average, or the arithmetic mean. The syntax for the AVERAGE function is:

AVERAGE(*number1,number2,...*)

Most of the time when you use the AVERAGE function *number* will be a range of cells. To calculate the average of a range of cells, Excel sums the values in the range, then divides by the number of *non-blank* cells in the range. Figure 4-6 shows the results of using the AVERAGE function on three ranges.

The AVERAGE Function   EX 135

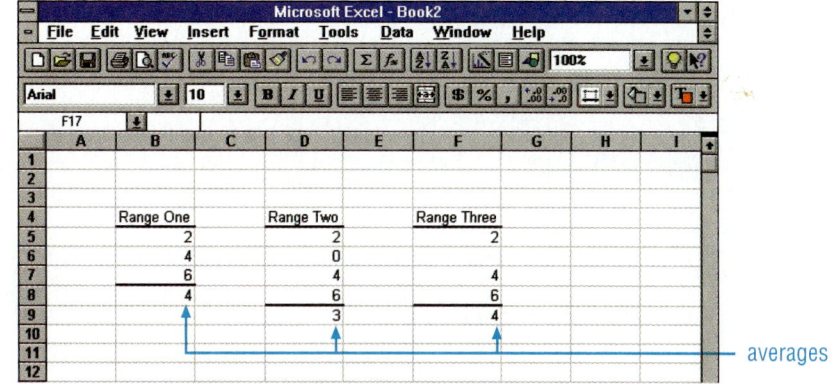

Figure 4-6
How the AVERAGE function handles zeros and blank cells

The first range has no blank cells or cells that contain zeros, so the sum of the numbers, 12, is divided by 3 to find the average. In the second range, the cells with zeros are counted, so the sum, 12, is divided by 4 to find the average. In the third range, the blank cells are not counted, so the sum, 12, is divided by 3 to find the average.

REFERENCE WINDOW

Using AVERAGE to Calculate the Average of the Numbers in a Range of Cells

- Click the cell where you want to display the result of the formula.
- Click the Function Wizard button, then select the statistical function AVERAGE.

  or

  Type =AVERAGE(to begin the function.
- Drag the pointer to outline the range of cells you want to average.
- Press [Enter] to complete the function.

Shabir wants to calculate the average of the boat loans listed in cells B5 through B16, and he wants to display the average in cell B19. Shabir is not certain about the syntax of the AVERAGE function. He decides to use the Function Wizard button because the Function Wizard dialog box shows the syntax for the AVERAGE function. This way Shabir can be sure he uses the correct syntax.

To enter the AVERAGE function into cell B19 using the Function Wizard button:

❶ Click cell **B19** to move to the cell where you want to enter the AVERAGE function.

❷ Click the **Function Wizard button** to display the Function Wizard - Step 1 of 2 dialog box. See Figure 4-7.

EX 136 TUTORIAL 4 Functions, Formulas, and Absolute References

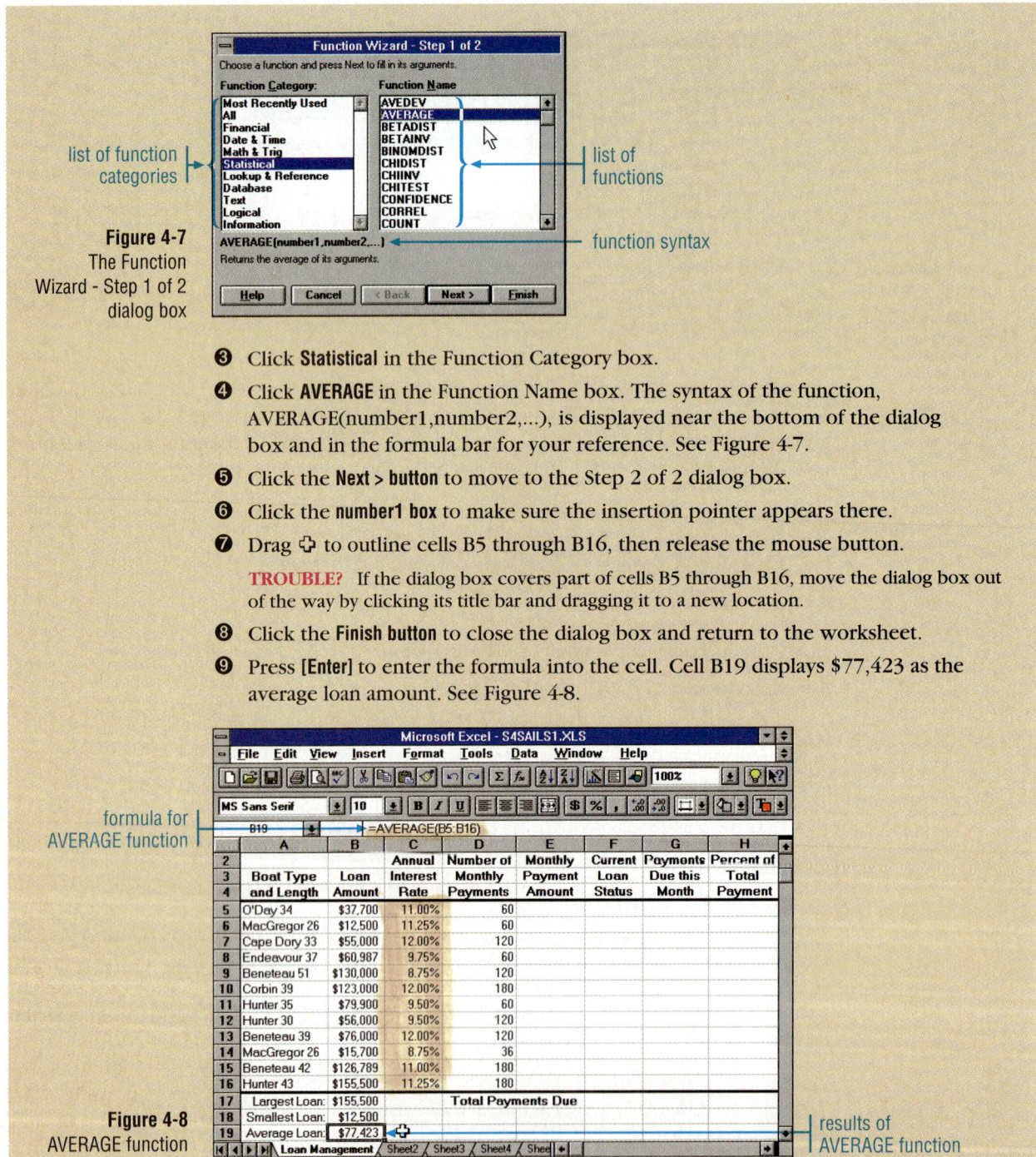

Figure 4-7
The Function Wizard - Step 1 of 2 dialog box

❸ Click **Statistical** in the Function Category box.

❹ Click **AVERAGE** in the Function Name box. The syntax of the function, AVERAGE(number1,number2,...), is displayed near the bottom of the dialog box and in the formula bar for your reference. See Figure 4-7.

❺ Click the **Next > button** to move to the Step 2 of 2 dialog box.

❻ Click the **number1 box** to make sure the insertion pointer appears there.

❼ Drag ✣ to outline cells B5 through B16, then release the mouse button.

   TROUBLE? If the dialog box covers part of cells B5 through B16, move the dialog box out of the way by clicking its title bar and dragging it to a new location.

❽ Click the **Finish button** to close the dialog box and return to the worksheet.

❾ Press **[Enter]** to enter the formula into the cell. Cell B19 displays $77,423 as the average loan amount. See Figure 4-8.

Figure 4-8
AVERAGE function pasted in cell B19

Next, Shabir consults his plan and decides to create a formula to calculate the monthly payment for each loan.

Calculating Loan Payments with the PMT Function

PMT is a financial function that calculates the periodic payment amount for money borrowed. For example, if you want to borrow $5,000 at 11% interest, you can use the PMT function to find out that your monthly payment would be $108.71 for five years.

The syntax of the PMT function is:

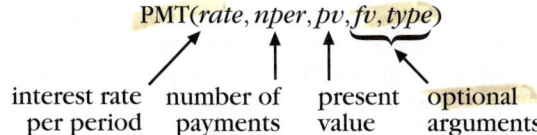

The last two arguments, *fv* and *type*, are optional; Shabir will not include them in the loan management worksheet. You can refer to the *Microsoft Excel On-line Help* if you want information about these two optional arguments.

The *rate* argument is the interest rate per period. Usually interest rates are expressed as annual rates. For example, a 10% interest rate means that if you borrow $1,000 for a year, you must pay back the $1,000 plus $100 interest—that's 10% of 1,000—at the end of the year.

The *nper* argument is the total number of payments required to pay back the loan.

The *pv* argument is the present value; in the case of a loan, this value is the total amount borrowed.

When you enter the arguments for the PMT function, you must be consistent about the units you use for *rate* and *nper*. For example, if you use the number of monthly payments for *nper*, then you must express the interest rate as the percentage per month. Usually, the loan payment period is monthly, but the interest is expressed as an annual rate. If you are repaying the loan in monthly installments, you need to divide the annual interest rate by 12 when you enter the rate as an argument for the PMT function.

To illustrate the PMT function, let's say that you wanted to know the monthly payment for a $5,000 loan at 11% annual interest that you must pay back in 36 months. You would use the PMT function in the formula:

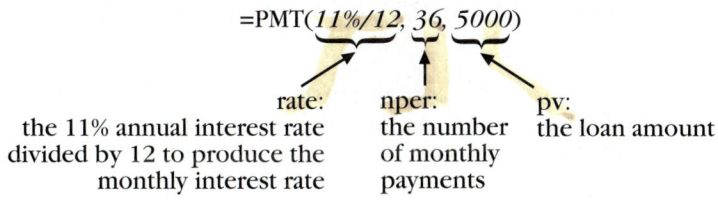

As another example, suppose you wanted to know the monthly payment for a $95,000 30-year loan at 9% (.09) interest. You would use the PMT function in the formula:

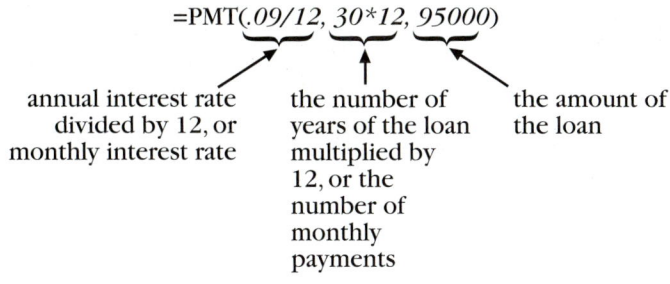

Excel displays the PMT function result as a negative number because you must pay it. Think of this as money that you subtract from your checkbook. If you prefer to display the payment amount as a positive number, place a minus sign in front of the PMT function.

> **REFERENCE WINDOW**
>
> ### Using PMT to Calculate a Monthly Payment
>
> These directions assume you are typing the function in the cell. Keep in mind that you can also use the Function Wizard button and then enter the arguments in the Step 2 of 2 dialog box.
>
> - Click the cell where you want to display the monthly payment amount.
> - Type =PMT(if you want the result displayed as a negative number.
>
>   or
>
>   Type =-PMT(if you want the result displayed as a positive number.
>
> - Type the annual interest rate, type %, then type /12 to divide it by 12 months.
> - Type a comma to separate the interest rate from the next argument.
> - Type the number of monthly payments that are required to pay back the loan, then type a comma to separate the number of payments from the next argument.
> - Type the amount of the loan, then press [Enter].
>
> Instead of typing the arguments, you can click the cells that contain the values you want to use for the arguments.

Shabir wants to display the monthly payment for the O'Day 34 loan in cell E5. The annual interest rate is in cell C5, but it must be divided by 12 to obtain the monthly interest rate. The number of periods is in cell D5, and the loan amount is in cell B5. Let's enter the =PMT(C5/12,D5,B5) formula for the O'Day 34 loan.

To calculate the monthly payment for the O'Day 34 loan:

1. Click cell **E5** to move to the cell where you want to enter the formula for the monthly payment.
2. Type **=PMT(** to begin the formula.
3. Click cell **C5** to specify the location of the annual interest rate.
4. Type **/12** to convert the annual interest rate to the monthly interest rate.
5. Type **,** (a comma) to separate the first argument from the second.
6. Click cell **D5** to specify the location of the number of payments.
7. Type **,** (a comma) to separate the second argument from the third.
8. Click cell **B5** to specify the location of the loan amount. See Figure 4-9.

Figure 4-9
Entering a formula using the PMT function

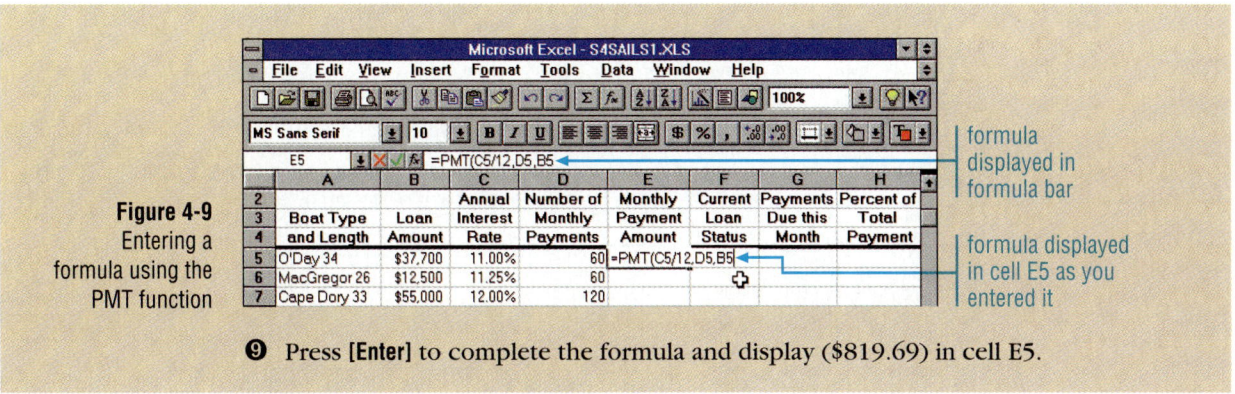

formula displayed in formula bar

formula displayed in cell E5 as you entered it

❾ Press **[Enter]** to complete the formula and display ($819.69) in cell E5.

As expected, the PMT function displays the payment as a negative number, in parentheses. (If you are using a color monitor, the number may also appear in red.) Shabir decides to change the formula to display the payment as a positive number. He uses the F2 function key to change the contents of cell E5 to =-PMT(C5/12,D5,B5).

To display the payment as a positive number:
❶ Make sure cell E5 is the active cell.
❷ Press **[F2]** to edit the formula in cell E5.
❸ Press **[Home]** to position the insertion point at the beginning of the formula.
❹ Press **[→]** to move the insertion point between the equal sign and the "P" in PMT.
❺ Type – (a minus sign). The formula is now =-PMT(C5/12,D5,B5).
❻ Press **[Enter]** to complete the edit. Cell E5 displays the positive value $819.69. On a color monitor, the value appears in black.

Shabir tests this formula by comparing the result to a table of loan payment amounts. He finds that the amount in cell E5 on his worksheet is correct. Now that he is confident he has used the PMT function correctly, he can copy the formula in cell E5 to calculate the payments for the rest of the loans.

To copy the PMT formula to cells E6 through E16:
❶ Make sure cell E5 is the active cell.
❷ Position the pointer over the fill handle in the lower-right corner of cell E5 until it changes to +.
❸ Drag the pointer to cell E16, then release the mouse button.
❹ Click any cell to remove the highlighting and view the payment amounts displayed in cells E5 through E16. See Figure 4-10.
   TROUBLE? If your formula did not copy to all the cells, repeat Steps 1 through 4.

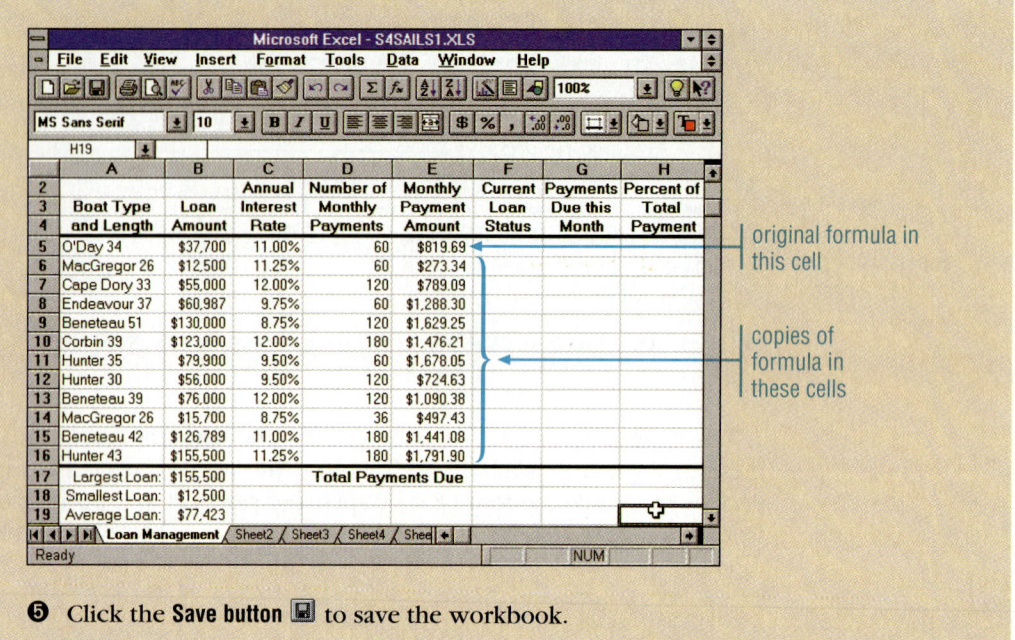

Figure 4-10
The payment formula copied from cell E5 to cells E6 through E16

⑤ Click the **Save button** to save the workbook.

Shabir considers his plan again. James wants a listing of all the boat loans, but he wants a sum of only those payments that he must make this month. He doesn't need to make payments on boat loans that he has already paid off; therefore, Shabir realizes that there is no need to sum the values in column E.

If you want to take a break and resume the tutorial at a later time, you can exit Excel by double-clicking the Control menu box in the upper-left corner of the screen. When you resume the tutorial, launch Excel, maximize the Microsoft Excel and Book1 windows, and place your Student Disk in the disk drive. Open the file S4SAILS1.XLS, then continue with the tutorial.

■   ■   ■

Shabir looks at the loan paperwork and finds that the O'Day 34, the Endeavour 37, and the Beneteau 51 loans have been paid in full. Shabir's plan is to type the word "Paid" in column F if a boat loan has been paid off.

To enter the current loan status:
① Click cell **F5** because this is where you want to enter "Paid" for the O'Day 34.
② Type **Paid** and press **[Enter]**.
③ Click cell **F8** because this is where you want to enter the status of the Endeavour 37.
④ Type **Paid** and press **[Enter]**.
⑤ If necessary, click cell **F9** because this is where you want to enter the status of the Beneteau 51.
⑥ Type **Paid** and press **[Enter]**.

The IF Function

There are times when the value you store or display in a cell depends on certain conditions. The **IF function** provides you with a way to specify the if-then-else logic required to calculate or display information based on one or more conditions.

An example of an if-then-else condition in Shabir's worksheet is: *if* the loan status is paid, *then* place a zero in the payment due column, otherwise (*else*) display the monthly payment amount in the payment due column (Figure 4-11).

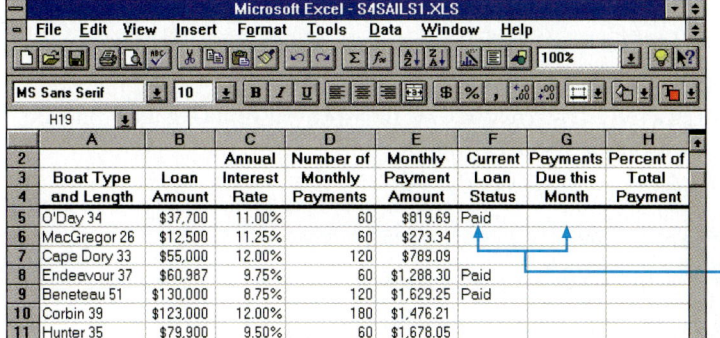

Figure 4-11
The conditions for displaying payments due this month

The syntax of the IF function is:

IF (*logical test*, *value if true*, *value if false*)

Excel evaluates this expression to determine if it is true or false

if the logical test is true, Excel uses this expression and displays the result

if the logical test is false, Excel uses this expression and displays the result

The *logical test* is any value or expression that Excel evaluates as true or false. For example, Excel evaluates the expression 2=2 as true when you use it for a logical test. Excel evaluates the expression 2=1 as false. Most expressions you use for logical tests will contain numbers or cell references separated by one of the comparison operators shown in Figure 4-12.

Type of Comparison	Comparison Operator Symbol
less than	<
greater than	>
less than or equal to	<=
greater than or equal to	>=
equal to	=
not equal to	<>

Figure 4-12
Comparison operators

Some examples of expressions are 2>3, B5=C3, and B8<=0. An expression can also include text. Note that you must put quotation marks around any text that you use in the IF function.

The *value if true* argument specifies what to display in the cell if the expression for the logical test is true.

The *value if false* argument specifies what to display in the cell if the expression for the logical test is false.

> **REFERENCE WINDOW**
>
> ### Using the IF Function to Specify the Conditions
>
> - These directions assume you are typing the function in the cell. Keep in mind that you can also use the Function Wizard button to select the logical function IF, then enter the arguments in the Step 2 of 2 dialog box.
> - Click the cell where you want to display the results of the formula that contains the IF function.
> - Type =IF(to begin the formula.
> - Type the *logical test*, then type a comma.
> - Type the specifications for *value if true*, then type a comma.
> - Type the specifications for *value if false*.
> - Press [Enter] to complete the formula.

Suppose you want Excel to display a warning message if the loan amount in cell B5 is greater than $150,000. You can use the formula:

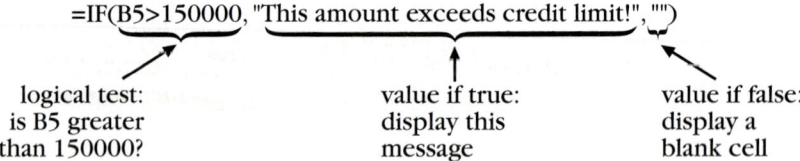

=IF(B5>150000, "This amount exceeds credit limit!", "")

logical test: is B5 greater than 150000?
value if true: display this message
value if false: display a blank cell

Notice the quotation marks around the text that contain the credit limit message and the quotation marks without any text, which will leave the cell blank. When you use text as an argument for the IF function, you *must* enclose it in quotation marks.

As another example, suppose you want to add a $100 bonus to the salary of any salesperson who sells more than $10,000 of merchandise. Look at Figure 4-13. The amount of merchandise sold by Sergio Armanti is in cell B9. Sergio's base salary is in cell C9.

The IF Function **EX 143**

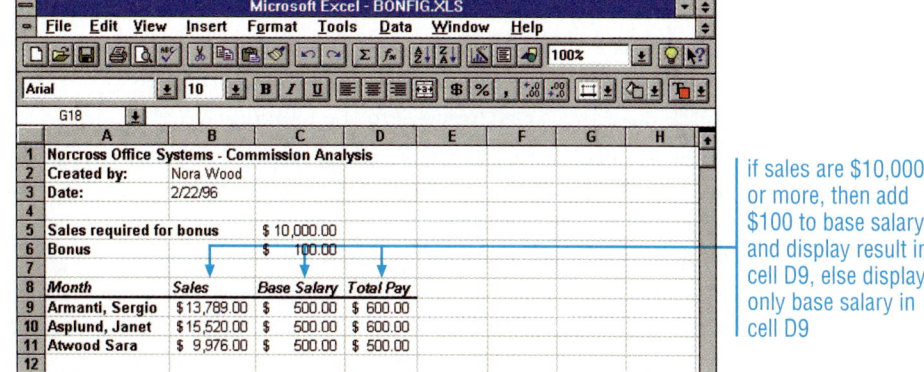

Figure 4-13
Conditions for awarding a bonus to Sergio Armanti

if sales are $10,000 or more, then add $100 to base salary and display result in cell D9, else display only base salary in cell D9

To calculate Sergio's total pay, including the bonus if he earned it, you would enter the formula =IF(B9>=10000,C9+100,C9) in cell D9. In this case if the amount sold in cell B9 is at least $10,000, Excel would add $100 to the base salary and display it in cell D9. If the amount sold in cell B9 is less than $10,000, Excel will display the base salary in cell D9.

Unlike the previous example that displayed text, the arguments for the IF function that calculates Sergio's bonus are all numeric, so you would not use quotation marks.

Now let's consider the formula Shabir needs to use. In cell G5 he wants to display the amount of the payment that is due. The conditions for this situation are: if the current loan status is "Paid," then put a zero in the payments due column, otherwise, put the monthly payment amount in the payments due column. Shabir's formula will be:

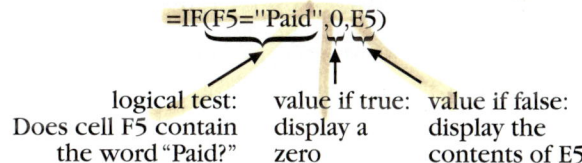

| logical test: | value if true: | value if false: |
| Does cell F5 contain the word "Paid?" | display a zero | display the contents of E5 |

If this formula works, Shabir expects to see a zero in cell G5 because the O'Day 34 loan is paid off. Let's see if the formula produces the results he expects. This time Shabir will use the Function Wizard button in the formula bar (instead of the Function Wizard button in the tool bar) to enter the formula.

To enter the formula containing the IF function in cell G5:
❶ Double-click cell **G5** to display the Function Wizard button in the formula bar. See Figure 4-14.

click the Function Wizard button in the formula bar to open the Function Wizard - Step 1 of 2 dialog box

Figure 4-14
The Function Wizard button in the formula bar

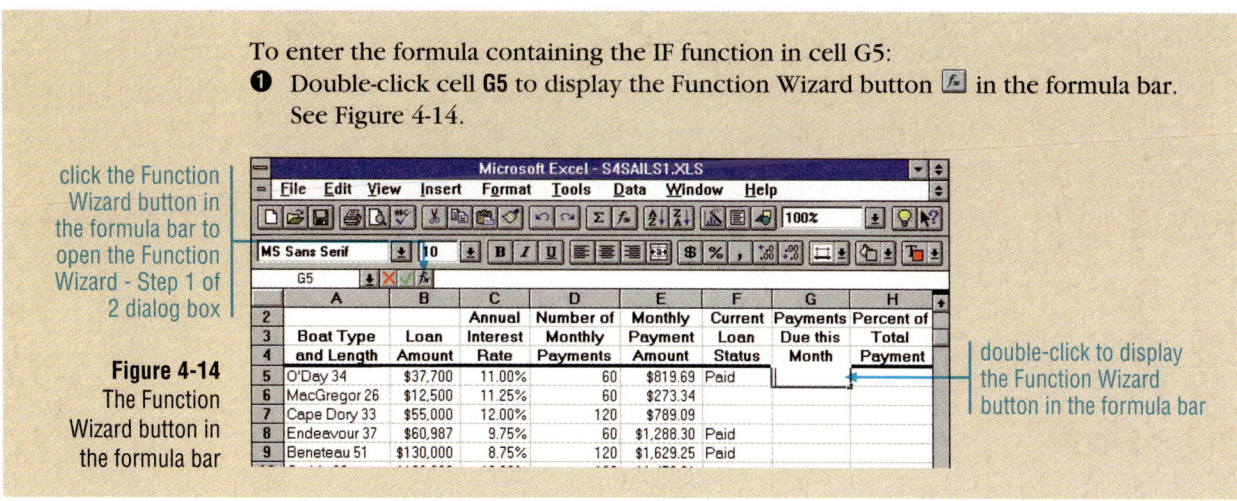

double-click to display the Function Wizard button in the formula bar

EX 144 TUTORIAL 4 Functions, Formulas, and Absolute References

❷ Click the **Function Wizard button** to open the Function Wizard - Step 1 of 2 dialog box.

❸ Click **Logical** in the Function Category box, then click **IF** in the Function Name box. Notice the function syntax displayed in the formula bar.

❹ Click the **Next > button** to move to the Function Wizard - Step 2 of 2 dialog box.

❺ Type **F5="Paid"** in the logical_test box. Make sure you type the quotation marks. (Notice that you do not have to type commas to separate arguments when using the Function Wizard dialog box.) Excel displays "True" in the box next to the logical_test box because cell F5 *does* contain the entry "Paid."

❻ Click the **value_if_true box** and type **0**. Make sure you type the number zero, and not the capital letter "O." The box next to the value_if_true box displays "0."

❼ Click the **value_if_false box** and type **E5**. The box next to the value_if_false box displays "816.6893498," which is the value in cell E5 displayed without formatting. See Figure 4-15.

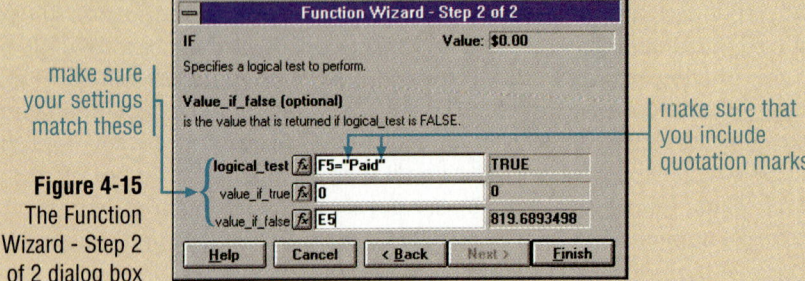

Figure 4-15
The Function Wizard - Step 2 of 2 dialog box

make sure your settings match these

make sure that you include quotation marks

❽ Click the **Finish button** to complete the formula and return to the worksheet. Then press **[Enter]** to enter the formula in the cell. Watch as $0.00 displays in cell G5.

TROUBLE? If you see the error message #NAME? in cell G5, look carefully at the formula displayed in the formula bar to see if you included the quotation marks around "Paid." Use the F2 key to edit the formula.

The formula produced the expected results, so Shabir decides to copy the formula to cells G6 through G16.

To copy the If formula to cells G6 through G16:

❶ Make sure that G5 is the active cell because it contains the formula you want to copy.

❷ Move the pointer over the fill handle until it turns into +.

❸ Drag the pointer to cell G16, then release the mouse button.

❹ Click any cell to remove the highlighting and view the results displayed in cells G5 through G16. See Figure 4-16.

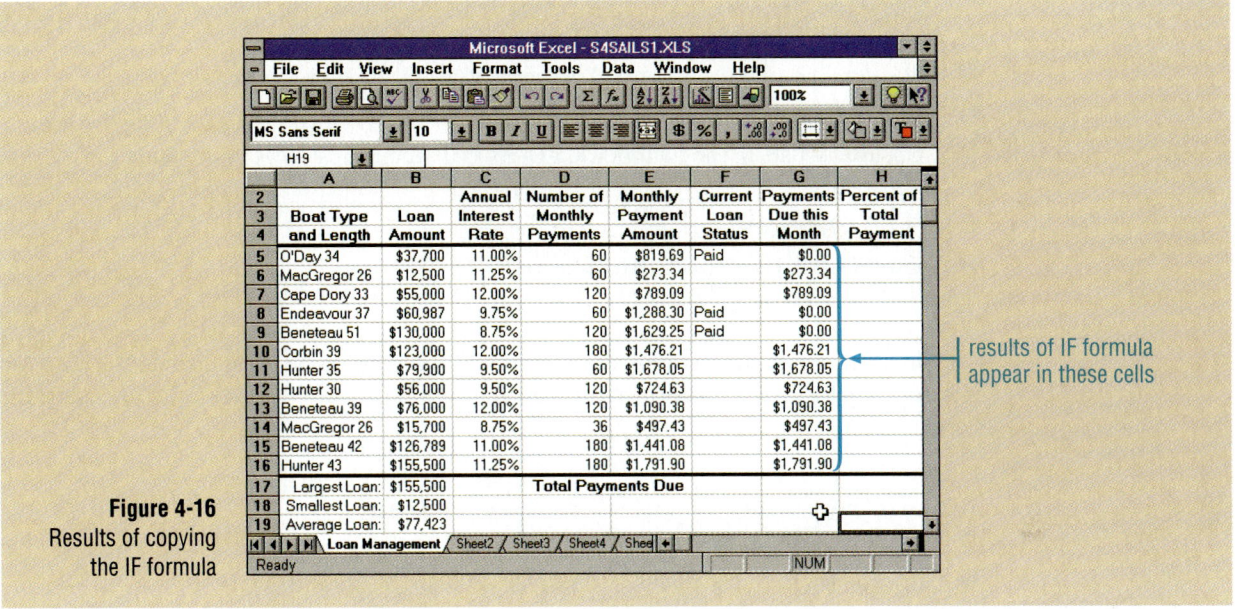

Figure 4-16
Results of copying the IF formula

Shabir carefully checks the results of the IF formulas in cells G5 through G16. He sees that the formulas produced zeros in cells G5, G8, and G9 because the loans for those boats are paid. In the other cells the IF formulas have correctly placed the same value as that displayed in column E. Shabir is satisfied that the formulas in column G are correct.

James wants a total of the payments due, so Shabir needs to sum the payments in column G. He plans to display the sum in cell G17.

To sum the payments due this month:
1. Click cell **G17** to move to the cell where you want to display the sum.
2. Click the **AutoSum button** .
3. Make sure cells G5 through G16 are outlined.
4. Press [Enter]. The amount $9,762.10 is displayed in cell G17.

Now Shabir looks at the label for the total payments. He wants the label to indicate the month and year for which the payment is calculated. He can use Excel's TODAY function to display the date.

Displaying and Formatting the Date with the TODAY Function

The **TODAY function** reads the computer system clock and displays the current date in the cell that contains the TODAY function. The syntax of the TODAY function is:

TODAY( )

The empty parentheses indicate that no arguments are required for this function. You enter the function by typing only "TODAY( )." As an alternative to typing the TODAY function, you can use the Function Wizard dialog box. Shabir wants the date displayed in cell F17.

EX 146   TUTORIAL 4   Functions, Formulas, and Absolute References

To enter the TODAY function in cell F17:
1. Click cell **F17** to move to the cell where you want to enter the function.
2. Click the **Function Wizard button** to open the Function Wizard - Step 1 of 2 dialog box.
3. Click **Date & Time** in the Function Category box, then click **Today** in the Function Name box.
4. Click the **Next > button** to move on to the Step 2 of 2 dialog box.
5. Press **[Enter]** to display the date in the cell.

Shabir wants to display only the month and the year, so he must change the date format for cell F17. He can format the cell that contains the TODAY function using the Format menu.

To format today's date to show only the month and year:
1. Make sure cell F17 is the active cell.
2. Click **Format**, then click **Cells...** to display the Format Cells dialog box.
3. Click the **Number tab**.
4. Click **Date** in the Category box.
5. Click **mmm-yy** in the Format Codes box to select the month-year format for the date.
6. Click the **OK button** to display the new date format.

The date doesn't look quite right. Shabir thinks it should be bold and aligned on the left side of the cell.

To bold the date and align it on the left side of the cell:
1. Make sure cell F17 is the active cell.
2. Click the **Bold button** on the toolbar.
3. Click the **Align Left button** on the toolbar. See Figure 4-17.

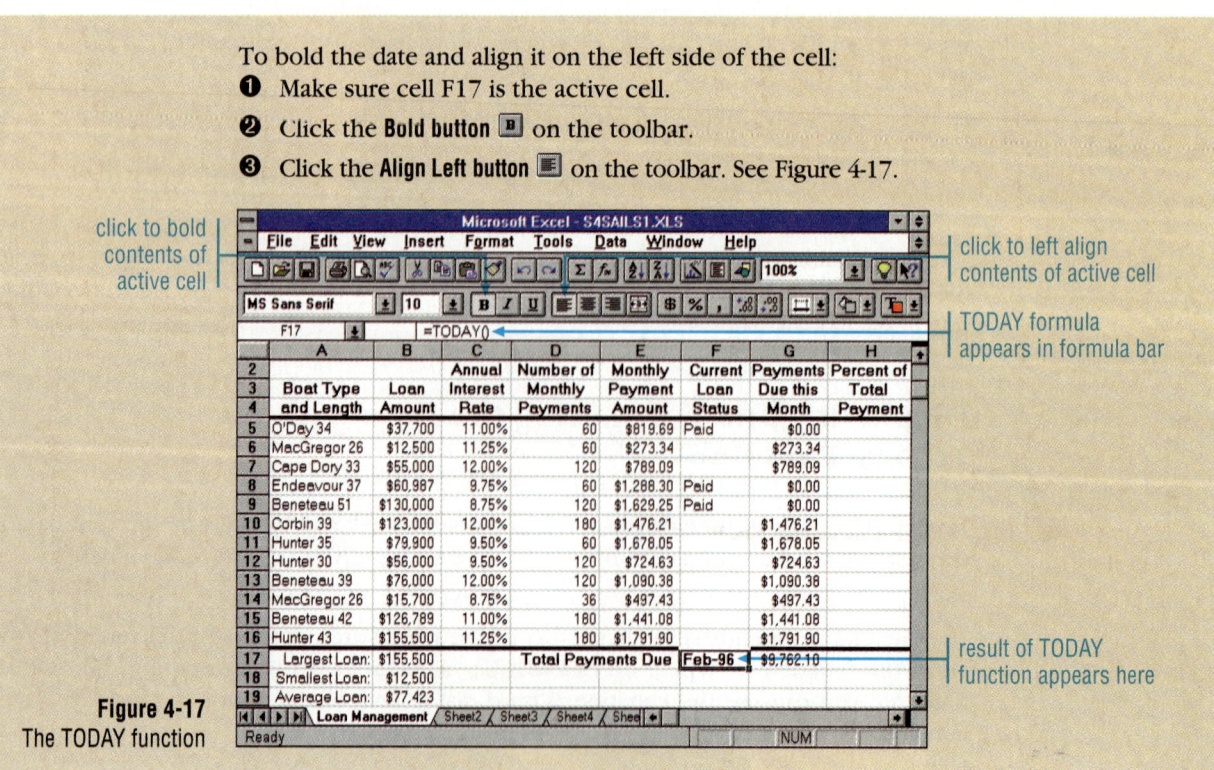

Figure 4-17
The TODAY function

Now Shabir consults his worksheet sketch and sees that he has only one column left to complete the worksheet. He wants column H to display the percent of the total payment that each individual loan payment represents. For example, if the total of all the loan payments is $10,000 and the O'Day payment is $1,000, the O'Day payment is 10% of the total payment. To do this calculation Shabir needs to divide each payment by the total payment, as shown in the equation:

percent of total payment = payment due this month / total payments due

Shabir decides to enter the formula =G5/G17 in cell H5.

To enter the formula to calculate the percent of total payment in cell H5:
❶ Click cell **H5** to move to the cell where you want to enter the formula.
❷ Type **=G5/G17** and press **[Enter]** to complete the formula and display 0.00% in cell H5.

Cell H5 seems to display the correct result. James is paying $0 for the O'Day loan, which is 0% of the $9,762.10 total. Next, Shabir decides to copy the formula to cells H6 through H16.

To copy the percent formula to cells H6 through H16:
❶ Make H5 the active cell. Then move the pointer over the fill handle in cell H5 until it changes to $+$.
❷ Drag the pointer to cell H16. Release the mouse button.
❸ Click any blank cell to remove the highlighting and view the message #DIV/0! displayed in cells H5 through H16.

Shabir knows something is wrong. Cells H6 through H16 display #DIV/0!, a message that means Excel was instructed to divide by zero, which is not possible. Shabir examines the formulas he copied into cells H6 through H16.

To examine the formulas in cells H6 through H16:
❶ Click cell **H6** and look at the formula displayed in the formula bar. The first relative reference changed from G5 in the original formula to G6 in the copied formula. That's correct because the loan amount for row 6 is in cell G6. The second reference changed from G17 in the original formula to G18, which is not correct. This formula should be =G6/G17 because the total of the payments is in cell G17.
❷ Look at the formulas in cells H7 through H16 and see how the relative references changed in each.

For a moment, Shabir is puzzled about the results, but then he remembers about relative and absolute references. Shabir realizes he should have used an absolute reference instead of a relative reference for cell G17 in the percent of total payment formula.

Absolute References

Sometimes when you copy a formula, you don't want Excel to automatically change all the cell references to reflect their new position in the worksheet. If you want a cell reference to point to the same location in the worksheet even when you copy it, you must use an absolute reference. An **absolute reference** is the row and column location of a cell that must not change if it is copied to other cells.

The reference to cell $G$17 is an absolute reference, whereas the reference to cell G17 is a relative reference. If you copy a formula that contains the absolute reference $G$17, the reference to $G$17 will not change. On the other hand, if you copy a formula containing the relative reference G17, the reference to G17 could change to G18, G19, G20 and so forth as it is copied to other cells.

To include an absolute reference in a formula, you can type the dollar sign when you type the cell reference, or you can use the F4 key to change the cell reference type. You can always edit a formula that contains the wrong cell reference type.

REFERENCE WINDOW

Editing Cell Reference Types

- Click the cell that contains the formula you want to edit.
- Press [F2] to begin editing in the formula bar.
- Use the arrow keys to move the insertion point to the cell reference you want to change.
- Press [F4] until the reference is correct.
- Press [Enter] to complete the edit.

Shabir used the wrong cell reference type when he entered the formula in cell H5. He should have used an absolute reference, instead of a relative reference, to indicate the location of the total payments. Now he must change the reference G17 to $G$17.

To change the formula in cell H5 from =G5/G17 to =G5/$G$17:

1. Click cell **H5** to move to the cell that contains the formula you want to edit.
2. Double-click the mouse button to edit the formula in the cell.
3. Make sure the insertion point is just to the right of the reference G17. See Figure 4-18.

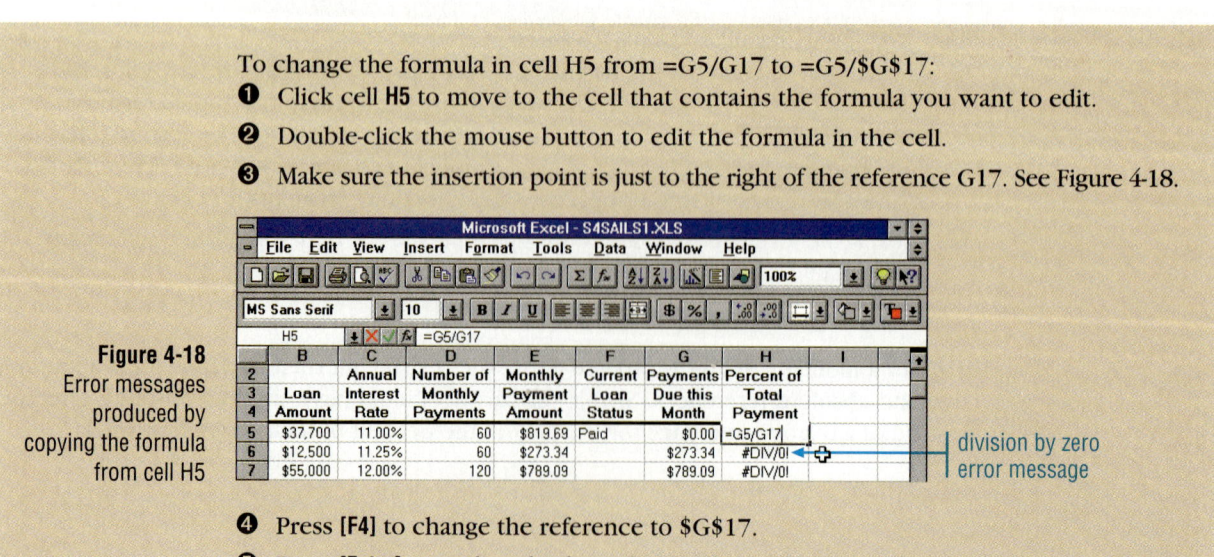

Figure 4-18
Error messages produced by copying the formula from cell H5

4. Press **[F4]** to change the reference to $G$17.
5. Press **[Enter]** to update the formula in cell H5.

Cell H5 still displays 0.00% as the result of the formula, which is correct, but the problem in Shabir's original formula did not surface until he copied it to cells H6 through H16. He copies the revised formula and checks to see if it produces the correct results.

To copy the revised formula from cell H5 to cells H6 through H16:

1. Make sure cell H5 is the active cell, because it contains the revised formula that you want to copy.
2. Move the pointer to the fill handle until it changes to +.
3. Drag the pointer to cell H16, then release the mouse button.
4. Click any cell to remove the highlighting and view the results of the formula. See Figure 4-19.

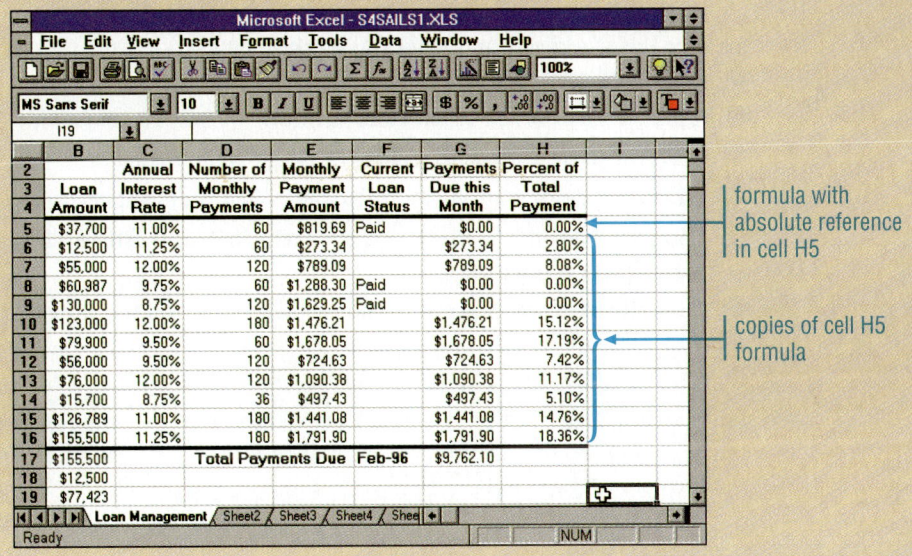

Figure 4-19
The results of copying the formula with an absolute reference

The revised formula works correctly and Shabir is pleased.

Shabir is just about to close the worksheet when James stops in the office. Shabir shows him the worksheet. James thinks the worksheet looks great, but notices that the MacGregor 26 loan in row 6 should be marked "Paid" because he just made the last payment a month ago. Shabir says it is easy to make the change and explains that the worksheet will recalculate the amount for the total payments due this month.

To change the loan status of the MacGregor 26:

❶ Click cell **F6** to make it the active cell.

❷ Type **Paid** and watch cell G17 as you press **[Enter]**.

As a result of changing the loan status, the amount in cell G6 changes to $0.00, the total payments due in cell G17 changes to $9,488.76, and Excel recalculates the percentages in column H. James is impressed. Now Shabir can save the workbook and then print the worksheet.

He wants to print the worksheet in landscape orientation, center it from left to right on the page, center it from top to bottom on the page, omit the row/column headings, and omit the cell gridlines.

To save the workbook and print the worksheet:

❶ Click the **Save button**.

❷ Click the **Print Preview button** to see how the worksheet will look when you print it.

❸ Click the **Setup... button** to display the Page Setup dialog box. Then click the **Page tab**.

❹ If landscape orientation is not selected, click the **Landscape button**.

❺ Click the **Margins tab**. Then click the **Horizontally** and **Vertically boxes** to center the worksheet on the page.

❻ Click the **Sheet tab**. Make sure the Gridlines box and the Row and Column Headings box are empty.

❼ Click the **OK button** to return to the print preview.

❽ Click the **Print... button**, then click the **OK button** on the Print dialog box to send the worksheet to the printer. The final printout for the loan management worksheet is shown in Figure 4-20.

Shabir Ahmad 2/7/96 S4SAILS1.XLS

Superior Sails Charter Company - Loan Management Worksheet

Boat Type and Length	Loan Amount	Annual Interest Rate	Number of Monthly Payments	Monthly Payment Amount	Current Loan Status	Payments Due this Month	Percent of Total Payment
O'Day 34	$37,700	11.00%	60	$819.69	Paid	$0.00	0.00%
MacGregor 26	$12,500	11.25%	60	$273.34	Paid	$0.00	0.00%
Cape Dory 33	$55,000	12.00%	120	$789.09		$789.09	8.32%
Endeavour 37	$60,987	9.75%	60	$1,288.30	Paid	$0.00	0.00%
Beneteau 51	$130,000	8.75%	120	$1,629.25	Paid	$0.00	0.00%
Corbin 39	$123,000	12.00%	180	$1,476.21		$1,476.21	15.56%
Hunter 35	$79,900	9.50%	60	$1,678.05		$1,678.05	17.68%
Hunter 30	$56,000	9.50%	120	$724.63		$724.63	7.64%
Beneteau 39	$76,000	12.00%	120	$1,090.38		$1,090.38	11.49%
MacGregor 26	$15,700	8.75%	36	$497.43		$497.43	5.24%
Beneteau 42	$126,789	11.00%	180	$1,441.08		$1,441.08	15.19%
Hunter 43	$155,500	11.25%	180	$1,791.90		$1,791.90	18.88%
				Total Payments Due	Feb-96	$9,488.76	

Largest Loan: $155,500
Smallest Loan: $12,500
Average Loan: $77,423

Page 1

Figure 4-20
Printout of loan management worksheet

9 Save your file once again, so it includes the page setup format you specified.

EX 152 TUTORIAL 4 Functions, Formulas, and Absolute References

If you want to take a break and resume the tutorial at a later time, you can exit Excel by double-clicking the Control menu box in the upper-left corner of the screen. When you resume the tutorial, launch Excel, maximize the Microsoft Excel and Book1 windows, and place your Student Disk in the disk drive. Open the file S4SAILS1.XLS, then continue with the tutorial.

■   ■   ■

Next, James wonders how much less his monthly payment would be if he refinanced some of the loans, so that instead of paying 12% interest he would pay 11%. Shabir shows him that this sort of what-if analysis is easy to do.

To change the interest rates and look at the effect on the total payment:

❶ Click cell **C7**, which contains one of the 12% interest rates.

❷ Type **11%** and press **[Enter]**. The total loan payment in cell G17 changes from $9,488.76 to $9,457.29.

❸ Click cell **C10**, which contains another of the 12% interest rates.

❹ Type **11%** and press **[Enter]**. The total loan payment in cell G17 changes to $9,379.10.

❺ Click cell **C13**, which contains another of the 12% interest rates.

❻ Type **11%** and press **[Enter]**. The total loan payment in cell G17 changes to $9,335.62.

James sees that he could save about $150 each month by refinancing the three loans that are at 12% interest. Now he wonders "what if" he bought a West Wight Potter 19 foot for $9,000 at 11% interest.

To add another boat to the list, Shabir must insert a row at the current location of row 17. Then he must copy the formulas to calculate the monthly payment amount, the payments due this month, and the percent of total payment to the new row.

To insert a row for the new boat and copy the necessary formulas:

❶ Click cell **A17** because you want to insert a new row at this location.

❷ Click **Insert**, click **Rows** to insert a blank row.

❸ Highlight cells A16 through H17, then release the mouse button.

❹ Click **Edit**, click **Fill**, then click **Down** to duplicate the formulas and data from row 16 to row 17. Click any cell to remove the highlighting and view the results. See Figure 4-21.

formulas and data from row 16 copied to row 17

10	Corbin 39	$123,000	11.00%	180	$1,398.01	$1,398.01	14.98%
11	Hunter 35	$79,900	9.50%	60	$1,678.05	$1,678.05	17.97%
12	Hunter 30	$56,000	9.50%	120	$724.63	$724.63	7.76%
13	Beneteau 39	$76,000	11.00%	120	$1,046.90	$1,046.90	11.21%
14	MacGregor 26	$15,700	8.75%	36	$497.43	$497.43	5.33%
15	Beneteau 42	$126,789	11.00%	180	$1,441.08	$1,441.08	15.44%
16	Hunter 43	$155,500	11.25%	180	$1,791.90	$1,791.90	19.19%
17	Hunter 43	$155,500	11.25%	180	$1,791.90	$1,791.90	19.19%
18	Largest Loan:	$155,500		Total Payments Due	Feb-96	$9,335.62	
19	Smallest Loan:	$12,500					

Figure 4-21 Duplicating a row

The Fill Down command copied the data, as well as the formulas, to row 17. That does not present a problem because Shabir can easily type over the copied data with the data for the West Wight Potter 19. Now Shabir fills in row 17 with the information for the West Wight Potter.

To change the data in row 17:
❶ Click cell **A17**, type **W W Potter 19** and press [→].
❷ Type **9000** as the loan amount and press [→].
❸ Type **11%** as the interest and press [→].
❹ Type **60** as the number of payments and press **[Enter]**. The monthly payment for this loan, $195.68, is displayed in cell E17.

Shabir and James look at the total payments due in cell G18, and they notice that something is wrong. The amount in this cell did not change to reflect the addition of the West Wight Potter. They look at the formulas in cells G18, B18, B19, and B20 to find out what happened.

To view the contents of cells G18, B18, B19, and B20:
❶ Click cell **G18** to make it the active cell. The formula for this cell appears in the formula bar as =SUM(G5:G16). The formula was not updated to include cell G17.
❷ Click cell **B18** and look at the formula that appears in the formula bar. The formula =MAX(B5:B16) was not updated to include B17.
❸ Click cell **B19** and look at the formula that appears in the formula bar. The formula =MIN(B5:B16) was not updated.
❹ Click cell **B20** and look at the formula that appears in the formula bar. The formula =AVERAGE(B5:B16) was not updated after row 17 was inserted.

It is obvious that these formulas need to be updated to include row 17. Shabir explains to James that if you add a row in the location of any of the current rows in a formula, the formula will update. *However, if you add a row that is not included in a formula, you must manually update the formulas to include the new row.*

The original range in these formulas was B5:B16. Shabir could have inserted a row in the current location of row 10, for example, and the range in the total payment formula would have "stretched" to include cells G5 through G17. But, Shabir inserted row 17, which was not within the original range, so he needs to manually update the formulas in cells G18, B18, B19, and B20.

To update the formulas in cells G18, B18, B19, and B20:
❶ Double-click cell **G18**, which contains the formula you want to change.
❷ Place I at the end of the formula and click. Then press **[Backspace]** to delete the 6.
❸ Type **7** and press **[Enter]**.
❹ Repeat Steps 2 through 4 so that the formulas in cells B18, B19, and B20 contain the argument (B5:B17). See Figure 4-22.

Figure 4-22
Manually updated formulas

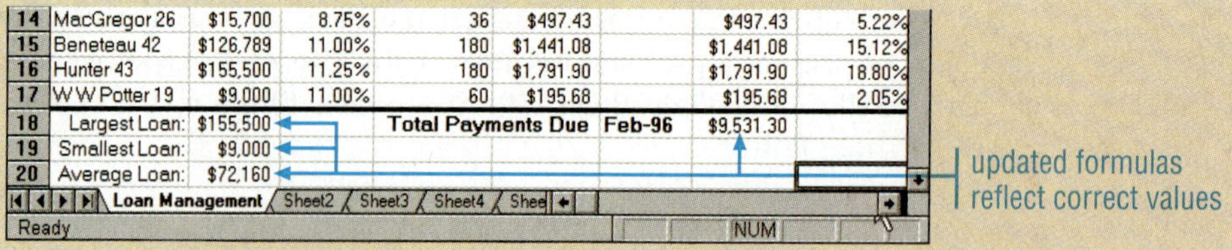

14	MacGregor 26	$15,700	8.75%	36	$497.43	$497.43	5.22%
15	Beneteau 42	$126,789	11.00%	180	$1,441.08	$1,441.08	15.12%
16	Hunter 43	$155,500	11.25%	180	$1,791.90	$1,791.90	18.80%
17	WW Potter 19	$9,000	11.00%	60	$195.68	$195.68	2.05%
18	Largest Loan:	$155,500		Total Payments Due	Feb-96	$9,531.30	
19	Smallest Loan:	$9,000					
20	Average Loan:	$72,160					

updated formulas reflect correct values

Now Shabir and James can see that the total loan payment would be $9,531.30 with the loan payment for a new West Wight Potter 19. The amount of the largest loan, shown in cell B18, did not change. The smallest loan, shown in cell B19, is now $9,000. The amount shown in cell B20 for the average loan changed from $77,423 to $72,160.

James now understands how important it is to check each formula to make sure it works. Shabir agrees and explains that there are many ways to test a worksheet to verify the accuracy of the results. For example, he can use test data or compare results with known values, such as those in loan payment tables.

James does not want a printout of the what-if analysis, so Shabir closes the workbook without saving it. Because he does not save the current version of the workbook, the version he has on disk will reflect the worksheet before he changed the interest rates from 12% to 11% and added the West Wight Potter.

To close the workbook without saving the what-if analysis:

❶ Double-click the **document window Control menu box**.

❷ Click the **No button** when you see the message "Save changes in S4SAILS1.XLS?"

❸ Exit Excel if you are not proceeding directly to the Tutorial Assignments.

To complete his loan management worksheet, Shabir used many Excel functions to simplify the formulas he entered. He was able to troubleshoot the problem he encountered when he copied the percent of total payment formula and ended up with a column of #DIV/0! error messages because he remembered that absolute references don't change when copied to other cells. Shabir is pleased that James was impressed by the capabilities of the worksheet to do what-if analyses.

Questions

1. List the Excel functions you used in this tutorial.
   a. Briefly explain what each function does.
   b. Write out the syntax for each function.
   c. Write a sample function in which you use cell references or constant numbers for the arguments.

E 2. Use the Function Wizard, or the Excel On-line Help to find one function for each category listed in Figure 4-4.
   a. Indicate the category to which this function belongs.
   b. List the function name.
   c. Write a short description of what this function does.

3. Write the definition of a function, then refer to Tutorial 1 and write out the definition of a formula. Explain the relationship between functions and formulas.
4. Explain the difference between the way the AVERAGE function handles zeros and the way it handles blank cells that are included in the range of cells to be averaged.
5. In the tutorial, Shabir thought that the MAX and MIN functions would be especially useful for large lists that changed frequently. Explain the advantage of using the MAX and MIN functions on such lists.
6. What are the advantages of using the Function Wizard dialog box instead of typing a function directly into a cell?
7. Write the formula you would use to calculate the monthly payment for a $150,000 30-year home loan at 8.75% annual interest.
8. Write the formula you would use to calculate the monthly payment for a $10,000 loan at 8% annual interest that you must pay back in 48 months.
9. Write the formula you would use to display the value $100 if cell A9 contains the word "Bonus," but display $0 if cell A9 is empty.
10. Write the formula you would use to display the message "Over budget" whenever the amount in cell B5 is greater than or equal to $800,000, but display the message "Budget OK" if the amount in cell B5 is less than $800,000.
11. Explain the difference between absolute and relative references.
12. What is the significance of the empty parentheses in the TODAY function?
13. Explain the meaning of the message #DIV/0!.
14. Which function key can you use to change the cell reference type from relative to absolute?

Tutorial Assignments

Launch Windows and Excel, if necessary, then complete the Tutorial Assignments and print the results for Tutorial Assignments 10 and 17.
1. Open the file T4SAILS1.XLS, then save it as S4SAILSR.XLS on your Student Disk. Shabir did not have the paperwork for the CSY Gulfstar 42 loan, so it was not included in the worksheet. The CSY Gulfstar 42 was purchased with a $183,000 loan at 9.75% (.0975) interest for 20 years.
2. Insert a blank row between the Hunter 30 and the Beneteau 39 at row 13.
   Hint: Because you are adding the row in the middle of the range specified for the function arguments, you will not need to adjust the SUM, MAX, MIN, and AVERAGE formulas.
3. Enter the name of the boat, CSY Gulfstar 42, in column A.
4. Enter the loan amount in cell B13, the interest rate in cell C13, and the number of monthly payments in cell D13.
5. In cell E13 use the PMT function to calculate the monthly payment.
6. In cell G13 use the IF function to display $0.00 if the loan is not paid, or display the loan payment if the loan is paid.
7. Copy the formula from cell H12 to cell H13 to calculate the percent of total payment.
8. Edit the header and replace Shabir's name with yours.
9. Save the revised workbook.
10. Print the worksheet in landscape orientation; center it from top to bottom and from left to right. Do not print cell borders or row/column headings.
11. Use a felt marker or pen to indicate on your printout which cells display different results after the addition of the CSY Gulfstar 42.
12. Return to the worksheet on your screen and enter the label "Largest Payment:" in cell A21; then in cell B21 enter the formula to find the largest loan payment in column G.

13. Enter the label "Smallest Payment:" in cell A22; then in cell B22 enter the formula to find the smallest loan payment in column G.
14. Enter the label "Average Interest Rate:" in cell A23; then in cell B23 enter the formula to calculate the average of the interest rates shown in column C.
15. Format the text in cells A21 through A23 to align on the right side of the cell, and adjust the column width, if necessary.
16. Save the revised workbook.
17. Use your customized print formulas module, S3MYMOD.XLM, to print the formulas for your worksheet.

Case Problems

1. Compiling Data on the U.S. Airline Industry

The editor of *Aviation Week and Space Technology* has asked Muriel Guzzetti to research the current status of the U.S. airline industry. Muriel collects information on the revenue-miles and passenger-miles for each of the major U.S. airlines. She wants to calculate the following summary information to use in the article:

- total revenue-miles for the U.S. airline industry
- total passenger-miles for the U.S. airline industry
- each airline's share of the total revenue-miles
- each airline's share of the total passenger-miles
- the average revenue-miles for U.S. airlines
- the average passenger-miles for U.S. airlines

Complete the following steps:

1. Open the workbook P4AIR.XLS, then save it as S4AIR.XLS on your Student Disk.
2. Use the SUM function to calculate the industry total revenue-miles in cell B14.
3. Use the SUM function to calculate the industry total passenger-miles in cell D14.
4. In cell C7, enter the formula to calculate American Airlines' share of the total industry revenue-miles using the following equation:

$$\frac{\text{American's share of total}}{\text{industry revenue-miles}} = \frac{\text{American's revenue-miles}}{\text{industry total revenue-miles}}$$

Hint: You are going to use this formula for the rest of the airlines, so consider which cell reference should be absolute.

5. Copy the formula from cell C7 to calculate each airline's share of the total industry revenue-miles.
6. In cell E7 enter the formula to calculate American Airlines' share of the total industry passenger-miles, then copy this formula for the other airlines.
7. In cell B15 use the AVERAGE function to calculate the average revenue-miles for the U.S. airline industry.
8. In cell D15 use the AVERAGE function to calculate the average passenger-miles for the U.S. airline industry.
9. Use the TODAY function to display the date in cell B3.
10. Enter your name in cell B2.
11. Format the worksheet so it is easier to read:
    a. Bold the titles and column headings.
    b. Center the title across the entire worksheet and center the column titles over each column.
    c. Add a border at the bottom of cells A6 through E6, and add a border at the top of cells A14 through E14.
    d. Format column B and column D to display numbers with commas; for example, the revenue-miles for American Airlines will display as 26,851 instead of 26851.
    e. Format columns C and E for percents that display two decimal places.

12. Save your workbook.
13. Make two printouts:
    a. Print the worksheet in portrait orientation, centered on the page, without cell gridlines or row/column headings.
    b. Print the formulas in landscape orientation, centered on the page, and include cell gridlines and row/column headings.

2. Commission Analysis at Norcross Office Systems

Maija Jansson is the sales manager for Norcross Office Systems, an office supply store. Maija is thinking of changing the commission structure to motivate the sales representatives to increase sales. Currently, sales representatives earn a monthly base salary of $500.00. In addition to the base salary, sales representatives earn a 6% (.06) commission on their total sales when their monthly sales volume is $6,000.00 or more.

To look at some options for changing the commission structure, Maija collected past payroll information for one of the employees, Jim Marley. Jim's monthly sales are typical of those of most of the Norcross sales representatives. Maija wants to design a worksheet that will help her look at how much money Jim would have earned in the past 12 months if the commission structure was different. Maija completed some of the worksheet and has asked you to help her finish it.

To complete the worksheet:

1. Open the workbook P4BONUS.XLS, then save it as S4BONUS.XLS on your Student Disk.
2. Enter your name in cell B2, then use the TODAY function to display the date in cell B3.
3. Enter the names of the months January through December in column A.
   Hint: Use the fill handle to automatically fill cells A9 through A20 with the names of the months.
4. In cell C9, enter a formula that uses the IF function to calculate Jim's bonus for January.
   For the *logical test* argument, enter the expression to check if Jim's sales are greater than or equal to the sales required for a commission in cell C5.
   For the *value if true* argument, multiply Jim's sales by the commission percent in cell C6.
   For the *value if false* argument, enter a zero.
5. Copy the formula from cell C9 to cells C10 through C20.
6. If your formulas produced zeros for every month, something is wrong. Examine the formula in cell C9 and determine which references need to be absolute. Edit the formula, then copy it again. Your formulas are correct if cell C18 shows that Jim earned a $433.56 commission.
7. In cell E9, enter a formula to calculate Jim's total pay for January. Calculate Jim's total pay by adding his commission to his base salary.
8. Copy the formula from cell E9 to cells E10 through E20.
9. In cell E21, use the SUM function to calculate Jim's total pay for the year.
10. Save the workbook.
11. Write out your answers to the following questions:
    a. How much did Jim earn in the last 12 months under the current commission structure?
    b. How much would Jim have earned last year if the commission was 8%?
    c. How much would Jim have earned in the last 12 months if the commission rate was 7%, but he had to make at least $6,500 in sales each month before he could earn a commission?

12. Print two versions of your worksheet:
    a. Print the worksheet showing what Jim would have earned if he had to sell $6,500 each month to earn a commission, and the commission was 7%. Center the worksheet on the page, but do not print cell gridlines or row/column headings.
    b. Display the formulas for the worksheet and adjust the column widths so there is no extra space. Print the formulas for the worksheet in portrait orientation. Print the entire worksheet on one page; include cell gridlines and row/column headings.

3. Calculating Car Loans at First Federal Bank

Paul Vagelos is a loan officer in the Consumer Loan Department of the First Federal Bank. Paul evaluates customer applications for car loans, and he wants to create a worksheet that will calculate the monthly payments, total payments, and total interest paid on a loan. Paul has finished most of the worksheet but needs to complete a few more sections. To complete the worksheet:

1. Open the workbook P4CAR1.XLS, then save it as S4CAR1.XLS on your Student Disk.
2. Enter a formula in cell B10 that uses the PMT function to calculate the monthly payment for the loan amount in cell B5, at the annual interest rate in cell B6, for the term in cell A10. Display the monthly payment as a positive amount.
3. Edit the formula in cell B10 so you use absolute references for any cell references that should not change when you copy the formula.
4. Copy the formula from cell B10 to cells B11 through B14.
5. Enter the formula in cell D10 to calculate the total interest using the following equation:

    total interest = total payments - loan amount
6. Edit the formula in cell D10 so you use absolute references for any cell references that should not change when you copy the formula.
7. Copy the formula from cell D10 to cells D11 through D14.
8. Type your name in cell B2, and enter the TODAY function in cell B3.
9. Make any formatting changes you think are appropriate to have a professional-looking worksheet.
10. Preview the printed worksheet. Make any page setup settings necessary to produce a professional-looking printout, then print the worksheet.
11. Save the workbook with formatting changes.
12. Use your customized print formulas module, S3MYMOD.XLM, to print the formulas for your worksheet.

TUTORIAL 5

Charts and Graphing

OBJECTIVES

In this tutorial you will:
- Plan and construct charts
- Create a pie chart, line chart, column chart, and 3-D column chart
- Identify the elements of the Excel chart
- Learn which type of chart will represent your data most effectively
- Select non-adjacent ranges
- Move a chart and change its size
- Add gridlines to a chart
- Change the format of chart lines
- Identify the differences between label text, attached text, and unattached text
- Add, edit, and format chart text
- Add pictures to a column chart
- Add color and borders to a chart
- Work with multiple sheets

Charting Sales Information

Cast Iron Concepts   Carl O'Brien is the assistant marketing director at Cast Iron Concepts, a distributor of traditional cast iron stoves. Carl is working on a new product catalog and his main concern is how much space to allocate for each product. In previous catalogs the Box Windsor stove was allocated one full page. The Star Windsor and the West Windsor stoves were each allocated a half page.

Carl has collected sales information about the three stove models, and he has discovered that Box Windsor stove sales have steadily decreased since 1991. Although the Box Windsor stove was the best-selling model during the 1980s, sales of Star Windsor stoves and West Windsor stoves have increased steadily and overtaken the Box Windsor sales. Carl believes that the space allocated to the Box Windsor stove should be reduced to a half page while the Star Windsor stove and the West Windsor stove should each have a full page.

Carl needs to convince the marketing director to change the space allocation in the new catalog, so he is preparing a presentation for the next department meeting. At the presentation Carl plans to show four charts that graphically illustrate the sales pattern of the Box Windsor, Star Windsor, and West Windsor stoves. Carl has stored the sales figures in a workbook named C5WINDSR.XLS. He will generate the charts from the data in the worksheet. Let's launch Windows, launch Excel, and then open Carl's worksheet.

To launch Excel, organize the desktop, and open the C5WINDSR.XLS workbook:
❶ Launch Excel following your usual procedure.
❷ Make sure your Student Disk is in the disk drive.
❸ Make sure the Microsoft Excel and Book1 windows are maximized.
❹ Click the **Open button** to display the Open dialog box.
❺ Double-click **C5WINDSR.XLS** in the File Name box to display the workbook.

Let's save the workbook using the filename S5WINDSR.XLS so the changes you make will be made to a copy of the file, not the original.

To save the workbook as S5WINDSR.XLS:
❶ Click **File**, then click **Save As...** to display the Save As dialog box.
❷ Type **S5WINDSR** using either uppercase or lowercase.
❸ Click the **OK button** to save the workbook under the new filename. When the save is complete, the new filename, S5WINDSR.XLS, appears in the title bar. See Figure 5-1.

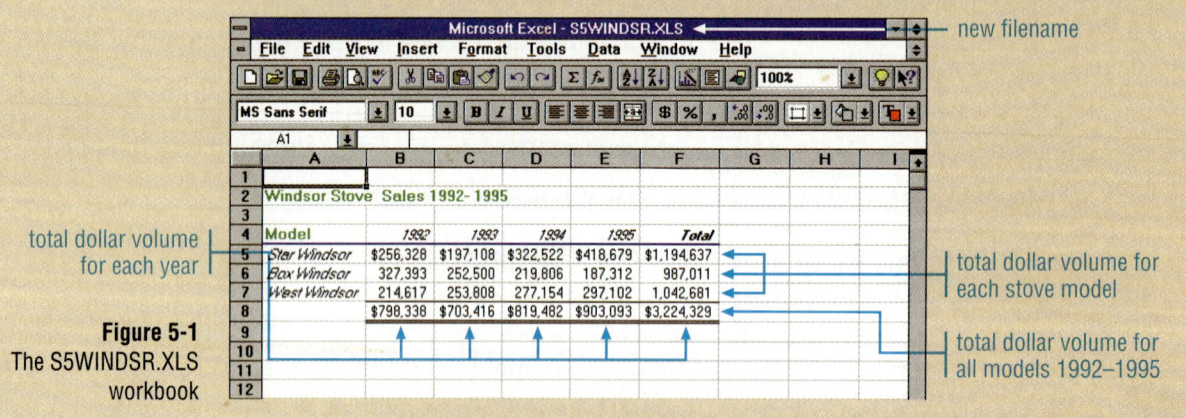

Figure 5-1
The S5WINDSR.XLS workbook

The worksheet shows the sales generated by each of the three Windsor stove models for the period 1992 through 1995. The total dollar volume during the four-year period for each model is displayed in column F. The total dollar volume for each year is displayed in row 8. Carl wants to make several charts that will help him convince the marketing director to change the catalog space allocated to each Windsor stove model. In this tutorial you will work with Carl as he plans and creates four charts for his presentation.

Excel Charts

As you learned in Tutorial 1, it is easy to graphically represent your worksheet data. You might think of these graphical representations as "graphs"; however, in Excel they are referred to as **charts**. Figure 5-2 shows the 15 **chart types** you can use to represent worksheet data. Of the 15 chart types, nine chart types produce two-dimensional (2-D) charts and six chart types produce three-dimensional (3-D) charts.

Icon	Chart Type	Purpose
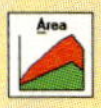	Area chart	Shows the magnitude of change over a period of time
	Bar chart	Shows comparisons between the data represented by each bar
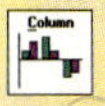	Column chart	Shows comparisons between the data represented by each column
	Line chart	Shows trends or changes over time
	Pie chart	Shows the proportion of parts to a whole
	Radar chart	Shows changes in data relative to a center point
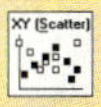	XY chart	Shows the pattern or relationship between sets of (x,y) data points
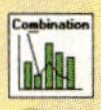	Combination chart	Shows how one set of data corresponds to another set by superimposing one chart type over another
	3-D Area chart	Shows the magnitude of each data series as a solid, three-dimensional shape
	3-D Bar chart	Similar to a 2-D Bar chart, but bars appear three-dimensional
	3 D Column chart	Shows three-dimensional columns and some formats show data on x-, y-, and z- axes
	3-D Line chart	Shows each chart line as a ribbon within a three-dimensional space
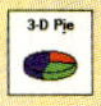	3-D Pie chart	Shows the proportion of parts to a whole, with emphasis on the data values in the front wedges
	3-D Surface chart	Shows the interrelationship between large amounts of data
	Doughnut chart	Shows the proportion of parts to whole

Figure 5-2
Excel chart types

Each chart type has several predefined **chart formats** that specify such format characteristics as gridlines, chart labels, axes, and so on. For example, the Area chart type has five predefined formats, as shown in Figure 5-3. You can find more information on chart types and formats in the *Microsoft Excel User's Guide*, in the Excel Help facility, and in the ChartWizard.

EX 162 TUTORIAL 5   Charts and Graphing

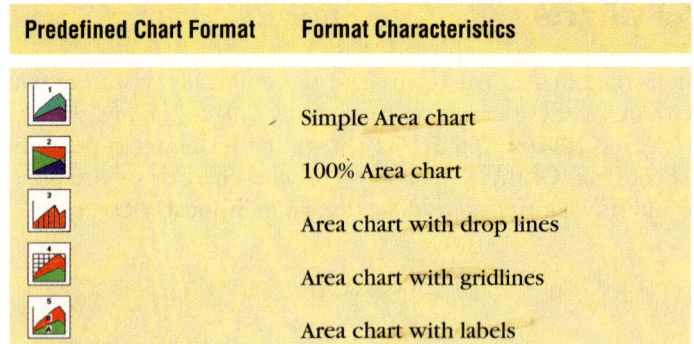

Figure 5-3
Predefined formats for the Area chart type

Figure 5-4 shows the elements of a typical Excel chart. It is particularly important to understand the Excel chart terminology so you can successfully construct and edit charts.

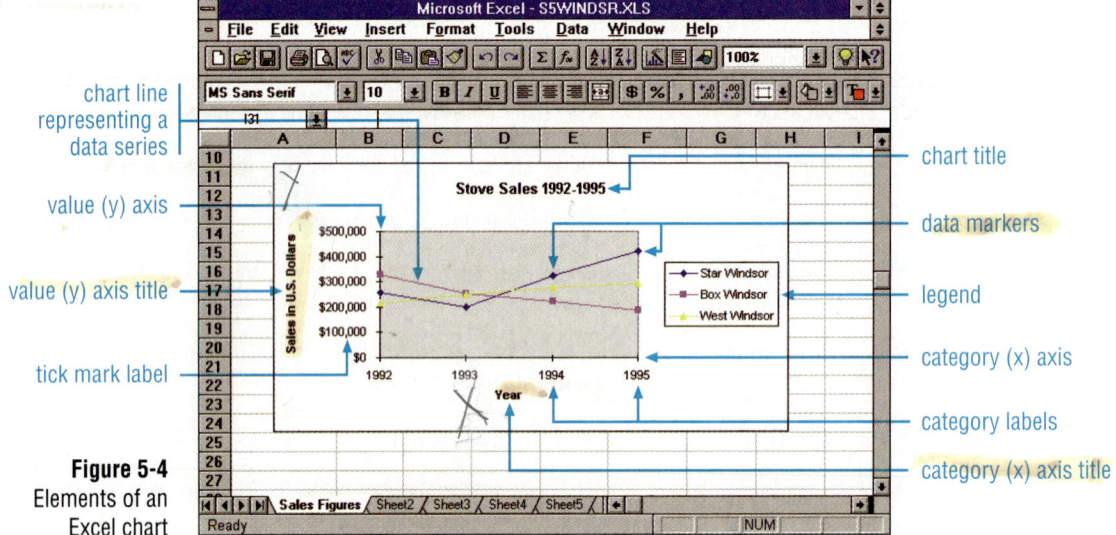

Figure 5-4
Elements of an Excel chart

The **chart title** identifies the chart. The horizontal axis of the chart is referred to as the **category axis** or the **x-axis**. The vertical axis is referred to as the **value axis** or the **y-axis**. Each axis on a chart can have a title that identifies the scale or categories of the chart data; in Figure 5-4 the x-axis title is "Year" and the y-axis title is "Sales in U.S. Dollars."

A **tick mark label** shows the scale for the y-axis. Excel automatically generates this scale based on the values selected for the chart. The **category names** or **category labels** correspond to the labels you use for the worksheet data and are usually displayed on the x-axis.

A **data point** is a single value in a cell in the worksheet. A **data marker** is a bar, area, wedge, or symbol that marks a single data point on a chart. For example, the 1995 sales of the Star Windsor stove in cell E5 of the worksheet on your screen is a data point. The small square on the chart line in Figure 5-4 that shows the 1995 sales of the Star Windsor stove is a data marker.

A **data series** is a group of related data points, such as the Star Windsor sales shown in cells B5 through E5 on your worksheet. On a chart such as the one in Figure 5-4, a data series is shown as a set of data markers connected by a chart line.

When you have more than one data series, your chart will contain more than one set of data markers. For example, Figure 5-4 has three chart lines, each representing a data series. When you show more than one data series on a chart, it is a good idea to use a **legend to** identify which data markers represent each data series. Figure 5-4 also shows the chart toolbar, which contains buttons for changing the chart type and some chart characteristics. You will use the menus instead of the chart toolbar in this tutorial, but don't be concerned if the chart toolbar appears in your Excel window.

Carl wants to show that the West Windsor and Star Windsor stove models generate a higher proportion of the total Windsor stove sales than the Box Windsor model. Because pie charts are an effective way to show the relationship of parts to the whole, Carl decides to use a pie chart to show the sales for each model as a percentage of total Windsor stove sales.

Carl knows that pie charts and 3-D pie charts illustrate the same relationships, but he decides to create a 3-D pie chart because he thinks it looks more professional. Since Carl will be creating a number of charts, he decides to put each chart on a separate sheet. This will allow him to switch quickly from one chart to the other, without having to scroll up and down through numerous charts. In the next set of steps, Carl renames Sheet2 "Pie Chart."

To rename Sheet2:
1. Double-click the **Sheet2 tab** to open the Rename Sheet dialog box.
2. Type **Pie Chart** in the Name box, then click the **OK button**. See Figure 5-5.

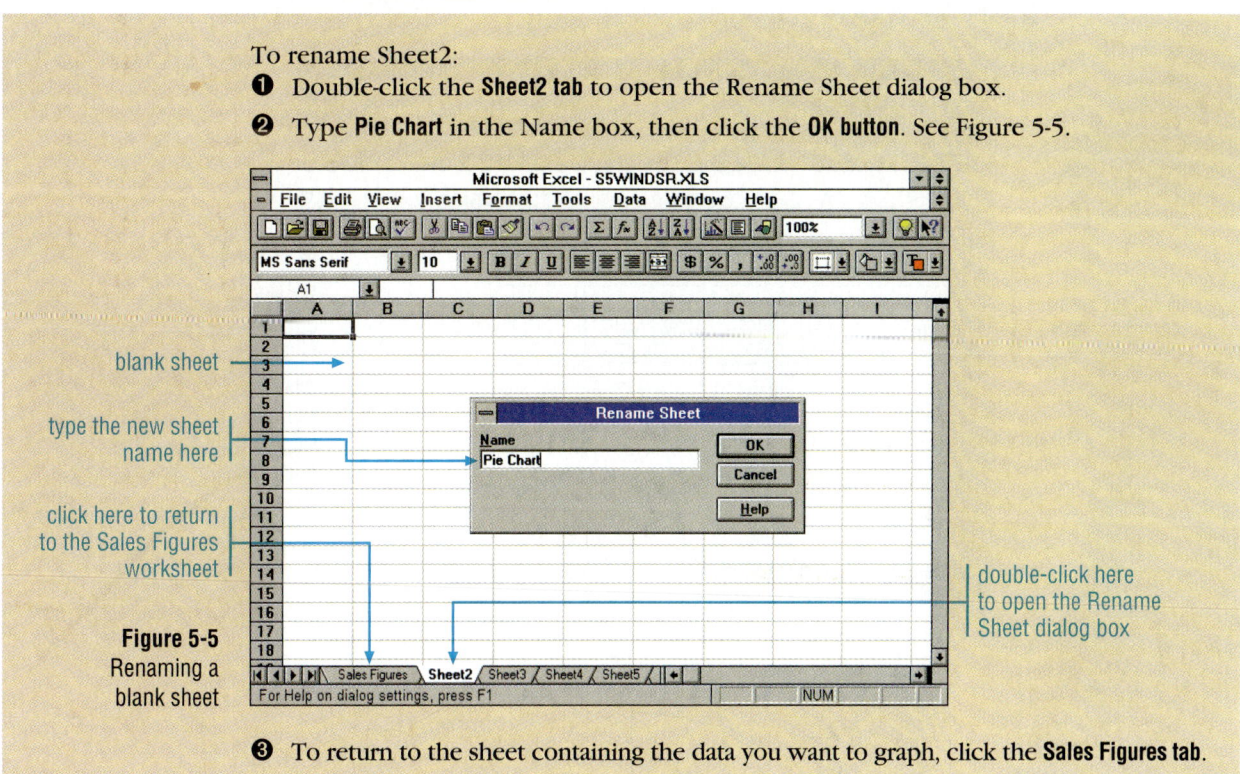

Figure 5-5 Renaming a blank sheet

3. To return to the sheet containing the data you want to graph, click the **Sales Figures tab**.

Now Carl is ready to create a pie chart on the Pie Chart sheet.

Creating a 3-D Pie Chart

A **pie chart** represents one data series by displaying each data point as a wedge. The size of the wedge represents the proportion of the data point in the total circle, or "pie." When you create a pie chart, you generally specify two ranges. Excel uses the first range for the category labels and the second range for the data series. Excel automatically calculates the percentage for each wedge, draws the wedge to reflect the percentage, and gives you the option of displaying the percentage as a label on the completed chart.

A 3-D pie chart shows a three-dimensional view of a pie chart. The 3-D representation adds visual interest and emphasizes the data points in the front wedges, or in any wedges that are pulled out, or "exploded," from the circle. Each wedge on an Excel 3-D pie chart can be colored or patterned, displayed with category labels, or labeled with its percentage relative to the whole pie.

Carl wants to create a 3-D pie chart to show the percentage of sales generated by each of the three Windsor stove models during 1995. He draws a sketch showing the way he wants the pie chart to look (Figure 5-6). The pie chart will have three wedges, one for each of the stove models. Carl wants each wedge labeled with the stove model and its percentage of the total sales. Because Carl doesn't know the percentages until Excel calculates them and displays them on the chart, he puts "__%" on his sketch where he wants the percentages to appear.

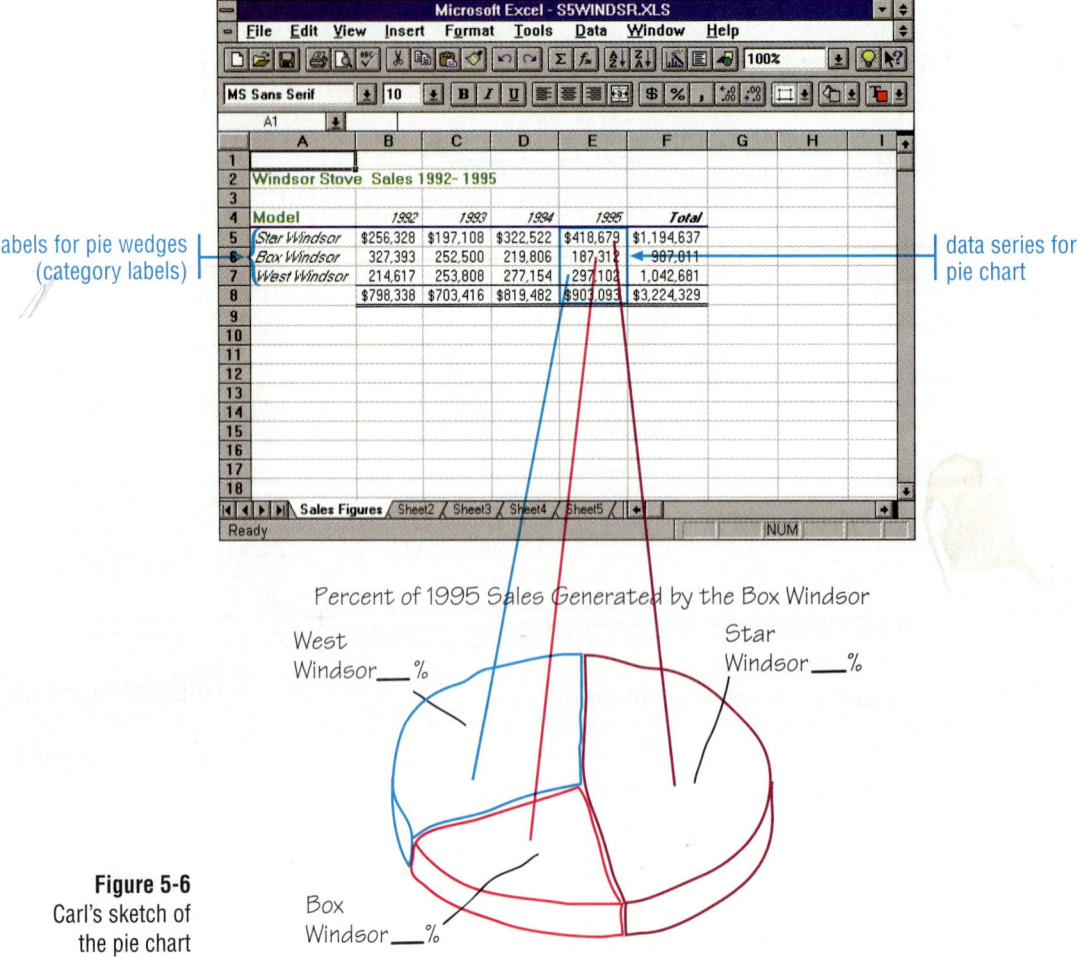

Figure 5-6
Carl's sketch of the pie chart

Carl's sketch shows roughly what he wants the chart to look like. It is difficult to envision exactly how a chart will appear until you know how the data series looks when it is plotted; therefore, it is not necessary to try to incorporate every detail on the chart sketch. As you construct the chart, you can take advantage of Excel's editing capabilities to try different formatting options until your chart looks just the way you want.

Carl refers back to his worksheet and notes in his sketch that the data labels for the pie wedges are in cells A5 through A7 and the data points representing the pie wedges are in cells E5 through E7. Carl must select these two ranges to tell the ChartWizard what he wants to chart, but he realizes that these ranges are not next to each other on the worksheet. He knows how to highlight a series of cells that are adjacent, but now he needs to select two separate ranges at the same time.

Selecting Non-adjacent Ranges

A **non-adjacent range** refers to a group of individual cells or ranges that are not next to each other. Selecting non-adjacent ranges is particularly useful when you construct charts because the cells that contain the data series and the data labels are often not next to each other on the worksheet. When you select non-adjacent ranges, the selected cells in each range are highlighted. You can then apply formats to the cells, clear the cells, or use them to construct a chart.

REFERENCE WINDOW

Selecting Non-adjacent Ranges

- Click the first cell or highlight the first range you want to select.
- Press and hold [Ctrl] while you click additional cells or highlight additional ranges.
- When you have selected all the cells you want to include, release [Ctrl].

To begin constructing the pie chart, Carl first selects the range A5:A7, which contains the data labels. Then he holds down the Control key while highlighting the range E5:E7, which contains the data points.

To select range A5:A7 and range E5:E7 in the Sales Figures sheet:

❶ Make sure the Sales Figures sheet is active. Highlight cells A5 through A7, then release the mouse button.

❷ Press and hold **[Ctrl]** while you highlight cells E5 through E7. Release **[Ctrl]**. Now two ranges are highlighted: A5:A7 and E5:E7.

TROUBLE? If you don't highlight the cells you want on your first try, click any cell to remove the highlighting, then go back to Step 1 and try again.

Now that Carl has selected the cells he wants to use for the pie chart, he uses the ChartWizard button to specify the chart type, chart format, and chart titles.

To create the pie chart using the ChartWizard:

❶ Click the **ChartWizard button** . The prompt "Drag in document to create chart" appears in the status bar. This prompt is asking you to specify where you want the chart to appear in the worksheet.

❷ Click the **Pie Chart tab** to select the sheet where you want the chart to appear.

❸ Move the ⁺ pointer to cell A1 to set the upper-left corner where the chart will appear.

❹ Hold down the mouse button and drag the pointer to cell F13 to outline the area where you want the chart to appear. Release the mouse button to display the ChartWizard - Step 1 of 5 dialog box. Now the dialog box appears over the Sales Figures sheet so you can correct the range address if necessary. See Figure 5-7.

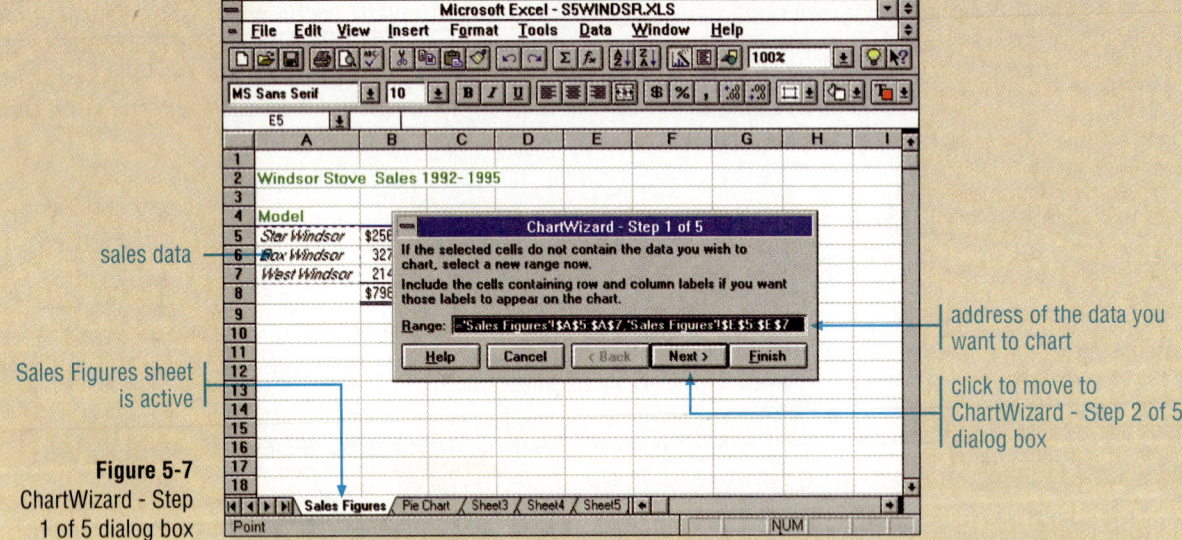

Figure 5-7
ChartWizard - Step 1 of 5 dialog box

Make sure the range is ='Sales Figures'!$A$5:$A$7,'Sales Figures'!$E$5:$E$7. These cell references are the absolute references of the ranges you selected in the previous set of steps. Note that the cell references also include the name of the sheet where the cells are located. The exclamation mark (!) indicates an absolute sheet reference.

TROUBLE? If the range displayed on your screen is not correct, type the necessary corrections in the Range box.

❺ Click the **Next > button** to display the ChartWizard - Step 2 of 5 dialog box.

❻ Double-click the **3-D Pie** chart type to display the ChartWizard - Step 3 of 5 dialog box.

❼ Double-click chart format **7** so your chart will display labels and percentages for each wedge. ChartWizard - Step 4 of 5 shows you a sample of the chart. See Figure 5-8.

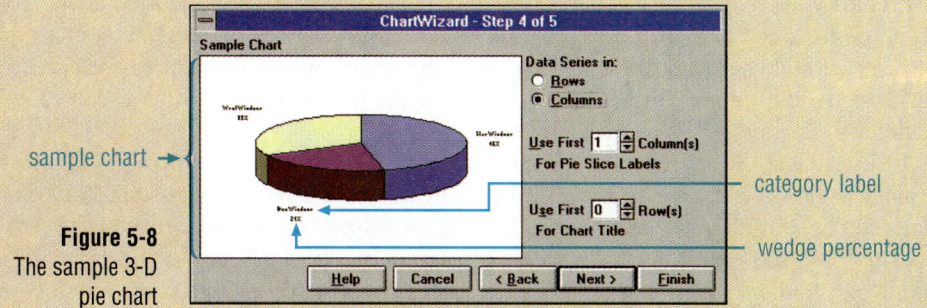

Figure 5-8
The sample 3-D pie chart

This looks right, so next you'll add a title to the chart.

❽ Click the **Next > button** to display the ChartWizard - Step 5 of 5 dialog box.

❾ Click the **Chart Title box**, then type **Percent of 1995 Sales Generated by the Box Windsor**. After a pause, Excel displays the new title in the Sample Chart box.

❿ Click the **Finish button** to complete the chart. The new chart, along with the chart toolbar, appears in the Pie Chart sheet. Use the scroll bars, if necessary, to view the entire chart on the worksheet. See Figure 5-9.

TROUBLE? If you have a monochrome monitor, the chart will be displayed in shades of gray instead of colors.

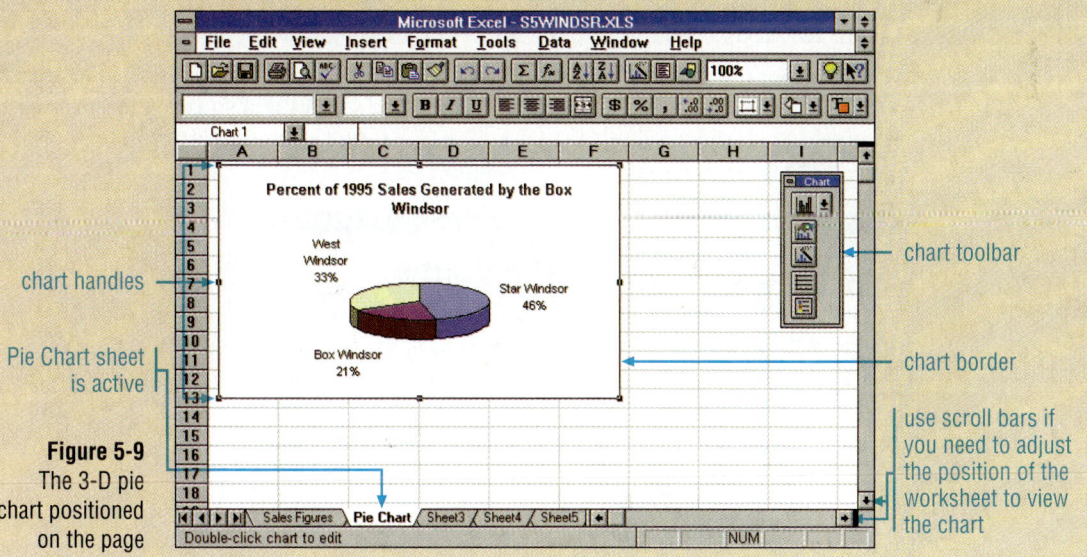

Figure 5-9
The 3-D pie chart positioned on the page

If your chart looks somewhat different from Figure 5-9, you might need to change the chart size, as explained later in this tutorial. For now, don't worry about the chart toolbar. You'll learn how to use it later in this tutorial.

Selecting and Activating the Chart

The chart you have created is called an embedded object or an embedded chart. To modify an embedded chart, you need to either select it or activate it. To select a chart, simply click once anywhere within the borders of the chart. When the chart is selected, Excel displays handles, eight small black squares, along the chart border. You can drag these handles to change the size of the chart.

You activate a chart by double-clicking anywhere within the borders of the chart. Usually, when the chart is activated, the chart border changes from a thin line to a thick colored (or gray) line. If the chart is too big to display on the screen without scrolling, you may see the entire activated chart displayed in a special chart window, with a title bar. Don't be concerned if you see one of your charts displayed in a chart window; it simply means you made your chart too big to fit in the worksheet window. Treat such a chart window just as you would an activated chart with a thick border.

Activating a chart gives you access to the chart commands on the menu bar. Also, when the chart is activated, you can double-click on any part of the chart to open a Format dialog box. Let's experiment with some of these techniques now.

To practice selecting and activating the chart:

❶ Make sure the Pie Chart sheet is active. Click anywhere outside the chart border to make sure the chart is *not* selected. The chart toolbar disappears, along with the square handles around the chart border.

❷ Click once anywhere within the chart border to select the chart. The chart toolbar appears, along with the square handles on the chart border.

❸ To activate the chart, double-click anywhere within the chart border. The chart border turns into a thick colored (or gray) line. Additional square handles might appear along the edge of the chart. The horizontal and vertical scroll bars disappear from the worksheet window. See Figure 5-10.

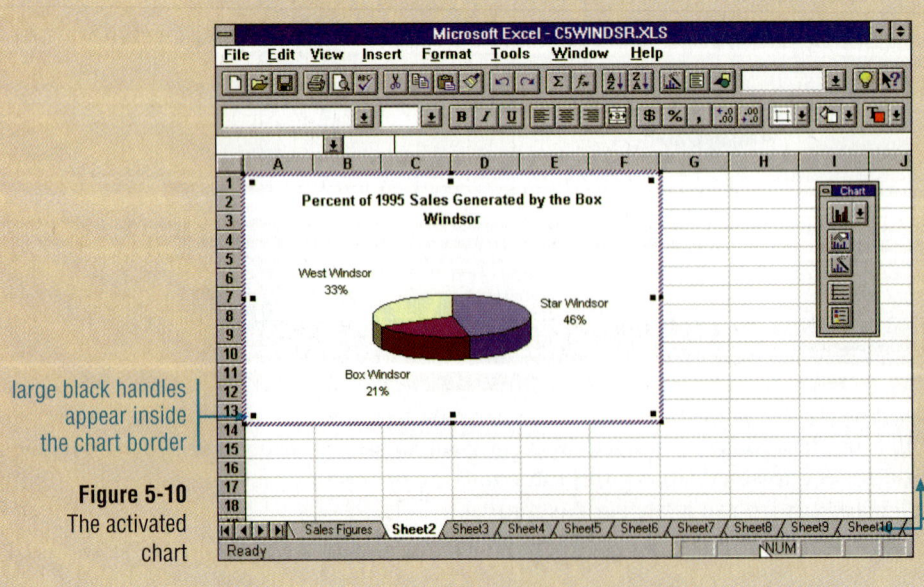

Figure 5-10
The activated chart

TROUBLE? If you don't see the large black handles as shown in Figure 5-10, try clicking the white area in the lower-right corner of the chart. If you see the chart displayed in a window with a menu bar, don't be concerned. Proceed with the following steps as if the chart were displayed within a thick border

Now that the chart is activated, you have access to the chart commands on the menu bar.

❹ Click **Format**. The Format menu displays the chart formatting options. Click **Format** again to close the Format menu.

❺ To open the Format Chart Area dialog box, double-click anywhere on the white space in the chart border. The Format Chart Area dialog box appears. See Figure 5-11.

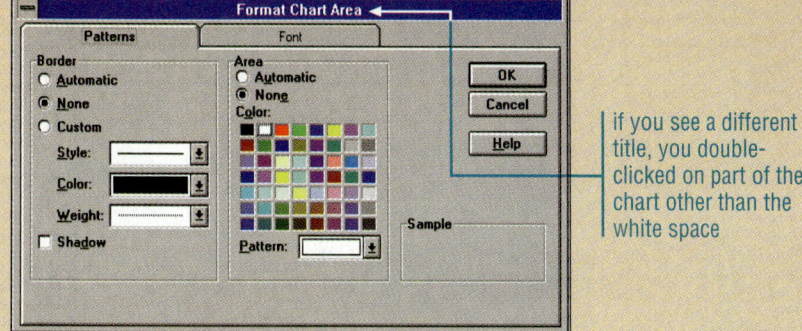

Figure 5-11
The Format Chart Area dialog box

if you see a different title, you double-clicked on part of the chart other than the white space

TROUBLE? If you see a dialog box with a slightly different title, don't worry—it simply means that you double-clicked on a part of the chart other than the white space. As a result, Excel displays the dialog box appropriate for that part of the chart.

❻ Click the **Cancel button** to close the dialog box and return to the Pie Chart sheet.

❼ Double-click anywhere outside the chart border to deactivate the chart. The chart border turns into a thin line without handles, and the chart toolbar disappears.

Now that you're familiar with selecting and activating a chart, you can help Carl modify the pie chart.

Moving and Changing the Size of a Chart

When you use the ChartWizard to create a chart, you drag the pointer to outline the area of the worksheet where you want the chart to appear. If the area you outlined is not large enough, Excel positions the chart elements as best as it can, but the text on the chart might break in odd places. For example, in Figure 5-9 the word "Windsor" appears on a separate line. You can increase the size of the chart to eliminate this problem.

To change the size of a chart, you first click the chart to select it. You can move the chart to another position on the worksheet by clicking anywhere inside the chart border and dragging the chart to the new location. Let's practice moving the chart and changing its size.

To move and change the size of the chart:

❶ Select the chart by clicking anywhere within the chart border. The black handles appear on the chart border.

❷ Position the pointer anywhere within the chart border, then hold down the mouse button and drag the chart two rows down. Release the mouse button to view the chart in its new position.

❸ Position the pointer over one of the handles on the right-hand chart border. Hold down the mouse button and drag the border one column to the right. Release the mouse button to view the new chart size.

❹ Adjust the size and position of your chart so it looks like Figure 5-12.

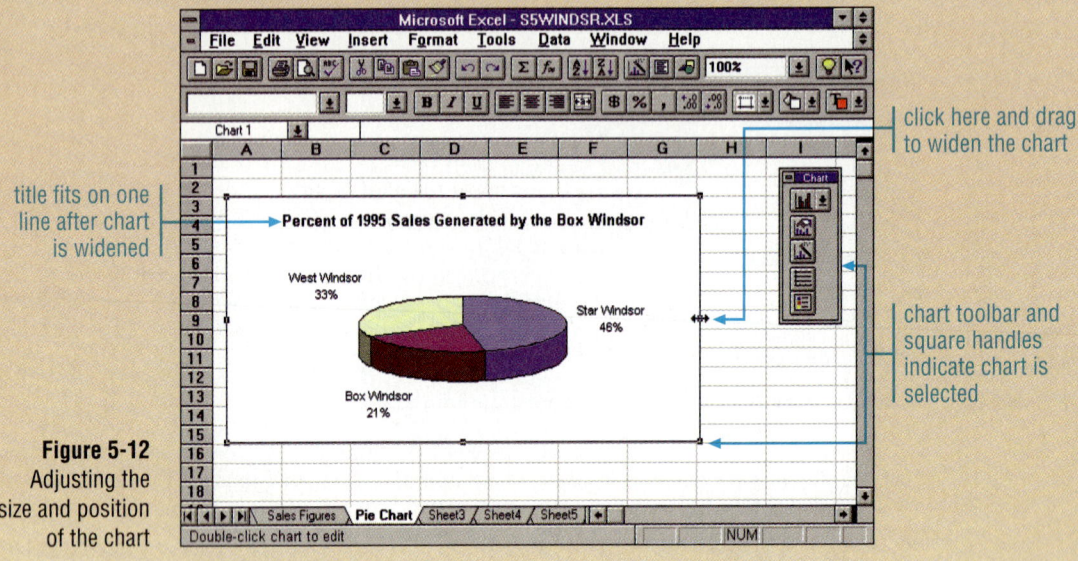

Figure 5-12 Adjusting the size and position of the chart

Carl decides to draw attention to the Box Windsor data by pulling out the wedge that represents its sales.

Pulling Out a Wedge of a Pie Chart

When the chart is activated, you can manipulate each part of the chart as you would any other Excel object. When you click a wedge of the pie chart, small black handles appear, showing you that the wedge is selected. You can then drag the wedge out of the circle or pull it back into the circle. Carl wants to pull out the wedge that represents sales for the Box Windsor stove.

To pull out the wedge that represents the Box Windsor stove sales:

❶ Double-click within the border of the chart to activate it. The border changes to a thick colored (or gray) line.

❷ Click the white space just inside the chart border to make sure the large black handles appear around the inside edge of the activated chart, as in Figure 5-10. These handles indicate that the entire chart border is selected.

❸ Click anywhere on the pie to select it. One square handle appears on each wedge of the pie.

❹ Now that the entire pie is selected, you can select one part of it, the Box Windsor Wedge. Position ▸ over the wedge that represents Box Windsor sales, then click to select the wedge. Handles now appear on this wedge only. See Figure 5-13.

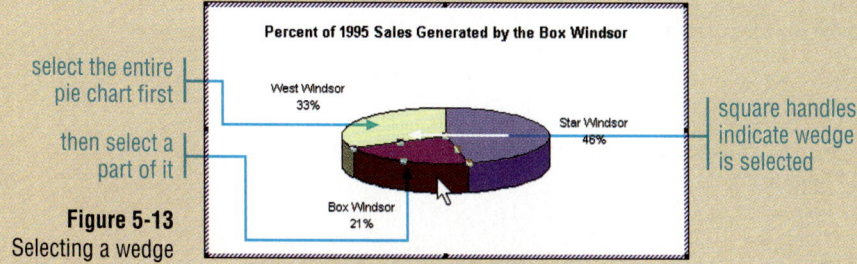

select the entire pie chart first
then select a part of it

Figure 5-13
Selecting a wedge

square handles indicate wedge is selected

TROUBLE? If the Box Windsor wedge is not selected, make sure the chart is activated and start again with Step 2. If you see the Format Chart Area dialog box, you accidentally double-clicked the activated chart. Click the Cancel button and start again with Step 2.

❺ Hold down the mouse button to drag the wedge away from the center of the pie chart. Notice that the wedge will only slide directly in or out. It will not move to the side.

❻ Move the wedge to the position shown in Figure 5-14.

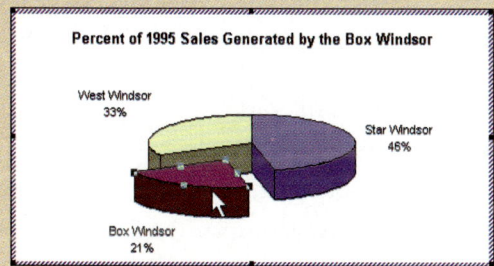

Figure 5-14
Moving a wedge

❼ Release the mouse button to leave the wedge in its new position.

The chart on Carl's screen shows that the Box Windsor stove sales generated the smallest percentage of the total Windsor stove sales in 1995. Carl studies the chart on his screen and decides to add patterns to two of the chart wedges for more visual interest.

Changing Chart Patterns

Excel provides a variety of patterns that you can apply to data markers. Patterns add visual interest to a chart, and they can be useful when you use a printer without color capability. Although your charts appear in color on a color monitor, if your printer does not have color capability Excel translates colors to shades of gray for the printout. Some colors, particularly some of the darker colors, are difficult to distinguish from each other when they are translated to gray shades and then printed. You can make your charts more readable by selecting a different pattern for each data marker.

To apply a pattern to a data marker, such as a wedge in a pie chart, activate the chart, select the data marker to which you want to apply a pattern, then select the pattern you want from the Patterns dialog box.

REFERENCE WINDOW

Selecting a Pattern for a Data Marker

Make sure the chart is activated.

- Select the wedge, or column data marker, to which you want to apply a pattern.
- Click Format, then click Selected Data Point... to display the Format Data Point dialog box.

or

Double-click the wedge or column marker to which you want to apply a pattern to display the Format Data Point dialog box.

- Click the Patterns tab, then click the Patterns box down arrow button to display a list of patterns.
- Click the pattern you want to apply, then click the OK button to close the dialog box.

Carl wants to apply a dot pattern to the Box Windsor wedge, a horizontal stripe pattern to the Star Windsor wedge, and a grid pattern to the West Windsor wedge.

To apply patterns to the wedges:

1. Make sure the chart is activated.
2. If necesary, select the Box Windsor wedge to display the small black handles.
3. Double-click the Box Windsor wedge to display the Format Data Point dialog box.

   TROUBLE? If you see a dialog box with a different title, then you didn't select the wedge before double-clicking. Close the dialog box and start again with Step 2.

4. Click the **Pattern box down arrow button** to display the patterns.
5. Click the sparse dot pattern to select it. See Figure 5-15.

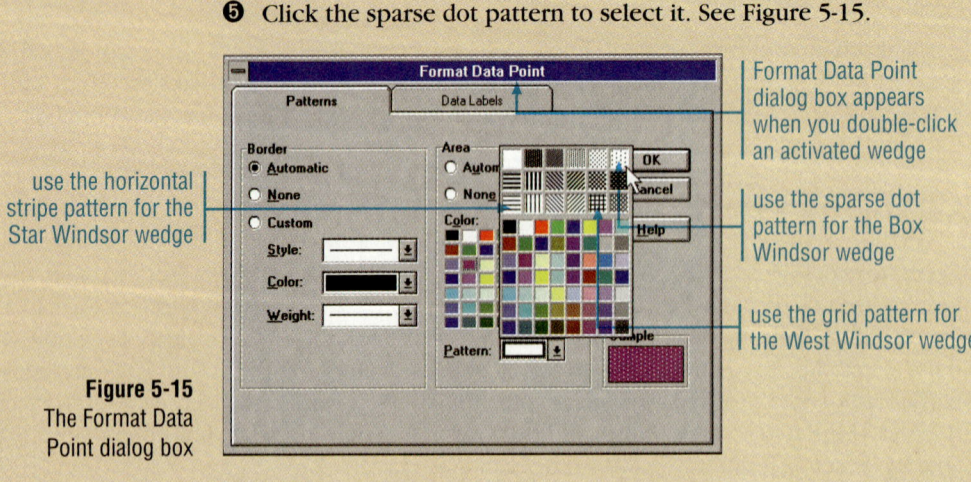

Figure 5-15
The Format Data Point dialog box

6. Click the **OK button** to close the dialog box and view the pattern.

❼ Repeat Steps 2 through 6 to select a horizontal stripe pattern for the Star Windsor wedge, and again to select a grid pattern for the West Windsor wedge. After you select patterns for the Star Windsor and West Windsor wedges, your chart should look like Figure 5-16.

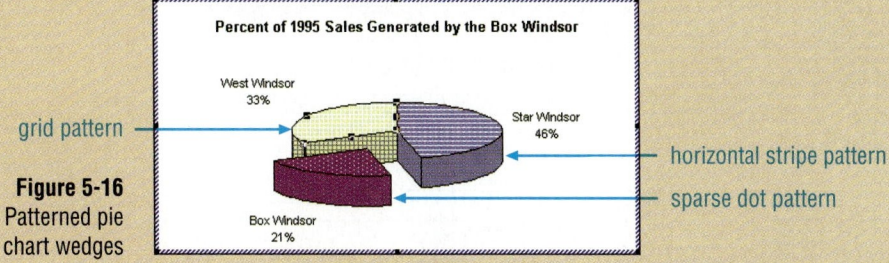

Figure 5-16
Patterned pie chart wedges

❽ To deactivate and deselect the chart, double-click anywhere outside the chart border.
❾ To return to the Sales Figures sheet, click the **Sales Figures tab**.

This chart is complete, so Carl saves the workbook with the new Pie Chart sheet.

❿ Click the **Save button**.

If you want to take a break and resume the tutorial at a later time, you can exit Excel by double-clicking the Control menu box in the upper-left corner of the screen. When you resume the tutorial, launch Excel, maximize the Microsoft Excel and Book1 windows, and place your Student Disk in the disk drive. Open the file S5WINDSR.XLS, then continue with the tutorial.

■   ■   ■

Carl wants to show the change in sales volume for each model during the period 1992 through 1995. He decides to create a line chart to illustrate this change. He begins by renaming a blank sheet, just as he did with the pie chart.

To rename Sheet3:
❶ Double-click the **Sheet3 tab** to open the Rename Sheet dialog box.
❷ Type **Line Chart** in the Name box, then click the **OK button**.
❸ To return to the sheet containing the data you want to graph, click the **Sales Figures tab**.

Creating a Line Chart

A **line chart** represents a data series by connecting each data point with a line. When you use a line chart to plot more than one data series, each data series is represented by one line on the chart. The primary use of a line chart is to show trends or changes over time. Generally, the category labels for the x-axis reflect the time periods for the data, such as days, months, or years. If you are charting more than one data series, make sure you use a legend to indicate which data series is represented by each line.

As with the pie chart, Carl begins by making a sketch of the line chart he wants to create. (Figure 5-17). He uses the years 1992, 1993, 1994, and 1995 for the category labels on the x-axis. The category labels are in row 4 of the worksheet.

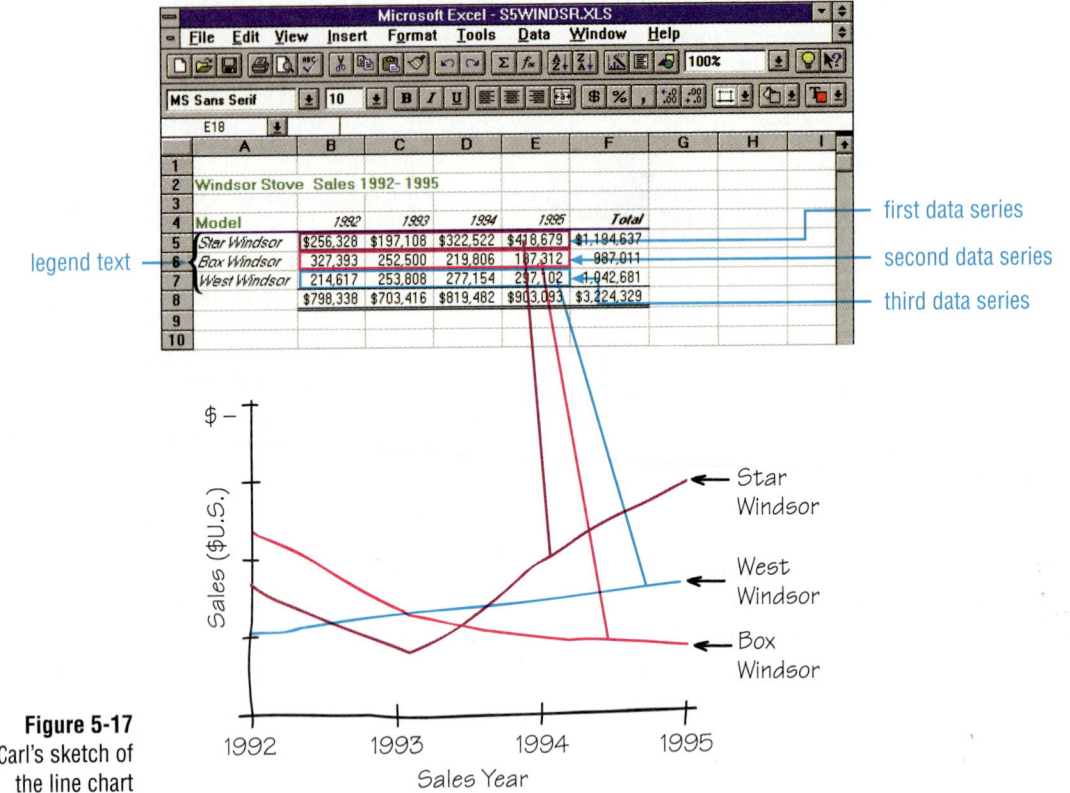

Figure 5-17
Carl's sketch of the line chart

The first chart line will show the Star Windsor sales for the four-year period. The values for this chart line are in row 5. The second chart line will show the Box Windsor sales for the four-year period. The values for the second chart line are in row 6. The third chart line will show the West Windsor sales for the four-year period. The values for the third chart line are in row 7.

Carl does not include any of the total sales figures from column F or row 8 in the chart. Carl knows that it would be confusing to show yearly sales and total sales on the same chart.

To highlight the chart range:
1. Click the **Sales Figures tab** to make sure the Sales Figures sheet is active.
2. Highlight cells A4 through E7, then release the mouse button. Make sure you have not highlighted any cells in column F or in row 8.

Now that he has highlighted the chart range, Carl uses the ChartWizard to create the line chart on the Line Chart sheet.

To create the line chart using the ChartWizard:

❶ Click the **ChartWizard button**.

❷ Click the **Line Chart tab** to display the Line Chart sheet.

❸ Drag the pointer to outline cells A1 through G14. Release the mouse button to display the ChartWizard - Step 1 of 5 dialog box.

❹ Make sure the Range box displays ='Sales Figures'!$A$4:$E$7, then click the **Next >** button to display the Chart Wizard - Step 2 of 5 dialog box.

TROUBLE? If the range shown on your screen is not ='Sales Figures'!$A$4:$E$7, drag the pointer to highlight the correct range on the Sales Figures sheet.

❺ Double-click the **Line** chart type to select the line chart and display the ChartWizard - Step 3 of 5 dialog box.

❻ Double-click chart format **1** to select the chart format with lines that connect data markers.

❼ When you see ChartWizard - Step 4 of 5, compare Carl's sketch in Figure 5-13 to the sample chart shown on your screen and in Figure 5-18. Even though the sample chart is too blurry to allow you to read all the text, it's clear that the chart is not turning out according to Carl's sketch.

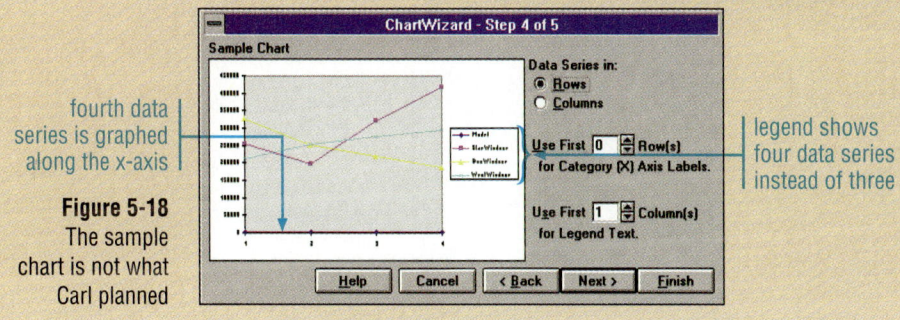

Figure 5-18
The sample chart is not what Carl planned

What's wrong with the sample chart? The legend for the sample chart on your screen shows four colored lines representing four data series: Model, Star Windsor, Box Windsor, and West Windsor. Carl's plan was to plot only three data series: the Box Windsor sales, the Star Windsor Sales, and the West Windsor sales.

The ChartWizard, however, plotted the range A4:F4 as an additional data series. The cells in this range contain the label "Model" and the values 1992, 1993, 1994, and 1995. These values are represented by the dark blue chart line that appears on the x-axis. Carl wants to use these values as labels instead of data, so he needs to revise the ChartWizard settings. Let's look at the options in the ChartWizard - Step 4 of 5 dialog box to find out how to do this.

The first dialog box option, "Data Series in:," lets you specify whether the data series are in rows or columns. Looking at Carl's sketch, you see that the data series are in rows. For example, the first line on the chart should plot the Star Windsor sales in row 5: $256,328; $197,108; $322,522; and $418,679. The Rows option button is selected in the dialog box. This is correct, so Carl does not need to change this setting.

The second dialog box option, "Use first __ Row(s) for Category (X) Axis Labels," lets you specify whether you want to use any rows as category labels for the x-axis. The first row that Carl highlighted for the chart contains the values 1992, 1993, 1994, and 1995. Carl wants to use these values as the category labels, so he needs to change the setting to 1. Before doing that, let's look at the last option in the dialog box.

The third dialog box option, "Use First __ columns for Legend Text" lets you specify whether you want to use any columns for the legend text. The first column that Carl highlighted for the chart was column A, which contains the name of each stove model. Carl wants to use the labels in this column as legend text so the chart clearly shows which line represents the sales data for each stove. Excel automatically selects the first column for the legend text. Carl does not need to change the setting for this option.

Carl needs to change the setting for the Category (X) Axis Labels, so that the values in the first row become the x-axis labels instead of the first data series. Let's do that now.

To use the first row for x-axis labels:

❶ Click the **up arrow button** for the Category (X) Axis Labels option to select 1 as the new setting. See Figure 5-19.

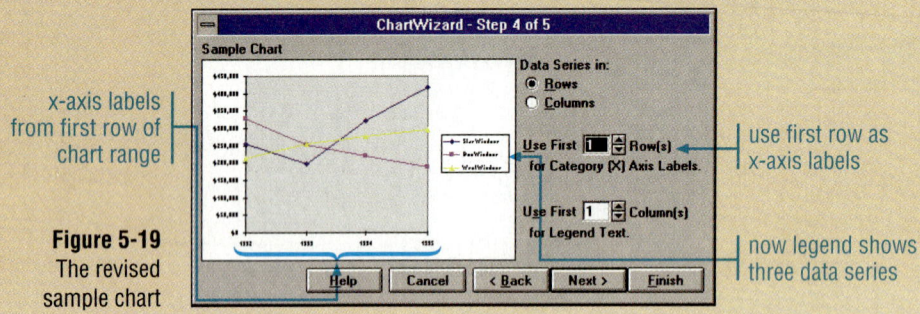

Figure 5-19
The revised sample chart

Carl likes the layout of the revised chart. The x-axis is labeled with the years, the legend box contains the labels for each stove model, and the chart displays one colored line for each stove model. Let's complete the chart by adding the chart title and the x-axis title.

To add the chart title and x-axis title:

❶ Click the **Next >** button to display the ChartWizard - Step 5 of 5 dialog box.

❷ Click the **Chart Title box**, then type **Sales by Model 1992–1995** as the chart title, but don't press [Enter]. You also need to type the x-axis title.

  TROUBLE? If you inadvertently pressed [Enter] and the ChartWizard disappeared, don't worry about it for now; just continue with Step 5.

❸ Press **[Tab]** to move the pointer to the Category (X) box.

❹ Type **Sales Year** and press **[Enter]** to complete the chart and display it on the Line Chart sheet. See Figure 5-20.

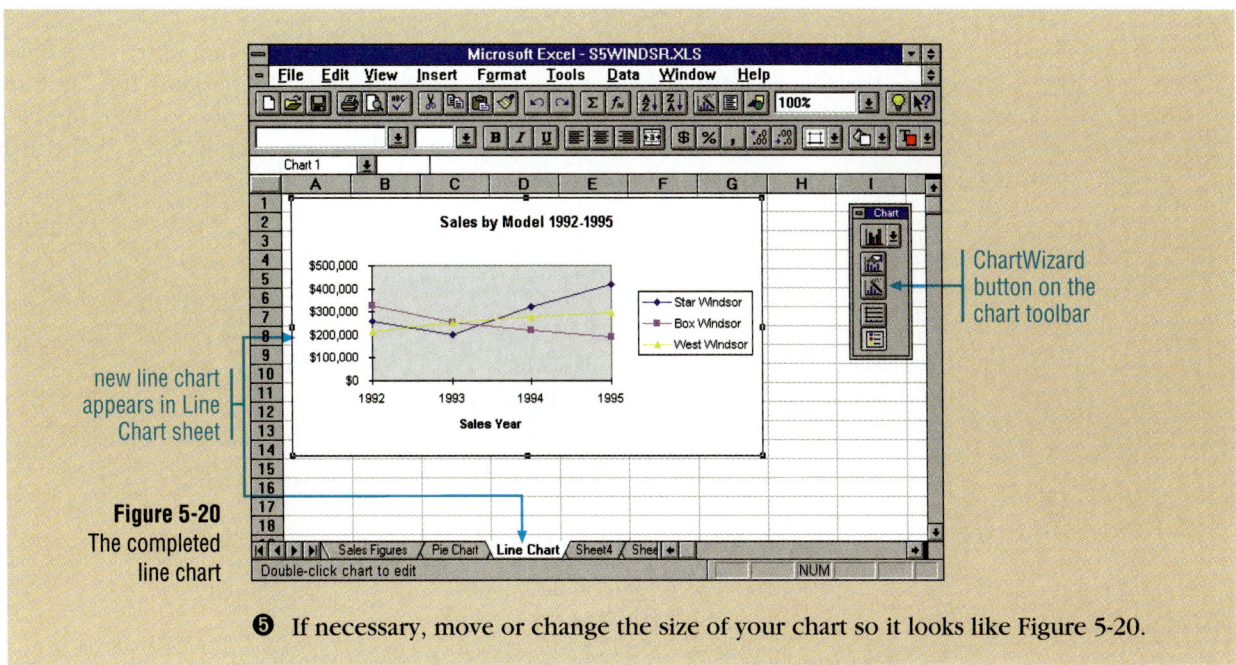

Figure 5-20
The completed line chart

5. If necessary, move or change the size of your chart so it looks like Figure 5-20.

Carl is concerned because the chart shows that the sales of the Star Windsor declined between 1992 and 1993. He thinks he could make a stronger point if he includes only the years 1993 through 1995 in the chart. But can he revise the chart without starting over?

Revising the Chart Data Series

After you create a chart, you might discover that you specified the wrong data range, or you might decide that your chart should display different data series. Whatever your reason, you do not need to start over if you want to revise the chart's data series.

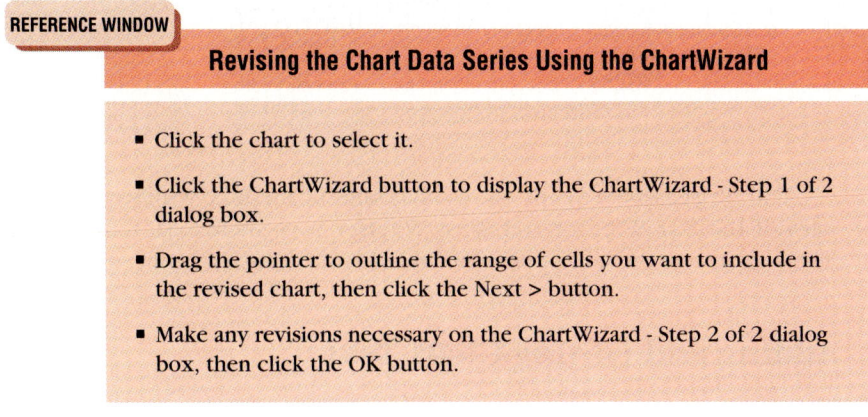

REFERENCE WINDOW

Revising the Chart Data Series Using the ChartWizard

- Click the chart to select it.
- Click the ChartWizard button to display the ChartWizard - Step 1 of 2 dialog box.
- Drag the pointer to outline the range of cells you want to include in the revised chart, then click the Next > button.
- Make any revisions necessary on the ChartWizard - Step 2 of 2 dialog box, then click the OK button.

Carl will use the ChartWizard to revise the data series for his line chart. This time, he'll use the ChartWizard button on the Chart toolbar. He wants to show the sales for each stove during the period 1993 through 1995, instead of the period 1992 through 1995. He examines his worksheet and sees that he needs to select range A4:A7 as the text for the legend and range C4:E7 as the data series.

To revise the line chart:

1. If the line chart is not selected, click it to display the small black handles.

2. Click the **ChartWizard button** on the chart toolbar to display the ChartWizard - Step 1 of 2 dialog box on the Sales Figures sheet. See Figure 5-20 for the location of the ChartWizard button on the Chart toolbar.

3. Highlight cells A4 through A7 for the first range, then release the mouse button.

   TROUBLE? If the ChartWizard dialog box hides the range you need to highlight, drag the title of the dialog box to a new location.

4. Press and hold **[Ctrl]** while you highlight cells C4 through E7.

5. Release the mouse button, then release [Ctrl].

6. Make sure the Range box displays
   ='Sales Figures'!$A$4:$A$7,'Sales Figures'!$C$4:$E$7, then click the
   Next > button to display the ChartWizard - Step 2 of 2 dialog box.

7. Look at the sample chart to verify that it now shows three years on the x-axis. (You probably can't actually read the labels, but you should be able to tell if they're displayed at all.) Don't worry if the dates are split onto two lines.

8. Click the **OK button** to close the ChartWizard dialog box and return to the Line Chart sheet. See Figure 5-21.

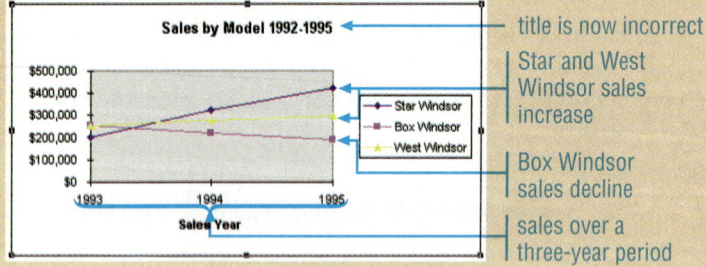

Figure 5-21
The revised line chart

- title is now incorrect
- Star and West Windsor sales increase
- Box Windsor sales decline
- sales over a three-year period

The revised chart clearly shows that sales of the Box Windsor have decreased, while sales of the Star Windsor and West Windsor have increased. Carl notices that he now needs to change the text of the chart title to reflect the revisions.

Adding and Editing Chart Text

Excel classifies the text on your charts into three categories: label text, attached text, or unattached text. **Label text** includes the category names, the tick mark labels, the x-axis labels, and the legend text. Label text is often derived from the cells on the worksheet and is usually specified using the ChartWizard or the Edit Series command on the Chart menu.

Adding and Editing Chart Text   EX 179

Attached text includes the chart title, the x-axis title, and the y-axis title. Attached text appears in a predefined position. You can edit attached text and move it by clicking and dragging. To add attached text, you use the Titles command on the Insert menu. To edit attached text, you click the text, then type the changes.

Unattached text includes text boxes or comments that you type on the chart. You can position unattached text anywhere on the chart. To add unattached text to a chart, you use the Text Box tool.

As noted earlier, Carl needs to change the chart title to reflect the revised data series. To do this he must activate the chart, select the chart title, then change "1992" to "1993."

To revise the chart title:

❶ Double-click the chart to activate it.

❷ Click the chart title to select it and display the gray border and small black handles. See Figure 5-22.

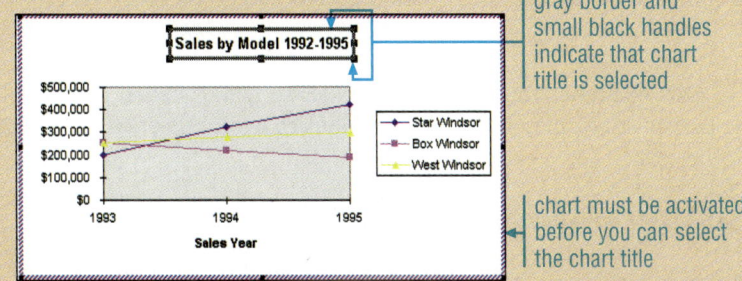

Figure 5-22
Revising the chart title

❸ Position the I-bar pointer in the chart title text box just to the right of "1992," then click to display the flashing insertion point.

❹ Press **[Backspace]** to delete the 2, then type **3** to change 1992 to 1993.

❺ Click anywhere on the chart to complete the change.

Carl checks his original sketch and notices that he forgot to include a y-axis title. He uses the Titles... command to add this title.

To add a y-axis title:

❶ Make sure the chart is still activated.

❷ Click **Insert**, then click **Titles...** to display the Titles dialog box.

❸ Click the **Value (Y) Axis option button** to indicate that you want to add a title for the y-axis.

❹ Click the **OK button** to close the Titles dialog box. Eight black handles and a gray border appear, surrounding the letter "Y" on the y-axis.

❺ Type **Sales ($U.S.)**. Notice that the letters appear in the formula bar as you type.

❻ Press **[Enter]** to add the y-axis title to the chart.

TROUBLE? If you need to revise the y-axis title after you press [Enter], make sure the title is selected, then type your revisions in the formula bar.

Now that the titles accurately describe the chart data, Carl sees that all he has left to do is format the chart labels.

Using Boldface for the Legend and Axis Labels

You can change the format of any chart text by using the Standard toolbar buttons or the Format menu. Each text item on a chart is an object; as with any object, you must click the object to select it before you can change it.

Carl looks at the chart and decides that it will look better if he bolds the legend text and the category labels along the x-axis.

To bold the legend text and the category labels:
1. Make sure the chart is still activated, then click the chart legend to select it and display the square black handles.
2. Click the **Bold button** to change the font in the chart legend to bold.
3. Click the **x-axis**, the bottom horizontal line of the chart. Two square handles appear on the x-axis.
4. Click to change the x-axis text to bold.

Carl examines the chart and decides to make several additional enhancements. First, he decides to display horizontal gridlines to make the chart easier to read.

Adding Horizontal Gridlines to a Chart

You can add horizontal gridlines to most types of 2-D and 3-D charts. Gridlines stretch from one axis across the chart to provide a visual guide for more easily estimating the value or category of each data marker. You can specify gridlines when you select the format for your chart using the ChartWizard, or you can add gridlines later by activating the chart and using the Gridlines... command from the Insert menu.

To add horizontal gridlines to the chart:
1. Make sure the chart is still activated, then click the **Horizontal Gridlines button** on the Chart toolbar. Horizontal gridlines appear on the chart. See Figure 5-23.

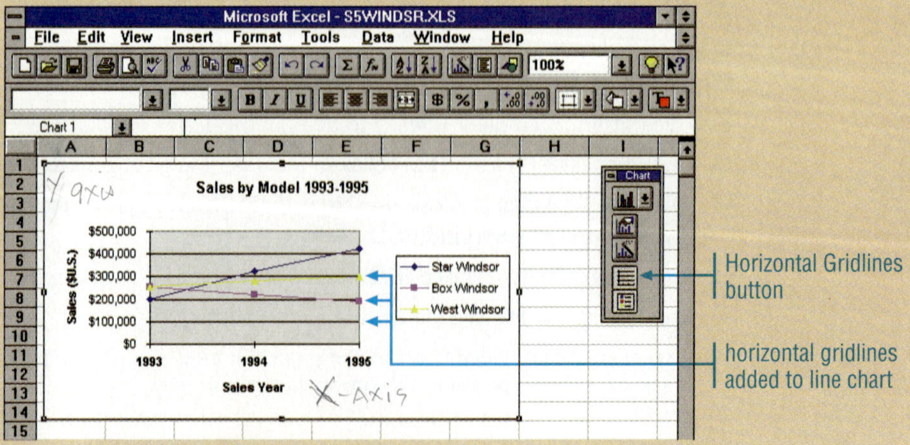

Figure 5-23
Adding horizontal gridlines

Next Carl wants to improve the appearance of the lines that represent data on the chart.

Formatting Chart Lines

You can change the format or appearance of the lines and data markers on a chart. In this case, Carl wants to make each chart line thicker. Excel provides a variety of line colors, line styles such as dashed lines and dotted lines, and line weights or thicknesses. Excel also provides a variety of data marker colors and styles, such as triangles, squares, and circles. As with any changes you make to a chart, the chart must be activated before you can change the appearance of the chart lines.

Each chart line is an object, so when you want to format a chart line, you must first select the chart line to display the handles. Once you select a chart line, you can apply formats using the Data Series dialog box.

To format the chart lines:

❶ Make sure the chart is still activated, then click the blue line that represents the sales trend for the Star Windsor stove. When the line is selected, handles appear. Also, the formula bar displays the address of the cells containing each data point represented on the line.

TROUBLE? If you are using a monochrome monitor, refer to Figure 5-24 for the location of the blue line.

❷ Click **Format**, click **Selected Data Series...**, then click the **Patterns tab** in the Format Data Series dialog box.

❸ Click the **Weight box down arrow button** to display the available line weights. Click the thickest line weight to select it.

❹ Click the **OK button** to make the changes.

❺ Repeat Steps 1 through 5, but select the pink line that represents Box Windsor sales.

❻ Repeat Steps 1 through 5, but select the yellow line that represents West Windsor sales.

❼ Click any empty area of the chart to deselect the line representing West Windsor sales. Your chart should look like Figure 5-24.

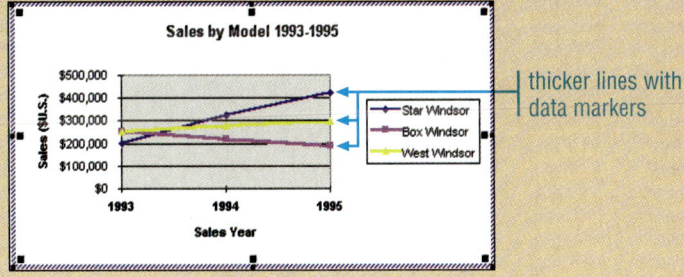

Figure 5-24
The completed line chart

❽ Click the **Save button** to save the workbook.

Carl is pleased with the line chart because it supports his argument for allocating less catalog space to the Box Windsor stove. Carl wants to drive his point home by creating a column chart that compares the total dollar sales for each model.

If you want to take a break and resume the tutorial at a later time, you can exit Excel by double-clicking the Control menu box in the upper-left corner of the screen. When you resume the tutorial, launch Excel, maximize the Microsoft Excel and Book1 windows, and place your Student Disk in the disk drive. Open the file S5WINDSR.XLS, then continue with the tutorial.

Creating a Column Chart

As you saw in Figure 5-2, Excel's **column chart** type uses vertical bars to represent data. You might want to call this a "column chart," but Excel has another chart type called a bar chart that uses horizontal bars to represent data. Both the column chart and the bar chart are excellent choices if you want to show comparisons. It is easy to construct either of these chart types with the ChartWizard.

Carl decides that he wants to make a column chart to compare the total sales of each stove model for the entire four-year period. Figure 5-25 shows Carl's sketch of this chart. He examines his worksheet and notes that the data labels are located in column A. The data series for the column chart is located in column F.

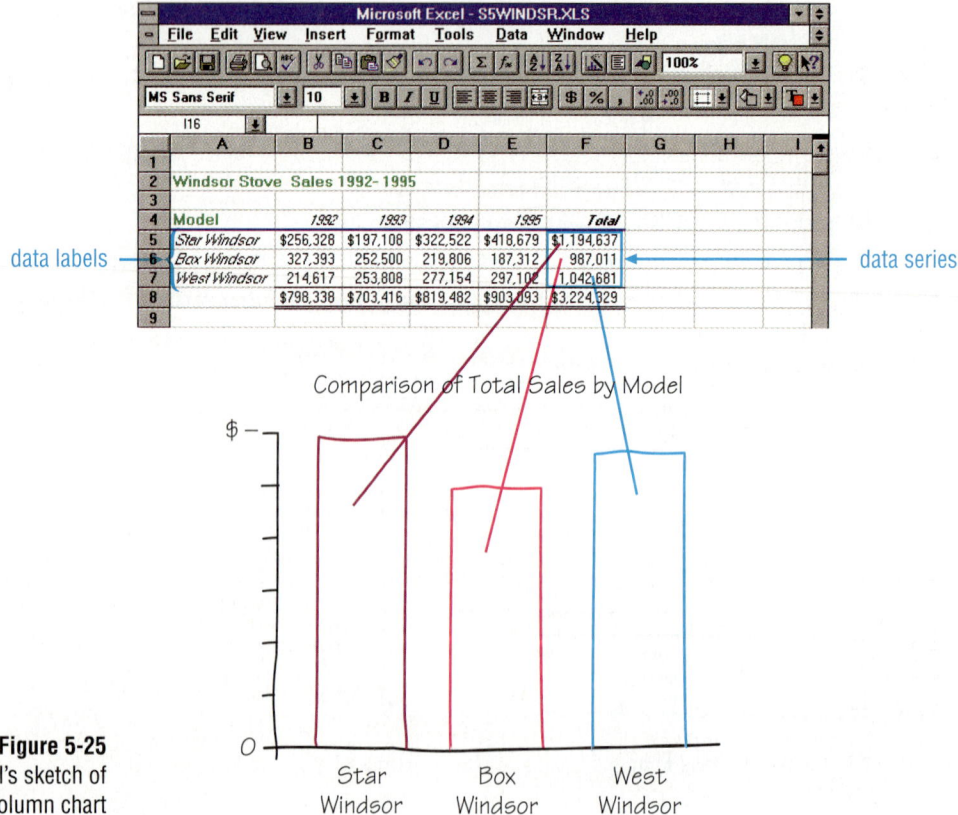

Figure 5-25
Carl's sketch of the column chart

To create the column chart, Carl renames a blank sheet. Then he selects the nonadjacent ranges that contain the data labels and the data series.

To rename Sheet4 and then select the non-adjacent ranges for the column chart:
1. Double-click the **Sheet4 tab** to open the Rename Sheet dialog box.
2. Type **Column Chart** in the Name box, then click the **OK button**.
3. To return to the sheet containing the data you want to graph, click the **Sales Figures tab**.
4. Highlight cells A5 through A7, which contain the labels for the chart.
5. Press and hold **[Ctrl]** while you highlight cells F5 through F7, which contain the data for the chart.
6. Release [Ctrl], then release the mouse button.

Next, Carl uses the ChartWizard to create a column chart in the Column Chart sheet.

To create the column chart:
1. Click the **ChartWizard tool**.
2. Click the **Column Chart tab** to activate the sheet where you want to create the chart.
3. Drag the pointer from cell A1 to cell G18 to outline the area where the chart should appear. Release the mouse button and the ChartWizard - Step 1 of 5 dialog box appears.
4. Make sure the range is ='Sales Figures'!$A$5:$A$7,'Sales Figures'!$F$5:$F$7, then click the **Next > button** to display the ChartWizard - Step 2 of 5 dialog box.
5. Double-click the **Column** chart type to display the chart formats.
6. Double-click chart format **2**. ChartWizard - Step 4 of 5 displays the sample chart.

Carl compares the sample chart to his sketch to make sure that the ChartWizard option buttons are set correctly. The chart appears to be what Carl expected, so he continues to the next step.

7. Click the **Next > button** to continue.
8. Click the **Chart Title** box, then type **Comparison of Total Sales by Model**.
9. Click the **Finish button** to complete the chart and view it on the worksheet. See Figure 5-26. Change the size of your chart, if necessary, so it looks like the figure.

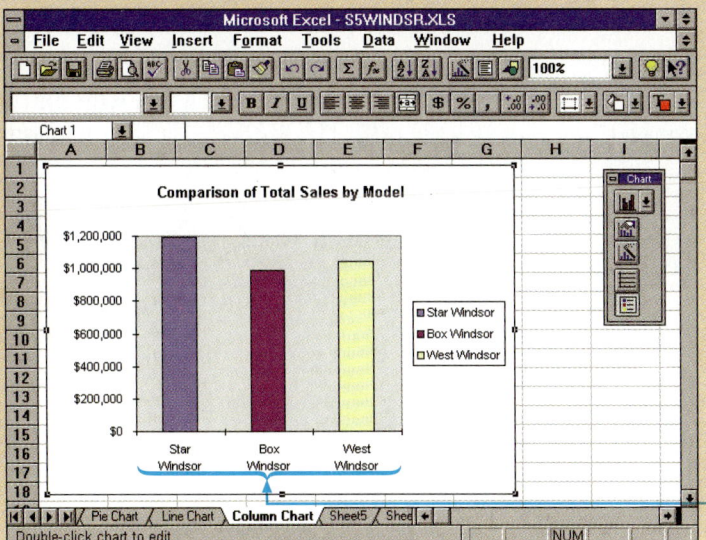

Figure 5-26
The column chart embedded in the worksheet

adjust the size of the chart if the labels are not formatted like this

Carl has heard that it is possible to use pictures instead of colored bars for bar charts and column charts in Excel. Carl decides to try using a picture in this chart.

Using Pictures in a Column Chart

When the ChartWizard creates a column or bar chart, it uses a plain bar as the data marker. You can add visual impact to your charts by using pictures or graphical objects instead of a plain bar. You can stretch or shrink these pictures to show the chart values, or you can create a stack of pictures to show the chart values.

REFERENCE WINDOW

Creating a Picture Chart

- Create a bar or column chart using the ChartWizard.
- Switch to the Windows application that contains the picture you want to use.
- Copy the picture to the Clipboard.
- Return to Excel.
- Select the data marker you want to replace with the picture.
- Click Edit, then click Paste.

Carl remembers that last month, one of the graphic artists in the marketing department created a picture of a stack of money to use in an advertisement. Carl thinks it would be clever to use the picture as the data marker in his column chart. Carl checks with the artist and learns that the filename for the picture is C5MONEY.PCX. His plan is to use the Windows Paintbrush application to open the picture, copy it to the Clipboard, then paste the picture into the columns of the Excel chart.

To copy the picture to the Clipboard:

❶ Press and hold [Alt] while you press [Tab] until a box with the title "Program Manager" appears. Release [Alt]. The Program Manager window appears.

❷ Locate the Accessories window.

TROUBLE? If you can't find the Accessories window, look for the Accessories group icon and double-click it. If you cannot see the Accessories window or group icon, click Window, then click Accessories.

Using Pictures in a Column Chart   **EX 185**

❸ Locate the Paintbrush icon in the Accessories window. Double-click the **Paintbrush icon** to start the Paintbrush application.

❹ On the Paintbrush menu bar, click **File**, then click **Open...** to display the Open dialog box. Make sure the Drives box displays the icon for the drive that contains your Student Disk.

❺ Click the **List Files of Type down arrow button**, then click **PCX files (*.PCX)**.

❻ Double-click **C5MONEY.PCX** to open the file that contains the picture Carl wants to use on the chart. See Figure 5-27.

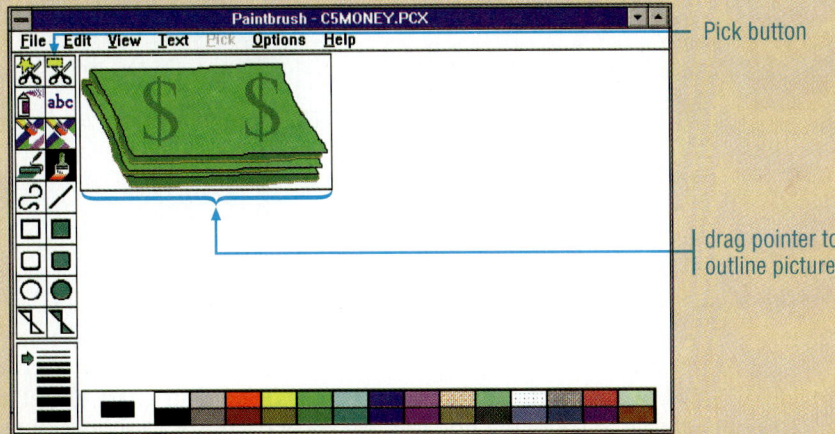

Figure 5-27
Copying the picture to the Clipboard

❼ Click the **Pick button** on the right column of the toolbar. Move the pointer to the drawing area; it changes to +.

❽ Position + in the upper-left corner of the picture. Drag the pointer to outline the picture. Release the mouse button.

❾ On the Paintbrush menu bar, click **Edit**, then click **Copy** to copy the picture to the Clipboard.

❿ Click **File**, then click **Exit** to exit Paintbrush. Minimize the Program Manager window to return to Excel.

TROUBLE? If you see the message "Do you want to save current changes?" click the No button. If you do not return to Excel, press [Alt][Tab] until you see the Excel box.

Now that the picture is on the Clipboard, Carl needs to select one of the columns of the chart, and use the Paste command to replace the plain bars with the picture.

To copy the picture to the column chart:

1. Make sure the entire chart is visible on the screen, then double-click the column chart to activate it.
2. Click any column in the chart. As a result, all three columns display handles.
3. Click **Edit**, then click **Paste** to paste the contents of the Clipboard into the columns. The picture of money appears in each column. See Figure 5-28. Notice that each picture is "stretched" to reflect the different values.

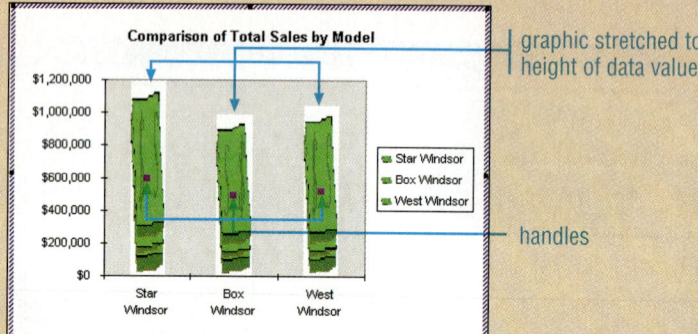

Figure 5-28
The picture chart with stretched graphics

When you paste a picture into a bar or column chart, Excel automatically stretches the picture to show the different values of each bar. Carl doesn't like the way the picture looks when it is stretched. He knows that Excel also provides a way to stack the pictures instead of stretching them, so he decides to try it.

Stretching and Stacking Pictures

The picture or graphical object you use as the data marker on a column chart can be either stretched or stacked to represent the height of the bar. Some pictures stretch well, whereas other pictures become very distorted and detract from, rather than add to, the impact of the chart. You should use your artistic judgment to decide whether to stretch or stack the pictures you use for data markers on your charts.

Carl thinks the money is too distorted when it is stretched, so he tries stacking it instead.

To stack the data marker picture:

1. If the handles have disappeared from the columns, click any column in the chart to select all columns.
2. Click **Format**, click **Selected Data Series...**, then click the **Patterns tab** in the Format Data Series dialog box.

❸ Click **Stack**.

❹ Click the **OK button** to apply the format. See Figure 5-29.

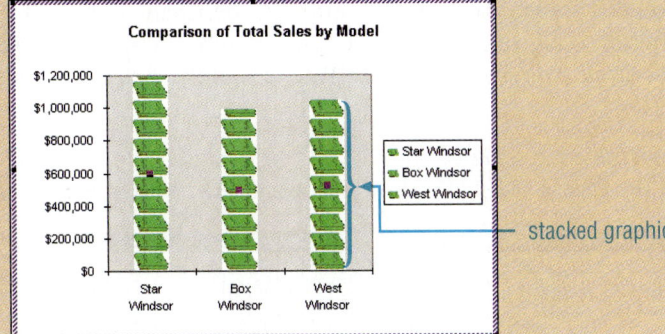

Figure 5-29
The picture chart with stacked graphics

Carl looks at the chart and decides that the stacked graphics effectively show that the Box Windsor stove has produced the lowest dollar volume of the three stove models. He notices that the chart title needs a box around it for emphasis.

Displaying the Title in a Colored Box with a Shadow

As mentioned earlier, the title on a chart is an object that you can select and then format using the menu options and toolbar buttons. To add emphasis to the title, Carl decides to fill the title area with green and then add a thick border around the title. To complete the title format, he creates a shadow effect under the title box.

To display the title in a colored box with a shadow:

❶ Click the title to select it and display the handles.

❷ Click **Format**, click **Selected Chart Title...**, then click the **Patterns tab** in the Format Chart Title dialog box.

❸ Click the **bright green box** in the top row of the Color palette.

TROUBLE? If you have a monochrome system, select a light gray shade.

❹ Click the **Weight box down arrow button** in the Border section to display a list of border weights.

❺ Click the thickest line in the list.

❻ Click **Shadow** to display a shadow under the title.

❼ Click the **OK button** to apply the format.

The chart looks better now that the title is emphasized. Now Carl notices that because all the column markers are identical in color, the chart legend is not necessary. The x-axis labels are sufficient to differentiate between the columns. The easiest way to delete the chart legend is to use the Legend button on the Chart toolbar. If you look closely at the Legend button now, you'll see that it appears to be two-dimensional, indicating that a legend *is* displayed. To remove the chart legend, simply click the Legend button.

To remove the chart legend:
❶ Click the **Legend button**. The chart legend disappears. See Figure 5-30.

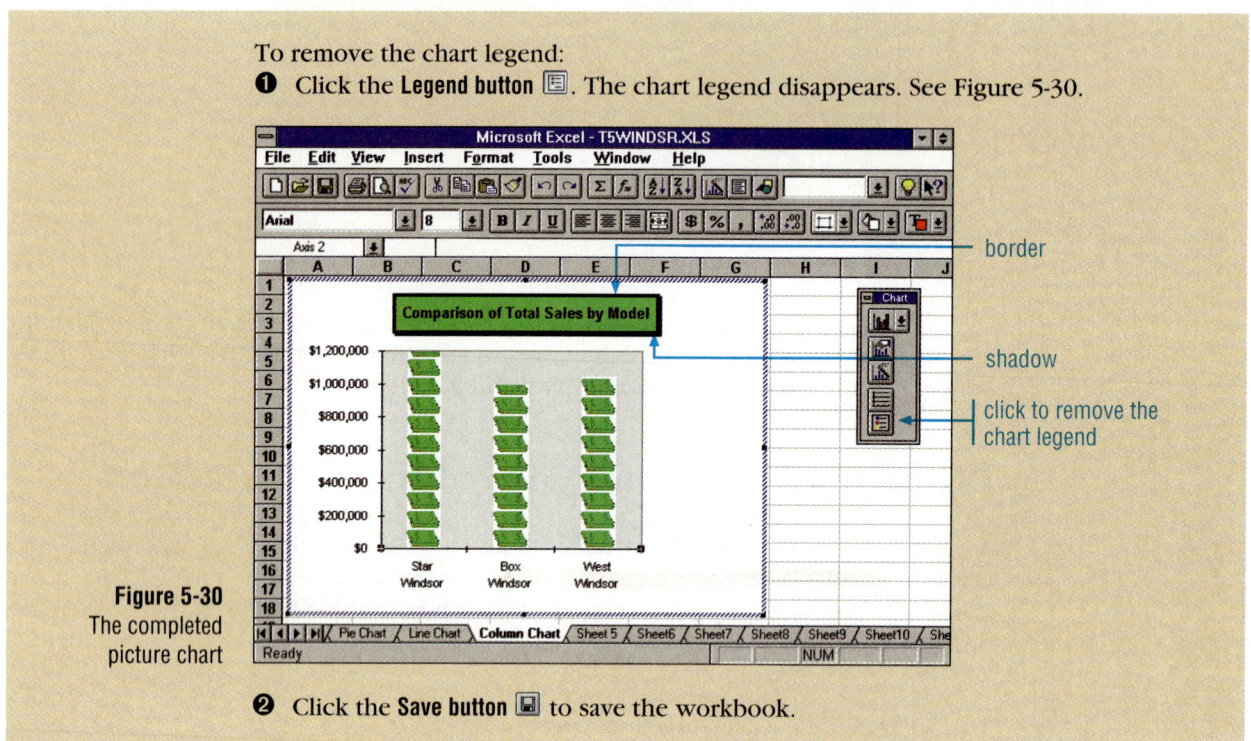

Figure 5-30
The completed picture chart

❷ Click the **Save button** to save the workbook.

The picture chart is complete. Now Carl decides to create a 3-D chart to show the sales figures for each of the three stove models from 1992 to 1995.

If you want to take a break and resume the tutorial at a later time, you can exit Excel by double-clicking the Control menu box in the upper-left corner of the screen. When you resume the tutorial, launch Excel, maximize the Microsoft Excel and Book1 windows, and place your Student Disk in the disk drive. Open the file S5WINDSR.XLS, then continue with the tutorial.

Creating a 3-D Column Chart

A 3-D column chart displays three-dimensional vertical bars plotted on either two or three axes. Excel provides eight different formats for 3-D column charts, as shown in Figure 5-31.

Predefined Chart Format	Format Characteristics
1	Column chart displayed on x, y axes using three-dimensional columns, no gridlines
2	Stacked three-dimensional columns on x, y axes, no gridlines
3	Columns stacked and proportioned to show relationship to 100% of the data series
4	Column chart displayed on x, y, z axes with x-axis and y-axis gridlines
5	Column chart displayed on x, y, z axes using three-dimensional columns, no gridlines
6	Column chart displayed on x, y, z axes using three-dimensional columns and showing gridlines
7	Column chart displayed on x, y, z axes with gridlines, using three-dimensional columns
8	Three-dimensional columns displayed on two-dimensional, x, y axes with gridlines

Figure 5-31
Predefined formats for 3-D column charts

Formats 1, 2, 3, and 4 convey the same information as 2-D column charts but with the added visual appeal of three-dimensional columns. Like their 2-D counterparts, 3-D formats 1, 2, 3, and 4 use two axes: the horizontal x-axis and the vertical y-axis. Formats 5, 6, and 7 display the data on three axes: the x-axis in the front of the chart, the y-axis on the side of the chart, and a vertical axis called the z-axis.

The three-dimensional arrangement of data on a chart with three axes makes it easier to view the data in different ways. For example, suppose you wanted to compare the number of employees in a company that work in clerical and managerial positions. Suppose you also were interested in the number of males and females in clerical and managerial positions. Figure 5-32 shows a 2-D column chart and a 3-D column chart that were created using the same data range. Both charts were designed to compare the number of male, female, clerical, and managerial employees.

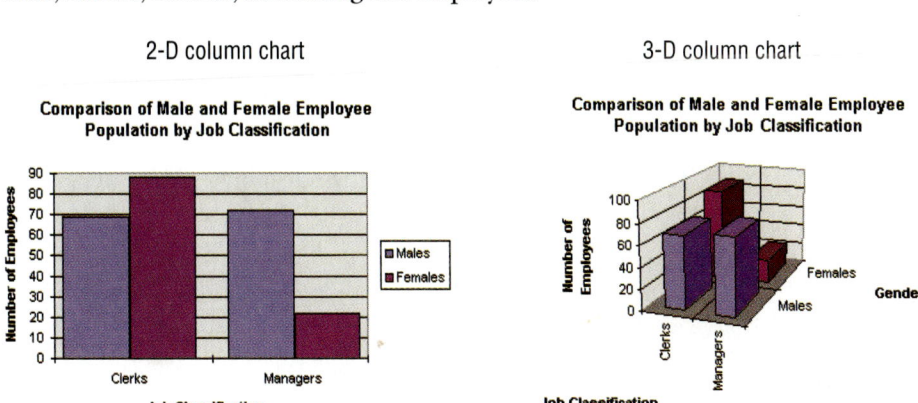

Figure 5-32
2-D and 3-D column charts

The 2-D chart in Figure 5-32 shows the comparison between the number of males and females by job classification. You can see clearly that there are more female clerical workers than males, and that there are fewer female managers. It is not as apparent in this chart that there are more men in clerical positions than in managerial positions. The 3-D column chart in Figure 5-32 shows comparisons based on both gender and job classification.

Carl wants to create a 3-D column chart to compare the sales data in two ways. He wants it to show the sales trends by model; for example, how the sales of the Star Windsor changed from 1992 to 1995. He also wants the chart to show sales by year; for example, the relative sales of each model in 1995. Carl thinks that a 3-D column chart will make it easier to examine the sales data by year or by model.

Carl's sketch of the 3-D column chart is shown in Figure 5-33, along with a note about the two relationships that he wants the chart to illustrate. It is not easy to draw a 3-D column chart by hand so Carl's sketch is not complete, but he tries to show what will appear on each of the three axes of the graph.

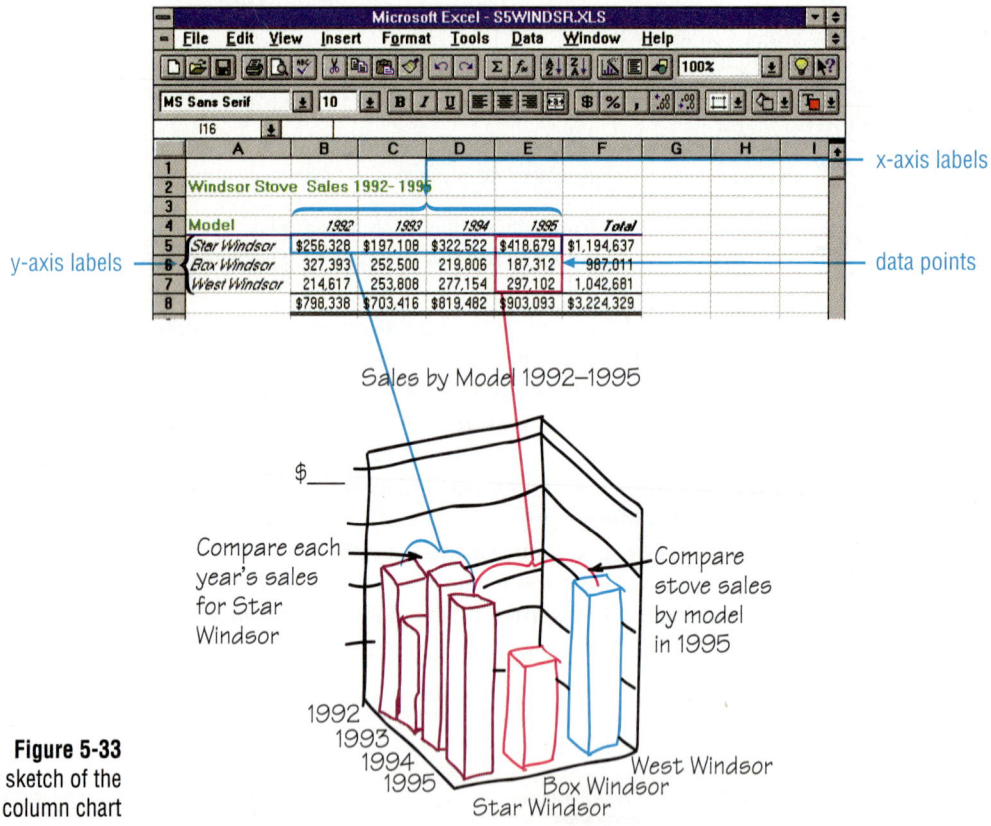

Figure 5-33
Carl's sketch of the 3-D column chart

Carl begins creating the chart by renaming a blank sheet and then selecting the range for the data series.

To rename a blank sheet and select the range for the 3-D column chart:
❶ Double-click the **Sheet5 tab** to open the Rename Sheet dialog box.

TROUBLE? If you can't see the Sheet5 tab, use the scroll arrows to the left of the sheet tabs to display the Sheet5 tab.

Creating a 3-D Column Chart **EX 191**

❷ Type **3-D Column Chart** in the Name box, then click the **OK button**.
❸ To return to the sheet containing the data you want to graph, click the **Sales Figures tab**.
❹ Highlight cells A4 through E7, then release the mouse button.

Next, Carl uses the ChartWizard to position the chart on the 3-D Column Chart sheet, select the chart type, select the chart format, and enter the chart text.

To create the chart using the ChartWizard:
❶ Click the **ChartWizard icon** 📊.
❷ Click the **3-D Column Chart tab** to activate the sheet where you want the chart to appear.
❸ Hold down the mouse button and drag the pointer from cell A1 to cell G15 to outline the range where you want the chart to appear. Release the mouse button and the ChartWizard - Step 1 of 5 dialog box appears.
❹ Make sure the range is ='Sales Figures'!$A$4:$E$7, then click the **Next > button** to display the ChartWizard - Step 2 of 5 dialog box.
❺ Double-click the **3-D Column chart type** to display the ChartWizard - Step 3 of 5 dialog box.
❻ Double-click chart format **6** to view the sample chart. See Figure 5-34.

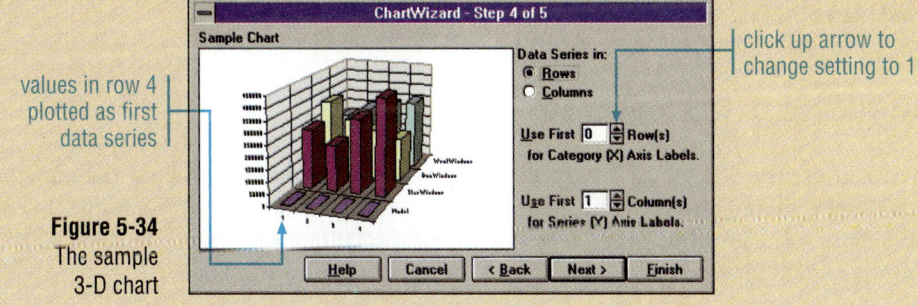

Figure 5-34
The sample 3-D chart

Compare the sample chart on your screen with Carl's sketch in Figure 5-33. The sample chart shows that Excel used the values in row 4 as the first data series. This is the same problem Carl encountered when he created the line chart. Carl must tell Excel to use the values in row 4 (the first row of the chart range) as x-axis labels, not as a data series.

To tell Excel to use the values in row 4 as x-axis labels:
❶ Click the **up arrow button** to change the Category (X) Axis Labels setting to 1.

Now the chart looks more like Carl's sketch. Let's add the title to complete the chart.

❷ Click the **Next > button** to continue to the next ChartWizard step.
❸ Click the **Chart Title box** to activate the flashing insertion point.
❹ Type **Sales by Model 1992–1995** and click the **Finish button** to complete the chart. See Figure 5-35.

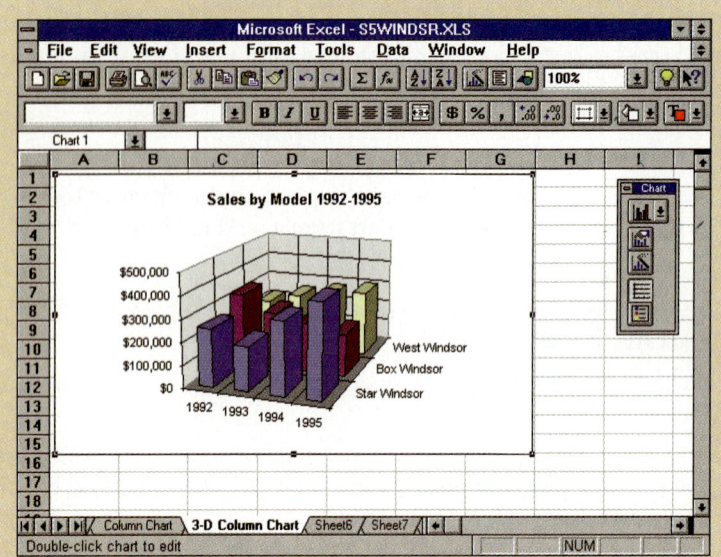

Figure 5-35
The 3-D column chart embedded in the worksheet

❺ If necessary, drag the handles to change the dimensions of the chart to display all the chart text.

Carl notices that some of the bars are hidden by other bars. He can fix this by rotating the chart.

Rotating a 3-D Column Chart

You can use the 3-D View dialog box on the Format menu to rotate a 3-D column chart by ten-degree increments in either a clockwise or counterclockwise direction. By rotating the chart you can display the clearest view of the columns or draw attention to the data from a certain viewpoint.

To rotate the chart:
❶ Double-click the 3-D column chart to activate the chart.
❷ Click **Format**, then click **3-D View...** to display the Format 3-D View dialog box. See Figure 5-36.

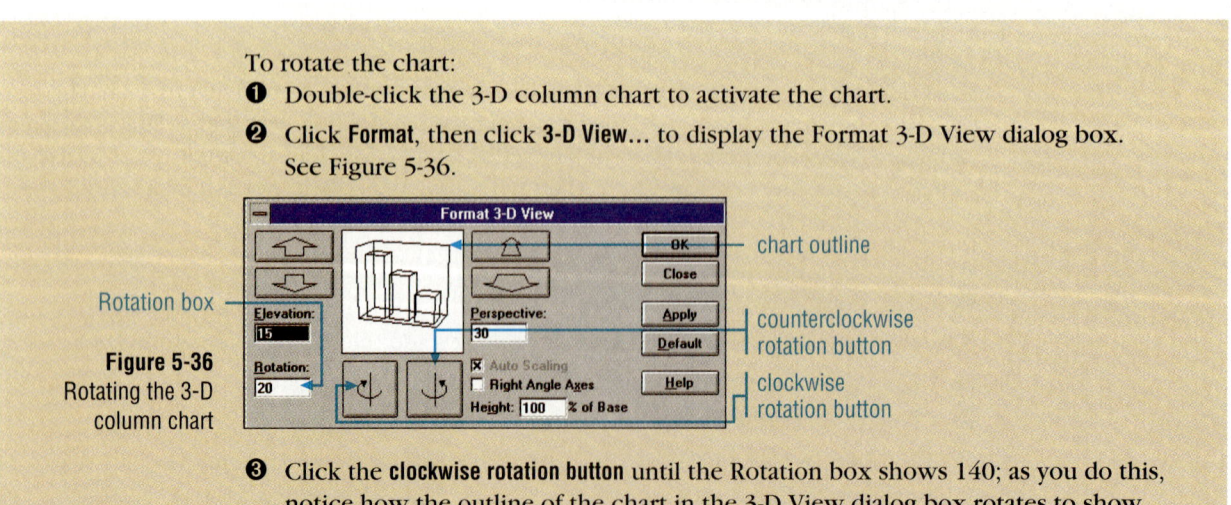

Figure 5-36
Rotating the 3-D column chart

❸ Click the **clockwise rotation button** until the Rotation box shows 140; as you do this, notice how the outline of the chart in the 3-D View dialog box rotates to show the new position.

❹ Click the **OK button** to apply the changes. The chart is now rotated to make it easier to see all the columns.

❺ Enlarge the chart by dragging the handle in the lower-right corner until you can see all the x- and y-axis labels displayed horizontally. You might need to drag the handle until part of the chart scrolls off the screen.

TROUBLE? If you enlarge the chart so that it scrolls off the screen, you may see the chart displayed in a chart window the next time you activate it. This is Excel's way of allowing you to view the entire chart without scrolling. You can treat the chart in the chart window exactly as you would an activated chart with a thick border.

Applying a Border Around a Chart

You can customize the border that appears around a chart by using the options in the Patterns dialog box. A border helps to define a chart and to make it visually appealing. For good visual balance, the weight of the chart border should be equivalent to the weight of the chart elements—a chart with vividly colored columns and large, bold text elements should have a thicker border than a line chart with a lighter text font. Carl wants to put a thick, black border around the 3-D column chart.

To apply a black border around the chart:

❶ Click any blank space in the upper-left corner of the chart window. Eight handles appear inside the chart border indicating that the chart border is selected.

❷ Click **Format**, click **Selected Chart Area...**, then click the **Patterns tab** in the Format Chart Area dialog box.

❸ Click the **Weight box down arrow button**, then click the thickest line.

❹ Click the **OK button** to apply the changes.

❺ Click anywhere outside the chart border to deactivate the chart.

❻ If necessary, use the black handles on the chart border to adjust the size of the chart so it looks like Figure 5-37.

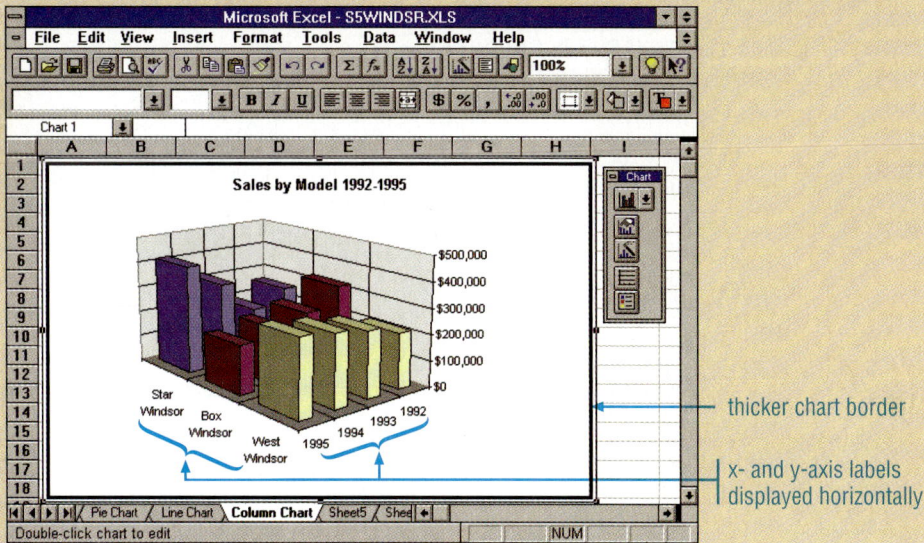

Figure 5-37
The completed 3-D column chart

The fourth chart is complete and Carl saves the workbook.

❼ Click the **Save button** 🖫 to save the workbook.

Previewing and Printing the Worksheet and Charts

Carl has four charts arranged vertically on four different sheets. What would the printed results look like? Carl uses the Print Preview button to find out.

To preview the 3-D Column chart before printing:

❶ Make sure the 3-D Column chart sheet is still on your screen.

❷ Click the **Print Preview button** 🔍 to preview the chart. The chart appears in the Print Preview window.

❸ If necessary, click the **Next button** to view the second page. (Don't worry if your chart doesn't fit on one page, you'll change the orientation to landscape in the next set of steps.)

Carl decides to use the scaling option in the Page Setup dialog box to enlarge the chart when it is printed. He also changes the orientation to landscape.

To adjust the Page Setup options:

❶ Click the **Setup... button** at the top of the Print Preview dialog box, then click the **Page tab** to display the Page Setup dialog box.

❷ Click **Landscape** to select landscape orientation.

❸ In the Scaling box, change Adjust to: to **125%**.

❹ Click the **Margins tab**.

❺ Click the **Horizontally box** and click the **Vertically box** to put an × in each box.

❻ Click the **sheet tab**.

❼ If an × appears in the Print Gridlines box, remove it so the gridlines will not appear on the printout.

❽ If an × appears in the Row & Column Headings box, remove it so the row and column headings will not appear on the printout.

❾ Click the **OK button** to return to the print preview and view the result of the revised page setup settings.

TROUBLE? If some of the chart text appears to be cut off, click the Zoom button to get a more accurate preview of the output.

❿ Click the **Close button** to return to the worksheet.

Now Carl will adjust the settings for the remaining sheets in the workbook.

Previewing and Printing the Worksheet and Charts   **EX 195**

To adjust the Page Setup options for the remaining sheets:

❶ Click the **Column Chart tab**. If necessary, use the scroll arrows on the sheet tab scroll bar to display the sheet tabs as you need them. See Figure 5-38.

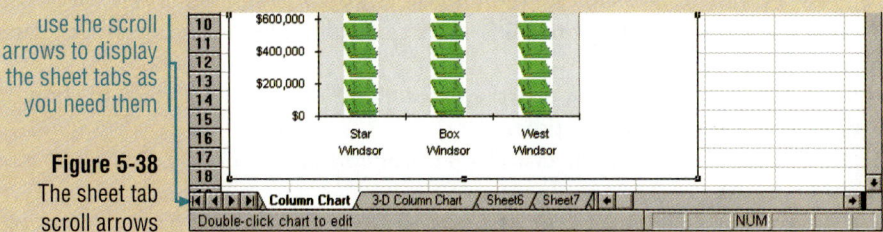

use the scroll arrows to display the sheet tabs as you need them

Figure 5-38
The sheet tab scroll arrows

❷ Click the **Print Preview button**, click the **Setup... button**, then click the **Page tab** to display the Page Setup dialog box.

❸ Click **Landscape** to select landscape orientation. In the Scaling box, change Adjust to: to **125%**.

❹ Click the **Margins tab**.

❺ Click the **Horizontally box** and click the **Vertically box** to put an × in each box.

❻ Click the **sheet tab**.

❼ If an × appears in the Print Gridlines box, remove it so the gridlines will not appear on the printout.

❽ If an × appears in the Row & Column Headings box, remove it so the row and column headings will not appear on the printout.

❾ Click the **OK button** to return to the print preview and view the result of the revised page setup settings, then click the **Close button** to return to the worksheet.

❿ Repeat Steps 2 through 9 for the Line Chart sheet, the Pie Chart sheet, and the Sales Figures sheet. Remember to use the scroll arrows on the sheet tab scroll bar to display the sheet tabs as you need them.

Carl likes the way his charts will print. He plans to print the charts on transparencies using a color printer. He will use an overhead projector to present the charts at the department meeting.

You do not need to print the charts from this tutorial now because you will have an opportunity to print them when you do the Tutorial Assignments. While Carl prints his charts, let's exit the print preview and save the workbook with the print specifications.

To exit the print preview and save the workbook:

❶ Click the **Save button**.

❷ Double-click the **document window Control menu box**.

❸ Exit Excel if you are not proceeding directly to the Tutorial Assignments.

In this tutorial Carl created a 3-D pie chart, a line chart, a column chart, and a 3-D column chart. He modified the charts by formatting text, adding titles, adding gridlines, formatting chart lines, adding a border, and selecting chart colors. He adjusted the page setup options to position each chart to create an effective set of color transparencies for his presentation.

Tips for Creating Charts

Excel includes many additional chart types, chart formats, and chart options. You will have an opportunity to use some of these in the Tutorial Assignments and Case Problems at the end of this tutorial. Here are some hints that should help you construct charts that effectively represent your data.

- Use a line chart, a 3-D line chart, an area chart, or a 3-D area chart to show trends or change over a period of time.
- Use a column chart, a bar chart, a 3-D column chart, or a 3-D bar chart to show comparisons.
- Use a pie chart or a 3-D pie chart to show the relationship or proportion of parts to a whole.
- Before you begin to construct a chart using Excel, locate the cell ranges on the worksheet that contain the data series you want to chart and locate the cell range that contains the x-axis labels. Then draw a sketch showing the x-axis, the x-axis title, the x-axis category labels, the y-axis, the y-axis title, y-axis labels, and the data series.
- Design the chart so that viewers can understand the main point at first glance. Too much detail can make a chart difficult to interpret.
- Chart consistent categories of data. For example, if you want to chart monthly income, do not include the year-to-date income as one of the data points.
- Every chart should have a descriptive title, a title for the x-axis, a title for the y-axis, and category labels.

Questions

1. Identify each of the numbered elements in Figure 5-39.

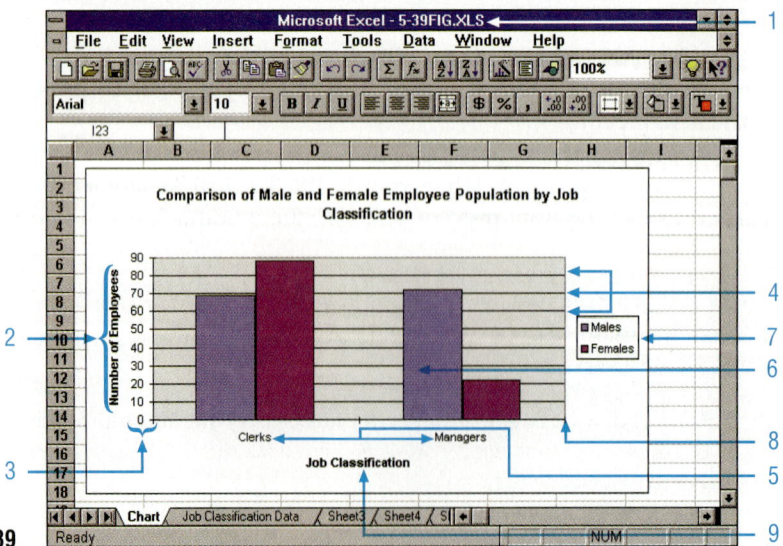

Figure 5-39

2. Write a one-sentence definition for each of the following terms:
   a. data point
   b. data marker
   c. data series
   d. non-adjacent range
3. Explain the difference between a chart type and a chart format.
4. List the chart types that are effective for showing change over time.
5. When do you need to activate a chart?
6. How many data series can you show using a pie chart?
7. List the chart types that are effective for showing comparisons.
8. Describe how Carl set up his workbook so each chart would be displayed on a separate sheet.
9. Suppose you wanted to use the data from Figure 5-1 to chart the sales trend for the Star Windsor stove.
   a. What range contains the category (x) axis labels?
   b. What range contains the data series?
   c. Would you include cell F5 in the data range? Why or why not?
   d. How many data series would you chart?
10. Describe the advantage of using a 3-D pie chart rather than a 2-D pie chart.
11. Explain how to rotate a 3-D chart.
12. Use your library resources to research the topic of graphing (called charting in Excel). Compile a one- to two-page list of tips for creating effective graphs (charts). Make sure you include a bibliography.
13. Look for examples of charts in magazines, books, or the textbooks you use for other courses. Select one chart and photocopy it.
    a. Label each of the chart components.
    b. Write a one-page evaluation of the effectiveness of the chart. Explain how the chart might be improved.

Tutorial Assignments

Carl wants to create a line chart that shows the change in total stove sales between 1992 and 1995. To do this:
1. Open the file T5WINDSR.XLS.
2. Save the file under the new name S5CHARTS.XLS.
3. Rename Sheet6 "Line Chart #2."
4. On the Sales Figures sheet highlight the non-adjacent ranges that contain the dates and the total sales.
5. Use the ChartWizard to create a chart positioned between rows 1 and 16 of the Line Chart #2 sheet.
6. Continue using the ChartWizard to select the Line chart type and format 2.
7. Use first row for the Category (X) Axis Labels at the prompt.
8. Enter "Total Stove Sales 1992–1995" as the chart title.
9. Activate the chart and make the chart line thicker.
10. Remove the chart legend.

Charts such as those Carl created in the tutorial are part of a series of related charts and, therefore, should have similar formats. To standardize the format of the charts that Carl created, do the following for each chart:
11. Put a box around the title of the chart.
12. Fill the title box with the bright green color and put a shadow under it.
13. Select yellow for the background color of the chart and put a thick border around the entire chart.
14. Bold all the text in the chart and adjust the chart size, as necessary, so that the chart text is formatted correctly.

After you have completed the format changes for each chart, do the following:
15. Revise the worksheet header so it includes your name, the filename, and the date.
16. Preview the new charts. Adjust the page setup options as necessary to print each chart centered on the page, enlarged to 125%, without gridlines.
17. Save the workbook, then select and print each chart. (You could choose the Entire Workbook option in the Print dialog box, and print the entire workbook at once, but you may have problems getting the charts to print properly.)

Case Problems

1. Charting Production Data at TekStar Electronics

Julia Backes is the Executive Assistant to the President of TekStar Electronics, a manufacturer of consumer electronics. Julia is compiling the yearly manufacturing reports. She has collected the production totals for each of TekStar's four manufacturing plants and has created a worksheet containing the production totals. Julia has asked you to help her create a 3-D pie chart and a column chart to accompany the report.

To help Julia create a 3-D pie chart showing the relative percentage of CD players produced at the four plants:
1. Open the file P5PROD.XLS.
2. Use the ChartWizard to create the 3-D pie chart on a separate sheet. Use chart format 7 to show the plant name and the percentage of CD players produced at that plant.
3. Enter "Total CD Player Production" as the chart title.
4. Adjust the size of the chart so that all the labels are displayed correctly.
5. Activate the chart and pull out the slice representing CD player production at the Madison plant.
6. Select patterns and colors for the chart that will give it visual impact when it is printed.
7. Save the workbook as S5PROD.XLS.

To help Julia create a column chart showing production totals for all four plants:
8. Use the ChartWizard to create the column chart. Use chart format 4 to show the production totals of VCRs, CD players, and TVs for each plant.
9. Enter "Total Production Quantities" as the chart title.
10. Adjust the size of the chart so that all labels are displayed correctly.
11. Put a shadowed box around the chart title.
12. Select patterns and colors to give the chart good visual impact.
13. Preview the worksheets. Adjust the size and position of the charts if necessary. Turn off row and column headings and cell gridlines.
14. Save the workbook as S5PROD.XLS.
15. Select and print each sheet in the workbook.

2. Showing Sales Trends at Bentley Twig Furniture

You are a marketing assistant at Bentley Twig Furniture, a small manufacturer of rustic furniture. Bentley's major products are rustic twig chairs, rockers, and tables. Your boss, Jack Armstrong, has asked you to create a line chart showing the sales of the three best-selling products during the period 1992 through 1995.

You have collected the necessary sales figures, entered them into a worksheet, and are ready to prepare the line chart.
1. Open the workbook P5TWIG.XLS.
2. Use the ChartWizard to prepare a line chart that shows the change in sales for the three best-selling items over the period 1992 through 1995. If you like, create the chart on the Sales Figures sheet, below the sales data. Use chart format 2.

3. Enter "Total Unit Sales 1992–1995" as the chart title.
4. Size the chart as necessary so that all the labels are displayed correctly.
5. Bold the x-axis and y-axis labels.
6. Change all the lines to a heavier line weight and assign each line a different data marker.
7. Add a shadow border around the entire chart.
8. Adjust the size and placement of the chart as needed.
9. Save the workbook with chart as S5TWIG.XLS.
10. Preview your work and make any changes necessary to position the printed worksheet and chart for the best visual impact.
11. Print the worksheet and chart.

3. Sales Comparisons at Trail Ridge Outfitters

You are working in the marketing department of Trail Ridge Outfitters, a manufacturer of camping equipment. Trail Ridge management is considering an expansion of its Canadian marketing efforts. You have been asked to prepare a chart showing the relative sales of major camping equipment items in the United States and Canada. You have prepared a simple worksheet containing the latest figures for Trail Ridge sales of camp stoves, sleeping bags, and tents in the U.S. and Canadian markets. You now want to prepare a 3-D column chart to illustrate the relative sales in each market.

1. Open the file P5CAMP.XLS.
2. Use the ChartWizard to create a 3-D column chart showing the relative sales in each market. Create the chart either on a separate sheet or on the Sales Figures sheet, below the sales data. Use 3-D column chart format 6.
3. Enter "U.S. and Canadian Unit Sales" as the chart title.
4. Adjust the size of the chart so the labels are displayed correctly.
5. Rotate the chart so that the Canadian figures are clearly visible.
6. Put a shadowed box around the chart title.
7. Change the x-, y-, and z-axis labels to boldface text.
8. Switch back to the worksheet and adjust the size of the chart so all titles are displayed correctly.
9. Preview the chart. If you created the chart on the Sales Figures sheet, you may need to adjust the size of the chart to fit the worksheet and chart on a single page.
10. Save the workbook as S5CAMP.XLS.
11. Print the worksheet and chart.

4. Duplicating a Printed Chart

Look through books, business magazines, or textbooks for your other courses to find an attractive chart. When you have selected a chart, photocopy it. Create a worksheet that contains the data displayed on the chart. You can estimate the data values that are plotted on the chart. Do your best to duplicate the chart you found. You might not be able to duplicate the chart fonts or colors exactly, but choose the closest available substitutes. When your chart is complete, save it, preview it, and print it. Submit the photocopy of the original chart as well as the printout of the chart you created.

TUTORIAL 6

Using Solver for Complex Problems

Determining the Most Profitable Product Mix

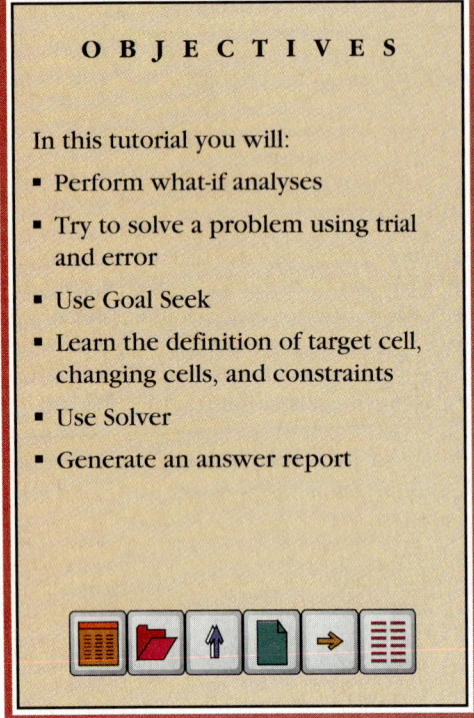

OBJECTIVES

In this tutorial you will:
- Perform what-if analyses
- Try to solve a problem using trial and error
- Use Goal Seek
- Learn the definition of target cell, changing cells, and constraints
- Use Solver
- Generate an answer report

CASE

Appliance Mart Superstore, Inc. Jordan Maki is the general manager of the Boulder, Colorado Appliance Mart Superstore. Keiko Nakamura, a management major at a nearby university, is just beginning a three-month internship at Appliance Mart.

Jordan has received information from GoldStar Corp. about special dealer pricing on selected models of GoldStar stoves, refrigerators, and microwave ovens. Refrigerator Model 5601, which usually costs $935 wholesale, is $875. The Gourmet Model S1200 stove, which usually costs $450 wholesale, is $420. And the popular Model 660 microwave oven, which usually costs $220 wholesale, is $195. This looks like a great opportunity to stock up on some fast-moving merchandise and to increase profits.

Jordan asks Keiko to recommend how many refrigerators they should order to take advantage of the special GoldStar pricing. Keiko returns to her desk to consider the problem and realizes she has very little information that will help her make a recommendation based on sound inventory-management principles. She begins to make a list of the information she needs.

Although she knows that the Model 5601 refrigerator usually costs $935 wholesale and that it is now $875, Keiko also needs to know the retail price of the refrigerator if she wants to justify her recommendation by showing the total profit Appliance Mart will make from selling the refrigerators from this order.

Next, Keiko needs to know if there are any customer orders for Model 5601 refrigerators. If there are, she should recommend to Jordan that he order at least the number of refrigerators required to fill the customer orders.

Keiko also needs to know if there is a limitation on Appliance Mart's warehouse space, which might affect the maximum number of refrigerators Jordan could order. If warehouse space is limited, she needs to know the size of each refrigerator so she can determine how many would fit into the available space.

Finally, Keiko wonders if Jordan has placed a limit on the funds available for the GoldStar order. Although he did not mention a limit, Keiko guesses that he probably has one in mind.

Keiko begins to gather the information she needs. The sales manager tells her that each Model 5601 refrigerator has a retail price of $1250 and that there are six existing customer orders. From the inventory manager she learns that each of these apartment-sized Model 5601 refrigerators requires 25 cubic feet of storage space.

Keiko is unable to find out what the warehouse space limitation might be because the warehouse manager is at lunch. Also, she can't track down Jordan to find out if there is a limit on the funds available for the GoldStar order. While she waits for the additional information she needs, Keiko thinks about how she would construct an Excel worksheet that could help her analyze inventory purchase decisions. Keiko develops the planning sheet shown in Figure 6-1. Then, she makes the worksheet sketch shown in Figure 6-2.

Worksheet Plan for GoldStar Order

My Goal:
Calculate how many Model 5601 refrigerators to order from GoldStar.

What results do I want to see?
The total cost of the order.
The total warehouse space required for the refrigerators.
The amount of profit from selling all the refrigerators on this order.

What information do I need?
The wholesale cost of each GoldStar Model 5601 refrigerator.
The retail price of each GoldStar Model 5601 refrigerator.
The number of customer orders for GoldStar Model 5601 refrigerators.
The amount of warehouse space available (in cubic feet).
The size (in cubic feet) of each GoldStar Model 5601 refrigerator.
The maximum amount of funds available for the order.

What calculations will I perform?
profit per unit = unit retail price − unit wholesale cost
total cost = unit wholesale cost * quantity to order
total profit = profit per unit * quantity to order
total cubic feet = cubic ft. per unit * quantity to order

Figure 6-1
Keiko's worksheet plan

Figure 6-2
Keiko's worksheet sketch

```
Appliance Mart Superstore
GoldStar Order Worksheet


                        Refrigerators
Unit Wholesale Cost     $875.00
Unit Retail Price       $1,250.00
Profit per Unit         ${profit per unit formula}
Cubic Ft. per Unit      ###

Customer Orders         6
Quantity to Order       ###

Total Cost              ${total cost formula}
Total Profit            ${total profit formula}
Total Cubic Feet        {total cubic feet formula}
```

Creating the Worksheet

Keiko begins by launching Excel.

To launch Excel and organize the desktop:

1. Launch Excel following your usual procedure.
2. Make sure your Student Disk is in drive A or B.
3. Make sure the Microsoft Excel and Book1 windows are maximized.

With Excel launched and the worksheet window maximized, Keiko starts the worksheet by entering the titles and labels.

To enter the worksheet titles and labels:

1. Click cell **A1**, type **Appliance Mart Superstore**, then press **[Enter]**.
2. Type **GoldStar Order Worksheet** in cell A2.
3. Click cell **B4**, then type **Refrigerators**.
4. Click cell **A5**, then type **Unit Wholesale Cost** and press **[Enter]**.

❺ Type the remaining labels in column A, as shown in Figure 6-3.

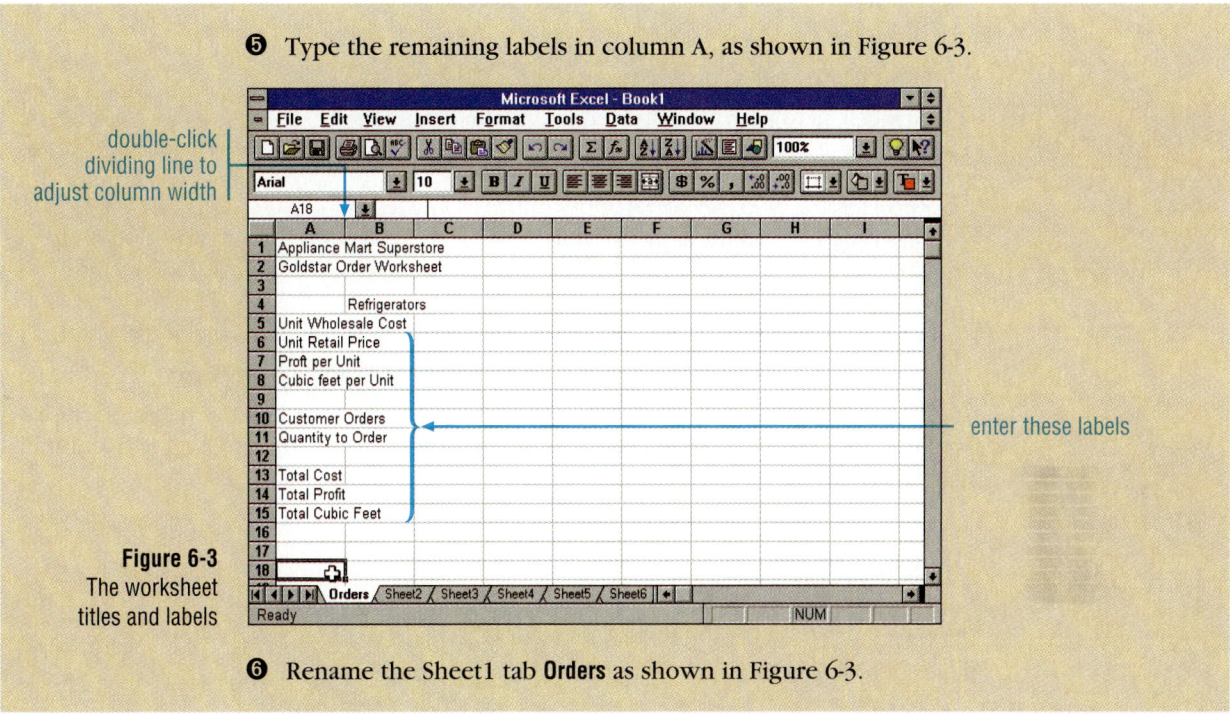

Figure 6-3
The worksheet titles and labels

❻ Rename the Sheet1 tab **Orders** as shown in Figure 6-3.

Keiko sees that she needs to adjust the width of column A because the labels spill into column B.

To adjust the width of column A:
❶ Double-click the dividing line between the headings for columns A and B. Column A adjusts to accommodate the longest label in the column.

Next, Keiko enters the starting values for the worksheet.

To enter the values into the worksheet:
❶ Click cell **B5**, then type **875** to specify the unit wholesale cost.
❷ Click cell **B6**, then type **1250** to specify the unit retail price.
❸ Click cell **B8**, then type **25** to specify the cubic feet per unit.
❹ Click cell **B10**, type **6** to specify the number of customer orders, then press **[Enter]**.

Now Keiko is ready to enter the formulas for the worksheet. The first formula on her planning sheet calculates the profit per unit, that is, how much money Appliance Mart will make on each refrigerator. The profit on a refrigerator unit is the retail price minus the wholesale cost:

profit per unit = unit retail price − unit wholesale cost

On the worksheet the unit retail price is in cell B6 and the unit wholesale cost is in cell B5, so the formula for cell B7 is =B6−B5.

To enter the formula for profit per unit:

❶ Click cell **B7**, then type = to begin the formula.

❷ Click cell **B6** to put this cell reference in the formula.

❸ Type – (a minus sign) to specify the subtraction operation.

❹ Click cell **B5** to put this cell in the formula.

❺ Press [Enter] to complete the formula. The value 375 appears as the profit per unit.

Next, in cell B13 Keiko enters the formula to calculate the total cost of the order:

*total cost = unit wholesale cost * quantity to order*

When Keiko enters this formula, she expects to see a zero as the result because on the current worksheet the value for quantity to order is blank, or zero, and 875 multiplied by 0 equals 0.

To enter the formula for total cost:

❶ Click cell **B13**, then type = to begin the formula.

❷ Click cell **B5**, type * and then click cell **B11**.

❸ Press [Enter] to complete the formula. A zero appears in cell B13.

Keiko sees that the formula for total profit should go in cell B14:

*total profit = profit per unit * quantity to order*

Keiko expects this formula to display a zero as the result until she enters a value for quantity to order.

To enter the formula for total profit:

❶ Click cell **B14**, then type = to begin the formula.

❷ Click cell **B7**, type * and then click cell **B11**.

❸ Press [Enter] to complete the formula. A zero appears in cell B14.

The formula that calculates total cubic feet goes in cell B15:

*total cubic feet = cubic ft. per unit * quantity to order*

As with the results of the two previous formulas, Keiko expects this formula to display a zero as the result until she enters a value other than zero for quantity to order.

To enter the formula for total cubic feet:

❶ Click cell **B15**, then type = to begin the formula.

❷ Click cell **B8**, type * and then click cell **B11**.

❸ Press [Enter] to complete the formula. A zero appears in cell B15.

Until now Keiko has not been concerned about the appearance of the worksheet. She doesn't plan to use the worksheet again after she calculates the number of refrigerators for this order. But upon consideration, she decides that it would be better to at least format the currency amounts to make the worksheet easier to read. Because the refrigerators are priced in whole dollar amounts, Keiko decides to use the currency format with no decimal places. Keiko highlights the non-adjacent ranges that contain currency amounts, then uses the Format menu to apply the appropriate currency format.

To format the currency amounts:
1. Highlight cells B5 through B7, then release the mouse button.
2. Press and hold [**Ctrl**] while you highlight cells B13 through B14.

   TROUBLE? If the highlighting on the range B5:B7 disappeared, you probably did not hold down [Ctrl]. Start again with Step 1 and make sure you hold down [Ctrl] until you have selected both ranges.

3. Release [Ctrl] and the mouse button.
4. Click **Format**, click **Cells...**, then click the **Number tab** in the Format Cells dialog box.
5. Click **Currency** in the Category box.
6. Click **$#,##0_);($#,##0)** in the Format Codes box, then click the **OK button** to apply the format to the selected ranges.
7. Click any cell to remove the highlighting. See Figure 6-4.

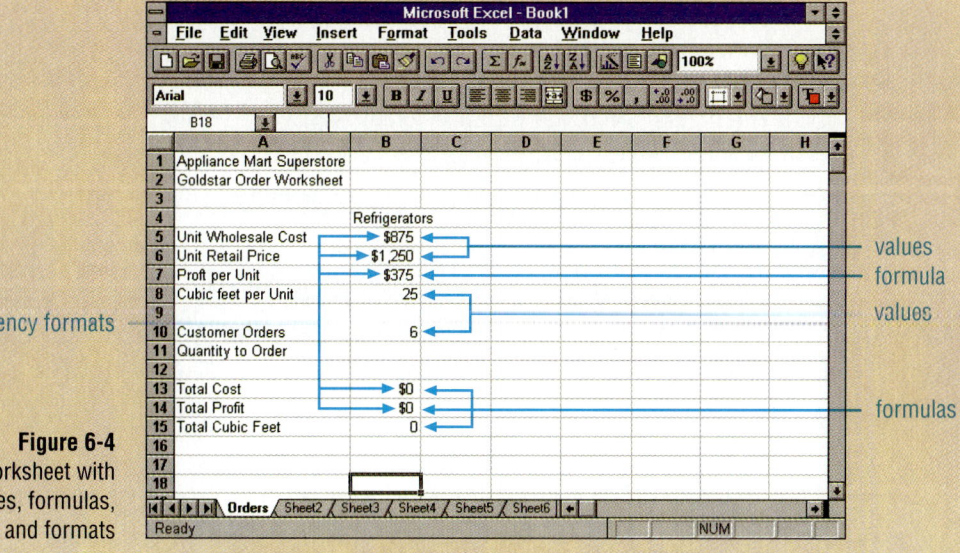

Figure 6-4
The worksheet with values, formulas, and formats

Keiko decides this is a good time to save the workbook.

To save the workbook:
1. Click the **Save button**.
2. Type **S6REF** for the filename of the workbook.
3. Make sure the Drives box displays the icon for the drive that contains your Student Disk.
4. Click the **OK button**. If you see a Summary Info box, click the **OK button**.

Performing What-If Analyses

The labels and formulas are completed, but Keiko has not yet received a call from the warehouse manager, so she doesn't know how much warehouse space is available. While she waits for the call, she decides to enter some values for the quantity to order to see how much profit Appliance Mart could potentially make when it sells the GoldStar refrigerators.

As mentioned in previous tutorials, this type of analysis—in which you change the value in one or more cells to see how it affects the results of the formulas—is often referred to as **what-if analysis**. When you perform a what-if analysis, you change the input values. Excel then recalculates the formulas and displays the results for the values you input.

Keiko plans to do a what-if analysis to answer the following question: "What if we order _____ refrigerators?" She could input the value 6 if she wanted to find out, "What if we order 6 refrigerators?" She could input the value 20 if she wanted to find out, "What if we order 20 refrigerators?" Excel will calculate the formulas in the worksheet using the input values, so Keiko will be able to see the total cost, total profit, and total cubic feet for an order of 6 or 20 refrigerators.

Keiko knows that there are customer orders for six GoldStar refrigerators. She decides that her first what-if analysis is to determine the total cost, the total profit, and the total cubic feet for an order of six refrigerators. To do this, she enters the value 6 in cell B11.

To enter the value 6 in cell B11:

❶ Click cell **B11** to make it the active cell.

❷ Type **6**, then press **[Enter]** and watch as Excel displays the results of recalculating the formulas. See Figure 6-5.

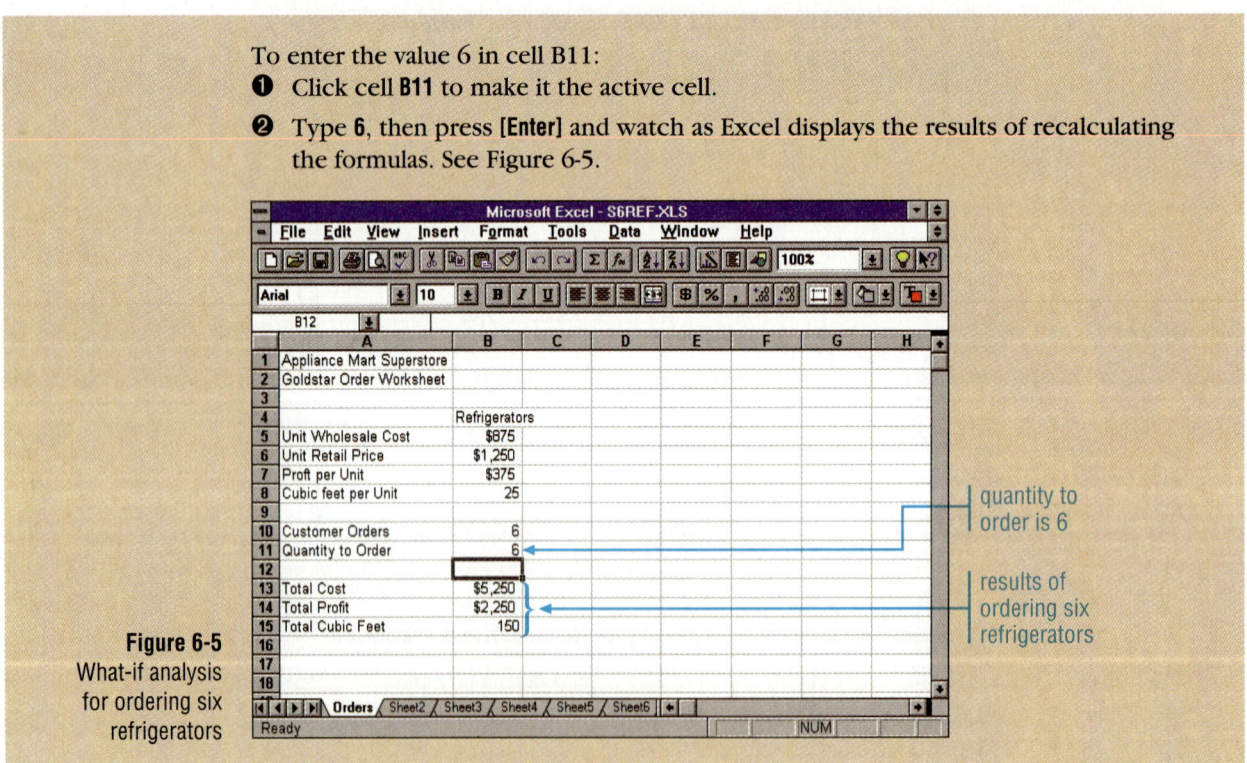

Figure 6-5
What-if analysis for ordering six refrigerators

Cell B13 shows that the total cost of an order for six refrigerators is $5,250. The total profit from this order, shown in cell B14, is $2,250. The six refrigerators will require 150 cubic feet of warehouse space, as shown by the value in cell B15.

Keiko knows that Appliance Mart usually keeps at least 20 GoldStar Model 5601 refrigerators in stock. She wants to know what the cost, profit, and space requirement would be for an order of 20 refrigerators. To determine this, she changes the value in cell B11 to 20.

To change the value in cell B11 to 20:

❶ Make sure cell B11 is the active cell, then type **20** and press **[Enter]**. Excel immediately shows that the total cost of this order is $17,500; the profit from selling the 20 refrigerators is $7,500; and the 20 refrigerators require 500 cubic feet of warehouse space.

Keiko is not sure if Jordan will approve an order for $17,500. She calls him, and he says that he would like to keep the order down to about $15,000. Soon after she talks to Jordan, Keiko receives a call from the warehouse manager who says that he has about 1,000 cubic feet of space for the refrigerators. Given these limitations, how many refrigerators should Keiko order?

Seeking a Solution by Trial and Error

When Keiko used her worksheet for the what-if analyses, she was interested in the results for the total cost, the total profit, and the total cubic feet, but she was not concerned with any limits that might affect these results. Now she knows that there are two limiting factors: Jordan does not want to spend more than $15,000 on the order, and the refrigerators on the order cannot require more than 1,000 cubic feet of warehouse space. She decides to modify the "goal" and "results" sections of her worksheet plan to reflect these limiting factors, as shown in Figure 6-6.

Worksheet Plan for GoldStar Order

My Goal:
Calculate how many Model 5601 refrigerators to order from GoldStar without exceeding cost and space limits.

What results do I want to see?
The total cost of the order does not exceed $15,000. $\leq = 60,000$ /45,000
The total warehouse space required for the refrigerators does not exceed 1000 cubic feet. $\leq = 1300$ /1400
The amount of profit from selling all the refrigerators on this order.

What information do I need?
The wholesale cost of each GoldStar Model 5601 refrigerator.
The retail price of each GoldStar Model 5601 refrigerator.
The number of customer orders for GoldStar Model 5601 refrigerators.
The amount of warehouse space available (in cubic feet).
The size (in cubic feet) of each GoldStar Model 5601 refrigerator.
The maximum amount of funds available for the order.

What calculations will I perform?
profit per unit = unit retail price – unit wholesale cost
total cost = unit wholesale cost * quantity to order
total profit = profit per unit * quantity to order
total cubic feet = cubic ft. per unit * quantity to order

Figure 6-6
Keiko's revised worksheet plan

Keiko now has a particular solution she is trying to reach. She wants the value for the total cost in cell B13 to be as close to $15,000 as possible without exceeding that number. She must also make sure the value for total cubic feet in cell B15 does not exceed 1,000. Keiko decides to adjust the value for quantity to order in cell B11 until the value for total cost in cell B13 is close to $15,000. This strategy is referred to as **trial and error** because she will "try" different entries and they will result in "errors" (solutions that are not optimal) until she enters the value that produces the result she wants.

To determine by trial and error the maximum number of units to purchase with available funds:

❶ Click cell **B11**, then type **10** and press **[Enter]**. This order would cost $8,750 and take up 250 cubic feet of storage. It appears that Keiko could order more than 10 units without exceeding the available funds and storage space.

❷ Click cell **B11**, then type **15** and press **[Enter]**. Cell B13 displays $13,125. It appears that Keiko can order more than 15 units and not exceed the two limitations.

❸ Click cell **B11**, then type **17** and press **[Enter]**. The total cost is $14,875.

With the total cost only $125 less than the $15,000 limit, Keiko recognizes that 17 is the maximum number of refrigerators Jordan can purchase with the available funds. Only 425 cubic feet are required for the 17 refrigerators, so the units will fit in the warehouse.

Just as Keiko arrives at this solution, Jordan calls to tell her that GoldStar has announced an additional discount on refrigerators purchased for this sale. With this additional discount, the wholesale cost of each Model 5601 refrigerator is only $850. Jordan also tells her that because of this price reduction, he has decided to allocate a total of $18,000 for the refrigerator order. He asks her to determine the maximum number of units that he can purchase at the new price.

Keiko begins by changing the value for unit wholesale cost in cell B5.

To make the change for the price reduction:

❶ Click cell **B5**, then type **850** and press **[Enter]**. The value for total cost in cell B13 changes to $14,450, which is far below the new order limit of $18,000.

Before she starts the trial-and-error process again, Keiko remembers an Excel feature called Goal Seek. She decides to use Goal Seek to find the solution to the new problem.

Using Goal Seek

Excel's **Goal Seek command** automates the trial-and-error process of changing one cell to make another cell display a specified result. Figure 6-7 illustrates a simplified worksheet showing the difference between what-if analysis and Goal Seek. With what-if analysis you change the *input values* in worksheet cells, then Excel uses these values to perform the calculation specified in a formula. With Goal Seek, you specify the *results* you want a formula to display, and Excel changes the input values that the formula uses.

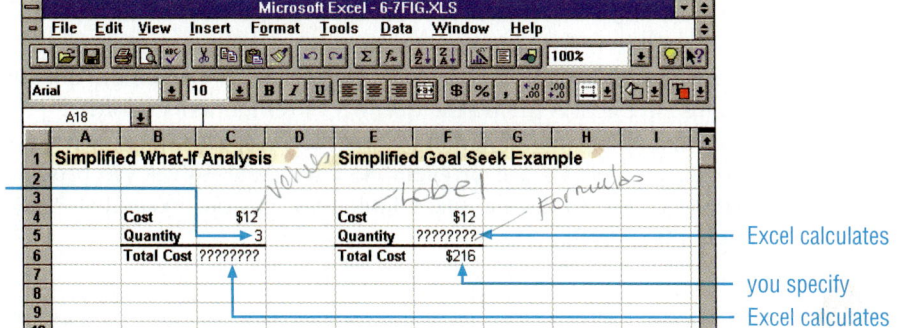

Figure 6-7
Simplified examples of what-if analysis and Goal Seek

Suppose you wanted to purchase some audio CDs that cost $12 each. You can ask the what-if question, "What would it cost if I buy _____ CDs?" In Figure 6-7 the what-if analysis is shown on the left side of the worksheet. To do the what-if analysis, you would enter values in cell C5. Each time you enter a value in this cell, Excel calculates the result of the formula =C4*C5, which multiplies the cost of a CD by the number you buy. As a result of doing the what-if analysis, Excel displays the cost of the CDs in cell C6.

The Goal Seek example is shown on the right side of the worksheet in Figure 6-7. If you have $216 to spend on CDs, you want $216 as the result of the formula in cell G6. You do not know the value you should enter in cell G5 to arrive at this result. You cannot just type $216 into cell G6 because it would erase the formula and would not change the value for quantity. To solve this problem using Goal Seek, you tell Excel to change the value in cell G5 to produce $216 in cell G6.

REFERENCE WINDOW

Using Goal Seek

- Set up the template for the worksheet with labels, formulas, and values.
- Click Tools, then click Goal Seek... to display the Goal Seek dialog box.
- Click the Set cell box, then click the cell where you want to display the result. This is a cell that contains a formula.
- Click the To value box, then type the value you want to see as the result.
- Click the By changing cell box, then click the cell that Excel can change to produce the result.
- Click the OK button.

Now what about the refrigerator order problem that Keiko is trying to solve? As you know, this problem has two limiting factors. First, the total cost of the order is limited to a maximum of $18,000. Second, the space required is limited to a maximum of 1,000 cubic feet. With Goal Seek, Keiko can set only one of these as the result. She decides that the most important result is to spend $18,000 or less on the entire order.

In addition to specifying the result, Keiko must specify which cell Excel can change to arrive at the result. She decides that Excel can change the quantity to order in cell B11 because her goal is to find the quantity of refrigerators to order.

What about the limitation on warehouse space? Excel will not consider this factor as it seeks a result for the problem. So after Excel solves the problem, Keiko will need to manually check that the space limitation was not exceeded. Let's see how Keiko uses Excel's Goal Seek.

To use Goal Seek to determine the number of refrigerators to order:

❶ Click **Tools**, then click **Goal Seek...** to display the Goal Seek dialog box.

❷ Move the Goal Seek dialog box so it doesn't hide any of the labels or values on your worksheet. See Figure 6-8.

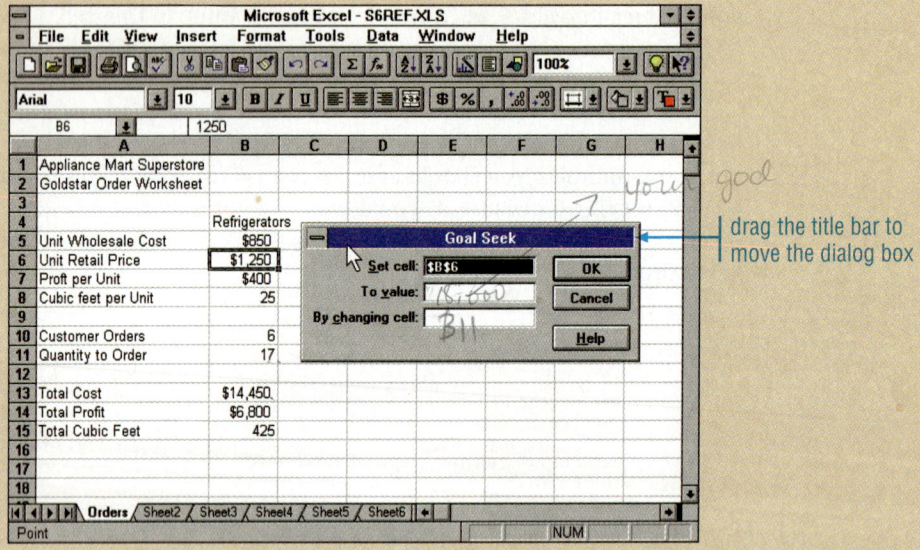

Figure 6-8
The Goal Seek dialog box

❸ The Set cell box is active, so click cell **B13** to indicate the cell where you want to display the result.

❹ Click the **To value box**, then type **18000** to indicate what the result should be.

⑤ Click the **By changing cell box**, then click cell **B11** to indicate that Goal Seek can change the value in cell B11 to arrive at the result. The dialog box should look like Figure 6-9.

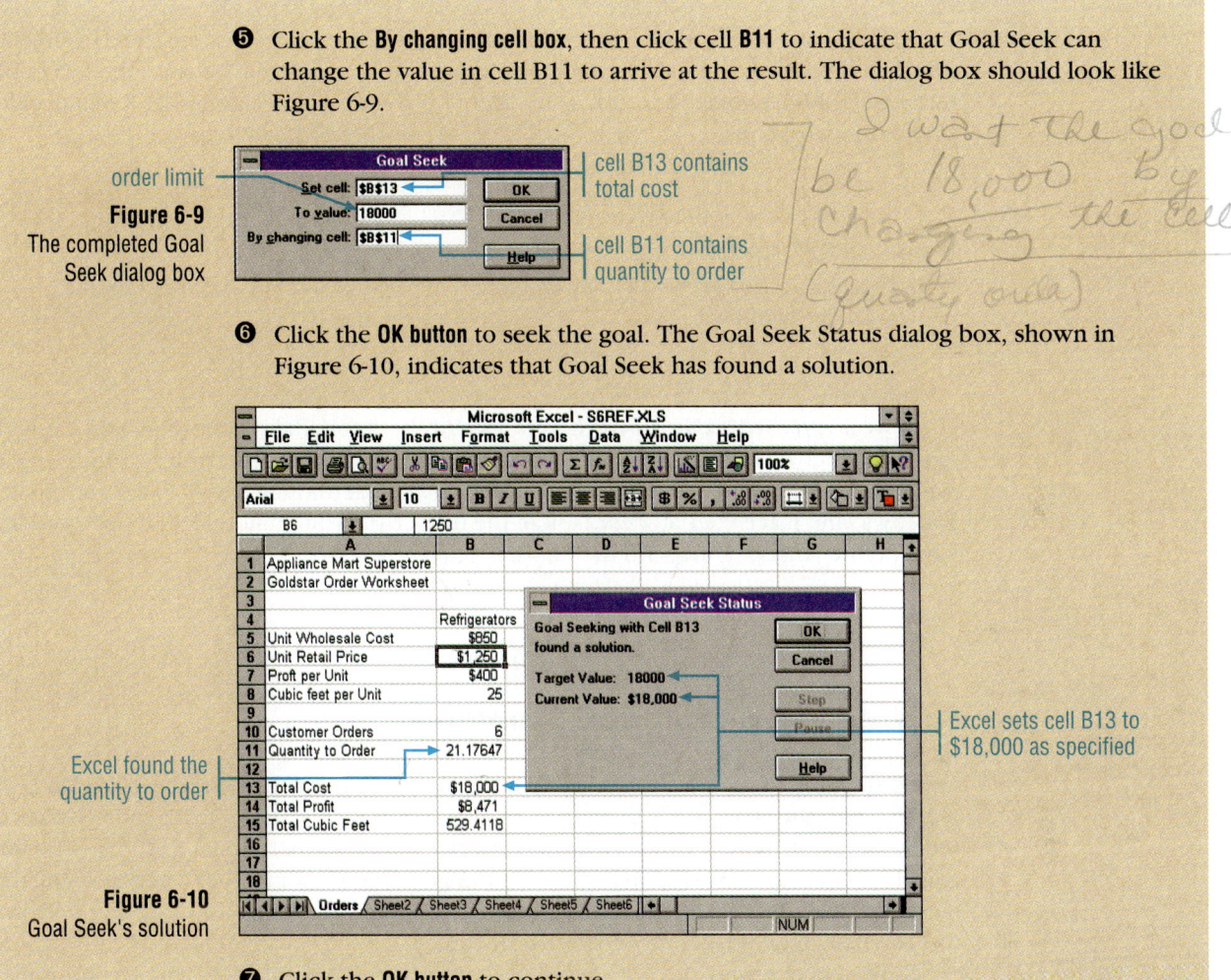

Figure 6-9
The completed Goal Seek dialog box

order limit → cell B13 contains total cost
cell B11 contains quantity to order

(handwritten: I want the goal to be 18,000 by changing the cell (quantity order))

⑥ Click the **OK button** to seek the goal. The Goal Seek Status dialog box, shown in Figure 6-10, indicates that Goal Seek has found a solution.

Excel found the quantity to order
Excel sets cell B13 to $18,000 as specified

Figure 6-10
Goal Seek's solution

⑦ Click the **OK button** to continue.

Look at the number in cell B11. Goal Seek determined that an order for 21.17647 refrigerators would use up all available funds. Keiko knows that she cannot order a fraction of a refrigerator, so she rounds this number down to 21 and manually changes it in the worksheet.

To change the number of refrigerators to 21:
① Click cell **B11**, which contains the number of refrigerators to order.
② Type **21** and press **[Enter]**.

Keiko looks at cell B15 to check the total cubic feet needed to store the 21 refrigerators. She is pleased to see that storage space will not be a problem because the 525 cubic feet required is less than the 1,000 cubic feet of warehouse space available. Keiko decides to save the workbook.

To save the workbook then close it:
1. Click the **Save button**.
2. Double-click the **Control menu box** on the menu bar (not the title bar) to close the worksheet window.

If you want to take a break and resume the tutorial at a later time, you can exit Excel by double-clicking the Control menu box in the upper-left corner of the screen. When you resume the tutorial, launch Excel, maximize the Microsoft Excel and Book1 windows, and place your Student Disk in the disk drive. You do not need to open a workbook before you continue with the tutorial.

Solving More Complex Problems

Jordan stops by to see how Keiko is doing, so she shows him the worksheet. Jordan is so pleased with the work she's done that he asks her to take charge of the entire GoldStar order. He explains that GoldStar has great prices on Gourmet Model S1200 stoves and Model 660 microwave ovens in addition to refrigerators. He wants Keiko to determine the most profitable mix of refrigerators, stoves, and microwave ovens to order. He tells her that she has a total budget of $50,000 for the order.

Keiko checks with the sales manager and learns that Appliance Mart has customer orders for 14 Gourmet Model S1200 stoves and 19 Model 660 microwave ovens. Keiko realizes that her solution must take into account the customer orders for six refrigerators, as well as the orders for the 14 stoves and 19 microwave ovens. Next, she calls the warehouse and learns that the products for the entire order must fit in 1,300 cubic feet of storage space. Keiko hopes that she can find an answer to this complex problem using Excel.

Keiko begins by creating columns on the worksheet for stoves and microwave ovens. Her revised worksheet is stored on your Student Disk as C6PROD2.XLS. Let's open this workbook, then save it under a new filename.

To open Keiko's enhanced workbook and save it under a new filename:
1. Click the **Open button** to display the Open dialog box.
2. Click **C6PROD2.XLS**, then click the **OK button** to open the workbook.
3. Click **File**, then click **Save As...** to display the Save As dialog box.
4. Type **S6PROD2**, then click the **OK button** to save the workbook under a different name. See Figure 6-11.

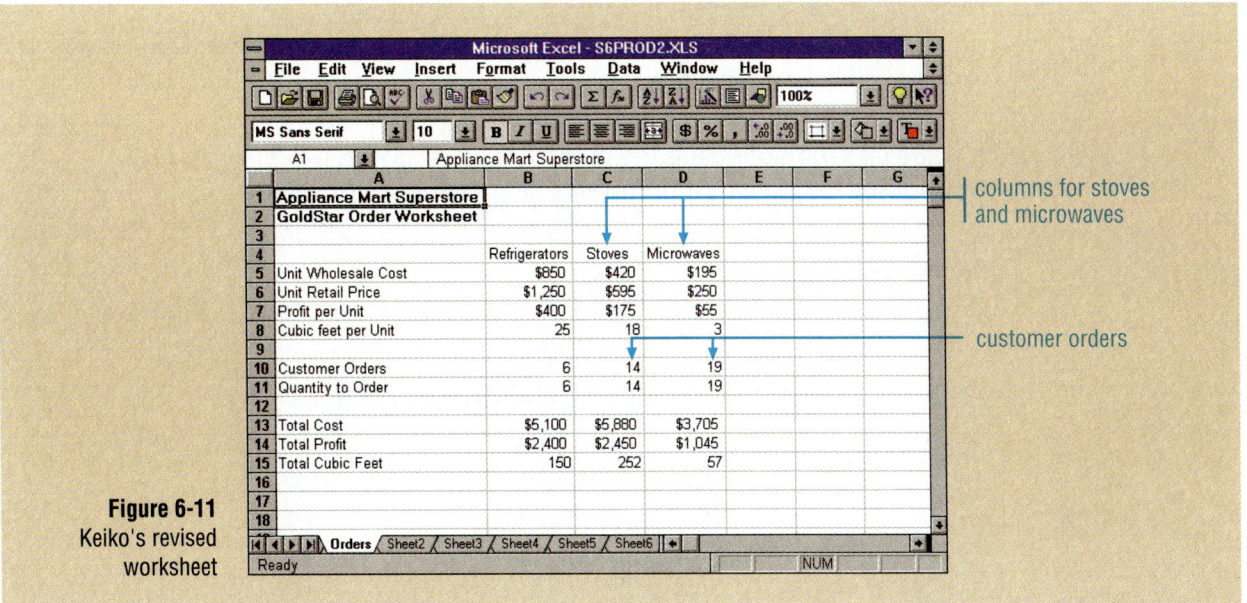

Figure 6-11
Keiko's revised worksheet

Notice that Keiko has added a column for stoves and a column for microwave ovens, each with the same format as the refrigerators column. She has also entered the unit wholesale cost, the unit retail price, and the customer orders for each product.

Keiko realizes that she needs to calculate the total order cost, the total order profit, and the total space required for all of the refrigerators, stoves, and microwave ovens on the order. First, she adds a label and a formula for the total order cost. She looks at the worksheet and determines that the total order cost will be the total of the contents of cells B13, C13, and D13.

To add the label and formula for total order cost:
1. Click cell **A17**, then type **TOTAL ORDER COST**.
2. Click cell **B17** because this is where you want to display the total order cost.
3. Type **=SUM(** to begin the formula.
4. Highlight cells B13 through D13, then press **[Enter]**. Cell B17 displays $14,685.

Next, Keiko enters the label and formula for the total order profit. The profit for the total order is the sum of the profit from the refrigerators, the stoves, and the microwave ovens on the order.

To enter the label and formula for the total order profit:
1. Click cell **A18**, then type **TOTAL ORDER PROFIT**.
2. Click cell **B18**.
3. Type **=SUM(** to begin the formula.
4. Highlight cells B14 through D14, then press **[Enter]** to complete the formula and display $5,895 in cell B18.

Keiko also needs to show the total space required for the refrigerators, stoves, and microwave ovens on the order.

To enter the label and formula for the total space required:
1. Click cell **A19**, then type **TOTAL SPACE REQUIRED**.
2. Click cell **B19**.
3. Type **=SUM(** to begin the formula.
4. Highlight cells B15 through D15, then press **[Enter]** to complete the formula and display 459 in cell B19. See Figure 6-12.

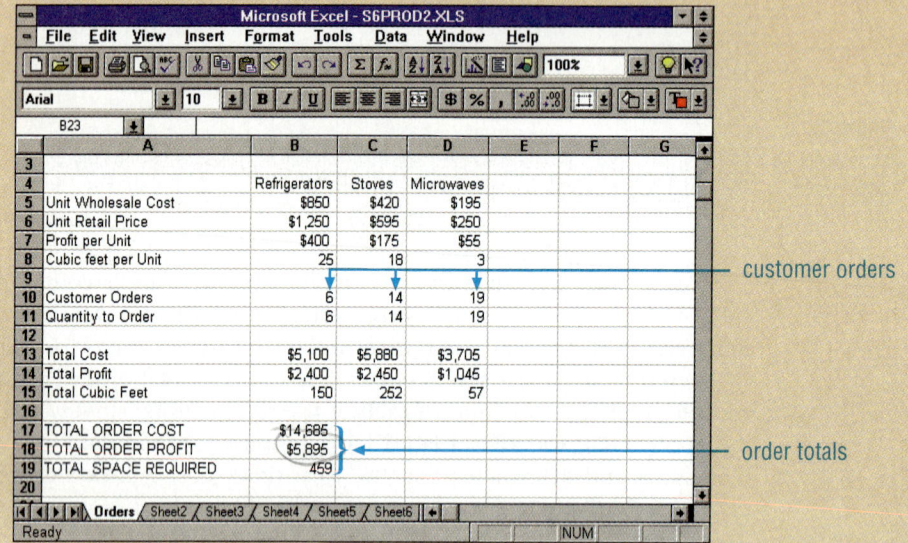

Figure 6-12
Order totals for customer orders

Keiko saves this new version of the workbook.

To save the workbook:
1. Click the **Save button**.

Formulating the Problem

Keiko needs to determine the mixture of refrigerators, stoves, and microwave ovens that will generate the greatest profit, assuming all units are sold. The total order cost cannot exceed $50,000, and the total space required cannot exceed 1,300 cubic feet.

Keiko considers using Goal Seek to determine how many of each appliance she should order. However, she realizes that Goal Seek is too limited for this task because it can change the contents of only one cell to find the solution. To determine how many to order of each appliance, three cells must change: cell B11, which contains the number of refrigerators; cell C11, which contains the number of stoves; and cell D11, which contains the number of microwave ovens.

Solving Complex Problems by Trial and Error

Since it appears that Goal Seek won't work, Keiko considers using trial and error to solve the problem manually. At first, this seems easy. Keiko's worksheet currently shows the result of ordering 6 refrigerators, 14 stoves, and 19 microwave ovens. The cost of this order would be $14,685 and the appliances would take up 459 cubic feet of storage space. If she places this order, she would not use the entire $50,000 or fill the storage space, so she can order additional appliances. But should she order more stoves, refrigerators, or microwave ovens?

Keiko can see from the values in cells B7, C7, and D7 that refrigerators generate the greatest profit, so she decides to purchase as many refrigerators as space and funds permit, then purchase stoves and microwave ovens to use up the remaining money and storage space. Let's follow Keiko as she attempts to manually solve the problem of what product mix will provide the most profit while still meeting the total order cost and space limitations.

To solve the product mix problem by trial and error:

❶ Keiko starts by ordering 50 refrigerators. Click cell **B11**, then type **50** and press **[Enter]**. The total order cost is $52,085 and the total space required is 1,559. There is not enough money or storage space for 50 refrigerators, so Keiko tries a smaller number.

❷ Click cell **B11**, then type **40** and press **[Enter]**. The total order cost is $43,585 and the total space required is 1,309. There is not quite enough space to store 40 refrigerators, so again Keiko tries a smaller number.

❸ Click cell **B11**, then type **39** and press **[Enter]**. The total order cost is $42,735 and the total space required is 1,284. There is sufficient money and space to order 39 units. The total profit from selling the appliances on this order would be $19,095.

Keiko sees that there is quite a bit of money left, but only 16 cubic feet of storage space. Microwave ovens require 3 cubic feet of space, so Keiko decides to purchase five more microwave ovens to use up the remaining space and some of the remaining money.

To add five more microwave ovens to the order:

❶ Click cell **D11**, then type **24** and press **[Enter]**. The total order profit increases to $19,370 with a total order cost of $43,710 and a total space requirement of 1,299 cubic feet.

Keiko looks at the worksheet and wonders if this is really the best answer. She used just about all of the available storage space but still has over $6,000 left. What would happen if she had ordered more microwave ovens and fewer refrigerators?

Keiko decides to test the effect of ordering only 35 refrigerators and as many microwave ovens as she can purchase with the remaining money.

To test the effect of ordering more microwave ovens instead of refrigerators:

❶ Click cell **B11**, then type **35** and press **[Enter]** to reduce the number of refrigerators.

❷ Click cell **D11**, then type **50** and press **[Enter]**. The total profit drops to $19,200, but the order would require only 1,277 cubic feet, leaving 23 cubic feet of remaining space. Since each microwave requires 3 cubic feet of storage, there seems to be room for seven more microwave ovens.

❸ Click cell **D11**, then type **57** and press **[Enter]**. Total profit increases to $19,585.

This is the best solution yet. It yields a profit of $19,585, compared to $19,370 for the previous solution. But Keiko is worried. There are so many combinations. It could take hours or even days to try them all. Keiko explains the problem to Jordan, who suggests that she try the Solver feature in Excel.

Keiko has not used Solver before, so she reads the section of the *Microsoft Excel User's Guide 2* that describes the Solver feature. It says:

> ...Microsoft Excel Solver answers questions such as, "What product price or promotion will maximize profit? How can I live within the budget? How fast can we grow without running out of cash?" Instead of guessing over and over, you can use Microsoft Excel Solver to find the best answer....

This seems to be just what Keiko needs to find the mix of products that will maximize the profit for the order.

Using Solver

When you use Solver, you must identify a target cell, the changing cells, and the constraints that apply to your problem. A **target cell** is a cell that you want to maximize, minimize, or change to a certain value by making changes to other cells. A **changing cell** is a cell that Excel changes to force the target cell to the desired result. A **constraint** is a value that limits the way the problem is solved. You specify the target cell, changing cells, and constraints using the Solver Parameters dialog box. The settings you make in this dialog box are referred to as the **parameters** for the problem.

> **REFERENCE WINDOW**
>
> ## Using Solver
>
> - Create a worksheet that contains the labels, values, and formulas for the problem you want to solve.
> - Click Tools, then click Solver to display the Solver parameters dialog box.
> - The Set Target Cell box must contain the cell reference for the target cell—the cell you want to maximize, minimize, or set to a certain value.
> - In the By Changing Cells box, list the cells that Excel can change to arrive at the solution.
> - Use the Add... button to add constraints that limit the changes Solver can make to the values in the cells.
> - Click the Solve button to generate a solution.
> - Click the OK button to return to the worksheet.

Keiko examines the worksheet and determines that the target cell on her order worksheet is cell B18. This cell displays the total order profit that will result from selling all the appliances on the order. She wants Excel to produce a solution that maximizes the total order profit.

Keiko determines that the changing cells—the cells Excel can change to reach the solution—are cells B11, C11, and D11. These cells contain the quantity to order for each appliance. These are the cells that Keiko changed when she tried to solve the problem manually.

The two major constraints for this problem are the $50,000 spending limit and the 1,300 cubic foot space limit. Let's see how Keiko initially sets up the parameters to solve this problem using Solver.

First, Keiko displays the Solver Parameters dialog box, specifies the target cell, and specifies the changing cells.

To set up the target cell and changing cells in Solver:

1. Click **Tools**, then click **Solver...** to display the Solver Parameters dialog box. Drag the dialog box to the upper-right corner of the screen so you can see the cells you need to set up the problem. See Figure 6-13.

EX 218 TUTORIAL 6 Using Solver for Complex Problems

click to maximize the total order profit

drag the dialog box to upper-right corner of screen

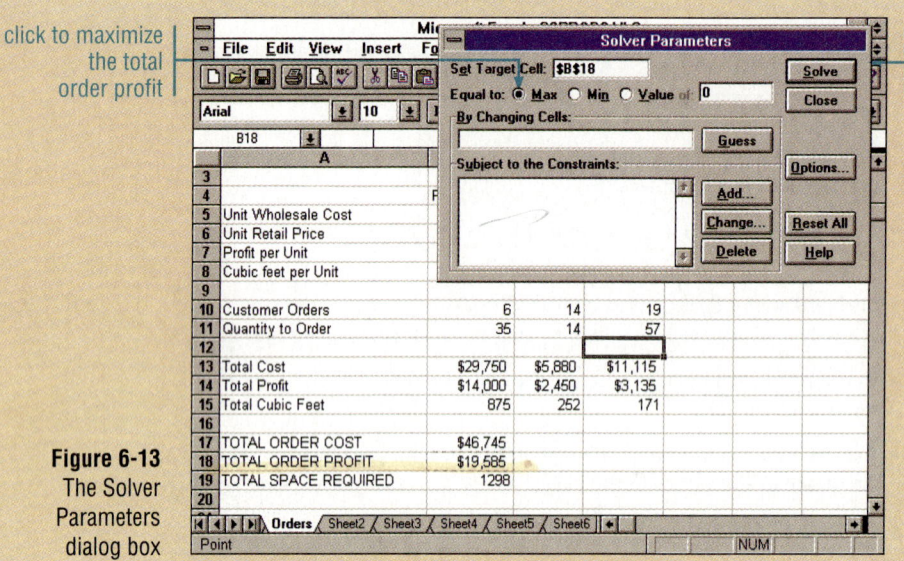

Figure 6-13
The Solver Parameters dialog box

❷ The Set Cell box is active, so click cell **B18** to select it as the target cell. See Figure 6-13.

❸ Click the **Max option button** to indicate that you want Solver to maximize the total order profit.

❹ Double-click the **By Changing Cells box** to highlight the current entry.

❺ Drag the pointer to outline cells **B11 through D11**, then release the mouse button. Notice that the range $B$11:$D$11 appears in the By Changing Cells box.

Keiko identifies the other parameters for Solver by entering the two constraints. The first constraint is that the total order cost must be less than or equal to $50,000, which can be expressed as B17<=50000. The second constraint is that the total space required must be less than or equal to 1,300 cubic feet, which can be expressed as B19<=1300.

To enter the constraints in Solver:

❶ Click the **Subject to the Constraints box**, then click the **Add... button** to display the Add Constraint dialog box.

❷ Click cell **B17** to place the cell reference $B$17 in the Cell Reference box.

❸ Click the **down arrow button** in the middle of the Add Constraint dialog box, then click the **<=** option from the list.

❹ Click the **Constraint box**, then type **50000**. The first constraint is now shown in the Add Constraint dialog box as $B$17<=50000. See Figure 6-14.

click cell B17 to select it as the cell reference

Figure 6-14
The Add Constraint dialog box

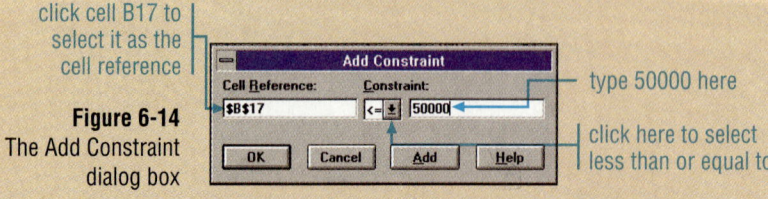

type 50000 here

click here to select less than or equal to

❺ Click the **Add button** to add another constraint.

❻ Click cell **B19** to place the cell reference $B$19 in the Cell Reference box.

❼ Click the **down arrow button** in the middle of the Add Constraint dialog box, then click the **<=** option from the list.

❽ Click the **Constraint box**, then type **1300**. The second constraint is now shown in the Add Constraint dialog box as $B$19<=1300.

❾ Click the **OK button** to return to the Solver Parameters dialog box. See Figure 6-15.

TROUBLE? If the constraints on your screen are not the same as those in Figure 6-15, click the Change... button if you need to change the cell references in a constraint, click the Add... button if you need to add a constraint, or click the Delete button if you need to delete a constraint.

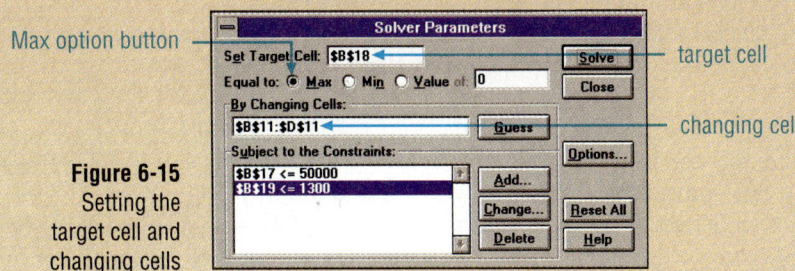

Figure 6-15
Setting the target cell and changing cells

Now that Keiko has specified the target cell, changing cells, and constraints, she is ready for Solver to look for a solution to the problem.

To generate the solution using Solver:

❶ Click the **Solve button**. After a short time, the Solver Results dialog box appears and displays the message, "Solver has converged to the current solution. All constraints are satisfied." See Figure 6-16.

TROUBLE? If you see the message, "The Set Target Cell Values do not Converge," in the Show Trial Solutions dialog box, click the Stop button. When the Solver Results dialog box appears, continue with the following steps. If you see "The Set Target Cell values do not converge," or any other message in the Solver Results dialog box, simply continue with the following steps.

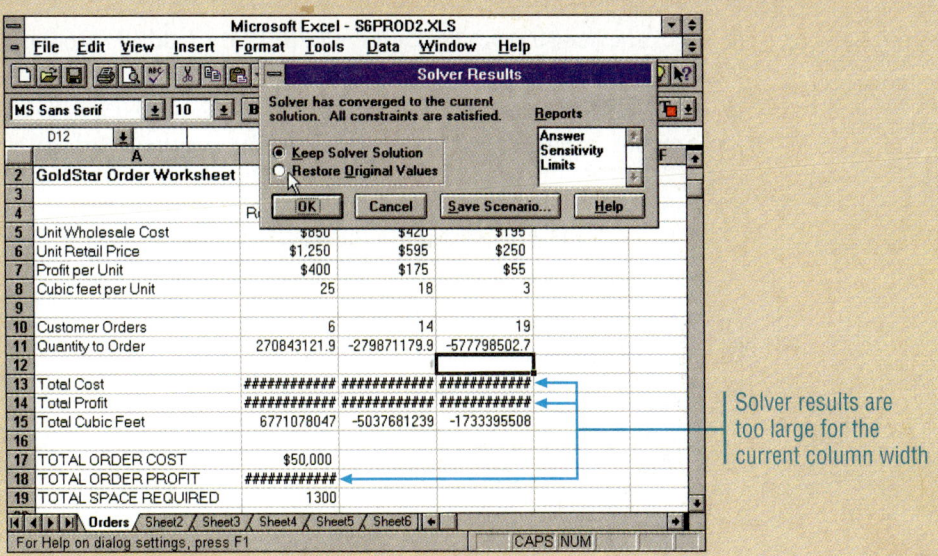

Figure 6-16
The Solver results

❷ If necessary, drag the dialog box out of the way to view the values Solver has produced so far as a solution to the problem.

Keiko sees that something is clearly wrong. In the current trial solution, Solver ordered a very large number of refrigerators and large negative numbers of stoves and microwave ovens. It did not order enough stoves or microwave ovens to fill the customer orders. Keiko decides to remove the values from the worksheet and start over.

To remove these values from the worksheet:
❶ Click **Restore Original Values**, then click the **OK button** to close the Solver dialog box. Solver restores the original values to the worksheet.

Keiko realizes that the two constraints she specified are not sufficient to solve the problem effectively. She must specify that Solver order enough refrigerators, stoves, and microwave ovens to fill customer orders. She will specify the following additional constraints:
- The number of refrigerators to order is greater than or equal to the customer orders for refrigerators: B11>=B10.
- The number of stoves to order is greater than or equal to the customer orders for stoves: C11>=C10.
- The number of microwave ovens to order is greater than or equal to the customer orders for microwave ovens: D11>=D10.

These constraints will also prevent Solver from ordering negative quantities because the order quantities are greater than zero. Let's add these three additional constraints to the Solver parameters.

To add a constraint forcing Solver to order enough refrigerators to fill customer orders:
❶ Click **Tools**, then click **Solver...** to display the Solver Parameters dialog box with the parameters you specified so far.
❷ Click the **Add... button** to display the Add Constraint dialog box.
❸ Click the **Cell Reference box**, then click cell **B11**.
❹ Click the **down arrow button** in the middle of the Add Constraint dialog box, then click the **>=** option from the list.
❺ Click the **Constraint box**, then click cell **B10** to indicate that the quantity to order must always be greater than or equal to the customer orders.

Next, let's add a constraint forcing Solver to order enough stoves to fill customer orders.

To add the constraint that C11>=C10:
❶ Click the **Add button** in the Add Constraint dialog box.
❷ Click the **Cell Reference box**, then click cell **C11**.

Using Solver   EX 221

❸ Click the **down arrow button** in the middle of the Add Constraint dialog box, then click the **>=** option from the list.

❹ Click the **Constraint box**, then click cell **C10** to indicate that the quantity to order must always be greater than or equal to the customer orders.

Now let's add a constraint forcing Solver to order enough microwave ovens to fill customer orders.

To add the constraint that D11>=D10:
❶ Click the **Add button** in the Add Constraint dialog box.
❷ Click the **Cell Reference box**, then click cell **D11**.
❸ Click the **down arrow button** in the middle of the Add Constraint dialog box, then click the **>=** option from the list.
❹ Click the **Constraint box**, then click cell **D10** to indicate that the quantity to order must always be greater than or equal to the customer orders.
❺ Click the **OK button** to return to the Solver Parameters dialog box. The revised constraints are shown in the Subject to the Constraints box. See Figure 6-17.

TROUBLE? If the constraints on your screen are not the same as those in Figure 6-17, click the Change... button if you need to change the cell references in a constraint, click the Add... button if you need to add a constraint, or click the Delete button if you need to delete a constraint.

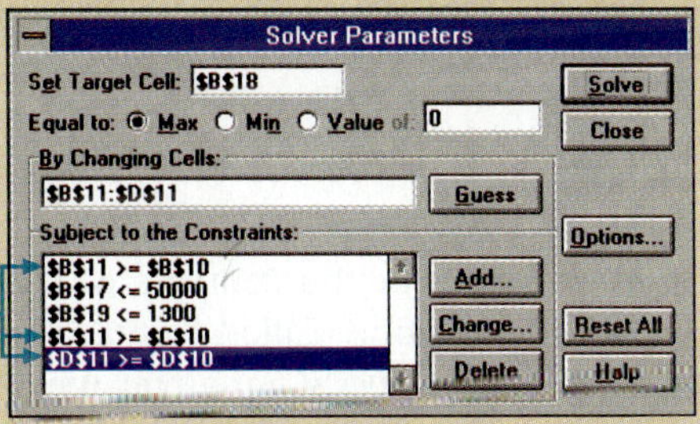

new constraints

Figure 6-17
The revised Solver parameters

Now, let's have Solver try again to find a solution, this time using the new set of constraints.

To activate Solver:

❶ Click the **Solve button** to solve the problem. This time the Solver dialog box message says, "Solver found a solution. All constraints and optimality conditions are satisfied."
❷ Click the **OK button** to view the solution on the worksheet. See Figure 6-18.

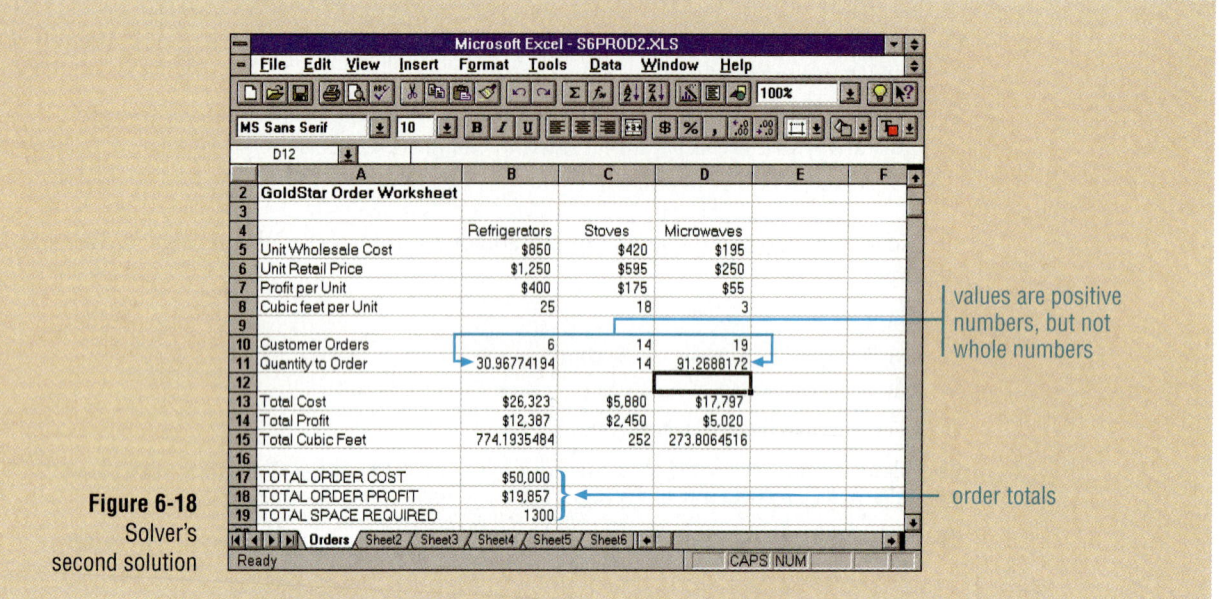

Figure 6-18
Solver's second solution

This solution is better. Solver did not order negative quantities, and it did order enough of each item to cover the customer orders.

However, Keiko notices yet another problem. Solver has ordered 30.96774194 refrigerators and 91.2688172 microwave ovens. Keiko decides that another constraint is needed to force Solver to order non-fractional unit quantities.

The Integer Constraint

In addition to constraints based on values or the contents of other cells, you can limit Solver to the use of integer values, commonly called "whole numbers," in the cells it changes to reach the solution. This is particularly important when a problem deals with items that exist as non-fractional units, such as refrigerators, stoves, and microwave ovens.

Keiko needs to specify that cells B11, C11, and D11 must contain integer values.

To specify integers in cells B11, C11, and D11:

❶ Click **Tools**, then click **Solver...** to display the Solver Parameters dialog box with the parameters you specified so far.

❷ Click the **Add... button** to display the Add Constraint dialog box.

❸ Drag the pointer to outline cells B11 through D11, then release the mouse button.

❹ Click the **down arrow button** in the middle of the Add Constraint dialog box, then click **int**. The word "integer" appears in the Constraint box, as shown in Figure 6-19.

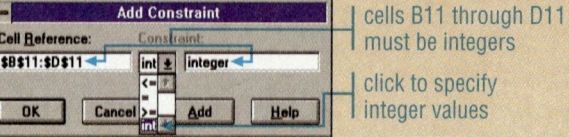

Figure 6-19
Setting the integer constraint

⑤ Click the **OK button** to return to the Solver Parameters dialog box.

⑥ Click the **Solve button** to solve the problem.

⑦ When the Solver dialog box appears, click the **OK button** to view the solution. See Figure 6-20.

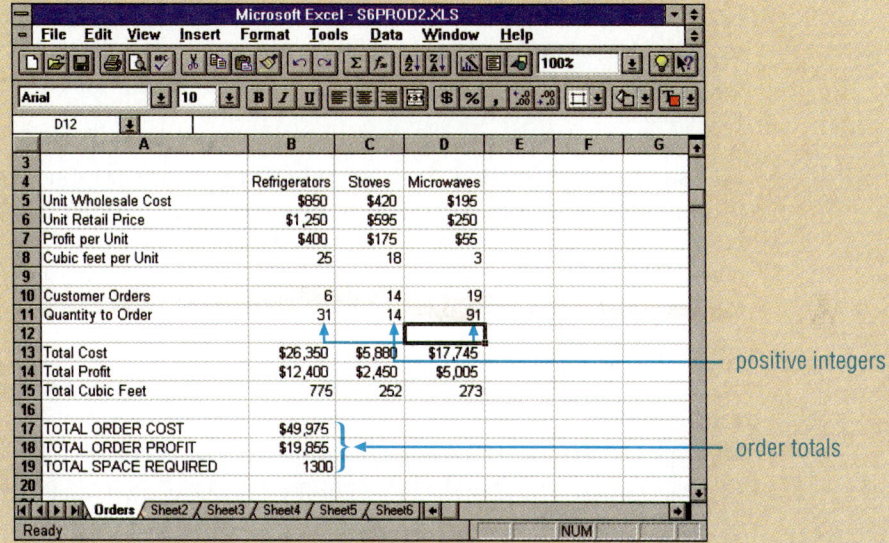

Figure 6-20
Solver's third solution

Solver indicates that Keiko should order 31 refrigerators, 14 stoves, and 91 microwave ovens. This solution uses all but $25 of the available funds and all of the available storage space. It also generates a total profit of $19,855.

Keiko understands that this might not be the ultimate solution because she has read in her Excel manual that Solver tries a limited number of combinations in its search for a solution. There is a small chance that the best solution might not be found. However, with all storage space used and only $25 left, Keiko is fairly certain that this solution must be very close to the optimal solution. Keiko decides to save the workbook.

To save the workbook:

❶ Click the **Save button**.

If you want to take a break and resume the tutorial at a later time, you can exit Excel by double-clicking the Control menu box in the upper-left corner of the screen. When you resume the tutorial, launch Excel, maximize the Microsoft Excel and Book1 windows, and place your Student Disk in the disk drive. Open the file S6PROD2.XLS, then continue with the tutorial.

Keiko decides to have Excel generate an answer report that shows the original values and the final values of the solution.

Generating an Answer Report

Solver can generate three different reports—an answer report, a sensitivity report, and a limits report—that provide additional information about the solution. The answer report is the most useful of the three because it summarizes the results of a successful solution by displaying information about the target cell, changing cells, and constraints. The report includes the original and final values for the target and changing cells, and the formulas that specify the constraints. Let's generate an answer report and examine the information it contains.

An answer report provides information on the process used to go from the original values to the final solution. To make sure that the answer report includes information on the entire process, Keiko decides to set the quantity to order back to the original values before she solves the problem again and generates the answer report. She only needs to change the values for refrigerators and microwave ovens because the current value for the quantity of stoves to order, 14, is the same as the original value.

To set the quantity to order back to the original values for refrigerators and microwave ovens:

❶ Click cell **B11**, then type **6** to enter the original quantity that Keiko had in this cell.

❷ Click cell **D11**, then type **19** to enter the original quantity that Keiko had in this cell.

❸ Press **[Enter]** to complete the entry.

Now Keiko uses Solver to solve the problem again and generate an answer report.

To solve the problem again and generate an answer report:

❶ Click **Tools**, then click **Solver...** to display the Solver Parameters dialog box with the setting you previously entered.

❷ Click the **Solve button** to solve the problem.

❸ When the Solver Results dialog box appears, click **Answer** in the Reports box. Make sure the Keep Solver Solution option button is selected. See Figure 6-21.

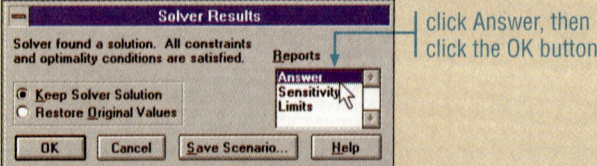

Figure 6-21
Generating an answer report

❹ Click the **OK button** to generate the answer report. The answer report appears on the screen briefly, then the original worksheet is displayed.

Solver places the answer report in a separate sheet called *Answer Report 1*.

The first time you generate an answer report for a problem, it is named Answer Report 1. The second report you create is called Answer Report 2, and so on. To view the answer report worksheet, click the Answer Report 1 tab.

To examine the answer report:

❶ Click the **Answer Report 1 tab** to display the answer report. Figure 6-22 shows a printout of the answer report. Your screen shows only part of the answer report; however, you can scroll the answer report to view it in its entirety.

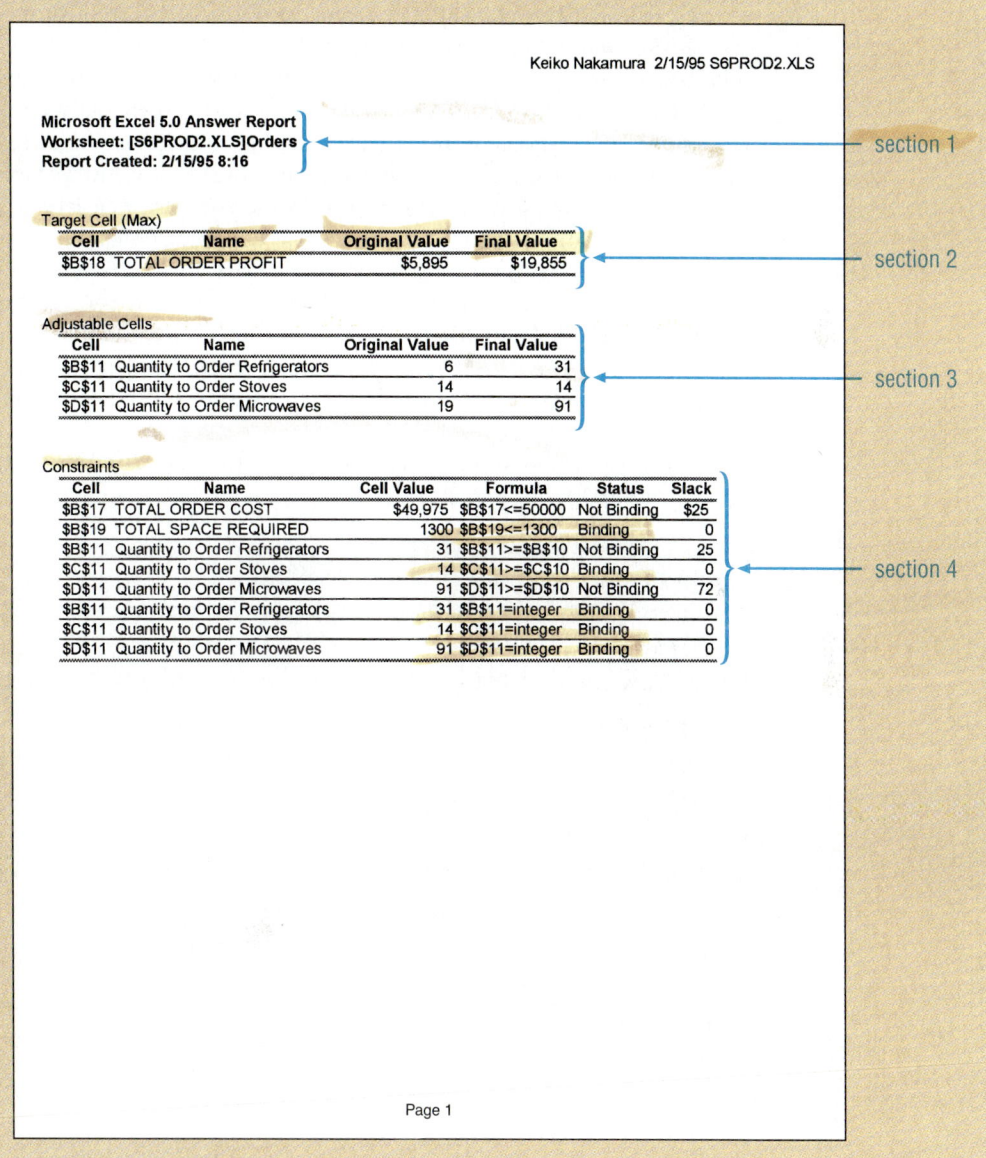

Figure 6-22
Printout of Keiko's answer report

Keiko notices that the answer report is divided into four sections. The first section includes titles, which indicate that this is an Excel answer report created from the Orders sheet in the S6PROD2.XLS workbook. The second section displays information about the target cell, including the location of the cell, the label for the cell, the original value of the cell, and the final value of the cell.

The third section displays information about the changing cells, referred to on the report as "Adjustable Cells." This section of the report shows the location, column or row label, the original value, and the final value of each cell.

The fourth section of the report displays information about the constraints. In addition to the location, label, and value of each constraint, this section shows the constraint formulas. The second column from the right shows the status of each constraint. The status of total order cost, quantity to order refrigerators, and quantity to order microwaves is listed as "Not Binding." **Not Binding means** that these constraints were not limiting factors in the solution. The status of the other constraints is listed as "Binding." **Binding** means that the final value in these cells was equal to the constraint value. For example, the total space required constraint was $B$19<=1300. In the solution, cell B19 is 1300, which is at the maximum limit of the constraint, so this was a binding constraint in the solution.

The last column on the right shows the slack for each constraint. The slack is the difference between the value in the cell and the value at the limit of the constraint. For example, the constraint for the total order cost was $50,000. In the solution the total order cost was $49,975. The difference, or slack, between these two numbers is $25. Binding constraints show a slack of zero. Constraints listed as not binding show the difference between the constraint limit and the final value.

Keiko decides to add a header as additional documentation, then print the answer report.

To add a header and print the answer report:

1. Click the **Print Preview button** to see how the answer report will look when you print it.
2. Click the **Setup... button** to display the Setup dialog box, then click the **Header/Footer tab**.
3. Click **Custom Header...** to display the Header dialog box.
4. Delete the header from the Center Section, then click the **Right Section** and type **Keiko Nakamura**. Press **[Spacebar]** to separate the name and date.
5. Click the **Date button**.
6. Press **[Spacebar]**, then click the **Filename button**. Don't be concerned if "&[File]" appears on a separate line.
7. Click the **OK button** to return to the Page Setup dialog box.
8. Click the **OK button** to return to the Print Preview screen.
9. Click the **Print... button** to open the Print dialog box.
10. Click the **OK button** to print the report.

Keiko saves the answer report, then closes the window containing the answer report.

To save the workbook with the new answer report worksheet:

1. Click the **Save button**.

Next, Keiko prints the orders worksheet.

To save and print the Orders worksheet:

❶ Click the **Orders tab**.

❷ Click the **Print Preview button** to see how your printout will look.

❸ Click the **Setup button** and adjust the settings in the Page Setup dialog box to produce a printout as in Figure 6-23. Check to make sure the header, is the same as in the Answer Report. Also, make sure the gridlines are turned off.

```
                                              Keiko Nakamura 2/15/95 S6PROD2.XLS

Appliance Mart Superstore
GoldStar Order Worksheet

                            Refrigerators   Stoves    Microwaves
Unit Wholesale Cost             $850        $420        $195
Unit Retail Price             $1,250        $595        $250
Profit per Unit                 $400        $175         $55
Cubic feet per Unit               25          18           3

Customer Orders                    6          14          19
Quantity to Order                 31          14          91

Total Cost                   $26,350      $5,880     $17,745
Total Profit                 $12,400      $2,450      $5,005
Total Cubic Feet                 775         252         273

TOTAL ORDER COST             $49,975
TOTAL ORDER PROFIT           $19,855
TOTAL SPACE REQUIRED           1300


                              Page 1
```

Figure 6-23
Keiko's final printed worksheet

❹ Click the **OK button** to return to the Print Preview window. When you are satisfied with the worksheet, click the **Print... button** to display the Print dialog box.

❺ Click the **OK button** to send the report to the printer. See Figure 6-23.

Keiko examines the printed worksheet and answer report to make sure they contain the correct information. She exits Excel and Windows and takes the printed reports to Jordan.

Questions

1. Describe the trial-and-error process.
2. In your own words, describe a what-if analysis.
3. Identify a typical business problem that could be solved using Excel's Goal Seek.
   a. Describe the problem.
   b. Sketch a worksheet that you would use to solve the problem.
   c. Which cell on your worksheet sketch is the set cell, or result cell?
   d. What value would you specify for the result?
   e. What cell can Excel change to produce the result?
4. Describe a typical business problem that could be solved using what-if analysis.
5. In your own words, describe Excel's Solver.
6. What is a changing cell?
7. What is a target cell?
8. What is a constraint?
9. What should you do if you do not want Solver to produce fractional numbers as the solution?
10. List three examples of Solver parameters.
11. Use the *Microsoft Excel User's Guide* or other reference material, such as business textbooks, to find information about *linear programming*.
    a. How does your reference define linear programming?
    b. How do you think linear programming relates to the topics covered in Tutorial 6?
    c. Provide a bibliography of the reference(s) you used for this question.
12. Eve Bowman is the manager of Southland Furniture store, and she is planning a New Year's Day sale. Eve has decided to slash prices 40% on folding tables and folding chairs. The store has only 75 square feet of space available to display and stock this merchandise. Each folding table costs $5, retails for $11, and takes up two square feet of space. Each chair costs $4, retails for $9, and takes up one square foot of space. The maximum amount allocated for purchasing the tables and chairs for the sale is $280. Eve doesn't think she can sell more than 40 chairs, but the demand for tables is virtually unlimited. Eve needs to know how many tables and how many chairs she should purchase in order to make the most profit.
    a. What is the goal in this problem?
    b. Which element of the problem would you specify for the changing cells if you used Solver to find a solution to this problem?
    c. List the constraints for this problem.
13. Joel Nieman is the advertising manager for a Chicago print shop. He is trying to determine how to best spend his advertising funds, but he wants to spend as little as he can to attract the attention of potential customers. He has two plans. The first plan is for a series of half-page ads in the *Chicago Tribune*. The second plan is for a series of 30-second ads on a local television channel. Each ad in the *Chicago Tribune* costs $1,150. Each television ad costs $600. Joel would like to reach at least 70% of the area business people and 30% of the area non-business people. The *Chicago Tribune* ads are typically read by 5% business people and 4% non-business people. The television ads are typically viewed by 5% business people and 3% non-business people in the Chicago area.
    a. What is the goal in this problem?
    b. Which element of the problem would you specify for the changing cells if you used Solver to find a solution to this problem?
    c. List the constraints for this problem.

14. Define the meaning of the following terms as they are used on an Excel answer report:
    a. adjustable cells
    b. binding
    c. slack

Tutorial Assignments

GoldStar offers Appliance Mart Superstore special pricing on dryers in addition to dishwashers, refrigerators, stoves, and microwave ovens. GoldStar dryers are available for $215 and require 11 cubic feet of storage space; the retail price is $385. There are no orders for GoldStar dryers at this time, but the sales manager thinks they will sell very well. Given funds of $75,000 and a storage space limit of 1,500 cubic feet for all the items on the order, what mix of products should Keiko order?

To help Keiko determine how many of each product to order, complete the following:
1. Open the file T6PROD4.XLS.
2. Save the file on your Student Disk as S6PROD4.XLS.
3. Enter the label "Dryers" in cell E4.
4. Enter the wholesale cost of a dryer in cell E5 and the retail price of a dryer in cell E6.
5. Enter the formula to calculate the profit for a dryer in cell E7.
6. Enter the cubic feet of storage required for a dryer in cell E8.
7. Enter the customer orders and the quantity to order.
8. Copy the formulas from the range D13:D15 to the range E13:E15.
9. Edit the formula in cell B17 so it includes the total cost of dryers.
10. Edit the formula in cell B18 so it includes the total profit from dryers.
11. Edit the formula in cell B19 so it includes the total cubic feet required for dryers.
12. Format the cells in column E as needed to match the format of the other columns.
13. Activate Solver and adjust the changing cells to $B$11:$E$11.
14. Change the integer constraint so all of the units sold must be integers.
15. Add a constraint so the quantity of dryers to order is greater than or equal to customer orders for dryers.
16. Change the constraint that limits the total order cost from $50,000 to $75,000.
17. Change the storage space constraint that limits total space required to 1500.
18. Use Solver to solve the problem and produce an answer report.
19. Modify the headers on the worksheet and on the answer report so they contain your name, the date, and the filename.
20. Preview the worksheet and the answer report and make format changes as needed.
21. Save the modified workbook.
22. Print the worksheet and the answer report.
23. Use your customized print formulas module, S3MYMOD.XLM, to print the formulas for the worksheet.

Case Problems

1. Ordering Products for a Furniture Sale at Home Furnishings WareHouse

Bruce Hsu is the assistant manager at Home Furnishings WareHouse, a retail furniture outlet. One of Home Furnishings WareHouse's suppliers is having a sales promotion featuring special prices on couches and chairs. Bruce has been asked to determine the mix of products that will generate the greatest profit within the limits of the available funds and display space. Bruce can spend up to $60,000 on the order, and display space is limited to 1,300 square feet. There are no customer orders for either couches or chairs, but the sales manager doesn't want Bruce to order more than 15 chairs.

Bruce has created a worksheet for this problem and has made several attempts to determine the solution manually. Bruce has asked you to help him use Solver to find the best solution.

To help Bruce use Solver to find the best solution:
1. Open the workbook P6FURN.XLS and maximize the worksheet window.
2. Save the file as S6FURN.XLS.
3. Set up the Solver parameters for this problem using the following hints:
    a. The target cell contains the value for total order profit. Solver should attempt to maximize this cell.
    b. The changing cells contain the quantity to order for couches and for chairs.
    c. The total order cost must be less than or equal to $60,000.
    d. The total space required must be less than or equal to 1300.
    e. You cannot order more than 15 chairs.
    f. You must order couches and chairs in whole units.
    g. You must order a positive number of couches and chairs.
4. Have Solver produce a solution.
5. Format the worksheet to give it a professional appearance.
6. Preview the worksheet and make any formatting changes necessary so your worksheet looks professional.
7. Save the workbook.
8. Print the worksheet, then use your customized print formulas module S3MYMOD.XLM to print the formulas you used to construct the worksheet.

2. Manufacturing Pontoon Boats at Robbins Pontoon Incorporated

Mike Chignell is the assistant to the director of manufacturing at Robbins Pontoon Incorporated. Robbins manufactures four different models of pontoon boats: All Purpose, Camping, Utility, and Fishing. Each of the four models is built on the same boat frame. A topside assembly is attached to the frame to create each model.

Robbins currently has 135 boat frames in stock and a limited number of the four different topside assemblies. Mike has been asked to determine the mix of models that will generate the greatest profit given the available frames and topside assemblies. Mike must also make sure he manufactures enough of each model to fill the customer orders. To help Mike use Solver to determine the best mix of models to manufacture:
1. Open the file P6BOATS.XLS and maximize the worksheet window.
2. Save the file as S6BOATS.XLS.
3. Set up the Solver parameters for this problem using the following hints:
    a. The target cell contains the value for the total profit from all models of pontoon boats. This should be maximized.
    b. The changing cells contain the values for the quantity to make for each boat model.
    c. The constraints should include the following limits:
        All Purpose boats to make <= available All Purpose assemblies
        Utility boats to make <= available Utility assemblies
        Camping boats to make <= available Camping assemblies
        Fishing boats to make <= available Fishing assemblies
        All Purpose boats to make >= customer orders for All Purpose boats
        Utility Boats to make >= customer orders for Utility Boats
        Camping Boats to make >= customer orders for Camping Boats
        Fishing Boats to make >= customer orders for Fishing Boats
        Total boats to make <= available frames
        Make only complete boats

4. Have Solver produce a solution.
5. Modify the heading of the worksheet so it contains your name, the date, and the filename.
6. Preview the printout and make any formatting changes necessary for a professional appearance.
7. Save the completed workbook.
8. Print the completed worksheet.

E 3. Scheduling Employees at Chipster's Pizza

Lisa Avner is the assistant manager at Chipster's Pizza, a popular pizza place located in Cedar Falls, Iowa. Chipster's is open every day from 5:00 PM to 1:00 AM. Friday and Saturday are the busiest nights. Sunday and Wednesday nights are moderately busy. Monday, Tuesday, and Thursday are the slowest nights.

It is Lisa's responsibility to devise a schedule that provides enough employees to meet the usual demand, without scheduling more employees than are needed for each shift. All of Chipster's employees work five consecutive days, then have two days off. This means Lisa can schedule employees for seven different shifts—the Sunday through Thursday shift, the Monday through Friday shift, the Tuesday through Saturday shift, and so forth.

Lisa has created a worksheet showing the number of employees scheduled for each of the seven shifts, the total hours scheduled for each day, the hours needed for each day, and the difference between the hours scheduled and the hours needed. Lisa has asked you to help her find the schedule that will result in enough employee hours to meet the daily demand without scheduling excess hours.

To help Lisa find the optimal schedule:
1. Open the workbook P6SCHED.XLS and maximize the worksheet window.
2. Save the workbook as S6SCHED.XLS.
3. The worksheet shows the current schedule. Cell B13 displays the current total of 560 scheduled hours. Cell B14 displays the current total of 448 needed hours. Cell B15 displays the current total of 112 excess scheduled hours.
4. Set up the Solver parameters to find a solution to the scheduling problem using the following hints:
   a. The target cell is B15, the difference between the total hours scheduled and the total hours needed. The solution should seek to minimize cell B15.
   b. The changing cells are B6:B12.
   c. Use the following constraints:
   Total Hours >= Hours Needed
   Workers Scheduled for each shift >= 0 (You must not schedule a negative number of workers for any shift.)
   Workers Scheduled for each shift = integer (You must schedule workers for the entire shift.)
   Difference for each day >= 0 (You must schedule enough workers so the total hours for each day minus the hours needed is greater than or equal to zero.)
5. Use Solver to generate a solution and an answer report.
6. Modify the headers on the worksheet and the answer report so they contain your name, the date, and the filename.
7. Save the workbook.
8. Preview and print the worksheet and the answer report.

TUTORIAL 7

Managing Data with Excel

Analyzing Personnel Data

OBJECTIVES

In this tutorial you will:
- Identify the elements of an Excel data list
- Sort data in a worksheet
- Query a list to find information
- Maintain a list with a data form
- Learn the difference between an internal and external database
- Filter records
- Create PivotTables on internal and external databases using Microsoft Query

CASE

North State University Sarah Magnussan is an administrative assistant to Ralph Long, the dean of the College of Business at North State University. The dean frequently asks Sarah to look up and summarize information about the College of Business faculty. To fulfill these requests more efficiently and accurately, Sarah has created an Excel worksheet that contains the names, academic rank, department, date hired, salary, and gender of each faculty member in the College of Business.

The College of Business is divided into two academic departments: the Management department and the Accounting department. Each faculty member holds an academic rank, such as professor or associate professor. Most faculty members are hired at the rank of instructor or assistant professor. After a period of time, the faculty member might be promoted to associate professor and then to full professor. Faculty salaries usually reflect the faculty member's rank and length of service in the department.

Sarah has become quite proficient using Excel to manage the data in her faculty worksheet. **Data management** refers to the tasks required to maintain and manipulate a collection of data. Data management tasks typically include entering data, updating current data, sorting data, searching for information, and creating reports.

In previous tutorials you learned how to use Excel to perform calculations using the numeric data or values you entered into worksheet cells. In this tutorial you will learn how to use Excel to manage numeric and non-numeric data. You will discover how easy it is to sort the information on a worksheet and how Excel can help you select or search for information. Later in the tutorial you will learn how to plan and create special tables based on the data you sorted and selected. Let's work along with Sarah as she uses Excel to manage the data in her faculty worksheet.

To launch Excel and organize the desktop:
1. Launch Windows and Excel.
2. Make sure your Student Disk is in the disk drive.
3. Make sure the Microsoft Excel and Sheet1 windows are maximized.

Sarah's file of faculty information is stored on your Student Disk as C7FACUL.XLS. Let's open that file, then save it under a different filename.

To open the C7FACUL.XLS workbook:
1. Click the **Open button** to display the Open dialog box.
2. Double-click **C7FACUL.XLS** in the File Name box to open the workbook.
   TROUBLE? If the file isn't in the file list, click the Drives down arrow button to display the drive where your student disk is located.
3. Click **File**, then click **Save As...** to display the Save As dialog box.
4. Save the workbook as **S7FACUL.XLS**.

Sarah's worksheet, shown as a split window view in Figure 7-1, contains a list of information, or data, about faculty members in the College of Business. A list of data like this is also referred to as a database. Information about individual faculty members is in rows 7 through 41. The information includes last name, first name, department, rank, date hired (STARTDATE), salary, and gender. The column titles in row 6 identify the information in each column. Each column in a database is known as a **field**. Each column heading is known as a **field name**. Each row in a database is known as a **record**.

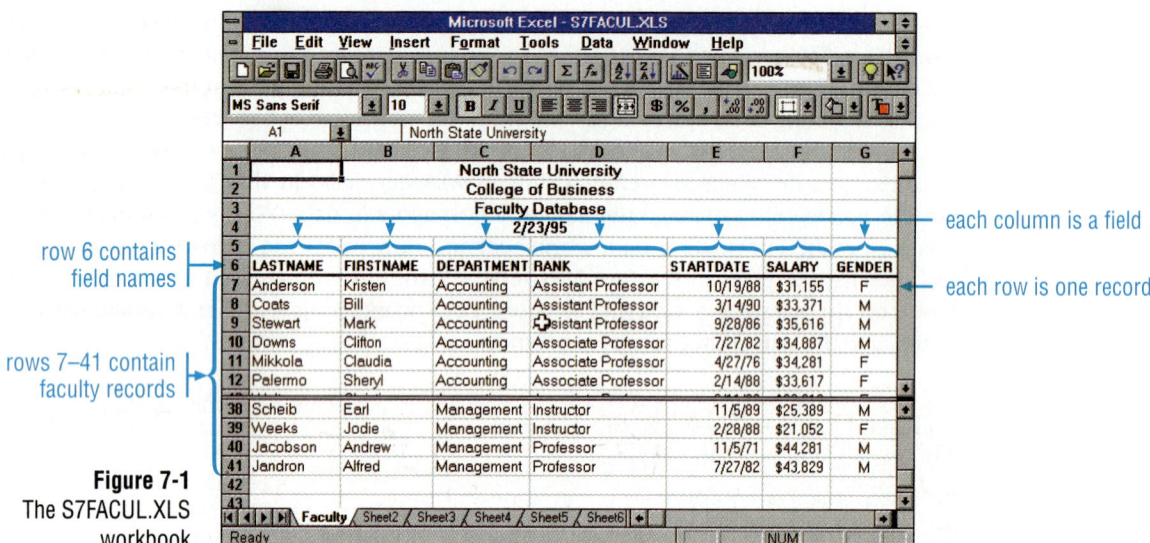

Figure 7-1
The S7FACUL.XLS workbook

As you can see in Figure 7-1, each row of Sarah's worksheet contains information about one faculty member. Another way to envision a list of data is as a set of cards or forms, like those shown in Figure 7-2. Here each card corresponds to one row (or record) on the Excel worksheet. Each entry line on a card corresponds to one column (or field) in the worksheet. As you progress through the tutorial, you will learn that you can view your data in rows and columns on the worksheet or in a format (called a data form) that is similar to a card file.

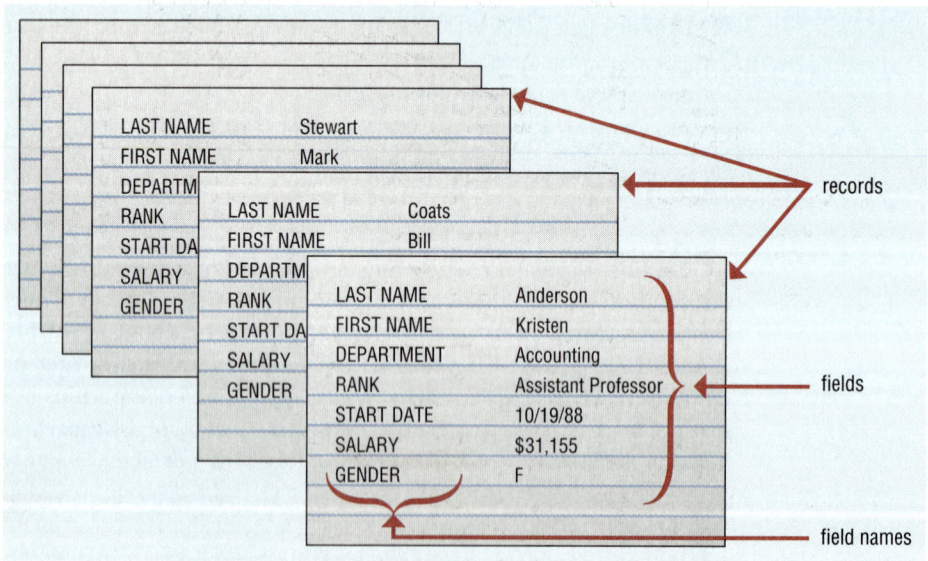

Figure 7-2
A card file representation of an Excel database

The dean has asked Sarah to provide him with a list of all faculty members in the College of Business, sorted in alphabetical order by last name. He also wants another list of all faculty members by rank with the faculty members sorted alphabetically by last name within each rank. Sarah knows she can use Excel's Sort command to create the lists the dean requested.

Sorting Data

When you sort a list, Excel arranges the rows of the list according to the contents of one or more columns. For example, in Sarah's worksheet you could sort the rows alphabetically according to the information contained in the DEPARTMENT column. The result would be a list in which all the rows containing information about faculty in the Accounting department would appear first, followed by all the rows containing information about the Management faculty. If you sorted the list by department, and then by rank, the result would be similar to Figure 7-3.

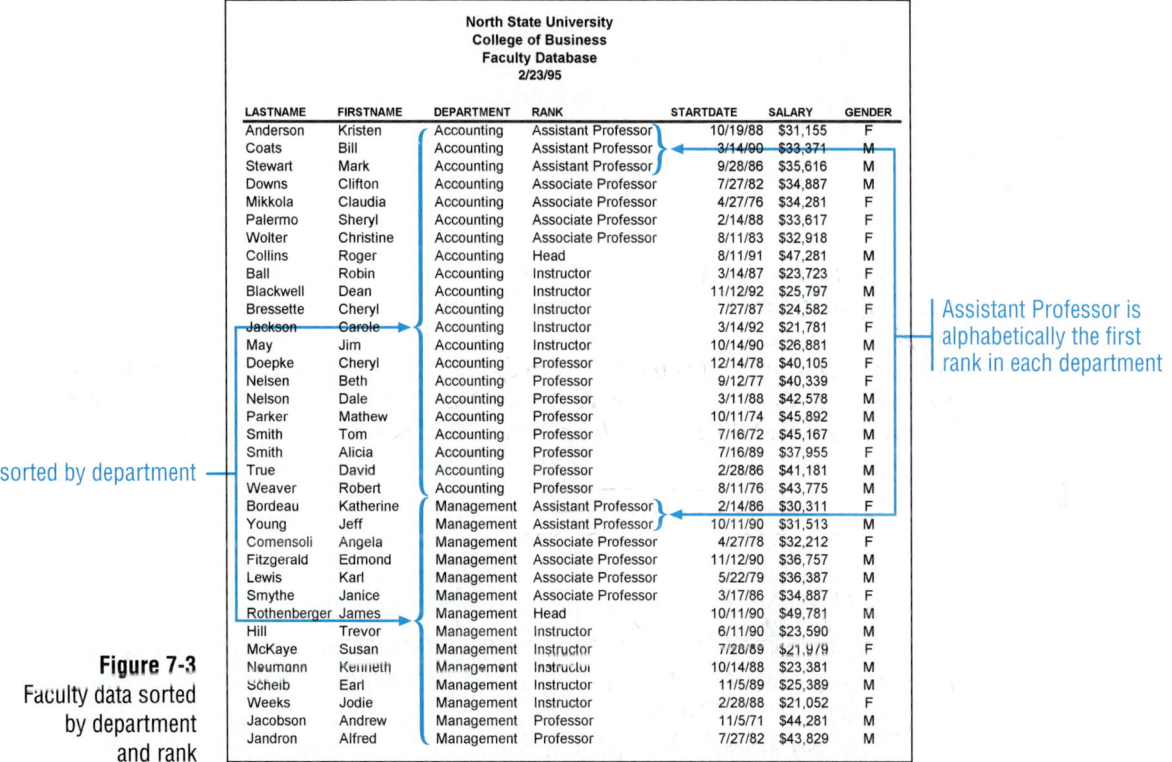

Figure 7-3
Faculty data sorted by department and rank

In Figure 7-3, the rows within the group of Accounting faculty are arranged alphabetically by rank, with the assistant professors listed first, then the associate professors, and so on. The same is true for the Management faculty rows.

To sort the data in an Excel worksheet, you highlight one cell within the list of data you want to sort. In this tutorial, you will always select the cell in the upper-left corner of the list (immediately under the column headings) because this cell is always visible on the screen. Excel automatically recognizes the rows of information as a collection of related data; it also recognizes the bolded text at the top of the list as column headings. You use the Sort command on the Data menu to specify the columns by which you want to sort. If you have a problem with a sort, use the Undo command to put the database back the way it was before the sort.

> **REFERENCE WINDOW**
>
> ### Sorting Rows in a Data List
>
> - Highlight any cell in the list.
> - Click Data, then click Sort... to display the Sort dialog box. The Sort By box is active.
> - Use the down arrow button to display the list of column headings and select the column by which you want to sort.
> - If you want to sort by a second column, click the Then By box and use the down arrow button to select the desired column heading.
> - If you want to sort by a third column, click the second Then By box and select the desired column heading.
> - Click the OK button to sort the list.

Sorting Data by One Column

The dean wants a list of faculty members sorted alphabetically by last name. To prepare this list, Sarah highlights any cell in the range A6:G41, which contains the column headings and the information she wants to sort. She then uses the Sort dialog box to specify that Excel should sort by the contents of the LASTNAME column.

To sort the records alphabetically by last name:

1. Click cell **A7**, which is the cell in the upper-left corner of the list. Remember that Excel will automatically recognize the adjacent rows and columns as a data list.

2. Click **Data**, then click **Sort...** to display the Sort dialog box. Note that Excel automatically selects the entire data list (but not the column headings) when it displays this dialog box.

3. Click the **Sort By down arrow button** to display the list of column headings. If LastName is not already displayed in the Sort By box, select **LastName** now.

4. Make sure the Ascending option button is selected. This tells Excel to arrange the rows alphabetically by last name from A to Z. (If you wanted to arrange the rows by last name from Z to A, you would click Descending.) Make sure the Header Row option is selected in the My List Has box. See Figure 7-4.

Sorting Data by One Column   EX 237

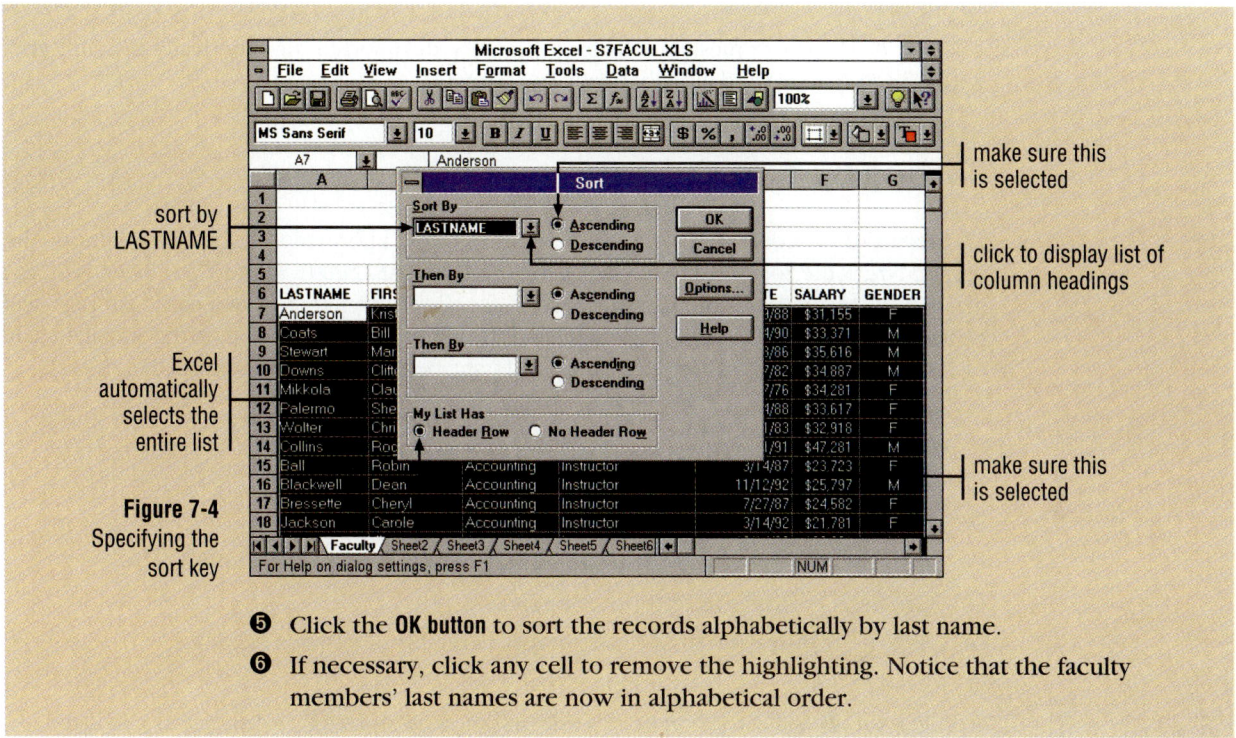

Figure 7-4 Specifying the sort key

- sort by LASTNAME
- Excel automatically selects the entire list
- make sure this is selected
- click to display list of column headings
- make sure this is selected

⑤ Click the **OK button** to sort the records alphabetically by last name.

⑥ If necessary, click any cell to remove the highlighting. Notice that the faculty members' last names are now in alphabetical order.

Sarah previews the worksheet, then prints it and gives it to the dean. Figure 7-5 shows Sarah's printed worksheet.

North State University
College of Business
Faculty Database
2/23/95

last names in alphabetical order

LASTNAME	FIRSTNAME	DEPARTMENT	RANK	STARTDATE	SALARY	GENDER
Anderson	Kristen	Accounting	Assistant Professor	10/19/88	$31,155	F
Ball	Robin	Accounting	Instructor	3/14/87	$23,723	F
Blackwell	Dean	Accounting	Instructor	11/12/92	$25,797	M
Bordeau	Katherine	Management	Assistant Professor	2/14/86	$30,311	F
Bressette	Cheryl	Accounting	Instructor	7/27/87	$24,582	F
Coats	Bill	Accounting	Assistant Professor	3/14/90	$33,371	M
Collins	Roger	Accounting	Head	8/11/91	$47,281	M
Comensoli	Angela	Management	Associate Professor	4/27/78	$32,212	F
Doepke	Cheryl	Accounting	Professor	12/14/78	$40,105	F
Downs	Clifton	Accounting	Associate Professor	7/27/82	$34,887	M
Fitzgerald	Edmond	Accounting	Associate Professor	11/12/90	$36,757	M
Hill	Trevor	Management	Instructor	6/11/90	$23,590	M
Jackson	Carole	Accounting	Instructor	3/14/92	$21,781	F
Jacobson	Andrew	Management	Professor	11/5/71	$44,281	M
Jandron	Alfred	Management	Professor	7/27/82	$43,829	M
Lewis	Karl	Management	Associate Professor	5/22/79	$36,387	M
May	Jim	Accounting	Instructor	10/14/90	$26,881	M
McKaye	Susan	Management	Instructor	7/28/89	$21,979	F
Mikkola	Claudia	Accounting	Associate Professor	4/27/76	$34,281	F
Nelsen	Beth	Accounting	Professor	9/12/77	$40,339	F
Nelson	Dale	Accounting	Professor	3/11/88	$42,578	M
Neumann	Kenneth	Management	Instructor	10/14/88	$23,381	M
Palermo	Sheryl	Accounting	Associate Professor	2/14/88	$33,617	F
Parker	Mathew	Accounting	Professor	10/11/74	$45,892	M
Rothenberger	James	Management	Head	10/11/90	$49,781	M
Scheib	Earl	Management	Instructor	11/5/89	$25,389	M
Smith	Tom	Accounting	Professor	7/16/72	$45,167	M
Smith	Alicia	Accounting	Professor	7/16/89	$37,955	F
Smythe	Janice	Management	Associate Professor	3/17/86	$34,887	F
Stewart	Mark	Accounting	Assistant Professor	9/28/86	$35,616	M
True	David	Accounting	Professor	2/28/86	$41,181	M
Weaver	Robert	Accounting	Professor	8/11/76	$43,775	M
Weeks	Jodie	Management	Instructor	2/28/88	$21,052	F
Wolter	Christine	Accounting	Associate Professor	8/11/83	$32,918	F
Young	Jeff	Management	Assistant Professor	10/11/90	$31,513	M

Figure 7-5 Printed list sorted by last name

The dean also requested a listing of faculty data sorted alphabetically by rank and, within each rank, sorted alphabetically by last name.

Sorting by Two Columns

To prepare the second list for the dean, Sarah sorts the information using two columns. She uses RANK as the Sort By entry in the dialog box, and LASTNAME as the Then By entry in the dialog box. As a result of the sort, the records for all faculty members of a particular rank will be listed together; within each rank, the faculty member records will be sorted alphabetically by last name. As usual with all Data commands, she begins by selecting one cell in the list.

To sort the faculty data by rank and then by last name:

❶ Click cell **A7**.

❷ Click **Data**, then click **Sort...** to display the Sort dialog box.

❸ Click the **Sort By down arrow button** to display the list of column headings.

❹ Click **RANK** to display it in the Sort By box.

❺ Click the **Then By down arrow button** to display the list of column headings.

❻ Click **LASTNAME** to display it in the Then By box.

❼ Click the **OK button** to sort the records first by rank and then by last name. Click any cell to remove the highlighting and view the newly sorted data.

Sarah then prints the report, shown in Figure 7-6.

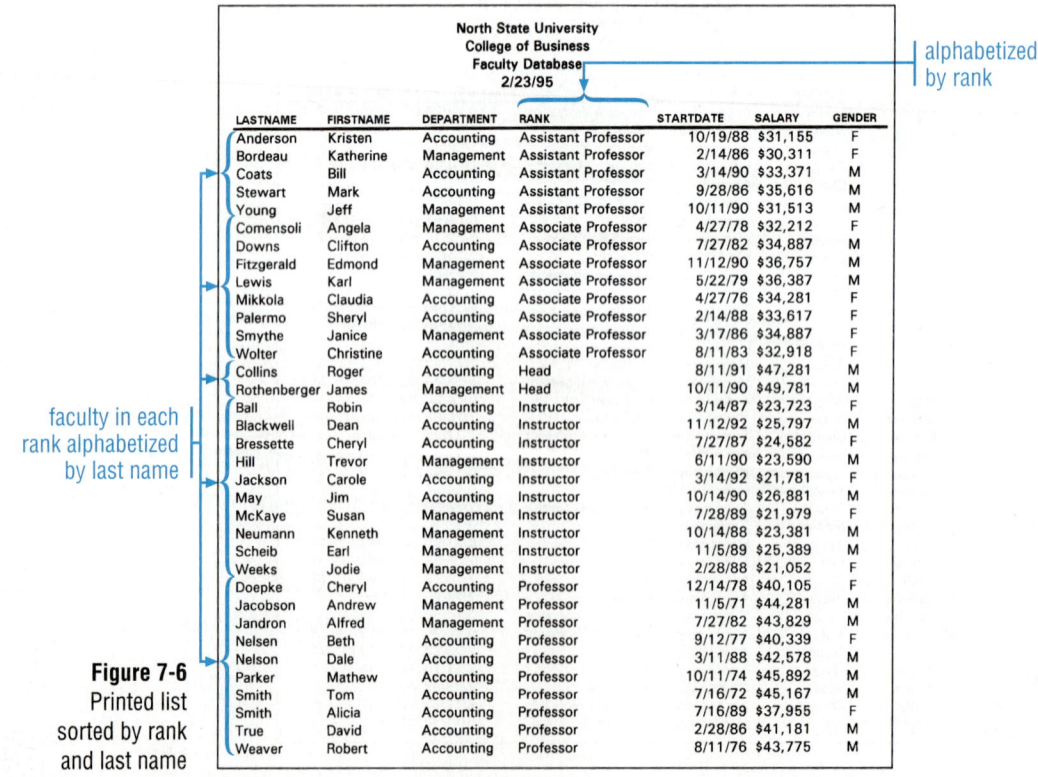

Figure 7-6
Printed list sorted by rank and last name

Excel performed this sort by first alphabetizing the ranks in column D—in effect, grouping the records by rank. All the assistant professors are grouped together, as are all the associate professors, department heads, instructors, and professors. Within each rank, Excel sorted the records alphabetically by last name. For example, within the assistant professor rank, Anderson is listed first, followed by Bordeau.

When Sarah uses the Excel Sort command, she works with the data using the row and column format in which it appears on the worksheet. Sarah finds it convenient to do other data management tasks using Excel's data form, which lets her view the data in a card file format.

Maintaining a List with Excel's Data Form

A **data form** is a dialog box that makes it easy to search for, view, edit, add, and delete rows (also known as records) in a list. A data form displays one record at a time, rather than the table of rows and columns you see on the worksheet.

Sarah uses the Form command now to display one record at a time. Just as she did when she performed a sort, Sarah begins by clicking any cell in the range A6:G41.

To display a data form:

❶ Click cell **A7**.

❷ Click **Data**, then click **Form...** to display the data form. The first record in the list is displayed, as shown in Figure 7-7. Note that the dialog box title, "Faculty," matches the name of the active sheet.

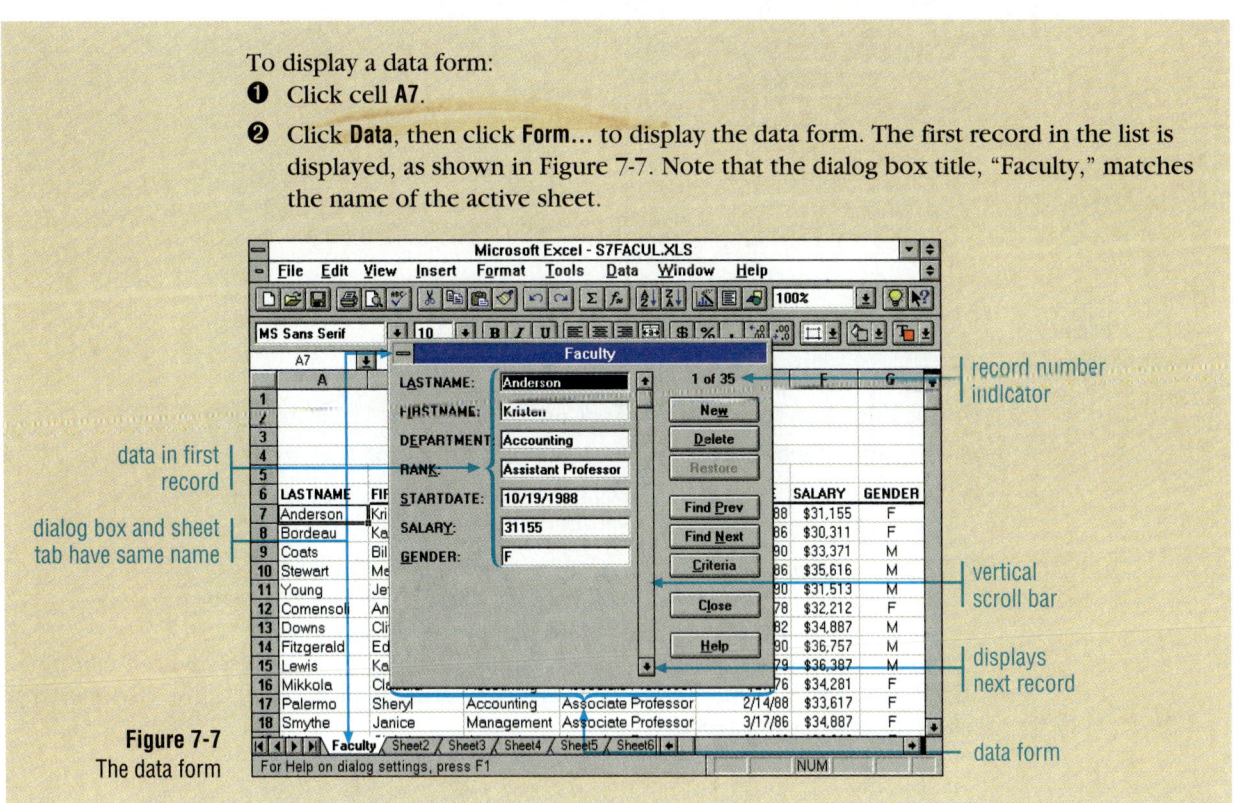

Figure 7-7
The data form

Sarah can use the data form to manually search through each of the records until she finds the one she wants, or she can have Excel search for the record she wants.

Manual Search

You can use the data form to manually scroll through the list one record at a time using the arrow buttons on the data form vertical scroll bar, or the Up Arrow and Down Arrow keys on the keyboard. You can also use the scroll box on the data form vertical scroll bar to move quickly to a particular record number.

The **record number indicator** in the upper-right corner of the data form indicates the number of the record displayed in the data form, and it shows the total number of records in the database. In Figure 7-7 the record indicator shows "1 of 35," indicating that the current record is the first record in the database and that there are 35 records in the database.

Let's practice using the scroll arrow buttons and arrow keys to scroll through the database records.

To practice manually scrolling through the database:

❶ Click the **down arrow button** at the bottom of the vertical scroll bar once or press [↓] once to display the next record in the database. The record number indicator shows that record 2 of 35 is displayed. See Figure 7-8.

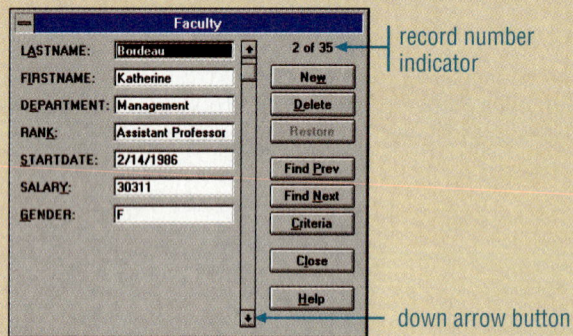

Figure 7-8
Record 2 of 35

❷ Click the **down arrow button** once or press [↓] once to display record 3 of 35.

❸ Click the **up arrow button** once or press [↑] once to scroll back to record 2 of 35.

❹ Drag the scroll box on the scroll bar until the record number indicator shows 18 of 35. Release the mouse button to display the contents of record 18.

❺ Drag the scroll box to the top of the scroll bar to display record 1 of 35.

With large lists of data, manually locating specific rows, or records, can take time. The alternative is to have Excel automatically search for records in the database that match the criteria you specify.

Criteria Search

You can use the Criteria button on the data form to have Excel search for a specific record or group of records. When you initiate a search, you specify the **search criteria**, or the instructions for the search. Excel starts from the current record and moves through the list searching for any records that match the search criteria. If it finds more than one match, Excel displays the first record that matches the search criteria. You use the Find Next button on the data form to display the next record that matches the search criteria. The Find Prev button displays the previous record that matches the search criteria.

The search is not *case sensitive*; that is, it does not matter if you use uppercase or lowercase when you enter the search criteria. For example, if you have a record with "Hill" as the last name, you can find it by entering "HILL" or "Hill" or "hill" as the search criteria.

> **REFERENCE WINDOW**
>
> **Searching for a Record Using the Data Form**
>
> - Click any cell in the data list.
> - Click Data, then click Form… to display the data form.
> - Make sure the data form displays the first record in the list so Excel starts searching at the beginning of the list.
> - Click the Criteria button.
> - Click the Clear button to clear any previous search criteria.
> - Enter the search criteria in the appropriate boxes. You can use uppercase or lowercase.
> - Click the Find Next button to display the next record that matches the search criteria.
> - Click the Find Prev button to display the previous record that matches the search criteria.

A criteria search is also referred to as a **query** because you use a criteria search to find the answers to questions, or **queries**, about the information in the database. Let's see how Sarah might query the faculty database.

Suppose Sarah wants to find the date that Trevor Hill started working at the College of Business. She can use the Criteria button to have Excel search for the record of the faculty member with a last name of "Hill." Then, when she finds the record, she needs only to look in the STARTDATE field to find out when he started.

To search for the record for Trevor Hill:
1. Make sure the record number indicator says 1 of 35.
2. Click the **Criteria button** to begin entering the criteria. Notice that some of the buttons change and the word "Criteria" appears in the upper-right corner of the dialog box.

❸ Click the **LASTNAME box**, then type **Hill**. See Figure 7-9.

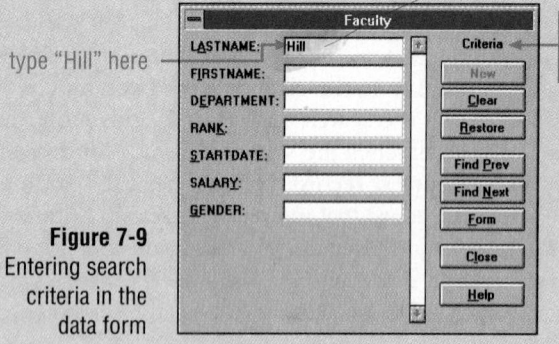

Figure 7-9
Entering search criteria in the data form

type "Hill" here

"Criteria" appears here when you are entering search criteria

will locate the record

❹ Click the **Find Next button** to display the first record that contains Hill as the last name. The record for Trevor Hill appears.

❺ Click the **Find Next button** again to see if there are any more records containing Hill as the last name. A beep indicates that no other records match the specified search criteria; therefore, no other faculty members have Hill as their last name.

Sarah can see from the record in the data form that Trevor started on 6/11/1990.

Next, suppose that Sarah needs to find the names of the female faculty members with the rank of professor. For this query, Sarah must enter two search criteria: RANK must be "Professor" and GENDER must be "F."

To view the records for all female professors:
❶ Click the **up arrow button** at the top of the scroll bar to display record 1 of 35.
❷ Click the **Criteria button**.
❸ Click the **Clear button** to clear the previous search criteria.
❹ Click the **RANK box**, then type **Professor**.
❺ Click the **GENDER box**, then type **F**.
❻ Click the **Find Next button** to view the record for the next female professor. Record 26 displays the information for Cheryl Doepke, a professor in the Accounting department.
❼ Click the **Find Next button** again to view the next record that matches the search criteria. Record 29 displays the information for Beth Nelsen, a professor in the Accounting department.
❽ Click the **Find Next button** again to view the next record. Record 33 displays the information for Alicia Smith, a professor in the Accounting department.
❾ Click the **Find Next button** again to view the next record. A beep indicates that no more records match the search criteria.

Sarah now knows that there are three female professors in the College of Business—Cheryl Doepke, Beth Nelsen, and Alicia Smith.

Next, suppose that Sarah wants to find out which faculty members started with the university before 1/1/1975. She can use the "less than" symbol (<) to specify that she wants to select faculty members whose start date is less than (earlier than) 1/1/1975.

To view the records for all faculty members who started before 1/1/1975:

❶ Click the **up arrow button** at the top of the scroll bar to display record 1 of 35.

❷ Click the **Criteria button**.

❸ Click the **Clear button** to clear the previous search criteria.

❹ Click the **STARTDATE box**, then type **<1/1/1975** to search for all faculty members who started before 1/1/1975. See Figure 7-10.

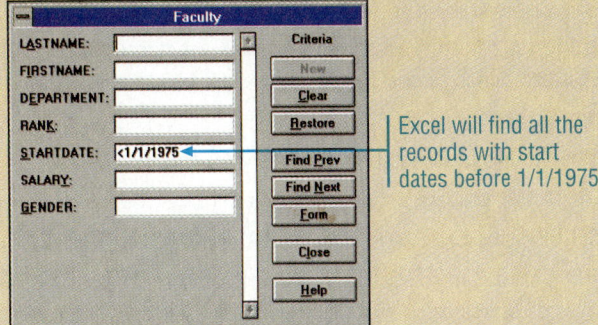

Figure 7-10
Searching for records by start date

❺ Click the **Find Next button** to view the record for the first faculty member who started before 1/1/1975. Record 27 displays the information for Andrew Jacobson, who started in the Management department on 11/5/1971.

❻ Click the **Find Next button** to view the record for the next faculty member who started before 1/1/1975. Record 31 displays the information for Mathew Parker, who started in the Accounting department on 10/11/1974.

❼ Click the **Find Next button** again to view the record for the next faculty member who started before 1/1/1975. Record 32 displays the information for Tom Smith, who started in the Accounting department on 7/16/1972.

❽ Click the **Find Next button** to view the record for the next faculty member who started before 1/1/1975. A beep indicates that no more records match the search criteria.

Now, suppose that on the way to work, Sarah heard part of a radio interview with a North State faculty member from the College of Business who recently won first place in a women's local 10K race. She remembers that her last name started with *Ne*, as in Nesbitt or Nelson. Sarah would like to use her database to find out who won the race. Because Sarah does not know the exact search criteria, she can use a wildcard to replace part of the search criteria.

Using Wildcards

Excel's data form allows you to use wildcards when you enter search criteria. A **wildcard** is a symbol that stands for one or more characters. The Excel data form recognizes two wildcards: the question mark and the asterisk.

You use the question mark (?) wildcard to represent any single character. For example, if you didn't know if a faculty member's last name was spelled Nels*e*n or Nels*o*n, you could specify Nels?n as the search criteria. The data form would display all records in which the last name started with *Nels*, followed by any single character, and then ending with *n*.

You can use the asterisk (*) wildcard to represent any group of characters. For example, if you use *Ne** as the search criteria for the last name field, Excel will find all the records with last names that begin with *Ne*, regardless of the letters that follow. If you use **son* as the search criteria for the last name field, Excel will find all the records with last names that end with *son*, regardless of the letters at the beginning of the last name.

Sarah decides to use the asterisk wildcard to find all the female faculty members whose last names start with the letters *Ne*.

To search for all female faculty members whose last names start with *Ne*:

1. Click the **up arrow button** at the top of the scroll bar to display record 1 of 35.
2. Click the **Criteria button**.
3. Click the **Clear button** to clear the previous search criteria.
4. Click the **LASTNAME box**, then type **Ne*** to select last names that start with *Ne*.
5. Click the **GENDER box**, then type **F** to limit the search to female faculty members.
6. Click the **Find Next button** to view the record for the first female faculty member whose last name starts with *Ne*. The record for Beth Nelsen is displayed. Beth could be the person who won the 10K race.
7. Click the **Find Next button** again to view the next record that matches the search criteria. A beep indicates that no more records match the search criteria.

Sarah found only one female faculty member whose last name starts with *Ne*, so Beth Nelsen must be the faculty member who won the women's 10K race.

Maintaining Data in a List

In addition to querying the list, you need to maintain the accuracy of the data by making changes, additions, or deletions. The process of maintaining the accuracy of the data is often referred to as **updating**.

Sarah goes through her in-basket and comes across a memo from the dean, announcing that Jim May, an instructor in the Accounting department, has resigned and that Martin Stein has been hired as his replacement. Sarah needs to update her faculty list to delete the record for Jim May and add a record for Martin Stein.

Deleting Records

The Delete button on the data form allows you to delete records in the database. To delete a record using the data form, you display the record, then click the Delete button. Deleted records are removed from the worksheet.

> **REFERENCE WINDOW**
>
> ### Deleting a Record Using the Data Form
>
> - Click any cell within the list.
> - Click Data, then click Form... to display the data form.
> - Scroll or search through the records to display the record you want to delete.
> - Click the Delete button.
> - Click the OK button to delete the record.

DATA/FORM/Delete

Sarah must locate the record for Jim May before she can delete it.

To locate and delete the record for Jim May:
1. Click the **up arrow button** at the top of the scroll bar to display record 1 of 35.
2. Click the **Criteria button**.
3. Click the **Clear button** to clear the previous query.
4. Click the **LASTNAME box**, then type **May** as the search criteria.
5. Click the **Find Next button** to display the first record that matches the search criteria. Jim May's record appears in the data form.
6. Click the **Delete button**.
7. When you see the message "Displayed record will be permanently deleted" click the **OK button**.

Excel deletes the row for Jim May from the worksheet. Sarah will check the worksheet to verify the deletion after she adds a new record and enters the information for Martin Stein.

Adding New Records

The New button on the data form adds a new blank row, or record, to the bottom of data list. If you want to keep your database in alphabetical order, you will need to sort it again after you add records.

REFERENCE WINDOW

Adding a Record Using the Data Form

- Click any cell within the list.
- Click Data, then click Form... to display the data form.
- Click the New button.
- Enter the information for the new record.
- Click the Close button or scroll to another record to save the new record.

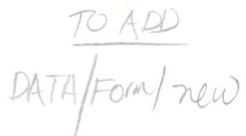

Work along with Sarah as she adds a record for Martin Stein to the database.

To add Martin Stein to the faculty database:

1. Click the **New button** to create a new record.
2. Type **Stein** in the LASTNAME box.
3. Press **[Tab]** to move to the FIRSTNAME box, then type **Martin**.
4. Press **[Tab]** to move to the DEPARTMENT box, then type **Accounting**.
5. Press **[Tab]** to move to the RANK box, then type **Instructor**.
6. Press **[Tab]** to move to the STARTDATE box, then type today's date using the format MM/DD/YYYY, for example, 2/23/1995.
7. Press **[Tab]** to move to the SALARY box, then type **20562**.
8. Press **[Tab]** to move to the GENDER box, then type **M**. Check that your form looks like Figure 7-11 before moving on to Step 9.

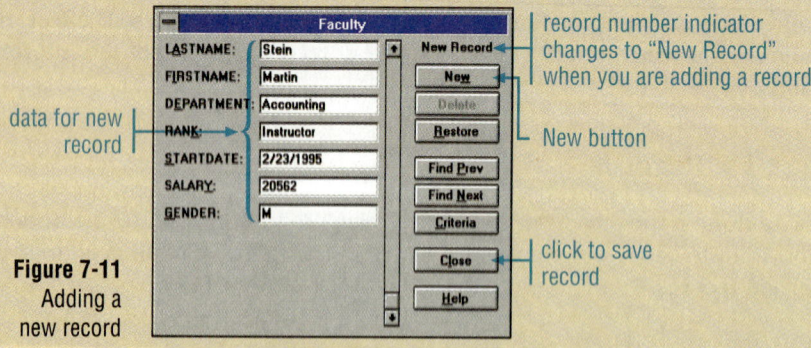

Figure 7-11
Adding a new record

TROUBLE? If you made a mistake, click the box you want to correct. Delete the incorrect entry, then type the correct entry.

9. Click the **Close button** to close the data form and save the record.

Sarah wants to verify that the record for Jim May was deleted and the record for Martin Stein was added; then she can save the worksheet.

To verify the record deletion for Jim May and the addition of Martin Stein and then save the worksheet:

❶ Scroll the worksheet and make sure the record for Jim May is gone.

❷ Scroll to the bottom of the worksheet and verify that row 41 now contains the record for Martin Stein.

❸ Click the **Save button** 🖬.

If you want to take a break and resume the tutorial later, you can exit Excel by double-clicking the Control menu box in the upper-left corner of the screen. When you resume the tutorial, launch Excel, maximize the Microsoft Excel and Sheet1 windows, and place your Student Disk in the disk drive. Open the file S7FACUL.XLS, then continue with the tutorial.

■   ■   ■

After lunch the dean returns from a meeting regarding equal pay for male and female faculty members. The dean wants to know if the male and female faculty members in the College of Business are receiving equivalent salaries. He asks Sarah to calculate the average pay for male and female faculty members in the College of Business.

Sarah thinks about the dean's request and decides that she can first list all the information for female faculty, then use the AVERAGE function to calculate the average salary. She will then list all the information for male faculty and calculate that average salary.

Filtering a List

In this tutorial you have manually scrolled through the list to find records, and you have used the data form Criteria button to search for records that match specific search criteria. When you use the data form, you can view only one record at a time, even if more than one record matches the search criteria. If you want to see a list of all the records that match the search criteria, you must filter the list.

The **Filter command** on the Data menu temporarily hides rows that do not match your search criteria. When Excel filters a list, the worksheet is in Filter mode. When you are in Filter mode, you can edit, format, chart and print your filtered list.

Excel offers two ways to filter a list. AutoFilter allows you to filter a list quickly based on one simple criteria at a time. For example, Sarah will use AutoFilter to display the records for all female faculty. Advanced Filter allows you to use more complicated criteria or several different criteria at once. For example, Sarah might use Advanced Filter if she wanted to display the records for all female faculty in the Accounting Department with salaries greater than $30,000. For now, you will only be concerned with AutoFilter. You will learn how to use Advanced Filter in the case problems at the end of this tutorial.

To use AutoFilter, simply click any cell within the list you want to filter. Then use the AutoFilter command on the Data menu to display down arrow buttons on each column heading in the data list. You can use the down arrow buttons to display lists of possible search criteria. Once you select a criteria, Excel displays only the rows that match your criteria. The row headings are displayed in blue to remind you that you are seeing only part of the entire data list. The down arrow button in the column you used as the search criteria also appears in blue. To display all the rows in the list (not just those that match your search criteria) use the blue down arrow button to select (All) as the search criteria. To remove the down arrow buttons, click AutoFilter on the Data menu again.

> **REFERENCE WINDOW**
>
> **Filtering a List with AutoFilter**
>
> - Click any cell within the list you want to filter.
> - Click Data, click Filter, then click AutoFilter to display the down arrow buttons on each column heading in the worksheet.
> - Click the down arrow button in the column you want to search to display a list of possible search criteria.
> - Click the desired search criteria.
> - Click Data, click Filter, then click AutoFilter again to remove the down arrow buttons from the column headings.

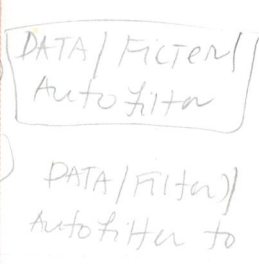

Now let's help Sarah use AutoFilter to display a list of all female faculty and then a list of all male faculty.

Using AutoFilter

The dean wants Sarah to find the average salary for female faculty members and for male faculty members. Sarah wants first to display the rows for female faculty members. As usual with data commands, she begins by clicking any cell within the data list.

To display the list of female faculty members:

❶ Click cell **A7**.

❷ Click **Data**, click **Filter**, then click **AutoFilter**. Down arrow buttons appear on each column label on the worksheet.

❸ Click the **down arrow button** in the Gender column (column G) to display a list of possible criteria. See Figure 7-12.

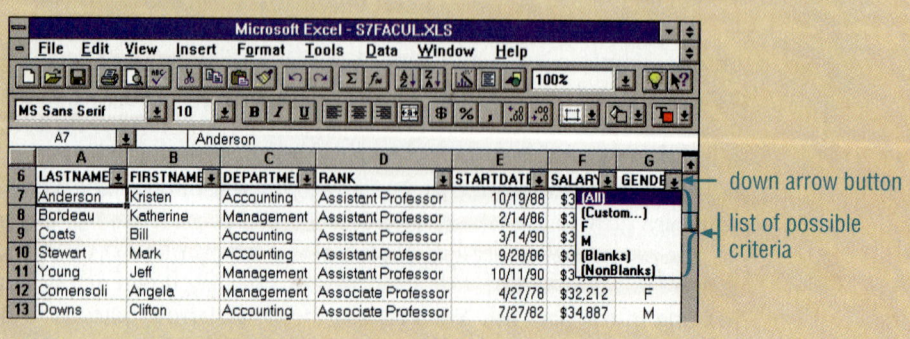

Figure 7-12
Filtering a list using AutoFilter

❹ Click **F** to display only those rows with an F in the Gender column. Excel displays the records for female faculty. The row headings and the down arrow button for column G are displayed in blue. Note that the row heading numbers are not consecutive because only the rows matching the search criteria are displayed. The Status Bar informs you that 15 of the 35 records matched the search criteria. See Figure 7-13.

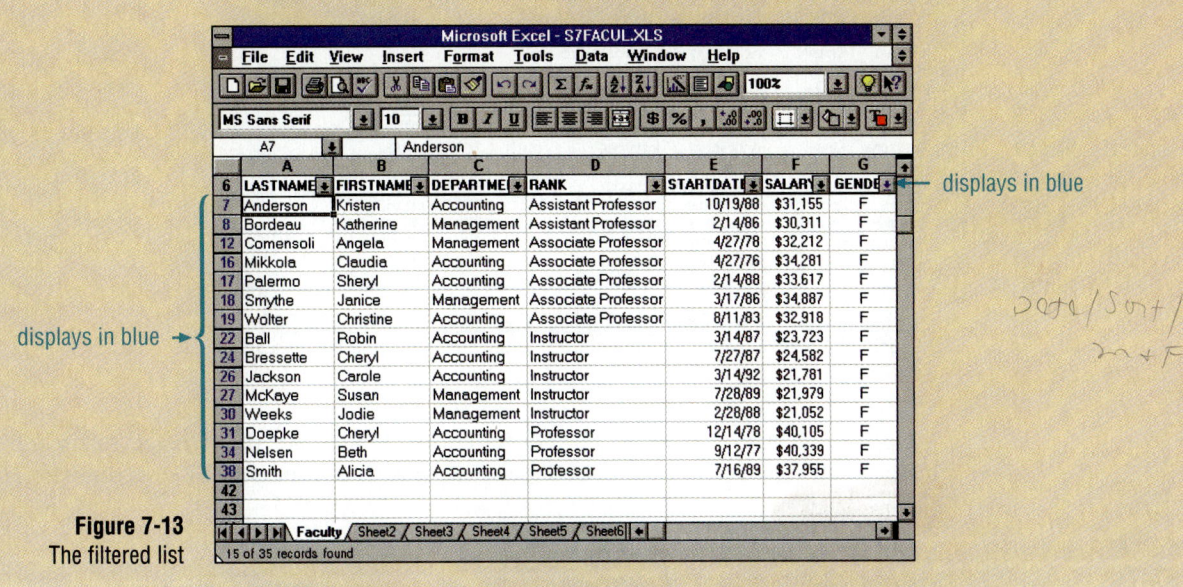

Figure 7-13
The filtered list

Sarah wants to keep a copy of the records for the female faculty, so she copies these rows to a blank sheet, adjusts the column width, and renames the sheet.

To copy the records for female faculty to a blank sheet:
❶ Highlight cells A6 through G38.
❷ Click the **Copy button**.
❸ Click the **Sheet2 tab** to display the blank Sheet2, then click cell A1 to begin inserting rows there.
❹ Click the **Paste button**. The records for the female faculty, along with the column headings, appear in the Sheet2 sheet. Note that Excel does not copy the AutoFilter down arrow buttons from the Faculty sheet.
❺ To format the columns so that all data is visible, click **Format**, click **Column**, then click **AutoFit Selection**.
❻ Click anywhere on the worksheet to remove the highlighting.
❼ Double-click the **Sheet2 tab** to display the Rename Sheet dialog box.
❽ Type **Female Faculty** in the name box, then click the **OK button** to return to the worksheet. See Figure 7-14.

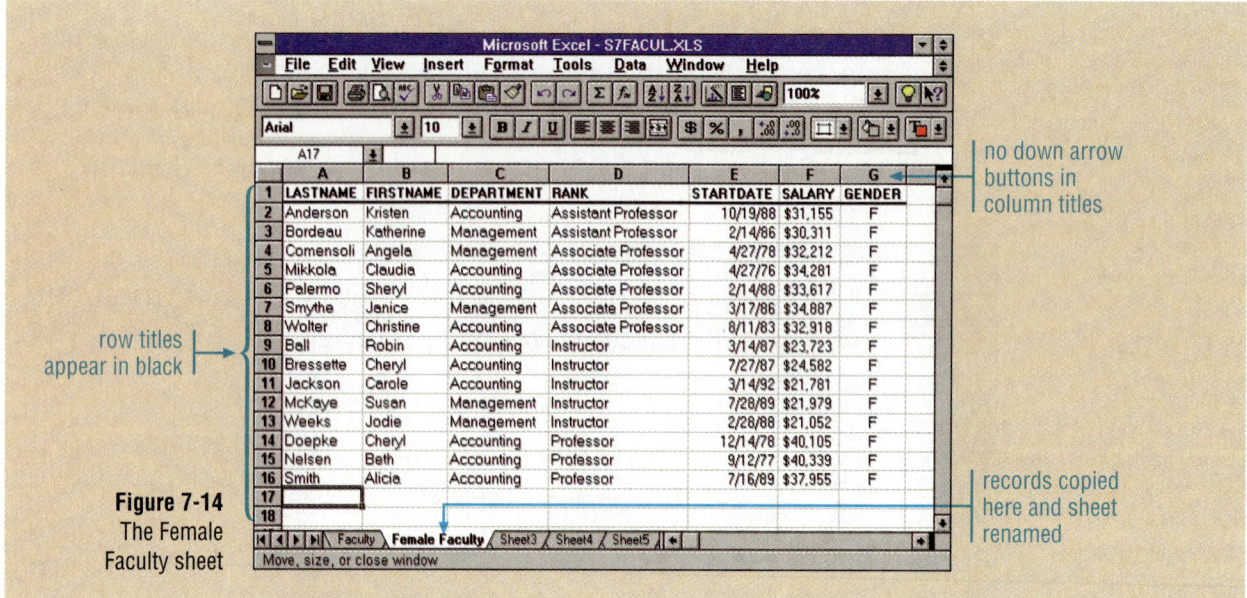

Figure 7-14
The Female Faculty sheet

Now Sarah can use the AVERAGE function to calculate the average salary for the female faculty members in the College of Business. She begins by entering the label "Average Salary."

To calculate the average salary for female faculty members in the College of Business:

❶ Click cell **E17** because this is where you want to enter the label.

❷ Type **Average Salary** and press **[Enter]**.

❸ Click cell **F17** because this is where you want to enter the AVERAGE function.

❹ Type **=AVERAGE(** to begin the formula. Don't forget to include the opening parenthesis.

❺ Select cells F2 through F16, the cells you want to average. When you see the range F2:F16 entered in the formula, release the mouse button.

❻ Press **[Enter]** to complete the calculation and display the average salary.

The worksheet shows that the average salary for female faculty members in the College of Business is $30,726. Next, Sarah notices that part of the "Average Salary" label has been cut off. She decides to format cells E17 and F17 to make them easier to read.

To format cells E17 and F17:

❶ Click cell **E17**, then click the **Align Right button** to display the entire label.

❷ Highlight cells E17 and F17, then click the **Bold button**. The label and the average salary value appear in bold.

❸ Click any cell to remove the highlighting. See Figure 7-15.

TROUBLE? If you need to widen the salary column to display the newly formatted average salary value, double-click the border between column headings F and G.

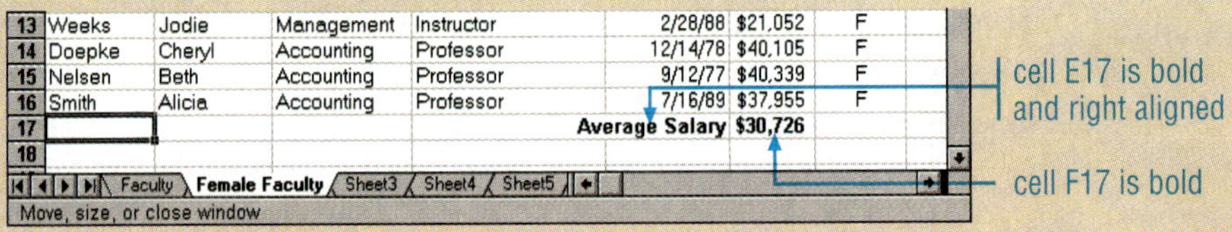

Figure 7-15
The formatted Average Salary label and value

13	Weeks	Jodie	Management	Instructor	2/28/88	F	$21,052
14	Doepke	Cheryl	Accounting	Professor	12/14/78	F	$40,105
15	Nelsen	Beth	Accounting	Professor	9/12/77	F	$40,339
16	Smith	Alicia	Accounting	Professor	7/16/89	F	$37,955
17					Average Salary		$30,726
18							

cell F17 is bold ───►
cell E17 is bold and right aligned ───►

Move, size, or close window

Now that she has created a separate worksheet for the female faculty, Sarah proceeds to create a separate worksheet for the male faculty. To do this, she simply changes the search criteria from "F" to "M" in the Faculty sheet. Then she copies the records for the male faculty to a separate sheet.

To display the records for all male faculty members:

1. Click the **Faculty tab** to display the Faculty sheet with the AutoFormat down arrow buttons. If necessary, click any cell to remove the highlighting.
2. Click the **blue down arrow button** in the Gender column (column G) to display the list of possible search criteria.

   TROUBLE? If the column headings aren't visible, scroll the worksheet until they are visible.

3. Click **M** to hide the records for female faculty and display the records for male faculty.

Now Sarah will copy the records for the male faculty to a new sheet. She'll format the sheet and calculate the the average salary, just as she did for the female faculty records.

To copy the records for male faculty to a new sheet:

1. Highlight cells A6 to G41, then click the **Copy button**.
2. Click the **Sheet3 tab** to display the blank Sheet3, then click cell **A1** to begin inserting rows there.
3. Click the **Paste button**. The records for the male faculty, along with the column headings, appear in Sheet3.
4. To format the columns so all the data is visible, make sure cells A6 through G21 are highlighted, click **Format**, click **Column**, then click **AutoFit Selection**.
5. Click anywhere on the worksheet to remove the highlighting.
6. Double-click the **Sheet3 tab**, then type **Male Faculty** in the Rename Sheet dialog box to rename the sheet. Click the **OK button** to return to the worksheet.

Now Sarah can use the AVERAGE function to calculate the average salary for the male faculty members in the College of Business. Once again, she begins by entering the label "Average Salary."

To calculate the average salary for male faculty members in the College of Business:

1. Click cell **E22** because this is where you want to enter the label.
2. Type **Average Salary**, then press **[Enter]**.

Filtering a List   EX 251

EX 252   TUTORIAL 7   Managing Data with Excel

It appears that the average salary for male faculty members in the College of Business is $36,551. This is significantly higher than the average female salary of $30,726. Sarah tells the dean the results of her calculations.

The dean thinks about the average salary figures for a while, then asks Sarah if there is any way to determine the average salary for males and females at *each rank*. The dean wants to compare the average salary of female instructors to the average salary of male instructors, the average salary of female assistant professors to the average salary of male assistant professors, and so on.

Sarah knows that she could calculate these figures by individually filtering the data for male and female faculty members of each rank, then calculating their average salary. This, however, would be very time-consuming because Sarah would need to copy the data and calculate the averages eight times. Instead, she decides to save time by using Excel's PivotTable Wizard to produce a table showing the average salaries for male and female faculty members at each rank.

Before Sarah can create the PivotTable, she needs to display all the records in the data list.

> To display all the records in the data list:
>
> ❶ Click the **Faculty tab** to return to the Faculty worksheet.
> ❷ Click the **blue down arrow button** in the Gender column (column G) to display the list of possible search criteria.
> ❸ Click **(All)** to display all the records in the list.
> ❹ Click **Data**, click **AutoFilter** to remove the down arrow buttons in the column headings.
> ❺ Click the **Save button** 🖫 to save the workbook.

If you want to take a break and resume the tutorial later, you can exit Excel by double-clicking the Control menu box in the upper-left corner of the screen. When you resume the tutorial, launch Excel, maximize the Microsoft Excel and Sheet1 windows, and place your Student Disk in the disk drive. Open the file S7FACUL.XLS, then continue with the tutorial.

■ ■ ■

> ❸ Click cell **F22** and type **=AVERAGE(** to begin the formula. Don't forget to include the opening parenthesis.
> ❹ Highlight **F2 through F21**, the cells you want to average.
> ❺ Press [**Enter**] to complete the calculation and display the average salary for male faculty, $36,551.
> ❻ Click cell **F22**, then click the **Align Right button** ▤ to display the entire label.
> ❼ Highlight cells **E22 and F22**, then click the **Bold button** **B**.
>
> **TROUBLE?** If you need to widen the salary column to display the newly formatted average salary value, double-click the the border between column headings F and G.
>
> ❽ Click the **Save button** 🖫 to save the workbook with the new sheets.

Using PivotTables

A PivotTable summarizes the contents of a database by automatically counting, averaging, or totaling the contents of selected fields. You could manually compile this information by doing a series of filters and calculations, but it's much easier to let the PivotTable Wizard do it for you. The PivotTable Wizard guides you through the steps for creating a PivotTable, just as the ChartWizard guided you through the steps for creating a chart. By following the directions in the PivotTable Wizard, you specify the column headings (or fields) you want to include in the PivotTable and indicate the calculations you want to perform on each field.

REFERENCE WINDOW

Generating a PivotTable

- Make sure all the rows in the data list are displayed.
- Click Data, then click PivotTable to start the PivotTable Wizard.
- Follow the PivotTable Wizard instructions to create a PivotTable on a separate sheet.
- Format and save the PivotTable.

Sarah considers the information that the dean wants and creates a PivotTable plan (Figure 7-16) and a PivotTable sketch (Figure 7-17). Sarah's plan and sketch will help her work with the PivotTable Wizard to produce the PivotTable she wants.

PivotTable Plan for Calculating Average Salaries

My Goal.
Create a table that compares female and male faculty salary averages for each academic rank.

What results do I want to see?
Average female salary for each rank.
Average male salary for each rank.
Overall average female salary.
Overall average male salary.
The average salary at each rank for males and females combined.

What information do I need?
The table rows will show the data for each RANK.
The table columns will show the data for each GENDER.
The table will show Grand Total values representing overall averages for faculty salaries.

What calculation method will I use for the values?
The SALARY values must be AVERAGED.

Figure 7-16
Sarah's PivotTable plan

Figure 7-17
Sarah's PivotTable sketch

Average Salaries in the College of Business by Rank and Gender			
	Female	Male	Grand Total
Assistant Professor	:	:	:
Associate Professor	:	:	:
Head	:	:	:
Instructor	:	:	:
Professor	:	:	:
Overall Average			

Now Sarah is ready to create a PivotTable summarizing the average faculty salaries. As usual with all data commands, she begins by clicking any cell within the data list.

To create a PivotTable:

❶ Click cell **A7**.

❷ Click **Data**, then click **PivotTable...** to display the PivotTable Wizard - Step 1 of 4 dialog box. See Figure 7-18.

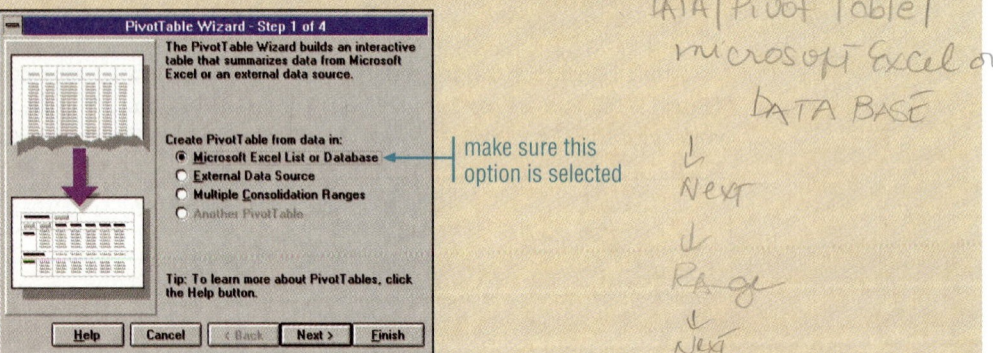

Figure 7-18
The PivotTable Wizard - Step 1 of 4 dialog box

❸ If necessary, click the **Microsoft Excel List or Database option button** to select it. This tells Excel that the data you want to use for the table is located in a Microsoft Excel workbook.

❹ Click the **Next > button** to display the PivotTable Wizard - Step 2 of 4 dialog box. Excel automatically recognizes the range A6:G41 as the the data list you want to use for the table. If your dialog box doesn't match the one in Figure 7-19, highlight cells A6 through G41 now.

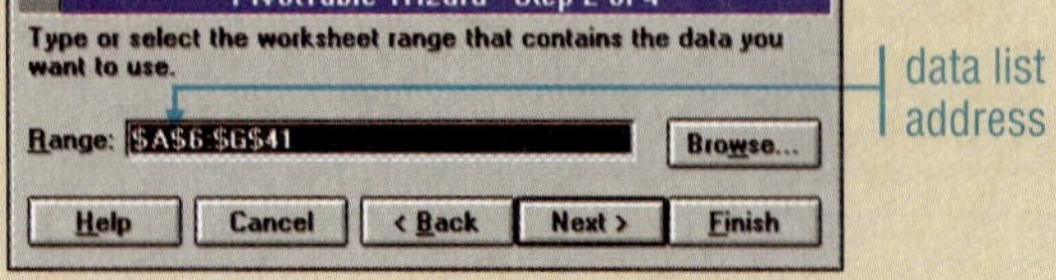

Figure 7-19
The PivotTable Wizard - Step 2 of 4 dialog box

❺ Click the **Next >** button to display the PivotTable Wizard - Step 3 of 4 dialog box, as shown in Figure 7-20.

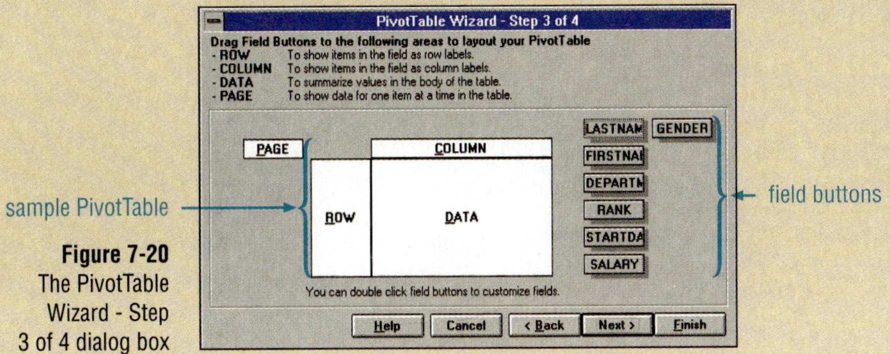

Figure 7-20
The PivotTable Wizard - Step 3 of 4 dialog box

Adding Row and Column Labels

The PivotTable Wizard - Step 3 of 4 dialog box lets you select the field buttons you want to use for the row and column labels in the PivotTable. You can click any of the field buttons on the right and drag them into the proper position on the sample PivotTable. Sarah's sketch shows that the row labels should list the faculty members' rank. The column labels should identify the gender.

To select RANK for the row labels and GENDER for the column labels:

❶ Click the **RANK button** and drag it to the ROW section of the sample PivotTable. When you release the mouse button, RANK appears in the row section of the sample PivotTable. See Figure 7-21.

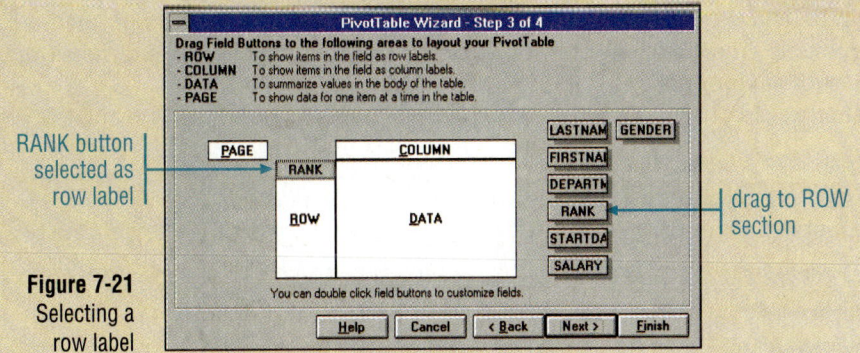

Figure 7-21
Selecting a row label

TROUBLE? If you add the wrong button, drag it back to its original position to the right of the sample PivotTable and start again with Step 1.

❷ Click the **GENDER button** and drag it to the Column section of the sample PivotTable. See Figure 7-22.

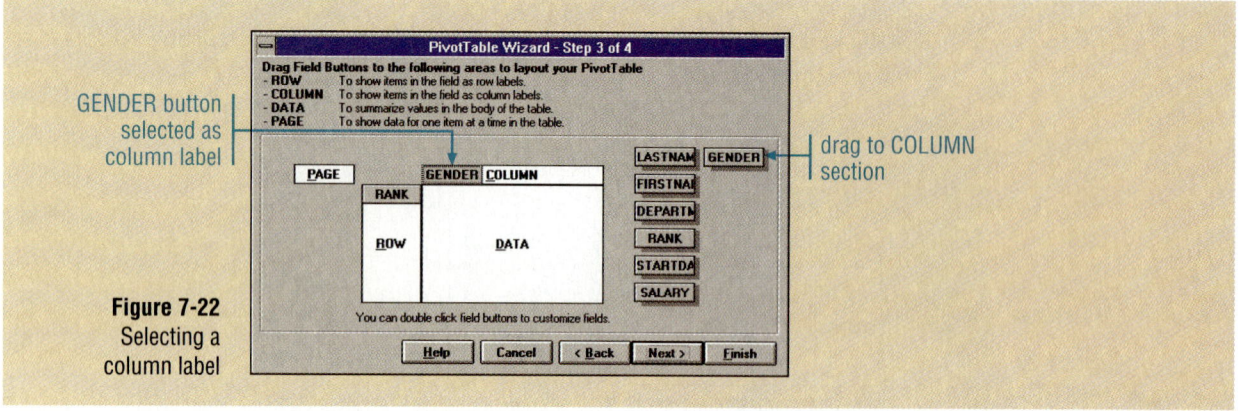

Figure 7-22
Selecting a column label

Selecting a Data Field for a PivotTable

The data fields you define for a PivotTable contain the data you want to count, total, average, and so forth. Sarah wants to average the salaries of the faculty members. Following her plan, she selects SALARY as the data field for the PivotTable.

To select the data field for the PivotTable:

❶ Click the **SALARY button** to the right of the sample PivotTable and drag it to the DATA section of the sample PivotTable. A Sum of SALARY button appears in the DATA section of the sample PivotTable.

Selecting a Calculation Method for a PivotTable

Unless you specify otherwise, the PivotTable Wizard will automatically *sum* the values in the data field. If you want the PivotTable to use a different calculation method, such as counting or averaging, you must double-click the data field button and select the calculation method you want.

In this case, Sarah is interested in the average salary rather than the total salary.

To select Average as the calculation method for the report:

❶ Double-click the **Sum of SALARY button** to display the PivotTable Field dialog box.
❷ Click **Average** in the Summarize by list box. See Figure 7-23.

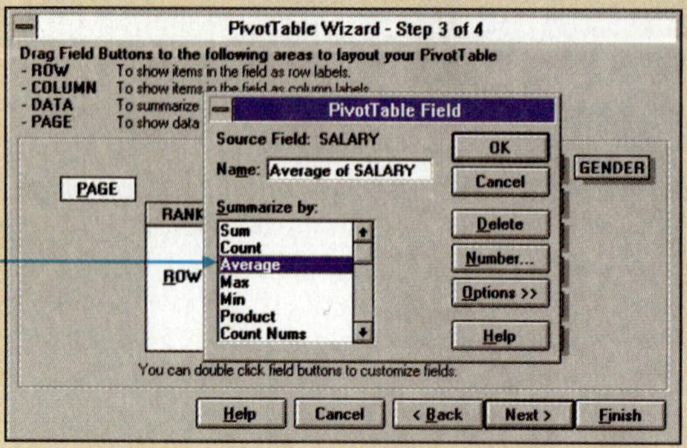

Figure 7-23
Selecting a calculation method

❸ Click the **OK button** to return to the PivotTable Wizard. An Average of SALARY button appears in the DATA section of the sample PivotTable.

❹ Click the **Next > button** to go to the PivotTable Wizard - Step 4 of 4 dialog box. See Figure 7-24.

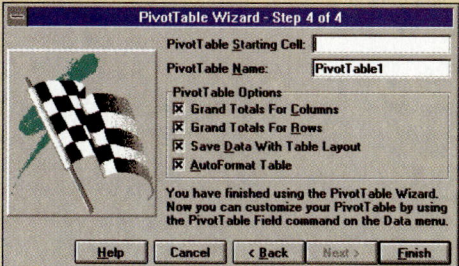

Figure 7-24
The PivotTable Wizard - Step 4 of 4 dialog box

In this final dialog box, Excel asks you where you would like to place the new PivotTable. Sarah decides to place the PivotTable in a separate sheet. She accepts the remaining default settings for the PivotTable.

To place the PivotTable in a separate sheet:
❶ Click the **PivotTable Starting Cell box**, then click the **Sheet4 tab** at the bottom of the screen. Sheet4! appears in the PivotTable Starting cell box. The dialog box is now displayed over the blank Sheet4.

❷ Click cell **A3** in Sheet4. You'll begin the PivotTable here, instead of in cell **A1**, in order to leave room for a title. The dialog box on your screen should now match Figure 7-25.

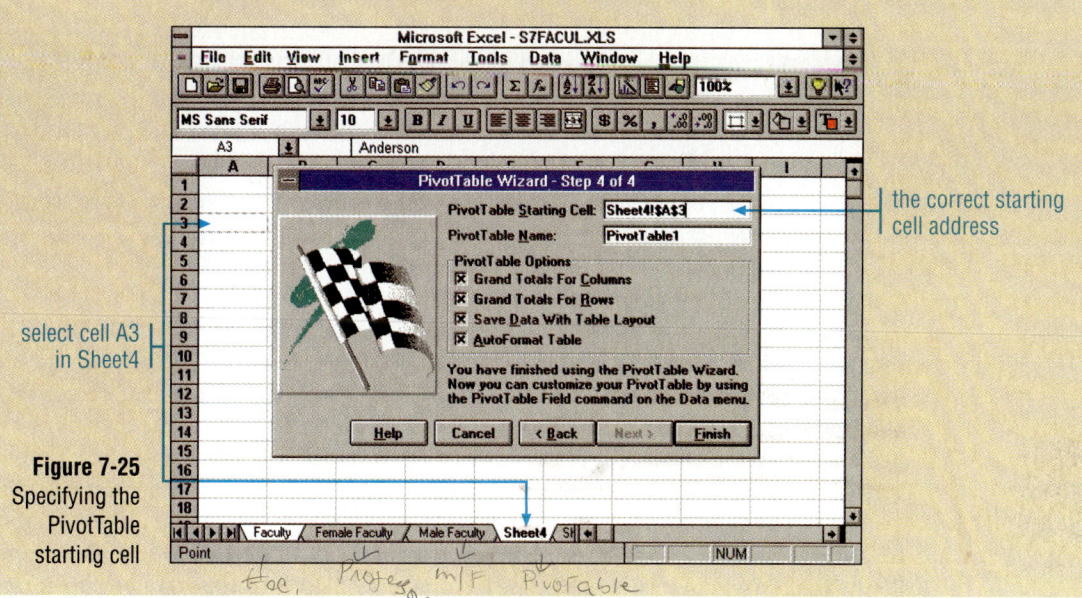

Figure 7-25
Specifying the PivotTable starting cell

Completing a PivotTable

With the row category, column category, data field, and calculation method defined, Sarah is ready to complete the PivotTable.

To complete the PivotTable:

❶ Check that the PivotTable options in the Step 4 of 4 dialog box match Figure 7-25.

❷ Click the **Finish button**. In a short time, the PivotTable appears in Sheet4 along with the Query and Pivot toolbar. See Figure 7-26.

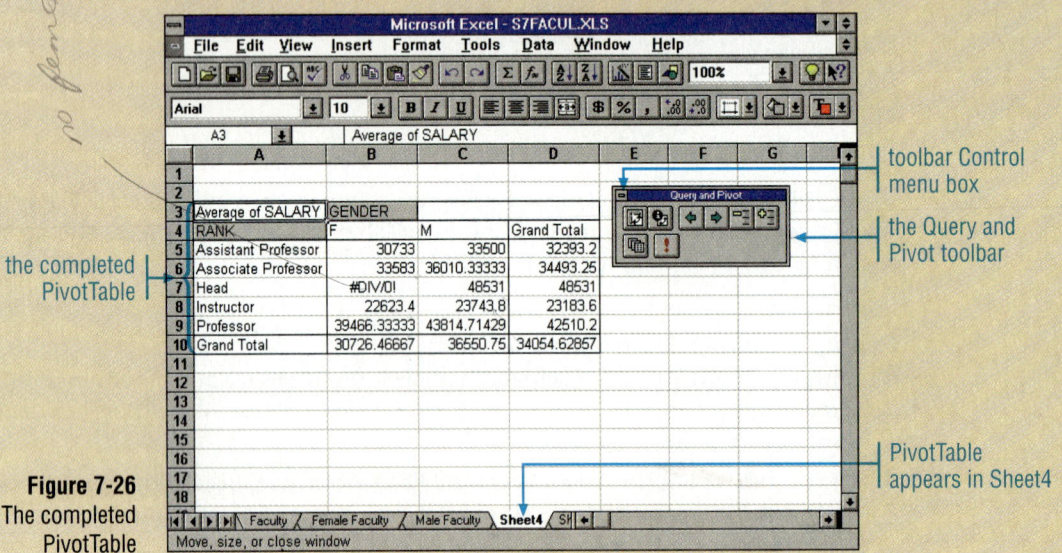

Figure 7-26
The completed PivotTable

TROUBLE? If the Query and Pivot toolbar does not appear, don't worry because you will not use the Query and Pivot toolbar in this tutorial. Skip Step 3 and continue with Step 4.

❸ The Query and Pivot toolbar provides quick options for performing some advanced PivotTable procedures. Because you won't be using the Query and Pivot toolbar in this tutorial, you can close it now by double-clicking its Control menu box.

❹ When you're certain your PivotTable matches Figure 7-26, click the **Save button** to save the workbook with the new PivotTable.

Sarah examines the PivotTable. She notices that cell B7 displays "#DIV/0!" This cell in the table is supposed to show the average salary of female department heads, but there are no female department heads. To calculate the average salary for this cell, Excel totaled the salaries for all female department heads ($0) and attempted to divide the total by the number of female department heads (0). Because dividing by zero is impossible, Excel displays the #DIV/0! message. You cannot delete this from the cell because it is part of the PivotTable.

The upper-left corner, cell A3, contains a description of the calculation method used to create the table. Cells B3 and A4 contain the field buttons. Once you've created a PivotTable, you can easily modify it by dragging field headings to new positions or by double-clicking on column headings to display the data in greater detail. You can also double-click on any of the data cells to display a filtered list of related records. Let's take a moment to explore some of these features now.

Using PivotTables   EX 259

To explore some features of the PivotTable:

❶ Make sure you saved the workbook in the previous set of steps.

❷ Click cell **B3** and drag the **GENDER button** to the left side of cell A5, below the RANK button. As you drag, the pointer changes to . When you release the mouse button, Excel changes, or pivots, the layout of the PivotTable, as shown in Figure 7-27.

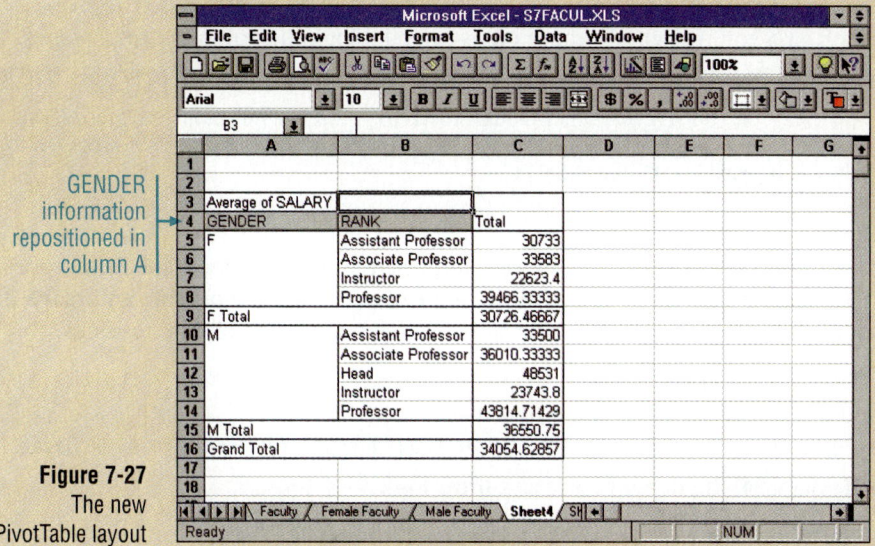

Figure 7-27
The new PivotTable layout

GENDER information repositioned in column A

TROUBLE? If your table doesn't look like Figure 7-27, you may have moved the GENDER button too far to the right. Click the Undo button and then repeat Step 2.

❸ Click the **Undo button** to return the PivotTable to its original layout. The Undo button is useful when the PivotTable doesn't turn out as you'd planned.

❹ Double-click cell **B5**, which is located at the intersection of the Female column and the Assistant Professor row to display a list of records for all female assistant professors. The records for Kristen Anderson and Katherine Bordeau appear in a separate sheet. Click any cell to remove the highlighting. See Figure 7-28.

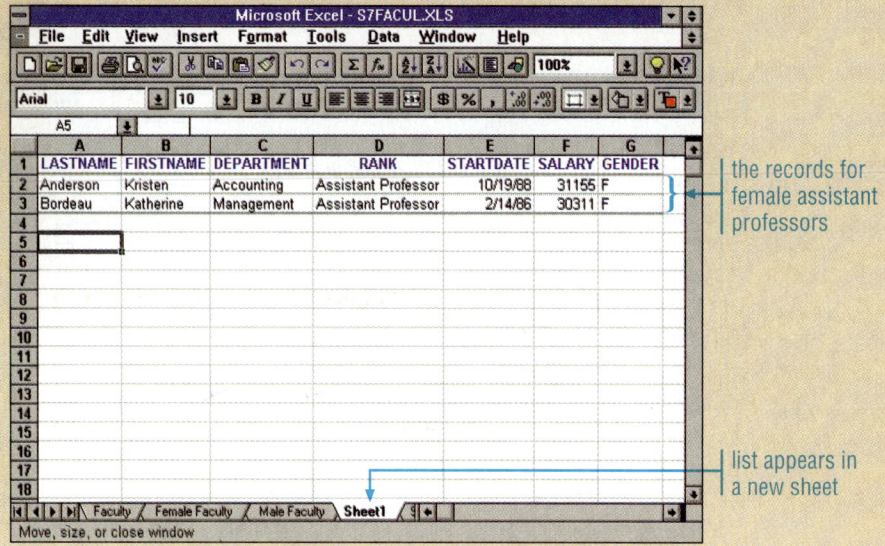

Figure 7-28
The list of female assistant professors

the records for female assistant professors

list appears in a new sheet

EX 260   TUTORIAL 7   Managing Data with Excel

⑤ Click **Edit**, then click **Delete Sheet** to delete the sheet with these records. When you see the message "Selected sheets will be permanently deleted. Continue?" click the **OK button**. Excel displays the PivotTable in Sheet4 again.

⑥ Try editing the contents of cells B5:D10. A dialog box appears informing you that you "Cannot change this part of a PivotTable."

⑦ Try editing the "Grand Total" labels in cells A10 or D4. A dialog box appears informing you that you "Cannot edit subtotal, block total or grand total names."

⑧ Check to make sure your PivotTable matches the original layout in Figure 7-26.

TROUBLE? If you've made other modifications to your PivotTable and can't return the PivotTable to its original layout, close the S7FACUL.XLS workbook and then reopen it to view the original PivotTable in Sheet4.

The PivotTable includes the desired information, but the labels and format are not the same as Sarah's sketch. To improve the appearance of the PivotTable and make it easier to understand, Sarah first adds a title and changes two of the column headings.

To add a title and change column headings:

❶ Click cell **A1**, then type **Average Salaries in the College of Business by Rank and Gender**.

❷ Click cell **B4**, then type **Female** and press **[→]**.

❸ Type **Male** in cell **C4** and press **[Enter]**.

Next, Sarah uses the AutoFormat command to improve the report format.

To improve the report format using AutoFormat:

❶ Highlight cells A3 through D10, then release the mouse button.

❷ Click **Format**, then click **AutoFormat...** to display the AutoFormat dialog box.

❸ Click **Accounting 3** in the Table Format box, then click the **OK button** to apply the format.

❹ Click cell **A1**, then click the **Bold button** to display the table title in bold. See Figure 7-29.

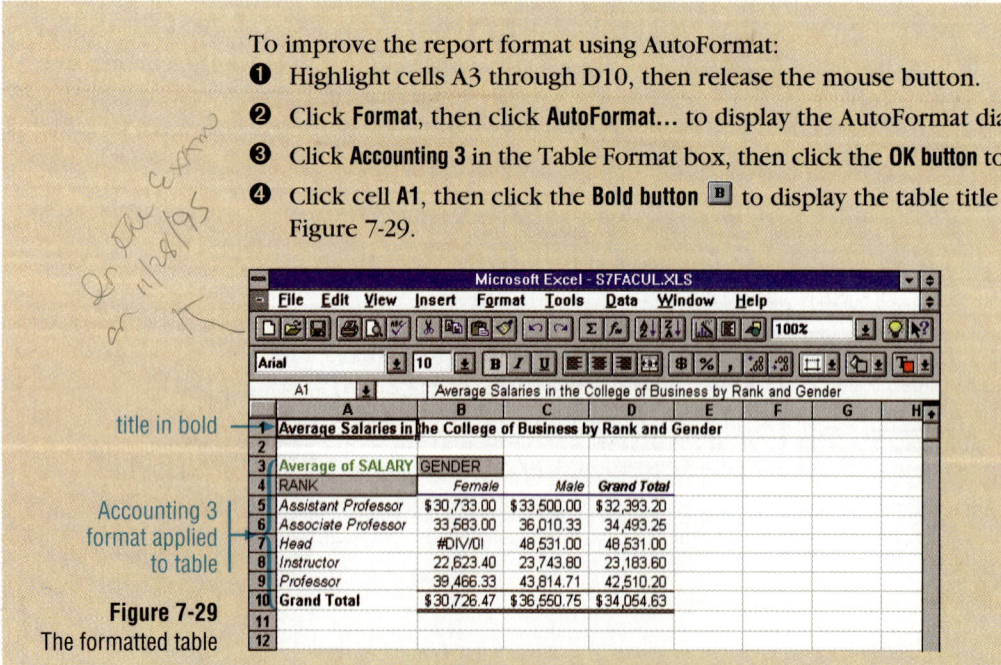

Figure 7-29
The formatted table

Now it is much easier to interpret the data. Cells B10 and C10 in the Grand Total row show the overall average salaries for males and females. The average salary for females at all ranks is $30,726.47, while the average salary for males at all ranks is $36,550.75. The male and female salaries displayed in columns B and C show that female faculty members at every rank are paid less than their male counterparts.

Sarah renames Sheet4, saves the workbook again with the formatted PivotTable, and then prints the PivotTable.

To rename Sheet4, save the workbook, and then print the PivotTable:

❶ Double-click the **Sheet4 tab**, then type **Average Salary** in the Rename Sheet dialog box. Click the **OK button** to close the dialog box.

❷ Click the **Save button** 🖫 to save the workbook with the newly formatted PivotTable.

❸ Click the **Print button** 🖨. Figure 7-30 shows the printed PivotTable.

Figure 7-30
The printed PivotTable

Average Salaries in the College of Business by Rank and Gender				
Average of SALARY	GENDER			
RANK	Female	Male	Grand Total	
Assistant Professor	$30,733.00	$33,500.00	$32,393.20	
Associate Professor	33,583.00	36,010.33	34,493.25	
Head	#DIV/0!	48,531.00	48,531.00	
Instructor	22,623.40	23,743.80	23,183.60	
Professor	39,466.33	43,814.71	42,510.20	
Grand Total	$30,726.47	$36,550.75	$34,054.63	

If you want to take a break and resume the tutorial later, you can exit Excel by double-clicking the Control menu box in the upper-left corner of the screen. When you resume the tutorial, launch Excel, maximize the Microsoft Excel and Sheet1 windows, and place your Student Disk in the disk drive. Open the S7FACUL.XLS workbook and continue with the tutorial.

■   ■   ■

The dean brings Sarah's PivotTable to his next meeting with the university's vice president. After some discussion, the vice president asks the dean to complete a salary analysis for faculty in all the colleges and departments at North State University. The vice president provides the dean with a disk containing a university-wide faculty database that was created, not with Excel, but with a database program called dBASE III Plus.

The dean calls Sarah and asks her if she can create PivotTables from a dBASE III file. Sarah says that she will be able to access the dBASE III file as an external database.

Internal and External Databases

Excel allows you to work with both internal and external databases. An **internal database** is a list of data that is part of the Excel worksheet you have open. An **external database** is not part of the open Excel worksheet. It can be an Excel worksheet, an ASCII file, or another application file such as dBASE. An **ASCII file** is a standard file type for exchanging information between different computers. A **dBASE file** is created using the dBASE III or dBASE IV database management software.

The capability to access external databases is very useful, especially if you want to find or summarize information from large databases that were created on a mainframe computer or with the popular dBASE database management software.

Creating a PivotTable from an External Database

The PivotTable Wizard can generate a PivotTable from an internal database or an external database. This feature enables you to analyze large databases that are created and maintained on a computer system other than your own or use databases that were created with software other than Excel. To access external databases, you must activate the MS Query add-in macro.

Activating the MS Query Add-In

An add-in adds features to the basic Excel spreadsheet command set installed with the software. The MS Query add-in modifies the Data menu, adding several new menu commands that give Excel the ability to work with external databases.

REFERENCE WINDOW

Activating the MS Query Add-In

- Click Tools, then click Add-Ins....
- Click the MS Query Add-In checkbox to insert an ×.

A number of add-in macros, such as MS Query, are included with the Excel software. Although they are usually installed when Excel is installed, the person who installed Excel on your computer might have decided to save disk space by not installing the add-in macros. If you cannot activate the MS Query add-in in the next set of steps, see your instructor or technical support person for assistance.

Sarah activates the MS Query add-in by using the Add-Ins command on the Tools menu.

To activate the MS Query add-in:

1. Click **Tools**, then click **Add-Ins...** to display the Add-Ins dialog box.
2. If you don't see an × in the MS Query Add-In checkbox, click the **MS Query Add-In checkbox** now to display an ×. See Figure 7-31.

Creating a PivotTable from an External Database **EX 263**

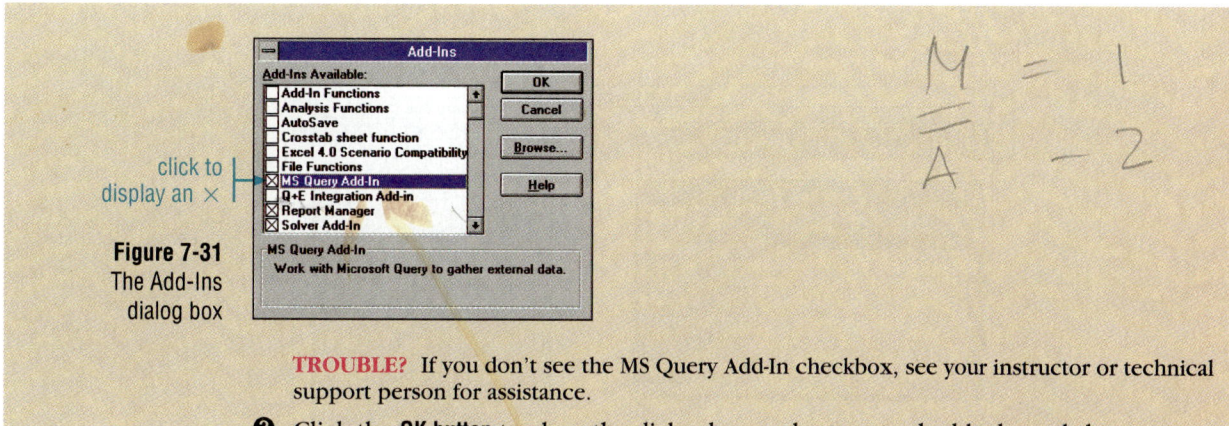

click to
display an ×

Figure 7-31
The Add-Ins
dialog box

TROUBLE? If you don't see the MS Query Add-In checkbox, see your instructor or technical support person for assistance.

❸ Click the **OK button** to close the dialog box and return to the blank worksheet.

Although the MS Query add-in macro does not appear to change the worksheet window, it does change the commands on the Data menu. Let's take a look.

To examine the changes in the Data menu:

❶ Click **Data** to view the Data menu. Note the command Get External Data. The MS Query add-in macro added this command to the menu.

❷ Click **Data** again to close the menu.

Using Microsoft Query

Now that Sarah has activated the MS Query Add-In macro, she can use Microsoft Query to access information in the university-wide faculty database. MS Query is a powerful application that you can use with Excel and with other data management applications. The Get External Data... command on the Data menu opens the MS Query application window. You can then use the MS Query commands to access data in external databases.

You can also open the MS Query window by using the PivotTable Wizard. Sarah will use this method now as she creates her PivotTable from the information in the university-wide faculty database. She wants to create the PivotTable in a separate sheet, so she begins by activating Sheet5.

To begin creating the university-wide faculty PivotTable:

❶ Use the sheet tab scroll arrows, if necessary, to display the Sheet5 tab. Then click the **Sheet5 tab** to display the blank Sheet5.

❷ Click **Data**, then click **PivotTable...** to display the PivotTable Wizard - Step 1 of 4 dialog box.

❸ Click the **External Data Source option button**, then click the **Next > button** to display the PivotTable Wizard - Step 2 of 4 dialog box.

❹ Click the **Get Data button**. After a pause, the Microsoft Query application window appears. You should see both the Select Data Source dialog box and the MS Query Cue Cards window. See Figure 7-32.

EX 264 TUTORIAL 7 Managing Data with Excel

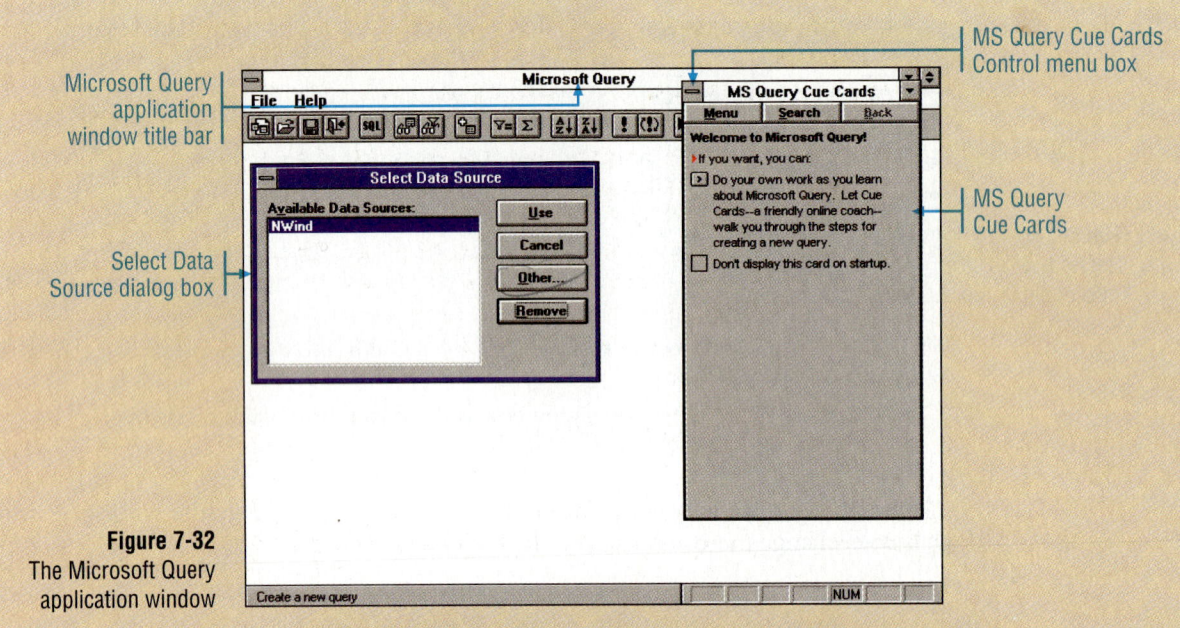

Figure 7-32
The Microsoft Query application window

TROUBLE? If your MS Query window is not maximized, don't worry about it now. You can maximize it later in this tutorial.

⑤ Take a moment to read the information in the MS Query Cue Card. The MS Query Cue Cards can take you through MS Query commands step by step. You'll have a chance to use them more extensively in the Tutorial Assignments and Case Problems. Because you won't be using the Cue Cards now, double-click the **MS Query Cue Cards Control menu box** to close the Cue Card window.

⑥ Click the **Other...** button in the Select Data Sources dialog box to display the ODBC dialog box, as shown in Figure 7-33.

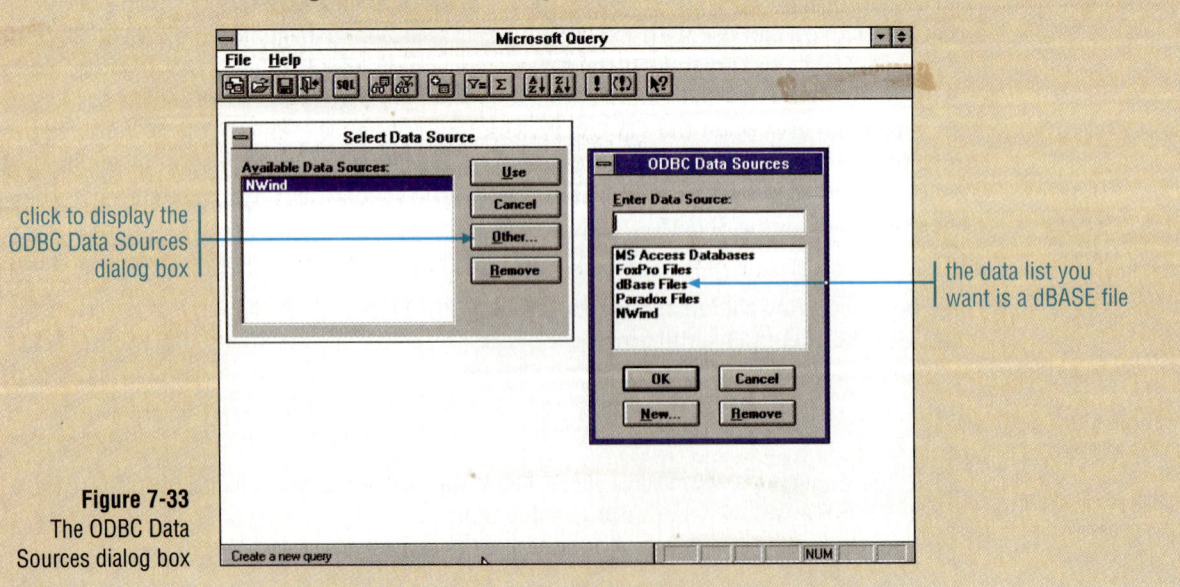

Figure 7-33
The ODBC Data Sources dialog box

❼ The university-wide faculty database is in a dBASE III external database, so click **dBase Files** in the list of data sources.

❽ Click **OK** to return to the Select Data Sources dialog box.

❾ Make sure dBase Files is selected in the list of Available Data Sources, then click the **Use button** to display the Add Tables dialog box.

Now that you've specified the type of external data (a dBASE file), you need to choose the database file containing the records you want to display. In MS Query terms, a database file is called a "table." Once you select a database file (or table), MS Query displays the field names (that is, the column headings) for the database. Then you can query the database to display the records you want to see. In this case, Sarah wants to see all the records in the university-wide faculty database contained in the C7FACUL.DBF file.

To display all the records in the university-wide faculty database:

❶ In the Drives box, select the drive containing your Student Disk.

❷ In the Table Name list box, click **C7FACUL.DBF**, then click the **Add button**.

❸ Click the **Close button** to close the dialog box and view the field names in the MS Query window.

❹ Maximize the Query1 window. If necessary, maximize the MS Query window too. See Figure 7-34.

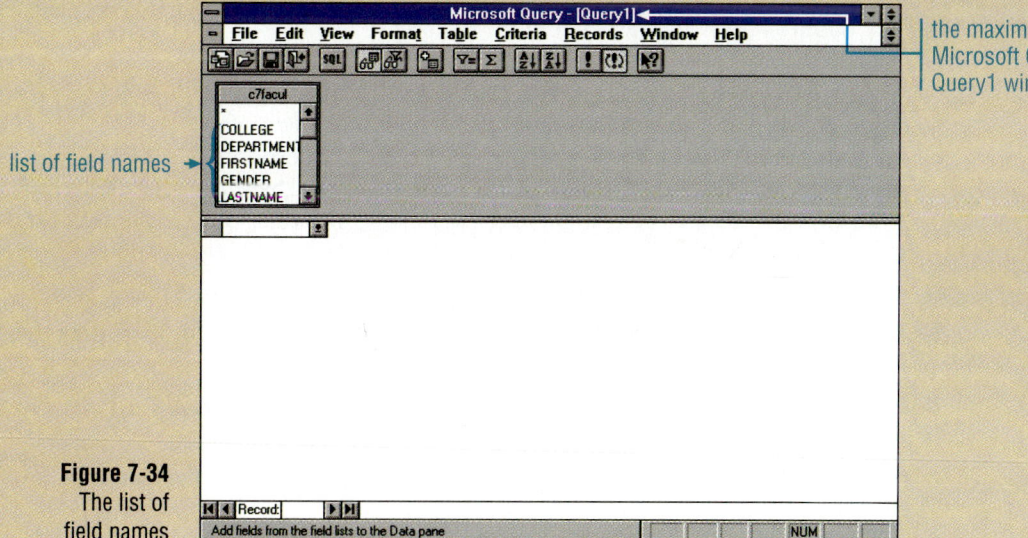

Figure 7-34
The list of field names

❺ Double-click * (asterisk) at the top of the list of field names (see Figure 7-34) to display all the records in the C7FACUL table. Figure 7-35 shows the records displayed in the MS Query window.

EX 266 TUTORIAL 7 Managing Data with Excel

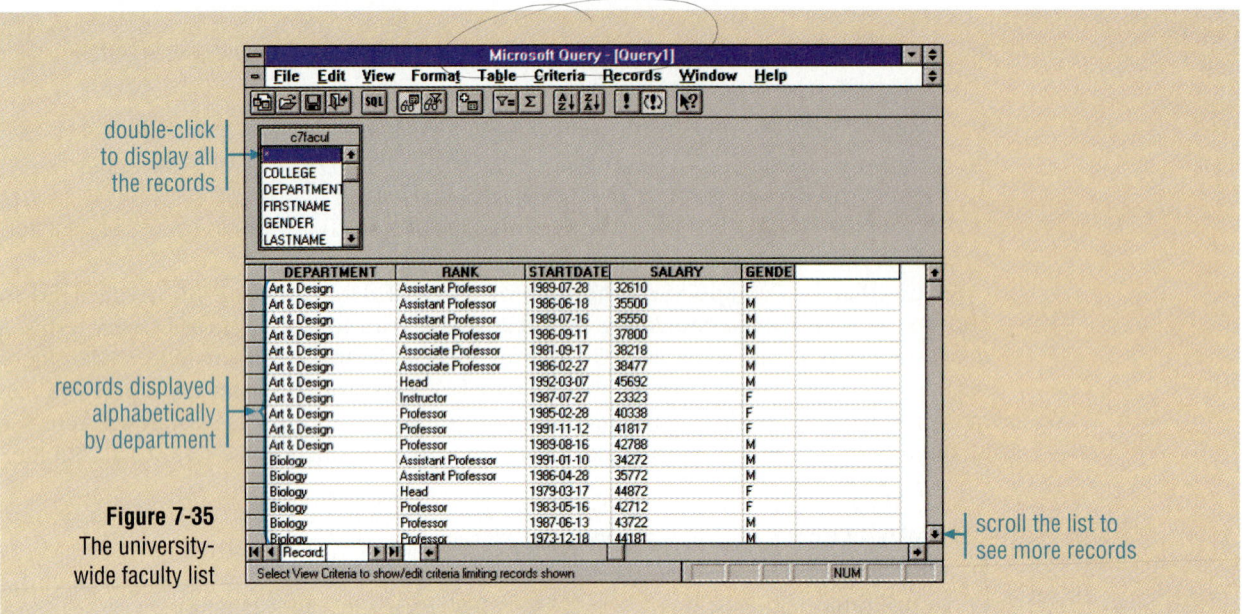

Figure 7-35
The university-wide faculty list

Now that you have retrieved the data you want to use for the PivotTable, you need to return the data to Microsoft Excel. Then you can continue creating the PivotTable with the PivotTable Wizard. To do this, Sarah uses the Return Data to Microsoft Excel command on the File menu. The university-wide PivotTable she creates will have the same layout as the College of Business PivotTable she created earlier. See Sarah's original sketch in Figure 7-17.

To return the data to Excel and finish creating the PivotTable:

❶ Click **File**, then click **Return Data to Microsoft Excel**. The Microsoft Query window closes and the PivotTable Wizard - Step 2 of 4 dialog box reappears in the Excel window. The message next to the Get Data button informs you that the data has been retrieved.

❷ Click the **Next >** button to display the PivotTable Wizard - Step 3 of 4 dialog box.

❸ Drag the **RANK button** to the ROW section of the sample PivotTable. Then drag the **GENDER button** to the COLUMN section of the sample PivotTable.

❹ Drag the **SALARY button** to the DATA section of the sample PivotTable.

❺ Double-click the **Sum of SALARY** field button to display the PivotTable Field dialog box. Click **Average** in the Summarize by box, then click the **OK button** to return to the PivotTable Wizard - Step 3 of 4 dialog box.

❻ Click the **Next >** button to display the PivotTable Wizard - Step 4 of 4 dialog box.

❼ Click the **PivotTable Starting Cell box**, then click cell **A3** in Sheet5 to display Sheet5!$A$3 in the PivotTable Starting Cell box.

❽ Click the **Finish button** to close the dialog box and view the completed PivotTable in the worksheet. See Figure 7-36.

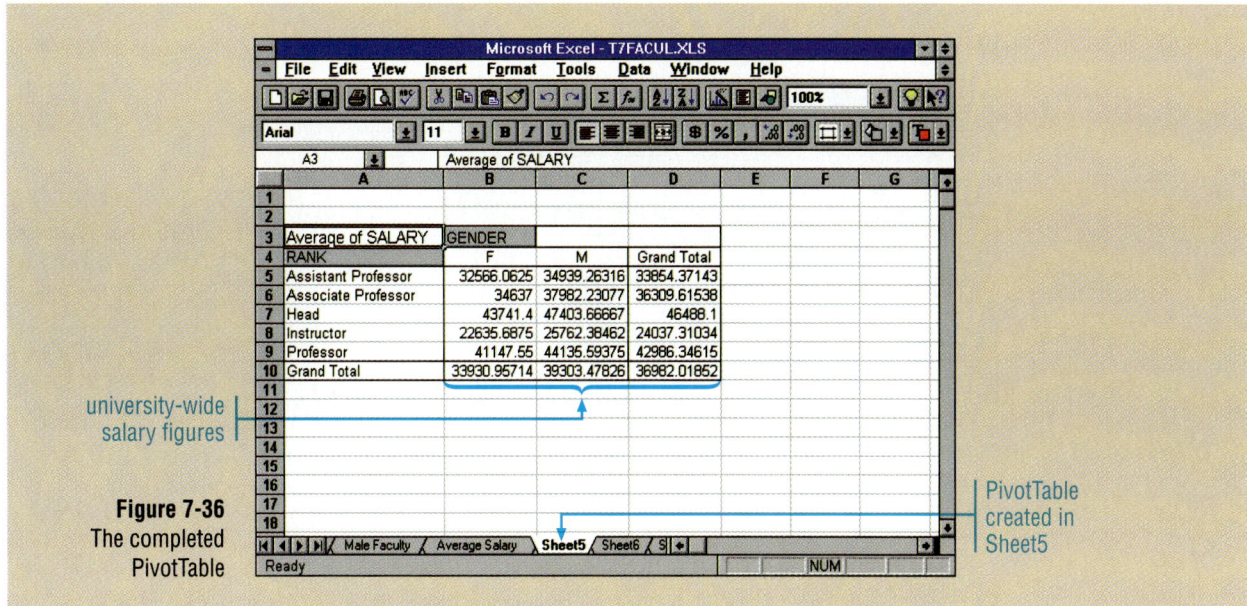

Figure 7-36
The completed PivotTable

The PivotTable is almost complete. All that remains is to enter the appropriate title and column headings. Finally, Sarah formats the PivotTable to make it easier to read.

To add a title to the PivotTable:
1. Click cell **A1** and type **North State University.**
2. Click cell **A2** and type **Average Salaries by Rank and Gender**.
3. Highlight cells A1 through D2.
4. Click the **Center Across Columns button** to center the titles.
5. Click the **Bold button** to display the titles in boldface.

Using her original sketch as a guide, Sarah enters more informative column titles for the report.

To enter the column titles:
1. Click cell **B4**, then type **Female** and press [→].
2. Type **Male** in cell C4 and press [**Enter**].

Sarah decides to use AutoFormat to apply the Accounting 3 format.

To format the PivotTable:
1. Highlight cells A3 through D10.
2. Click **Format**, then click **AutoFormat...** to display the AutoFormat dialog box.
3. Click **Accounting 3** in the Table Format box, then click the **OK button** to apply the format.

❹ Click any cell to remove the highlighting. See Figure 7-37.

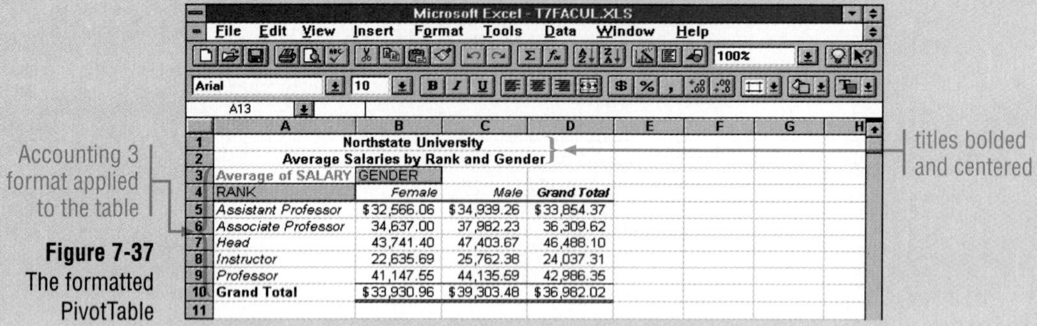

Accounting 3 format applied to the table

titles bolded and centered

Figure 7-37
The formatted PivotTable

Sarah renames Sheet5 and then saves the workbook with the new PivotTable.

To rename Sheet5 and save the workbook:
❶ Double-click the **Sheet5 tab**, then type **Average Salary (Univ.)**. Click the **OK button** to close the dialog box.
❷ Click the **Save button**.

Finally, Sarah previews the report, prints a copy for the dean, and then closes the workbook.

To preview and print the PivotTable, then close the workbook:
❶ Click the **Print Preview button** to preview the report.
❷ Click the **Setup... button** to display the Page Setup dialog box.
❸ Click the **Margins tab**. If the Horizontally box is empty, click it so that the report will be centered between the right and left margins.
❹ Click the **Sheet tab**. If necessary, click the Cell Gridlines box to remove the ×.
❺ Click the **OK button** to close the Page Setup dialog box and look at the revised print preview.
❻ Click the **Print... button** to display the Print dialog box.
❼ Click the **OK button** on the Print dialog box to print the PivotTable, shown in Figure 7-38.

North State University
Average Salaries by Rank and Gender

Average of SALARY	GENDER		
RANK	Female	Male	Grand Total
Assistant Professor	$32,566.06	$34,939.26	$33,854.37
Associate Professor	34,637.00	37,982.23	36,309.62
Head	43,741.40	47,403.67	46,488.10
Instructor	22,635.69	25,762.38	24,037.31
Professor	41,147.55	44,135.59	42,986.35
Grand Total	$33,930.96	$39,303.48	$36,982.02

Figure 7-38
The printed university-wide PivotTable

Now that Sarah has printed the report, she can close the workbook and exit Excel.

To close the workbook and exit Excel:
1. Click the **Save button** to save the workbook with the new print settings.
2. Click **File**, then click **Close** to close the S7FACUL.XLS workbook.
3. Click **File**, then click **Exit** to exit Excel.

The dean is very impressed with Sarah's work. The report provides exactly the information he needs for his meeting with the university's vice president.

Questions

1. What is an Excel data list?
2. A row within a data list is often referred to as a _____.
3. A column within a data list is often referred to as a _____.
4. A data list is often referred to as a _____.
5. The following list was sorted using three columns. Which column was used as the first column to sort by? Which column was used as the next column to sort by? Which column was used as the third column to sort by?

   CLASS,   LASTNAME,   FIRSTNAME
   EN211,   Baker,   Joseph
   EN211,   Smith,   Carol Ann
   EN211,   Smith,   Jim
   SP312,   Andrews,   Carole
   SP312,   Casselman,   Timothy

6. What is a data form?
7. You can use the _____ button on a data form to enter information that determines which records will be found when you click the Find Next or Find Prev buttons.
8. You can use the _____ wildcard to represent any group of characters.
9. Arranging the rows in a list according to the contents of a particular column is known as _____ a list.
10. Explain how to filter a list using AutoFilter.
11. How is an external database different from an internal database?
12. Which add-in is required if you want to create a PivotTable on an external database?
13. Name two types of files that can be accessed as external databases with Excel.

Tutorial Assignments

Write your answers to Tutorial Assignments 2, 3, and 4. Print the worksheet for Tutorial Assignment 10. Open the workbook T7FACUL.XLS on your Student Disk and complete the following:
1. Use the New button on the data form to add the following information for a new faculty member. *Hint:* Remember to select any cell in the list before using commands on the Data menu.

a. Last name = Gerety
   b. First name = Estelle
   c. Department = Management
   d. Rank = Assistant Professor
   e. Start date = Today's date
   f. Salary = 32454
   g. Gender = F
2. Use the data form to determine how many faculty members hold the rank of professor in the Management department.
3. Use the data form to determine how many female faculty members earn more than $35,000 per year.
4. Use the data form to determine how many faculty members hold the rank of associate professor in the College of Business.
5. Close the data form.
6. Use the AutoFilter command in the Data menu to display the down arrow buttons in the column headings.
7. Select cell A7, in the LASTNAME column. Use the Sort Descending button to arrange the records in reverse alphabetical order (from Z to A) by last name. Then use the Sort Ascending button to arrange the records in alphabetical order (from A to Z) by last name.
8. Click the SALARY down arrow button, and select (Custom...). Then use the Custom AutoFilter dialog box to display the rows where SALARY is greater than $40,105, or less than $30,311. *Hint:* Use the down arrow buttons in the dialog box to select the appropriate symbols and salary figures. Also, make sure to select the Or option button.
9. Preview the worksheet and make any necessary format changes.
10. Save the workbook as S7NAMES.XLS on your Student Disk.
11. Print the worksheet.

Case Problems

1. Creating a List of Discontinued Inventory Items at OfficeMart Business Supplies

You are an assistant buyer at OfficeMart Business Supplies, a business supply retail store. Your boss, Ellen Kerrigan, has created an Excel workbook containing the product and pricing information for inventory items purchased from each primary vendor.

Ellen is preparing her monthly order for EB Wholesale Office Supplies, one of Office Mart's suppliers. Ellen has asked you to print a list of all back-ordered EB Wholesale products so she can include them on the order. She would also like a list of all discontinued items so she can remove those items from the catalogue.

Open the file P7INVENT.XLS on your Student Disk and complete the following:
1. Use the AutoFilter command on the Data menu to insert the down arrow buttons on the column headings.
2. Filter the list to display only the records for back-ordered items. Refer to the status codes listed at the top of the worksheet.
3. Print the records for back-ordered items (including the column headings).
4. Preview the worksheet and make any necessary formatting changes.
5. Print the records for the back-ordered items.

6. Filter the list again to display only the records for discontinued items.
7. Print the records for discontinued items.
8. Save the workbook as S7INVENT.XLS on your Student Disk.

2. Creating a Current Membership List for Shih Tzu Fanciers of America

Jennifer Santarelli is the membership coordinator for the Shih Tzu Fanciers of America, a non-profit organization for owners, fanciers, and breeders of Shih Tzu dogs. The organization maintains a membership list in dBASE format. The list includes the first name, last name, address, city, state, and zip code for approximately 1,000 current members.

The board of the Shih Tzu Fanciers of America (STFA) has asked Jennifer to prepare a report on the current membership, showing the number of members in each state and the total current membership.

It's been some time since Jennifer used the database features in Excel. She has tried to create the report but has run into trouble, so she asks you to help her use the PivotTable Wizard to create the PivotTable.

1. Open a new workbook and activate the PivotTable Wizard.
2. Choose the External Data Source option, then in the PivotTable Wizard - Step 2 of 4 dialog box click the Get Data button to start MS Query.
3. Use the MS Query Cue Card to remind yourself how to access external data. Begin by clicking the [>] button on the MS Query Cue Card. Then follow the directions to learn more about MS Query. You can leave the cue card on the screen as you proceed with the following steps. If necessary, drag the cue card to a new location.
4. Select dBase Files as your data source. When you see the Add Tables dialog box, select the external database P7MEMBR.DBF from your Student Disk.
5. Display all the records in the database, then return the data to Microsoft Excel.
6. Select STATE as the ROW category.
7. Do not select a COLUMN category.
8. Select STATE as the DATA field. Because STATE is a non-numeric field, the PivotTable Wizard will automatically count the number of records in each state.
9. Complete the PivotTable, using cell A3 in the blank sheet as the Starting Cell.
10. Add the title "Shih Tzu Fanciers of America, Current Membership by State," then format the PivotTable.
11. Preview the worksheet and use the Page Setup dialog box to print the PivotTable at 85% of Normal Size. Make sure the PivotTable will print on one page.
12. Save the workbook as S7STATES.XLS on your Student Disk.
13. Print the PivotTable.

3. Creating an Invitation List for Shih Tzu Fanciers of America

The New Mexico Chapter of the STFA is planning a Shih Tzu Fanciers picnic lunch. They want to invite all STFA members in nearby states, and they have asked Jennifer to send them a list of all current members in the surrounding states. Help Jennifer use Advanced Filter to filter the membership list and create a list of records for all members who live in the surrounding states. As you may recall, Advanced Filter allows you to filter a list using several criteria at once. To use Advanced Filter you'll need to create a special range called a criteria range. You enter the critieria you want to use in your search in the criteria range. But first, you begin by importing the external database into Excel 5.0.

1. Open a new workbook.
2. Use the Get External Data... on the Data menu to activate MS Query.

3. Select the external database P7MEMBR.DBF from your Student Disk and then return the data to Microsoft Excel. When you see the Get External Data dialog box, make sure the Keep Query Definition and the Include Field Names options are selected. Use Sheet1, cell A1 as the destination.
4. Bold the labels in row 1 so Excel readily identifies them as column labels.
5. Create the criteria range by making a copy of the column labels (in cells A1:F1) and then pasting them in cells H1:M1.
6. Enter the criteria you want to use for your search. In this case, you want to find all the records for New Mexico, Arizona, Colorado, and Texas. Enter NM in cell L2, AZ in cell L3, CO in cell L4, and TX in cell L5.
7. Click any cell in the data list, then use the Advanced Filter command on the Data menu to display the Advanced Filter dialog box.
8. Make sure the range address for the data list ($A$1:$F$1044) is displayed in the List Range box.
9. Enter the address of the criteria range by clicking the criteria range box and then selecting the criteria range (H1:M5) in the worksheet.
10. Make sure the Filter the list, in-place option box is selected, then click the OK button.
11. Use the Sort command on the Data menu to sort the records by zip code and then by last name.
12. Copy the records to Sheet2, then widen the columns using AutoFit Selection, then rename Sheet2 "Mail List."
13. Redisplay all the records in Sheet1 by clicking Data, clicking Filter, then clicking Show All.
14. Rename Sheet1 "Membership List."
15. Save the workbook as S7MAIL.XLS on your Student Disk.
16. Preview and print the Mail List sheet. *Hint:* Print in landscape orientation and scale to 90% to fit complete records on each page.

TUTORIAL 8

Working with Multiple Worksheets

Creating a Consolidated Cash Flow Statement

OBJECTIVES

In this tutorial you will:

- Organize a workbook
- Document a workbook using a documentation sheet
- Reference cells and ranges in other worksheets
- Use the VLOOKUP function
- Insert, delete, and copy a worksheet
- Insert and move a chart sheet
- Define and use names
- Use the Go To command
- Use the ROUND function to eliminate apparent errors caused by rounding
- Work with a group of worksheets

CASE

Johnson International Johnson International, whose headquarters are in Madison, Wisconsin, produces and sells sporting goods. The company operates in both the United States and Great Britain, and is best known for its golf products. Bill McDougal is an assistant to the comptroller. It is November 1, 1996, and Bill is working on the budget for 1997. Bill has projected sales forecasts, accounts receivable collection rates, and production information for both countries. Bill will use this information to prepare his budgets for the upcoming year.

As part of the budgeting process, Bill must prepare a **consolidated**, or combined, cash flow budget. A **cash flow budget** shows when a company will receive and spend cash, and when a company will need to borrow money to cover costs. Thus, a **consolidated cash flow budget** combines two or more cash flow budgets. Bill will combine the numbers from the budgets for the United States and Great Britain, each of which is located on separate sheets, to produce a consolidated cash flow budget, which also will appear on its own sheet and show totals for the entire company.

Before Bill can consolidate the cash flow budget, he needs to complete a few other tasks. First, he must enter formulas that determine how much money the Great Britain operation will need to borrow during 1997. Second, he wants to add a chart that compares the interest rates at which Johnson International can borrow money in each country. Third, Bill must convert the Great Britain budget (currently stated in pounds) to U.S. dollars so he can calculate the consolidated cash flow budget in dollars. Finally, Bill will consolidate the worksheets.

In this tutorial, you will learn more about organizing multiple worksheets and using formulas that refer to multiple worksheets. Let's work with Bill as he uses Excel to create a consolidated cash flow statement.

Effective Workbook Organization

As you learned in Tutorial 2, worksheets must be well planned, carefully built, thoroughly tested, and comprehensively documented. Because workbooks often contain many worksheets, workbooks also need to be planned, built, tested, and documented.

Bill is creating his cash flow budget in a workbook named C8CASH.XLS. Let's look at the work he has completed so far.

To launch Excel, organize the workspace, and open the C8CASH.XLS workbook:

❶ Launch Windows and Excel.

❷ Make sure your Student Disk is in the disk drive.

❸ Make sure the Microsoft Excel and Book1 windows are maximized.

❹ Click the **Open button** to display the Open dialog box.

❺ Double-click **C8CASH.XLS** in the File Name box to open the workbook. See Figure 8-1.

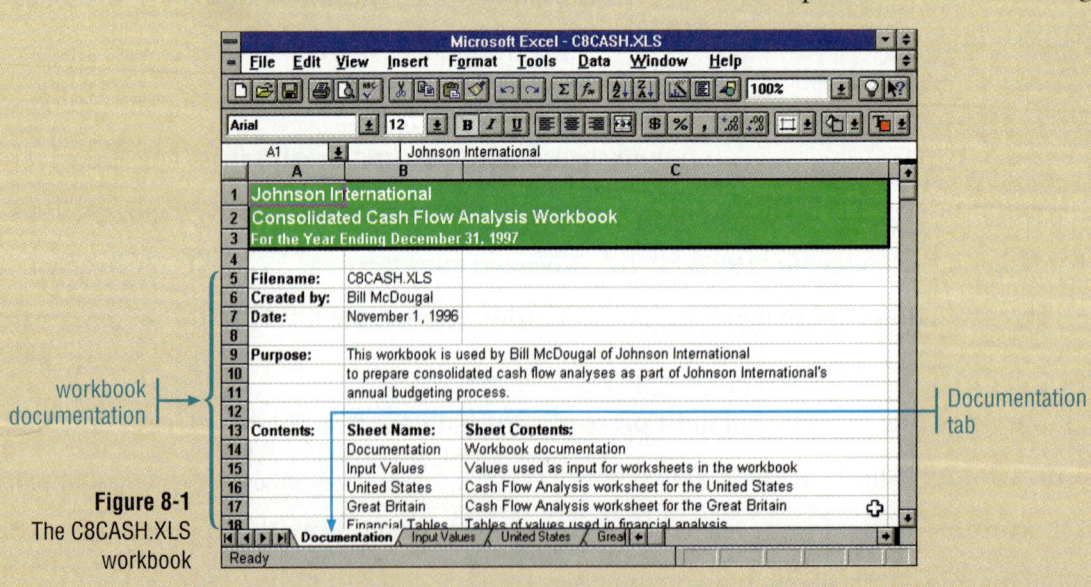

Figure 8-1
The C8CASH.XLS workbook

TROUBLE? If the file isn't in the file list, click the Drives down arrow button to display the drive in which your Student Disk is located.

Using a Documentation Worksheet in a Workbook

The first worksheet, named "Documentation," contains Bill's workbook documentation. Bill knows that when using multiple worksheets, it is a good idea to develop a workbook plan and document it in the first workbook sheet. Bill's plan for the workbook is shown in Figure 8-2.

Workbook Plan for the Johnson International Consolidated Cash Flow Analysis Workbook

My Goal:
To develop a workbook to prepare and analyze the annual consolidated cash flow budget for Johnson International

What workbook sheets will I use?

Type	Name	Contents
Worksheet	Documentation	Workbook documentation
Worksheet	Input Values	Values used as input for other worksheets
Worksheet	United States	Cash Flow Analysis for the United States operation
Worksheet	Great Britain	Cash Flow Analysis for the Great Britain operation
Worksheet	Financial Tables	Tables of values used in financial analysis
Chart	Interest Rates	Chart comparing interest rates

Figure 8-2
The workbook plan

Notice that Bill specified the types of sheets he will use. Bill plans to use two types of sheets—a worksheet and a chart sheet. A **chart sheet** contains a single chart, or graph. Bill will use a chart sheet to create his graph of interest rates.

The Documentation sheet lists the five sheets that are currently in the workbook plus the chart sheet that Bill will add to the workbook. Bill has named each sheet and described its contents.

To view the contents of the Documentation sheet:

❶ Make sure the Documentation sheet is the active worksheet. If it isn't, click the **Documentation tab**.

❷ Scroll the worksheet until you see rows 13 through 19.

Notice that the information Bill entered into the Documentation sheet follows the workbook plan shown in Figure 8-2.

EX 276   TUTORIAL 8   Working with Multiple Worksheets

The Documentation sheet tells you what you will find in each sheet in the workbook. The Input Values worksheet contains values that Bill will use for calculations in the workbook. The United States sheet contains Bill's cash flow analysis for Johnson International's operations in the U.S., and the Great Britain sheet contains the cash flow analysis for the Great Britain operations. The Financial Tables worksheet contains values needed to calculate the amount of money the company might need to borrow in a particular month. The Interest Rates chart sheet, which Bill has not created yet, will contain a chart comparing interest rates in the United States and Great Britain.

Let's save the workbook under the name S8CASH.XLS, so your changes do not alter the original file. When working with multiple worksheets, it's helpful to make A1 the active cell in each worksheet before saving the workbook. That way, when you switch between sheets, you'll know exactly where you are in the new worksheet.

To save the workbook as S8CASH.XLS:

❶ Make sure the Documentation sheet is the active worksheet.

❷ Double-click cell **B5**, change the filename to **S8CASH.XLS**, then press **[Enter]**.

❸ Press **[Ctrl][Home]** to make cell A1 the active cell.

❹ Click **File**, then click **Save As...** to display the Save As dialog box.

❺ Save the workbook as **S8CASH.XLS**.

Now that you understand the workbook's Documentation sheet, let's look at how a cash flow budget is organized. To make the worksheet easier to read as you scroll, you will freeze the row and column labels using the Freeze Panes command on the Window menu.

To view the United States cash flow budget:

❶ Click the **United States tab** to display the worksheet that contains Bill's cash flow budget for the United States.

❷ Click cell **B6** to make it the active cell.

❸ Click **Window**, then click **Freeze Panes** to freeze all the columns to the left of the active cell and all the rows above the active cell. A printout of this worksheet is shown in Figure 8-3.

Johnson International
Cash Flow Analysis - United States
For the Year Ending December 31, 1997

Values in Dollars	JAN	FEB	MAR	APR	MAY	JUN	JUL	AUG	SEP	OCT	NOV	DEC	YEAR
Cash Balance - Beginning	$50,000	$51,269	$76,456	$89,644	$89,413	$87,513	$79,775	$54,025	$54,166	$50,543	$50,410	$56,114	$50,000
Add Cash Receipts:													
Sales	$137,500	$125,000	$125,000	$137,500	$150,000	$175,000	$150,000	$156,250	$162,500	$168,750	$181,250	$193,750	$1,862,500
Cash Receipts:													
0-30 Days	$100,750	$89,375	$81,250	$81,250	$89,375	$97,500	$113,750	$97,500	$101,563	$105,625	$109,688	$117,813	$1,185,438
31-60 Days	37,500	38,750	34,375	31,250	31,250	34,375	37,500	43,750	37,500	39,063	40,625	42,188	448,125
61-90 Days	14,500	15,000	15,500	13,750	12,500	12,500	13,750	15,000	17,500	15,000	15,625	16,250	176,875
Total Cash Receipts	$152,750	$143,125	$131,125	$126,250	$133,125	$144,375	$165,000	$156,250	$156,563	$159,688	$165,938	$176,250	$1,810,438
Total Cash Available	$202,750	$194,394	$207,581	$215,894	$222,538	$231,888	$244,775	$210,275	$210,728	$210,231	$216,347	$232,364	$1,860,438
Less Expenditures:													
Direct Materials	$13,200	$12,000	$12,000	$13,200	$14,400	$16,800	$14,400	$15,000	$15,600	$16,200	$17,400	$18,600	178,800
Direct Labor	35,063	31,875	31,875	35,063	38,250	44,625	38,250	39,844	41,438	43,031	46,219	49,406	474,938
Production Overhead	43,844	42,813	42,813	43,844	44,875	46,938	44,875	45,391	45,906	46,422	47,453	48,484	543,656
Selling	20,625	18,750	18,750	20,625	22,500	26,250	22,500	23,438	24,375	25,313	27,188	29,063	279,375
Administration	13,750	12,500	12,500	13,750	15,000	17,500	15,000	15,625	16,250	16,875	18,125	19,375	186,250
Equipment Purchases							50,000	25,000					75,000
Dividends	25,000						25,000						50,000
Total Expenditures	$151,481	$117,938	$117,938	$126,481	$135,025	$152,113	$210,025	$164,297	$143,569	$147,841	$156,384	$164,928	$1,788,019
Cash Available less Expenditures	$51,269	$76,456	$89,644	$89,413	$87,513	$79,775	$34,750	$45,978	$67,159	$62,390	$59,963	$67,436	$72,419
Financing:													
Loan Balance - Beginning	$0	$0	$0	$0	$0	$0	$0	$20,000	$30,000	$15,016	$3,714	$0	$0
Add Borrowings (beginning of month)	0	0	0	0	0	0	20,000	10,000	0	0	0	0	30,000
Less Repayments (end of month)	0	0	0	0	0	0	0	0	14,984	11,301	3,714	0	30,000
Loan Balance - Ending	$0	$0	$0	$0	$0	$0	$20,000	$30,000	$15,016	$3,714	$0	$0	$0
Interest (paid on average balance)	0	0	0	0	0	0	725	1,813	1,632	679	135	0	4,983
Financing Expenditures	$0	$0	$0	$0	$0	$0	$725	$1,813	$16,616	$11,980	$3,849	$0	$34,983
Cash Balance - Ending	$51,269	$76,456	$89,644	$89,413	$87,513	$79,775	$34,025	$54,166	$50,543	$50,410	$56,114	$67,436	$67,436

Notes:
1. Borrowings must be in increments shown on Financing Tables worksheet. Borrowings must cover any projected monthly deficit plus the required minimum cash balance.
2. Financing Expenditures = Repayments plus interest expenditures.
3. Ending Cash Balance = Beginning cash balance plus borrowings less financing expenditures.

Figure 8-3
The printed United States worksheet

Now that the Freeze Panes command is activated, when you scroll vertically through the worksheet the column labels (in row 5) remain frozen in place. When you scroll horizontally, the row labels (in column A) remain frozen in place. This makes it much easier to read the worksheet as you scroll.

The cash flow budget worksheet contains the section labels shown in Figure 8-4. You don't need to understand every detail of the worksheet, but you should familiarize yourself with its general organization.

Section	Purpose
Cash Balance - Beginning	The amount of cash on hand at the beginning of the month.
Add Cash Receipts	Receipts from accounts receivable collected during the month are added to the Cash Balance to get the **Total Cash Available** during the month
Less Expenditures	Cash expenditures during the month are listed and summed to get the **Total Expenditures** for the month.
Cash Available less Expenditures	The cash surplus or shortage after the cash expenditures.
Financing	Each Johnson International unit must borrow money when necessary to cover costs. The unit must have enough cash to cover a required minimum cash balance for the next month *plus* any **Interest** on the average loan balance during the month. **Repayments** are made only when there is a **Loan Balance** greater than $0.00 and enough **Cash Available less Expenditures** to make a repayment, cover the **Interest**, and maintain the **Required Minimum Cash Balance** for the next month.
Cash Balance - Ending	This is equal to **Cash Available less Expenditures** plus **Borrowings** less **Financing Expenditures** (**Repayments** and **Interest**). This becomes the **Cash Balance - Beginning** for the next month.

Figure 8-4
Cash flow analysis organization

To inspect the United States cash flow analysis:
1. Scroll through the United States worksheet and compare your worksheet to the worksheet in Figure 8-3.
2. Press **[Ctrl][Home]** to make cell B6 the active cell. Notice that when the Freeze Panes command is activated, pressing [Ctrl][Home] moves you to the upper-left cell of the unfrozen range of cells.

Bill's first task is to complete the Great Britain worksheet by entering the formulas that calculate how much money (if any) the company should borrow each month.

How does Johnson International decide if the company needs to borrow money? The basic idea is simple. The company must have enough money at the beginning of a month to meet the company's cash needs for that month. If it doesn't, the company borrows money.

The actual calculations in the worksheet are more complicated, but they follow the same principle. If the cash balance at the beginning of a month is forecast to be less than a critical value, the company borrows money. The value that management has chosen as the critical value is stored in the Input Values worksheet.

An important principle of effective workbook organization is to *always display input values in a separate worksheet or area of a worksheet*. Never "bury" input values within formulas. You'll find it much easier to change the input values when they are displayed in a separate area.

Now, let's find the critical beginning cash balance for Johnson International.

To view the Input Values worksheet in the workbook:

❶ Click the **Input Values tab** to display the worksheet that contains the input values for Johnson International. You'll use several of the values on this sheet as you create formulas in this tutorial. Right now, though, we are interested only in the amount of cash the company must have available. See Figure 8-5.

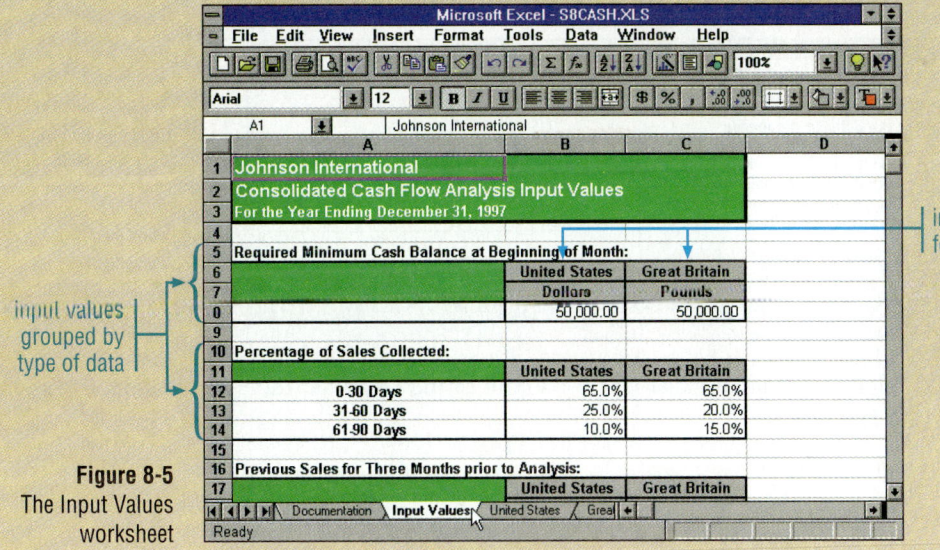

Figure 8-5
The Input Values worksheet

The section labeled "Required Minimum Cash Balance at Beginning of Month:" shows that the critical beginning cash balance for the United States is $50,000.00 (in cell B8), and the critical value for Great Britain is 50,000.00 pounds (in cell C8).

The formula that calculates the amount of money to borrow will appear in the Great Britain worksheet, but will use values in the Financial Tables worksheet. Let's look at the Great Britain and Financial Tables worksheets now.

To view the Great Britain and Financial Tables worksheets:

1. Click the **Great Britain tab** to display the worksheet that contains Bill's cash budget for Great Britain. This worksheet has the same design as the United States worksheet. As you did earlier, click cell **B6** to make it the active cell, click **Window**, then click **Freeze Panes**.

2. Scroll the worksheet until you see rows 26 through 36. The Cash Available less Expenditures entries are in row 26 followed by the Financing section.

3. Click cell **B30**. Notice that the cell is blank. This is the first cell in which Bill needs to enter a formula. See Figure 8-6.

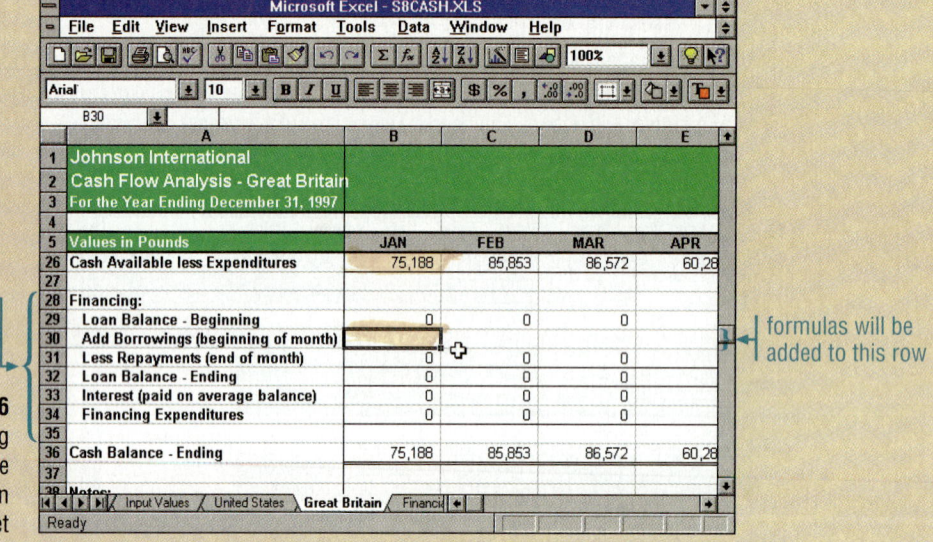

Figure 8-6
The Financing section of the Great Britain worksheet

4. Click the **Financial Tables tab**. A printout of the Financial Tables worksheet is shown in Figure 8-7.

Effective Workbook Organization **EX 281**

Johnson International
Financing Tables
For the Year Ending December 31, 1997

AMOUNT TO BORROW:

United States (in Dollars):

If Cash Available less Expenditures is:		Borrow:
At least:	But less than:	
($1,000,000.00)	($500,000.00)	$1,050,000.00
($500,000.00)	($250,000.00)	$550,000.00
($250,000.00)	($200,000.00)	$275,000.00
($200,000.00)	($175,000.00)	$250,000.00
($175,000.00)	($150,000.00)	$225,000.00
($150,000.00)	($125,000.00)	$200,000.00
($125,000.00)	($100,000.00)	$175,000.00
($100,000.00)	($75,000.00)	$150,000.00
($75,000.00)	($50,000.00)	$125,000.00
($50,000.00)	($40,000.00)	$100,000.00
($40,000.00)	($30,000.00)	$90,000.00
($30,000.00)	($20,000.00)	$80,000.00
($20,000.00)	($10,000.00)	$70,000.00
($10,000.00)	$0.00	$60,000.00
$0.00	$10,000.00	$50,000.00
$10,000.00	$20,000.00	$40,000.00
$20,000.00	$30,000.00	$30,000.00
$30,000.00	$40,000.00	$20,000.00
$40,000.00	$50,000.00	$10,000.00
$50,000.00		$0.00

Highlighted
10000 + 40000 = 50,000 always

Great Britain (in Pounds):

If Cash Available less Expenditures is:		Borrow:
At least:	But less than:	
(1,000,000)	(500,000)	1,050,000
(500,000)	(250,000)	550,000
(250,000)	(200,000)	275,000
(200,000)	(175,000)	250,000
(175,000)	(150,000)	225,000
(150,000)	(125,000)	200,000
(125,000)	(100,000)	175,000
(100,000)	(75,000)	150,000
(75,000)	(50,000)	125,000
(50,000)	(40,000)	100,000
(40,000)	(30,000)	90,000
(30,000)	(20,000)	80,000
(20,000)	(10,000)	70,000
(10,000)	0	60,000
0	10,000	50,000
10,000	20,000	40,000
20,000	30,000	30,000
30,000	40,000	20,000
40,000	50,000	10,000
50,000		0

Figure 8-7
The printed Financial Tables worksheet

❺ Scroll through the Financial Tables worksheet and compare it to Figure 8-7. You see two tables, one for each country; each table shows how much money the company should borrow when the Cash Available less Expenditures for a month falls within a certain range. Negative numbers are displayed in parentheses.

❻ Scroll the worksheet until rows 31 through 48 are visible and you see Great Britain's financial table.

Bill's formula to calculate the amount of money that the Great Britain unit needs to borrow will appear in the Great Britain worksheet but will use values in the Financial Tables worksheet. To accomplish this, Bill will need to write a formula in one worksheet, in this case the Great Britain worksheet, that refers to, or *references*, cells in other worksheets in the workbook.

Referencing Cells and Ranges in Other Worksheets

You need to follow some basic rules when referencing cells in other worksheets. If the worksheet name does *not* contain a space, use the worksheet name followed by an exclamation point (!). For example, Documentation!B6 references the cell B6 in the Documentation worksheet.

If the worksheet name contains a space, enclose the name in single quotation marks (' ') followed by an exclamation point (!). For example 'Financial Tables'!A10:C29 requires single quotation marks because of the space between Financial and Tables.

A **3-D reference** is a reference to the same worksheet range in two or more worksheets. To create a 3-D reference, use a sheet range (the names of the first and last worksheets separated by a colon) followed by a worksheet range (the cell references within one worksheet). For example, 'United States:Great Britain'!B6:M6 refers to the worksheet range B6:M6 in both the United States sheet and the Great Britain sheet. Notice that single quotation marks enclose the sheet range, not individual sheet names; 'United States:Great Britain' is correct, but 'United States':'Great Britain' is not and will cause Excel to display an error message.

REFERENCE WINDOW

Referencing Cells and Ranges in Other Worksheets

- If a sheet name does not contain a space, use the worksheet name followed by an exclamation point (!), followed by the range or cell address. For example, Sheet1!C36.

- If a worksheet name contains a space, enclose the name in single quotation marks followed by an exclamation point (!). For example, 'Sheet One'!C36.

- To create a 3-D reference (a reference to the same worksheet range in two or more worksheets), use a sheet range (the names of the first and last worksheets separated by a colon) followed by a worksheet range (the cell references within one worksheet). For example, 'Sheet One:Sheet Two'!C36:E45.

Because Bill will reference a table of values in the Financial Tables worksheet, his formula on the Great Britain worksheet will contain the reference:

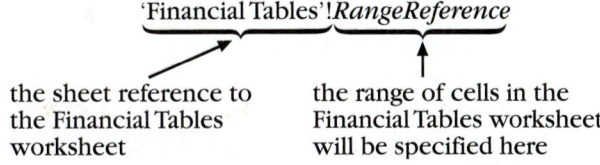

Bill needs to write a formula in the Great Britain worksheet that will check the Cash Available less Expenditures value for the month in row 26, and then look up this value in the Great Britain table on the Financial Tables worksheet to determine how much, if any, Johnson International needs to borrow. To do this, Bill will use a LOOKUP function in his formula.

LOOKUP Functions

LOOKUP functions, as the name implies, are functions that find, or look up, a value in a worksheet, and then display, or return, another value associated with the original value. You do the same thing when, for example, you look up Jenny Smith's name in a phone book to find her phone number. The phone number is a value associated with the original value of Jenny Smith, and is what you want to see.

Bill will look up information using the VLOOKUP function. V indicates that the information you're searching through is arranged vertically, in columns. (You'll learn about the HLOOKUP function—or Horizontal LOOKUP—in a case at the end of this tutorial.) When you use the VLOOKUP function, the worksheet range you search through is called the **lookup table**. In order to locate a value in the lookup table, Excel compares an input value, called the **lookup value**, to other values that you provide. You enter these values, called **compare values**, in the leftmost column of the lookup table. Values that are associated with these compare values are in the other columns of the lookup table and are the values that can be displayed or returned in the worksheet.

The syntax of the VLOOKUP function is:

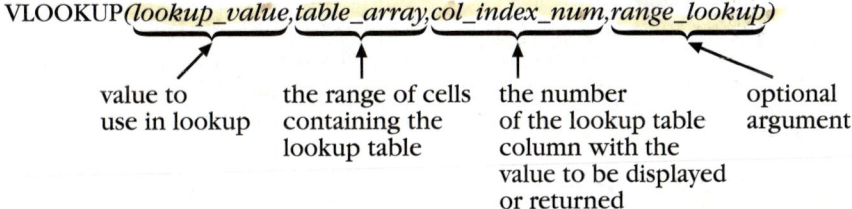

The *lookup_value* is the input value or cell reference of the input value you are trying to match and is located in the list of compare values in the leftmost column of the lookup table. You must list compare values in ascending order, from smallest to largest. Listing negative numbers can be tricky. Remember that –125,000 is a larger (more positive) number than –150,000. For example, on the Financial Tables worksheet, the negative value ($1,000,000.00) comes before the larger negative value ($500,000.00). Recall that Excel displays negative currency numbers in parentheses.

The *table_array* is the range of cells that contain the lookup table. The compare values are in the leftmost column of this range.

The *col_index_num* is the column number in the lookup table that contains the value you want displayed in (or returned to) the cell in which you entered the formula with the VLOOKUP function. The columns in the lookup table are labeled consecutively. The leftmost column is column 1, the next column to the right is column 2, and so on. If you enter a column number less than 1, Excel displays a #VALUE! error value. If you enter a column number greater than the number of columns in the lookup table, Excel displays a #REF! error value.

The *range_lookup* is an optional argument you use to tell Excel whether or not it can find an approximate match for the *lookup_value* in the compare values. For this argument, you enter a logical value of TRUE or FALSE. If you leave out this argument or indicate TRUE, Excel will find an approximate match (the first row where the *lookup_value* is greater than or equal to the compare value). If you indicate FALSE, Excel will find an exact match in the compare values.

> **REFERENCE WINDOW**
>
> ### Using VLOOKUP to Display Values Found in a Lookup Table
>
> These steps assume you are typing the function in the cell. Keep in mind that you can also use the Function Wizard button and select the LOOKUP & REFERENCE function. Then enter the arguments in the Step 2 of 2 dialog box.
>
> - Create the lookup table in a worksheet: Place the compare values in the leftmost column. Add columns of associated values to the right of this column.
> - Click the cell where you want to display the results of the formula that contains the VLOOKUP function.
> - Type =VLOOKUP(to begin the formula.
> - Type the *lookup_value*, type a comma, type the *table_array*, type a comma, then type the *col_index_num*.
> - If the *lookup_value* must find an exact match in the lookup column, type a comma, then type the word FALSE as the *range_lookup* value.
> - Press [Enter] to complete the formula.

Now let's consider the formula Bill will use in the Great Britain worksheet. The first formula will check the value of Cash Available less Expenditures in cell B26 of the Great Britain worksheet. It will then look up this value in the Great Britain lookup table on the Financial Tables worksheet to determine how much to borrow. The lookup table is in range A34:C53 on the Financial Tables worksheet (this range does *not* include column labels) and is shown in part in Figure 8-8.

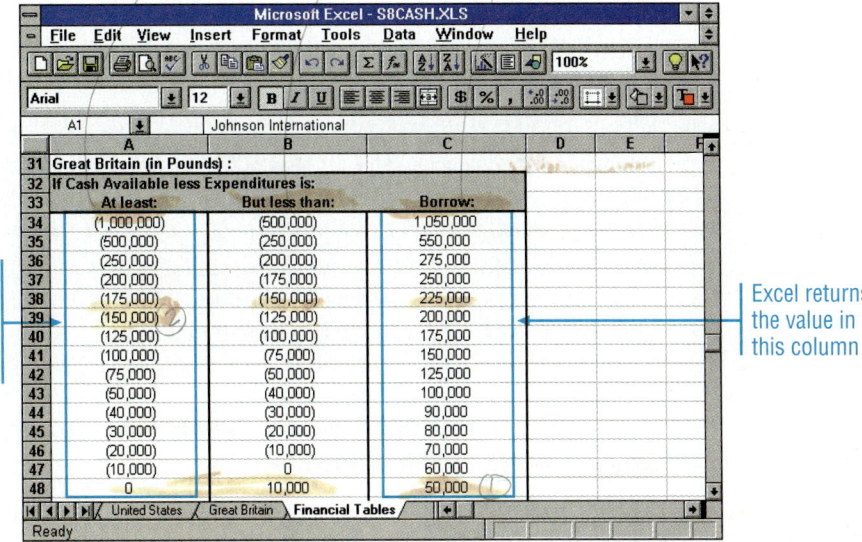

Figure 8-8
Rows 34 through 48 of the Great Britain lookup table

the VLOOKUP function compares the lookup value to the compare values in this column

Excel returns the value in this column

In this case, the lookup value does not have to match the compare values exactly. The compare values are in one column labeled "At least:." The lookup value is located on the Great Britain sheet. Bill's LOOKUP formula will select the first row where the lookup value (in the Great Britain worksheet) is greater than or equal to the compare value. Bill has listed the next compare value in the column labeled "But less than:" so that he can easily read the range of possible lookup values that cause Excel to select a certain row. For example, Excel will select row 48 if the Cash Available less Expenditures value in cell B26 (on the Great Britain sheet) is *greater than or equal* to 0 pounds but *less than* 10,000 pounds. Similarly, Excel will select row 39 if the value in cell B26 (on the Great Britain sheet) is *greater than or equal* to –150,000 pounds but *less than* –125,000 pounds.

Bill has left cell B53 on the Financial Tables worksheet blank (You can scroll to cell B53 to see for yourself) because Excel selects rows based only on the value in column A (the compare values column), and will select row 53 for all values greater than 50,000 pounds.

When you create lookup tables that don't require an exact match of the lookup value, it is a good idea to set up the lookup tables as shown in Figure 8-8 so you can identify easily the ranges of lookup value associated with each row in the table.

Bill wants his LOOKUP formula to return the value in the column labeled "Borrow:," which indicates how much Johnson International needs to borrow. The *col_index_num* for this column is 3. Because the *lookup_value* argument does not require an exact match in the compare values, Bill can omit the *range_lookup* argument. Because Bill is referencing this lookup table range from the Great Britain worksheet, the correct range reference is 'Financial Tables'!A34:C53. Bill also needs to copy this formula to other cells in the Great Britain worksheet, so he must use an absolute reference for the lookup table.

Putting this information together, the formula Bill needs to use is: =VLOOKUP(B26, 'Financial Tables'!$A$34:$C$53,3).

EX 286 TUTORIAL 8 Working with Multiple Worksheets

To use VLOOKUP to determine the amount to borrow:

1. Press **[Ctrl][Home]** to make cell A1 the active cell on the Financial Tables worksheet.
2. Click the **Great Britain tab**.
3. Make sure cell B30 is still the active cell.
4. Type **=VLOOKUP(B26,'Financial Tables'!$A$34:$C$53,3)** and then press **[Enter]**. (Make sure you include single quotation marks around the sheet reference; also, make sure you type an exclamation point after the last single quotation mark.)

Because cell 'Great Britain'!B26 contains the value 75,188 pounds and this value is greater than 50,000 pounds, there is no need for Johnson International to borrow any money this month. The value 0 appears in cell B30.

Now that Bill has created the formula in cell B30, he can copy this formula to the other cells in row 30 that require a similar formula.

To copy the formula:

1. Click cell **B30**, then click the **Copy button**.
2. Highlight the range **C30:M30**, then press **[Enter]** to complete the copy.
3. Click any cell to remove the highlighting.
4. Scroll through the months to see the results. Notice that the Johnson International Great Britain organization will need to start borrowing in June, and will have a loan balance of 30,514 pounds at the end of the year. See Figure 8-9.

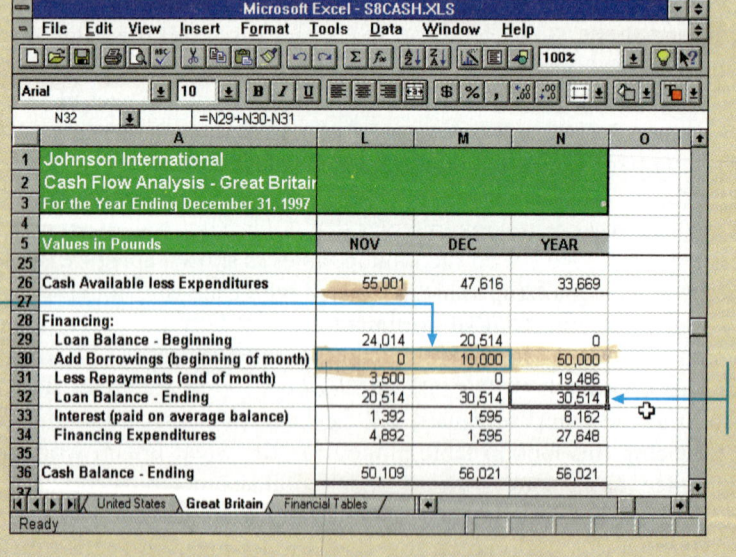

Figure 8-9
The ending loan balance for the Great Britain unit

these cells contain formulas using the VLOOKUP function

the Great Britain unit will owe 30,514 pounds at the end of the year

5. Press **[Ctrl][Home]**, then click the **Save button** to save the workbook.

Bill has completed the Great Britain worksheet. He can now convert the values on the Great Britain worksheet to dollars. Then he can use the dollar values to create the consolidated cash flow worksheet.

Modifying the Documentation Worksheet

To consolidate the cash flow budgets, Bill needs two new worksheets—one to convert pounds to dollars and one for the consolidation. He modifies his workbook plan to reflect these additions, as shown in Figure 8-10. Bill will use the name "Great Britain ($)" to identify the Great Britain cash flow analysis converted to dollars and the name "Consolidation" to identify the worksheet containing the consolidated cash flow analysis. Notice how the dollar sign ($) is used to distinguish the Great Britain worksheet in dollars ("Great Britain ($)") from the Great Britain worksheet in pounds ("Great Britain").

Workbook Plan for the Johnson International Consolidated Cash Flow Analysis Workbook

My Goal:
To develop a workbook to prepare and analyze the annual consolidated cash flow budget for Johnson International

What workbook sheets will I use?

Type	Name	Contents
Worksheet	Documentation	Workbook documentation
Worksheet	Input Values	Values used as input for other worksheets
Worksheet	Consolidation	Consolidated Cash Flow Analysis
Worksheet	United States	Cash Flow Analysis for the United States operation
Worksheet	Great Britain ($)	Cash Flow Analysis for Great Britain in dollars
Worksheet	Great Britain	Cash Flow Analysis for the Great Britain operation
Worksheet	Financial Tables	Tables of values used in financial analysis
Chart	Interest Rates	Chart comparing interest rates

Figure 8-10
The revised workbook plan

Bill knows that it is important to keep documentation up to date, so he takes time to enter the new sheet names on the Documentation worksheet.

To modify the Documentation worksheet:

1. Click the **Documentation tab**.
2. Right-click row heading **16** to select the row and display the Shortcut menu. (Recall that "right-click" means to click the right mouse button.)
3. Click **Insert**.
4. Right-click row heading **18** to select the row and display the Shortcut menu, then click **Insert**.
5. Type **Consolidation** in cell **B16**.
6. Type **Consolidated Cash Flow Analysis worksheet** in cell **C16**.

⦿ Type **Great Britain ($)** in cell B18 and type **Cash Flow Analysis worksheet for Great Britain in Dollars** in cell C18. Your worksheet should look like Figure 8-11.

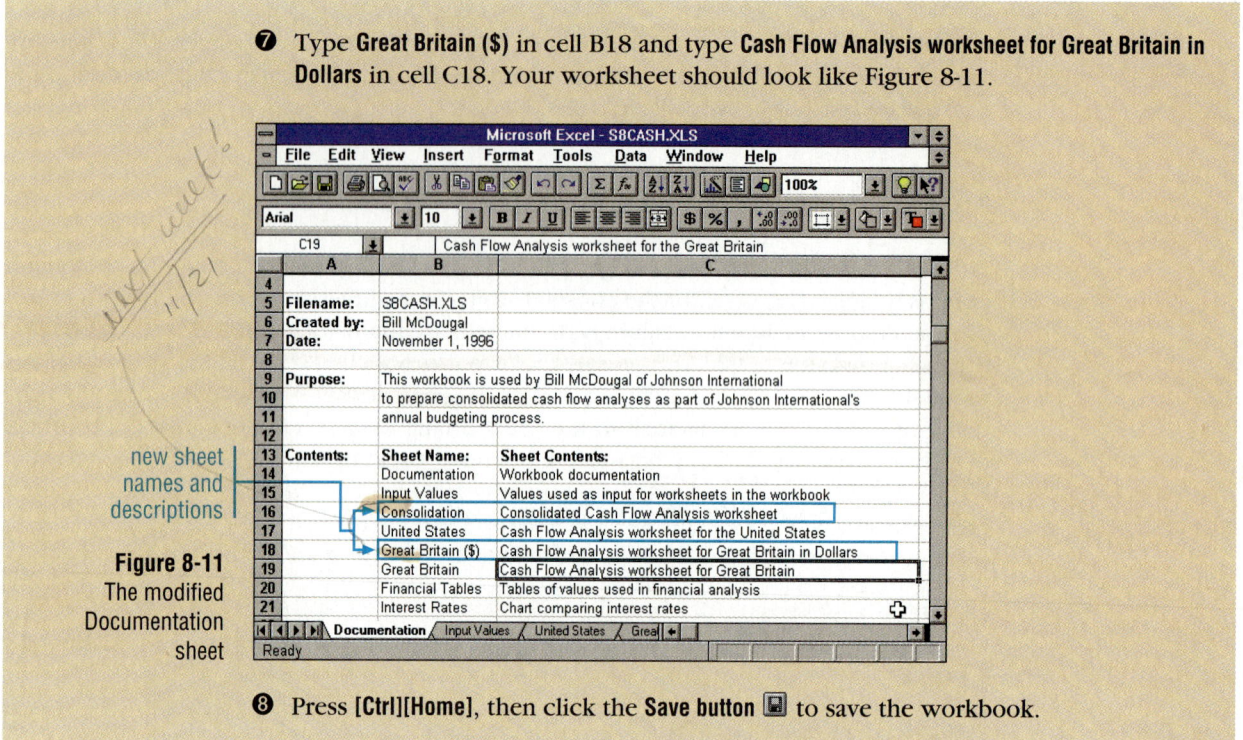

Figure 8-11
The modified Documentation sheet

⦿ Press **[Ctrl][Home]**, then click the **Save button** to save the workbook.

Bill is ready to create the Great Britain ($) worksheet, which will contain the British pound figures on the Great Britain worksheet converted to U.S. dollars. To do this, he will need to insert a new worksheet into the workbook.

Inserting, Deleting, Moving, and Copying Workbook Sheets

Excel makes it easy to insert new sheets into a workbook.

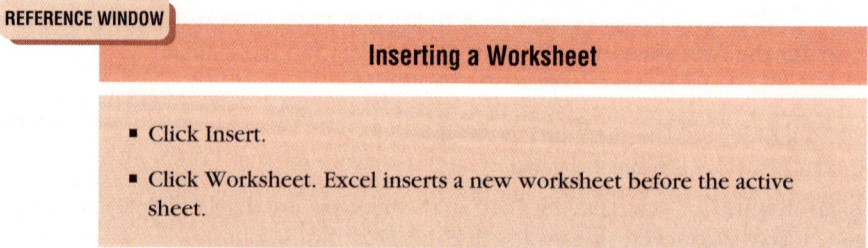

REFERENCE WINDOW

Inserting a Worksheet

- Click Insert.
- Click Worksheet. Excel inserts a new worksheet before the active sheet.

You can easily delete a sheet from a workbook, but after you delete a sheet you *cannot* recover it—the Undo command will *not* undelete a deleted sheet!

Inserting, Deleting, Moving, and Copying Workbook Sheets **EX 289**

> **REFERENCE WINDOW**
>
> ### Deleting a Sheet
>
> - Click the tab of the sheet you want to delete.
> - Click Edit, then click Delete Sheet.

Bill decides to insert a new worksheet for the Great Britain dollar values between the United States and Great Britain sheets so that he can keep the worksheets expressed in dollars next to each other.

To insert the new worksheet:

1. Click the **Great Britain tab** to insert the new worksheet between the United States worksheet and the Great Britain worksheet.

2. Click **Insert**, then click **Worksheet** to insert the new worksheet named Sheet1. See Figure 8-12.

Figure 8-12
The new worksheet

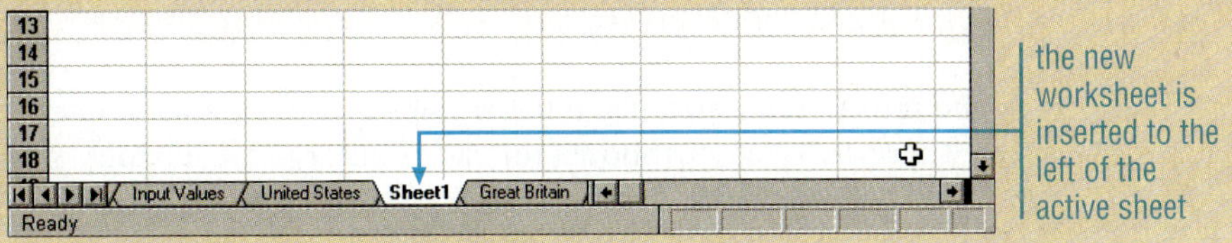

the new worksheet is inserted to the left of the active sheet

Bill realizes he's made a mistake. If he uses a new, blank worksheet, he will have to rebuild the worksheet from scratch. It is easier to copy an existing worksheet. Bill decides to delete the new sheet and make a copy of the United States worksheet, which he can modify to become the Great Britain ($) worksheet.

To delete the Sheet1 worksheet:

1. Make sure Sheet1 is the active worksheet.

2. Click **Edit**, then click **Delete Sheet**.

3. The message "Selected sheets will be permanently deleted. Continue?" appears. Check again to make sure that Sheet1 is the active worksheet, then click the **OK button**.

   TROUBLE? If you deleted the wrong sheet, click File, then click Save As… and save the workbook as S8DELETE.XLS. Then re-open the S8CASH.XLS workbook (you saved this copy just before inserting and deleting Sheet1). Continue with the tutorial using the S8CASH.XLS workbook.

Inserting the worksheet reminds Bill that he needs to create a chart that compares interest rates. Bill wants to add a chart sheet to the workbook instead of putting the chart on a worksheet. He'll do this now and create the Great Britain ($) sheet later.

Inserting a Chart Sheet

A chart sheet is a sheet that contains only a chart. Using a chart sheet allows you to view a chart quickly by clicking the chart sheet tab. The menu options on a chart sheet are similar to the menu options you see after double-clicking a chart on a regular worksheet.

> **REFERENCE WINDOW**
>
> **Inserting a Chart Sheet**
>
> - Highlight the range you want to chart.
> - Click Insert, click Chart, then click As New Sheet.
> - Follow the ChartWizard instructions to create your chart. The new chart sheet is inserted to the left of the active sheet.

The Johnson International interest rates that Bill wants to chart are on the Input Values sheet. There are two rates shown for each country—the country's **prime rate**, which is the rate banks charge their best, least-risky customers; and the Johnson International rate, which is the prime rate plus one percent.

To insert the chart sheet and create the chart with ChartWizard:

❶ Click the **Input Values tab** to make Input Values the active worksheet.

❷ Highlight the range A24:C26.

❸ Click **Insert**, click **Chart**, then click **As New Sheet**. The ChartWizard - Step 1 of 5 dialog box appears with $A$24:$C$26 highlighted in the Range text box.

TROUBLE? If the range is not $A$24:$C$26, edit the range until it is correct.

❹ Click the **Next >** button. The ChartWizard - Step 2 of 5 dialog box appears with the Column chart type selected.

TROUBLE? If the Column chart type is not selected, click the Column chart type to select it.

❺ Click the **Next >** button. The ChartWizard - Step 3 of 5 dialog box appears.

Inserting, Deleting, Moving, and Copying Workbook Sheets   EX 291

❻ Click format **1**, then click the **Next >** button. The ChartWizard - Step 4 of 5 dialog box appears.

❼ Make sure that the Rows button is selected, and that the number 1 appears in both the Category (X) Axis Labels and Legend text boxes, then click the **Next >** button. The ChartWizard - Step 5 of 5 dialog box appears.

❽ Click the **Chart Title text box** to make it active, then type **INTEREST RATES**.

❾ Click the **Finish** button. The new chart sheet appears before the Input Values sheet. See Figure 8-13.

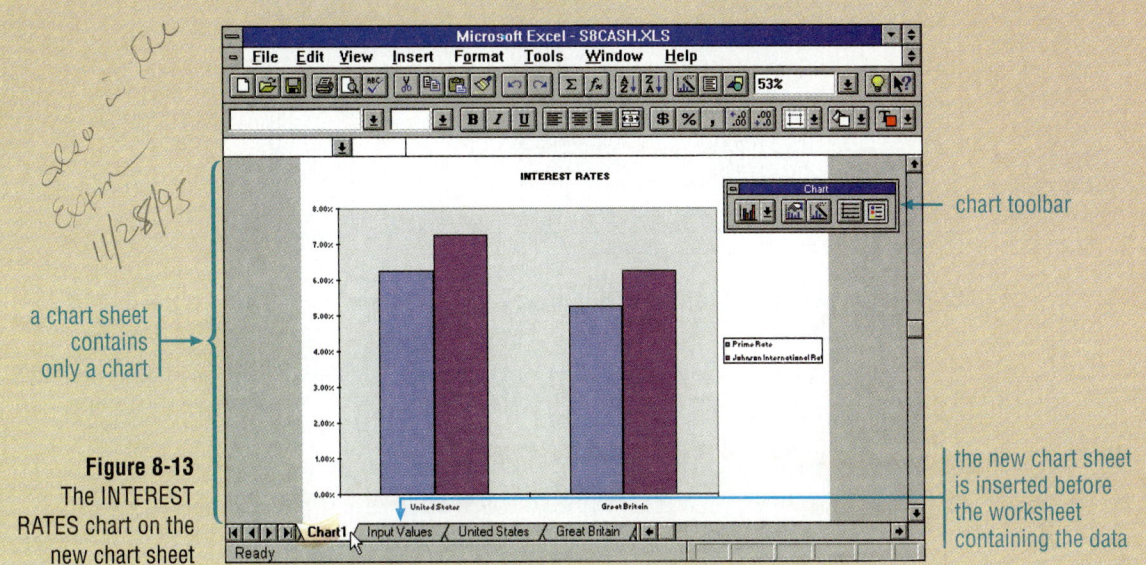

Figure 8-13
The INTEREST RATES chart on the new chart sheet

❿ Double-click the **Chart1 tab** to display the Rename Sheet dialog box. Type **Interest Rates Chart** and then click the **OK button**. The new sheet name appears on the sheet tab.

The Interest Rates chart shows that the interest rates in the United States are slightly higher than those in Great Britain. The difference between the prime rate and the company's rate for both countries is also clearly visible.

Bill likes the chart, but dislikes where the chart sheet is located in the workbook. Bill wants the Interest Rates Chart to be the last sheet in the workbook.

Moving a Sheet

You can move a sheet easily by dragging its sheet tab to a new location.

To move the Interest Rates Chart sheet to the end of the workbook:
❶ Drag the **Interest Rates Chart tab** to the right of the Financial Tables tab. When you drag the sheet tab, the pointer changes to 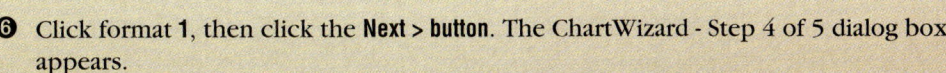 and a black triangle shows where the sheet will be placed. See Figure 8-14.

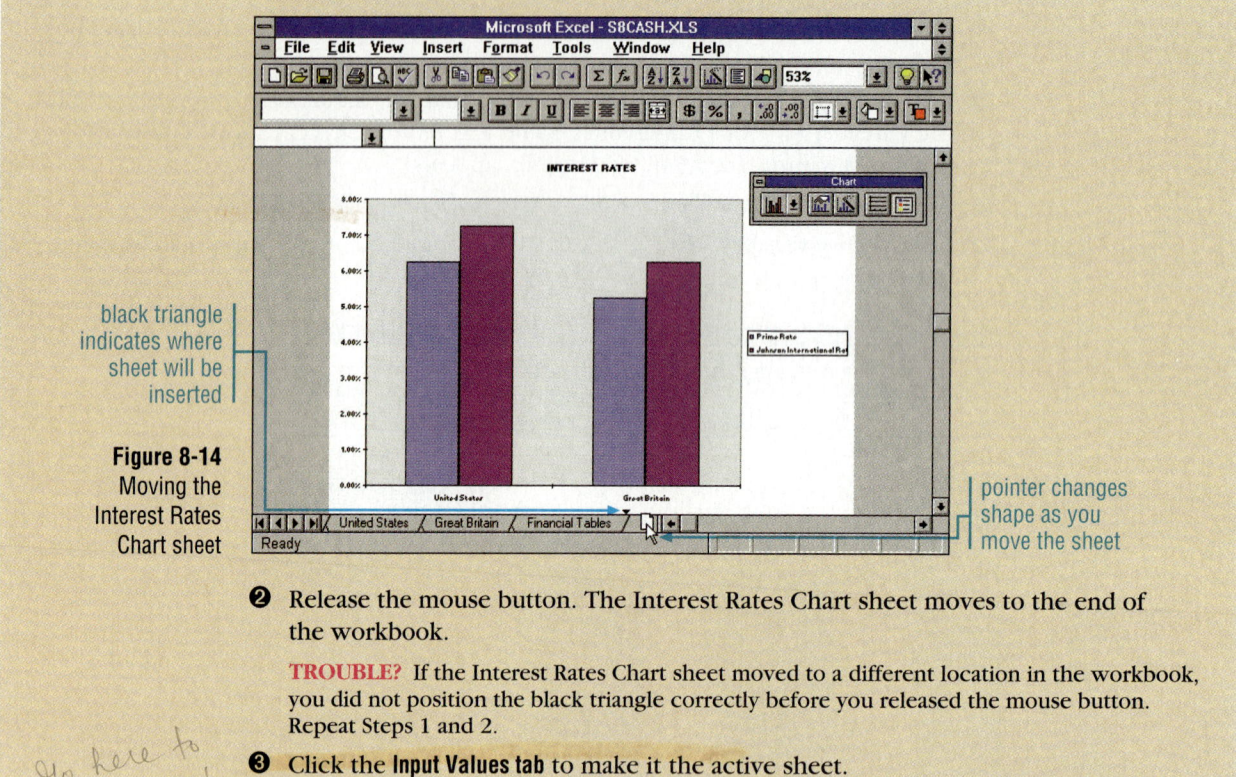

black triangle indicates where sheet will be inserted

Figure 8-14
Moving the Interest Rates Chart sheet

pointer changes shape as you move the sheet

❷ Release the mouse button. The Interest Rates Chart sheet moves to the end of the workbook.

TROUBLE? If the Interest Rates Chart sheet moved to a different location in the workbook, you did not position the black triangle correctly before you released the mouse button. Repeat Steps 1 and 2.

❸ Click the **Input Values tab** to make it the active sheet.

❹ Press **[Ctrl][Home]**, then click the **Save button** 🖫 to save the workbook.

Copying a Sheet

You can easily copy a sheet by holding down the Control key as you drag tab of the sheet you want to copy to the location where you want it to appear.

Bill is ready to create the Great Britain ($) worksheet, which will contain the values from the Great Britain sheet converted from pounds to dollars. Bill decides to copy the United States sheet using the mouse. He will then modify the copy to create the Great Britain ($) worksheet.

To create the Great Britain ($) worksheet:

❶ Click the **United States tab**.

❷ Press and hold **[Ctrl]** while dragging the United States tab until the black triangle appears between the United States and Great Britain tabs. When you drag the sheet tab, the pointer changes to 🖫 and a black triangle shows where the sheet will be placed. See Figure 8-15.

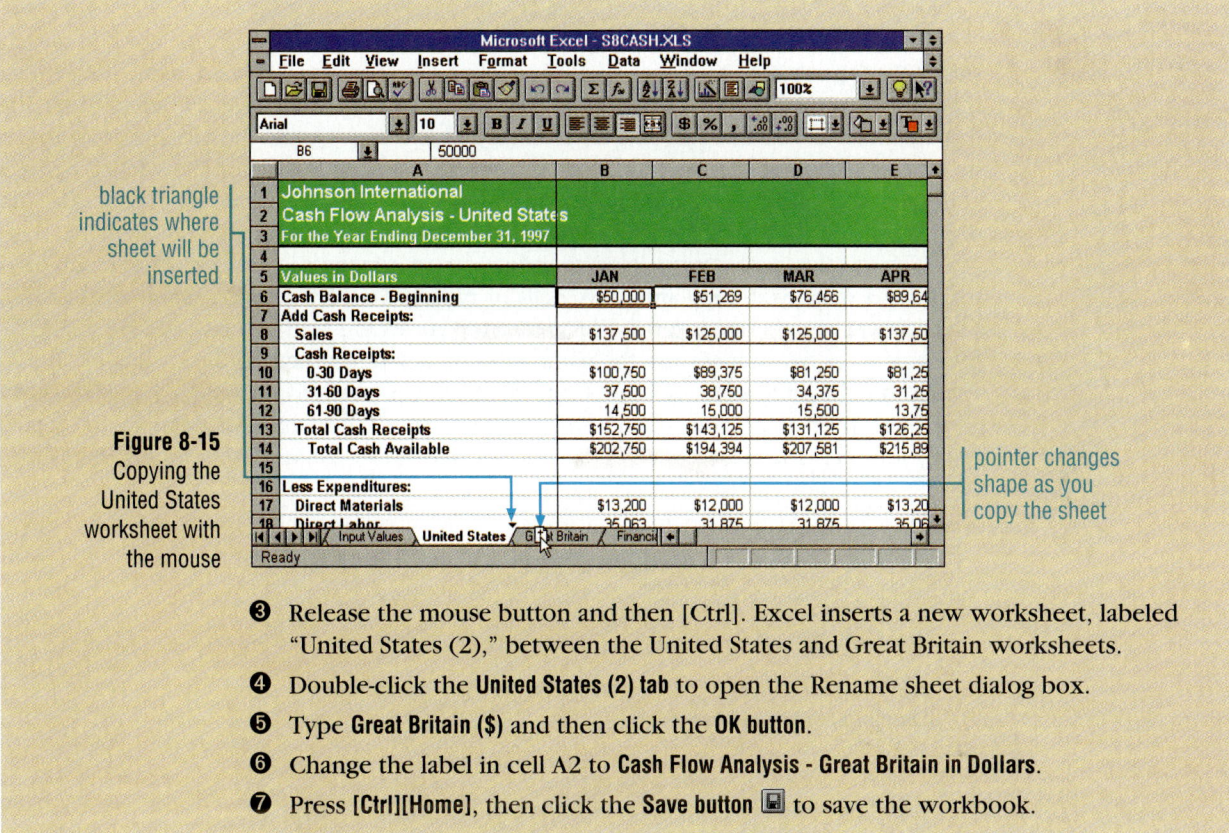

Figure 8-15
Copying the United States worksheet with the mouse

3. Release the mouse button and then [Ctrl]. Excel inserts a new worksheet, labeled "United States (2)," between the United States and Great Britain worksheets.

4. Double-click the **United States (2) tab** to open the Rename sheet dialog box.

5. Type **Great Britain ($)** and then click the **OK button**.

6. Change the label in cell A2 to **Cash Flow Analysis - Great Britain in Dollars**.

7. Press **[Ctrl][Home]**, then click the **Save button** to save the workbook.

Now that Bill has created the Great Britain ($) worksheet, he must convert the figures on the Great Britain worksheet from pounds to dollars. To do this, Bill must use a currency exchange rate. A **currency exchange rate** is the value that a country's currency is multiplied by in order to convert the value to U.S. dollars. The rate for converting pounds to dollars is currently 1.4751, the value in cell C36 of the Input Values worksheet. An exchange rate of 1.4751 means that each pound is equal to $1.4751. Therefore:

$$2{,}000 \text{ pounds} = 1.4751 * 2{,}000 = \$2{,}950.20$$

The formula Bill creates using the currency exchange rate will replace the values currently in the worksheet. To make his formula easier to understand, Bill decides to use a name to identify the cell containing the currency exchange rate.

Defining and Using Names

Excel allows you to define a **name** for a cell or a range of cells. (Other spreadsheet software often use the term "range name.") Names are easier to remember than cell or range addresses and make formulas easier to read. Also, when you enter a cell or range address in a formula, you can click the name box down arrow button in the formula bar and select a named range from a list of the names you have created.

You will find names very useful when you are printing. Often you will have several ranges in your spreadsheet that you need to print regularly. Excel can print selected ranges as well as entire worksheets. You simply indicate the name of the range you want to print instead of its address.

To define a name, select the range and either type the name in the name box (on the left side of the formula bar) or choose the Name Define command on the Insert menu. (Remember that a range can consist of a single cell.) Names can contain as many as 255 characters. The first character in a name must be a letter or an underscore (_), and the other characters can be letters, numbers, periods (.), or underscores (_). Spaces are not allowed, so periods and underscores are often used as separators in names (for example, Cost.of.Goods.Sold or Cost_of_Goods_Sold). You can use both uppercase and lowercase letters in names.

Excel creates names with absolute references to a range so that correct referencing is maintained when you copy and move cells or ranges. You can create a **book-level name**, which refers to only one range in the workbook. For example, if you give cell B7 in Sheet1 the name Sales, you cannot use the name Sales on any other sheet in the workbook. If you want to use the same name on more than one sheet, you need to create a **sheet-level name**. To define a sheet-level name, use the sheet name as part of the name. For example, if you give cell B7 in Sheet1 the name Sheet1!Sales, you can give cell B7 in Sheet2 the name Sheet2!Sales.

> **REFERENCE WINDOW**
>
> ### Defining a Name
>
> - Click or highlight the cell or range you want to name.
> - Click the name box on the formula bar, then type the name in the name box and press [Enter].
>
> or
>
> Click Insert, click Name, then click Define... to display the Define Name dialog box. Then type the name in the Names in Workbook text box and click the OK button.

Bill is ready to create a name for the range containing the exchange rate.

To create a name for the exchange rate range:
1. Click the **Input Values tab**.
2. Click cell **C36**.
3. Click **Insert**, click **Name**, then click **Define...** to open the Define Name dialog box. See Figure 8-16. Notice that Excel suggests using the name Great_Britain, which is the column label above the exchange rate.

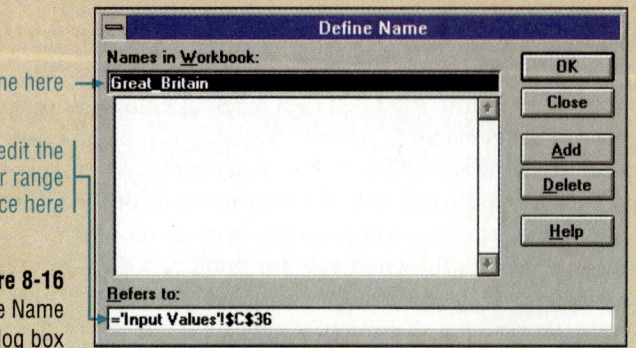

Figure 8-16
The Define Name dialog box

type name here →
you can edit the cell or range reference here

Insert/Name/Define (to automatically convert exchange rate)

Using the Go To Command

④ Type **ExchangeRate** in the Names in Workbook text box.
⑤ Click the **OK button** to close the dialog box.
⑥ Press **[Ctrl][Home]**, then click the **Save button** .

Bill tests the name using Excel's Go To command to make sure it is defined correctly.

Using the Go To Command

You can move quickly to any named cell or range in the workbook using [F5] or the Go To command on the Edit menu.

REFERENCE WINDOW

Using the Go To Command

- Press [F5] to open the Go To dialog box.

  or

  Click Edit, then click Go To... to open the Go To dialog box.
- Click the desired name in the Go to list.
- Click the OK button.

To use Go To to move to the range named ExchangeRate:
① Click **Edit**, then click **Go To...** to display the Go To dialog box.
② Click **ExchangeRate**. See Figure 8-17.

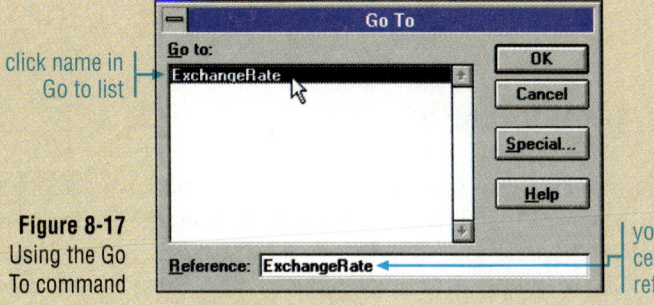

Figure 8-17
Using the Go To command

click name in Go to list

you can type a cell or range reference here

TROUBLE? Don't be concerned if you see other cell addresses in the Go to list. Excel adds cell references to the Go to list whenever the Go To command is used.

③ Click the **OK button**. Cell C36 is selected.

You can also use the names in the name box drop-down list to move to a named cell or range.

To use the name ExchangeRate in the name box to move to the named cell:

❶ Press **[Ctrl][Home]** to make cell A1 the active cell.

❷ Click the **Documentation tab**.

❸ Click the **name box down arrow button** to display the list of named cells and ranges. See Figure 8-18.

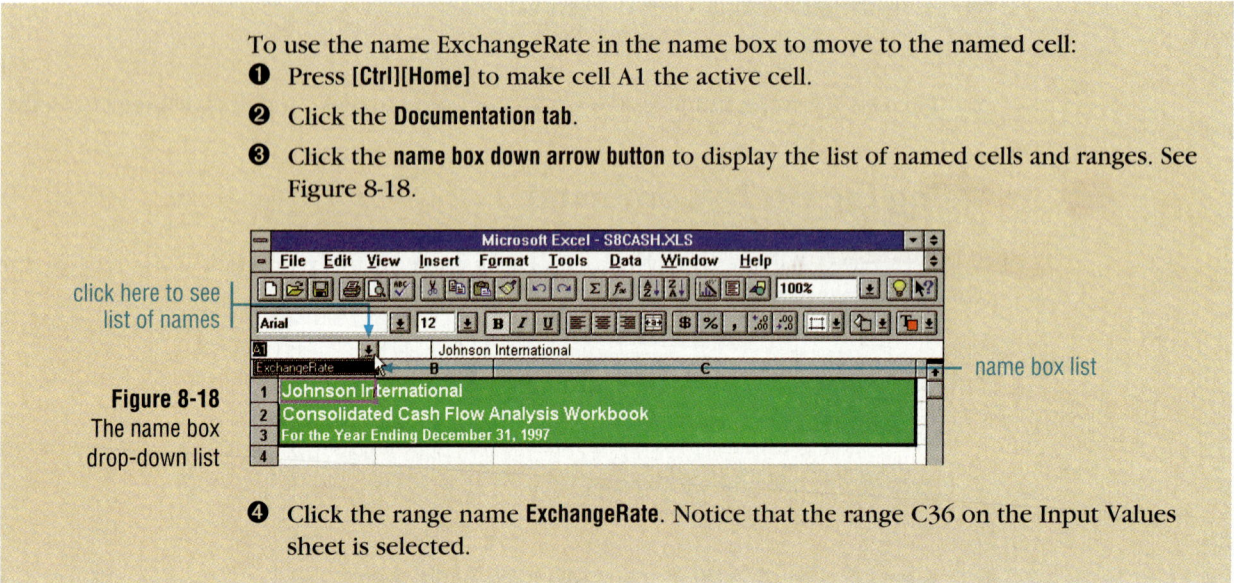

Figure 8-18
The name box drop-down list

❹ Click the range name **ExchangeRate**. Notice that the range C36 on the Input Values sheet is selected.

Now Bill will use the named range in his formulas to calculate the converted currency values.

If you want to take a break and resume the tutorial at a later time, you can exit Excel by double-clicking the Control menu box in the upper-left corner of the screen. When you resume the tutorial, launch Excel, maximize the Microsoft Excel and Book1 windows, and place your Student Disk in the disk drive. Open the file S8CASH.XLS, then continue with the tutorial.

Using the Exchange Rates

The values in the Great Britain ($) worksheet will be in U.S. dollars. To calculate the dollar values in the Great Britain ($) worksheet, Bill must multiply the values in the Great Britain worksheet by the exchange rate in cell C36 (now named ExchangeRate) in the Input Values worksheet. For example, to use the value in cell 'Great Britain'!B6 to calculate the value in cell 'Great Britain($)'!B6, Bill will use the formula:

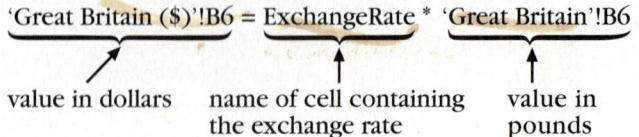

Keep in mind that Bill needs to multiply only the values in the Great Britain worksheet by the exchange rate. The formulas in the Great Britain ($) worksheet will then use the new dollar values to calculate the totals in U.S. dollars. Bill starts by entering the formula for cell B6.

Using the Exchange Rates EX 297

To calculate the value in cell B6 of the Great Britain ($) worksheet:
1. Click the **Great Britain ($) tab**. (Make sure to click the correct tab. Do *not* click the Great Britain tab.)
2. Click cell **B6**.
3. Type **=** to begin the formula.
4. Click the **name box down arrow button**, then click the name **ExchangeRate**. The Input Values sheet appears on the screen, with the "ExchangeRate" range, cell C36, selected. This allows you to verify that you chose the correct name in the name box. The formula you are creating remains in the formula bar.
5. In the formula bar, type ***'Great Britain'!B6** and press **[Enter]**. The Great Britain ($) worksheet reappears.
6. Click cell **B6** to make it the active cell. Cell B6 in the Great Britain ($) worksheet now shows the dollar value ($88,506) of cell B6 in the Great Britain worksheet. See Figure 8-19.

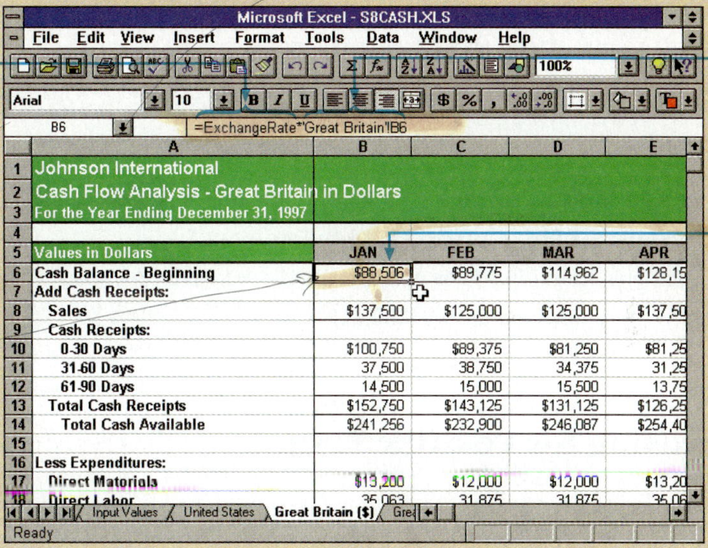

Figure 8-19
The converted pound amount in dollars

Now Bill enters the other formulas needed to complete the worksheet.

To calculate the other values in the Great Britain ($) worksheet:
1. Make sure that the Great Britain ($) worksheet is the active sheet.
2. Click cell **B8**.
3. Type **=** to begin the formula.
4. Click the **name box down arrow button**, then click the name **ExchangeRate**. Again, the Input Values sheet appears with the ExchangeRate range, cell C36, selected.
5. Type ***'Great Britain'!B8** and press **[Enter]**. The Great Britain ($) sheet reappears.
6. Click cell **B8** to make it the active cell. Cell B8 of the Great Britain ($) worksheet now shows the dollar value of $129,071.

❼ Click the **Copy button**.

❽ Select range **C8:M8**, then press **[Enter]**. Click any cell to remove the highlight. All the formulas in row 8 are now correct.

You could continue creating the formulas for the Great Britain ($) worksheet, but this would take quite a while. Instead, let's close the S8CASH.XLS workbook and open the C8CASH2.XLS workbook, in which all the formulas are already entered. Then we'll save the C8CASH2.XLS workbook as S8CASH2.XLS and continue with the tutorial.

To close the S8CASH.XLS workbook and open the C8CASH2.XLS workbook:

❶ Press **[Ctrl][Home]**.

❷ Click the **Documentation tab**, then click the **Save button**.

❸ Click **File**, then click **Close** to close the S8CASH.XLS workbook.

❹ Click the **Open button**.

❺ Double-click **C8CASH2.XLS** in the File Name box to display the workbook.

TROUBLE? If the file isn't in the file list, click the Drives down arrow button to display the drive in which your Student Disk is located.

❻ Make sure the Documentation sheet is the active worksheet

❼ Double-click cell **B5** then change the filename to **S8CASH2.XLS**.

❽ Press **[Ctrl][Home]** to make cell A1 the active cell.

❾ Click **File**, then click **Save As...** to display the Save As dialog box.

❿ Save the workbook as **S8CASH2.XLS**.

Checking for Possible Errors

You should always check your work carefully for errors. In a complex spreadsheet, such as this one, it is easy to make mistakes.

Now that Bill has converted pounds to dollars, he decides to review the conversions in the Great Britain ($) worksheet to make sure everything is correct.

To review the Great Britain ($) worksheet:

❶ Click the **Great Britain ($) tab**.

❷ Click cell **B6**.

❸ Check the calculations for Total Cash Receipts and Total Cash Available in January. Total Cash Receipts, $119,852 + $29,502 + $19,914, does equal $169,268. Total Cash Available, $88,506 + $169,268, does equal $257,774.

❹ Check the calculations for Total Cash Receipts and Total Cash Available in February, as shown in Figure 8-20. There is a problem here. Total Cash Receipts, $83,896 + $36,878 + $22,127, equals $142,901 not $142,900, as displayed in cell C13.

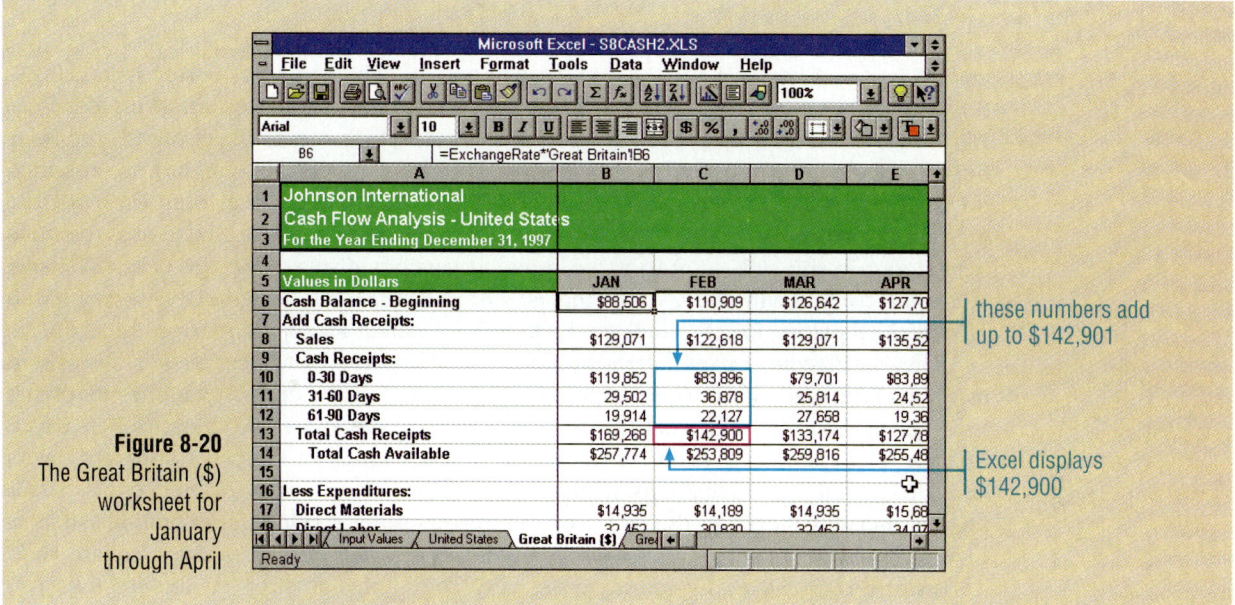

Figure 8-20
The Great Britain ($) worksheet for January through April

Bill finds the same type of error in the calculations of Total Cash Receipts for March, July, and September. It occurs again in some of the Total Expenses calculations (January, for example).

How is this happening? Bill has always relied on his Excel workbook to perform accurate calculations, but the Great Britain ($) worksheet seems to be filled with errors. Bill realizes that he has encountered apparent errors caused by rounding.

Apparent Errors Caused by Rounding

Apparent errors caused by rounding are discrepancies that occur when a cell's formatting causes the displayed number to be rounded to fewer digits than are actually stored in the cell. When this happens, your worksheet might tell you that 2 + 2 = 5, as shown in Figure 8-21.

Figure 8-21
Apparent errors caused by rounding

In Figure 8-21, notice that the actual number stored in the worksheet cells C7, C8, D7, and D8 is 2.4. When you add 2.4 and 2.4 you get 4.8, which appears correctly in cell C9. But what happens when cells are formatted so that no decimal places are displayed? Cells D7 though D9 are formatted to zero decimal places, which means Excel rounds the numbers to fit the reduced number of decimal places. (Numbers 0 through 4 are rounded down, and numbers 5 through 9 are rounded up.) Therefore, Excel rounds downs the number 2.4, stored in cells D7 and D8, to 2. When summing the cells, Excel uses the numbers stored in the cells (2.4), not the rounded versions displayed in the cells (2). Excel stores the correct sum of 2.4 + 2.4 (that is, 4.8) in cell D9, but because D9 is formatted to zero decimal places, Excel rounds up 4.8 to 5. The result is an apparent error, 2 + 2 = 5.

This is called an apparent error because it only *appears* that Excel made a mistake. In fact, Excel has the correct (unrounded) number stored in the cell. (Remember that what is displayed in a cell and what is stored in a cell are not the same thing; the displayed number does not always show all the decimal places stored in the cell.) Apparent errors occur frequently in calculations whose values are displayed with fewer decimal places than are actually stored in the cell. Apparent errors often result from operations such as division, multiplication by fractions or percentages, squaring, and taking a square root. Apparent errors caused by rounding are very common, but often go undetected. You should always check for apparent rounding errors in your worksheets.

Bill realizes that when he multiplied the values in the Great Britain worksheet by the currency exchange rate of 1.4751, he created a situation in which the worksheet displayed fewer decimal places than were actually stored. For example, the 0-30 days cash receipts amount in January in cell 'Great Britain ($)'!B10 is actually $119,851.8750, but when rounded to zero decimals it appears as $119,852.

Bill knows that he can eliminate the apparent errors in his workbook by using the ROUND function to make the values stored in the worksheet match the values displayed.

The ROUND Function and Nesting Functions

ROUND is a mathematical function that rounds a number, or the result of a calculation, to a specified number of decimal places. Excel then uses the rounded value in further calculations. The syntax of the ROUND function is:

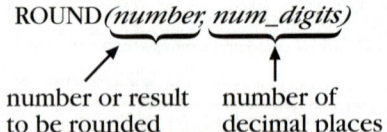

ROUND*(number, num_digits)*

number or result to be rounded   number of decimal places

Number can be a number, such as 7.8365112, or the result of formula such as (345*2)/15 or PMT(B5/12,B6,B7). If you are rounding the result of a formula that uses a function, then you are using one function as part of an argument of another function. This is known as **nesting functions**.

Num_digits is the number of decimals places that you want to round the number or result to. Generally, you round to the same number of decimal places that you used when you formatted the cell containing the formula.

Bill needs to round the values in the Great Britain ($) worksheet to zero decimal places. For example, cell 'Great Britain ($)'!B6 contains the formula =ExchangeRate*'Great Britain'!B6. This formula is the *number* for the ROUND function. Bill will edit the formula in cell 'Great Britain ($)'!B6 to include the ROUND function, and the final result is the formula:

ROUND(ExchangeRate*'Great Britain'!B6,0)

- the results of this formula need to be rounded
- the results will be rounded to 0 decimal places

[handwritten note: Nesting Formula]
[handwritten note: will be rounded to no decimal places]

REFERENCE WINDOW

Using ROUND to Round the Stored Results of a Formula to the Desired Number of Decimals

These directions assume you are using the ROUND function to round the result of a formula. Keep in mind that you can also use the ROUND function to round a simple value in a cell.

- Click the cell in which you want to enter the ROUND function.
- In the formula bar, click to the right of the equal sign (=).
- Type ROUND(to begin adding the ROUND function to the formula.
- Press [End] to move the insertion point to the end of the formula.
- Type a comma to separate the arguments.
- Type the number of decimal places to which you want the result rounded.
- Type) to complete the formula.
- Press [Enter] to enter the formula into the worksheet.

Bill edits the formula in cell 'Great Britain ($)'!B6 to include the ROUND function.

To add the ROUND function to the formula in cell 'Great Britain ($)'!B6:

1. Make sure that the Great Britain ($) worksheet is active.
2. Make sure rows 1 through 17 are visible.
3. Click cell **B6**.
4. In the formula bar, click to the right of the equal sign (=). *[handwritten note: Put your cursor after the Equal sign]*

❺ Type **ROUND(** to begin adding the ROUND function to the formula.

❻ Press **[End]** to move the insertion pointer to the end of the formula.

❼ Type **,0)** and then compare your work to the edited formula shown in Figure 8-22.

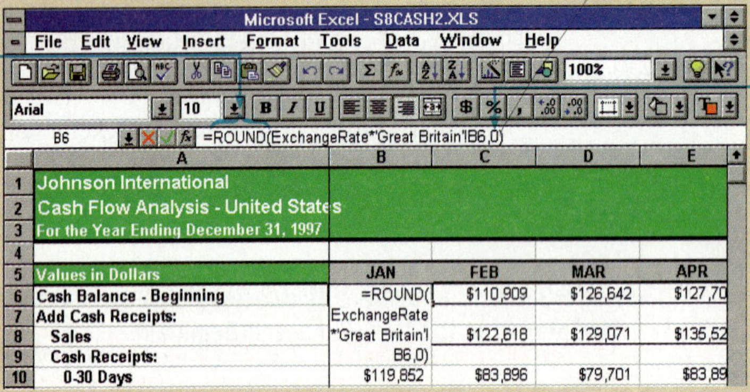

Figure 8-22
The edited formula with the ROUND function added

add ROUND(to beginning of formula

add ,0) to end of formula

❽ Press **[Enter]** to enter the formula into the worksheet. Cell B6 displays the value $88,506.

Bill edits the formula in cell B8 to include the ROUND function, and then copies the modified formula to cells C8 through M8.

To add the ROUND function to the formulas in cells 'Great Britain ($)'!B8:M8:

❶ Double-click cell **B8** in the Great Britain ($) worksheet.

❷ Follow the directions in the previous set of steps to add the ROUND function to the formula in cell B8. The result of the formula is $129,071.

❸ Click cell **B8**, then click the **Copy button** on the toolbar.

❹ Highlight the range **C8:M8**.

❺ Press **[Enter]**. The formula is copied to cells C8 through M8.

❻ Click any cell to remove the highlighting.

TROUBLE? If your formula did not copy to all the cells, repeat Steps 3 through 6.

Again, you could continue creating the formulas for the Great Britain ($) worksheet, but this would take quite a while. Let's close the S8CASH2.XLS workbook and open the C8CASH3.XLS workbook, which has all the formulas entered for you. Then we'll save the C8CASH3.XLS workbook as S8CASH3.XLS and continue with the tutorial.

To close the S8CASH2.XLS workbook and open the C8CASH3.XLS workbook:

❶ Press **[Ctrl][Home]**.

❷ Click the **Documentation tab**, then click the **Save button**.

❸ Click **File**, then click **Close** to close the S8CASH2.XLS workbook.

❹ Click the **Open button**.

Creating the Consolidation Worksheet   EX 303

❺ Double-click **C8CASH3.XLS** in the File Name box to display the workbook.

TROUBLE? If the file isn't in the file list, click the Drives down arrow button to display the drive in which your Student Disk is located.

❻ Make sure the Documentation sheet is the active worksheet.

❼ Double-click cell **B5**, then change the filename to **S8CASH3.XLS**.

❽ Press **[Ctrl][Home]** to make cell A1 the active cell.

❾ Click **File**, then click **Save As...** to display the Save As dialog box, then save the workbook as **S8CASH3.XLS**.

❿ Click the **Great Britain ($) tab**.

Bill sees that the Total Cash Receipts figure for February is now $142,901 instead of $142,900. The ROUND function solved the problem of the apparent errors due to rounding in his Great Britain ($) worksheets.

So far Bill has created his interest rates chart, completed the Great Britain worksheet, and converted the Great Britain cash flow analysis from pounds to dollars. Now he's ready to create the consolidated cash flow worksheet.

If you want to take a break and resume the tutorial at a later time, you can exit Excel by double-clicking the Control menu box in the upper-left corner of the screen. When you resume the tutorial, launch Excel, maximize the Microsoft Excel and Book1 windows, and place your Student Disk in the disk drive. Open the file S8CASH3.XLS, then continue with the tutorial.

■   ■   ■

Creating the Consolidation Worksheet

Bill is ready to consolidate, or combine, the information in the United States and Great Britain ($) cash flow analyses into a cash flow analysis for the entire company. The consolidated cash flow analysis will be on a worksheet named Consolidation. To create the Consolidation worksheet, Bill inserts a copy of the United States worksheet between the Input Values worksheet and the United States worksheet. He then edits the copy to create the Consolidation worksheet.

To insert the Consolidation worksheet:

❶ Click the **United States tab**.

❷ Click **Edit**, then click **Move or Copy Sheet...** to open the Move or Copy dialog box.

❸ In the Before Sheet list box, click **United States**.

❹ Click the **Create a Copy checkbox**.

❺ Click the **OK button**. Excel inserts a new worksheet, United States (2), between the Input Values and United States worksheets

❻ Double-click the **United States (2) tab** to display the Rename Sheet dialog box.

❼ Type **Consolidation** in the text box, then click the **OK button**.

⑧ Double-click cell **A2**.

⑨ Change the label to **Cash Flow Analysis - Consolidated** and then press **[Enter]**.

⑩ Press **[Ctrl][Home]**, then click the **Save button** to save the workbook.

Bill is ready to enter the consolidation formulas in the Consolidation worksheet. These formulas will add the values in the United States and Great Britain ($) worksheets.

Entering the Consolidation Formulas

Excel's multi-sheet format makes it easy to combine multiple worksheets by adding the values in the corresponding cells. In this case, Bill will add the values in corresponding cells in the United States and Great Britain ($) worksheets. For example, to calculate the consolidated Cash Balance - Beginning value in cell Consolidation!B6, he'll add the values in cell B6 of the United States and Great Britain ($) worksheets. The formula in cell Consolidation!B6 will be ='United States'!B6+'Great Britain ($)'!B6, as shown in Figure 8-23.

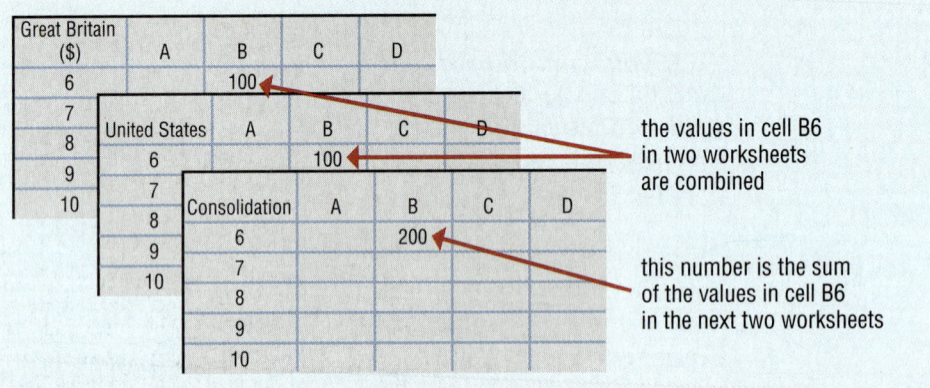

Figure 8-23
Calculating the consolidated Cash Balance - Beginning

Bill enters the formula for the consolidated Cash Balance - Beginning into cell Consolidated!B6.

To calculate the consolidated value in cell B6 of the Consolidation worksheet:

❶ Make sure that the Consolidation worksheet is the active sheet. If it isn't, click the **Consolidation tab**.

❷ Click cell **B6**, then type the formula **='United States'!B6+'Great Britain ($)'!B6** and press **[Enter]**. (Remember to type single quotation marks around the sheet names and make sure to place the exclamation points outside the single quotation marks.) The combined value ($138,506) of the dollar values in cell B6 of the United States and Great Britain ($) worksheets appears in cell Consolidated!B6. See Figure 8-24.

Entering the Consolidation Formulas   **EX 305**

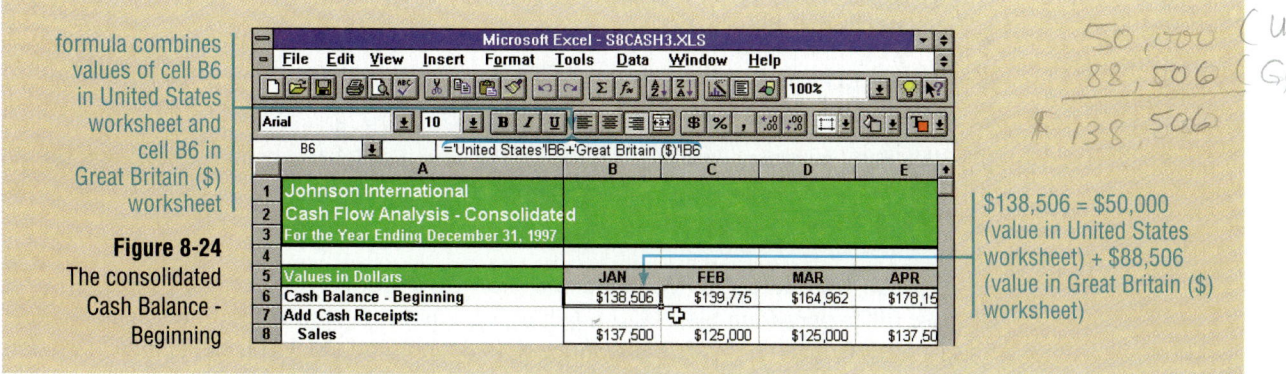

Figure 8-24
The consolidated Cash Balance - Beginning

formula combines values of cell B6 in United States worksheet and cell B6 in Great Britain ($) worksheet

$138,506 = $50,000 (value in United States worksheet) + $88,506 (value in Great Britain ($) worksheet)

Now Bill enters the consolidation formulas into the other cells on the Consolidated worksheet.

To calculate the other values in the Consolidated worksheet:

❶ Click cell **B8**.

❷ Type **'United States'!B8 +'Great Britain ($)'!B8** and press **[Enter]**. The combined value ($266,571) of the dollar values in cell B8 of the United States and Great Britain ($) worksheets appears in cell Consolidated:B8.

❸ Click cell **B8** to make it the active cell.

❹ Click the **Copy button**.

❺ Select the range **C8:M8**, then press **[Enter]**.

❻ Click any cell to remove the highlighting.

TROUBLE? If your formula did not copy to all the cells, repeat Steps 3 through 6.

Again, you could continue typing the formulas for the Consolidation worksheet, but this would take quite a bit of time. Let's close the S8CASH3.XLS workbook and open the C8CASH4.XLS workbook, which has all the consolidation formulas in place. Then we'll save the C8CASH4.XLS workbook as S8CASH4.XLS and continue with the tutorial.

To close the S8CASH3.XLS workbook and open the C8CASH4.XLS workbook:

❶ Press **[Ctrl][Home]**.

❷ Click the **Documentation tab**.

❸ Click the **Save button**, click **File**, then click **Close** to close the S8CASH3.XLS workbook.

❹ Click the **Open button**.

❺ Double-click **C8CASH4.XLS** in the File Name box to display the workbook.

TROUBLE? If the file isn't in the file list, click the Drives down arrow button to display the drive in which your Student Disk is located.

❻ Make sure the Documentation sheet is the active worksheet.

❼ Double-click cell **B5**, then change the filename to **S8CASH4.XLS** and press **[Enter]**.

❽ Press **[Ctrl][Home]** to make cell A1 the active cell.

❾ Click **File**, then click **Save As...** to display the Save As dialog box and save the workbook as **S8CASH4.XLS**.

Bill has completed his consolidated cash flow budget for Johnson International. Because Bill is preparing his 1997 budget in November, 1996, Bill might revise his budget figures until January 1, 1997. Bill decides to add a note on the worksheets indicating that the worksheets will be final on (that is, no further changes will be made after) January 1, 1997. Bill wants to add this note at the bottom of each cash analysis worksheet. He could do this one worksheet at a time, but Excel makes it easy to work on more than one worksheet simultaneously. Bill will select a group of worksheets and add his note to all the cash analysis worksheets at once.

Working with a Group of Worksheets

You can make a **group selection** of two or more worksheets. To select a group of worksheets that are next to each other, click the sheet tab for the first worksheet you want in the group, then press and hold the Shift key and click the sheet tab for the last worksheet you want in the group. To select a group of nonadjacent sheets, click the sheet tab for the first worksheet you want in the group, then press and hold the Control key and click the sheet tab for each of the other worksheets you want in the group. The word "[Group]" is added to the title bar when you are using a group selection, and all sheet tabs of the worksheets in the group are white. You must use the mouse to select a group; there is no equivalent menu command. The set of sheets in the group is known as a **sheet range**. To ungroup sheets, simply press and hold the Control key while you click each tab in the sheet range.

REFERENCE WINDOW

Grouping and Ungrouping Worksheets

To group two or more adjacent worksheets:

- Click the sheet tab for the first worksheet you want in the group.
- Press and hold [Shift] while you click the sheet tab for the last worksheet you want in the group.

To group two or more non-adjacent worksheets:

- Click the sheet tab for the first worksheet you want in the group.
- Press and hold [Ctrl] while you click the sheet tab for each of the other worksheets you want in the group.

To ungroup worksheets:

- Press and hold [Ctrl] while you click the sheet tab in the sheet range.

Bill adds a note to all the sheets in the sheet range so that other users of the workbook will know that the figures are final as of January 1, 1997.

To add the note to the sheet range Consolidation:Great Britain:

❶ Click the **Consolidation tab**. Use the scroll arrow buttons to scroll through the sheet tabs until you see the Great Britain tab.

❷ Press and hold **[Shift]** while clicking the **Great Britain tab**. All the sheet tabs in the sheet range Consolidated:Great Britain are highlighted and the label [Group] appears in the title bar. See Figure 8-25.

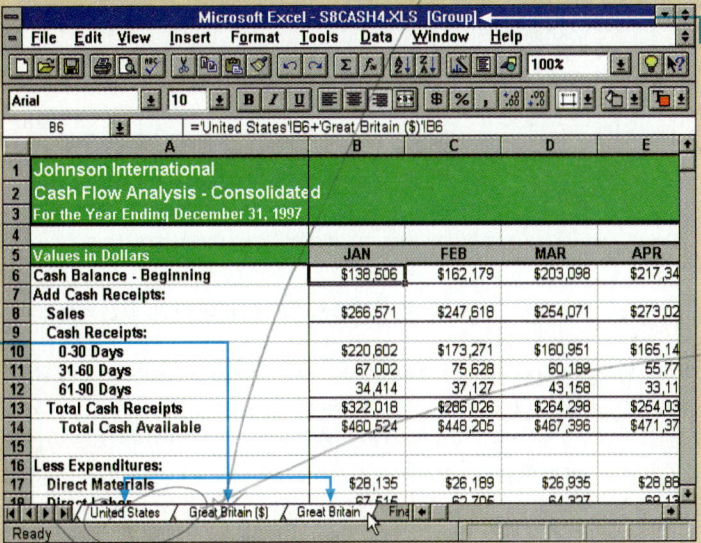

Figure 8-25
The group selection Consolidated: Great Britain

❸ Use the scroll arrow buttons to scroll through the sheet tabs until you see the Consolidation tab. Notice that the name appears in bold to show that this is the active sheet in the sheet range.

Now that you have grouped the sheets you can type a note in the first sheet; the note will appear in all the other sheets in the group.

❹ Scroll the worksheet until you see row 42, then click cell **A42** to make it the active cell.

❺ Press **[Spacebar]** three times, then type **4. The numbers in this worksheet are final as of January 1, 1997.** (include two spaces before the word The and include the periods after 4 and 1997). Press **[Enter]**.

❻ Click the **Great Britain tab** to make Great Britain the active sheet. Scroll down the worksheet until you see row 42. The note has also been entered into cell A42 of the Great Britain worksheet. See Figure 8-26.

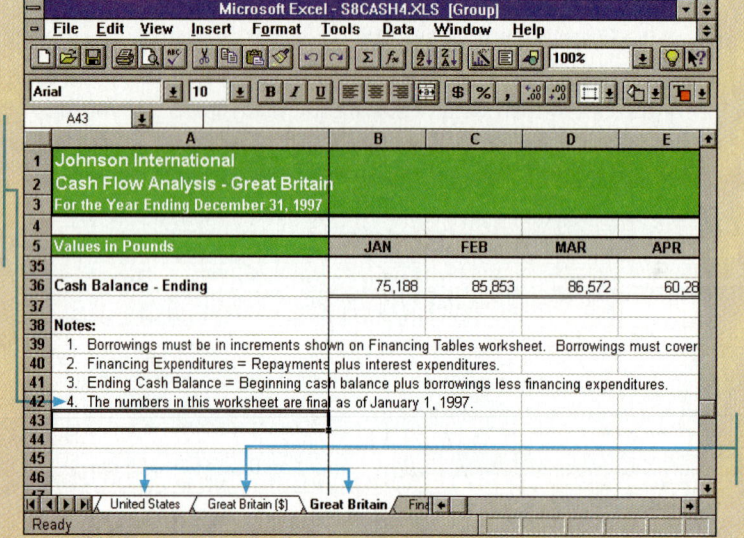

Figure 8-26
The note in the Great Britain worksheet

this note was typed into the Consolidation worksheet while Consolidation was part of a group

note is also entered in other worksheets in the group

❼ Press **[Ctrl][Home]**. Check some of the other worksheets in the group to see that the note was also added to those worksheets. In each sheet, press **[Ctrl][Home]** to keep B6 the active cell before moving to another worksheet.

❽ Click the **Consolidation tab**. Press and hold **[Ctrl]** while clicking the other sheet tabs in the group (United States through Great Britain) to remove them from the group. After you click the Great Britain tab, the word "[Group]" is removed from the title bar and you have ended the group selection. Press **[Ctrl][Home]**.

❾ Click the **Documentation tab**, then click the **Save button** 🖫 to save the workbook.

❿ Exit Excel if you are not proceeding directly to the Tutorial Assignments.

Bill has finished consolidating the cash flow budgets for Johnson International. The workbook he has created contains important information that management will use when making decisions in the coming year. In the next tutorial Bill will analyze the information contained in his cash flow workbook using what-if analysis and Scenario Manager. For now, though, he closes the workbook and exits Excel.

Questions

1. What four activities are required to create an effective worksheet?
2. Describe how to organize a workbook effectively.
3. How do you reference cells and ranges in other worksheets?
4. Describe how to use the VLOOKUP functions.
E 5. How does the HLOOKUP function work?
6. How do you insert a worksheet into a workbook?
7. How do you insert a chart sheet into a workbook?
8. How do you delete a sheet from a workbook?
9. How do you move a sheet in a workbook?
10. How do you copy a sheet?
11. Describe how the Freeze Panes command works.
12. What is a name?
13. Why do you use names?
14. How do you define a name?
15. Why should you check your worksheet carefully for errors?
16. What is an apparent error caused by rounding?
17. How do you use the ROUND function to correct apparent errors caused by rounding?
18. What does consolidating a group of worksheets mean?
19. How do you do a consolidation in Excel?
20. What is a group selection?
21. How do you select a group of worksheets?
E 22. The Johnson International Cash Flow Analysis dealt with expenditures. What is the difference between an expenditure and an expense? Which is used on the company's Income Statements?
E 23. Use the resources of your library to find information about the budgeting process for a manufacturing company. What budgets and pro forma financial statements are prepared in the budgeting process? What is the purpose of each?
24. What does the term consolidation mean when applied to a budget? How does Excel's workbook structure make it easy to create a consolidation?

Tutorial Assignments

Johnson International has split its United States operation into two regions: United States - West and United States - East. Bill needs to modify his workbook to reflect these changes. He'll also add new exchange rate data to the workbook.

1. Based on the workbook plan in Figure 8-10, draw a revised workbook plan that indicates that the United States - West worksheet and the United States - East worksheet will be inserted between the Consolidation and Great Britain ($) worksheets.
2. Open the workbook T8CASH5.XLS, then save it as S8CASH5.XLS on your Student Disk.

To modify the Documentation worksheet:

3. Change the filename in cell B5 to S8CASH5.XLS.
4. Column B currently has a column width of 15.00. Increase the column width to 18.00.
5. Column C currently has a column width of 55.00. Increase the column width to 57.00.
6. Insert a new row 18.
7. Change the sheet name in cell B17 to "United States - West" and change the sheet contents in cell C17 to "Cash flow analysis for the western United States."

8. In cell B18 enter the sheet name "United States - East" and in cell C18 enter the sheet contents "Cash flow analysis for the eastern United States."
9. Return to cell A1, then save the workbook.

To create the United States - West and the United States - East worksheets:

10. Change the sheet name United States to "United States - West."
11. In cell A2, change the worksheet title to "Cash Flow Analysis - Western United States."
12. Press [Ctrl][Home], then save the workbook.
13. Insert a new worksheet by inserting a copy of the United States - West worksheet between the United States - West and Great Britain ($) worksheets.
14. Name the new sheet "United States - East."
15. In cell A2, change the worksheet title to "Cash Flow Analysis - Eastern United States."
16. Enter the following sales figures in row 8 of the United States - East worksheet:

January	$135,000
February	$120,000
March	$125,000
April	$130,000
May	$150,000
June	$160,000
July	$180,000
August	$160,000
September	$155,000
October	$165,000
November	$175,000
December	$200,000

17. Scroll through the worksheet to examine the effects of these sales figures. In particular, look at the Financing section in rows 28 through 34. How much money does the eastern region of United States Johnson International borrow during the year? What is the loan balance at end of the year? How much does the eastern region unit pay in financing expenditures during the year? Write a memo to your instructor reporting these figures.
18. Press [Ctrl][Home], then save the workbook.

To modify the Consolidation worksheet:

19. Click the Consolidation tab, then change the formula in cell B6 to include the Cash Balance - Beginning value in the United States - East worksheet in the consolidation formula. (Note that Excel automatically changed the sheet name "United States" to "United States - West." The new formula is:
    ='United States - West'!B6+'United States - East'!B6+'Great Britain ($)'!B6
20. If necessary, convert the other formulas in the Consolidation worksheet to include the values from the United States - East worksheet. *Hint*: You need to convert the formulas in these ranges: B8:M8, B10:M10, B11:M11, B12:M12, B17:M17, B18:M18, B19:M19, B20:M20, B21:M21, B22:M22, B23:M23, B29:M29, B30:M30, B31:M31, and B33:M33.
21. Press [Ctrl][Home].
22. Click the Documentation tab, then save the workbook.
23. Print the Documentation sheet, the Consolidation sheet (in landscape orientation), the United States - East sheet (in landscape orientation), and the Financial Tables sheet. Do not print row and column borders, or gridlines. Center your printouts horizontally and include a right-aligned header with your name, the filename, the sheet name, and the date. Do not use a footer. Each printout should fit on its own page.
24. Click the Documentation tab, then save and close the workbook.
25. Turn in your workbook plan, memos, and printouts to your instructor.

Case Problems

1. Linking Budgeting Processes at Greenbridge Corporation

Sheila Thompson, the controller at Greenbridge Corporation, is completing her annual budgeting process. As part of the process, Sheila has prepared two Excel workbooks: a sales forecast workbook and a cash flow budget workbook. The cash flow budget uses the sales values calculated in the sales forecast workbook. Sheila wants you to help her link the two workbooks, so that updates to the forecast are automatically moved to the cash flow budget.

To link the workbooks:

1. Open the Cash Flow Budget workbook P8QCASH.XLS, then save it as S8QCASH.XLS on your Student Disk.
2. On the Documentation worksheet in the S8QCASH.XLS workbook, change the filename in cell B5 to S8QCASH.XLS, and change the name in cell B6 to your name.
3. Open the Sales Forecast workbook P8QFORE.XLS, then save it as S8QFORE.XLS on your Student Disk.
4. On the Documentation worksheet in the S8QFORE.XLS workbook, change the filename in cell B5 to S8QFORE.XLS and the name in cell B6 to your name.
5. Link the S8QFORE.XLS workbook to S8QCASH.XLS workbook by creating formulas in the Cash Flow worksheet in the S8QCASH.XLS workbook that refer to the Forecast worksheet in the S8QFORE.XLS workbook:
   a. Click Window, then click S8QCASH.XLS to switch to the S8QCASH.XLS workbook.
   b. Click cell 'Cash Flow'!B8 in the S8QCASH.XLS workbook.
   c. Enter a formula that tells Excel to read the contents of Forecast!B8 in the S8QFORE.XLS workbook and display them in cell 'Cash Flow'!B8 in the S8QCASH.XLS workbook. To do this, include the workbook name in brackets at the start of the cell reference: =[S8QFORE.XLS]Forecast!$B$8.
   d. Create the formulas to link cells 'Cash Flow'!C8:E8 in the S8QCASH.XLS workbook to cells Forecast!C8:E8 in the S8QFORE.XLS workbook.
   e. Save both workbooks.
   f. In the S8QFORE.XLS workbook, change the Expected Sales in Units to 17,000 for QTR 1, 18,000 for QTR 2, 19,000 for QTR 3 and 20,000 for QTR 4.
   g. Check the values in the Cash Flow worksheet in the S8QCASH.XLS workbook to see the updated values.
6. Print the Forecast sheet (in landscape) from the S8QFORE.XLS workbook. Print the Cash Flow worksheet (in landscape) from the S8QCASH.XLS workbook. Do not print row and column borders, or gridlines. Center your printouts horizontally and include a right-aligned header with your name, the filename, the sheet name, and the date. Do not use a footer. Each worksheet should fit on its own page.
7. Save and close the S8QFORE.XLS workbook. Make sure you close this workbook first!
8. Save and close the S8QCASH.XLS workbook.
9. Turn in your workbook plan, memos, and printouts to your instructor.

2. Looking Up Area Code Locations at Telephone Access, Inc.

Dan Ryder owns and operates Telephone Access, Inc., a telemarketing firm. Dan contracts telemarketing services with various businesses and then conducts telephone marketing campaigns. Dan's telemarketing staff needs an easy way to determine the geographical location of an area code. Dan responded to this need by creating an Excel workbook. However, Dan can't figure out how to use a LOOKUP function to show the location of an area code, and has asked you to help him.

Complete the following steps:

1. Open the Area Code workbook P8ACODE.XLS, then save it as S8ACODE.XLS on your Student Disk.
2. On the Documentation worksheet in the S8ACODE.XLS workbook, change the filename in cell B5 to S8ACODE.XLS and the name in cell B6 to your name, then save the workbook.
3. On the Area Codes worksheet in the S8ACODE.XLS workbook, name the range E6:F147 "CodesTable." (Do not include quotation marks in the name.)
4. Using the name you defined in Step 3, create a formula in cell B8 that looks up an area code entered in cell B6 on the table in range E6:F147 and returns the location shown in column F.
5. Area code 206 is currently in cell B6. What location uses this area code?
6. Enter area code 303 into cell B6. What location uses this area code?
7. Use Excel's Help system to learn about the HLOOKUP function. Did the formula you created in Step 4 use an HLOOKUP function or a VLOOKUP function? Why did you select the one you used?
8. Dan has not completely entered all locations for the area codes. Using a phone book, add the locations for area codes 304 thorough 308 to the table. Enter area code 307 into cell B6 to check that the new locations show up correctly.
9. Save the workbook.
10. Turn in a copy of your workbook on disk to your instructor.

3. A Consolidated Production Budget for Johnson International

Before Bill McDougal of Johnson International created the cash flow budget and analysis that you worked with in this tutorial, Sarah Miles had to forecast the monthly sales figures for each month and create the production budget for each unit of Johnson International. The production budget for each country consists of (1) a direct materials section, (2) a direct labor section, and (3) a production overhead section. Sarah created an Excel workbook that contains her production budgets. She included a Documentation worksheet, an Input Values worksheet, and Production Budgets worksheets for the United States and Great Britain.

Sarah has hired you to help her prepare the consolidated production budgets for Johnson International:

1. Based on the workbook plan in Figure 8-2, draw a revised workbook plan that shows a Consolidation worksheet and a Great Britain ($) worksheet.
2. Open the workbook P8PROD.XLS, then save it as S8PROD.XLS on your Student Disk.
3. On the Documentation worksheet, change the filename in cell B5 to S8PROD.XLS.

4. Change the name in cell B6 to your name.
5. Change the documentation to include a Consolidation worksheet and a Great Britain ($) worksheet.
6. Make a copy of the United States worksheet. Place it between the Input Values worksheet and the United States worksheet. Rename the sheet "Consolidation."
7. Make a second copy of the United States worksheet. Place it between the United States worksheet and the Great Britain worksheet. Rename the sheet "Great Britain ($)."
8. Save the workbook.
9. On the Great Britain ($) worksheet, change the title in cell A2 to "Production Budgets - Great Britain in Dollars."
10. Convert the *currency values* in the worksheet to dollars by multiplying the pound value in the Great Britain worksheet by the currency exchange rate on the Input Values worksheet. Use the ROUND function in your conversion formulas to guard against apparent errors due to rounding.
11. On the Consolidation worksheet, change the title in cell A2 to "Consolidated Production Budgets."
12. Consolidate the budgets for the United States and Great Britain by following these steps:
    a. *Sum the dollar currency values* in the two worksheets for the following items:
       Expected Sales in Units   (row 6)
       Fixed Overhead Cost   (row 30)
       Depreciation   (row 32)

    b. Average the values in the two worksheets for the following items (Use the ROUND function in your conversion formulas to guard against apparent errors due to rounding):
       Selling Price per Unit   (row 7)
       Direct Materials:
          Raw Materials per Unit (pounds)   (row 14)
          Raw Materials Cost per Pound   (row 16)
       Direct Labor:
          Direct Labor per Unit (hours)   (row 21)
          Direct Labor Cost per Hour   (row 23)
       Production Overhead:
          Variable Overhead Rate per Hour   (row 28)
13. Click the Documentation tab, then save the workbook.
14. Print the Documentation sheet, the Consolidation sheet (in landscape), and the Great Britain ($) sheet (in landscape). Do not print row and column borders or gridlines. Center your printouts horizontally, and include a right-aligned header with your name, the filename, the sheet name, and the date. Do not use a footer. Each printout should fit on its own page.
15. Save and close the S8PROD.XLS workbook.
16. Turn in your workbook plan, memos, and printouts to your instructor.

TUTORIAL 9

Data Tables and Scenario Management

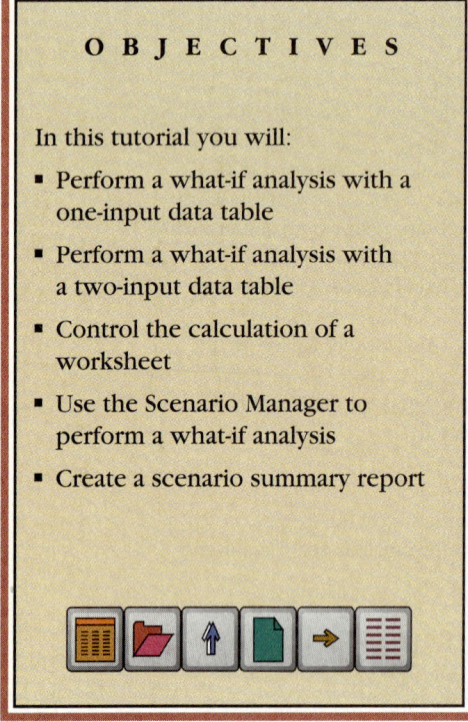

OBJECTIVES

In this tutorial you will:
- Perform a what-if analysis with a one-input data table
- Perform a what-if analysis with a two-input data table
- Control the calculation of a worksheet
- Use the Scenario Manager to perform a what-if analysis
- Create a scenario summary report

Analyzing a Consolidated Cash Flow Statement with a What-If Analysis

 Johnson International (II) Bill McDougal, an assistant to the comptroller of Johnson International, is helping prepare the company's annual budget for the upcoming year, 1997. In Tutorial 8, you helped him create a consolidated cash flow analysis for the company. Now Bill wants to use what-if analysis to see the effects of interest rate fluctuations on the company's cash flow during the year. Bill will use data tables and the Excel Scenario Manager to analyze his budget.

Bill is creating his what-if analysis in a workbook named C9CASH6.XLS. Let's take a look at the work he has completed so far.

To launch Excel, organize the workspace, and open the C9CASH6.XLS workbook:
1. Launch Windows and Excel.
2. Make sure your Student Disk is in the disk drive.
3. Make sure the Microsoft Excel and Book1 windows are maximized.
4. Click the **Open button**.
5. Double-click **C9CASH6.XLS** in the File Name box to open the workbook. See Figure 9-1.

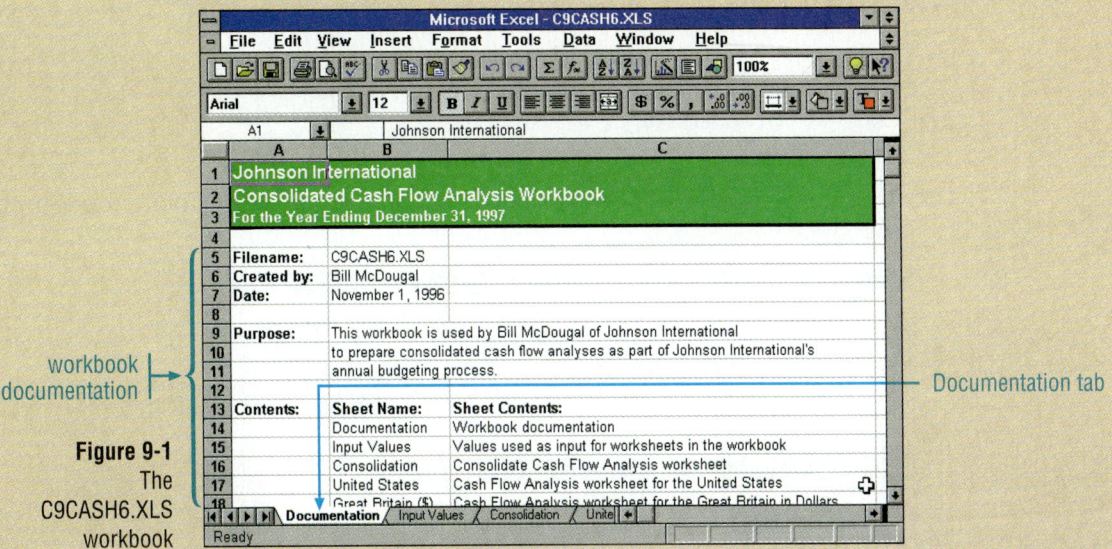

Figure 9-1 The C9CASH6.XLS workbook

TROUBLE? If the file isn't in the file list, click the Drives down arrow button to display the drive where your Student Disk is located.

Let's save the workbook under the name S9CASH6.XLS, so that your changes will not alter the original file.

To save the workbook as S9CASH6.XLS:
1. Make sure the Documentation sheet is active.
2. Double-click cell **B5**, change the filename to **S9CASH6.XLS**, then press **[Enter]**.
3. Press **[Ctrl][Home]** to make cell A1 the active cell.
4. Click **File**, then click **Save As...** to display the Save As dialog box.
5. Save the workbook as **S9CASH6.XLS**.

Bill wants to see the effects of changing interest rates on the cash flow analysis. To do this, he will do a what-if analysis similar to the one you learned about in Tutorial 6. This time, however, he will use some new tools, including one-input and two-input data tables and the Scenario Manager.

Bill wants to explore the effects of changing interest rates upon Johnson International's cash flow budget. He is particularly interested in how changes in the interest rates will affect the company's ending loan balance, total interest payments, and annual financing charges. To start, Bill decides to use data tables to see the effects of changing interest rates on annual financing charges.

Data Tables

The **prime rate** is the rate at which commercial banks lend money to their "best" corporate customers. Johnson International is not large enough to obtain loans at the prime rate, but the banks have agreed to loan money to Johnson International at interest rates of 1.0% above the prime rate. As the prime rates vary in the United States and Great Britain, Johnson International's interest rates will vary. The prime rates for the United States and Great Britain and the interest rates for Johnson International are on the Input Values worksheet.

To view the interest rates on the Input Values worksheet:

❶ Click the **Input Values tab**.

❷ Scroll until you see rows 22 through 38.

❸ The interest rates are in the Interest Rate on Borrowings section of the worksheet. See Figure 9-2.

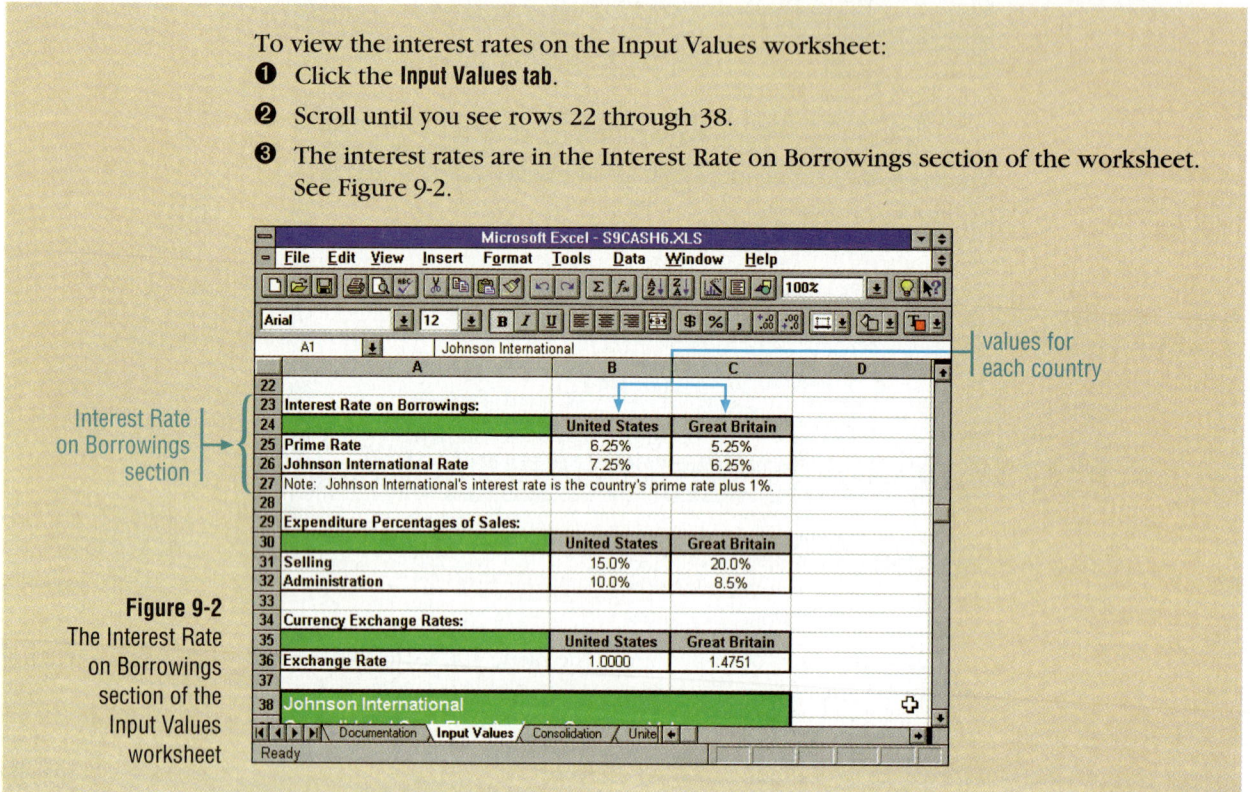

Figure 9-2
The Interest Rate on Borrowings section of the Input Values worksheet

Bill wants to see the effects of changing interest rates on Johnson International's cash flow. He could substitute different prime rates on the Input Values worksheet (in cells B25 and C25) and see the effect on the worksheet values, as you learned in Tutorial 6. Instead, Bill decides to use a data table, which will allow him to display his results in an easy-to-read format.

There are two types of data tables—one-input and two-input data tables. As the names imply, a **one-input data table** allows you to vary the value stored in one input cell. A **two-input data table** allows you to change the value stored in two input cells.

One-Input Data Tables

The format of a one-input data table is shown in Figure 9-3.

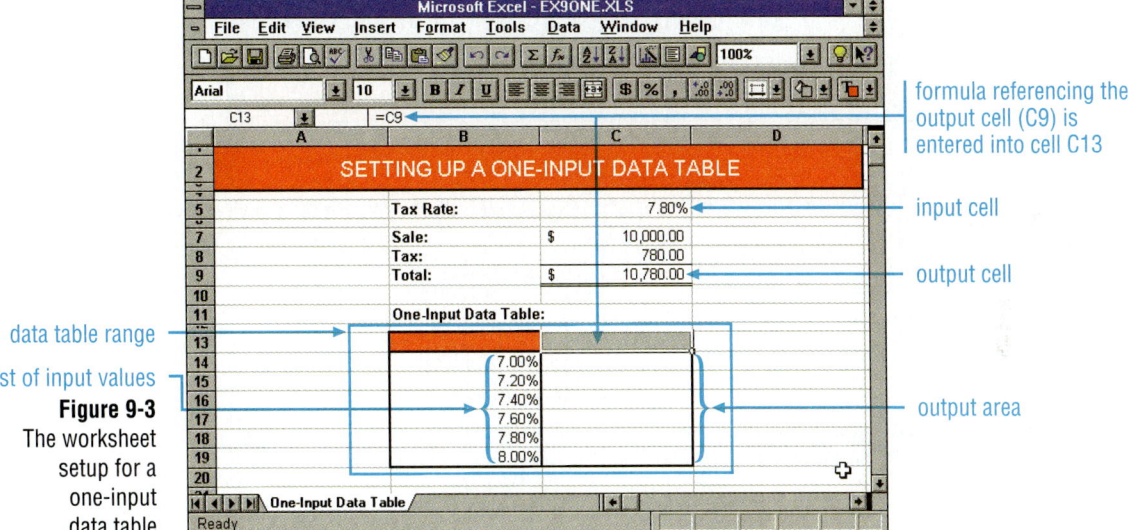

Figure 9-3 The worksheet setup for a one-input data table

The input table in the figure is designed to calculate a sales total for a variety of tax rates. The data table range includes the list of possible tax rates (input values), a formula referencing the output cell, and the output area (the column of cells to the right of the list of possible input cell values). In this case, the output cell contains a formula calculating the total sale (=C7+C8). The formula in the output cell depends, in turn, on a formula in cell C8. The formula in cell C8 (=C7*C5) calculates the tax using the tax rate in the input cell. The output area remains blank until you use the Table command on the Data menu.

After you select the Table command, Excel begins substituting the possible tax rates (the input values) into cell C5 (the input cell). Then, it uses the formulas in cells C8 and C9 to calculate the sales total for each tax rate. Instead of actually displaying the sales total in cell C9, Excel displays the sales total for each tax rate in the output area of the data table.

Note that cell C13 contains a formula referencing the output cell (cell C9). This formula tells Excel to display the results of the calculations in the output area. You see the results of the formula in C9, but not in C13 because cell C13 is formatted as hidden. When you format a cell as hidden, the contents are stored but not displayed. It's a good idea to use the hidden format for the output formula; although Excel needs the formula to calculate the table, you don't need to see the value in the table. The fewer numbers you have displayed in the table, the easier it is to read.

Figure 9-4 shows the calculated table, with output values displayed in the output area.

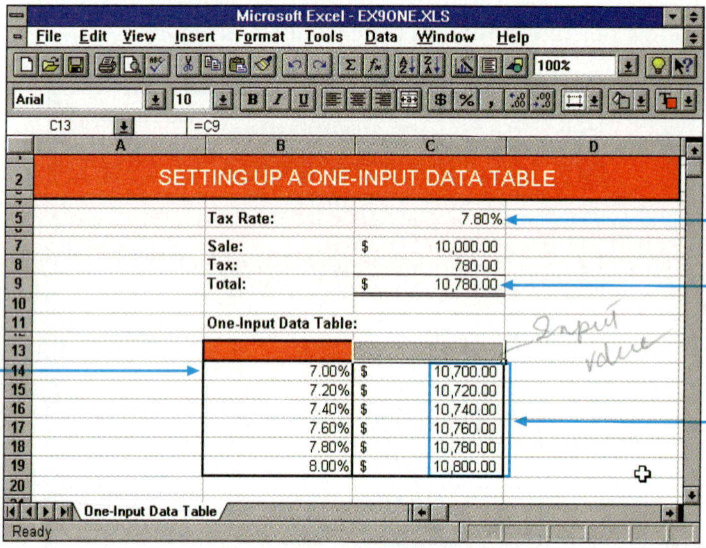

Figure 9-4
The one-input data table

Annotations on figure:
- input cell (pointing to 7.80% Tax Rate)
- output cell (pointing to $10,780.00 Total)
- output values (pointing to the column of calculated values)
- when the input value of 7.00% is entered into the input cell, the output value of $10,700.00 is calculated
- Input values (handwritten, pointing to the input values column)

Spreadsheet contents:
- Cell reference: C13 = C9
- Title (row 2): SETTING UP A ONE-INPUT DATA TABLE
- Tax Rate: 7.80%
- Sale: $10,000.00
- Tax: 780.00
- Total: $10,780.00
- One-Input Data Table:

Input	Output
7.00%	$10,700.00
7.20%	$10,720.00
7.40%	$10,740.00
7.60%	$10,760.00
7.80%	$10,780.00
8.00%	$10,800.00

Bill began creating his one-input data table at the bottom of the Input Values worksheet. His data table has the same structure as the table in Figures 9-3 and 9-4, but his input table will require an output formula that refers to a cell on another sheet.

To view the one-input data table:

❶ Make sure Input Values is still the active sheet.

❷ Scroll until you see rows 48 through 64.

Bill will list his input values (the possible interest rates) in column A, and Excel will place the calculated results (the annual financial expenditures) in column B. He decides to try interest rates of 5.0% to 9.5%, entered in increments of .5%. He has already labeled the input values as interest rates.

Bill is interested in the effect of changing interest rates on the total annual financing expenditures, which is displayed in Consolidation!N34. That means he will use a formula referring to Consolidation!N34 as his output formula. The input cell is the cell containing the United States interest rate, 'Input Values'!B26. When Bill uses the Table command, Excel will begin substituting the input values (the possible interest rates) into the input cell. Then Excel will use the interest rates to recalculate the Consolidation worksheet. Finally, it will display the resulting financial expenditures (from Consolidation!N34) in the output area.

To create the list of interest rates (the input values):

❶ Click cell **A55**, then type **.05** and press **[Enter]**.

❷ Click cell **A56**, type **.055** and press **[Enter]**.

❸ Highlight the range A55:A56, then drag the fill handle to extend the range to A64. When you release the mouse button, Excel fills the range with the list of interest rates; each rate is .5% greater than the preceding one.

❹ With the range A55:A64 still highlighted, click the **Percent Style button** on the formatting toolbar.

❺ Click the **Increase Decimal button** on the formatting toolbar twice to display the percentages with two decimal places.

Bill is interested in how changing interest rates affect the total annual financing expenditures, displayed in Consolidation!N34. He references this cell in the output formula.

To create the output cell reference formula:

❶ Click cell **B54**.

❷ Type **=Consolidation!$N$34** and then press **[Enter]**.

Now that you have entered the output formula, you will hide the contents of the cell.

❸ Right-click cell **B54** to display the Shortcut menu, then click **Format Cells...** to display the Format Cells dialog box.

❹ If necessary, click the **Number tab** to display the Number options.

❺ Click **Custom** in the Category box.

❻ Delete the current contents of the Code text box and type ;;; (three semi-colons). This code tells Excel to format the cell as hidden.

❼ Click the **OK button**. The setup for the Table command is complete. See Figure 9-5.

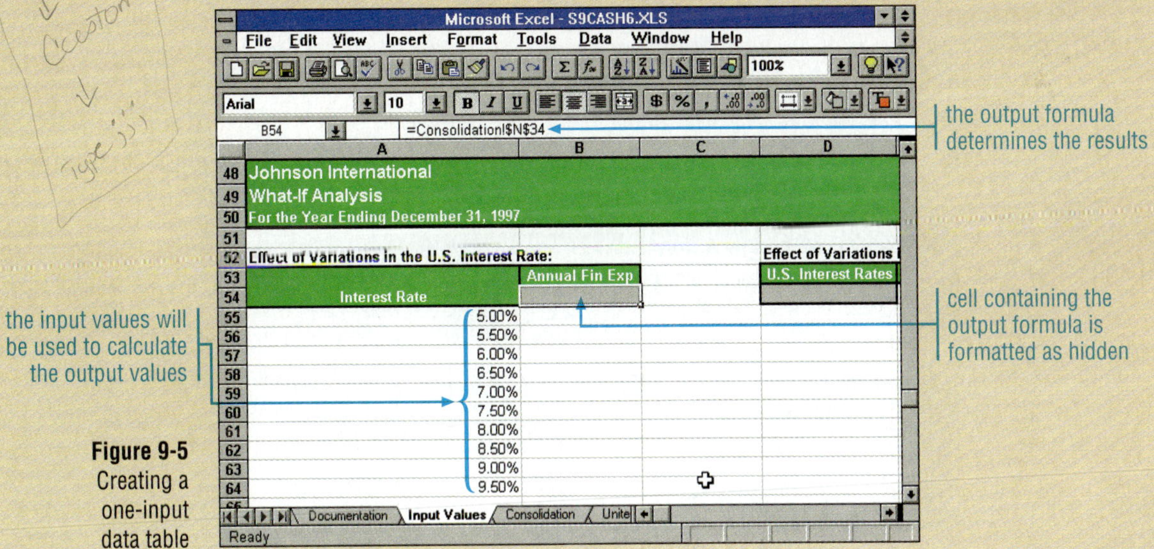

Figure 9-5
Creating a one-input data table

TROUBLE? If your worksheet doesn't match Figure 9-5, make the necessary changes by repeating the appropriate steps.

Now Bill uses the Table command on the Data menu to calculate the output values for the table.

To calculate the output values using the Table command:

❶ Highlight the range A54:B64. Make sure this range includes cell A54, which contains the Interest Rate label, and blank cells B55 through B64. Check your highlighted range carefully.

❷ Click **Data**, then click **Table...**. The Table dialog box appears. See Figure 9-6.

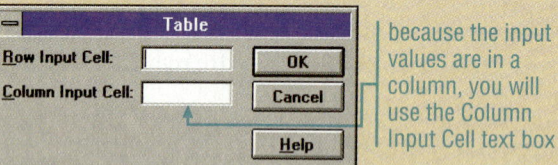

Figure 9-6
The Table dialog box

because the input values are in a column, you will use the Column Input Cell text box

❸ Click the **Column Input Cell text box** because the input values are in a column (specifically, column A in the range A55:A64).

❹ The input cell is cell 'Input Values'!$B$26, which contains the United States interest rate. Type **'Input Values'!$B$26** in the Column Input Cell text box.

❺ Click the **OK button**. Excel calculates the output values for the what-if table and enters them in the worksheet. (This calculation might take a while, especially on slower 386SX or 386DX computers.)

Bill wants to be consistent when he displays currency amounts on his worksheet.

To format the range B55:B64 as currency with two decimal places:

❶ Highlight cells B55 through B64.

❷ Click the **Currency Style button** 🔘.

❸ Click cell **C64** or any other cell to remove the highlighting. The completed one-input data table appears with the correct currency format. See Figure 9-7.

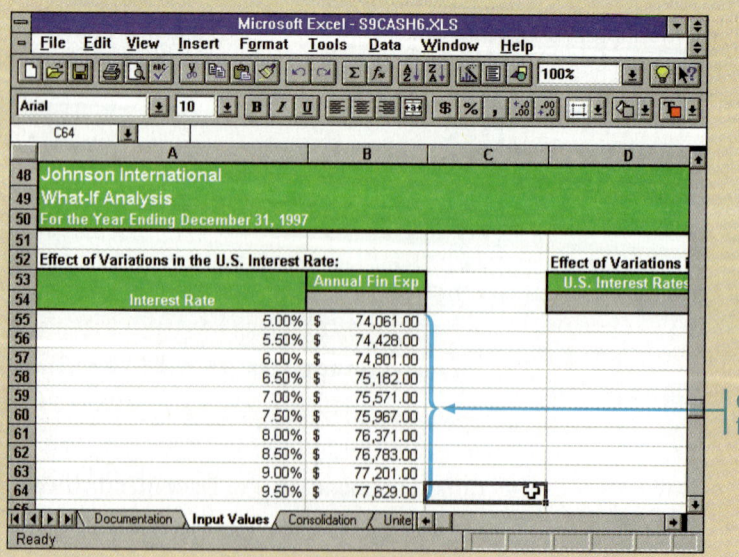

Figure 9-7
The one-input data table with output

output results formatted as currency

Johnson International's current U.S. interest rate is 7.25%, and total annual financing expenditures are $75,769.00. If Johnson International's U.S. interest rate falls to 5.00%, Bill can expect financing expenditures to drop to $74,061.00. On the other hand, if the rate climbs to 9.50%, financing expenditures will increase to $77,629.00. Bill sees that variations in the U.S. interest rate of plus or minus 2.25% will vary financing expenditures by plus or minus approximately $2,000.

Of course, Bill knows that the interest rates in Great Britain will also vary. To take the variations in the Great Britain rate into account, Bill decides to use a two-input data table.

Two-Input Data Tables

As the name implies, a two-input data table allows you to specify two sets of input values for Excel to use to calculate the results in the data table. The setup of a two-way data table is shown in Figure 9-8.

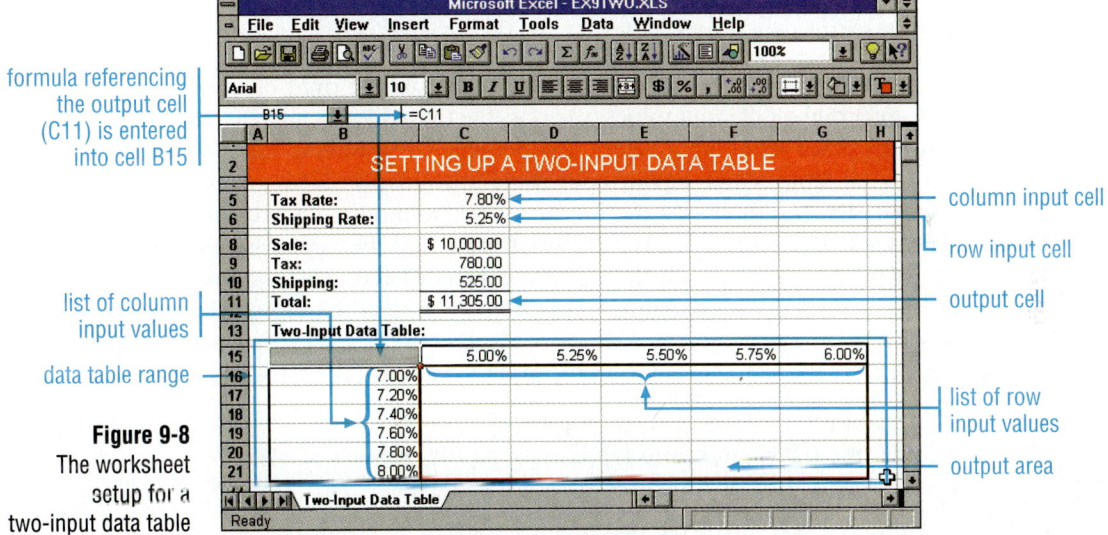

Figure 9-8
The worksheet setup for a two-input data table

In the figure, one set of input values (the possible tax rates) is in a column, as it was in the one-input data table. The other set of input values (the possible shipping rates) is in a row at the top of the table. Cell B15 contains a formula referencing the output cell (the total in cell C11). Again, this reference formula is formatted as hidden. After you use the Table command, Excel begins to substitute each pair of input values in two input cells on the worksheet. (In this case, the input cells are cells C5, which contains the tax rate, and C6, which contains the shipping rate.) Excel then uses the input values to calculate the possible totals (using the formula in cell C11). Finally, Excel displays the results (the possible totals) in the output area.

The rectangular data table range includes the list of possible input cell values, the output cell reference formula, and the output area (the range of cells to the right of and below the lists of possible input cell values). As before, the output area remains blank until the Table command on the Data menu is used; then it is filled with output values as shown in Figure 9-9.

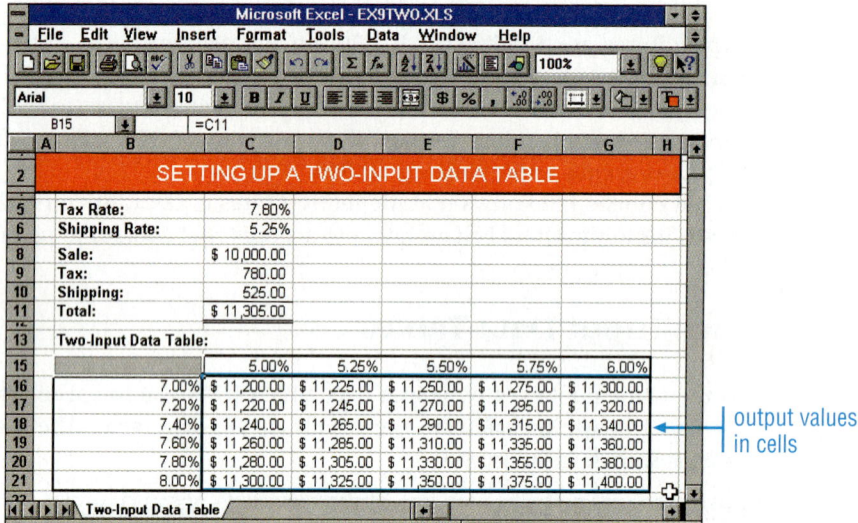

Figure 9-9
The two-input data table

Bill began creating his two-input data table to the right of the one-input data table. He'll enter one set of input values (the possible United States interest rates) in a column. He'll enter the other set of input values (the possible Great Britain interest rates) in a row at the top of the table. Once again, he'll use Consolidation!N34—which displays the Total Financial Expenditures—as the output cell. The input cells are the cells containing the United States interest rate ('Input Values'!B26) and the Great Britain interest rate ('Input Values'!C26). After you use the Table command, Excel will begin to substitute each pair of input values in the two input cells. Excel then uses the input values to recalculate the Consolidation worksheet. Finally, Excel displays the possible financial expenditures in the output area. Bill starts by entering the input values into the table.

To enter the U.S. interest rate values into the two-input data table:

❶ Scroll until you see the range D49 through K64.

❷ Click cell **D55**, then type **.05** and press **[Enter]**.

❸ In cell D56, type **.055** and press **[Enter]**.

❹ Highlight the range D55:D56, then drag the fill handle to extend the range to D64. When you release the mouse button, Excel fills the range with the list of interest rates, each rate .5% greater than the preceding rate.

❺ With the range D55:D64 still highlighted, click the **Percent Style button** on the formatting toolbar.

❻ Click the **Increase Decimal button** on the formatting toolbar twice to display each percentage with two decimal places.

Now Bill enters the values for the British interest rate. Because British interest rates vary less than U.S. interest rates, he decides to use a range of input values from 5.50% to 7.00%.

To enter the British interest rate input values into the two-input data table:

❶ Click cell **E54**, then type **.055** and press **[Enter]**.

❷ Click cell **F54**, then type **.0575** and press **[Enter]**.

❸ Highlight the range E54:F54, then drag the fill handle to extend the range to K54.

❹ Highlight the range E54:K54, then click the **Percent Style button** on the formatting toolbar.

❺ Click the **Increase Decimal button** on the formatting toolbar twice to display each percentage with two decimal places.

❻ Click the **Center button** on the formatting toolbar to center the displayed percentages.

❼ Click any cell to remove the highlight.

Again, Bill wants to see how changing interest rates affect the total annual financing expenditures, displayed in cell Consolidation!N34. He uses a reference to this cell as his output formula.

To create the output cell reference formula:

❶ Click cell **D54**.

❷ Type **=Consolidation!$N$34** and press **[Enter]**. Now you'll format this cell as hidden.

❸ Right-click cell **D54** to display the Shortcut menu, then click **Format Cells...**.

❹ If necessary, click the **Number tab** to display the Number options.

❺ Click **Custom** in the Category box.

❻ Delete the contents of the Code text box and type ;;; (three semi-colons).

❼ Click the **OK button**. The setup for the Table command is complete. See Figure 9-10.

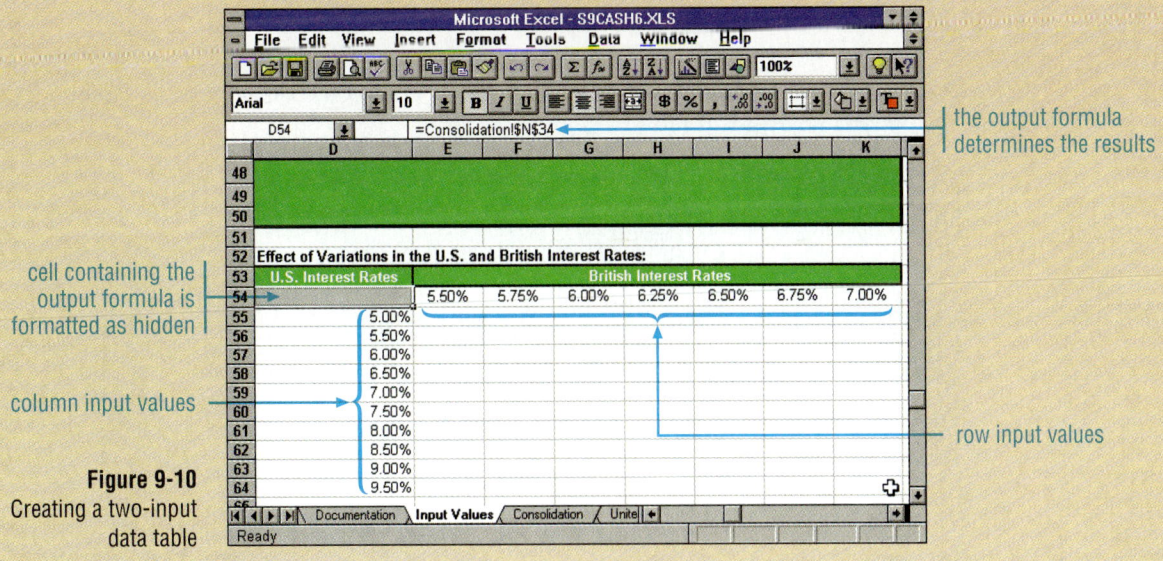

Figure 9-10
Creating a two-input data table

cell containing the output formula is formatted as hidden

column input values

the output formula determines the results

row input values

TROUBLE? If your worksheet doesn't match Figure 9-10, make the necessary changes by repeating the appropriate steps.

Now Bill uses the Table command on the Data menu to calculate the output values for the table.

To calculate the output values using the Table command:

❶ Highlight the range D54:K64. Make sure this range includes cell D54, which contains the formula, and blank cells E55 through K64. Check your highlighted range carefully and repeat Step 1 if necessary.

❷ Click **Data**, then click **Table...**. The Table dialog box appears.

❸ Make sure the Row Input Cell text box is active.

❹ Type 'Input Values'!$C$26 in the Row input cell text box. Cell 'Input Values'!$C$26 contains the British interest rate for Johnson International.

❺ Click the **Column Input Cell text box** to make it active.

❻ Type 'Input Values'!$B$26 in the Column input cell text box. Cell 'Input Values'!$B$26 contains the United States interest rate for Johnson International.

❼ Click the **OK button**. Excel calculates the output values for the what-if table, and enters them in the worksheet. (This calculation might take quite a while, especially on slower 386SX or 386DX computers.)

Again, Bill wants to make the currency format consistent in the what-if table and in the worksheet.

To format the range E55:K64 as currency with no decimal places:

❶ Highlight cells E55 through K64.

❷ Click the **Currency Style button** 🔲. Pound symbols appear in the cells, indicating that the newly formatted values are too wide for the current cell width. You'll fix this problem in Step 3.

❸ Click the **Decrease Decimal button** 🔲 twice.

❹ Click any cell to remove the highlighting. The completed two-input data table appears. See Figure 9-11.

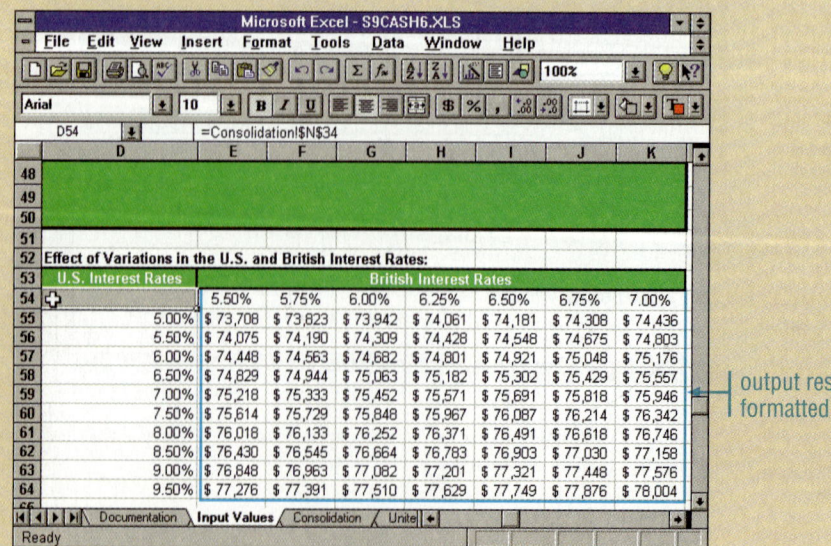

Figure 9-11
The two-input data table with output

Johnson International's current U.S. interest rate is 7.25%, its current British interest rate is 6.25%, and the total annual financing expenditures are $75,769. If Johnson International's U.S. interest rate falls to 5.00% and the British rate falls to 5.50%, Bill can expect the financing expenditures (in cell E55) to drop to $73,708. On the other hand, if the U.S. rate climbs to 9.50% and the British rate goes to 7.00%, the financing expenditures (in cell K64) will go up to $78,004. The table details the total annual financing expenditures for various combinations of interest rates, and allows Bill to see the effects of variations in the two interest rates.

Controlling the Recalculation of a Worksheet with Tables

Usually, worksheets in a workbook are automatically recalculated each time you enter a new value, label, or formula, and each time you save. Recalculating one-input and two-input data tables can take a long time and slow down your use of the worksheet. You can control recalculation two ways. **Manual calculation** turns off automatic calculation and allows Excel to recalculate the workbook only when you press [F9]. **Automatic Except Tables calculation** allows Excel to recalculate everything in the workbook except the tables, ensuring that all non-table numbers are current and correct. Excel recalculates one- and two-input data tables only when you press [F9].

Bill decides to set the workbook to Automatic Except Tables calculation.

To set Automatic Except Tables calculation:
1. Click **Tools**, then click **Options...** to open the Options dialog box.
2. Click the **Calculation tab** to display the calculation options. See Figure 9-12.

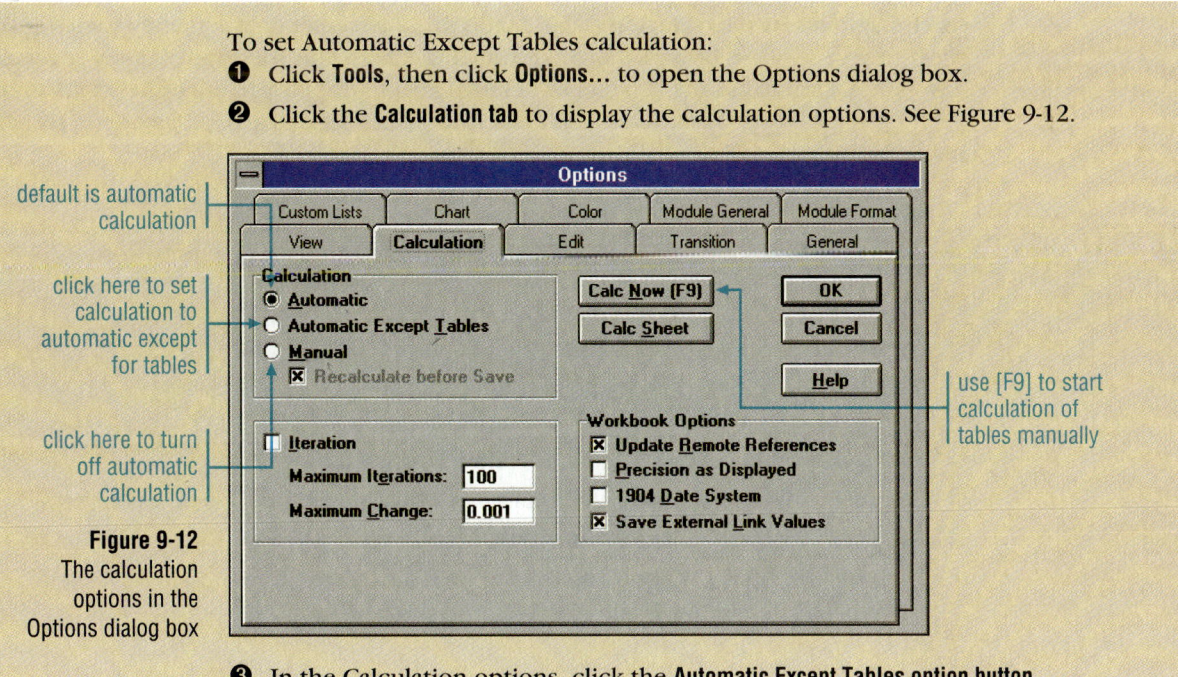

Figure 9-12
The calculation options in the Options dialog box

3. In the Calculation options, click the **Automatic Except Tables option button**.
4. Click the **OK button**.

Now the data tables will be recalculated only when Bill presses [F9]. He can enter new values and formulas without waiting for the data tables to be recalculated.

Bill used a two-input data table to see the effects of varying two interest rates upon the cash flow analysis. He can use the data table to analyze one output variable. If Bill wants to see the effects of changing interest rates on more than one output variable, he can use Excel's Scenario Manager.

Using Scenario Manager in What-If Analysis

Excel's **Scenario Manager** allows you to store sets of input values along with an identifying name. Each named set of values is called a **scenario**. When you create a scenario, you specify the input cells, or **changing cells**. After you create a number of scenarios, you can switch easily among them to make comparisons. The Scenario Manager substitutes the set of input values in the changing cells, recalculates the worksheet, and then displays output values you specify. The output values are displayed in **result cells**. You can summarize the scenarios in a **scenario summary report** if the result cells are on the *same worksheet* as the changing cells. One way to work around this limitation in a workbook with several worksheets is to use a set of result cells that copy the output values on other sheets.

Bill wants to see the effects of changing interest rates on three output values on the Consolidation worksheet: ending loan balance, total interest paid, and financing expenditures. He wants to display these values in result cells on the Input Values sheet (the same sheet that contains the changing cells). To do this, he has set up a summary values area—consisting of result cells and the corresponding labels—on the Input Values sheet. Bill now enters formulas in the result cells, telling Excel to display the values he wants to see. Then he names each result cell. (He'll use the names later when he creates a scenario summary report.)

To set up the summary values area:

❶ Make sure the Input Values sheet is active.

❷ Scroll until you see the range A38:D45.

❸ Click cell **B43**, then type **=Consolidation!N32** and press **[Enter]**.

❹ Click cell **B43**, click the **name box**, then type the name **LoanBalanceEnding** and press **[Enter]**.

❺ Click cell **B44**, then type **=Consolidation!N33** and press **[Enter]**.

❻ Click cell **B44**, click the **name box**, then type **TotalInterestPaid** and press **[Enter]**.

❼ Click cell **B45**, then type **=Consolidation!N34** and press **[Enter]**.

❽ Click cell **B45**, click the **name box**, then type **FinancingExpenditures** and press **[Enter]**. The worksheet appears as shown in Figure 9-13.

Using Scenario Manager in What-If Analysis **EX 327**

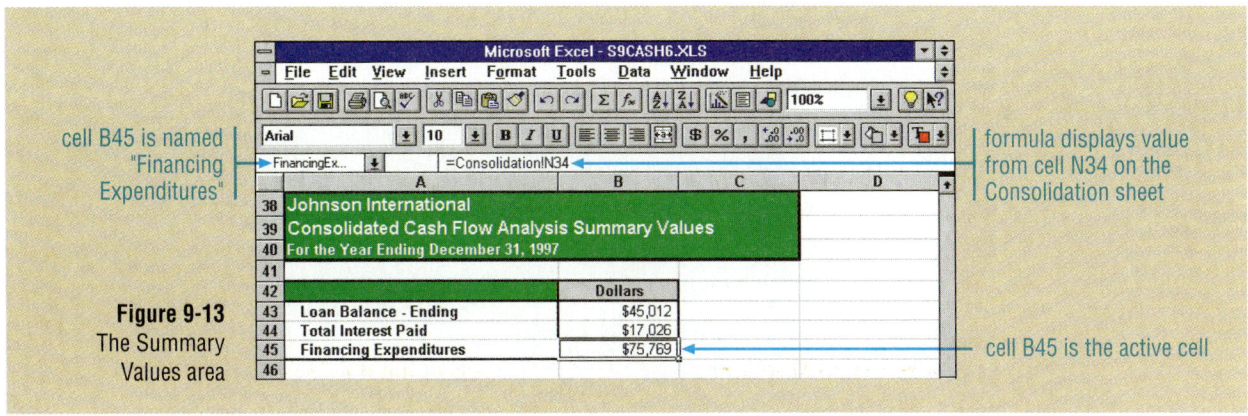

Figure 9-13
The Summary Values area

Now Bill creates his scenarios. He starts with the current values in the worksheet, which he'll call the "Most Likely" scenario.

To enter the Most Likely scenario in the Scenario Manager:
❶ Click **Tools**, then click **Scenarios…** to display the Scenario Manager dialog box. See Figure 9-14.

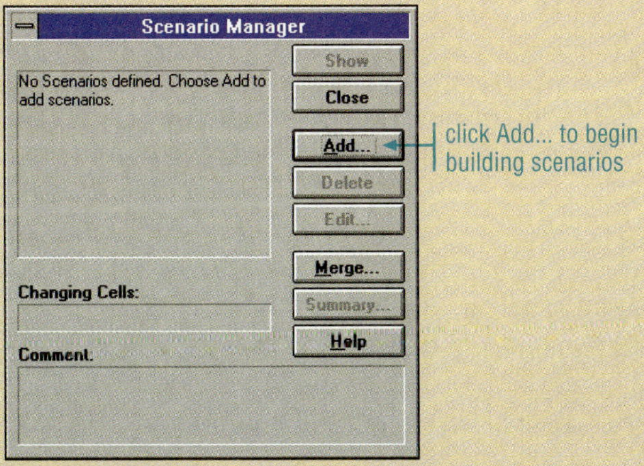

Figure 9-14
The Scenario Manager dialog box

❷ Click the **Add…** button to display the Add Scenario dialog box. See Figure 9-15.

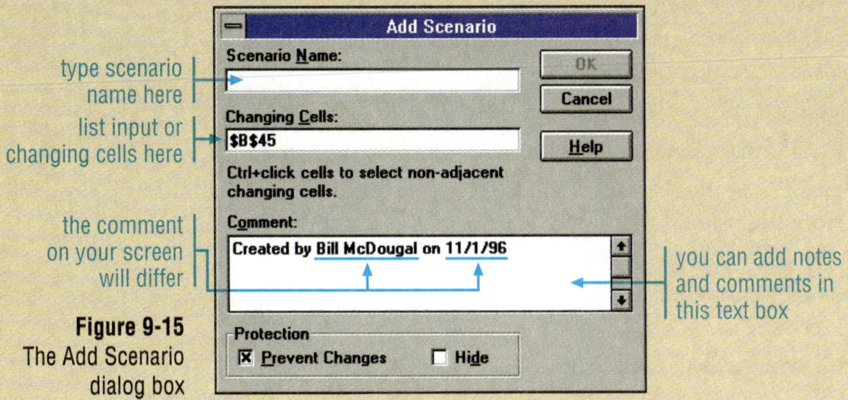

Figure 9-15
The Add Scenario dialog box

❸ In the Scenario Name text box, type **Most Likely**.

❹ Click the **Changing Cells text box** to make it active.

Bill will use cells B25 through C25, which contain the prime rates for each country, because changing cells must contain *values*, not formulas.

❺ Delete the reference in the Changing Cells text box, then type **$B$25:$C$25**.

❻ Click the **OK button**. The Scenario Values dialog box, which contains the current values of the two changing cells, appears. See Figure 9-16.

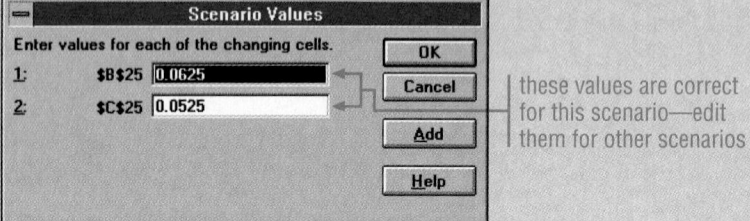

Figure 9-16
The Scenario Values dialog box

❼ Click the **OK button** to accept the scenario and return to the Scenario Manager dialog box.

Bill wants to create two more scenarios—a "Worst Case" scenario and a "Best Case" scenario. In the worst-case scenario, prime rates will increase by 2.00% in each country, increasing Johnson International's costs. In the best-case scenario, interest rates will decrease by 1.00% in each country, decreasing Johnson International's costs. Bill adds these scenarios.

To enter the Worst Case and Best Case scenarios in the Scenario Manager:

❶ Click the **Add... button**.

❷ Type **Worst Case** in the Scenario Name text box.

❸ You do not need to change the addresses of the changing cells, so click the **OK button**. The Scenario Values dialog box appears.

❹ Edit the values in the Scenario Values dialog box to increase the interest rates by 2.00%: the values in the text boxes labeled $B$25 and $C$25 should read **0.0825** and **0.0725**, respectively.

❺ Click the **Add... button** to accept this scenario and return to the Add Scenario dialog box to create the next scenario.

❻ Type **Best Case** in the Scenario Name text box.

❼ Click the **OK button** to display the Scenario Values dialog box.

❽ Edit the values in the Scenario Values dialog box to decrease the interest rates by 1.00% from the original values: the values in the text boxes labeled $B$25 and $C$25 should read **0.0525** and **0.0425**, respectively.

❾ Click the **OK button** to accept this scenario and return to the Scenario Manager dialog box.

❿ Click the **Close button** to close the Scenario Manager.

Bill uses the Scenario Manager to review the results of each scenario.

To use the Scenario Manager:

❶ Scroll until you see rows 38 through 46 at the bottom of the window.

❷ Click **Tools**, then click **Scenarios...** to display the Scenario Manager dialog box. Drag the Scenario Manager dialog box to the upper-right corner of the screen to allow you to see the results cells (B43:B45).

❸ In the Scenarios list, click **Worst Case**, then click the **Show button**. Excel enters the worst-case values into the worksheet and recalculates the worksheet. The output results show that in the worst-case scenario, Johnson International will have an ending loan balance of $48,733, pay $23,463 in interest, and have financing expenditures of $78,485. See Figure 9-17.

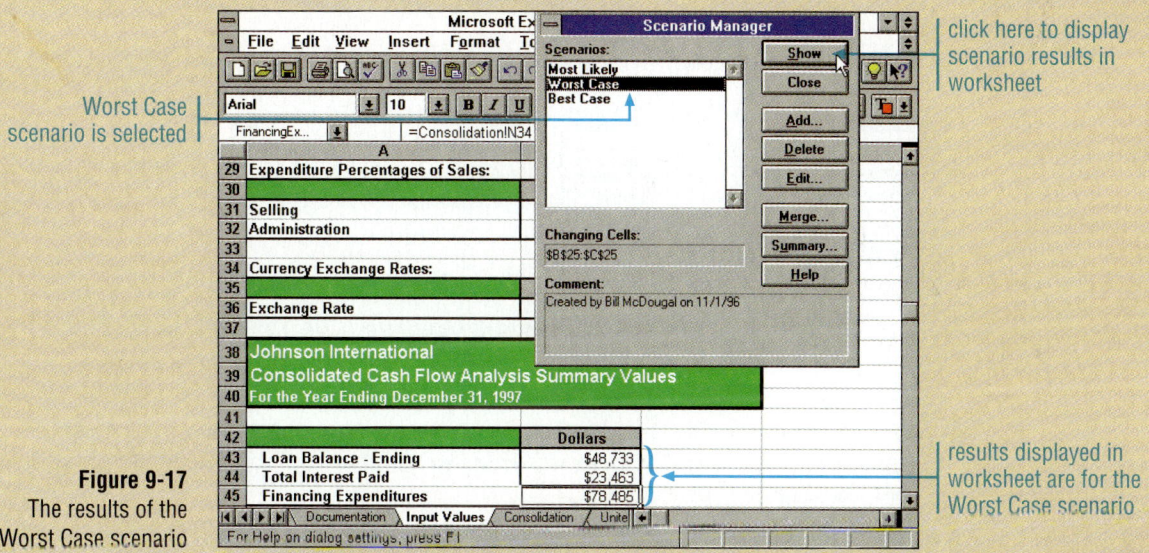

Figure 9-17
The results of the Worst Case scenario

❹ In the Scenarios list, click **Best Case**, then click the **Show button**. Excel enters the best-case values into the worksheet, recalculates the worksheet, and displays the output values in the result cells. In the best-case scenario, Johnson International will have an ending loan balance of $43,260, pay $14,033 in interest, and have financing expenditures of $74,528.

❺ In the Scenarios list, click **Most Likely**, then click the **Show button**. Excel enters Bill's original values into the worksheet, recalculates the worksheet, and displays the original output values shown in the result cells: an ending loan balance of $45,012, interest of $17,026, and financing expenditures of $75,769.

❻ Click the **Close button** to close the Scenario Manager.

❼ Click the **Save button** 🖫 to save the workbook.

Bill decides to create a summary report showing results of the three scenarios.

Scenario Summary Reports

You can view the results of one scenario at a time by using the Scenario Manager to display the results in the workbook (as you just did). To see the results of all the scenarios at once, you can create a scenario summary report.

A scenario summary report shows all the scenario input values and the values of selected results cells. (Recall that to create a scenario summary report the changing cells must be on the same worksheet as the results cells.) The scenario summary report will appear on a new sheet in the workbook.

To create a scenario summary report:

❶ Click **Tools**, then click **Scenarios...** to display the Scenario Manager dialog box. The Scenario Manager dialog box appears in its previous position in the upper-right corner of the screen.

❷ Click the **Summary button**. The Scenario Summary dialog box appears. See Figure 9-18.

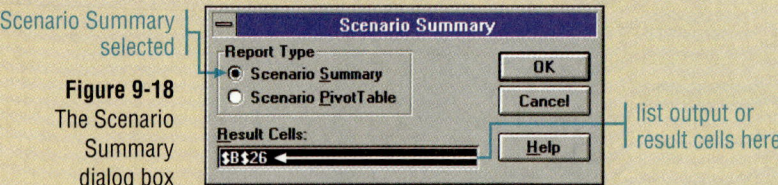

Figure 9-18
The Scenario Summary dialog box

❸ Type **$B$43:$B$45** in the Results Cells text box. This is the range of the three results cells for the ending loan balance (B43), the interest payments (B44), and the financing expenditures (B45).

❹ Click the **OK button**. Excel creates the scenario summary report on a worksheet named Scenario Summary. Drag the Scenario Summary tab to the end of the workbook. See Figure 9-19.

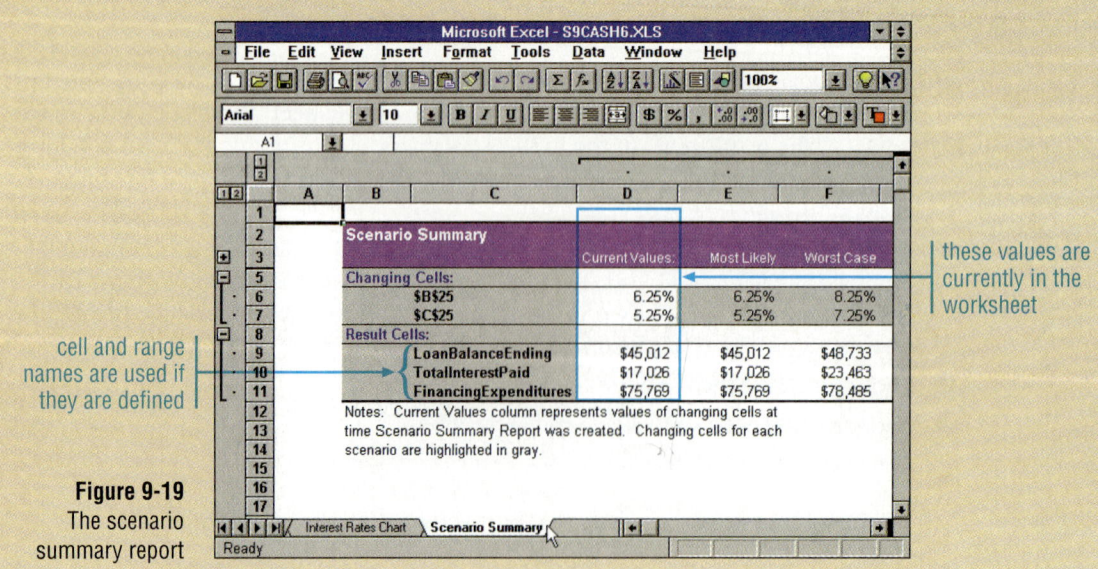

Figure 9-19
The scenario summary report

⑤ Scroll through the scenario summary report and compare the values shown with the input and result values you saw earlier in this tutorial. Notice the names you created identify the result cells and that all scenarios are listed, as are the values currently in the workbook. Press **[Ctrl][Home]**.

⑥ Click the **Input Values tab**, then press **[Ctrl][Home]**.

⑦ Click the **Documentation tab**, then press **[Ctrl][Home]**.

⑧ Click the **Save button** to save the workbook.

⑨ Click **File**, then click **Close** to close the S9CASH6.XLS workbook.

⑩ Exit Excel if you are not proceeding directly to the Tutorial Assignments.

Bill has completed his what-if analysis. The information in the one-input data table, the two-input data table, and the scenario summary report provide the information he needs to prepare for variations in the interest rates for each country in which Johnson International operates. Bill is done for the day, and exits Excel.

Questions

1. What is a one-input data table?
2. What is a two-input data table?
3. How does a two-input data table differ from a one-input data table?
4. How do you control the recalculation of a worksheet?
5. What effect does choosing the Automatic Except Tables calculation option have on the workbook?
6. What is the Scenario Manager?
7. Describe a situation in which you would use the Scenario Manager.
8. What are changing cells?
9. What are result cells?
10. How do you display a scenario?
11. How do you create a scenario summary report?

12. The scenario summary report is a worksheet that has been outlined by Excel's outlining feature. Use the Excel Help system to find out more about outlining and how it works.

Tutorial Assignments

Bill wants to add another scenario to his what-if analysis. This is the Even Worse Case scenario, and changes interest rates to 9.25% for the United States and 8.25% for Great Britain.

1. Open the workbook T9CASH7.XLS, then save it as S9CASH7.XLS on your Student Disk.

To modify the Documentation worksheet:

2. Change the filename in cell B5 to S9CASH7.XLS.

To modify the Input Values worksheet:

3. Click the Input Values tab, then scroll until you see the Cash Flow Analysis Summary Values section at the bottom of the screen. Click cell B45.

4. Using the Scenario Manager, add the Even Worse Case scenario to the set of scenarios. In the Scenario Manager dialog box, change the Comment text to: Created by *your name* on 11/7/95.
5. Use the Scenario Manager dialog box to show the results of the four scenarios. Write a memo to your instructor listing the input values and results for each scenario.
6. Delete the current scenario summary report sheet.
7. Create a new scenario summary report, then move the Scenario Summary sheet to the end of the workbook.
8. Save the workbook.
9. Print the Scenario Summary sheet.
10. Click the Documentation tab, save the workbook, then close the workbook.
11. Submit your memo and printout to your instructor.

Case Problems

1. Capital Budgeting at Campobasso Construction Company

Gerald DeRito works in the finance department at Campobasso Construction Company. Part of Gerald's job is to help client companies evaluate the profitability of potential projects. To do this, Gerald uses a financial technique known as capital budgeting.

Capital budgeting compares the cash expenditures and receipts associated with a project. This comparison includes expenditures and revenues for each year during the life-cycle of the project. Because the calculations can be complex, Gerald has created an Excel workbook to help him evaluate each project.

Input values for an evaluation include the client company's tax rate and cost of capital (the interest rate the client company will pay to borrow money to pay for the project). Critical output values are the project's Net Present Value (NPV) and Internal Rate of Return (IRR). If the Net Present Value (NPV) of the project is greater than $0.00, the client company should do the project. The Internal Rate of Return (IRR) is the cost of capital that would give a $0.00 NPV, and if the IRR is greater than the cost of capital, the client company should do the project.

Gerald wants you to help evaluate a possible project for a client company. He has already calculated the NPV and IRR, but he is concerned about the effects of variation in the client company's tax rate and cost of capital. He wants you to do a what-if analysis to determine the possible effects of changes on these input variables.

Open the file P9CAPBDG.XLS on your Student Disk and do the following:
1. Save the Capital Budgeting workbook as S9CAPBDG.XLS on your Student Disk.
2. On the Documentation worksheet, change the filename in cell B4 to S9CAPBDG.XLS.
3. Change the name in cell B5 to your name.
4. Change the date in cell B6 to the current date.
5. Use cells B9 and B10 to complete the statement of purpose for the workbook.
6. Make cell A1 the active cell, then save the workbook.
7. Look at the values and calculations in the Project Budget worksheet. The Cash Flow After Taxes (CFAT) values in row 16 are used in the final calculation of the NPV and IRR.
8. Create a one-input data table on the Input Values worksheet to see the effects of changes in the cost of capital in the range A23:B34.
    a. In cells A24:A34, enter the possible cost of capital values starting at .10 and ending at .20, then format these values as percentages with one decimal place.
    b. In cell B23, enter a formula referring to the Net Present Value cell, B15. Hide the contents of this cell.

c. Use the Table command on the Data menu to create the table. *Hint*: The input values are in a column, the input cell is B10.
d. At what cost of capital (if any) should you stop recommending that the client company do this project?
9. Create a two-input data table to see the effects of changes in the cost of capital and the tax rate in the range D23:K34.
   a. In cells D24:D34, enter the possible cost of capital values of .10 to .20, then format these values as percentages with one decimal place.
   b. In cells E23:K34, enter possible cost of capital values of .30, .32, .34, .36, .38, .40, and .42. Format these values as percentages with one decimal place.
   c. In cell D23, put a formula referring to the Net Present Value cell, B15. Hide the contents of this cell.
   d. Use the Table command on the Data menu to create the table. *Hint*: The tax rate input values are in a row, the row input cell is B9, the cost of capital input values are in a column, the column input cell is B10.
   e. At what combination(s) of cost of capital and tax rate (if any) should you stop recommending that the client company do this project?
10. Bob needs to do a what-if scenario analysis. He will use tax rate (B9) and cost of capital (B10) as changing cells, and Net Present Value (NPV) and Internal Rate of Return (B15:B16) as results cells.
    a. Name cell B9 "TaxRate," cell B10 "CostOfCapital," cell B15 "NPV," and cell B16 "IRR."
    b. Create the following three scenarios:

Scenario	Tax Rate (B9)	Cost of Capital (B10)
Worst Case	.45	.18
Most Likely	.36	.12
Best Case	.33	.11

   c. Use the Scenario Manager to print a scenario summary. Move the Scenario Summary sheet to the end of the workbook. Change the width of column A to 3.00.
11. Print all the pages in the workbook. Do not print row and column borders or gridlines. Center your printouts horizontally and include a right-aligned header with your name, the filename, the sheet name, and the date. Do not use a footer. Each printout should fit on its own page.
12. Save and close the S9CAPBDG.XLS workbook.
13. Submit your printouts to your instructor.

2. Break-Even Analysis at Merriman Manufacturing

Every year the Still River County Chamber of Commerce hosts the "All The Way To The Bay" race. The race starts on the snowy slopes of Mount Jefferson and ends on the waters of Rainy Bay. Each six-person team consists of a cross-country skier, a bicyclist, a canoe team (two people), a cross-country runner, and a kayaker. The event has become very popular in the area, and has even attracted some national publicity.

Barbara Stevenson of Merriman Manufacturing has been asked to produce a sweatshirt commemorating this year's race. The sweatshirt will be given to race participants and sold to spectators. Barbara is enthusiastic, but wants to make sure that her company will not lose money on the deal. She is preparing a break-even analysis.

A break-even analysis compares total revenues to total costs to determine the minimum number of items (the break-even point) that must be sold to make enough revenue to cover the costs of producing a product (that is, to break even).

Barbara believes that there is a market for 300,000 sweatshirts. Barbara has put together an Excel workbook for her break-even analysis, and according to her analysis, she will make a profit of $450,000 if she produces and sells 300,000 sweatshirts. She is worried, however, about how variations in production costs and sweatshirt sales will affect the profitability of the project. She has asked you to do a what-if analysis.

1. Open the Break-Even Analysis workbook P9BRKEVN.XLS, then save it as S9BRKEVN.XLS on your Student Disk.
2. On the Documentation worksheet in the S9BRKEVN.XLS workbook, change the filename in cell B4 to S9BRKEVN.XLS.
3. Change the name in cell B5 to your name.
4. Change the date in cell B6 to the current date.
5. Use cells B9 and B10 to complete the statement of purpose for the workbook.
6. Make cell A1 the active cell, then save the workbook.
7. Look at the Break-Even Analysis worksheet to see the values and calculations used in the worksheet. Then look at the Break-Even Chart to see how the numbers in the Break-Even Analysis can be used to graphically show the break-even point.
8. On the Input Values worksheet, create a one-input data table to see the effects of changes in the variable cost per unit in range A21:B32.
   a. In cells A22:A32, enter the possible variable cost per unit values of $5.00 to $10.00 in increments of .50, then format these values as currency with two decimal places.
   b. In cell B21, put a formula referring to the break-even point cell, B14. Hide the contents of this cell.
   c. Use the Table command on the Data menu to create the table. *Hint*: The input values are in a column, the correct break-even point at $5.00 per unit is 175,000, and at $10.00 per unit there is a #DIV/0! error message. The #DIV/0! error message occurs at the variable cost of $10.00 per unit because there is no profit if the price is also $10.00 per unit ($10.00 − $10.00 = $0.00).
   d. The break-even point is calculated as:

   Break-Even point = Fixed costs / Profit per unit

   What happens to the break-even point as the variable cost per unit increases? Explain why this happens.
9. Create a two-input data table to see the effects of changes in the variable cost per unit and the fixed costs in range D21:K32.
   a. In cells D22:D32, enter the possible variable cost per unit values of $5.00 to $10.00, then format these values as currency with two decimal places.
   b. In cells E21:J21, enter the fixed cost values of $750,000, $800,000, $850,000 and so on through $1,000,000, then format these values with no decimal places.
   c. In cell D23, enter a formula referring to the break-even point cell, B14. Hide the contents of this cell.
   d. Use the Table command on the Data menu to create the table. Format the output values as currency with no decimal places and widen the columns as necessary. *Hint*: The fixed-cost input values are in a row, the variable cost per unit values are in a column.
   e. If Barbara's sales forecast of 300,000 sweatshirts is correct, the break-even point must be less than 300,000 for her to make a profit. What combination of variable cost per unit and fixed costs results in a break-even point of less than 300,000 units?
   f. Barbara's sales forecast of 300,000 sweatshirts is correct. Also, Barbara has just determined that fixed costs will be $900,000 and the variable cost per unit will be $7.50. Based on the two-input data table, should Barbara produce the sweatshirts?

10. Barbara wants you to do a what-if scenario analysis. She wants you to use fixed costs (B5), variable cost per unit (B6) and price per unit (B7) as changing cells, and profit at 300,000 units sold (B13) and break-even point (B14) as results cells.
    a. Name cell B5 "FixedCosts," cell B6 "VariableCost," cell B7 "Price," cell B13 "Profit," and cell B14 "BreakEvenPoint."
    b. Create the following three scenarios:

Scenario	Fixed Costs (B5)	Variable Cost (B6)	Price (B7)
Worst Case	$950,000	$7.25	$9.00
Most Likely	$875,000	$5.50	$10.00
Best Case	$750,000	$5.25	$11.00

   c. Use the scenario manager to print a scenario summary. Move the Scenario Summary sheet to the end of the workbook. Change the width of column A to 3.00.
11. Print all the pages in the workbook. Do not print row and column borders or gridlines. Center your printouts horizontally and include a right-aligned header with your name, the filename, the sheet name, and the date. Do not use a footer. Each printout should fit on its own page.
12. Save and close the S9BRKEVN.XLS workbook.
13. Submit your printouts to your instructor.

3. Ordering Stereo Components for a Sale at the Incredible Sound Company

Bob Nakamoto owns the Incredible Sound Company, which sells stereo and home video components and systems. Bob buys some of his items from the wholesale supplier Stereo Warehouse. Stereo Warehouse has offered Bob special prices on High End Stereo's model 4625 receiver and model 412 speakers (sold only in pairs). To take advantage of the prices, Bob has decided to have a sale. Bob must decide whether to order receivers or speakers or both. He decides to do a what-if analysis. Bob has $5,000 to spend on sales merchandise. He currently has orders for five receivers and three pairs of speakers. He has limited storage space of 200 cubic feet. Each receiver needs five cubic feet, and each pair of speakers needs eight cubic feet.

1. Open the workbook P9STEREO.XLS, then save it as S9STEREO.XLS on your Student Disk.
2. On the Documentation worksheet, change the filename in cell B4 to S9STEREO.XLS, change the name in cell B5 to your name, and change the date in cell B6 to the current date.
3. Complete the statement of purpose for the workbook.
4. On the Receivers worksheet, create a one-input data table in the range D4:E16.
    a. In cells D5:D16, enter order quantities of 10 to 21.
    b. In cell E4, enter a formula referring to the total cost cell, B13. Hide the contents of this cell.
    c. Use the Table command on the Data menu to create the table. (*Hint*: The input values are in a column.) How many receivers can Bob order with the amount of money he has available?
5. On the Two Products worksheet, create a two-input data table in the range F5:N17.
    a. In cells F6:F17, enter speaker order quantities of 5 to 16.
    b. In cells G5:N5, enter receiver order quantities of 5 to 12.
    c. In cell F5, enter a formula referring to the total total cost, cell D13. Hide the contents of this cell.

d. Use the Table command on the Data menu to create the table. (*Hint*: The speaker input values are in a row, the receiver input values are in a column.) What combinations of receivers and speakers can Bob order with the amount of money he has available?

6. Bob needs to do a what-if scenario analysis. He will use customer order quantities (B10 and C10) and product order quantities (B11 and C11) as changing cells, and total total cost, total total profit, and total total cubic feet (D13:D15) as results cells.
   a. Name cell D13 "TotalTotalCost," cell D14 "TotalTotalProfit," and cell D15 "TotalTotalCubicFeet."
   b. Create the following three scenarios:

	Receivers		Speakers	
Scenario	Customer Orders (B10)	Product Orders (B11)	Customer Orders (C10)	Product Orders (C11)
Worst Case	3	10	3	5
Most Likely	5	10	4	5
Best Case	10	10	5	5

   c. Do *not* print a scenario summary report at this time.

7. Use Solver, which you studied in Tutorial 6, to find an optimal solution for this situation.
   a. The target cells contain the total total profit, which Solver should maximize.
   b. The changing cells contain the quantity of receivers and speakers to order.
   c. The total total order cost must be less than or equal to $5,000.
   d. The total storage space (total cubic feet) must be less than or equal to 200 cubic feet.
   e. You must order at least as many receivers and speakers as are currently on order, and this number must be a positive number or zero.
   f. You must order in whole units.

E 8. After Solver has found the optimal solution, click the Save Scenario... button in the Solver Results dialog box. Name the scenario "Solver Solution."

9. Use the Scenario Manager to print a scenario summary. Move the Scenario Summary sheet to the end of the workbook. Notice that Solver's solution is included as one of the scenarios.

10. Print all the pages in the workbook. Do not print row and column borders or gridlines. Center your printouts horizontally and include a right-aligned header with your name, the filename, the sheet name, and the date. Do not use a footer. Each printout should fit on its own page.

11. Save and close the S9STEREO.XLS workbook.

12. Submit your printouts to your instructor.

TUTORIAL 10

Integrating Excel with Other Windows Applications

OBJECTIVES

In this tutorial you will:
- Transfer or share data among applications using Object Embedding and Linking (OLE)
- Transfer or share data among applications using Dynamic Data Exchange (DDE)
- Use MS Query to retrieve data from a database
- Create multi-table queries using MS Query
- Group data in categories in a PivotTable
- Use Excel as an object server and an object client

Data Analysis Using MS Query

J. J. Svensen J. J. Svensen, located in Boulder, Colorado, sells outdoor recreational clothing for hikers, campers, and skiers by mail order only. Founded by the avid sportsman Jacob J. Svensen in the late 1940s, the company is still owned and operated by the Svensen family. Heather Svensen, Jacob's daughter, is president and CEO. The company's merchandise is known and respected throughout the United States.

Jennifer Skelstad, the sales manager, prepares quarterly sales reports that are used to monitor the company's current performance. The reports include regional and company-wide sales figures, as well as sales figures for individual items listed in the company catalog. Jennifer's next report will contain several paragraphs of text, a diagram illustrating the structure of the sales department, a PivotTable analyzing the sales information, and the complete list of products in the J. J. Svenson catalog. Because the sales report is circulated widely among management, Jennifer wants it to look as professional as possible.

Jennifer will need more than one Windows application to create the sales report. She'll use **MS Query** to retrieve the sales data and catalog list from a Microsoft Access database. She'll use Paintbrush to create the diagram and Microsoft Excel to analyze that sales data and create the PivotTable. Finally, she'll use the word processing application Microsoft Write to combine all the elements of the report and print the final document.

Each Application Has Its Purpose

Most application programs are written to do one type of task efficiently. You use a **word processing program**, such as Microsoft Word or Write, or WordPerfect, to create and edit memos, letters, and reports. In this tutorial, we'll use Write as the word processor. The Write software is included with Microsoft Windows, so it should be available regardless of what word processor you normally use.

A **database program**, also called a **database management system** or **DBMS**, is used primarily for storing large quantities of data (facts) about people, places, and things, and for creating reports summarizing that data. Examples of database programs include Borland's dBASE IV and Paradox, and Microsoft's Fox Pro and Access. J. J. Svensen uses Access.

As you know, **spreadsheet software**, such as Microsoft Excel, is useful for analyzing data and creating charts. Unlike a database, which is highly structured, spreadsheet software allows you flexibility in placing labels, values, and equations so you can be creative in arranging your analyses and, in turn, your problem solving.

Graphics software, such as Microsoft Paintbrush and CorelDRAW, lets you create a wide variety of graphic images. A **presentation graphics program**, such as Microsoft Power Point or Lotus Freelance Plus, helps you prepare and use slides, transparencies, and handouts for business presentations.

Transferring and Sharing Data Among Windows Applications

To transfer or share data among applications, Jennifer will use pasting, linking, embedding, and querying an external database. Before you can help Jennifer create the report, you need to learn the basics about pasting, linking, and embedding. (You learned about querying external databases using MS Query in Tutorial 7.)

Pasting Data

You can **paste** material—usually text—from one application to another the same way you paste material within an application. For example, you can paste a column heading from an Excel worksheet into a Write document, format the pasted text in Write, and use it as the title of your document. You *move* material from one application to the other using Cut and Paste commands, and you *copy* material using Copy and Paste commands. See Figure 10-1.

JUL	AUG	SEP	OCT	NOV	DEC	TOTAL ANNUAL
$79,775	$54,025	$54,166	$50,543	$50,410	$56,114	553,000
$150,000	$156,250	$162,500	$168,750	$181,250	$193,750	$1,862,550
$113,750	$97,500	$101,563	$105,625	$109,688	$117,813	$1,865,437
37,500	43,750	37,500	39,063	40,625	42,188	$448,000
13,750	15,000	17,500	15,000	15,625	16,250	$176,425
$165,000	$156,250	$156,563	$159,688	$165,938	$176,250	$1,810,788
$244,775	$210,275	$210,728	$210,231	$216,347	$232,364	$1,860,743

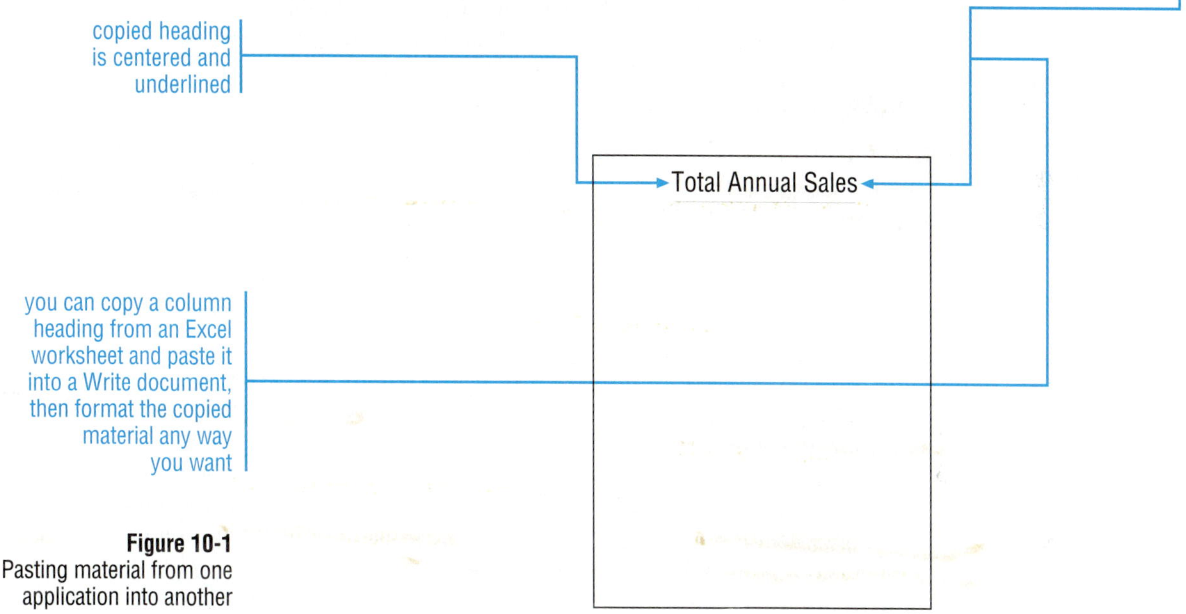

copied heading is centered and underlined

Total Annual Sales

you can copy a column heading from an Excel worksheet and paste it into a Write document, then format the copied material any way you want

Figure 10-1
Pasting material from one application into another

Because you are already familiar with the Copy and Paste commands, you will not copy and paste text in this tutorial. You will use the Paste command in the Case Problems.

Embedding Data

You embed material using **Object Linking and Embedding (OLE)**. An **object** is a package of data or information. For example, workbooks or documents you create in those applications are objects. OLE (pronounced oh-LAY) allows you to copy an object from one application into another. For example, you can copy an image from Paintbrush and embed it in a Write document. The application containing the original material is the **source** or **server application**, and the application in which you place the copy is the **client application**. A copied object is said to be **embedded** because it exists as a separate object within the document or worksheet in the client application. The embedded copy is *not* linked to the original document or worksheet, which means that changes in the original are *not* made in the copy. You can edit the embedded copy using the tools and commands of the source application.

The ability to use the tools and commands of the source application differentiates embedding from pasting. When you embed one object within another, you directly access the source application by double-clicking the embedded object, allowing you to edit the embedded object quickly and easily.

You edit an embedded object in one of two ways, depending on the application you are using and the version of OLE it supports. For example, assume you have an Excel PivotTable embedded in a Write document, and that you have not launched Excel. Write supports only OLE 1.0, which means that to edit the PivotTable, you simply double-click the PivotTable. This launches Excel; the PivotTable appears in the Excel window, ready for you to edit. In Microsoft Word for Windows 6.0 and Excel 5.0, which support OLE 2.0, double-clicking an embedded object does not actually launch the source application. Instead, the border of the embedded object darkens, and the menus and toolbars of the client application change to the menus of the source application. In either case, double-clicking an embedded object gives you direct access to the source application's commands and tools.

Linking Data

You can also link material using Object Linking and Embedding (OLE). When you **link** material, any changes you make to the object in the source document are also made to the copy in the client application. For example, you can link the PivotTable in the Write document to the PivotTable in the Excel workbook. Then, every time you launch Excel and revise the PivotTable, you *automatically* revise the PivotTable in the Write document. As with an embedded object, you can always double-click a linked object to directly access the source application.

Don't be confused by the fact that you generally use Copy and Paste commands to embed and link objects. When you copy an object (such as a PivotTable) and then switch to the client application, the Paste command in the client application will give you an opportunity to embed or link the object, or it will automatically embed the object. (Exactly what happens depends on the application and the version of OLE you are using.) If you merely copy some text and paste it in the client application, you are allowed only a simple paste (without links to the source application).

Let's see how Jennifer transfers and shares data as she writes her sales analysis report. We'll discuss each method as Jennifer uses it. She has already started entering the text of the report in Write. Let's take a look at what she's done so far.

To launch Write:

❶ Launch Windows following your usual procedure.

❷ Make sure your Student Disk is in the disk drive.

❸ If the Program Manager is not the active application, press **[Ctrl][Esc]**. The Task List dialog box appears. See Figure 10-2.

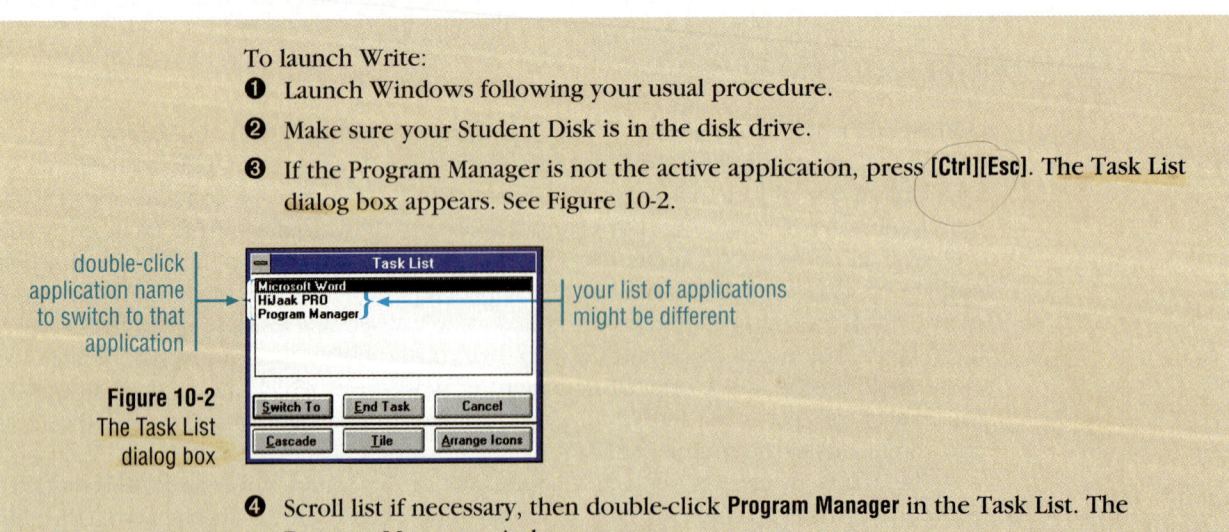

Figure 10-2
The Task List dialog box

double-click application name to switch to that application

your list of applications might be different

❹ Scroll list if necessary, then double-click **Program Manager** in the Task List. The Program Manager window appears.

Transferring and Sharing Data Among Windows Applications   **EX 341**

❺ If the Accessories group window is not open, double-click the **Accessories group icon** to open the Accessories group window. See Figure 10-3

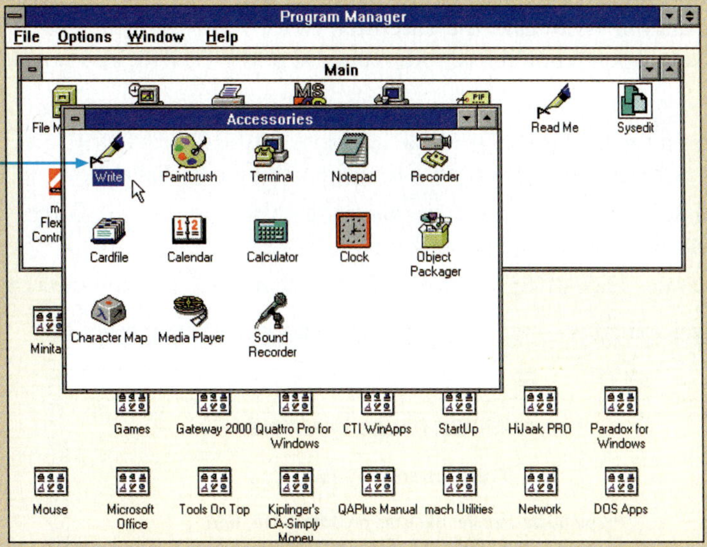

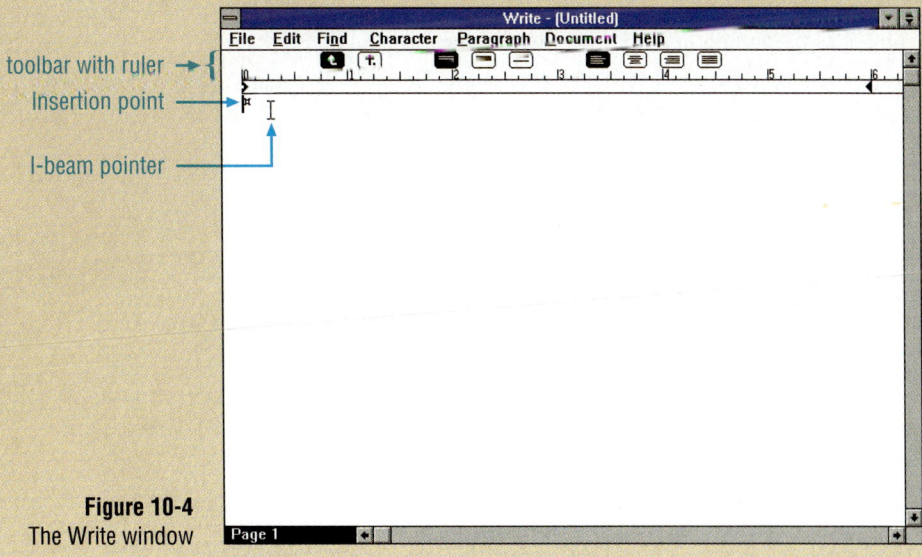

Figure 10-3
The Accesories group window

TROUBLE? If there is no Accessories group in your Program Manager, ask your instructor or technical support person for assistance.

❻ In the Accessories group window, double-click the **Write icon** to open Write.

TROUBLE? If there is no Write icon in your Accessories group, ask your instructor or technical support person for assistance.

❼ Click the **Write application window Maximize button**.

❽ Click **Document**, then click **Ruler On**. The Write application window appears. See Figure 10-4.

Figure 10-4
The Write window

Because Windows applications have standard menu systems and keyboard shortcuts, you can use many of the same menu commands you learned using Excel. For example, to open a file in Write, use the Open... command on the File menu, as you do in Excel. Filenames in Write have the extension .WRI.

Let's open Jennifer's report, named C10REPRT.WRI, and save it under a new name.

To open the C10REPRT.WRI file and save it as S10REPRT.WRI:
1. Click **File**, then click **Open...** to display the Open dialog box.
2. If necessary, click the **Drives down arrow button** next to the Drives box and then click the drive containing your Student Disk.
3. Double-click **C10REPRT.WRI** in the File Name box to open the report. See Figure 10-5.

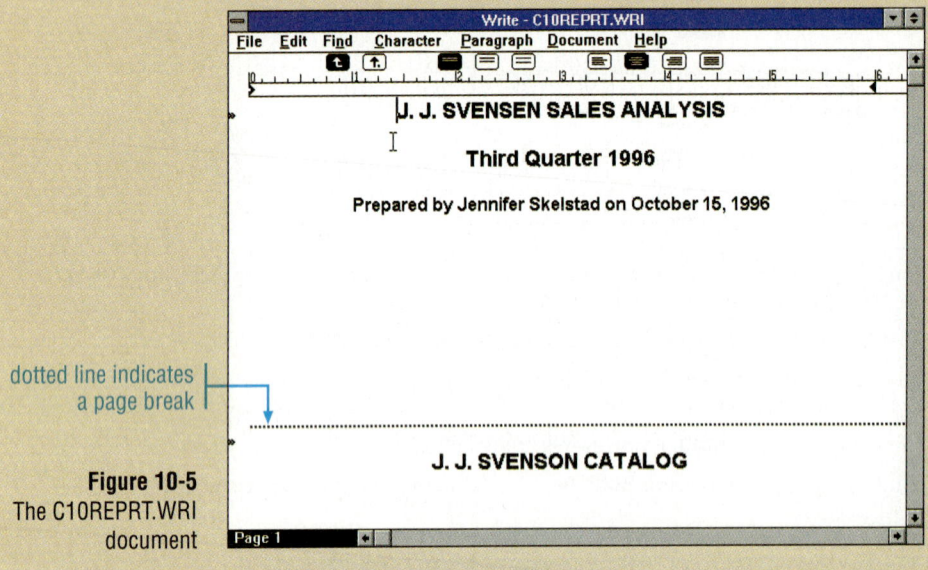

Figure 10-5
The C10REPRT.WRI document

dotted line indicates a page break

4. Click **File**, then click **Save As...** to display the Save As dialog box.
5. Change the filename to **S10REPRT.WRI**, then click the **OK button**.

Jennifer has already created her organization diagram in Paintbrush. Now she will use Copy and Paste commands to embed the graphic in her report

To embed the sales department organization diagram in the report:
1. Press **[Ctrl][Esc]** to display the Task List, then double-click **Program Manager** to switch to the Program Manager window.
2. If the Accessories group window is not open, double-click the **Accessories group icon** to open the Accessories window, then double-click the **Paintbrush icon** to open Paintbrush.

    TROUBLE? If there is no Accessories group in your Program Manager, or no Paintbrush icon in your Accessories group, ask your instructor or technical support person for assistance.
3. Click the **Paintbrush window Maximize button**. Paintbrush appears. See Figure 10-6.

Transferring and Sharing Data Among Windows Applications **EX 343**

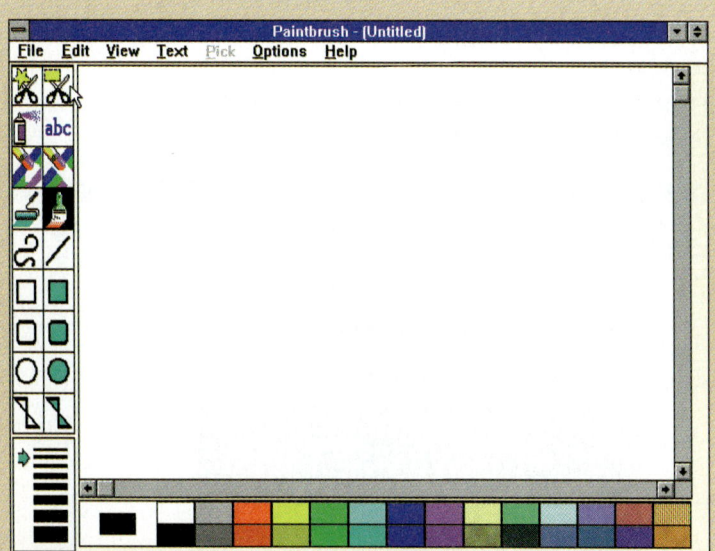

Figure 10-6
The Paintbrush window

❹ Click **File**, then click **Open...** to display the Open dialog box. If necessary, click the **Down arrow button** next to the Drives box and then click the drive containing your Student Disk. Double-click **C10SALES.BMP** to open the file containing the organization chart.

❺ Click the **Pick button** ✂, then click and drag the outline to form a rectangular area around the organization chart. See Figure 10-7.

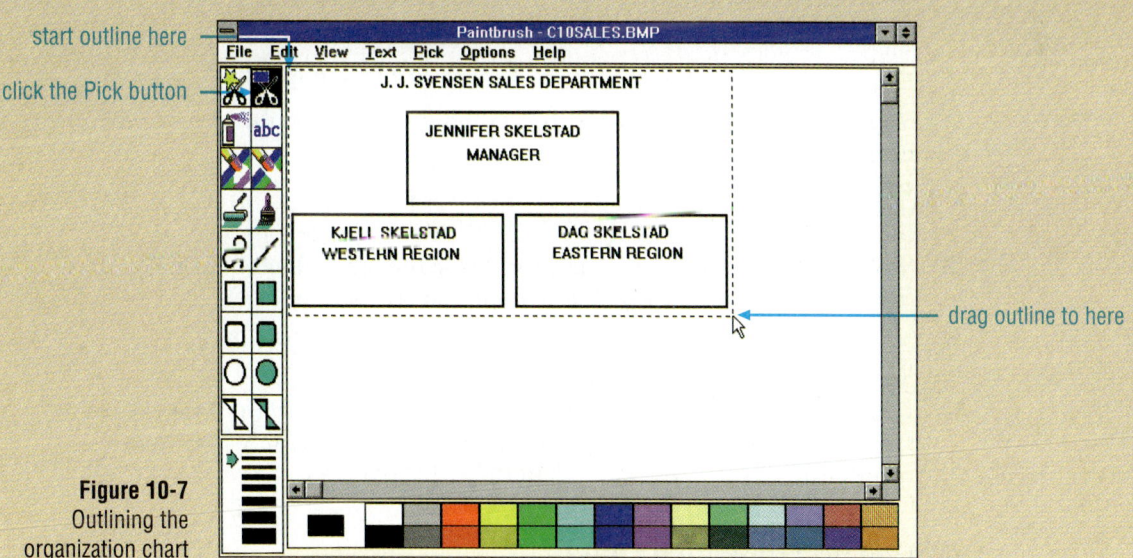

Figure 10-7
Outlining the organization chart

❻ Click **Edit**, then click **Copy**.

❼ Press **[Ctrl][Esc]** to display the Task List dialog box, then double-click **Write - S10REPRT.WR1** in the Task List. The Write window appears. Maximize the window, if necessary.

❽ Click the pointer at the end of the line "Prepared by Jennifer Skelstad on October 15, 1996," then press **[Enter]** twice to move the insertion pointer to the second blank line below the heading.

EX 344 TUTORIAL 10 Integrating Excel with Other Windows Applications

❾ Click **Edit** in the Write window, then click **Paste...** to paste the organization chart into the report.

❿ Click anywhere in the organization chart to highlight the chart, then click the **Center button** 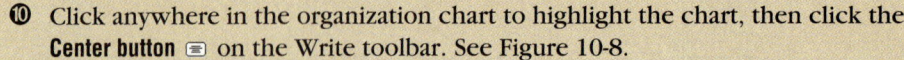 on the Write toolbar. See Figure 10-8.

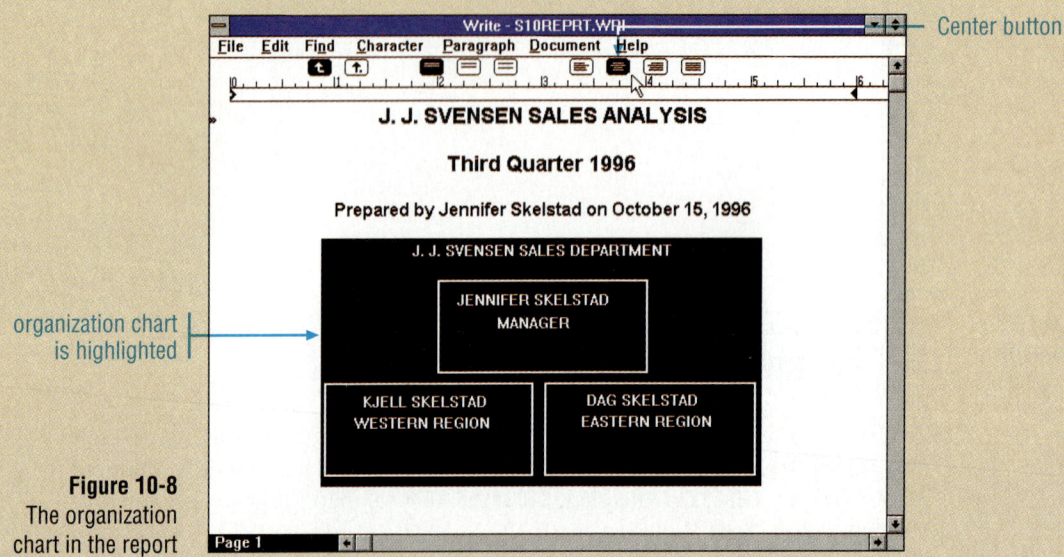

Figure 10-8
The organization chart in the report

TROUBLE? If the organization chart appears in a Paintbrush window, you *double-clicked* the organization chart in Write. Double-click the Paintbrush application Control menu box to close the Paintbrush window, then repeat Step 10.

Now that Jennifer has pasted the graphic image into the report, she closes the Paintbrush window.

To close the Paintbrush window:
❶ Press **[Ctrl][Esc]** to display the Task List dialog box, then double-click **Paintbrush - C10SALES.BMP** to switch to the Paintbrush window.
❷ Double-click the **Paintbrush application Control menu box** to close the Paintbrush window.
❸ If the Write window is not active, press **[Ctrl][Esc]** to display the Task List dialog box, then double-click **Write - C10REPRT.WR1** to switch to the Write window.

Editing an Embedded Object

When you paste a graphic image from Paintbrush, Windows treats the image as a picture object and embeds it in the client application document using OLE. Recall that an embedded object is *not* linked to the original—which means that changes to the original object will *not* affect the embedded copy.

> **REFERENCE WINDOW**
>
> ### Editing an Embedded Object Using OLE
>
> - Double-click the embedded object.
> - Edit the object in the source application (OLE 1.0) or use the source application's toolbars and menus (OLE 2.0).
> - Click File, then click Exit. If the Exit command appears in a modified form such as "Exit and Return," click the modified Exit command.

Jennifer doesn't need to edit the organization chart, but let's take a moment to see how OLE activates the source application for an embedded object.

To edit the picture object in Paintbrush:

❶ Double-click the **organization chart**. The Paintbrush application is launched with the organization chart open. See Figure 10-9. The size and placement of your Paintbrush window might differ from the figure.

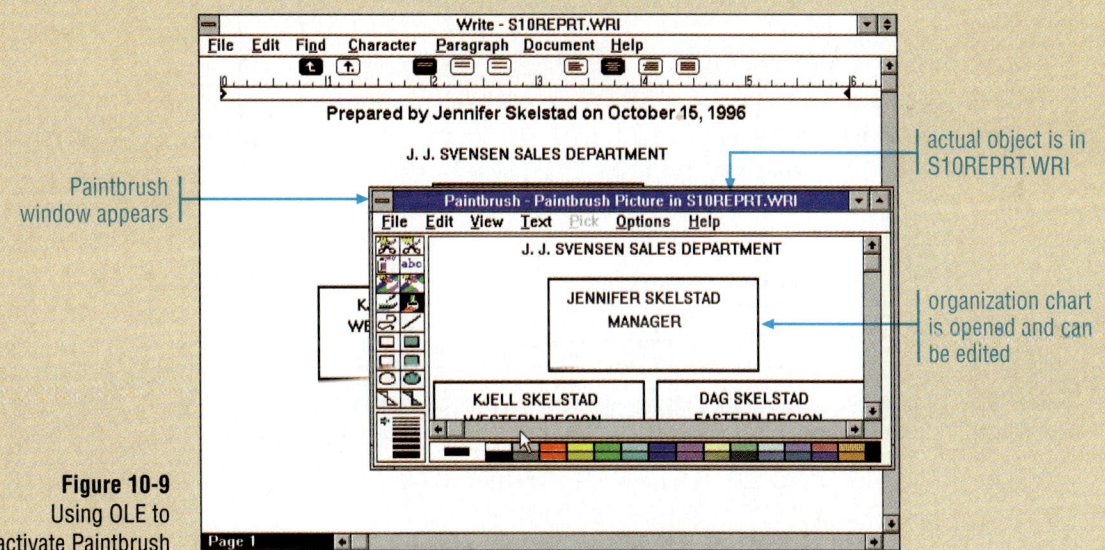

Figure 10-9
Using OLE to activate Paintbrush

❷ If you wanted to edit the organization chart, you could do it now, but there's no need. In the Paintbrush menu, click **File** and then click **Exit & Return to S10REPRT.WR1**.

Jennifer needs to organize her Excel workbook before continuing with her report, so she decides to close the report and temporarily exit Write.

To close the S10REPRT.WR1 file and exit Write:
❶ Click **File**, then click **Save**.
❷ Click **File**, then click **Exit**.

Now Jennifer needs to analyze the sales data and compile the catalog list for her report. She knows that sales and catalog information are stored in a Microsoft Access database. Jennifer decides to launch Excel and then use MS Query and the PivotTable Wizard to retrieve and analyze the sales and catalog information. Then she can transfer the sales analysis and catalog list to her Write document.

Jennifer has already created the workbook and the documentation she'll need for the sales report. Let's open this workbook now.

To launch Excel, organize the workspace, and open the C10SALES.XLS workbook:
1. Launch Excel following your usual procedure.
2. Make sure the Microsoft Excel and Book1 windows are maximized.
3. Click the **Open button** to display the Open dialog box.
4. Double-click **C10SALES.XLS** in the File Name box to open the workbook. See Figure 10-10.

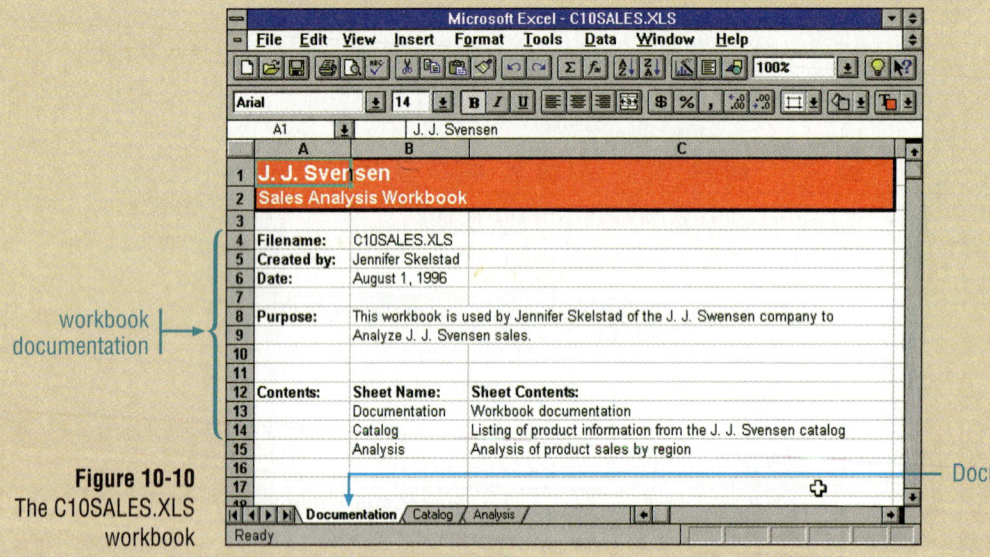

Figure 10-10
The C10SALES.XLS workbook

TROUBLE? If the file isn't in the File Name list, click the Drives down arrow button to display the drive in which your Student Disk is located.

Let's save the workbook under the name S10SALES.XLS, so that your changes do not alter the original file.

To save the workbook as S10SALES.XLS:
1. Make sure the Documentation sheet is the active worksheet.
2. Double-click cell **B4**, change the filename to **S10SALES.XLS**, then press **[Enter]**.
3. Press **[Ctrl][Home]** to make cell A1 the active cell.
4. Click **File**, then click **Save As...** to display the Save As dialog box.
5. Save the workbook as **S10SALES.XLS**.

There are three worksheets in Jennifer's workbook: Documentation, Catalog, and Analysis. The Documentation sheet contains the workbook documentation. Notice how the information Jennifer has entered into the Documentation sheet follows the documentation methods you studied in Tutorial 8. The Catalog and Analysis sheets are currently blank. Jennifer will add data and information to them when she creates her sales analysis in Excel.

Next, Jennifer will query the relational database Microsoft Access and, after finding the data she needs, place the data in the Excel workbook. Let's take a moment to learn more about queries and relational databases.

How Relational Databases Work

A **query** is a question you ask about the data in a database. For example, Jennifer wants to include a catalog list in her report. To get this list, she will ask the question, What products are listed in the J. J. Svensen catalog? The answer to this question will be the catalog list she needs for her report.

To query a relational database, you need to understand how a relational database like Access works. As you learned in Tutorial 7, in an Excel database, a **record** is the set of data for a single person, place, or thing stored in a worksheet row. The data relating to each characteristic of the person, place, or thing are stored in columns, called **fields**. Each column is labeled with a **field name**. The actual data value in a field is called the **field value**.

Relational databases have the same database structure—based on fields and records. What is called a list on an Excel worksheet is called a **table** in a relational database. Each table in a relational database has a **table name**.

For example, one table in the J. J. Svensen database is the CUSTOMER table, which stores data such as the first name, last name, and address of each customer in the credit program. The CUSTOMER table is shown in Figure 10-11.

table name — CUSTOMER
field names

CUST_ID#	LAST_NAME	FIRST_NAME	ADDRESS	CITY	STATE	ZIP	PHONE
C00001	Svensen	Heather	276 Westview Drive	Boulder	CO	80303	(303)-478-8823
C00002	Skelstad	Jennifer	1178 35th Street	Boulder	CO	80303	(303)-478-2299
C00003	Johnson	Doug	1568 North Glencoe St	Denver	CO	80222	(303)-789-8533
C00004	Bauer	Judith	3402 Arizona Stree	San Diego	CA	92110	(619)-778-3434
C00005	Troutman	Carl	977 Mountain View Avenue North	San Bernardino	CA	92410	(805)-455-7256
C00006	Winfield	Donald	2366 Clearview Circle SW	Topeka	KS	66619	(913)-223-8257

records

Figure 10-11
The CUSTOMER table structure

In Figure 10-11, each record consists of the data stored in the eight fields: CUST_ID#, LAST_NAME, FIRST_NAME, etc. Each record in the table is identified by a unique value in one of the fields. This field is called the **primary key** for the table. In CUSTOMER, the CUST_ID# field is the primary key. Each record in CUSTOMER contains a unique CUST_ID# value to identify the customer. For example, Judith Bauer is identified by the CUST_ID# C00004.

Primary keys help avoid confusion between records. There might be more than one customer named Judith Bauer, and there might be more than one customer with Judith Bauer's address (her husband for instance), but there is only one customer with the ID number C00004.

The J. J. Svensen Database

A relational database often contains more than one table. The J. J. Svensen database consists of the five tables listed in Figure 10-12.

Figure 10-12
The J. J. Svensen database

Table Name	Contents
CATALOG	Data about each product
STAFF	Data about each employee
CUSTOMER	Data about each customer
ORDER	Data about each order
ITEM	Data about each product in each order

The complete set of tables with some records in each table is shown in Figure 10-13.

CATALOG

CATALOG_ID#	BRAND	CATEGORY	TYPE	DESCRIPTION	PRICE
M00001	J. J. Svensen	Multiple	Parka	Nylon Shell	$70.00
M00002	J. J. Svensen	Multiple	Parka	Gore-Tex Shell	$125.00
M00003	J. J. Svensen	Multiple	Parka	Nylon Insulated	$115.00
M00004	J. J. Svensen	Multiple	Parka	Gore-Tex Insulated	$165.00
M00005	J. J. Svensen	Multiple	Parka	Nylon Down-filled	$250.00
M00006	J. J. Svensen	Multiple	Parka	Gore-Tex Down-filled	$290.00
M00007	J. J. Svensen	Skiing	Parka	Nylon Down-filled Coverall	$350.00
M00008	J. J. Svensen	Skiing	Parka	Gore-Tex Down-filled Coverall	$390.00
M00009	McKinley	Multiple	Parka	Nylon Down-filled	$270.00
M00010	McKinley	Multiple	Parka	Gore-Tex Down-filled	$320.00

STAFF

STAFF_ID#	LAST_NAME	FIRST_NAME	DATE_HIRED
S00001	Svensen	J. J.	9/1/48
S00002	Svensen	Heather	9/1/68
S00003	Svensen	Eric	3/1/72
S00004	Skelstad	Jennifer	9/15/86
S00005	Skelstad	Kjell	9/15/88
S00006	Skelstad	Dag	3/1/92

CUSTOMER

CUST_ID#	LAST_NAME	FIRST_NAME	ADDRESS	CITY	STATE	ZIP	PHONE
C00001	Svensen	Heather	276 Westview Drive	Boulder	CO	80303	(303)-478-8823
C00002	Skelstad	Jennifer	1178 35th Street	Boulder	CO	80303	(303)-478-2299
C00003	Johnson	Doug	1568 North Glencoe St	Denver	CO	80222	(303)-789-8533
C00004	Bauer	Judith	3402 Arizona Stree	San Diego	CA	92110	(619)-778-3434
C00005	Troutman	Carl	977 Mountain View Avenue North	San Bernardino	CA	92410	(805)-455-7526
C00006	Winfield	Donald	2366 Clearview Circle SW	Topeka	KS	66619	(913)-223-8257

ORDER

ORDER_ID#	CUST_ID#	DATE	REGION	STAFF_ID#
R00001	C00003	7/15/96	Western	S00003
R00002	C00004	7/15/96	Western	S00005
R00003	C00005	7/25/96	Western	S00006
R00004	C00006	7/27/96	Western	S00005
R00005	C00007	8/1/96	Eastern	S00006

ITEM

ORDER_ID#	ITEM_ID#	QUANTITY	CATALOG_ID#
R00001	1	2	M00002
R00001	2	1	M00012
R00001	3	1	M00028
R00002	1	1	M00038
R00002	2	2	M00044
R00002	3	6	M00033
R00002	4	1	M00028

Figure 10-13
The tables in the J. J. Svensen database

The tables in a relational database are linked by values in **common fields**, fields that are common to two or more tables. These links between tables allow us to find the information we need in a database. For example, the order items in the ITEM table are linked to the order items in the ORDER table by the ORDER_ID# field in both tables. Similarly, we know which customer placed the order by the CUST_ID# in both the CUSTOMER and ORDER tables. In Figure 10-14, the ORDER table shows that the order ORDER_ID# = R00006 was placed by customer CUST_ID# = C00008. Looking in the common field CUST_ID# in the CUSTOMER table, we find that the customer with CUST_ID# = C00008 is Scott Ehren.

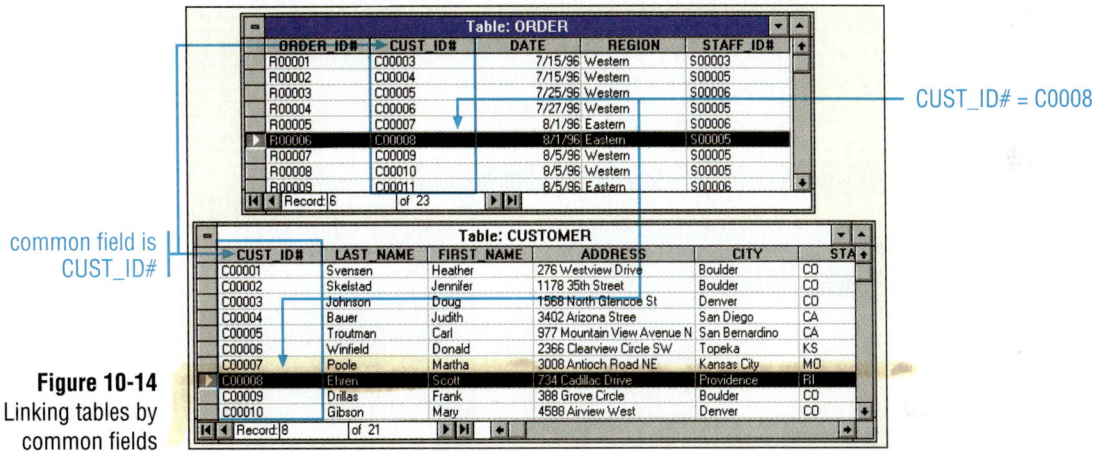

Figure 10-14
Linking tables by common fields

The relationships between tables in the SVENSEN database are illustrated in Figure 10-15. In Figure 10-15, each table is represented by a **field list**, or list of the fields in the table.

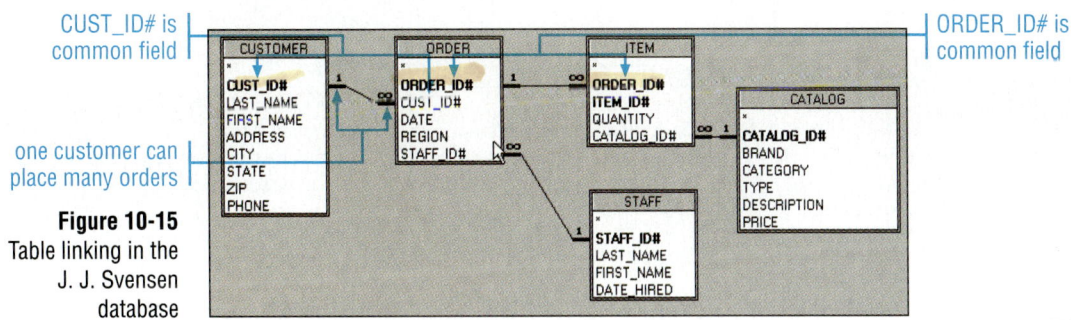

Figure 10-15
Table linking in the J. J. Svensen database

Now that you understand the structure of a relational database, you can help Jennifer query the database using MS Query.

Using Microsoft Query

As you learned in Tutorial 7, MS Query allows you to retrieve information from a database application and place it in your workbook. Jennifer needs to retrieve a list of products from the CATALOG table in the database and place the data in the Catalog sheet in her workbook. She begins by selecting the Catalog sheet. Then she launches MS Query.

To launch MS Query:

❶ Click the **Catalog tab**.

❷ Click **Data**, then click **Get External Data...**. The MS Query window appears. Don't worry if your MS Query window is not maximized. You'll get a chance to maximize it later in this tutorial. See Figure 10-16.

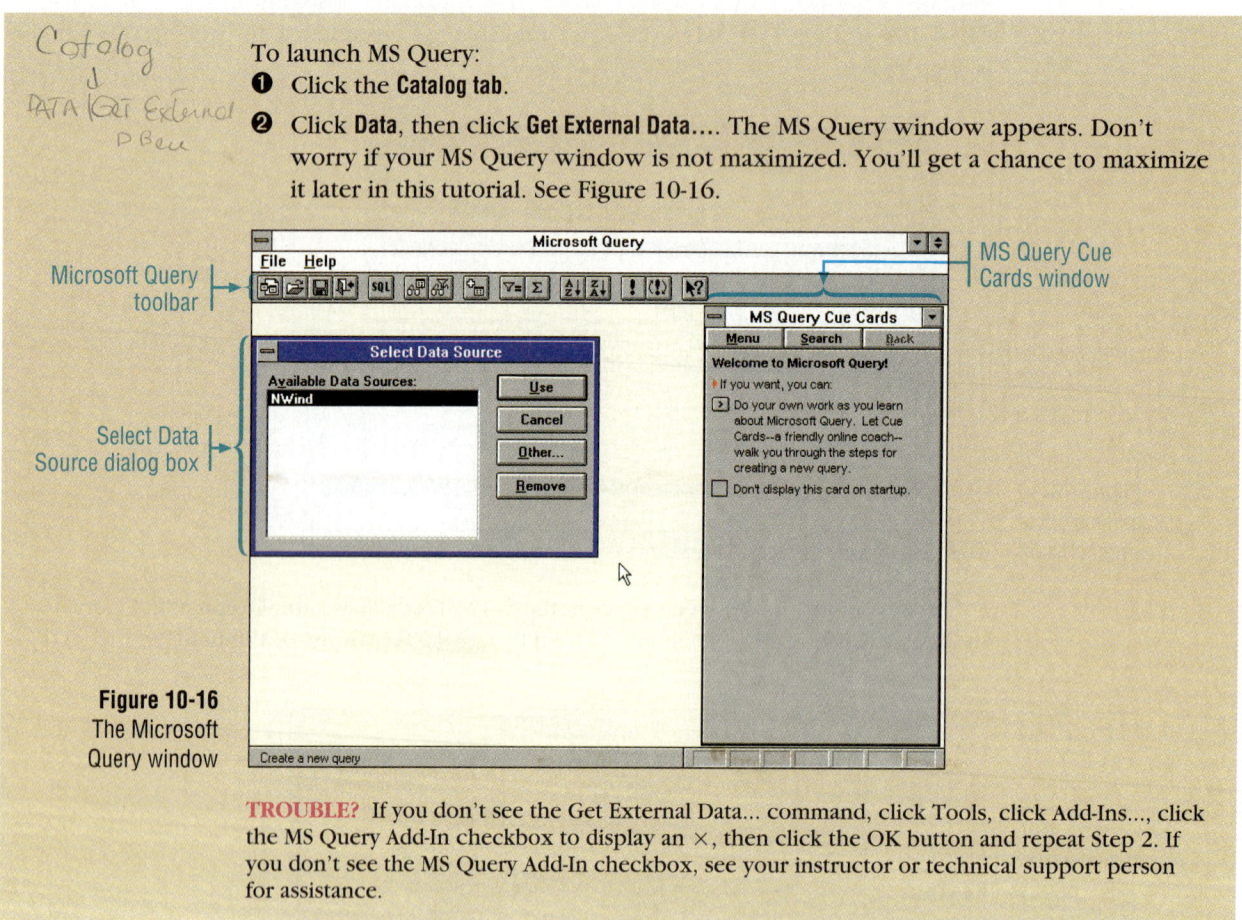

Figure 10-16
The Microsoft Query window

TROUBLE? If you don't see the Get External Data... command, click Tools, click Add-Ins..., click the MS Query Add-In checkbox to display an ×, then click the OK button and repeat Step 2. If you don't see the MS Query Add-In checkbox, see your instructor or technical support person for assistance.

You saw the MS Query window in Tutorial 7, but let's take a closer look at it now.

MS Query Cue Cards

When you launch MS Query, the MS Query window appears with the Select Data Source dialog box open and the MS Query Cue Cards window displayed. You can use the Cue Cards to help you perform a query. When the MS Query Cue Cards window is open, it is visible on top of the Microsoft Query window.

MS Query Cue Cards   **EX 351**

REFERENCE WINDOW

Opening and Closing MS Query Cue Cards

- Click Cue Cards in the Help menu to open the MS Query Cue Cards window.
- Double-click the MS Query Cue Cards Control menu box to close the MS Query Cue Cards window.

Let's use the MS Query Cue Cards to see how a query is defined.

To use the MS Query Cue Cards:

❶ Click the **Menu button** in the MS Query Cue Cards window to display the MS Query Cue Cards menu. The menu appears. See Figure 10-17.

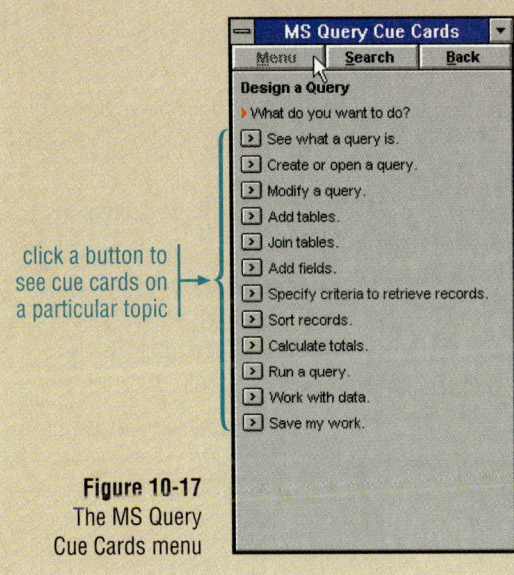

click a button to see cue cards on a particular topic

Figure 10-17
The MS Query Cue Cards menu

❷ Click the **See what a query is button** to display the What Is A Query? cue card. See Figure 10-18.

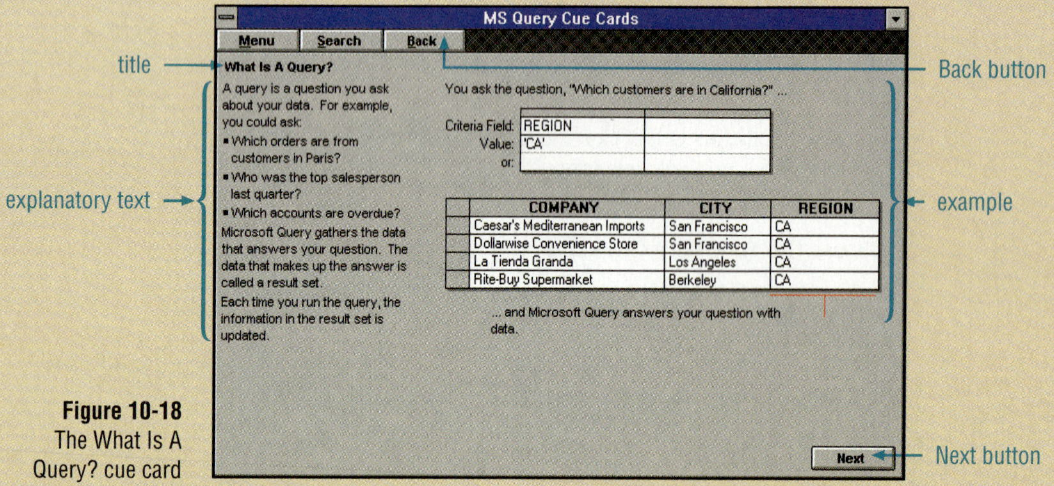

Figure 10-18
The What Is A Query? cue card

❸ Read the information on the cue card, then click the **Next button** to display the Why Use Querys? cue card.

❹ You can return to a previously viewed cue card using the Back button. Click the **Back button** to return to the What Is A Query cue card, then click the **Next button** to return to the Why Use Querys? cue card.

❺ Read the information on the Why Use Querys? cue card, then click the **Next button** to display the An Example of a Query cue card.

❻ Read the information on the An Example of a Query cue card, then click the **Next button** to return to the MS Query Cue Cards menu.

❼ You won't need the Cue Cards to proceed, so double-click the **MS Query Cue Cards Control menu box** to close the MS Query Cue Cards window.

The Microsoft Query Toolbar

When you launch MS Query from within Excel, the Query toolbar appears as shown in Figure 10-19.

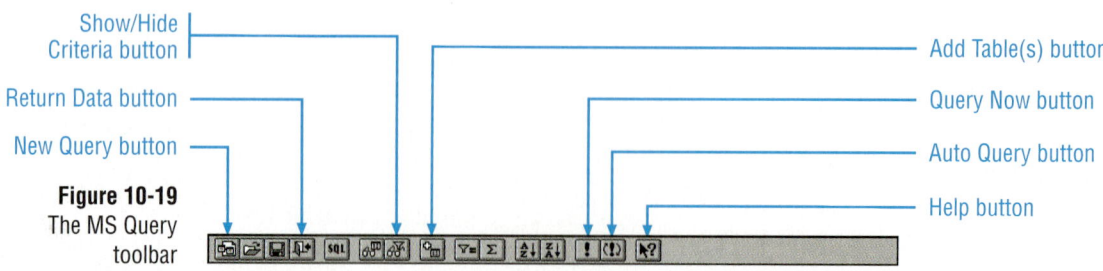

Figure 10-19
The MS Query toolbar

The toolbar buttons make it easy to perform tasks in MS Query. You will use only a few buttons in this tutorial. The New Query button opens the Select Data Source dialog box. The **Return Data button** sends the results of the query back to Excel. The **Show/Hide Criteria button** controls whether or not the Criteria pane is displayed in an MS Query window. (You'll learn more about the Criteria pane later in this tutorial.) The **Query Now button** performs the query. The **Auto Query button** controls whether or not MS Query automatically performs the query, and the **Help button** gives you access to MS Query Help.

Before Jennifer can create her query, she must first select her data source.

Selecting a Data Source

When you create a new query you have to select a data source for the query, telling MS Query the type of database file you want to work with.

> **REFERENCE WINDOW**
>
> ### Selecting a Data Source
>
> - If the Select Data Source dialog box is not already on the screen, click the New Query button (or click File, then click New Query...) to display the Select Data Source dialog box.
> - If the data source you want to use is *not* listed in the Available Data Sources list, click the Other... button to display the ODBC Data Sources dialog box.
> - Double-click the Data Source you want to use in the Enter Data Source list.
> - If you select MS Access Databases in the Enter Data Source list, the Select Database dialog box is displayed. Double-click the filename of the Access database you want to use.
> - Click the Use button in the Select Data Source dialog box.

Because the J. J. Svensen data is stored in an Access database, Jennifer chooses Access as her data source. Then she'll select the J. J. Svensen database, which is named SVENSEN.MDB.

To select the J. J. Svensen database:

❶ Click the **Other... button** in the Select Data Source dialog box to display the OBDC Data Sources dialog box.

❷ Click **MS Access Databases** in the Enter Data Source list. See Figure 10-20.

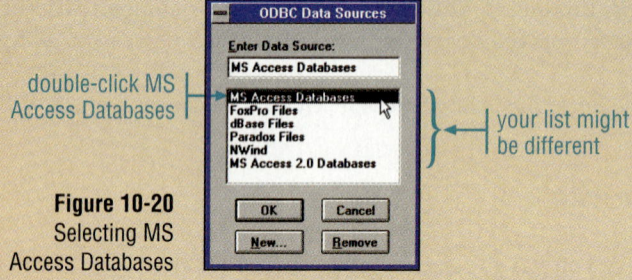

double-click MS Access Databases

your list might be different

Figure 10-20
Selecting MS Access Databases

❸ Click the **OK button** to open the Select Database dialog box. If necessary, click the Drives down arrow button and select the drive in which your Student Disk is located.

❹ Click **SVENSEN.MDB** in the Database Name list, then click the **OK button**. The Select Data Source dialog box reappears with MS Access Databases highlighted in the Available Data Sources list.

❺ Click the **Use button** in the Select Data Source dialog box. A query window appears with the Add Tables dialog box open. See Figure 10-21.

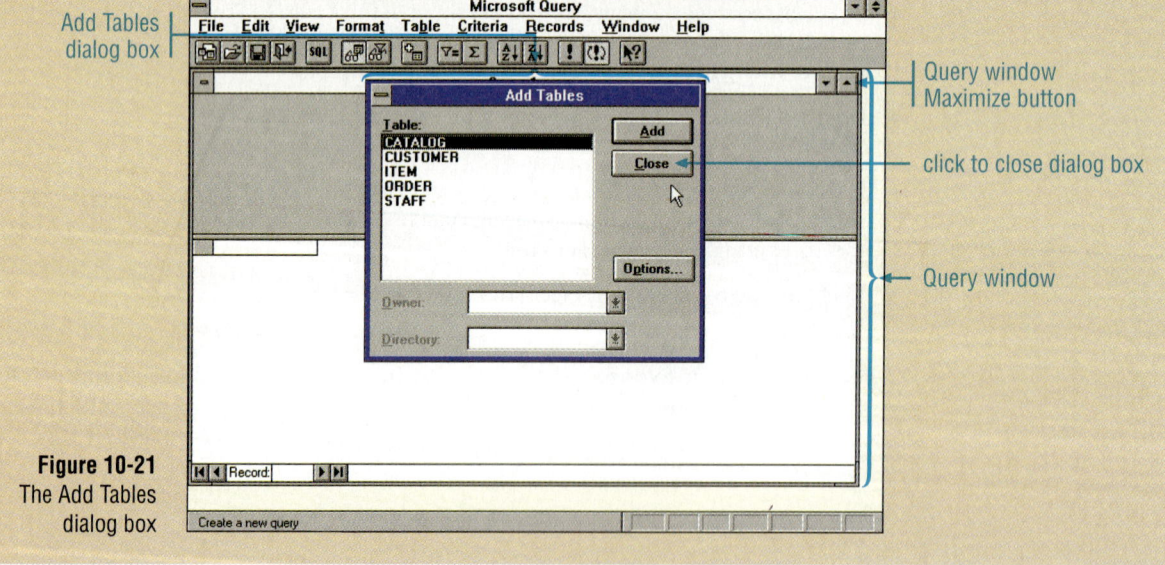

Add Tables dialog box

Query window Maximize button

click to close dialog box

Query window

Figure 10-21
The Add Tables dialog box

❻ You could select the tables to be included in the query at this time, but you'll do that later in this tutorial. Click the **Close button** to close the Add Tables dialog box, leaving the Query1 window active.

❼ If your Microsoft Query application window is *not* maximized, click the **Microsoft Query window Maximize button**.

❽ Click the **Query1 window Maximize button**. (See Figure 10-21.)

❾ Click the **Show/Hide Criteria button** to display the Criteria Pane. See Figure 10-22.

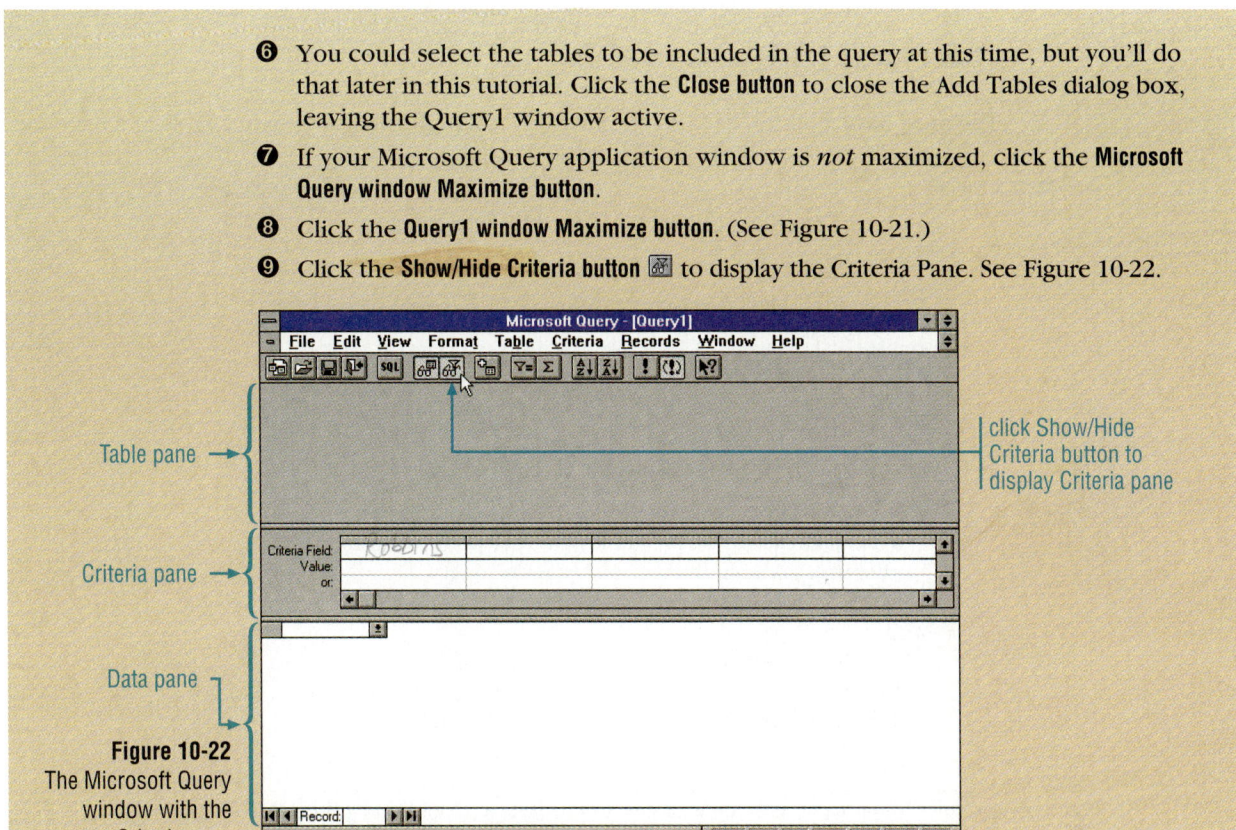

Figure 10-22
The Microsoft Query window with the Criteria pane

The Query1 window contains three partitions, or panes: the Table pane, the Criteria pane, and the Data pane. The tables you use in your query are displayed in the Table pane. You enter your search criteria in the Criteria pane. The **criteria** are the values you want MS Query to search for. For example, to ask the question "Did anyone with the last name 'Robbins' place an order with J. J. Svenson?" you would enter "Robbins" as your criteria and then ask MS Query to search for all records that match this criteria. The answer to your question—in this case, all the records for customers named Robbins—is the **result set**. The result set is displayed in the Data pane.

Jennifer is now ready to create the query that lists the contents of the J. J. Svensen catalog.

Querying Only One Table

The most basic queries, like the one Jennifer will perform, use only one table in a database.

> **REFERENCE WINDOW**
>
> **Creating a Query that Uses Only One Table**
>
> - Click the Add Table(s) button to display the Add Tables dialog box.
> - Double-click the name of the table you want to query (or click the table name, then click the Add button).
> - Click the Close button.
> - Select the fields you want to include in the query results:
>
>   Double-click the field names of each field you want in the query in the table field list in the Table pane. Select the fields in the order that you want them displayed in the query.
>
>   *or*
>
>   Drag the field names from the table field list in the Table pane to the blank column field name box in the Data pane. Select the fields in the order that you want them displayed in the query.
>
>   *or*
>
>   If you want to include all fields in the query, double-click the asterisk at the top of the table field list in the Table pane. The fields will be displayed in same order as in the table.
>
> - To specify criteria, drag the field name from the table field list in the Table pane to a blank criteria field name box in the Criteria pane, then enter the value or condition in the text boxes below the field name.
> - If the Automatic Query option is on (indicated by a depressed Auto Query button on the toolbar), the results of the query (the result set) are immediately displayed in the Data pane. If the Automatic Query option is not on, click the Query Now button (or click Query Now in the Records menu).
> - To return the query results to Excel, click the Return Data button.

Jennifer's query will use only one table, the CATALOG table. She'll add the CATALOG table to the Table pane using the Add Tables dialog box.

To list the J. J. Svensen catalog query:

❶ Click the **Add Table(s) button** to display the Add Tables dialog box. See Figure 10-23.

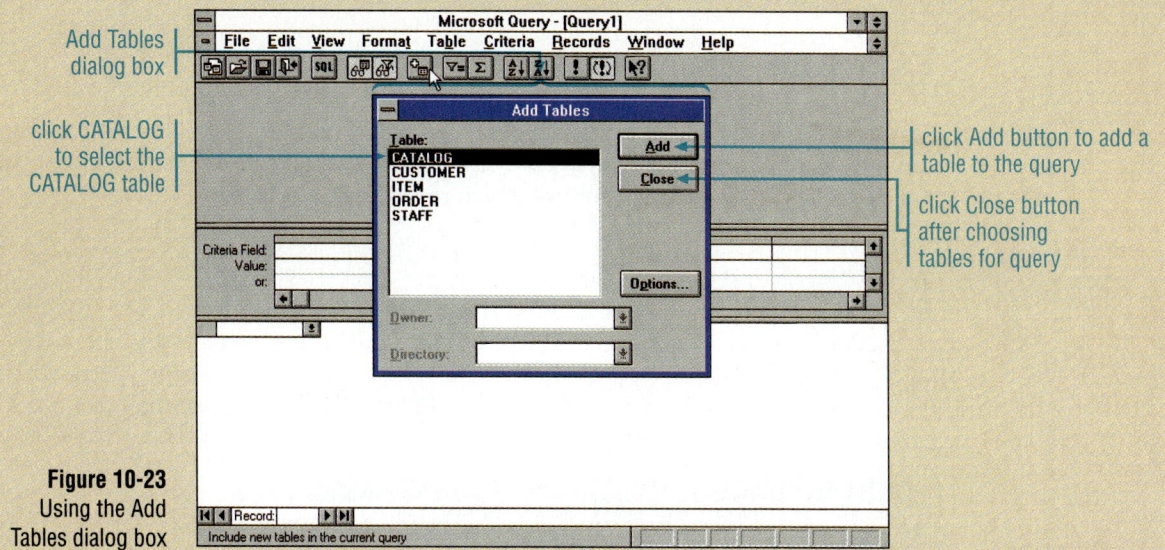

Figure 10-23
Using the Add Tables dialog box

❷ Click **CATALOG** in the Table list, then click the **Add button**. The CATALOG table appears as a field list in the Tables pane.

❸ Click the **Close button**.

❹ To display all the fields in the table, double-click the ***** (asterisk) at the top of the CATALOG field list. The result of the query—all the records in the table—appears in the Data pane. Use the horizontal scroll bar to scroll to the leftmost column in the Data pane. See Figure 10-24.

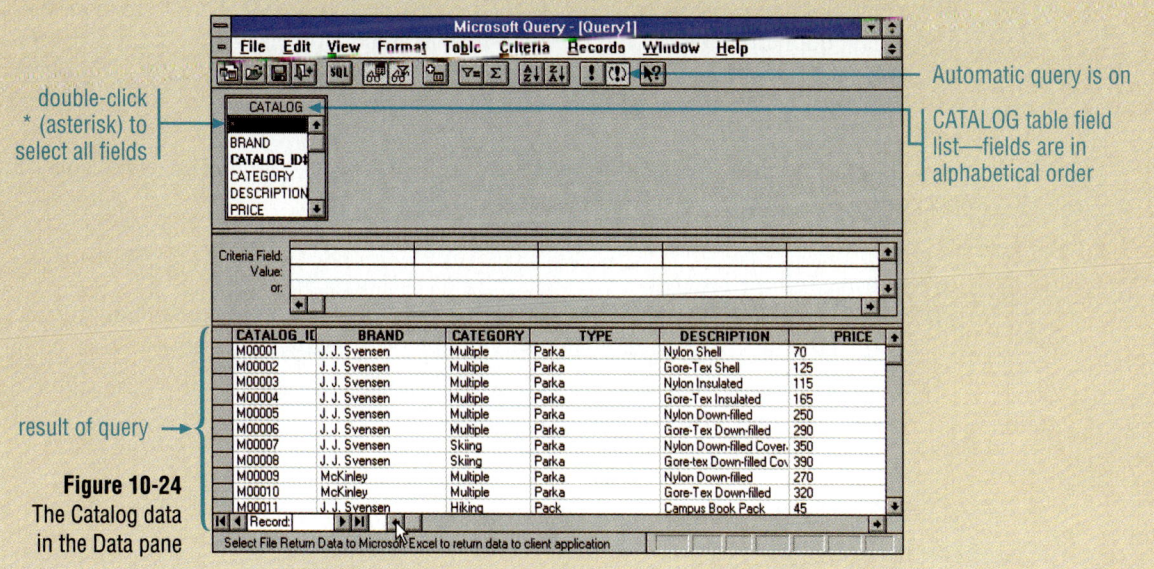

Figure 10-24
The Catalog data in the Data pane

Jennifer's query asked for a list of all the products in the CATALOG table. She could have asked for a partial list of the products, for example only the parkas, by creating a criteria for the query.

Using the Criteria Pane

Criteria are values you enter to tell MS Query what records to look for. For example, if Jennifer wants to find only parkas in the CATALOG table, she enters the criteria *parka*. Let's use the Criteria pane to control which records are displayed.

To use criteria to select only parkas:
❶ Scroll through the CATALOG field list until you see the field name TYPE. Drag the field name **TYPE** from the CATALOG field list to the first Criteria Field cell in the Criteria pane. As you drag the field name, the pointer changes shape. When you release the mouse button, the field name TYPE appears in the cell along with a down arrow button. See Figure 10-25.

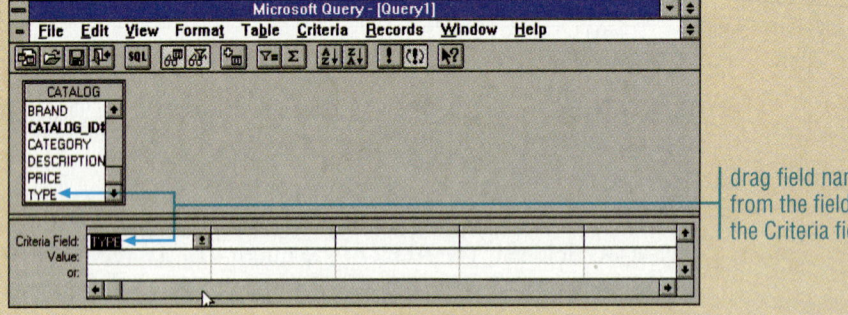

Figure 10-25
Dragging the field name to the Criteria pane

drag field name TYPE from the field list to the Criteria field

❷ Click the Value cell directly below the field name TYPE. Type **'Parka'** (include the single quotation marks), then press **[Enter]**. MS Query displays only the records for parkas.

Because Jennifer needs a complete list of the products, you'll need to redisplay all the records (not just the records for parkas).

To redisplay all the records:
❶ In the Criteria pane, move the pointer to the top of the column containing the TYPE criteria. The pointer changes to a thick black arrow.
❷ Click to select the column, then press **[Del]** to delete the column from the Criteria pane. MS Query restores the original query.

Now Jennifer needs to return the results of the query to Excel.

To return the results of the query to Excel:

❶ Click the **Return Data button** to copy the data to Excel. The Excel window appears with the Get External Data dialog box displayed. Notice that Keep Query Definition and Include Field Names options are checked. The Keep Query Definition option tells Excel to store a copy of the query with the Excel workbook, allowing you to easily update the query results at a later time. The Include Field Names option allows you to list the field names from the query results in the Excel worksheet.

❷ Click the **OK button**.

❸ The Catalog sheet appears with the catalog data. Press **[Ctrl][Home]** to remove the highlighting. The Catalog sheet appears. See Figure 10-26.

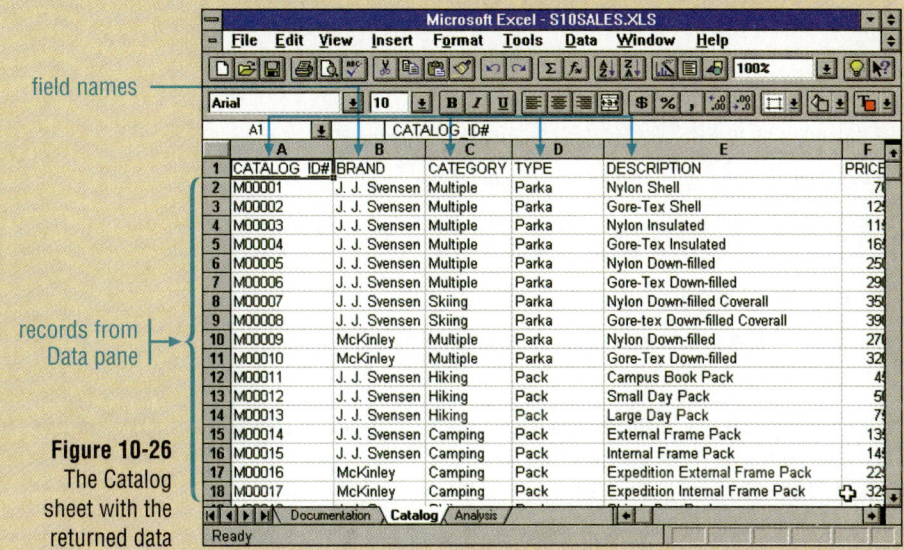

Figure 10-26
The Catalog sheet with the returned data

❹ Format the data in column F as Currency with two decimal places, and adjust the width of column F so that the prices are properly displayed.

❺ Press **[Ctrl][Home]**, then click the **Save button** to save the workbook.

❻ Press **[Ctrl][Esc]** to display the Task List dialog box, then double-click **Microsoft Query** to switch to MS query.

❼ Click **File** in the MS Query menu, then click **Exit** to close MS Query.

❽ If Excel is not the active application, press **[Ctrl][Esc]** to display the Task List dialog box, then double-click **Microsoft Excel - S10SALES.XLS** to switch to Excel.

Jennifer now has the catalog list data she needs for her report. Because the Keep Query Definition box was checked (in Step 1 above), changes to the CATALOG table in the original Access database are reflected in the Excel worksheet. Excel and MS Query use Dynamic Data Exchange to link the result set in MS Query to the copy of the result set in the Excel worksheet.

How Dynamic Data Exchange (DDE) Works

Dynamic Data Exchange (DDE) places material in a client application that is linked to material in a source (or server) application. When the original data changes, so does the linked copy. To edit linked data, you must work within the source document in the server application.

The changes to the copy in the client application (in this case, Excel) are not made automatically. You need to update, or refresh, the result set in the client application whenever you edit the data in the source application. In Excel, you use the Get External Data... command on the Data menu to update the result set.

REFERENCE WINDOW

Updating a Result Set in Excel

- Click any cell in the Excel result set you want to update.
- Click Data, then click Get External Data....
- Click the Refresh button. MS Query is launched if it is not open, and the updated result set is returned to Excel.
- Return to the MS Query window and exit MS Query.
- Return to Excel to see the updated result set.

Let's assume that Jennifer's assistant has just added a new item to the catalog list in the Access database. This means that Jennifer must update her result set in the Catalog sheet to include the new product.

To update the result set:
1. Make sure the Catalog sheet is active.
2. Click cell **A1**.
3. Click **Data**, then click **Get External Data...**. The Get External Data dialog box appears.
4. Click the **Refresh button**. Updating the result set might take a couple of minutes, depending on your computer.
5. When the update is complete, the result set is highlighted. Press **[Ctrl][Home]** to remove the highlighting.
6. Click the **Save button** to save the workbook.
7. Press **[Ctrl][Esc]** to display the Task List dialog box, then double-click **Microsoft Query** to switch to MS Query.
8. In the MS Query menu, click **File**, then click **Exit** to close MS Query.
9. If Excel is not the active application, press **[Ctrl][Esc]** to display the Task List dialog box, then double-click **Microsoft Excel - S10SALES.XLS** to switch to Excel.

Jennifer has completed creating the catalog list for her report. Her next task is to retrieve and analyze the sales data using the PivotTable Wizard. Then she'll transfer the catalog list and the PivotTable to her Write document.

If you want to take a break and resume the tutorial at a later time, you can exit Excel by double-clicking the Control menu box in the upper-left corner of the screen. When you resume the tutorial, launch Excel, maximize the Microsoft Excel and Book1 windows, and place your Student Disk in the disk drive. Open the file S10SALES.XLS, then continue with the tutorial.

Querying More Than One Table

Jennifer wants to analyze J. J. Svensen sales by tallying the total sales of each item in the catalog for both sales regions. Jennifer will use an Excel PivotTable, which you learned about in Tutorial 7, to create her analysis. She will use MS Query to retrieve data she needs for the PivotTable from the Svensen database.

For this query Jennifer needs to combine data from *three* tables: ORDER, ITEM, and CATALOG.

To create a query that combines data from more than one table, the tables in the query must be linked using the common fields in the tables. The matching data from each of the linked tables are linked and displayed together in the query results.

For example, if John Ehren calls with a question about his last order, you need to combine the data on John Ehren in the CUSTOMER table with the data on the orders he's made from the ORDER table using the link between the CUSTOMER and ORDER tables, which is the common field CUST_ID#. The result will be data on John Ehren (from the CUSTOMER table) and every order he's made (from the ORDERS table). Figure 10-27 shows the results.

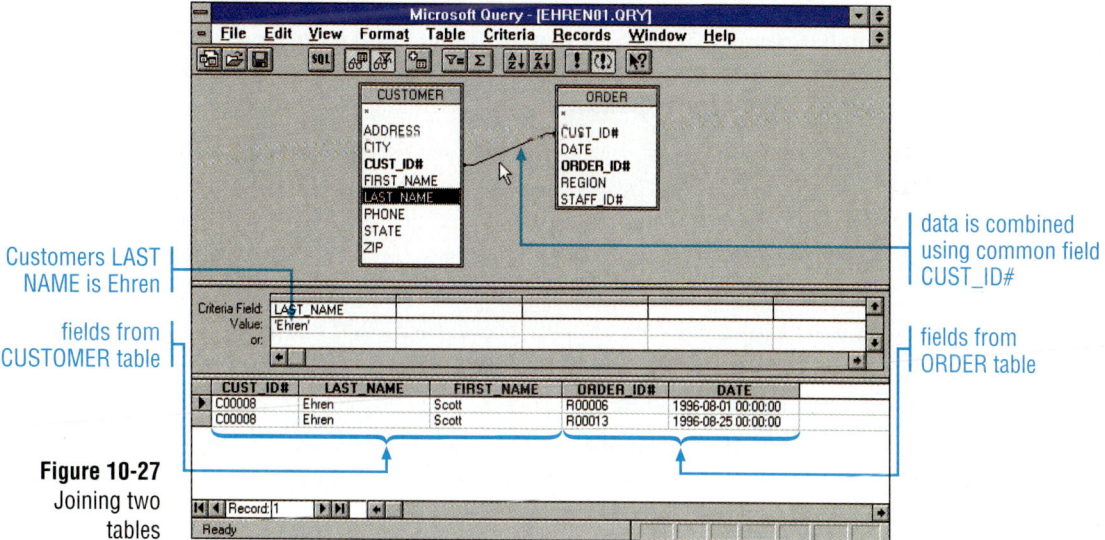

Figure 10-27 Joining two tables

In a properly constructed database, such as the J. J. Svenson database, the links between tables are already established and appear in the Table Pane when you select your tables. See Figure 10-27.

When creating a query with two or more tables you must select the fields from each table that you want to appear in the result set.

> **REFERENCE WINDOW**
>
> ### Creating a Query that Uses Two or More Tables
>
> - Click the Add Tables button on the MS Query toolbar to display the Add Tables dialog box.
> - Click the name of each table you want to query, then click the Add button until all tables are listed.
> - Click the Close button.
> - Double-click the field names of each field you want to include in the query or drag the field names to a blank field name box. (The field names are located in the table field lists in the Table pane.) Select the fields in the order that you want them displayed in the query.
> - To specify criteria, drag field names from the Table pane to a blank criteria cell in the Criteria pane, then enter the value or condition in the text boxes below the field name.
> - If the Automatic Query option is on (indicated by a depressed Auto Query button on the toolbar), the results of the query are displayed immediately in the Data pane. If the Automatic Query option is not on, click the Query Now button (or click Query Now in the Records menu).
> - To return the query results to Excel, click the Return Data button.

Jennifer wants to know, How many of each product were sold in each region? The answer to this question will be the data Jennifer needs to create a PivotTable.

Jennifer starts the PivotTable Wizard.

To start creating the PivotTable:

❶ Make sure the Catalog sheet is active.

❷ Click **Data**, then click **PivotTable...** to display the PivotTable Wizard - Step 1 of 4 dialog box.

❸ Click the **External Data Source option button**, then click the **Next >** button to display the PivotTable Wizard - Step 2 of 4 dialog box.

❹ Click the **Get Data...** button. The Microsoft Query window appears.

❺ Double-click the **MS Query Cue Cards Control menu box** to close the Cue Cards window.

❻ Make sure the drive containing your Student Disk is selected, then double-click **MS Access Databases** in the Available Data Sources list of the Select Data Source dialog box.

❼ Click **SVENSEN.MDB** in the Database Name list, then click the **OK button**. The Select Data Source dialog box reappears briefly with MS Access Databases highlighted in the Available Data Sources list, then a query window appears with the Add Tables dialog box on top.

Now Jennifer selects the tables she needs for her query. She needs to combine data from the ORDER, ITEM, and CATALOG tables.

To add the ORDER, ITEM, and CATALOG tables to the query:
1. Click **ORDER** in the Add Tables dialog box, then click the **Add button** to add the ORDER table to the query. The ORDER table appears in the Table pane.
2. Click **ITEM**, then click the Add button to add the ITEM table to the query. The ITEM table appears in the Table pane.
3. Click **CATALOG**, then click the Add button to add the CATALOG table to the query. The CATALOG table appears in the Table pane.
4. Click the **Close button**, then maximize the Query1 window. See Figure 10-28. Notice the links between the common fields.

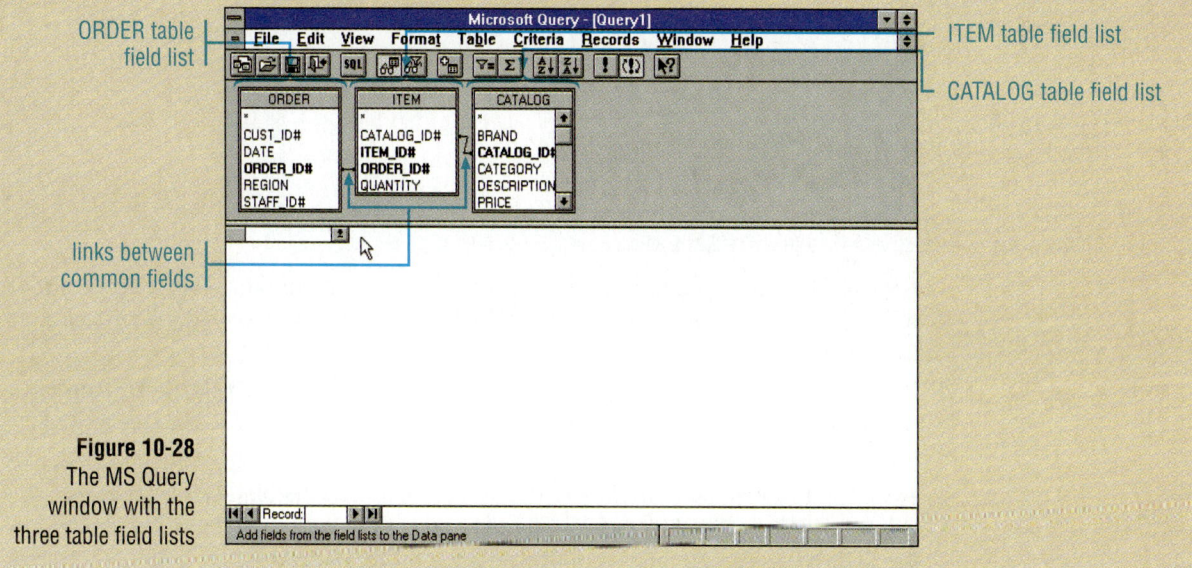

Figure 10-28
The MS Query window with the three table field lists

Now Jennifer can create her query. Jennifer wants all the data in each field, not just data matching certain criteria. She does not have to specify any criteria, so there is no need to open the Criteria pane.

To build the query:

❶ From the ORDER table, drag the ORDER_ID# field name to the blank text box in the Data pane. The ORDER_ID# field is added to the query, and the results are shown in the Data pane. A new, blank column appears in the Data pane. See Figure 10-29.

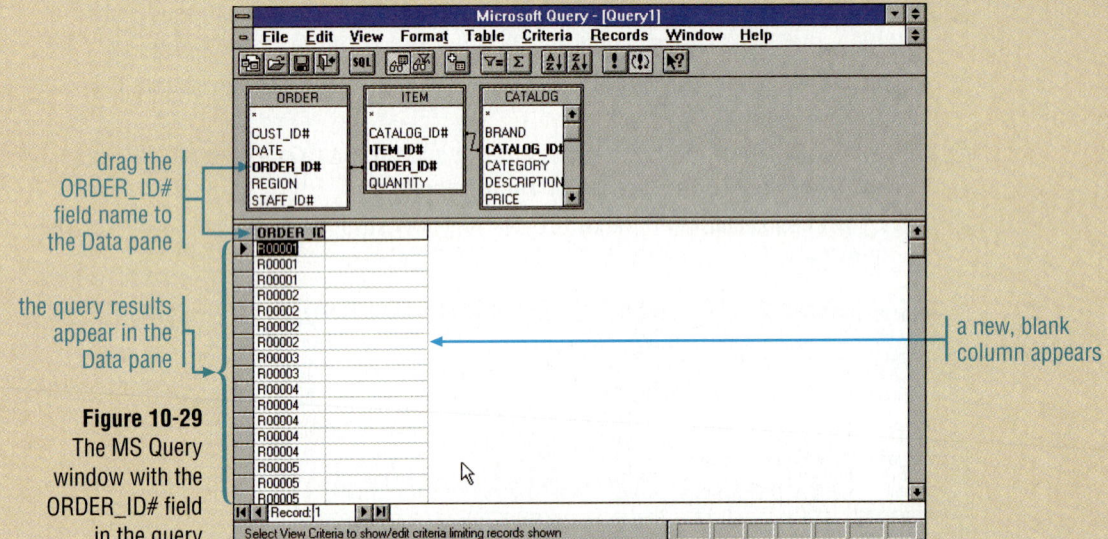

drag the ORDER_ID# field name to the Data pane

the query results appear in the Data pane

a new, blank column appears

Figure 10-29
The MS Query window with the ORDER_ID# field in the query

Because the Auto Query button is depressed, MS Query automatically executes the query as you create it. The result set changes with each field or criteria you add to the query.

❷ From the ORDER table, drag the REGION field name to the text box at the top of the blank column in the Data pane. The REGION field is added to the query, and the results are updated in the Data pane.

❸ From the ITEM table, drag the ITEM_ID# field name to the blank column in the Data pane. The ITEM_ID# field is added to the query, and the results are updated in the Data pane. A new, blank column appears in the Data pane.

❹ From the ITEM table, drag the QUANTITY field name to the blank column in the Data pane. The QUANTITY field is added to the query, and the results are updated in the Data pane.

❺ From the CATALOG table, drag the CATALOG_ID# field name to the blank column in the Data pane. The CATALOG_ID# field is added to the query, and the results are updated in the Data pane.

❻ In the CATALOG table, scroll until you see the TYPE field name, then drag it to the blank column in the Data pane. The TYPE field is added to the query, and the results are shown in the Data pane. The MS Query window appears as shown in Figure 10-30.

Querying More Than One Table   **EX 365**

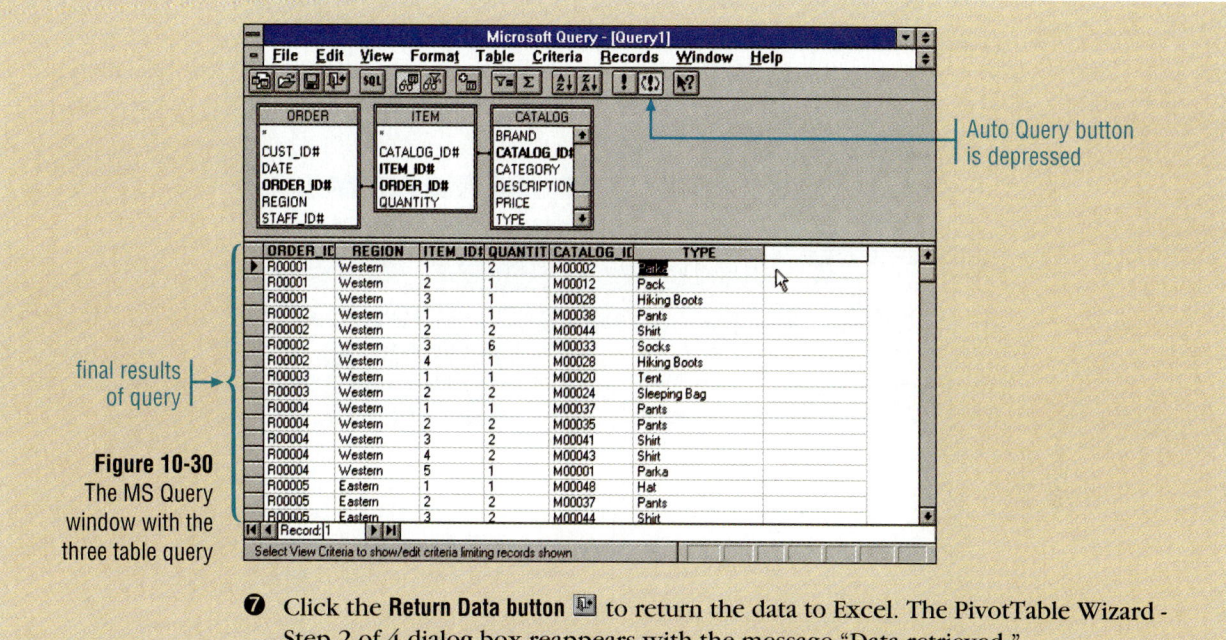

Figure 10-30
The MS Query window with the three table query

➐ Click the **Return Data button** to return the data to Excel. The PivotTable Wizard - Step 2 of 4 dialog box reappears with the message "Data retrieved."

Now that Jennifer has retrieved the data, she can finish creating her PivotTable. She wants her PivotTable to show the regional sales for each product, so she will use product type and regions to form the rows and columns of the PivotTable.

To complete the pivot table:
➊ Click the **Next > button**. After a pause the PivotTable Wizard - Step 3 of 4 dialog box appears.
➋ Click the **REGION button** and drag it to the COLUMN section of the sample PivotTable.
➌ Click the **TYPE button** and drag it to the ROW section of the sample PivotTable.
➍ Click the **QUANTITY button** and drag it to the DATA section of the sample PivotTable. The PivotTable Wizard automatically sums the values in the data field and displays Sum of QUANTITY.
➎ Click the **Next > button**. The PivotTable Wizard - Step 4 of 4 dialog box appears.
➏ Click the **PivotTable Starting Cell text box**, click the **Analysis tab**, then click cell **A4** to display the cell address Analysis!$A$4 in the PivotTable Starting Cell box.
➐ Click the **PivotTable Name text box**, and change the text to **SalesAnalysis**.

8. Click the **Finish button** to close the dialog box. The completed PivotTable appears in the Analysis worksheet. See Figure 10-31. You do not need to close MS Query. When you create a PivotTable, MS Query automatically closes after the result set is returned to Excel.

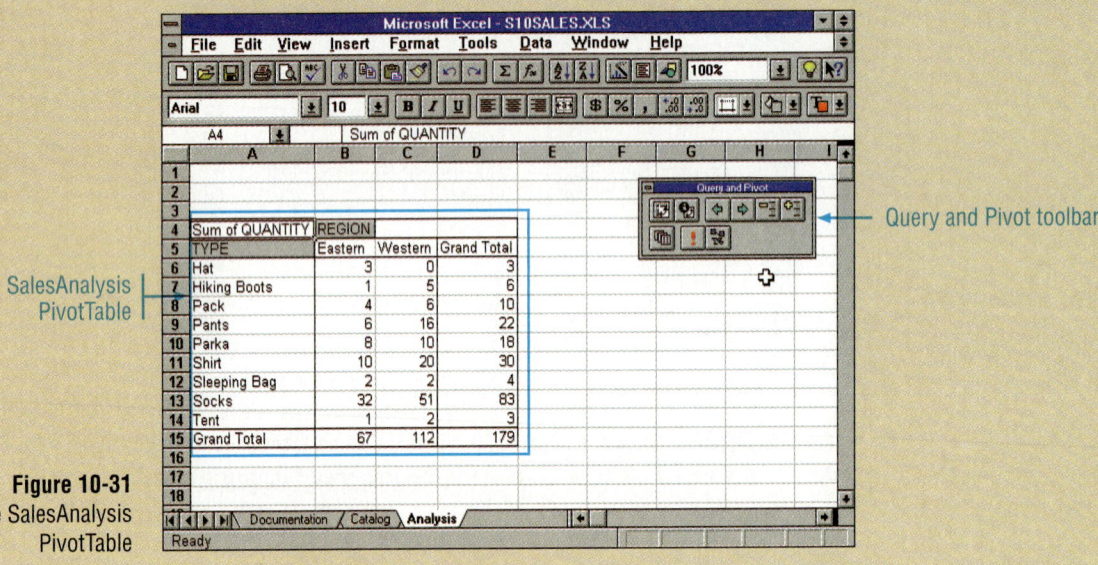

Figure 10-31
The SalesAnalysis PivotTable

TROUBLE? If you don't see the Query and Pivot toolbar, right-click the toolbar to display the Toolbar menu. Click Toolbars..., click the Query & Pivot checkbox, then click the OK button.

The J. J. Svensen management traditionally groups the products into three categories: Clothing, which contains data on hats, pants, parkas, and shirts; Boots and Socks, which contains data on hiking boots and socks; and Camping, which contains data on packs, sleeping bags, and tents. To complete her analysis in the PivotTable, Jennifer needs to group the products into these categories. She can do this using the tools in the Query and Pivot toolbar.

Grouping PivotTable Data

The Query and Pivot toolbar provides a set of tools for modifying PivotTables. See Figure 10-32.

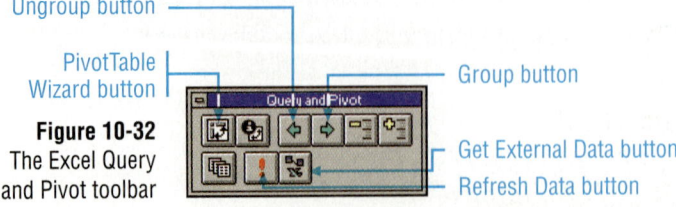

Figure 10-32
The Excel Query and Pivot toolbar

The **PivotTable Wizard button** starts the PivotTable Wizard, which allows you to create or modify a PivotTable. You use the **Ungroup** and **Group buttons** to create or delete groups of field categories in the PivotTable. You use the **Refresh Data** and **Get External Data... buttons** to update a query. You see the Get External Data button... on the toolbar only when you create a PivotTable using the Get External Data... command.

Jennifer will use the Group Button on the Query and Pivot toolbar to create her product groupings.

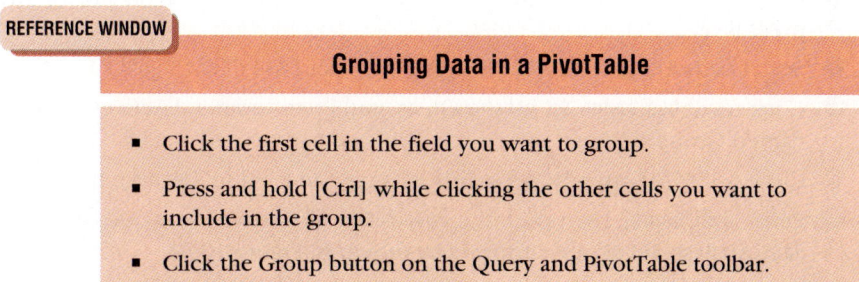

REFERENCE WINDOW

Grouping Data in a PivotTable

- Click the first cell in the field you want to group.
- Press and hold [Ctrl] while clicking the other cells you want to include in the group.
- Click the Group button on the Query and PivotTable toolbar.

Jennifer is ready to group the products into the three categories: Clothing, Boots and Socks, and Camping.

To group the items in the SalesAnalysis PivotTable:

❶ Select the nonadjacent cells **A6** (Hat), **A9** (Pants), **A10** (Parka), and **A11** (Shirt).

TROUBLE? Recall that to select nonadjacent cells you press and hold [Ctrl] while you select the cells with the mouse.

❷ Click the **Group button** on the Query and Pivot toolbar. A new field button labeled TYPE2 is added to the table, and Hat, Pants, Parka, and Shirt are grouped as part of a group named Group1. See Figure 10-33.

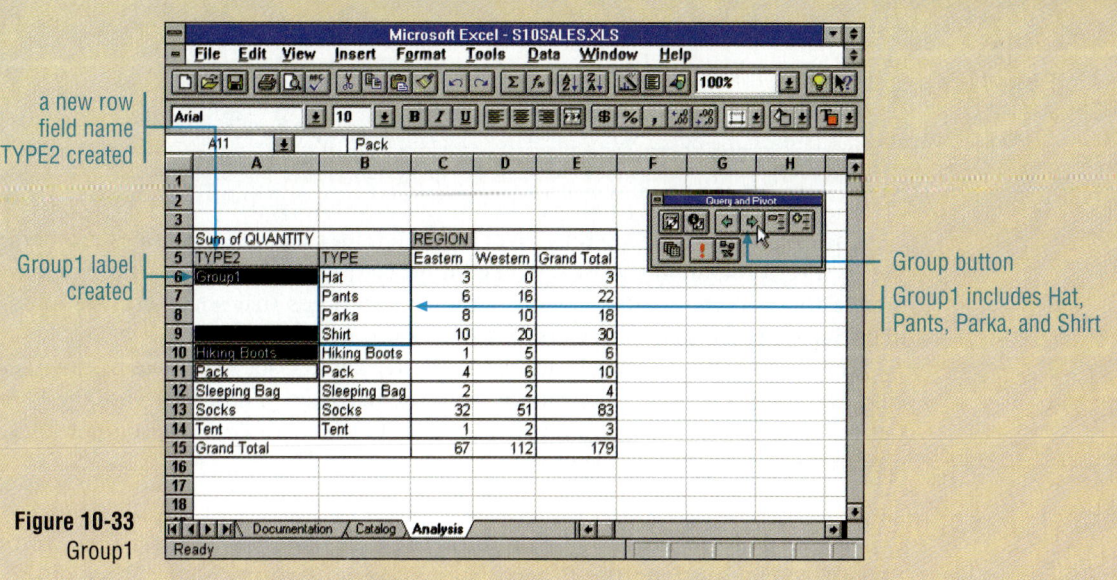

Figure 10-33
Group1

❸ Click cell **A6** (Group1), press [F2], change the label to **Clothing**, and then press [Enter].

TROUBLE? If the PivotTable became smaller by two rows and the labels Hat, Parka, and Shirt in Column B disappeared, you double-clicked cell A6. To edit a cell in a PivotTable you must click only once, then press [F2]. To continue, double-click cell A6 to expand the PivotTable, then press [F2] to edit the label.

❹ Select cells **A10** (Hiking Boots) and **A13** (Socks).

⑤ Click the **Group button** on the Query and Pivot toolbar. Excel creates a new group named Group2.

⑥ Click cell **A10** (Group2), press **[F2]**, change the label to **Boots and Socks**, then press **[Enter]**.

⑦ Select cells **A12** (Pack), **A13** (Sleeping Bag), and **A14** (Tent).

⑧ Click the **Group button** on the Query and Pivot toolbar. Excel creates a new group named Group3.

⑨ Click cell **A12** (Group3), press **[F2]**, change the label to **Camping**, then press **[Enter]**.

⑩ Press **[Ctrl][Home]**, then click the **Save button** to save the workbook. The SalesAnalysis PivotTable appears as shown in Figure 10-34.

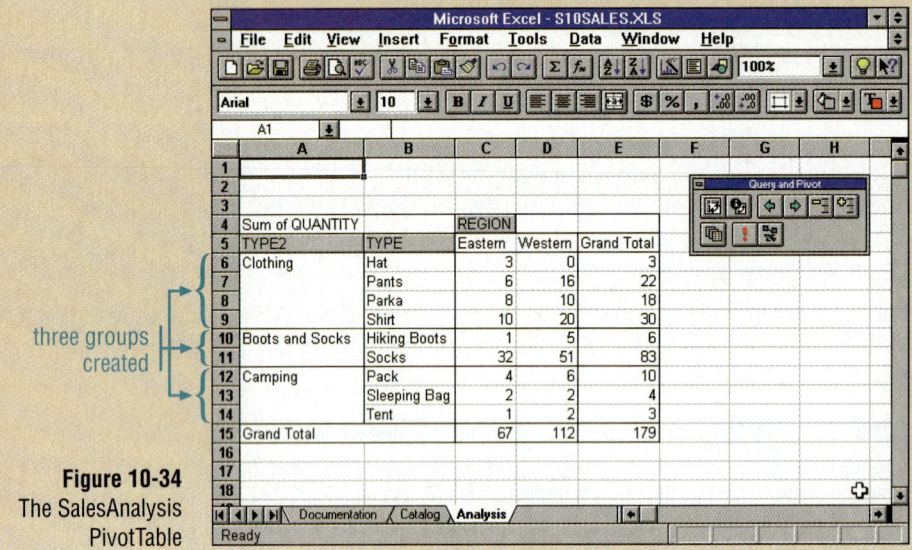

Figure 10-34
The SalesAnalysis PivotTable

Looking at the SalesAnalysis PivotTable, Jennifer can see that sales are better in the Western region than in the Eastern region. In fact, sales in the Western region are almost double those in the Eastern region. Jennifer also notes that socks are the most popular item. She will mention these facts in her sales report.

The data in the PivotTable are linked by Dynamic Data Exchange to the Access database, so the next time her assistant updates the database, Jennifer can use the Refresh button on the Query and Pivot toolbar to update her PivotTable, ensuring her sales analysis uses the most current sales figures.

If you want to take a break and resume the tutorial at a later time, you can exit Excel by double-clicking the Control menu box in the upper-left corner of the screen. When you resume the tutorial, launch Excel, maximize the Microsoft Excel and Book1 windows, and place your Student Disk in the disk drive. Open the file S10SALES.XLS, then continue with the tutorial.

Jennifer is ready to complete her sales report. She needs to write the text of the report and transfer the catalog list and PivotTable to the Write document. To save time, we'll open a file that contains Jennifer's finished text. After opening the file C10RPRT2.WRI we'll save it as S10RPRT2.WRI.

To launch Write and open the sales report:

❶ Press **[Ctrl][Esc]** to access the Task List dialog box, then double-click **Program Manager** in the Task List. The Program Manager window appears. In the Accessories group, double-click the **Write icon** to open Write.

❷ Click the **Write application window Maximize button**.

❸ Click **Document**, then click **Ruler On**.

❹ Click **File**, then click **Open...** to display the Open dialog box. If necessary, click the **Drives down arrow button** and select the drive in which your Student Disk is located.

❺ Double-click **C10RPRT2.WRI** in the File Name box to display the report.

❻ Click **File**, then click **Save As...** to display the Save As dialog box.

❼ Change the filename to **S10RPRT2.WRI**, then click the **OK button**.

❽ Scroll through the report. Read the explanatory material Jennifer has written.

The text of Jennifer's report explains the results of her sales analysis. Now Jennifer will add the catalog list and the PivotTable to her report. She could use the Paste command on the Edit menu to paste the catalog list in the report, producing an unformatted copy of the catalog list with no links or connections to the original data. But Jennifer knows that sales figures are occasionally corrected when discrepancies or incomplete data are discovered, so she decides to create a link between the numbers in her report and the numbers in the Excel worksheet. Then, if she updates the numbers in the worksheet (using the Refresh command on the Data menu for the catalog list and the Refresh button on the Query and Pivot toolbar for the PivotTable), the numbers in the report will be updated automatically via the links. She will use OLE to link her Excel workbook file to her Write sales report file.

Using Object Linking and Embedding (OLE) to Link Files

You have used Object Linking and Embedding (OLE) to embed data. Now, you'll use OLE to link data. Remember that OLE copies source material from a server application to a document in a client application. Changes made to the original document are reflected in the linked copy. You edit linked data by activating the source application, the same way you edited embedded data.

Jennifer will use the copy and paste link commands to add the catalog list to page two of the sales report. Excel is the source application because the information Jennifer is looking for is on the Catalog sheet of an Excel workbook. Write is the client application because Jennifer will paste the information in a Write document.

> **REFERENCE WINDOW**
>
> ### Using Excel as an OLE Server for a Write Document
>
> - Launch Excel and open or create the workbook you want to link.
> - Launch Write and open or create the document where you will place the linked material.
> - Select the range in the Excel workbook that you want to link to the Write document.
> - Click the Copy button to copy the information to the Clipboard.
> - In the Write document, position the insertion point where you want to insert the linked material.
> - Click Edit, then click Paste Link....

Jennifer wants to place the catalog list on the second page of her report, titled J. J. Svensen Catalog.

To copy the catalog list from the Excel workbook and paste it as a linked object in the Write document:

1. Press **[Ctrl][Esc]** to open the Task List dialog box, then double-click **Microsoft Excel - S10SALES.XLS** in the Task List. The Excel window appears.

2. Click the **Catalog tab** to display the Catalog worksheet.

3. Highlight the range A1:F49, which contains the data you want to include in the sales report.

4. Click the **Copy button**. Excel copies the data to the Clipboard. Now you can return to the Write application window and paste the data in the sales report.

5. Press **[Ctrl][Esc]** to display the Task List dialog box and then double-click **Write - S10RPRT2.WRI**. The Write window appears.

6. Scroll down until a dashed line representing a page break appears. The title "J. J. Svensen Catalog" appears just below the page break. Click at the end of the title, then press **[Enter]** twice to move the insertion point to the second blank line below the title.

⏺ Click **Edit**, then click **Paste Link....** The data is copied from the Clipboard into the document as a linked object. See Figure 10-35.

this Excel worksheet object is linked to the data in the Catalog worksheet

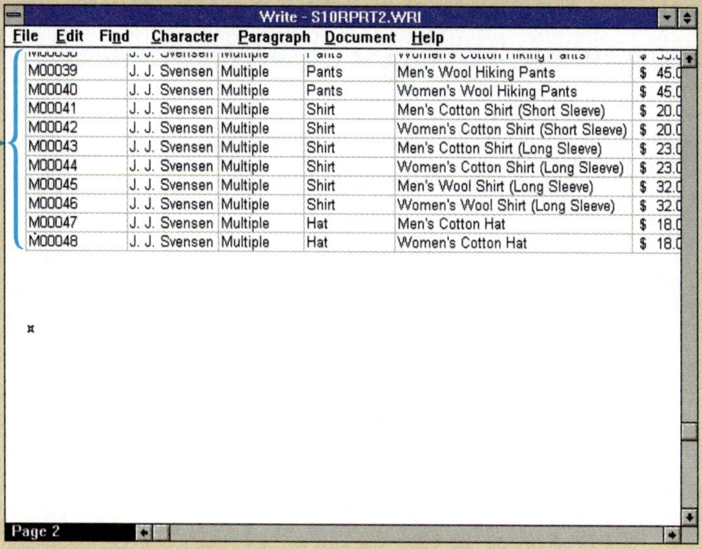

Figure 10-35
The catalog data in the report

Now you need to clear the Copy command in Excel.

⏺ Press **[Ctrl][Esc]** to display the Task List dialog box, then double-click **Microsoft Excel - S10SALES.XLS** in the Task List. Notice that the marquee, the moving dashes that surround the highlighted range, is still running and the message "Select destination and press ENTER or choose Paste" is still displayed in the status line. Press **[Esc]** to end the Copy command (this also deletes the contents of the Clipboard), then press **[Ctrl][Home]**.

⏺ Press **[Ctrl][Esc]** to display the Task List dialog box and then double-click **Write - S10RPRT2.WRI**. The Write window appears with the catalog list in place.

Jennifer has just created a link between her report and the Excel S9SALES.XLS workbook using Object Linking and Embedding (OLE). The next time her assistant updates the Access database, Jennifer will refresh the data in her Excel workbook. When she refreshes the data in the workbook, the changes will automatically show up in her Write document.

Jennifer now adds the PivotTable to her report using an OLE link.

To add the PivotTable analysis to the report:

⏺ In the Write window, press **[Ctrl][Home]** to return to the beginning of the report.

⏺ Press **[Ctrl][Esc]** to display the Task List dialog box, then double-click **Microsoft Excel - S10SALES.XLS**.

⏺ Click the **Analysis tab** to display the Analysis worksheet, then highlight the range A4:E15, which contains the PivotTable.

⏺ Click the **Copy button**. Excel copies the range to the Clipboard.

⏺ Press **[Ctrl][Esc]** to display the Task List dialog box and then double-click **Write - S10RPRT2.WRI** to display the Write window.

⏺ Click two lines below the second paragraph of the report text on page one.

7. Click **Edit**, then click **Paste Link....** The PivotTable is inserted in the document as a linked object.

8. Scroll until you see the report and the PivotTable. See Figure 10-36.

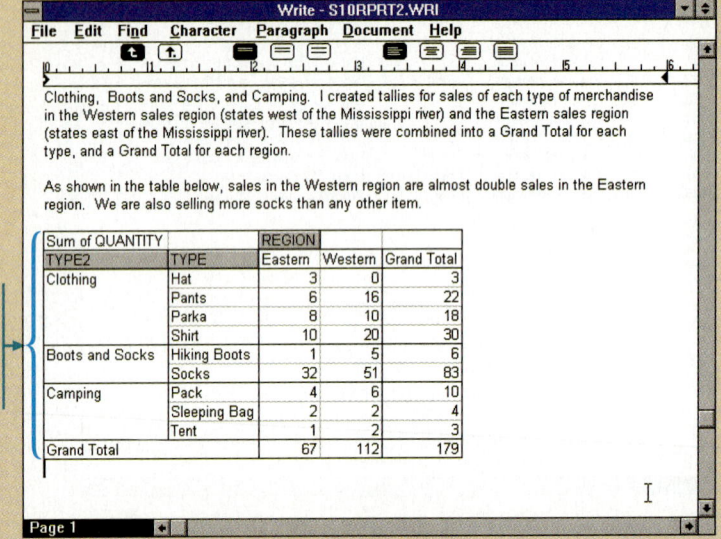

this is another Excel worksheet object linked to the data in the Analysis worksheet

Figure 10-36
The PivotTable analysis in the sales report

9. Press **[Ctrl][Esc]** to display the Task List dialog box, then double-click **Microsoft Excel - S10SALES.XLS** in the Task List. Press **[Esc]** to end the Copy command, then press **[Ctrl][Home]**.

10. Press **[Ctrl][Esc]** to display the Task List dialog box and then double-click **Write - S10RPRT2.WRI**. Click **File**, then click **Save** to save the Write file S10RPRT2.WRI.

Using Excel as an OLE Client and Paintbrush as an OLE Server

To have the J. J. Svensen sales department organization diagram handy in case she wants to use it as a graphic on future worksheets, Jennifer decides to add the diagram to her workbook. This means she will use Excel as an OLE client.

In the previous section you used Excel as an OLE server (or source application). When you embed and link OLE objects from other applications in an Excel Workbook, you use Excel as an OLE client. In fact, you already used Excel as an OLE client in Tutorial 5, when you used the Paintbrush money picture in the bar chart.

Using Object Linking and Embedding (OLE) to Link Files   **EX 373**

> **REFERENCE WINDOW**
>
> ### Using Excel as an OLE Client for a Paintbrush Graphic Image
>
> - Launch Paintbrush and open or create the graphic image you want to link.
> - Launch Excel and open or create the worksheet in which you will place the linked material.
> - In Paintbrush, select the image you want to link to the Excel worksheet.
> - Click Edit, then click Copy... to copy the image to the Clipboard.
> - In Excel, click the cell in the upper-left corner of the range in which you want to insert the image.
> - Click Edit, then click Paste Special....
> - Click the Paste Link button in the Paste Special dialog box.
> - Click the OK button.

Now Jennifer adds the diagrams to her workbook.

To add the sales department organization chart to the workbook:

❶ Press **[Ctrl][Esc]** to display the Task List dialog box, then double-click **Microsoft Excel - S10SALES.XLS** in the Task List.

❷ Make sure the Analysis sheet is active. Click **Insert**, then click **Worksheet** to insert a new worksheet. Drag the new sheet tab to the end of the workbook and name the new worksheet **OrganizationChart**.

❸ Press **[Ctrl][Esc]** to display the Task List dialog box and then double-click **Program Manager**. If the Accessories group window is not open, double-click the **Accessories group icon** to open the Accessories window, then double-click the **Paintbrush icon** to open Paintbrush.

❹ Click the **Paintbrush window Maximize button**.

❺ Click **File**, then click **Open...** to display the Open dialog box. If necessary, switch to the drive containing your Student Disk. Double-click **C10SALES.BMP** to display the organization diagram.

❻ Click the **Pick button** and then drag the pointer to outline a rectangular area around the organization diagram. Click **Edit**, then click **Copy...**.

❼ Press **[Ctrl][Esc]** to display the Task List dialog box, then double-click **Microsoft Excel - S10SALES.XLS** in the Task List. The Excel window appears.

EX 374 T U T O R I A L 10 Integrating Excel with Other Windows Applications

❽ Click **Edit**, then click **Paste Special...** to display the Paste Special dialog box. See Figure 10-37.

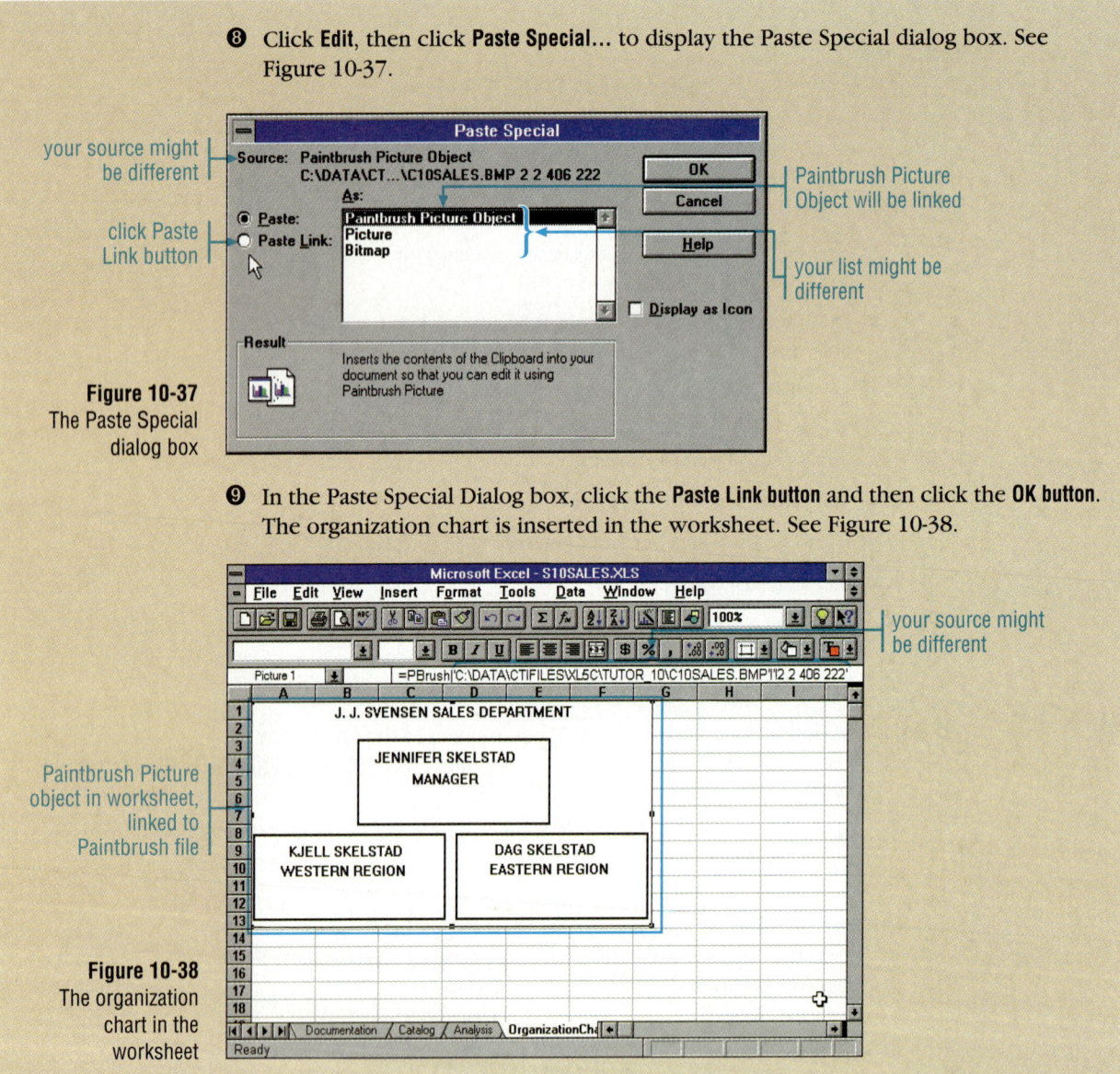

Figure 10-37
The Paste Special dialog box

❾ In the Paste Special Dialog box, click the **Paste Link button** and then click the **OK button**. The organization chart is inserted in the worksheet. See Figure 10-38.

Figure 10-38
The organization chart in the worksheet

❿ Click the **Save button**.

Now Jennifer needs to close Paintbrush. She has finished using her Excel workbook, so she can close Excel.

To close Paintbrush, and save and close the workbook:

❶ Press **[Ctrl][Esc]** to display the Task List dialog box, then double-click **Paintbrush - C10SALES.BMP** in the Task List.

❷ Click **File**, then click **Exit** to close Paintbrush.

❸ Press **[Ctrl][Esc]** to display the Task List dialog box, then double-click **Microsoft Excel - S10SALES.XLS** in the Task List.

❹ Click the **Documentation tab**.

❺ Click the **Save button** 🖫 to save the workbook. Click **File**, then click **Close** to close the S10SALES.XLS workbook.

Jennifer has completed her sales analysis report. She is ready to print the report and give it to Heather.

To print the sales analysis report:

❶ Press **[Ctrl][Esc]** to display the Task List dialog box and then double-click **Write - S10RPRT2.WRI** to display the Write window.

❷ Click **File**, click **Print...**, then click the **OK button** to print the report. The printed report is shown in Figure 10-39.

J. J. SVENSEN SALES ANALYSIS

Third Quarter 1996

Prepared by Jennifer Skelstad on October 15, 1996

J. J. SVENSEN SALES DEPARTMENT

```
            JENNIFER SKELSTAD
                 MANAGER

   KJELL SKELSTAD         DAG SKELSTAD
   WESTERN REGION         EASTERN REGION
```

The final sales figures are now available for July, August and September, 1996. I tallied the sales in units for each type of merchandise according to the type listed in the J. J. Svensen catalog (see attached catalog listing). I also grouped the merchandise into three categories called Clothing, Boots and Socks, and Camping. I created tallies for sales of each type of merchandise in the Western sales region (states west of the Mississippi river) and the Eastern sales region (states east of the Mississippi river). These tallies were combined into a Grand Total for each type, and a Grand Total for each region.

As shown in the table below, sales in the Western region are almost double sales in the Eastern region. We are also selling more socks than any other item.

Sum of QUANTITY		REGION		
TYPE2	TYPE	Eastern	Western	Grand Total
Clothing	Hat	3	0	3
	Pants	6	16	22
	Parka	8	10	18
	Shirt	10	20	30
Boots and Socks	Hiking Boots	1	5	6
	Socks	32	51	83
Camping	Pack	4	6	10
	Sleeping Bag	2	2	4
	Tent	1	2	3
Grand Total		67	112	179

Figure 10-39
Jennifer's printed sales analysis report (page 1)

Figure 10-39
Jennifer's printed sales analysis report (page 2)

J. J. SVENSON CATALOG

CATALOG_ID#	BRAND	CATEGORY	TYPE	DESCRIPTION	PRICE
M00001	J. J. Svensen	Multiple	Parka	Nylon Shell	$ 70.00
M00002	J. J. Svensen	Multiple	Parka	Gore-Tex Shell	$125.00
M00003	J. J. Svensen	Multiple	Parka	Nylon Insulated	$115.00
M00004	J. J. Svensen	Multiple	Parka	Gore-Tex Insulated	$165.00
M00005	J. J. Svensen	Multiple	Parka	Nylon Down-filled	$250.00
M00006	J. J. Svensen	Multiple	Parka	Gore-Tex Down-filled	$290.00
M00007	J. J. Svensen	Skiing	Parka	Nylon Down-filled Coverall	$350.00
M00008	J. J. Svensen	Skiing	Parka	Gore-tex Down-filled Coverall	$390.00
M00009	McKinley	Multiple	Parka	Nylon Down-filled	$270.00
M00010	McKinley	Multiple	Parka	Gore-Tex Down-filled	$320.00
M00011	J. J. Svensen	Hiking	Pack	Campus Book Pack	$ 45.00
M00012	J. J. Svensen	Hiking	Pack	Small Day Pack	$ 50.00
M00013	J. J. Svensen	Hiking	Pack	Large Day Pack	$ 75.00
M00014	J. J. Svensen	Camping	Pack	External Frame Pack	$135.00
M00015	J. J. Svensen	Camping	Pack	Internal Frame Pack	$145.00
M00016	McKinley	Camping	Pack	Expedition External Frame Pack	$225.00
M00017	McKinley	Camping	Pack	Expedition Internal Frame Pack	$325.00
M00018	J. J. Svensen	Skiing	Pack	Skier's Day Pack	$125.00
M00019	J. J. Svensen	Camping	Tent	Dome for Two (2 person)	$125.00
M00020	J. J. Svensen	Camping	Tent	Dome for Four (4 person)	$175.00
M00021	J. J. Svensen	Camping	Tent	Dome for Six (6 person)	$225.00
M00022	McKinley	Camping	Tent	Expedition Geodesic (4 person)	$250.00
M00023	J. J. Svensen	Camping	Sleeping Bag	ThinFilSulate Three Season	$150.00
M00024	J. J. Svensen	Camping	Sleeping Bag	Goose Down Three Season	$185.00
M00025	J. J. Svensen	Camping	Sleeping Bag	Goose Down Minus 20	$245.00
M00026	McKinley	Camping	Sleeping Bag	Goose Down Extreme	$275.00
M00027	J. J. Svensen	Multiple	Hiking Boots	Day Hiker	$ 75.00
M00028	J. J. Svensen	Multiple	Hiking Boots	Backpacker Light	$ 95.00
M00029	J. J. Svensen	Multiple	Hiking Boots	Backpacker Medium	$120.00
M00030	J. J. Svensen	Multiple	Hiking Boots	Backpacker Heavy	$175.00
M00031	McKinley	Multiple	Hiking Boots	Expedition Heavy	$225.00
M00032	J. J. Svensen	Multiple	Socks	Inner liners	$ 4.50
M00033	J. J. Svensen	Multiple	Socks	Wool Hikers	$ 9.00
M00034	J. J. Svensen	Skiing	Socks	Wool Skiers	$ 9.00
M00035	J. J. Svensen	Multiple	Pants	Men's Cotton Hiking Shorts	$ 27.50
M00036	J. J. Svensen	Multiple	Pants	Women's Cotton Hiking Shorts	$ 27.50
M00037	J. J. Svensen	Multiple	Pants	Men's Cotton Hiking Pants	$ 35.00
M00038	J. J. Svensen	Multiple	Pants	Women's Cotton Hiking Pants	$ 35.00
M00039	J. J. Svensen	Multiple	Pants	Men's Wool Hiking Pants	$ 45.00
M00040	J. J. Svensen	Multiple	Pants	Women's Wool Hiking Pants	$ 45.00
M00041	J. J. Svensen	Multiple	Shirt	Men's Cotton Shirt (Short Sleeve)	$ 20.00
M00042	J. J. Svensen	Multiple	Shirt	Women's Cotton Shirt (Short Sleeve)	$ 20.00
M00043	J. J. Svensen	Multiple	Shirt	Men's Cotton Shirt (Long Sleeve)	$ 23.00
M00044	J. J. Svensen	Multiple	Shirt	Women's Cotton Shirt (Long Sleeve)	$ 23.00
M00045	J. J. Svensen	Multiple	Shirt	Men's Wool Shirt (Long Sleeve)	$ 32.00
M00046	J. J. Svensen	Multiple	Shirt	Women's Wool Shirt (Long Sleeve)	$ 32.00
M00047	J. J. Svensen	Multiple	Hat	Men's Cotton Hat	$ 18.00
M00048	J. J. Svensen	Multiple	Hat	Women's Cotton Hat	$ 18.00

Now Jennifer saves her report and exits Write.

To save the report and exit Write:

❶ Click **File**, then click **Save** to save the Write file S10RPRT2.WRI.

❷ Click **File**, then click **Exit** to exit the Write program.

Keeping Linked Files Together

When you use OLE and DDE to share data among applications you need to be aware of which files you must keep together to properly maintain links. Because a file with embedded data contains a complete copy of the embedded data, you do not need to keep it with other files. The linked files, however, must be kept together for the links to function properly. If you give a copy of a linked file to someone else (on disk or via e-mail), you must also include copies of all the files that the file is linked to. For example, if Jennifer wanted to give a copy of her report to Heather, she would have to include:

- S10RPRT2.WR1—the Write file containing the sales report
- S10SALES.XLS—the Excel workbook containing her analysis
- SVENSEN.MDB—the Microsoft Access 1.1 file containing the J. J. Svensen database
- C10SALE.BMP—the Paintbrush file containing the organization chart

The catalog list and PivotTable in the Write file are linked to the Excel workbook via OLE. The Excel file in turn is linked to the Microsoft Access file via DDE and MS Query. The Excel file is also linked to the Paintbrush file via OLE.

Notice that the S10RPRT2.WR1 itself does *not* need to be accompanied by the C10SALES.BMP file, because the organization diagram is *embedded* in S10RPT2.WR1. But the organization diagram in the S10SALES.XLS file is linked to the C10SALES.BMP file, so the C10SALES.BMP file must accompany the S10SALES.XLS file.

Jennifer has completed her report. She takes the printed report along with the associated files on disk to Heather.

Questions

1. Describe two situations in which you might want to share data among two or more applications.
2. Name the four basic types of applications used in this tutorial and describe the basic purpose of each.
3. Define the following components of a relational database:
    a. table
    b. primary key
    c. common field
4. When you combine data from two tables in a query you are performing a _____.
5. Name the three panes in the MS Query window. What is the purpose of each?
6. How do you use MS Query when creating a PivotTable?
7. The _____ command copies material to the Windows clipboard.
8. What is the difference between the Paste command and the Paste Link command?
9. What is the difference between embedding and linking?
10. When sharing data between applications using OLE, what is a server application and what is a client application?

Tutorial Assignments

Jennifer Skelstad asked you to help her perform a further analysis using the J. J. Svensen database. She needs to prepare a report showing how the sales staff is performing. The report should include a list of all the staff at J. J. Svenson and a numerical analysis of sales by region for the members of the sales department.

She wants you to use MS Query to retrieve the required data. She also asked you to write the report for her.

1. Launch Excel, if necessary, and maximize the Excel window.
2. Open the T10SALE2.XLS file. A dialog box will appear once or twice with the message: "This document contains links. Re-establish links?" Click the Yes button each time. Excel re-establishes the links between the Excel workbook and the Access database, and between the Excel workbook and the Paintbrush application.
3. Check to see if Paintbrush was launched while the links were re-established. Was Paintbrush launched? If Paintbrush was launched, close it.
4. Save the file as S10SALE2.XLS.
5. On the Documentation worksheet, change the filename in cell B4 to S10SALE2.XLS.
6. Insert two new worksheets at the end of the workbook. Name one "Staff" and the other "Sales by Staff."
7. On the Staff worksheet, use MS Query to create a list of the staff at J. J. Svensen for Jennifer's report. *Hint*: This is a one-table query using only the STAFF table, and no criteria are needed.
8. Save the workbook.
9. Print the Staff worksheet (in portrait orientation). Do not print row and column borders or gridlines. Center your printouts horizontally, and include a right-aligned header with your name, the filename, the sheet name, and the date. Do not use a footer. Each printout should fit on its own page.
10. On the Sales by Staff worksheet, create a PivotTable named SalesByStaff that uses staff names as the row field and region as the column field. Limit the staff in the query to the three people in the Sales department: Jennifer Skelstad, Kjell Skelstad, and Dag Skelstad.
    Hint: Only two of the three members of the sales staff have made sales, so you will see only two names listed in your query results.
    Hint: This is a three-table query using the STAFF, ORDER, and ITEM tables. Be careful to include the following in your query:
    a. Use Last Name, First Name, Region, Order_ID#, Item_ID#, and Quantity.
    b. Use the Criteria pane to enter criteria. Use Last Name and First Name as criteria fields, and use three lines of criteria to enter the three names.
    Hint: The PivotTable uses Last Name and First Name as row labels, Region as the column label, and Sum of Quantity as the data.
11. Create a new chart sheet named Sales Chart and create a chart based on the Sales by Staff PivotTable on the sheet. Move the sheet to the end of the workbook.
12. Save the workbook.
13. Print the Sales by Staff worksheet (in portrait orientation) and the Sales Chart chart sheet. Do not print row and column borders or gridlines. Center your printouts horizontally, and include a right-aligned header with your name, the filename, the sheet name, and the date. Do not use a footer. Each printout should fit on its own page.

14. Launch Write and, if necessary, maximize the Write window.

E 15. Write a report describing the performances of the sales staff. How much has each person sold? Who has sold the most? How do sales vary with region? In your report, use OLE to include the list of staff on the Staff sheet and the SalesByStaff PivotTable on the Sales by Staff sheet. In your report, use OLE to include the Sales Chart.

16. Save this report as S10RPRT3.WRI.
17. Print a copy of the report.
18. Exit Write.
19. Return to Excel. Make Documentation the active sheet, save your workbook again, then close the workbook.
20. Submit your printouts to your instructor.
21. Prepare a disk labeled "J. J. Svensen Files" that contains the S10SALE2.XLS file and all necessary files to properly maintain the links between files. Submit this disk to your instructor.

Case Problems

1. Reporting Income at Crawdad Fishing Supplies

Joseph Simpson of Crawdad Fishing Supplies is responsible for reporting financial results to upper-level management. He has prepared an Excel workbook that contains the company's income statement for the year and is ready to write his report using Write. He has asked you to help him link his worksheet to his report.

1. Open the workbook P10INC.XLS. Save it as S10INC.XLS on your Student Disk.
2. On the Documentation sheet, change the filename in cell B5 to S10INC.XLS, change the name in cell B6 to your name, and enter the date you complete this case problem in cell B7. If necessary, adjust column widths.

To help Joseph create a report in Write:

3. Launch Write, maximize the Write window, and display the ruler and toolbar.
4. Copy the titles for the report from cells A1:A3 on the Titles sheet in the S10INC.XLS workbook to the top of the Write document. *Hint*. Highlight only cells A1:A3, then use the Copy and Paste commands. This is a copy and paste, not an embedding or a linking. Make sure you return to Excel to end the Copy command after you paste the titles into the Write document.
5. Use the Center button to center the titles.

 6. Use the Bold command on the Character menu to format the titles in boldface.

 7. Select the Enlarge Font command on the Character menu *twice* to enlarge the size of the titles.

8. Write a report for management analyzing the income statement. Discuss the variations in revenues, expenses, and net income during the four quarters.
9. In your report, use OLE to add the income statement from the Income Statement worksheet.
10. Save the report as S10INC.WRI.
11. Print the report.
12. Exit Write.

Joseph has asked you to create a picture of a fishing boat for the company's logo and add it to the Excel workbook S10INC.XLS. To create a picture and place it in the workbook:

13. Return to Excel.
14. Insert a new worksheet at the end of the workbook. Label it "Artwork."

E 15. Create an embedded Paintbrush picture object on the new worksheet:
   a. Click Insert, then click Object... to open the Object dialog box.
   b. In the CreateNew tab of the Object dialog box, double-click Paintbrush Picture in the Object Type list. The Paintbrush application is opened, ready for your artwork.

E c. Create a picture in Paintbrush. Experiment and use the Paintbrush Help system to guide you.
   d. To return the picture to Excel, click File, then click Exit and Return to S10INC.XLS. When you see the message "The command you have chosen will close the connection between this open embedded object and S10INC.XLS. Do you want to update the open embedded object before proceeding?" Click the Yes button. You return to Excel and can view the embedded picture in the worksheet.
16. Save the workbook.
17. Print the Artwork sheet in landscape orientation. Do not print row and column borders or gridlines. Center your printout horizontally and include a right-aligned header with your name, the filename, the sheet name, and the date. Do not use a footer. The printout should fit on its own page.
18. Close the workbook
19. Submit your printouts to your instructor.

2. Ordering Parts at Shinohara Electronics

Amy Takahara works at Shinohara Electronics, a manufacturer of consumer electronic products. She is responsible for maintaining adequate inventory of the parts used in the manufacturing process. Most parts are available from more than one vendor. Amy wants to do an analysis of how part orders are distributed among vendors to see if there are patterns in Shinohara's parts purchases. The inventory database is a Microsoft Access database. Because she is unfamiliar with queries in Access and MS Query, she has asked you to help her.

1. Open the workbook P10INV.XLS. Save it as S10INV.XLS on your Student Disk.
2. On the Documentation worksheet, change the filename in cell B5 to S10INV.XLS, change the name in cell B6 to your name, and enter the date you complete this case problem in cell B7. If necessary, adjust column widths.
3. Switch to the Inventory Analysis worksheet.
4. Make cell A5 the active cell.
5. Use MS Query to create a PivotTable showing how many of each part have been purchased from each supplier:
   a. Start the PivotTable Wizard and choose External Data Source.
   b. In the PivotTable Wizard - Step 2 of 4 dialog box, click the Get Data... button to start MS Query.
   c. In MS Query, use the database file P10INV.MDB, which contains three tables: ORDER, PARTS, and VENDOR. Add all three tables to the query in the following order: PARTS, ORDER, and VENDOR.
   d. Use the DESCRIPTION field from PARTS, the QUANTITY field from ORDER, and the NAME field from VENDOR in your query.
   e. In the PivotTable, DESCRIPTION is the row variable, NAME is the column variable, and Sum of QUANTITY is the data variable. The name of the PivotTable is VendorAnalysis.
6. Save the workbook
7. Launch Write, maximize the Write window and display the ruler and toolbar.
8. Write a report that introduces the analysis in the PivotTable.
9. In your report, use OLE to include the PivotTable from the Inventory Analysis worksheet.
10. Save the report as S10INV.WRI.

11. Print a copy of the report.
12. Exit Write.
13. Return to Excel and save the workbook.
14. In the S10INV.XLS workbook, print the Inventory Analysis sheet in landscape orientation. Do not print row and column borders or gridlines. Center your printout horizontally and include a right-aligned header with your name, the filename, the sheet name, and the date. Do not use a footer. The printout should fit on its own page.
15. Close the workbook.
16. Submit your printout to your instructor.

3. Tracking Shipments at Redmond-Wheeler Express

Sarah Cunningham works at Redmond-Wheeler Express, an express shipping company located in the Pacific Northwest. She is responsible for tracking shipments and sending invoices to the shippers. She wants to prepare a report on the use of the company's services. The company database is a Microsoft Access database. She has asked you to help her because she is unfamiliar with queries in Access and MS Query.

1. Open the workbook P10SHIP.XLS. Save it as S10SHIP.XLS on your Student Disk.
2. On the Documentation worksheet, change the filename in cell B5 to S10SHIP.XLS, change the name in cell B6 to your name, and enter the date you complete this case problem in cell B7. If necessary, adjust column widths.
3. Complete the Purpose statement in cells B10 and B11.
4. Switch to the Analysis worksheet.
5. Make cell A5 the active cell.
6. Use MS Query to create a PivotTable showing how many shipments went from each customer to each destination.
   a. Start the PivotTable Wizard and choose External Data Source.
   b. In the PivotTable Wizard - Step 2 of 4 dialog box, click the Get Data... button to start MS Query.
   c. In MS Query, use the database file P10SHIP.MDB, which contains three tables: INVOICE, CUSTOMER, and SHIPMENT. Add both tables to the query in the following order: CUSTOMER and SHIPMENT.
   d. Use the CUSTOMER_NAME field from CUSTOMER, the DESTINATION field from SHIPMENT, and the INVOICE_ID# field from SHIPMENT in your query.
   e. In the PivotTable, CUSTOMER is the row variable, DESTINATION is the column variable, and Count of INVOICE_ID# is the data variable. The name of the PivotTable is ShipmentAnalysis. *Hint:* To select count instead of sum as the calculation for the data, you can: (1) set INVOICE_ID# as the data variable; (2) double-click the label sum of INVOICE_ID# to open the PivotTable Field dialog box; and (3) double-click count in the Summarize by list box.
7. Save the workbook.
8. Launch Write, maximize the Write window, and display the ruler and toolbar.
9. Write a report that introduces the analysis in the PivotTable.
10. Save the report as S10SHIP.WRI.
11. Print the report, then exit Write.
12. You could use OLE to add a copy of the PivotTable to the report, but the PivotTable is too large to fit easily on a Write page. Instead, return to Excel and print the Analysis sheet in landscape orientation. Do not print row and column borders or gridlines. Center your printout horizontally and include a right-aligned header with your name, the filename, the sheet name, and the date. Do not use a footer. Attach this printout to your report.
13. Close the workbook.
14. Submit your report with the attached printout to your instructor.

T U T O R I A L   1 1

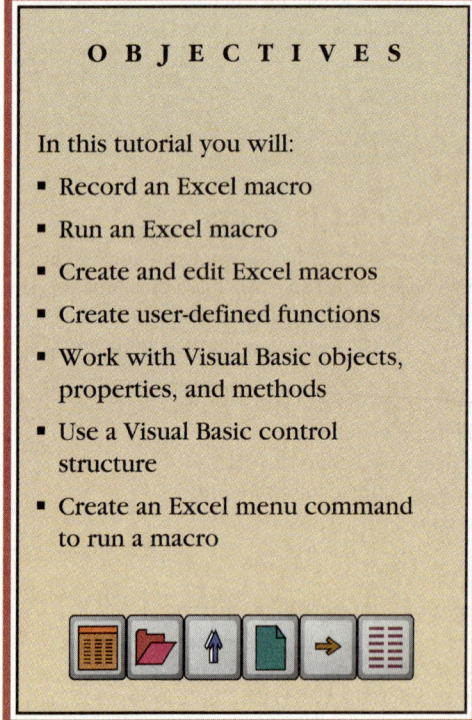

OBJECTIVES

In this tutorial you will:
- Record an Excel macro
- Run an Excel macro
- Create and edit Excel macros
- Create user-defined functions
- Work with Visual Basic objects, properties, and methods
- Use a Visual Basic control structure
- Create an Excel menu command to run a macro

Application Development with Macros and Visual Basic

Building a Quality Control System Using Statistical Process Control

CASE

Shared Resources, Inc. Shared Resources is a recycling company located in the southwestern United States. The firm recycles aluminum, glass, plastic, and paper, and sells the recycled material to companies that use it to produce products as diverse as lawn chairs and plastic bags. The secret to Shared Resources' success is a patented sorting process that allows it to sift through tons of household trash to recover recyclable material quickly and inexpensively. The company's clients do not have to sort recyclable material into separate containers; Shared Resources sorts everything for them. Because of its sorting process, Shared Resources, which is privately owned, has become profitable while many government-run recycling programs continue to lose money.

Shared Resources can stay profitable, however, only as long as the company can maintain a high ratio of sellable recovered material (recyclable glass, plastic, etc.) to collected unsorted material (collected trash). The company recovers approximately 40 pounds of sellable recovered material for each 100 pounds of unsorted trash. This 40% recovery ratio is crucial to Shared Resources' profitability.

Building a Quality Control System Using Statistical Process Control   EX 383

Owner and President Donna Taliesin has asked Chief Financial Officer Andrew Cisneros to create a quality control system to monitor Shared Resources' recovery ratio.

Andrew has begun creating a quality control system workbook. In this tutorial, we'll work with Andrew as he implements a quality control system using **statistical process control (SPC)** techniques (mathematical techniques for monitoring and controlling production processes) such as process control charts. Because Andrew updates control charts frequently, he plans to automate the task using a Visual Basic macro module. He will also use Visual Basic to automate other tasks such as printing worksheets. You used a Visual Basic macro module in Tutorial 3; in this tutorial you will create your own macro module.

Andrew has named the workbook C11QC.XLS. Let's open this workbook now.

To launch Excel, organize the workspace, and open the C11QC.XLS workbook:

❶ Launch Windows and Excel following your usual procedure.

❷ Make sure your Student Disk is in the disk drive.

❸ Make sure the Microsoft Excel and Book1 windows are maximized.

❹ Click the **Open button** to display the Open dialog box.

❺ Double-click **C11QC.XLS** in the File Name box to open the workbook. See Figure 11-1.

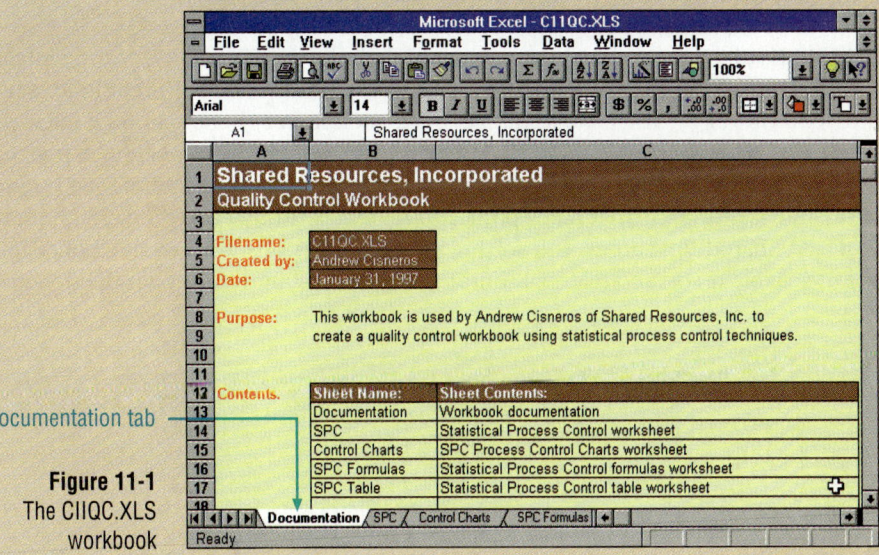

Figure 11-1
The C11QC.XLS workbook

TROUBLE? If the file isn't in the file list, click the Drives down arrow button to display the drive in which your Student Disk is located.

❻ Make sure the Documentation sheet is the active worksheet. Notice that the information Andrew entered into the Documentation sheet follows the documentation methods you studied in Tutorial 8.

Let's save the workbook under the name S11QC.XLS so your changes do not alter the original file.

To save the workbook as S11QC.XLS:

❶ In the Documentation sheet, double-click cell **B4**, change the filename to **S11QC.XLS**, then press **[Enter]**.

❷ Press **[Ctrl][Home]** to make cell A1 the active cell.

❸ Click **File**, then click **Save As...** to display the Save As dialog box.

❹ Save the workbook as **S11QC.XLS**.

There are five worksheets in Andrew's workbook: Documentation, SPC, Control Charts, SPC Formulas, and SPC Table. As you know, the Documentation sheet contains the workbook documentation. You'll work with the other sheets in the workbook as you learn about statistical process control.

Statistical Process Control (SPC)

Quality control refers to many concepts and techniques that are used to maintain standards of quality during a production process. One quality control technique, statistical process control (SPC), uses statistical sampling techniques (taught in introductory business statistics classes) to determine if a process is performing as expected. A **process** is a series of actions that takes input and converts it to output. For example, an automobile assembly line is a process that takes parts and materials (input) and converts them to cars (output). At Shared Resources, the sorting process takes unsorted trash (input) and converts it to sellable recovered material (output). Figure 11-2 illustrates a production process.

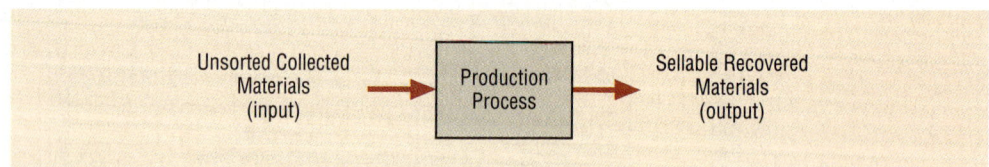

Figure 11-2
A production process

If a process is working correctly, the output should conform to a quality control standard. For example, in the automobile manufacturing process, the headlights should be a certain distance apart. This distance is the quality control standard for headlight placement. At Shared Resources, the quality control standard requires 40 pounds of sellable recovered materials for every 100 pounds of unsorted trash.

Maintaining quality control standards is difficult because output from processes usually has some **variation**—that is, the output doesn't always match the standard exactly. For example, on an assembly line, the distance between automobile headlights should be 36 inches. But in actuality, it might be 35.92 inches or 36.04 inches. Similarly, Shared Resources might recover 39.8 pounds from one 100-pound batch of trash and 41.1 pounds from the next.

To monitor the sorting process, Shared Resources could measure the output from every 100 pounds of trash, but this would slow down the production process a lot. Instead, Shared Resources takes periodic samples. Once each day, the output from three 100-pound batches is weighed. The results are recorded on the SPC worksheet in the workbook.

Let's take a look at the SPC worksheet.

To view the SPC worksheet:
① Click the **SPC tab** to display Andrew's SPC worksheet. See Figure 11-3.

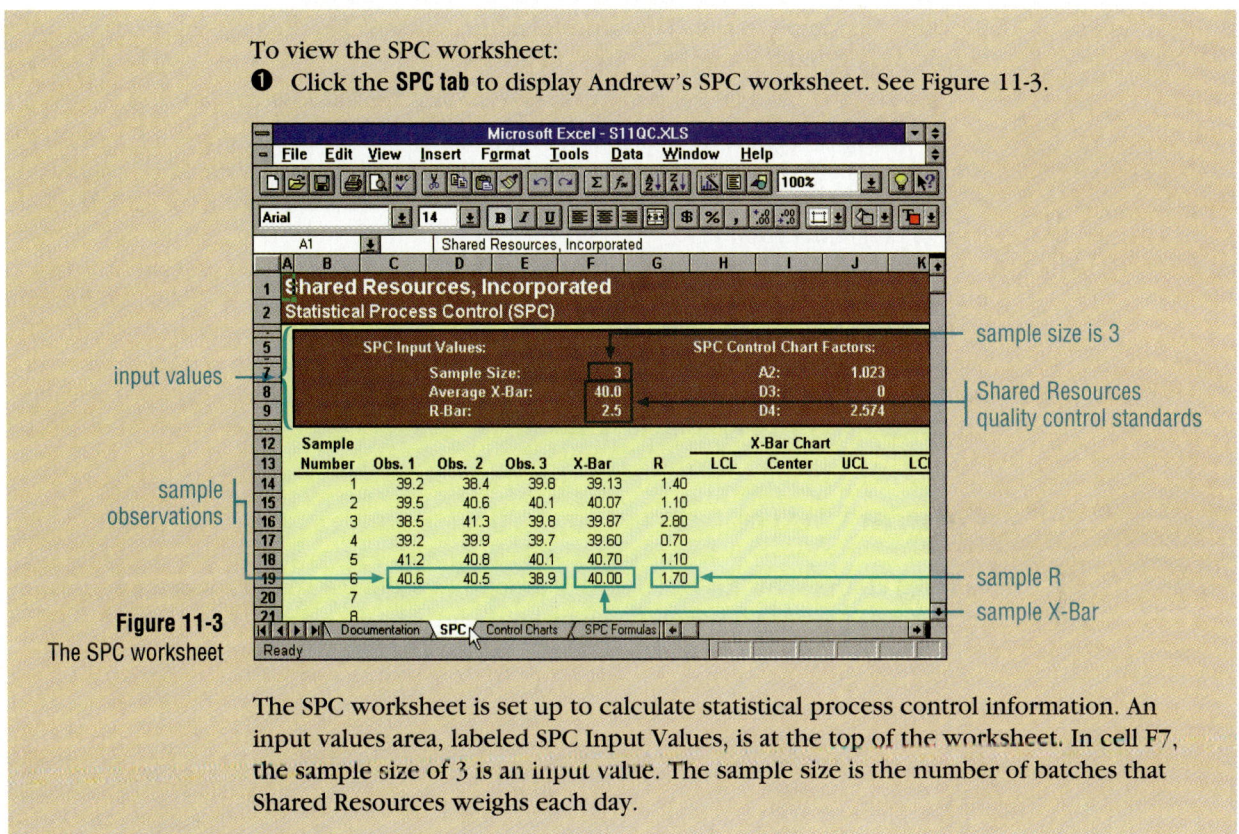

Figure 11-3
The SPC worksheet

The SPC worksheet is set up to calculate statistical process control information. An input values area, labeled SPC Input Values, is at the top of the worksheet. In cell F7, the sample size of 3 is an input value. The sample size is the number of batches that Shared Resources weighs each day.

The three weights from each day are recorded as observations in the worksheet. For example, the three weights from yesterday (the day of the last sample was taken) are 40.6 pounds, 40.5 pounds, and 38.9 pounds. These values are recorded as the observations for sample number 6, in cells C19:E19.

These three values are used to calculate an average weight for the day. In SPC terms, an average is called an **X-Bar**, and appears in column F. (Statistics often uses the notation "X" for an observation.) The average for yesterday is X-Bar = (40.6 + 40.5 + 38.9)/3 = 40.00 pounds, which is the value in cell F19.

Shared Resources' quality control standards are entered as values in the SPC Input Values area. As shown by the Average X-Bar value of 40.0 in cell F8, the average of the X-Bars for the daily samples should be close to 40 pounds. This means that *over time* the X-Bars from the samples should average 40.0. This does not mean that the average of the X-Bars in the worksheet is *always* 40.0.

We must allow for **reasonable variation** (an acceptable variation above or below the quality control standard) in the output from each process. If the process variation is *within* the acceptable variation, the process is said to be **in control**; if the process variation is *beyond* the acceptable variation, the process is said to be **out of control**. When the process is out of control, we need to stop the process and correct any problems.

For example, suppose that reasonable variation for the distance between headlights is 0.50 inches greater than or less than the standard 36.00 inches. If the actual distance we measure is 36.75 inches, then variation is 36.75 − 36.00 = 0.75 inches, which is greater than the allowed 0.50 inches. The process is out of control and needs to be fixed.

On the SPC worksheet, there is a value by which you can measure a variation in the process: the sample range. The **sample range**, or range, is the difference between the largest weight and the smallest weight in the sample:

Range = Maximum observation − Minimum observation

The sample range is notated as **R** and appears in column G. The range for yesterday is R = (40.6 − 38.9) = 1.70, and this value is in cell G19. The allowable variation is shown by the R-Bar (the average Range in cell F9), and is 2.5. This means that a sample range *cannot be greater than* 2.5.

However, the sample range only tells you the greatest possible difference between maximum and minimum observations. It does *not* tell you how far an X-Bar can be from 40.0 pounds and still have the process in control. Looking at the observations on the SPC sheet, you cannot tell if the process is in control or out of control. To come up with a definite answer, you need to use an SPC control chart, which makes it easy to see when a process has exceeded reasonable variation.

Control Charts

Control charts show the behavior of a process over time. A control chart for monitoring the distance between headlights is shown in Figure 11-4.

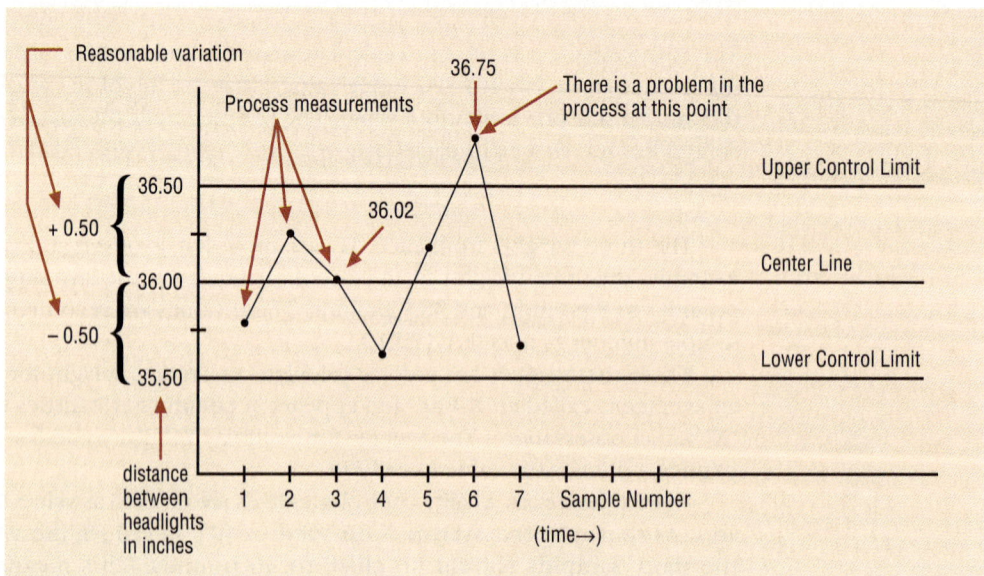

Figure 11-4
A control chart

The **center line** on a control chart shows the quality control standard of a measurement. The **control limits** show the limits of the reasonable variation. The lower control limit (LCL) specifies the smallest acceptable value and the upper control limit (UCL) specifies the largest acceptable value.

You might expect to see a headlight measurement on the chart for each car produced (that is, for each unit of output). But taking these measurements would be time-consuming and would dramatically slow down production. Instead, a sample of several cars is taken at regular intervals and averaged. This average distance between headlights (X-Bar) for the sample is recorded on the control chart as a process measurement. For example, a sample of five cars is selected and the distances between the headlights of each car in the sample is measured. This results in the following five values in inches: 35.8, 36.1, 36.2, 35.9, and 36.1. The average distance between the headlights for this sample is X-Bar = (35.8 + 36.1 + 36.2 +35.9 + 36.1)/5 = 180.1/5 = 36.02. The average distance of 36.02 appears as the third point on the control chart.

There are several types of control charts, as shown in Figure 11-5. The type of chart you use depends on the type of data you can collect.

Figure 11-5 Types of control charts

Type of Control Chart	Based on	Symbol for Measurement on Control Chart
X-Bar chart	Sample average	X-Bar
R chart	Sample range	R
p chart	Sample proportion	p

The control chart in Figure 11-4 is an X-Bar chart since it is based on sample averages. You use an X-Bar chart when you are controlling a process based on a measurement such as a distance or weight.

An R chart, used to control variation in a process, is always used in conjunction with an X-Bar chart.

You use a p chart when you are monitoring a process based on the percentage of bad or defective products that the process produces. For example, if you are producing radios and 50 out of 1000 are defective, then p = 50/1000 = .05, and .05 * 100% = 5%, indicating that 5% of the radios are defective. You will create an R-Bar chart and a p chart in the Tutorial Assignments at the end of this tutorial.

Andrew needs to measure the average pounds of sellable recovered materials per 100 pounds of unsorted trash. Because he is working with a sample average, he will create an X-Bar chart for the Shared Resources quality control program. As you have already seen, Andrew has created an SPC worksheet to calculate the necessary numbers for his control chart.

Let's take another look at that worksheet.

To view the SPC worksheet:

❶ Make sure the SPC worksheet is still active.

Andrew collected the observations for six samples and recorded the observations in the worksheet. Based on the sample observations, he calculated an X-Bar (sample average) and R (sample range) for each sample. See Figure 11-6.

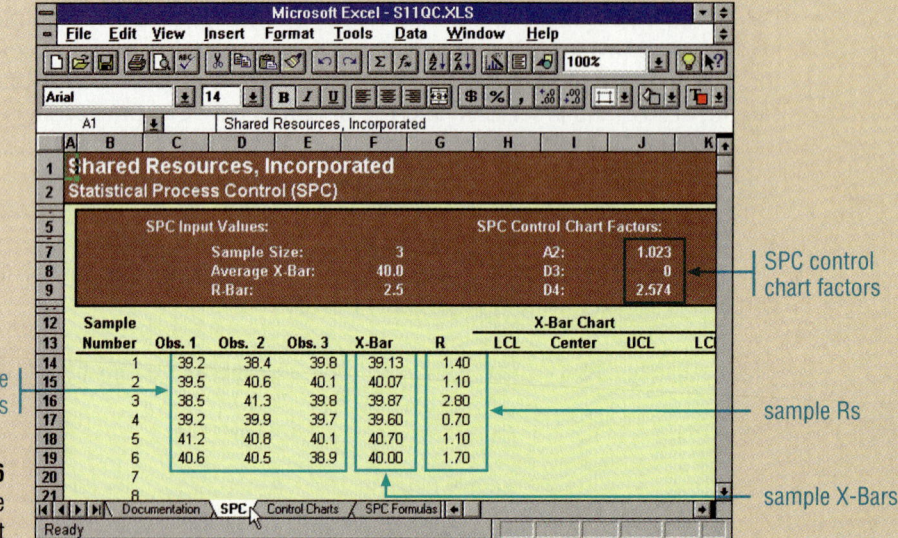

Figure 11-6
The samples in the SPC worksheet

Notice that Andrew also has an input area labeled SPC Control Chart Factors.

Factors are numbers that help calculate center line and control limit values for control charts. Andrew used a lookup function to obtain the SPC control chart factors from the SPC Table worksheet. You will use the A2 factor for the X-Bar chart in this tutorial and the D3 and D4 factors for your R chart in the Tutorial Assignments. You don't need to understand all the calculations involving control chart factors, but notice that the value of these factors depends on the sample size. Let's look at the SPC Table, which lists all the possible factors for various sample sizes.

❷ Click the **SPC Table tab** (at the end of the workbook) to display the SPC Table worksheet. See Figure 11-7.

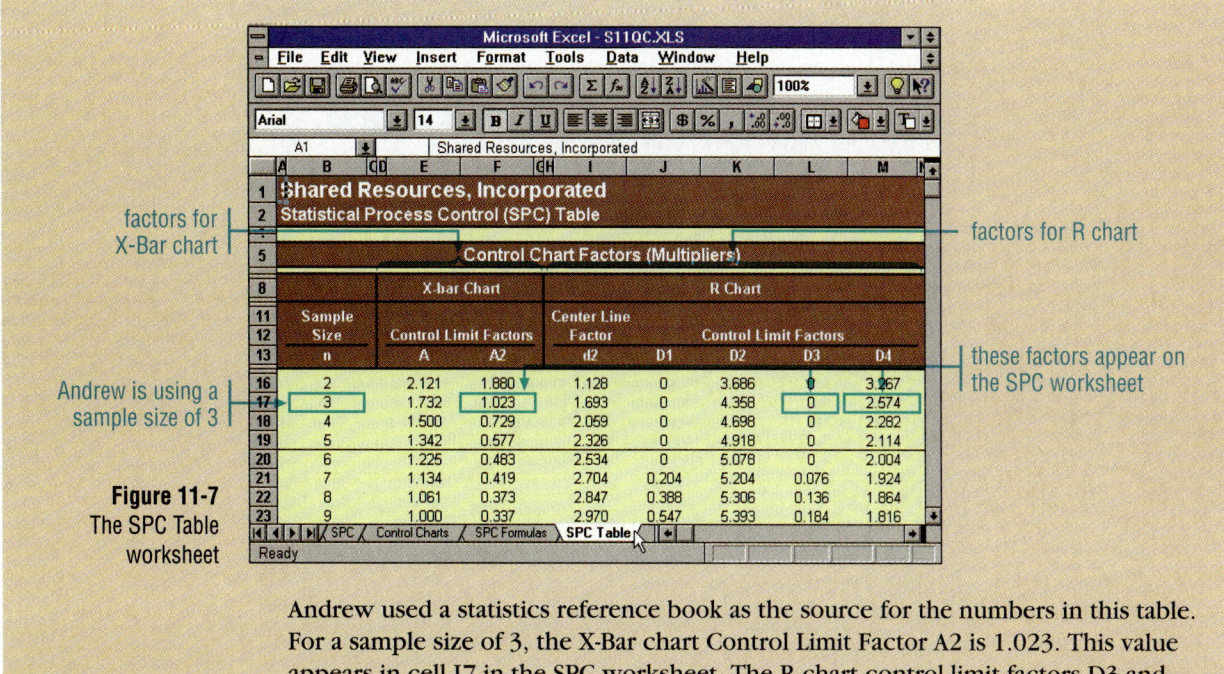

Figure 11-7
The SPC Table worksheet

Andrew used a statistics reference book as the source for the numbers in this table. For a sample size of 3, the X-Bar chart Control Limit Factor A2 is 1.023. This value appears in cell J7 in the SPC worksheet. The R chart control limit factors D3 and D4 (0 and 2.574 respectively) also appear in the SPC worksheet. Let's see how the control chart factors change when you change the sample size in the SPC worksheet.

❸ Click the **SPC tab**.

❹ Click cell **F7** to make it the active cell, then type **5** and press **[Enter]** to change the sample size to 5. Notice that the SPC control chart factor in cell A2 changed with the change in sample size. Excel looked up the new value, 0.577, in the SPC Table worksheet.

❺ Click cell **F7**, then type **3** and press **[Enter]** to restore the original SPC control chart factors.

The formulas Andrew will use to calculate the center line and control limits are on the SPC Formulas worksheet. Let's take a look at this worksheet.

To view the SPC Formulas worksheet:
1. Click the **SPC Formulas tab**. See Figure 11-8.

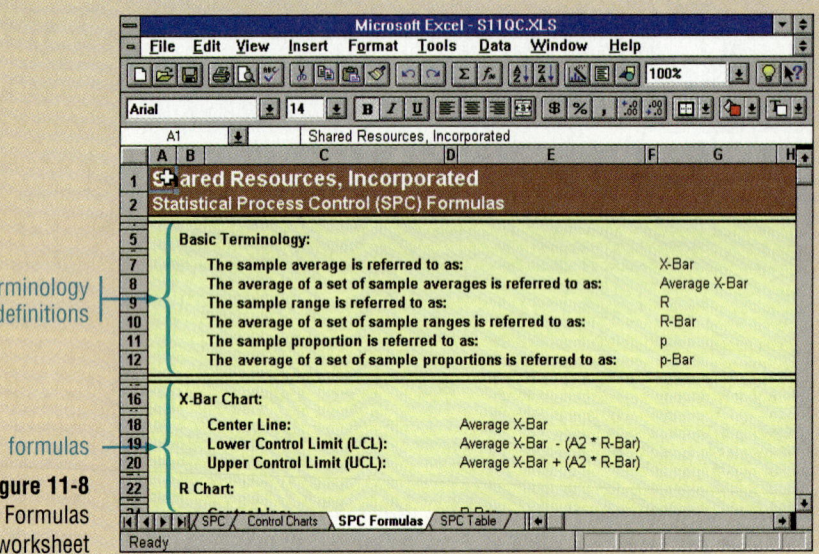

Figure 11-8
The SPC Formulas worksheet

Notice that Andrew has included definitions of statistical terms as well as the formulas he needs for calculating the control chart center lines and control limits. Again, you don't need to understand every detail of the SPC formulas, but you should have a general idea of how they work.

Andrew's first task is to print copies of both the SPC Formulas worksheet and the SPC Table worksheet to give to other Shared Resources employees. Because he has to print these worksheets regularly, Andrew decides to create an Excel macro to automate the task.

Macros vs. Procedures vs. Modules

As you recall from Tutorial 3, a macro automatically performs a series of steps, such as menu commands selection and keystrokes. You used a macro in Tutorial 3 to print cell formulas. To create a macro you record the steps as you perform them or you write the commands in Visual Basic programming language, which will perform the steps. First, you will record a macro. Later, you will work with a series of commands that would be difficult to record because they require input from the user.

Whether you create a macro by recording a series of steps or by writing commands, your macro is stored in a Visual Basic module, a sheet that contains only Visual Basic commands. The MyMod macro you customized in Tutorial 3 was stored as a series of Visual Basic commands in a module named Print Module. You edit a module sheet much like you edit a document in a word processor. You can delete characters using the Backspace and Delete keys, you can toggle between insert mode (the normal mode) and overtype mode using the Insert key, and you can use Excel's Cut, Copy, and Paste buttons on the toolbar.

A module is one type of macro sheet. Besides modules, the two other types of macro sheets are dialog sheets, which contain user-created dialog boxes, and Microsoft Excel 4.0 macro sheets, which contain macros written in the Excel 4.0 macro programming language. Earlier versions of Excel (previous to Excel 5.0) used a macro programming language that was very different from Visual Basic. Because Microsoft plans to use Visual Basic in all future Microsoft applications, we will use only Visual Basic modules in this tutorial.

Figure 11-9 shows the types of sheets that you can use in an Excel workbook.

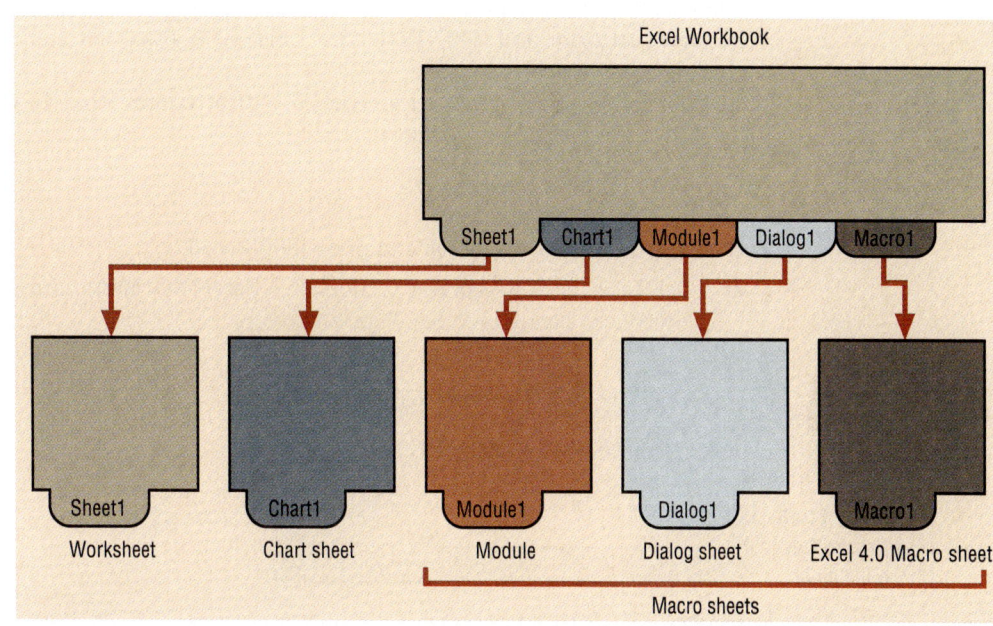

Figure 11-9
Excel workbook sheets

Andrew decides to record a macro that will print the SPC Formulas worksheet and the SPC Tables worksheet.

Recording a Macro

Although you used a macro in Tutorial 3, you haven't yet created an entirely new macro. Of the two ways to create a macro, recording a macro is by far the easiest.

REFERENCE WINDOW

Recording an Excel Macro

- Click Tools, click Record Macro, then click Record New Macro... to display the Record New Macro dialog box.

- In the Macro Name text box, type the name for the macro. Macro names must start with a letter and can contain only letters, numbers, and the underscore character.

- In the Description text box, type a description of the macro (press [Enter] to start a new line).

- Click the OK button. The macro recorder starts running, and a toolbar containing the Stop Macro button appears.

- Perform the steps that you want the macro to automate. Each time you perform a step, it is recorded as part of the macro.

- Click the Stop Macro button to finish the macro recording process. The recorded macro appears on a module sheet in the workbook. (If there is no module sheet in the workbook, Excel inserts one; if there is a module sheet in the workbook, Excel adds the macro to the existing sheet.)

Andrew has named the ranges he wants to print on the SPC Formulas and SPC Table worksheets: 'SPC Formulas'!$A$1:$H$34 (named SPCFormulas) contains the SPC formulas he wants to print and 'SPC Table'!$A$1:$N$42 (named SPCTable) contains the control chart factors he wants to print.

Using the range names to indicate the print ranges (that is, the ranges he wants to print), Andrew records his macro.

To start the macro recorder:
1. Click the **Documentation tab** and press **[Ctrl][Home]**.
2. Click **Tools**, click **Record Macro**, then click **Record New Macro...** to display the Record New Macro dialog box. See Figure 11-10.

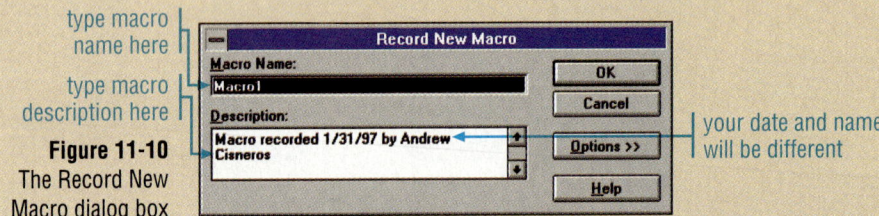

Figure 11-10
The Record New Macro dialog box

Notice that Excel provides a default name, Macro1, and a description indicating when the macro was recorded and by whom.

3. In the Macro Name text box, type **PrintSPCInformation**. Note that spaces are not allowed in macro names.
4. Press **[Tab]** to move the cursor to the Description text box.
5. Move the insertion point to the end of the current description and press **[Enter]** to start a new line. Type **This macro prints the SPC formulas and SPC Table**.
6. Click the **OK button**. The macro recorder starts running, and the Stop toolbar appears containing the Stop Macro button. See Figure 11-11.

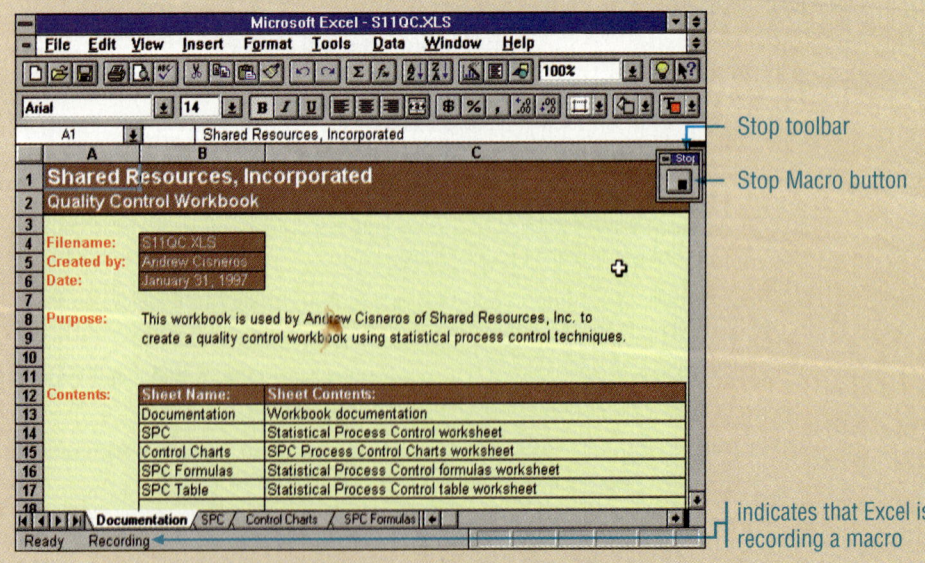

Figure 11-11
The Stop Macro button on the Stop toolbar

Andrew has named the macro, created it's description, and started the macro recorder. Now he's ready to perform the steps that he wants the macro to automate.

To record the PrintSPCInformation macro:
1. Click the **SPC Formulas tab** to make SPC Formulas the active worksheet.
2. Press **[F5]** to display the Go To dialog box.
3. Click the range name **SPCFormulas**, then click the **OK button**. The SPC Formulas sheet appears with the SPCFormulas range highlighted.
4. Click the **Print button**. Excel prints the SPC formulas.
5. Press **[Ctrl][Home]** to make 'SPC Formulas'!A1 the active cell.
6. Click the **SPC Table tab** to make SPC Table the active sheet.
7. Press **[F5]** to display the Go To dialog box, click the range name **SPCTable**, then click the **OK button**. The SPC Table sheet appears with the SPCTable range highlighted.
8. Click the **Print button**. The SPC Table is printed.
9. Press **[Ctrl][Home]** to make 'SPC Table'!A1 the active cell.
10. Click the **Stop Macro button** on the Stop toolbar to finish recording the macro.

Andrew has completed recording his macro. There was no module sheet in the workbook, so Excel inserted one and named it Module1. The Visual Basic code for the macro is recorded on this sheet. Let's look at the macro code.

To view the PrintSPCInformation macro:
1. Scroll through the sheet tabs, if necessary, then click the **Module1 tab**. The recorded PrintSPCInformation macro appears. See Figure 11-12.

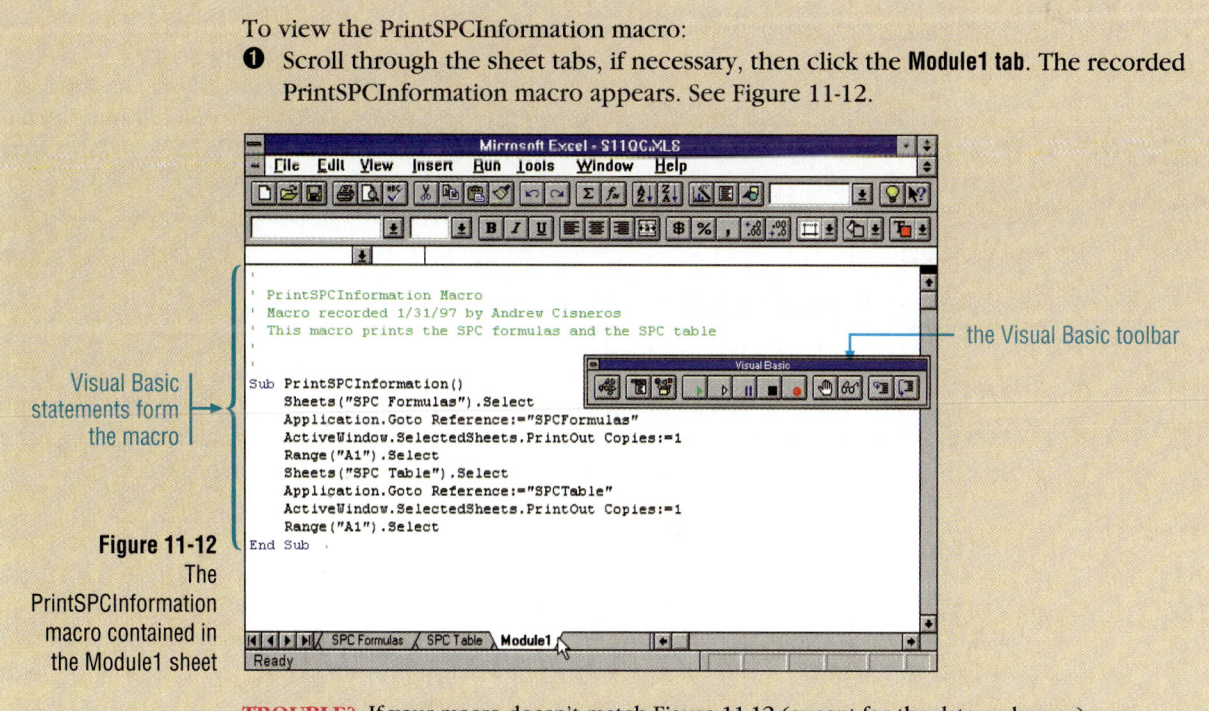

Figure 11-12
The PrintSPCInformation macro contained in the Module1 sheet

TROUBLE? If your macro doesn't match Figure 11-12 (except for the date and name), you might have made an error in recording the macro. Edit your macro until it matches Figure 11-12

EX 394 TUTORIAL 11 Application Development with Macros and Visual Basic

> ❷ Double-click the **Module1 tab** to display the Rename Sheet dialog box.
>
> ❸ Change the sheet name to **Print SPC Reports Module**, then click the **OK button**.
>
> ❹ Click the **Save button** 🖫 to save the workbook.

The Print SPC Reports Module contains the Visual Basic code for the PrintSPCInformation macro, and the Visual Basic toolbar appears. The menu bar displays the Visual Basic menus.

We'll discuss Visual Basic code and some of the Visual Basic menu commands later in this tutorial. Let's take a look at the Visual Basic toolbar now.

The Visual Basic Toolbar

The Visual Basic toolbar, shown in Figure 11-13, simplifies working with macros and Visual Basic.

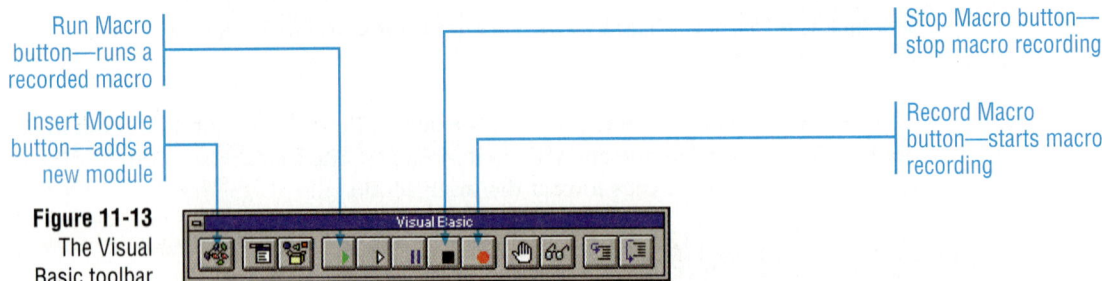

Figure 11-13
The Visual Basic toolbar

In this tutorial, you will use only a few of the buttons on the Visual Basic toolbar. The Insert Module button adds a new module to the workbook. The Run Macro button runs recorded macros. The Record Macro button lets you record macros, like the Record New Macro... command on the Tools menu. The Stop Macro button stops macro recording.

Andrew takes a moment to look at the set of Visual Basic statements he has created.

Using Visual Basic

Visual Basic is a programming language and, like all programming languages, has a set of statements, or lines, containing **keywords** (words that have a special meaning) that you use within a **syntax** (or order) to create commands that the computer can execute. If you do not use valid keywords or the correct syntax, your macro will not work.

Visual Basic Comments

Andrew notices that the first lines in the macro start with an apostrophe (') and include information about the macro. In Visual Basic, a line beginning with an apostrophe is called a comment. On color monitors, comments appear in green.

A **Visual Basic comment** is a statement that documents a macro. It is ignored when the macro is run. When you record a macro, Excel automatically includes the macro name and the information you typed in the Description text box in the Record New Macro dialog box as comments. Some Visual Basic comments are shown in Figure 11-14.

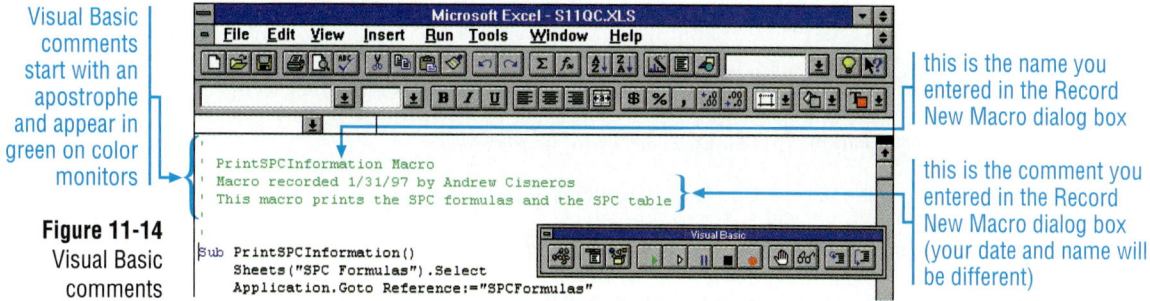

Figure 11-14
Visual Basic comments

Andrew notices that the first line in the macro without an apostrophe begins with the word Sub. On a color monitor, Sub appears in blue.

Visual Basic Sub Procedures

A Visual Basic macro is also called a **sub procedure**. In traditional programming languages, the **main procedure** controls the overall program execution and calls upon sub procedures to carry out specialized tasks such as printing worksheets. A sub procedure must begin with a Sub statement, followed by the sub procedure name, and ending with a set of parentheses. Sub procedures must end with an End Sub statement. Sub procedures have the following structure:

```
Sub SubProcedureName ()
    <Visual Basic statements>
End Sub
```

This structure can be seen in Andrew's PrintReports macro, as shown in Figure 11-15.

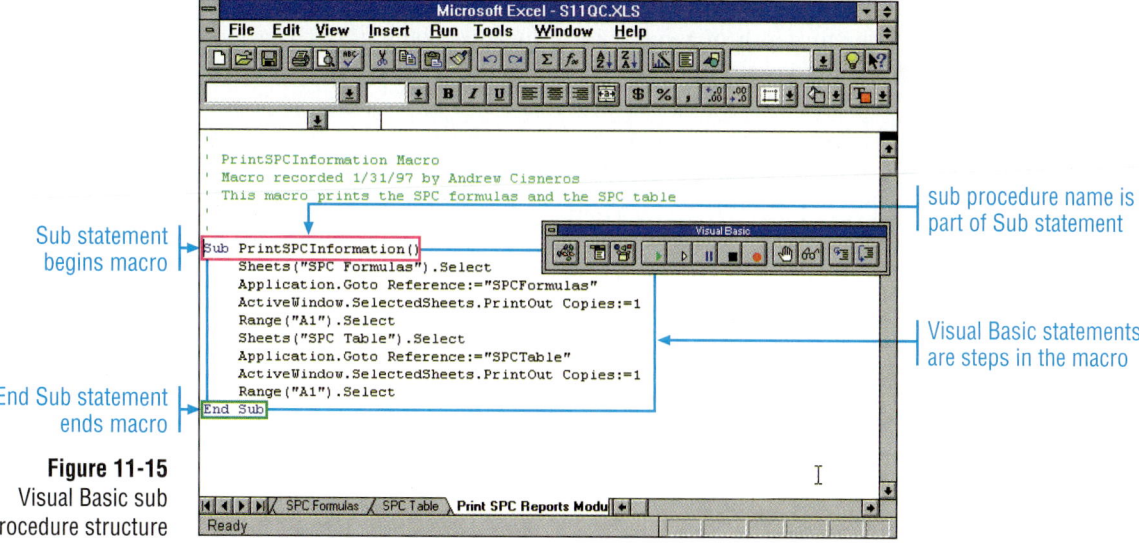

Figure 11-15
Visual Basic sub procedure structure

Visual Basic Objects, Properties, and Methods

The Visual Basic statements that make up a sub procedure refer to various objects. The term **object** is general, and refers to such things as workbooks, worksheets, ranges, and menus. (Because a cell is considered a range, there is no such thing as a cell object.) Examples of Visual Basic objects are shown in Figure 11-16.

Object	Refers to
Application	The Excel application as a whole
Workbook	One Excel workbook
Workbooks	A group of Excel workbooks
Sheets	A group of sheets in a workbook (can include worksheets, charts, modules, and dialog sheets)
Worksheet	One worksheet in a workbook
Worksheets	A group of worksheets in a workbook
Module	One Visual Basic module in a workbook
Modules	A group of Visual Basic modules in a workbook
Range	A cell or group of cells in a worksheet
Chart	One chart in a workbook
Charts	A group of charts in a workbook

Figure 11-16
Visual Basic objects

Objects can contain other objects. For example, a workbook contains worksheets, and a worksheet contains ranges. Excel is the application object, which contains workbooks.

Visual Basic objects have **properties**, or characteristics, whose property settings can be changed. For example, a range is an object with a ColumnWidth property. You can set the column width of a range by using the ColumnWidth property. Examples of Visual Basic properties are shown in Figure 11-17.

Object	Some Associated Properties	Refers to
Application	ActiveCell	Which cell is the active cell?
	ActiveSheet	Which sheet is the active sheet?
	DisplayFormulaBar	Is the formula bar displayed?
Workbook	ActiveSheet	Which sheet in the workbook is active?
	Saved	Have changes been made to the workbook since it was last saved?
Worksheet	Name	What is the name of the worksheet?
	StandardHeight	What is the default row height?
	StandardWidth	What is the default column width?
Range	Border	What are the settings of the border around the range?
	RowHeight	What is the height of the row in the range?
	ColumnWidth	What is the width of the column in the range?
Chart	HasLegend	Does the chart have a legend?

Figure 11-17 Visual Basic properties

The following sub procedure selects the object named Sheet1—that is, it makes Sheet1 the active sheet. It then sets the column width properties for columns C through E to 15.

```
Sub SetWidth()
    Sheets("Sheet1").Select
    Range(Columns("C"), Columns("E")).ColumnWidth = 15
End Sub
```

In this SetWidth sub procedure, we **set**, or changed, the property setting to 15. The Visual Basic syntax for setting a property setting is:

object.property = expression

In the SetWidth sub procedure, `Range(Columns("C"), Columns("E"))` is the object, `ColumnWidth` is the property, and `15` (the column width setting) is the expression. Notice that a period separates the object and the property.

We could also write a sub routine that would **return** a column width (that is, test to determine the current column width setting). The Visual Basic syntax for returning a property value is:

variable = object.property

Note that the syntax includes a `variable`. You'll learn more about variables later in this tutorial.

The following sub procedure checks the width of column C in Sheet1 and displays it in a dialog box called a message box:

```
Sub ColumnCWidth()
    Sheets("Sheet1").Select
    WidthOfColumnC = Range(Columns("C"),Columns("C")).ColumnWidth
    MsgBox ("The width of Column C is: " & WidthOfColumnC)
End Sub
```

In this ColumnCWidth sub procedure, `WidthOfColumnC` is the variable, `Range(Columns("C"),Columns("C"))` is the object, and `ColumnWidth` is the property.

In addition to properties, Visual Basic objects have methods associated with them. **Methods** are actions that the objects can perform. A method is similar to an Excel command. Examples of Visual Basic methods are shown in Figure 11-18.

Object	Some Associated Methods	Action
Workbook	Close	Closes the workbook
	Save	Saves the workbook
	UpdateLink	Updates a DDE or OLE link
Worksheet	Calculate	Recalculates the worksheet
	Move	Moves the worksheet to another location in the workbook
	PrintOut	Prints the worksheet
	Select	Selects the worksheet
Range	BorderAround	Adds a border around the range
	Cells	Defines the cells in the range
	Clear	Clears the cells in the range
	Select	Selects the range
Chart	CheckSpelling	Checks the spelling of the chart
	Select	Selects a chart

Figure 11-18
Visual Basic methods

The Visual Basic syntax for a method is:

object.method argumentlist

Note that the syntax includes an argument list. An **argument** is a constant, variable, or expression that provides the method with needed information. (You've used arguments in Excel functions before.) For example, in the formula =SUM(C2:C10) the range C2:C10 is the argument. Visual Basic arguments are always listed at the end of a Visual Basic statement.

You have already seen an example of a method in the sub procedure that selects Sheet1 and then sets the column width for columns C through E. Once again, that sub procedure is:

```
Sub SetWidth()
    Sheets("Sheet1").Select
    Range(Columns("C"), Columns("E")).ColumnWidth = 15
End Sub
```

The sub procedure uses a method to make Sheet1 the active worksheet. Here the method or command is `Select`, which is the same action as clicking on the Sheet1 tab. `Sheets("Sheet1")` is the object. There are no arguments.

Looking at his recorded macro, Andrew recognizes the Visual Basic objects, properties, and methods he has recorded. See Figure 11-19.

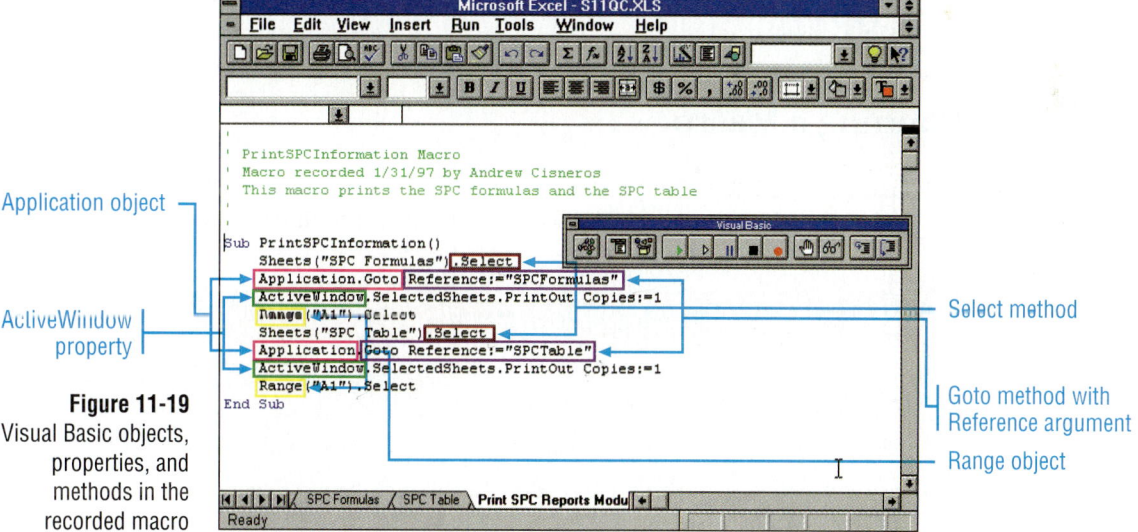

Figure 11-19
Visual Basic objects, properties, and methods in the recorded macro

Figure 11-20 describes each Visual Basic statement in the macro.

Figure 11-20
The Visual Basic statements in the recorded macro

Statement	Action
`Sub PrintSPCInformation`	Beginning of macro
`    Sheets ("SPC Formulas").Select`	Makes SPC Formulas the active sheet
`    Application.Goto Reference:="SPCFormulas"`	Highlights the range named SPCFormulas
`ActiveWindow.SelectedSheets.PrintOut Copies:=1`	Prints the SPC Formulas
`    Range("A1").Select`	Makes cell A1 the active cell
`    Sheets ("SPC Table").Select`	Makes SPC Table the active sheet
`    Application.Goto Reference:="SPCTable"`	Highlights the range named SPCTable
`ActiveWindow.SelectedSheets.PrintOut Copies:=1`	Prints the SPC Table
`    Range("A1").Select`	Makes cell A1 the active cell
`End Sub`	End of macro

Now that Andrew has recorded the macro, he can use it to print the SPC Formulas and the SPC Table.

Running a Macro

As you learned in Tutorial 3, you can run an Excel macro using the Macro... command on the Tools menu. If the module sheet is active, there are additional ways to run a macro.

REFERENCE WINDOW

Running an Excel Macro

When any type of sheet is the active sheet:

- Click Tools, then click Macro... to display the Macro dialog box.
- In the Macro Name/Reference box, click the name of the macro you want to run.
- Click the Run button.

When a module sheet is the active sheet:

- Click at the beginning of the Sub statement to place the insertion point before the word Sub.
- Click the Run Macro button on the Visual Basic toolbar.

  or

  Click Run, then click Start.

  or

  Press [F5].

Andrew runs his macro to make sure it operates properly.

To run the PrintSPCInformation macro:

❶ Move the insertion point in front of the word Sub in the Sub statement.

❷ Click the **Run Macro button** on the Visual Basic toolbar. (Make sure you click the Run Macro button not the Step Macro button.) The PrintSPCInformation macro runs and the SPC Formulas and the SPC Table are printed.

TROUBLE? If you get a Macro Error message or a "Sub or Function not defined" dialog box, there is an error in your Visual Basic code. For an error message, click the End button. For the dialog box, click the OK button. Then edit your macro to match Figure 11-19, save the workbook, and run the macro again.

❸ Click the **Print SPC Reports Module tab** so that the Print SPC Reports module is active.

❹ Click the **Save button** to save the workbook.

Now that Andrew has completed the macros to print the SPC Formulas and Table, he returns to the SPC calculations on the SPC worksheet. He needs to calculate the center line and control limits for the X-Bar chart. He starts by calculating the center line.

If you want to take a break and resume the tutorial at a later time, you can exit Excel by double-clicking the Control menu box in the upper-left corner of the screen. When you resume the tutorial, launch Excel, maximize the Microsoft Excel and Book1 windows, and place your Student Disk in the disk drive. Open the file S11QC.XLS, then continue with the tutorial.

Calculating the Control Chart Center Line

The formulas for the X-Bar chart are on the SPC Formulas worksheet, which you have printed. Looking at the formulas, Andrew sees that the center line for an X-Bar chart is the Average X-Bar. For Andrew's X-Bar chart, the Average X-Bar is the Shared Resources control standard of 40.0. This value is in cell F8 of the SPC worksheet.

In cell I14 of the SPC worksheet, Andrew enters a reference to cell F8 to establish the center line value. He then copies this formula to the other cells in column I.

To calculate the center line value for the X-Bar chart:

❶ Click the **SPC tab** to make the SPC worksheet the active sheet.

❷ Click cell **I14** to make it the active cell.

❸ Type **=$F$8** to create an absolute reference the Average X-Bar value in cell F8, then press **[Enter]**. The Average X-Bar value, 40.0, appears in cell I14.

❹ Click cell **I14**, then click the **Copy button**.

❺ Highlight cells I15 through I38, then press **[Enter]**. The center line value is copied to these cells.

❻ Press **[Ctrl][Home]**, then click the **Save button**.

Andrew is ready to calculate the control limits. He could create Excel formulas to do this, but decides to create two Excel user-defined functions to do the calculations for him, making it easier to repeat this task in the future.

User-Defined Functions

You are familiar with built-in Excel functions such as SUM or AVERAGE that use values in the worksheet to perform calculations and return a value. A **user-defined function** is a function that you, the user, create using Visual Basic. It is similar to a macro because you create it using a Visual Basic procedure, but unlike a macro, a user-defined function takes values from a worksheet as input and returns a value to a worksheet as output.

User-defined functions must begin with a statement containing the word "Function," followed by the function name and set of parentheses enclosing the arguments. User-defined functions must end with an End Function statement. This gives user-defined functions the following structure:

```
Function FunctionName (Arguments)
    <Visual Basic statements>
End Function
```

Andrew must create one user-defined function to calculate the X-Bar chart lower control limit, and a second user-defined function to calculate the X-Bar chart upper control limit. He starts with the formula for the lower control limit, named XBarLCL.

According to the formula on the SPC Formulas worksheet, the lower control limit equals the average X-Bar minus the A2 factor multiplied by R-Bar:

Lower Control Limit = Average X-Bar – (A2 * R-Bar)

The Average X-Bar, A2, and R-Bar values must be supplied by the user. This means that the XBarLCL function needs three input arguments, which Andrew calls AverageXBar, A2, and Rbar.

Andrew also decides to put his function on a new module sheet named SPC Functions.

To begin creating the XBarLCL user-defined function:

1. Click the **Print SPC Reports Module tab**.
2. Click the **Insert Module button** on the Visual Basic toolbar. A new module named Module2 is added to the workbook in front of the Print SPC Reports Module.
3. Drag the **Module2 tab** to the right of the Print SPC Reports Module tab to move the Module2 sheet to the end of the workbook.
4. Double-click the **Module2 tab** to display the Rename Sheet dialog box. Type **SPC Functions**, then click the **OK button**. The new name appears on the sheet tab.

Andrew begins his function by entering comments to identify it.

❺ Make sure the cursor is in the upper-left corner of the blank sheet, then type ' (apostrophe) and press [Enter] to move to the second line. On a color monitor, the apostrophe turns green after you press [Enter].

❻ In the second line, type ' **XBarLCL Function** (make sure you include a space between the apostrophe and the letter X) and then press [Enter]. Notice that the spacing between letters adjusts slightly after you press [Enter]. On a color monitor, the comment changes to green after you press [Enter].

❼ Continue typing the following comments. Remember to include the apostrophe at the beginning of each line, and notice that there are some blank lines in the comments, the lines that contain only an apostrophe at the beginning. Substitute the current date and your name where appropriate. You might need to drag the toolbar out of the way while you're entering text.

```
' Function written 1/31/97 by Andrew Cisneros.
' This function calculates the X-Bar chart lower control limit.
'
'
```

Now that you have entered the comments, you are ready to enter the function itself. The function takes the AverageXBar, A2, and Rbar values as input, uses these values to calculate the XBarLCL value, and returns the XBarLCL value to the worksheet.

To enter the XBarLCL function:

❶ Type **Function XBarLCL(AverageXBar, A2, RBar)** and press [Enter]. Do not type spaces between the arguments of the function. After you press [Enter], the "Function" turns blue on a color monitor and the spacing between the arguments adjusts slightly.

❷ Press [Tab] to indent the second line of the function. Type **XBarLCL=AverageXBar−(A2*RBar)** and press [Enter]. Do not include spaces. The spacing between the parts of the formula adjusts slightly after you press [Enter].

❸ Press [Backspace] to un-indent the third line of the function. Type **End Function** and press [Enter].

❹ Compare your work to the complete function. See Figure 11-21.

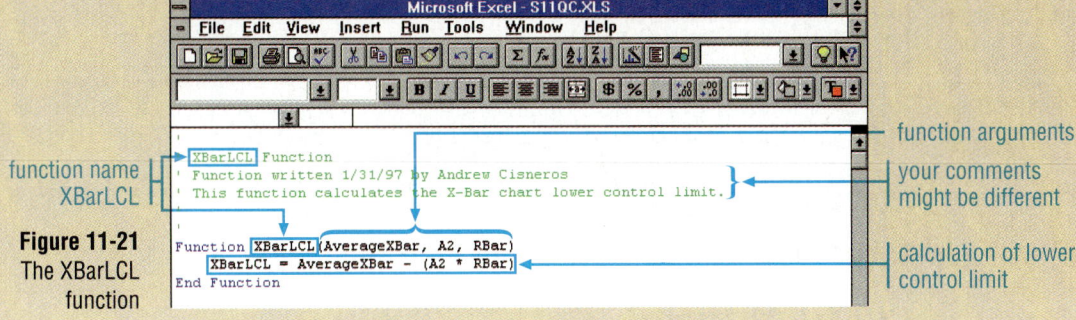

Figure 11-21 The XBarLCL function

TROUBLE? If your screen does not match Figure 11-21 (except for the current date and your name), edit the function until it does.

⑤ Click the **Save button** to save the workbook.

Now Andrew copies the XBarLCL function and edits it to create his XBarUCL function. The XBarUCL function will calculate the upper control limit for the X-Bar chart. The upper control limit equals the Average X-Bar plus the A2 factor multiplied by R-Bar:

Upper Control Limit = Average X-Bar + (A2 * R-Bar)

To create the XBarUCL:

① Make sure the SPC Functions module is active.

② Drag the pointer to highlight the entire XBarLCL function, including the comments at the beginning of the function. Make sure you include the first apostrophe in the first blank line.

③ Click the **Copy button**.

④ Press [↓] to remove the highlight and move the insertion point to the beginning of a new line, then press **[Enter]** to insert a blank row.

⑤ Click the **Paste button**. A copy of the function appears in the module.

⑥ Edit the function to match the XBarUCL function shown in Figure 11-22.

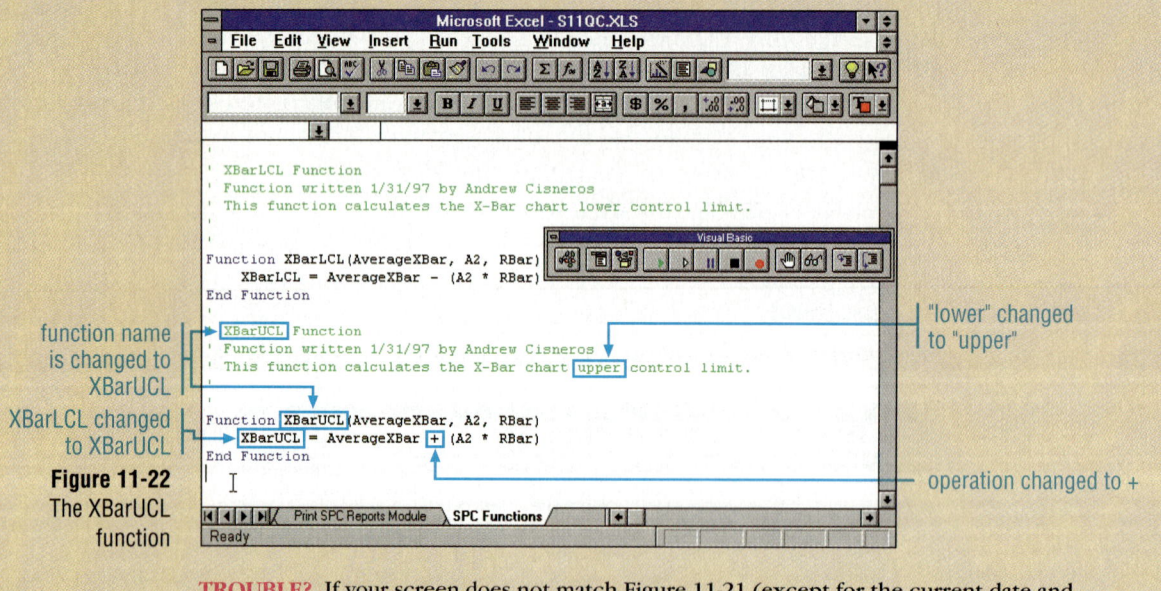

Figure 11-22 The XBarUCL function

TROUBLE? If your screen does not match Figure 11-21 (except for the current date and your name), edit the function until it does.

⑦ Click the **Save button** to save the workbook.

Now that Andrew has created his function, he can use it just as he would any other Excel function. He returns to the SPC worksheet and uses his user-defined functions to calculate the control limits.

Calculating the Control Chart Control Limits

The functions Andrew wrote to calculate the control limits reference the Average X-Bar value in cell F8, the A2 factor in cell J7, and the R-Bar value in cell F9 of the SPC worksheet. Andrew will use absolute references to these cells so he can copy the formula later.

To calculate the lower control limit for the X-Bar chart:

❶ Click the **SPC tab** to make the SPC worksheet the active sheet.

❷ Click cell **H14** to make it the active cell.

❸ Type **=XBarLCL($F$8,$J$7,$F$9)** and press [Enter]. The lower control limit value of 37.44 appears in cell H14.

❹ Click cell **H14**. See Figure 11-23.

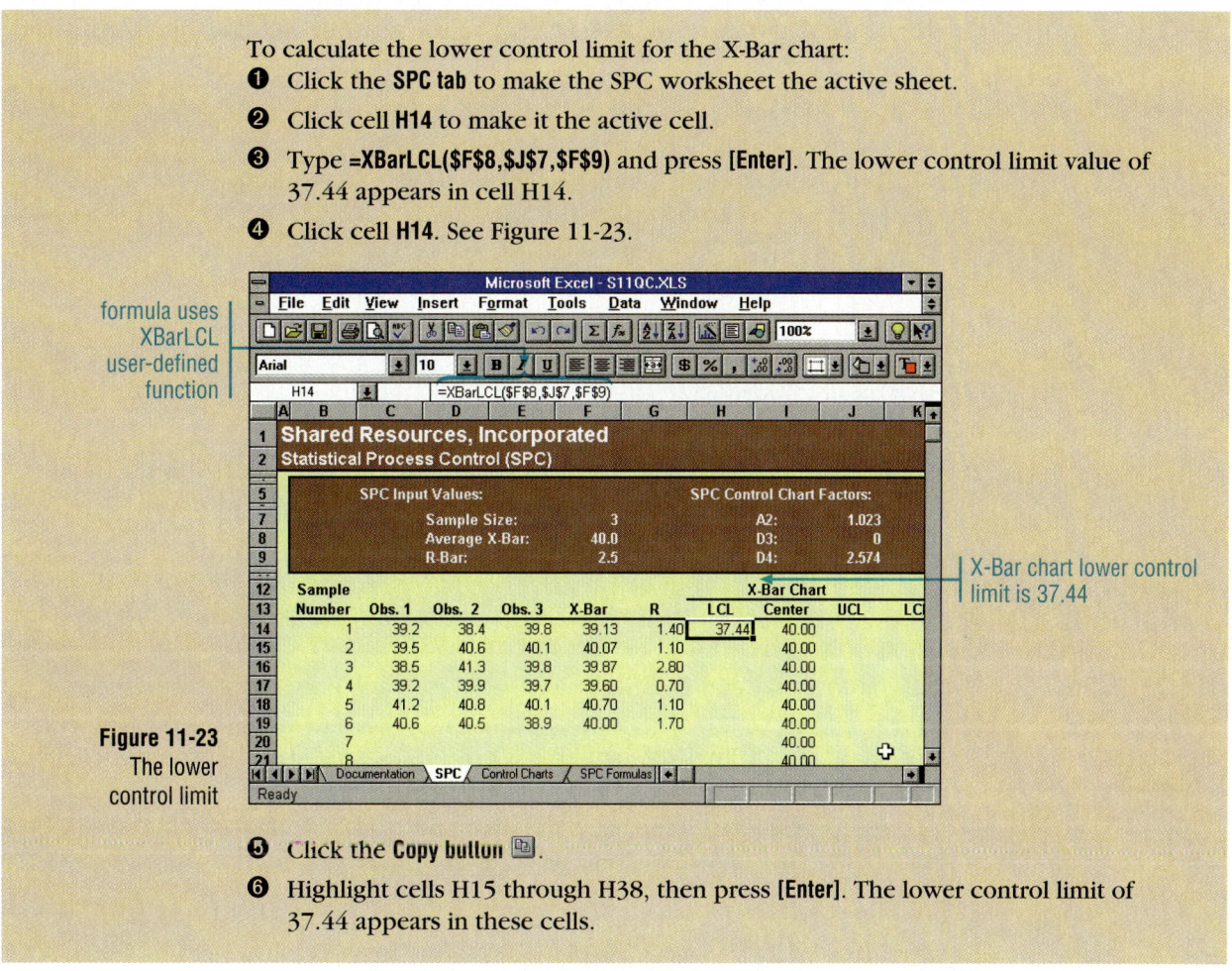

Figure 11-23
The lower control limit

❺ Click the **Copy button**.

❻ Highlight cells H15 through H38, then press [Enter]. The lower control limit of 37.44 appears in these cells.

Now Andrew calculates the upper control limit using his XBarUCL function.

To calculate the upper control limits for the X-Bar chart:

❶ Click cell **J14** to make it the active cell.

❷ Type **=XBarUCL($F$8,$J$7,$F$9)** and press [Enter]. The upper control limit value of 42.56 appears.

❸ Click cell **J14**, then click the **Copy button**.

❹ Highlight cells J15 through J38, then press [Enter]. The upper control limit value of 42.56 appears in these cells.

❺ Press [Ctrl][Home], then click the **Save button**.

Andrew's goal is to create an X-Bar chart to help monitor Shared Resources' materials recovery process. So far, he has calculated the center line and the control limits for the X-Bar chart using the user-defined functions he created on the SPC module. Andrew can now create the X-Bar chart itself. This chart will use data from the SPC worksheet. The X-Bar chart will appear on the Control Charts worksheet. Andrew starts by highlighting the worksheet ranges that will be represented in the chart. He includes rows 14 through 38 in the chart range so the chart will automatically update when he adds new observation data.

To select the worksheet ranges for the X-Bar chart:
❶ Drag the pointer to highlight cells B14 through B38.
❷ Press and hold [**Ctrl**] while you highlight cells F14:F38 and cells H14:J38.

Now Andrew uses ChartWizard to create the X-Bar chart.

To create the X-Bar chart:
❶ Click the **ChartWizard button**.
❷ Click the **Control Charts tab** to open the Control Charts sheet.
❸ Drag the pointer to outline the range A3:I17, then release the mouse button to display the ChartWizard - Step 1 of 5 dialog box. Make sure the range is =SPC!$B$14:$B$38,SPC!$F$14:$F$38,SPC!$H$14:$J$38.
❹ Click the **Next > button** to display the ChartWizard - Step 2 of 5 dialog box.
❺ Click the **XY (Scatter) chart type**, then click the **Next > button** to display the Chart Wizard - Step 3 of 5 dialog box.
❻ Click format **2**. Click the **Next > button** to display the ChartWizard - Step 4 of 5 dialog box.
❼ Make sure that the Columns option button is selected, and that 1 is in the Columns box and 0 is in the Row(s) box, then click the **Next > button**. The ChartWizard - Step 5 of 5 dialog box appears.
❽ Click the **Chart Title text box** to make it active, type **X-Bar Chart**, then click the **Finish button**. The chart sheet appears. See Figure 11-24.

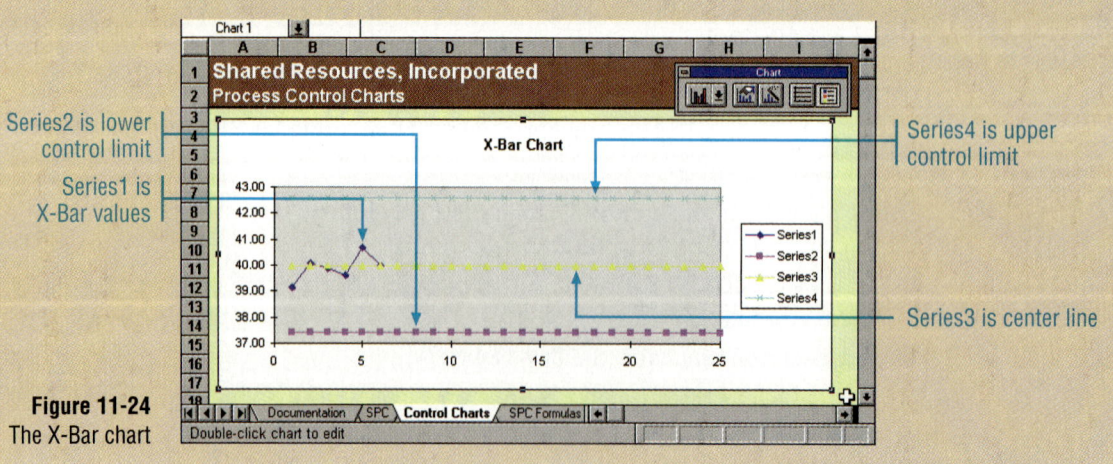

Figure 11-24 The X-Bar chart

Next, Andrew formats the X-Bar chart. He knows that in the future, some X-Bar measurements might fall above the upper control limit, or below the lower control limit. To allow for this possibility, he decides to adjust the y-axis to show a greater range of data values. He'll also format the data series to remove the data markers from the center line and control limits. First, Andrew adjusts the y-axis values.

To format the y-axis of the X-Bar chart:
1. Double-click the **X-Bar Chart** to activate it.
2. Double-click the **y-axis**. The Format Axis dialog box appears.
3. Click the **Scale tab**. The scale settings appear.
4. Click each of the Auto boxes to remove the check mark.
5. Now Andrew adjusts the y-axis values to display a larger range on the y-axis: Click the **Minimum text box** to select it, change the minimum scale value to **35**, then press **[Tab]** to move between text boxes and change the maximum to **45**, the major unit to **5.0**, the minor unit to **1.0**, and the X-axis crosses the Y-axis to **35**. Then click the **OK button**.

Now Andrew formats the data series. He selects new colors for the data series and then removes the data markers for the center line and control limits. These lines do not need data markers because they are reference lines.

To format the data series of the X-Bar chart:
1. Double-click the line in the chart representing the **Series1 data series** (not the Series1 label in the legend). The Format Data Series dialog box appears.
2. Click the **Name and Values tab**. The name and values settings appear. Click the **Name text box** and type **Sample X-Bar**.
3. Click the **OK button**. Sample X-Bar appears in the legend in place of the name Series1.
4. Double-click the **Series2 line** to display the Format Data Series dialog box.
5. If necessary, click the **Name and Values tab**, then click the **Name text box** and type **Lower Control Limit**.
6. Click the **Patterns tab**.
7. In the Line settings, click the **Custom option button**, then click the **Color box down arrow button** to display the color palette. In the color palette, click the red square. If you have a monochrome monitor, click the black square in the upper-left corner of the palette. See Figure 11-25.

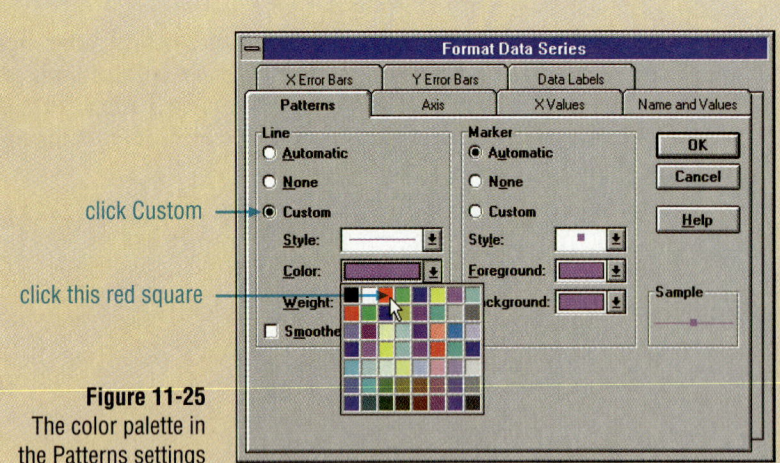

Figure 11-25
The color palette in the Patterns settings

click Custom

click this red square

8. In the Marker settings, click the **None option button**.
9. Click the **OK button**.
10. Repeat Steps 4 through 9 for the Series3 and Series4 lines. Name Series3 "Center Line"; use the color black (first square in the first row of the palette) with no markers. Name Series4 "Upper Control Limit"; use the color green (the second square in the second row of the palette) with no markers. (If you have a monochrome monitor, use the same black square you used for the lower control limit). Then, double-click cell **A1** to deactivate the chart. The chart appears as shown in Figure 11-26.

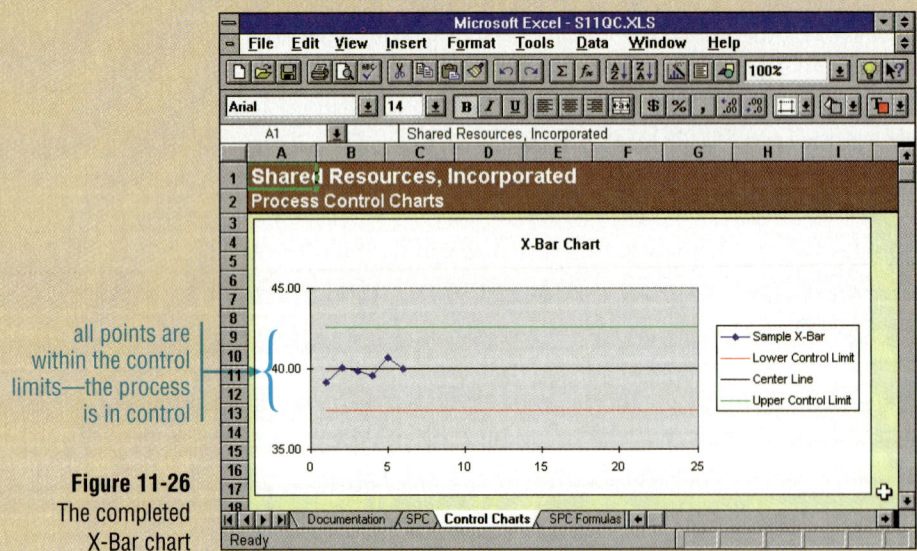

all points are within the control limits—the process is in control

Figure 11-26
The completed X-Bar chart

TROUBLE? If your chart doesn't match the chart in Figure 11-26, edit your chart until it does.

Remember that the purpose of a control chart is to provide an easy way to monitor a process. If all the sample X-Bars are within the control limits, the process is in control. Looking at the X-Bar chart, Andrew can see that all the sample X-Bars are within the control limits. The Shared Resources production process is in control. Andrew saves the workbook. Because you will be using a new workbook in the following sections of the tutorial, you will also close your workbook.

To save the workbook:
❶ Click the **Documentation tab**, then press **[Ctrl][Home]**.
❷ Click the **Save button** 🖫.
❸ Click **File**, then click **Close** to close the S11QC.XLS workbook.

If you want to take a break and resume the tutorial at a later time, you can exit Excel by double-clicking the Control menu box in the upper-left corner of the screen. When you resume the tutorial, launch Excel, maximize the Microsoft Excel and Book1 windows, and place your Student Disk in the disk drive. You do not need to open a workbook to continue with the tutorial.

■   ■   ■

In addition to the X-Bar chart, Andrew created a macro to print two worksheets providing information about calculations in the X-Bar chart, and two user-defined formulas that he used in the calculation of the control limits for the X-Bar chart.

Andrew now needs to update the workbook and the X-Bar chart after new sample data are obtained from the materials recovery process. Because this happens daily, Andrew decided to write a Visual Basic procedure to automate adding new sample results to the SPC worksheet and updating the X-Bar.

Andrew's procedure is in the C11QC2.XLS workbook. Let's open that workbook and save it as S11QC2.XLS.

To open the workbook:
❶ Click the **Open button** 📂 to display the Open dialog box.
❷ Double-click **C11QC2.XLS** in the File Name box to display the workbook.
  TROUBLE? If the file isn't in the file list, click the Drives down arrow button to display the drive in which your Student Disk is located.
❸ Make sure the Documentation sheet is the active worksheet.
❹ Double-click cell **B4**, change the filename to **S11QC2.XLS**, then press **[Enter]**.
❺ Press **[Ctrl][Home]** to make cell A1 the active cell.
❻ Click **File**, then click **Save As...** to display the Save As dialog box.
❼ Save the workbook as **S11QC2.XLS**.

To understand the steps that Andrew wants to automate, let's work with him as he manually enters one new sample.

The new sample will be sample 7 in the SPC worksheet, and the observations for the sample are 39.8, 39.5 and 40.2. Andrew enters these numbers into the SPC worksheet and then calculates the sample 7 X-Bar and R values.

To enter the sample observations and calculate X-Bar and R:
1. Click the **SPC tab**.
2. Click cell **C20**.
3. Type **39.8** and press **[Enter]**.
4. Click cell **D20**. Type **39.5** and press **[Enter]**.
5. Click cell **E20**. Type **40.2** and press **[Enter]**.
6. Highlight the range F19:G19, then click the **Copy button**.
7. Highlight the range F20:G20, then press **[Enter]** to complete copying the formulas for calculating X-Bar and R. The values for X-Bar and R for the new sample are calculated as 39.83 and 0.70 respectively, and appear in the worksheet. See Figure 11-27.

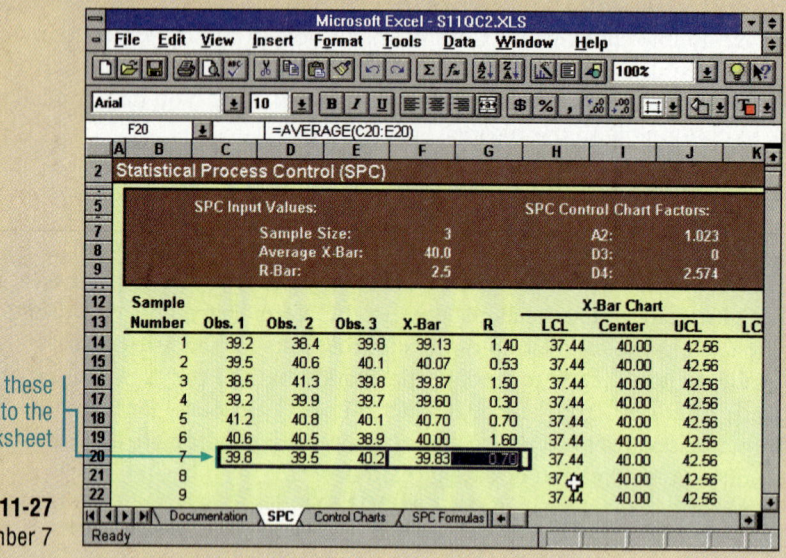

Figure 11-27
Sample number 7

TROUBLE? If your X-Bar and R values don't match those in Figure 11-27, you might have entered an observation value incorrectly. Check the values you entered.

Because you included rows 14 through 38 in the chart range, the X-Bar chart automatically updated when you added new observation data to row 20. Let's take a look at the X-Bar chart and see if the process measurements are still within control limits.

To view the X-Bar chart:
1. Click the **Control Charts tab**. The X-Bar chart with the new X-Bar value is shown in Figure 11-28.

Writing Visual Basic Procedures **EX 411**

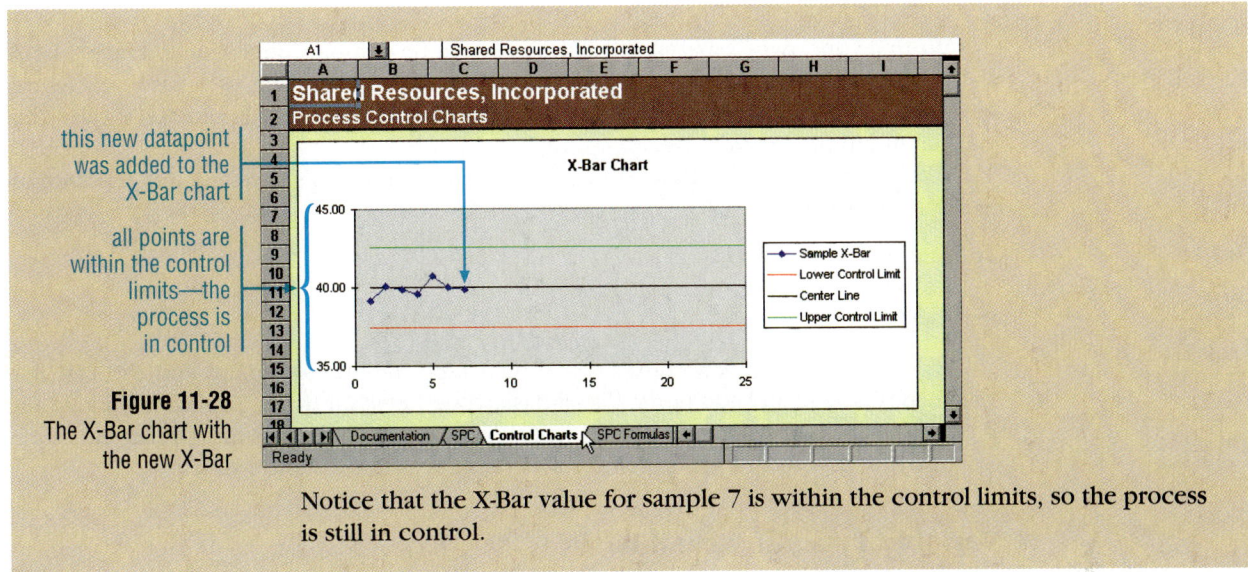

Figure 11-28
The X-Bar chart with the new X-Bar

- this new datapoint was added to the X-Bar chart
- all points are within the control limits—the process is in control

Notice that the X-Bar value for sample 7 is within the control limits, so the process is still in control.

Andrew wants to automate the steps to enter the sample observations and calculate the X-Bar and R values. These steps require user input and can't be recorded easily with the macro recorder, so Andrew has written a Visual Basic procedure to allow for user input.

Writing Visual Basic Procedures

You can write Visual Basic procedures on any module sheet. Andrew's procedure, named SPCSample, is on the SPC Sample module of the workbook.

To view the SPCSample procedure:

❶ Click the **SPC Sample Module tab**.

❷ The SPCSample procedure is shown in Figure 11-29.

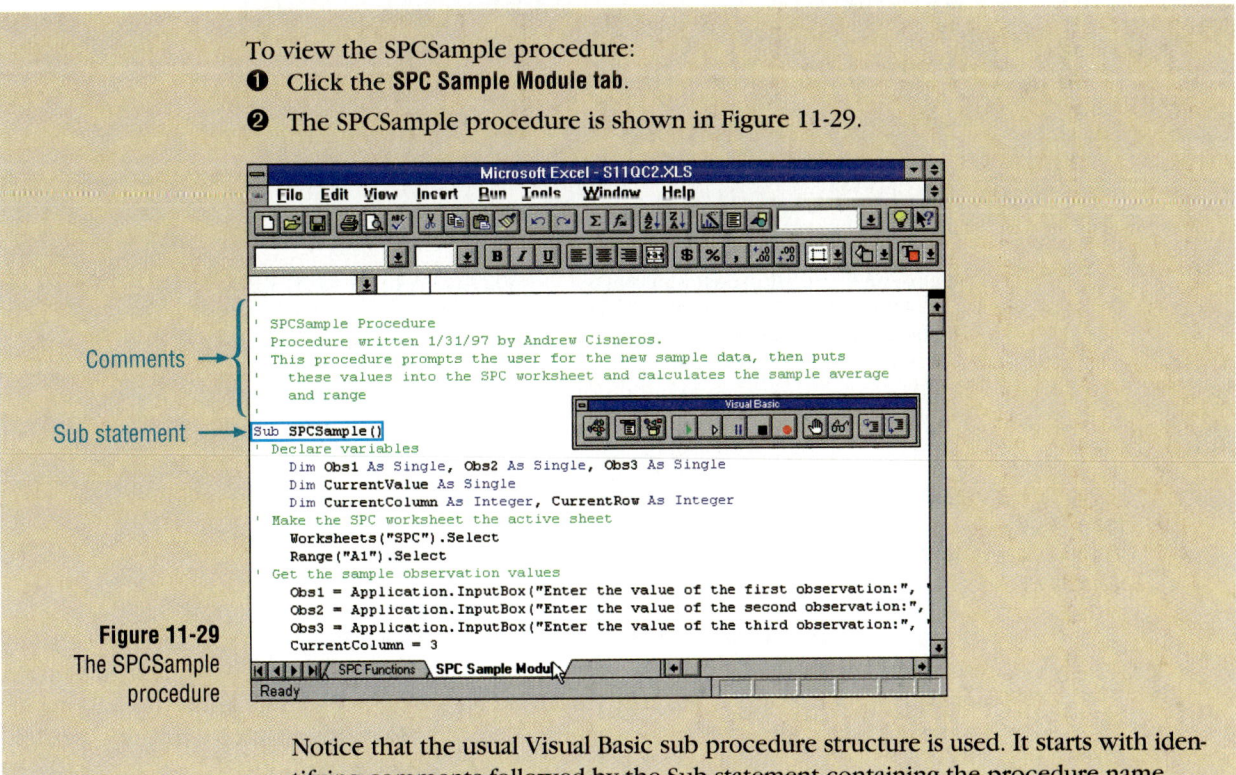

Figure 11-29
The SPCSample procedure

- Comments
- Sub statement

Notice that the usual Visual Basic sub procedure structure is used. It starts with identifying comments followed by the Sub statement containing the procedure name.

Writing your own Visual Basic procedures can be complex, and it would take a book as long as this one to cover the topic thoroughly. Instead of trying to write a procedure, let's look at Andrew's procedure and learn about some of the tools and techniques that you can use in procedures.

Like macros, all Visual Basic procedures begin with a Sub statement and end with an End Sub statement:

```
Sub ProcedureName()
    <Visual Basic statement>
End Sub
```

When you write a procedure, you should type the Sub statement and the End Sub statement first and add additional Visual Basic code between them. This will maintain the proper Visual Basic structure, and you will not forget to add the End Sub statement.

The first new technique that Andrew uses is declaring variable types.

Variable Types in Visual Basic

Variables store data for procedures and user-defined functions just like cells store data in a worksheet. Variables always have identifying variable names. (For example, we used a variable named `XbarLCL` in the XBarLCL function.) They can store numbers or labels, called character strings. A variable that can store information about whether a condition is true or false is called a **Boolean variable**. When we talk about the information stored in a variable, we often refer to the value of a variable or we say that a variable is set to a particular value. There are several types of variables, some of which are illustrated in Figure 11-30.

Variable Type	Data Value Range
Variant	Depends on the data
Boolean	True or False
Integer	–32,768 to +32,767
Long (Long Integer)	–2,147,483,648 to +2,147,483,647
Single (single-precision floating point)	–3.402823E38 to +3.402823E38
Double (double-precision floating point)	–1.79769313486232E308 to +1.79769313486232E308
Currency	–922,337,203,685,477.5808 to +922,337,203,685,477.5808
Date	January 1, 0100 to December 31, 9999
String	up to 65,535 Characters

Figure 11-30
Visual Basic variable types

So far, Andrew has used Visual Basic variables without worrying about their types. If you do not declare the type of variable you are using, Visual Basic declares the variable as a variant type automatically. A **variant variable** changes type, depending on the information stored in it. When `XbarLCL` was assigned a number, Visual Basic made it a numeric variable.

Your Visual Basic procedures will run more efficiently if you specify the type of variable you want. You declare variable types using the Visual Basic Dim statement, which has the syntax:

```
Dim VariableName As VariableType
```

Andrew's SPCSample procedure begins with the declaration of variables shown in Figure 11-31.

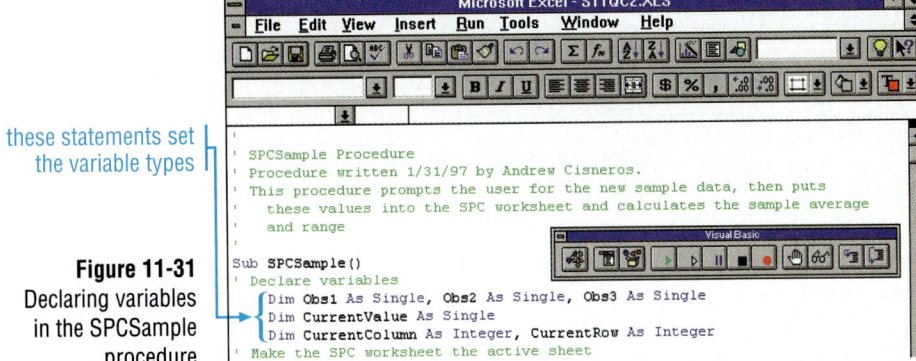

Figure 11-31
Declaring variables in the SPCSample procedure

these statements set the variable types

Andrew uses the variables `Obs1`, `Obs2`, and `Obs3` to store the observation values. He declares these variables as single-precision floating point numbers because they require decimal places. Andrew uses the variable `CurrentValue` to store the value of the active cell. He also declares this variable as single-precision floating point numbers because the numbers stored here have decimal places. Andrew uses the variables `CurrentColumn` and `CurrentRow` to store the location of the active cell. He declares these variables as integers because they don't require decimal places. Note the use of comments to identify the purposes of the statements. It is helpful to use comments liberally so that a user can identify easily the purpose of the procedure.

Selecting a Worksheet and an Active Cell

The next set of Visual Basic statements in Andrew's procedure make the SPC worksheet the active sheet and cell A1 the active cell. To do this, Andrew uses the `Select` method with `Worksheets` and `Range` objects:

```
' Make the SPC worksheet the active sheet
    Worksheets("SPC").Select
    Range("A1").Select
```

Prompting for User Input

Unlike a simple macro, a procedure allows you to prompt the user for input. The procedure then stores the input as a variable. (In this case, the procedure will store the input in the variables `Obs1`, `Obs2`, and `Obs3`.) To allow for user input, you use the `InputBox` method with the `Application` object.

EX 414 TUTORIAL 11 Application Development with Macros and Visual Basic

Andrew has used this technique in his SPCSample procedure.

To view the InputBox method:

❶ Scroll the SPCSample procedure in the SPC Sample Module sheet until you see all of the section that starts with the comment **Get the sample observation values**. Drag the Visual Basic toolbar to another part of the window if it blocks your view of the statements in the section. See Figure 11-32.

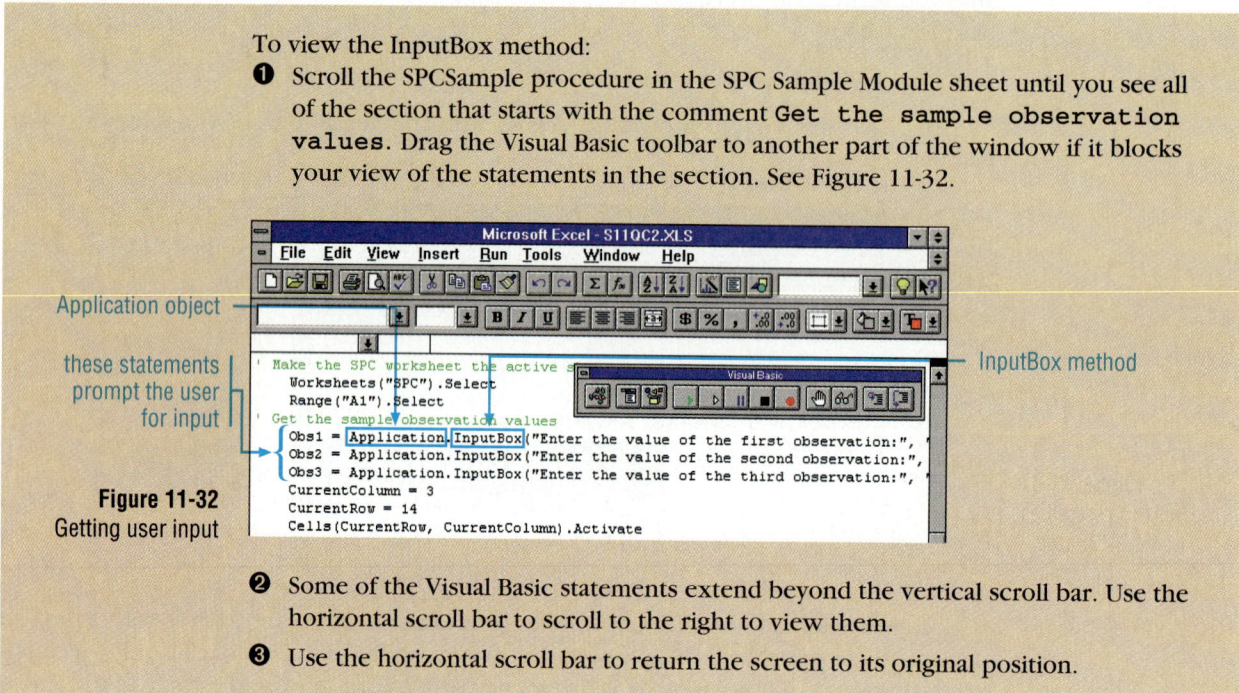

Figure 11-32
Getting user input

❷ Some of the Visual Basic statements extend beyond the vertical scroll bar. Use the horizontal scroll bar to scroll to the right to view them.

❸ Use the horizontal scroll bar to return the screen to its original position.

The statement that begins **Obs1 = Application.InputBox ("Enter the value of the first observation:"** will display the dialog box (an Input Box) when the SPCSample procedure is run. See Figure 11-33.

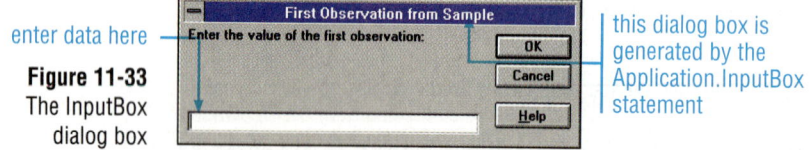

Figure 11-33
The InputBox
dialog box

The Input Box method allows you to prompt a user for a value or label. Visual Basic then stores the information in a variable. For example, in Andrew's procedure the variable **Obs1** in the following statement stores the value entered by the user:

`Obs1 = Application.InputBox()`

After the user enters the three observation values, the values should be displayed in the worksheet. The next part of the procedure finds blank worksheet cells in which to display the new observation values.

Andrew's procedure first makes cell C14 in the SPC worksheet the active cell. This is done by the statements:

```
CurrentColumn = 3
CurrentRow = 14
Cells(CurrentRow, CurrentColumn).Activate
```

The variable `CurrentColumn` is set to 3, which refers to the third column in the worksheet, column C. The variable `CurrentRow` is set to 14. Using these values, the statement `Cells(CurrentRow, CurrentColumn).Activate` becomes `Cells(14, 3).Activate`, which tells Excel to make cell C14 the active cell.

The next statement in Andrew's procedure is:

`CurrentValue = Cells(CurrentRow, CurrentColumn).Value`

This sets the value of the variable `CurrentValue` equal to the contents of cell C14.

To find the row in which to place the new observations, Andrew has to find the first blank cell in column C. Because a blank cell is numerically equal to a value of zero, Andrew's procedure can determine if the cell is blank by testing to see if its value is equal to zero.

To do this, Andrew uses a Visual Basic control structure.

Visual Basic Control Structures

A **control structure** controls the actions of a program based on the value of a variable or on whether or not a certain condition exists. The **If...Then...Else control structure** tests a condition or a set of conditions and performs actions based on whether or not the conditions are true. For example, suppose you find a car you want to buy. If the dealer will sell it to you for less than $10,000, you'll buy it, otherwise you won't. This might remind you of the IF function you worked with in Tutorial 4—*if* the price is less than $10,000, *then* you'll buy the car, *else* you won't buy it.

The logic of the If...Then...Else statement is shown in Figure 11-34.

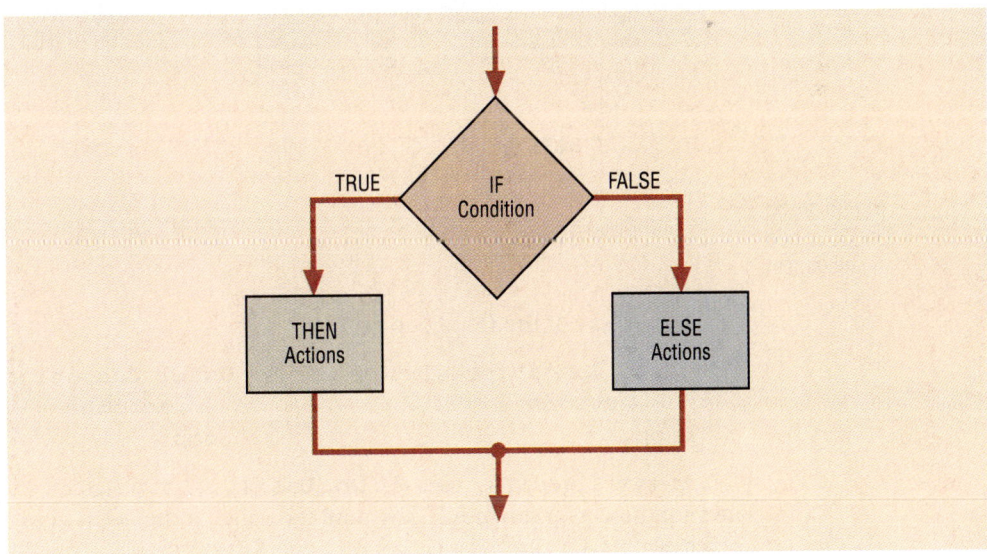

Figure 11-34
The If...Then...Else statement

The syntax of the If...Then...Else statement is:

```
If Condition1 Then
        Action1
    Else Action2
EndIf
```

Another Visual Basic control structure is the Do...Loop. The **Do...Loop control structure** allows you to repeat an action based on whether a condition is true or false. There are two variations of this statement. The **Do While...Loop** repeats an action as long as the condition is *true*. For example, you drive your car as long as it is true that you've got enough gasoline. When this condition stops being true, you're out of gasoline and you buy more or your car stops running. A Visual Basic statement of `Do While VariableX < 100` tells Visual Basic to repeat a set of steps as long as it is true that the value of `VariableX` is less than 100.

On the other hand, the **Do Until...Loop** repeats an action as long as the condition is *false*. For example, you keep washing dishes as long as it is false that all the dishes are clean. When this condition becomes true, all the dishes are clean and you stop. A Visual Basic statement of `Do Until VariableX < 100` tells Visual Basic to repeat a set of steps as long as it is false that the value of `VariableX` is less than 100; it continues repeating the steps until VariableX is less than 100.

Figure 11-35 illustrates the logic of the Do While...Loop and the Do Until...Loop statements.

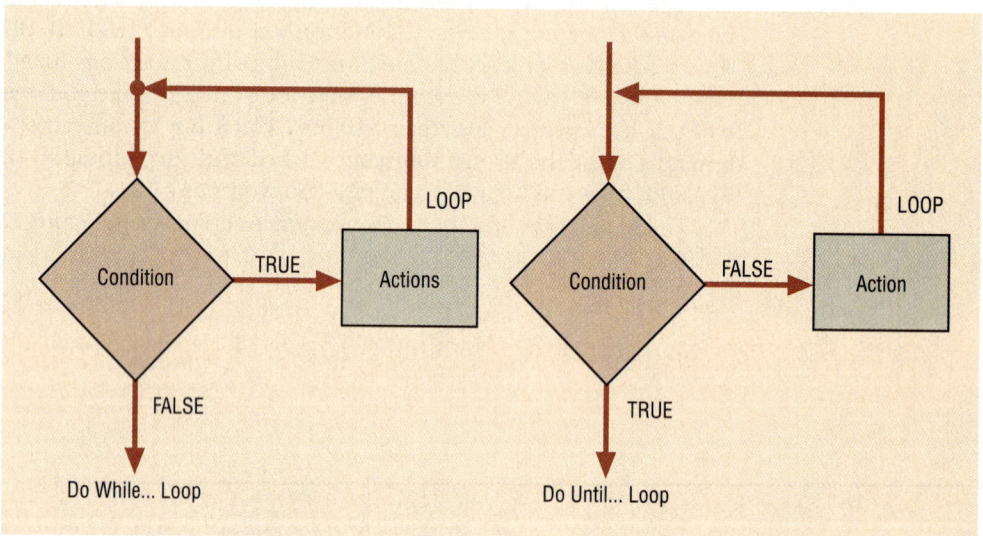

Figure 11-35
The Do...Loop statement

The syntax of the Do...Loop statements is:

```
Do While ConditionIsTrue         Do Until ConditionIsTrue
      Actions                          Actions
Loop                             Loop
```

Andrew's procedure uses the `Do Until...Loop` statement to repeat the action of moving the cursor down one row until the value of the cell is zero (that is, until the cursor reaches a blank cell).

```
Do Until CurrentValue = 0
  CurrentRow = CurrentRow + 1
  CurrentValue = Cells(CurrentRow,CurrentColumn).Value
Loop
```

When the first blank cell is found in column C, the cell becomes the active cell with the statement:

```
Cells(CurrentRow, CurrentColumn).Activate
```

Now that the proper row has been located, Andrew's procedure enters the observation values into the cells. Let's scroll the module so we can see the rest of the code in the procedure:

To view the rest of the SPCSample procedure:

❶ Scroll the SPCSample procedure in the SPC Sample Module sheet until you see all the statements in the section that starts with the comment **Put the sample observation values into the SPC worksheet** and ends with the **End Sub** statement. Move the Visual Basic toolbar to another part of the window, if necessary, to see the statements in the section. See Figure 11-36.

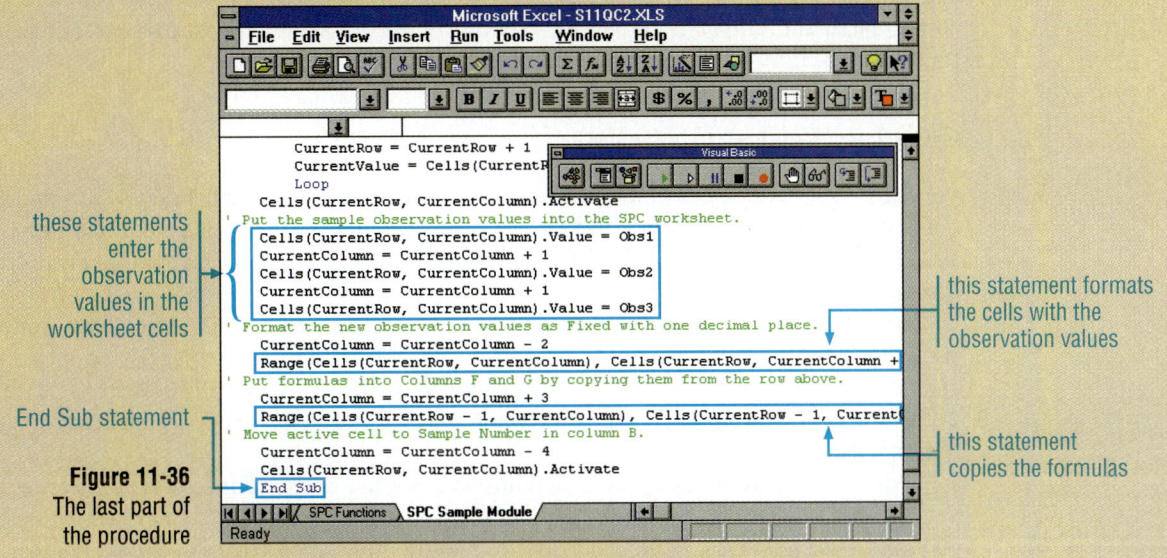

Figure 11-36
The last part of the procedure

❷ Some of the Visual Basic statements extend beyond the vertical scroll bar. Use the horizontal scroll bar to scroll to the right to view them.

❸ Use the horizontal scroll bar to return the screen to its original position.

Entering Values into Worksheet Cells

Andrew's procedure uses the Value method to enter the observation values into the SPC worksheet. After each value is entered, the active cell is moved one column to the right. The Visual Basic statements that accomplish this are:

```
' Put the sample observation values into the SPC worksheet.
    Cells(CurrentRow, CurrentColumn).Value =  Obs1
    CurrentColumn = CurrentColumn + 1
    Cells(CurrentRow, CurrentColumn).Value = Obs2
    CurrentColumn = CurrentColumn + 1
    Cells(CurrentRow, CurrentColumn).Value = Obs3
```

Formatting Worksheet Cells

You can format cells using the NumberFormat property. Andrew's procedure moves the active cell back to column C with the statement `CurrentColumn = CurrentColumn - 2`, and then uses the NumberFormat property to format the observation values as fixed (no commas, no dollar signs) with one decimal place.

The Visual Basic statement that formats the cells is `Range(Cells(CurrentRow, CurrentColumn), Cells(CurrentRow, CurrentColumn + 2)) .NumberFormat = "0.0"`.

Now the X-Bar and R values must be calculated. Remember that when we added a new sample manually, we did these calculations by copying the formulas from the row above. Andrew's procedure also creates the formulas by copying them from the row above. First, the cursor is moved to column G by the statement `CurrentColumn = CurrentColumn + 3`, then the formulas are copied.

Copying Worksheet Cells

You can copy worksheet cells using the Copy method. The Visual Basic statement that copies the cells is `Range(Cells(CurrentRow - 1, CurrentColumn), Cells(CurrentRow - 1, CurrentColumn + 1)).Copy (Cells(CurrentRow, CurrentColumn))`.

Andrew's procedure ends by moving the active cell to column B, the column Andrew chose to identify the new sample's number. The Visual Basic statements that move the cursor and make the cell active are `CurrentColumn = CurrentColumn - 4` and `Cells(CurrentRow,CurrentColumn).Activate`. The procedure ends with the required `End Sub` statement.

Now that we know how the procedure is designed, let's see it in action. Andrew has a set of new sample data. Observation 1 is 40.2, observation 2 is 39.7, and observation 3 is 40.8. Let's use the SPCSample procedure to add the new sample data to the worksheet.

To run the SPCSamples procedure:

❶ Click the **SPC tab** to make the SPC worksheet active.

❷ Click **Tools**, click **Macro...**, then double-click the macro name **SPCSample** in the Macro Name/Reference list in the Macro dialog box.

❸ When you are prompted for the first input value, type **40.2** in the text box, then click the **OK button**.

❹ When you are prompted for the second input value, type **39.7** in the text box, then click the **OK button**.

❺ When you are prompted for the second input value, type **40.8** in the text box, then click the **OK button**.

❻ The new sample data appears in the worksheet. See Figure 11-37.

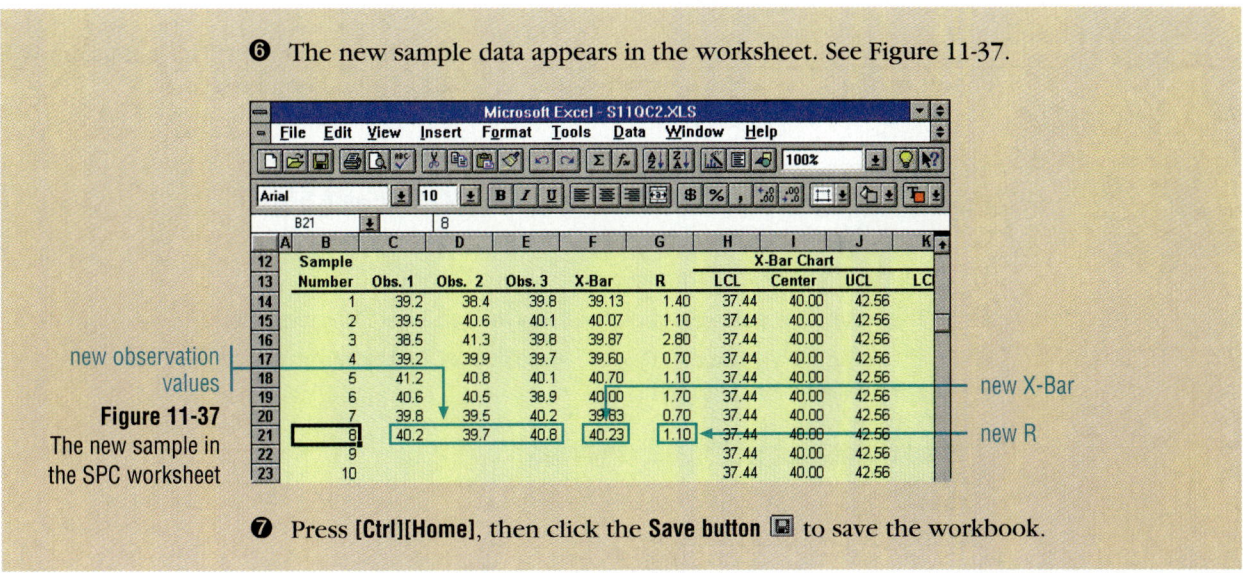

Figure 11-37
The new sample in the SPC worksheet

❼ Press **[Ctrl][Home]**, then click the **Save button** to save the workbook.

Now that Andrew's procedure to add new sample data is working, he adds a command to the Tools menu to run the procedure.

Adding a Command to the Tools Menu to Run the Macro

After you create a macro that you plan to use regularly, it is helpful to add a command to the Tools menu to allow you to run your macro quickly and easily.

REFERENCE WINDOW

Adding a Command to the Tools Menu to Run an Excel Macro

- Click Tools, then click Macro... to display the Macro dialog box.
- In the Macro Name/Reference box, click the name of the macro.
- Click the Options button to display the Macro Options dialog box.
- In the Assign To settings, click the Menu Item on Tools Menu checkbox, then click the Menu Item on Tools Menu text box and type the command name as you want it to appear on the Tools menu.
- Click the OK button on the Macro Options dialog box.
- Click the Close button on the Macro Dialog box.

Andrew adds an "Add SPC Sample" command to the tools menu. This command will appear on the Tools menu only when the S11QC2.XLS workbook is open.

To add the Add SPC Sample command to the Tools menu:

❶ Click **Tools**, then click **Macro...** to display the Macro dialog box.

❷ Click **SPCSample** in the Macro Name/Reference box.

❸ Click the **Options button** to display the Macro Options dialog box.

❹ In the Assign To settings, click the **Menu Item on Tools Menu checkbox**.

❺ In the Assign To settings, click the **Menu Item on Tools Menu text box**, then type **Add SPC Sample**. See Figure 11-38.

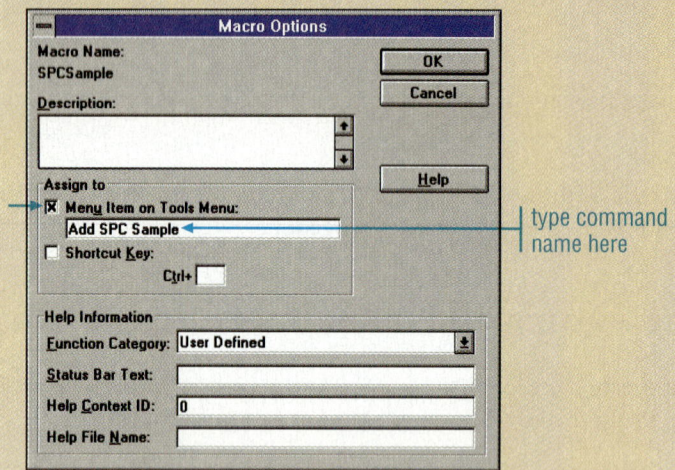

Figure 11-38
The Macro Options dialog box

❻ Click the **OK button** in the Macro Options dialog box.

❼ Click the **Close button** in the Macro dialog box.

Andrew has just received a new set of sample observations. Observation 1 is 39.2, observation 2 is 39.8, and observation 3 is 39.4. He uses his Add SPC Sample command to add the sample data to the SPC worksheet.

To use the Add SPC Sample Command:

❶ Click **Tools**. The Tools menu appears with the Add SPC Sample command at the bottom of the menu. See Figure 11-39.

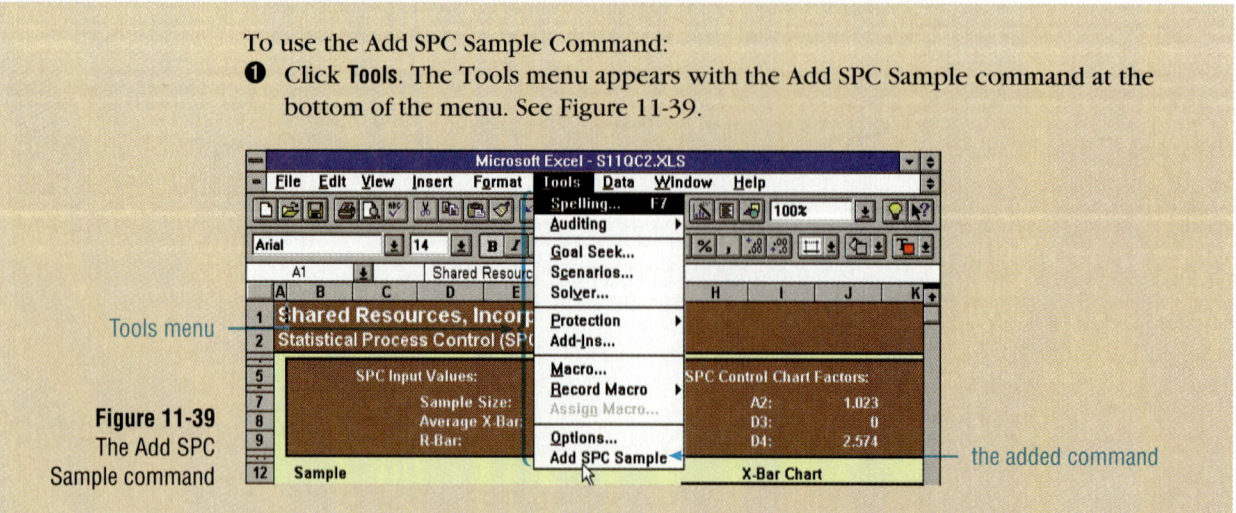

Figure 11-39
The Add SPC Sample command

Adding a Command to the Tools Menu to Run the Macro **EX 421**

❷ Click **Add SPC Sample**.

❸ Use the dialog boxes to enter **39.2**, **39.8**, and **39.4** as the input values.

❹ Press **[Ctrl][Home]**, then click the **Save button** to save the workbook.

The new sample has been added to the SPC worksheet. But to evaluate the results of the sample, Andrew needs to check the X-Bar chart to see if the process is still in control.

To check the X-Bar chart:

❶ Click the **Contol Charts tab**. The X-Bar chart now appears. See Figure 11-40.

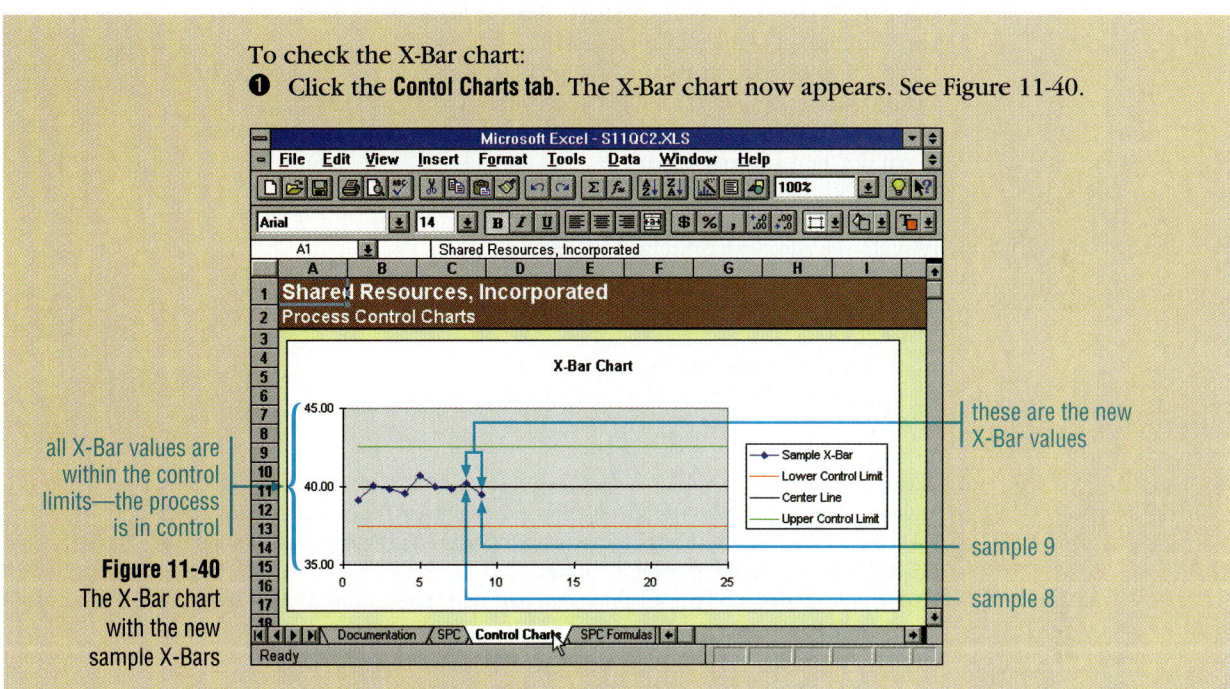

Figure 11-40
The X-Bar chart with the new sample X-Bars

all X-Bar values are within the control limits—the process is in control

these are the new X-Bar values

sample 9

sample 8

The X-Bar chart shows that the sample X-Bars are within the control limits, so the process is in control. This indicates that the Shared Resources materials recovery process is working, and that Shared Resources is recovering enough materials to remain profitable. The X-Bar chart provides Shared Resources' management an easy way to monitor the materials recovery process, and Andrew's macro, user-defined functions and SPCSample procedure provide powerful tools that allow new sample data be added easily to the workbook. Andrew closes his workbook.

To close the workbook:

❶ Click the **Documentation tab**.

❷ Press **[Ctrl][Home]**, then click the Save button to save the workbook.

❸ Click **File**, then click **Close** to close the S11QC2.XLS workbook.

❹ Exit Excel if you are not proceding directly to the Tutorial Assignments.

Questions

1. What is an Excel macro?
2. What is a Visual Basic procedure?
3. Discuss the relationship between macros and procedures.
4. What is the advantage of recording a macro instead of writing one? When would you want to write a macro instead of recording one?
5. What are the five types of Excel sheets that can be used in a workbook. Give a brief description of the purpose of each.
6. What is the difference between a sub procedure and a user-defined function?
7. Define objects, properties, and methods. Give two examples of each.
8. What is a Visual Basic control structure? Sketch a flow chart that illustrates:
    a. an If...Then...Else statement
    b. a Do While...Loop statement
    c. a Do Until...Loop statement
9. How do you run a macro from the Tools menu?
10. Describe how an SPC control chart works. In your discussion, define the following terms:
    a. Center line
    b. Lower control limit (LCL)
    c. Upper control limit (UCL)
    d. In control
    e. Out of control
11. In the Microsoft Help System, click Programming with Visual Basic in the Microsoft Excel Help Contents to open the Visual Basic Reference. In the Visual Basic Reference, find and print the topic "Understanding Visual Basic Objects in Microsoft Excel." Using this information:
    a. Define and describe the terms "container" and "collection" as they apply to Visual Basic.
    b. Define and discuss a "property that returns an object."
    c. Define and discuss a "method that returns an object."
12. In the Microsoft Help System, click Programming with Visual Basic in the Microsoft Excel Help Contents to open the Visual Basic Reference. In the Visual Basic Reference, find and print the topics "Range Object," "RowHeight Property," and the example for the "RowHeight Property." Using this material, write (on paper, not using Excel) a macro that will set the row height of rows 4 through 10 to 21.00.

Tutorial Assignments

1. Launch Excel, if necessary, and maximize the Excel window.
2. Open the T11QC3.XLS file.
3. Save the file as S11QC3.XLS.
4. On the Documentation sheet, change the filename in cell B4 to S11QC3.XLS.
5. Edit the contents by adding sheet names and sheet contents to bring the documentation up to date.

6. On the Print SPC Reports Module sheet, create a macro that prints only the SPC Formulas.
   a. Copy the PrintSPCInformation macro to serve as a model.
   b. Edit the copy to create a macro named PrintSPCFormulas. *Hint*: You need to edit the comments and the sub procedure name and delete the four lines that print the SPC Table.
7. Create a macro that prints only the SPC Table.
   a. Copy the PrintSPCInformation macro to serve as a model.
   b. Edit the copy to create a macro named PrintSPCTable. *Hint*: You need to edit the comments and the sub procedure name and delete the four lines that print the SPC Formulas.
8. Use the PrintSPCFormulas macro and the PrintSPCTable macro to print the SPC Formulas and the SPC Table.
9. Switch to the SPC Functions worksheet.
10. Based on the formulas in the SPC Formulas sheet, write these three user-defined functions (*Hint*: These formulas use the same basic structure as those in the tutorial.):
    a. RCenter, which calculates the center line for an R chart.
    b. RLCL, which calculates the lower control limit for an R chart.
    c. RUCL, which calculates the upper control limit for an R chart.
11. Switch to the SPC worksheet.
12. Using your user-defined functions, calculate the LCL, center line, and UCL for the R chart (*Hint*: These worksheet formulas use the same basic structure as those in the tutorial). Copy your formulas to all of the 25 rows where samples can be entered in the worksheet.
13. Switch to the Control Charts worksheet.
14. Create an R chart in cells A19 through I33 (*Hint*: You need to use the ranges B14:B38, G14:G38, K14:M38). Label it R chart, and format it similarly to the X-Bar chart you created in the tutorial.
15. To be in control, a process must be in control on both the X-Bar chart (which checks the value of the product variable being measured) and the R Chart (which checks the variability of the product variable being measured). Is the Shared Resources production process under control?
16. Use your library to find references on quality control and statistical process control. Write a short paper explaining the statement made in Tutorial Assignment 15, that a process must be in control on both the X-Bar chart and the R chart to be in control. In your paper, show what it means if the process is in control according to one chart but not the other. Make sure you consider both possibilities.
17. Print the worksheet with both charts on it. Do not print row and column borders or gridlines. Center your printouts horizontally and include a right-aligned header with your name, the filename, the sheet name, and the date. Do not use a footer. Each printout should fit on its own page.
18. Print the Documentation sheet and the SPC sheet. Do not print row and column borders or gridlines. Center your printouts horizontally and include a right-aligned header with your name, the filename, the sheet name, and the date. Do not use a footer. Each printout should fit on its own page.
19. Submit your printouts and your written answers for Assignments 15 and 16 to your instructor.

Case Problems

1. Quality Control Using p Charts at Ten Mile Creek Manufacturing

Ten Mile Creek Manufacturing produces spare parts for agricultural equipment. Like other manufacturers, the company uses statistical process control as part of its quality control program. Susan McConnell is the director of Ten Mile Creek's quality control program and she is concerned with the amount of defective parts produced by the production process. She has asked you to help set up a p chart to monitor the percentage of defectives in samples of 500 units.

She has created an Excel workbook, but needs you to create the statistical process control worksheet and p chart. A p chart uses an average percentage defective, called p-Bar, as the basis of the chart. The center line is equal to p-Bar. The formulas for the control limits are more complicated:

$$\text{Lower Control Limit} = (\text{p-Bar}) - \left(3 * \sqrt{\frac{(\text{p-Bar}) * (1 - (\text{p-Bar}))}{n}}\right)$$

$$\text{Upper Control Limit} = (\text{p-Bar}) + \left(3 * \sqrt{\frac{(\text{p-Bar}) * (1 - (\text{p-Bar}))}{n}}\right)$$

Susan has asked you to write user-defined functions for the control limits so that she can use them easily in other worksheets.

1. Open the Quality Control workbook P11QCP.XLS, then save it as S11QCP.XLS on your Student Disk.
2. On the Documentation sheet in the S11QCP.XLS workbook, change the filename in cell B4 to S11QCP.XLS.
3. Enter your name in cell B5.
4. Add the current date to cell B6.

Create a user-defined function to calculate the control limits:

5. Insert a module sheet, then move it to the end of the workbook.
6. Name the module sheet SPC Functions Module.
7. Visual Basic's Sqr function calculates a square root. Read about this function in Excel's Help system. Make sure you study the examples.
8. Write a user-defined function named PLCL to calculate the p chart lower control limit. *Hint*: This formula uses the same basic structure as those in the tutorial.
9. Write a user-defined function named PUCL to calculate the p chart upper control limit. *Hint*: This formula uses the same basic structure as those in the tutorial.
10. On the Documentation sheet, update the documentation to include the new sheet.
11. On the SPC worksheet in the S11QCP.XLS workbook, enter an Excel formula that uses your PLCL function to calculate the p chart lower control limit in cell F14. *Hint*: Use absolute references so you can copy the formula.
12. Copy the lower control limit formula to cells F15 through F38.
13. In cell G14, enter an Excel formula to calculate the p chart center line. *Hint*: Use an absolute reference so you can copy the formula.
14. Copy the lower control limit formula to cells G15 through G38.
15. In cell H14, enter an Excel formula that uses your PUCL function to calculate the p chart upper control limit. *Hint*: Use absolute references so you can copy the formula.
16. Copy the lower control limit formula to cells H15 through H38.
17. Save the workbook.
18. On the Contol Charts worksheet, create the p chart. *Hint*: Use the steps in the tutorial as a guide for creating the X-Bar chart.
19. Based on the p chart, decide whether or not the process is in control. Write a memo to Susan in which you explain your conclusion.

20. Print the Documentation sheet, the SPC worksheet, and the Control Charts sheet. Do not print row and column borders or gridlines. Center your printouts horizontally and include a right-aligned header with your name, the filename, the sheet name, and the date. Do not use a footer. Each printout should fit on its own page.
21. Save and close the S11QCP.XLS workbook.
22. Submit your memo and printouts to your instructor.

2. Inventory Management at Wescott Manufacturing

Sarah Johnson works in the production department of Wescott Manufacturing. The production department handles its own purchasing, and Sarah helps with production inventories and materials purchases. She is concerned about ordering the most cost-effective order quantity, known as an Economic Order Quantity, or EOQ. Sarah has asked you to help her write a user-defined formula to calculate the EOQs.

1. Open the Inventory Management workbook P11INV.XLS, then save it as S11INV.XLS on your Student Disk.
2. On the Documentation worksheet in the S11INV.XLS workbook, change the filename in cell B4 to S11INV.XLS.
3. Enter your name in cell B5.
4. Add the current date to cell B6.

To create the EOQ user-defined function:

5. Insert a module sheet, then move it to the end of the workbook.
6. Name the module sheet EOQ Functions Module.
7. Write a user-defined function named EOQ to calculate an EOQ. The formula for an EOQ is:

$$EOQ = \sqrt{(2 * Annual\ Demand * Ordering\ Cost)/Holding\ Cost}$$

Hint: Visual Basic's Sqr function calculates a square root. If necessary, read about this function in Excel's Help system; make sure you study the examples.

8. On the Documentation sheet, update the documentation to include the new sheet.
9. On the Inventory worksheet, enter an Excel formula to calculate the holding cost in cell D8. The formula for calculating holding cost is:

$$holding\ cost = price * holding\ cost\ rate$$

Hint: Use an absolute reference to the holding cost rate so you can copy the formula.

10. Copy the holding cost formula to cells D9 through D12.
11. In cell F8, enter an Excel formula to calculate the EOQ that uses your user-defined EOQ function.
12. Copy the EOQ formula to cells F9 through F12.
13. Click the Documentation sheet tab, then save the workbook.
14. Print the Documentation sheet, the Inventory sheet, and the EOQ Functions module. Do not print row and column borders or gridlines. Center your printouts horizontally and include a right-aligned header with your name, the filename, the sheet name, and the date. Do not use a footer. Each printout should fit on its own page.
15. Save and close the S11INV.XLS notebook.
16. Submit your printouts to your instructor.

3. Financial Management at Emerald Computer Peripherals.

Ryan Fairchild works in the finance section of Emerald Computer Peripherals, a company the produces and sells personal computer add-on products such as modems. Part of his job is to create and print the financial statements of the company.

Ryan has prepared the statements in an Excel workbook and is ready to print them. Ryan has defined three worksheet ranges to be printed. Their names are FinancialSummary, IncomeStatement, and BalanceSheet.

He has decided that he wants to automate the printing process, and has asked you to help him create the necessary Excel macros or Visual Basic procedures.

1. Open the Financial Management workbook P11FIN.XLS, then save it as S11FIN.XLS on your Student Disk.
2. On the Documentation worksheet, change the filename in cell B4 to S11FIN.XLS.
3. Enter your name in cell B5.
4. Add the current date to cell B6.

To create the PrintReports macro:

5. Use Excel's macro recorder to record a macro to print all three sheets in the order (1) Financial Summary, (2) Income Statement, and (3) Balance Sheet.
6. Rename your new module sheet "PrintReports module" and, if necessary, move it to the end of the workbook.
7. On the PrintReports module, create three additional macros by copying the original macro three times and editing the copies. Each macro will print one of the three sheets. Name the macros: PrintSummary, PrintIncomeStatment, and PrintBalanceSheet.
8. Save the workbook.
9. Add commands to the Tools menu to run each of the four macros. Name the commands: Print Statements, Print Summary, Print I/S, and Print B/S.
10. Set the print settings on the three statement pages so you do not print row and column borders or gridlines; center your printouts horizontally; and include a right-aligned header with your name, the filename, the sheet name, and the date. Do not use a footer. Each printout should fit on its own page.
11. Using the commands on the Tools menu, use your macros to: (1) print all three sheets at one time, and (2) print each sheet individually.
12. Click the Documentation tab, then save the workbook.
13. Close the S11FIN.XLS workbook.
14. Submit your printouts to your instructor.

ADDITIONAL CASES

Additional Case 1

Sales Invoicing for Island Dreamz Shoppe

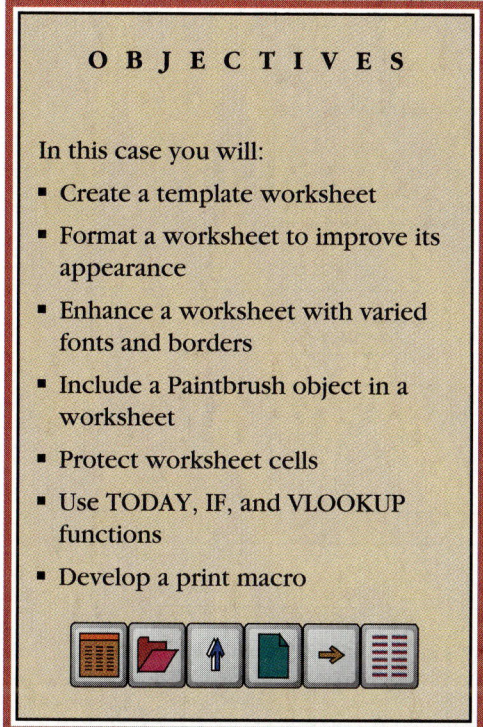

OBJECTIVES

In this case you will:
- Create a template worksheet
- Format a worksheet to improve its appearance
- Enhance a worksheet with varied fonts and borders
- Include a Paintbrush object in a worksheet
- Protect worksheet cells
- Use TODAY, IF, and VLOOKUP functions
- Develop a print macro

Island Dreamz Shoppe Like many entrepreneurs, Nicole Richardson discovered the old-fashioned way to make money: choose something you like to do, keep costs low and quality high, and make teamwork a priority. This principle has led to the success of her Island Dreamz Shoppe, a gift gallery that features crafts of artist from the Caribbean whose jewelry, paintings, and embroidered giftware capture the spirit of the islands.

Since the gallery opened two years ago, business has been brisk. At the request of many of her customers, Nicole has expanded her business to include mail orders. When customers visit the Shoppe, Nicole gives them a catalog to take home. Many customers find it more convenient to order items after they return home than to cram extra gifts into an already overstuffed suitcase.

On a good day, Nicole receives about a dozen phone calls from customers wanting to place orders. With so few calls, she doesn't need a full-blown order-entry system, but she would like to automate her invoice preparation. She decides to create an Excel workbook with a documentation sheet and a template worksheet for her sales invoices. After she creates the template, all she needs to do is enter the data for each order and print the invoice.

ADDITIONAL CASES Additional Case 1

Nicole has recently completed a paper invoice for an order from Rachel Nottingham, shown in Figure 1. Using this invoice as a model to identify the labels, formulas, and format she wants to use in her template worksheet, Nicole prepares her planning analysis sheet (Figure 2). The calculations she needs in the template include the current date, the unit price for each item ordered times the quantity ordered (the extended price), the total amount for all items, the sales tax, the shipping amount, and the total amount of the order.

Island Dreamz Shoppe
1001 Anchor Cove
Montego Bay, Jamaica, B.W.I.

Date	24-Nov-95
Invoice No	1097

Name: Rachel Nottingham
Address: 2741 Landsdowne Road
City: Victoria, BC   Postal Code: V8R 3P6
Country: Canada

Item #	Description	Quantity	Unit Price	Extended Price
21	Summer Beach Scene	3	$25.00	$75.00
27	Sea Scape Watch	2	36.00	72.00
47	Spanish Ducat Key Chain	1	12.00	12.00
63	Raindrop Crew Neck T-shirt	2	14.00	28.00
67	Stone-washed Twill Jacket	3	54.00	162.00

	Total Sale	$349.00
	Sales Tax	24.43
	Shipping	25.00
	TOTAL	**$398.43**

	Payment Method
	Check
	Visa
X	MasterCard
	Discover
	American Express
Credit Card #	4799123456789000

Expiration	03/97

Thank you for your order!

Figure 1
Island Dreamz Shoppe sales invoice

Using her planning analysis sheet and the original paper invoice, Nicole sketches the template she wants to create with Excel (Figure 3). For each item ordered, she plans to enter the item number, description, quantity, and unit price. She wants Excel to do the calculations described in her planning analysis sheet (Figure 2). The circled numbers are guides to help you relate Nicole's sketch to the required calculations.

Sales Invoicing for Island Dreamz Shoppe **EX 429**

Planning Analysis Sheet

<u>My goal:</u>
Develop a template worksheet for preparing sales invoices

<u>What results do I want to see?</u>
A sales invoice for each order

<u>What information do I need?</u>
Customer name and address
Item number and quantity to be shipped
Lookup description in product table ❶
Lookup unit price for item in product table ❷
Method of payment

<u>What calculations will I perform?</u>
1. Extended price ❸ = quantity * unit price
2. Total sale ❹ = sum of extended price
3. Sales tax ❺ = total sale * 7%
4. Shipping ❻ = if total sale is less than $200 then $15, otherwise $25
5. Total ❼ = total sale + sales tax + shipping

Figure 2
Nicole's planning analysis

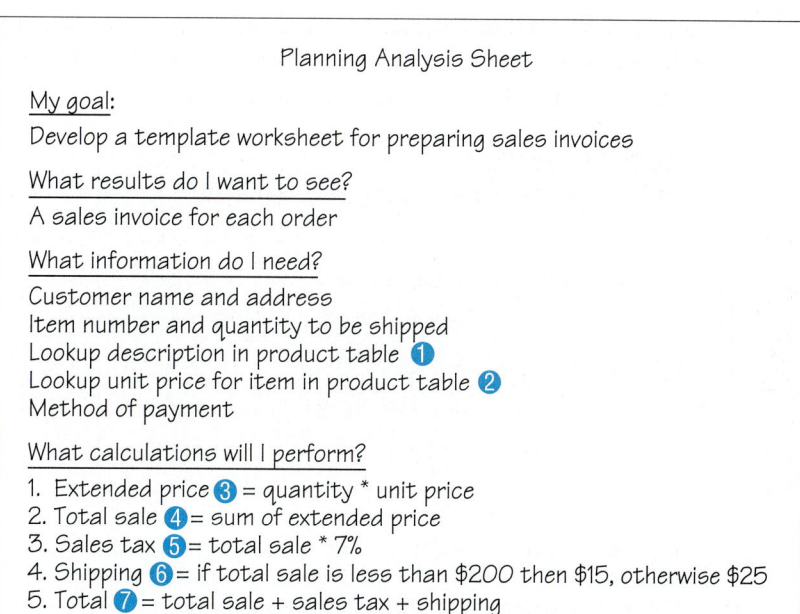

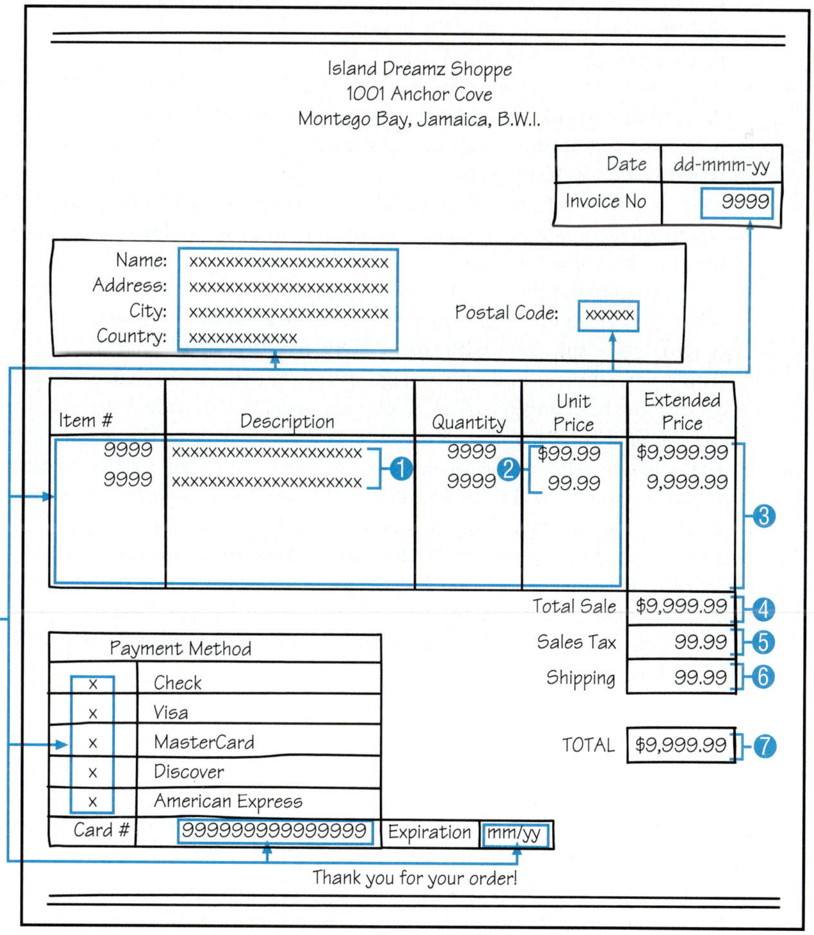

Figure 3
Nicole's sketch of her template worksheet

Nicole also sketches a table that lists the items Island Dreamz sells (Figure 4). The table includes the number, product description, and unit price of each product.

Figure 4
Island Dreamz product table

Item #	Description	Unit Price
21	Summer Beach Scene	25.00
27	Sea Scape Watch	36.00
31	Victorian Walking Stick	28.00
47	Spanish Ducat Key Chain	12.00
63	Raindrop Crew Neck T-shirt	14.00
67	Stone-washed Twill Jacket	54.00
78	Island Can Coolers	6.00

Help Nicole create a sales invoice template worksheet.

1. Create the sales invoice for Island Dreamz by entering the labels for the invoice template worksheet. Adjust the column widths as necessary. The placement of the labels should correspond to Nicole's sketch, but does not need to match exactly. Include a documentation sheet in the sales invoice workbook.
2. Enter the formulas specified by Figure 2 in the worksheet. Obtain the date from the computer's clock using the appropriate function.
3. Format the cells as shown in Figure 3. Remember to format the cell containing the expiration date as a label. Also, note that the first cell in the Unit Price and Extended Price columns is formatted differently than the rest of the cells in those columns.
4. Add fonts and borders as shown in Figure 1. Save your sales invoice template workbook as SC1IDS1.XLS.
5. Launch Paintbrush and open the XC1IDS1.BMP file, which contains the Island Dreamz logo. Paste the logo on the invoice as shown in Figure 1. Remove the line that surrounds the logo.
6. On a separate module sheet named "Macro," create a macro for printing the invoice. Add a command named "Print Invoice" to the Tools menu to run the macro. Name the sheet with the sales invoice "Invoice."
7. Apply protection as indicated in Figure 3 so that only those cells in which data are entered can be changed. Put the worksheet in protected mode. Make sure you remember the password. Before entering any data, save the revised template worksheet.
8. Test the operation of the worksheet by entering the data for the order shown in Figure 1. Note how the values in the Extended Price column are calculated automatically as you enter the data. Use the macro to print this invoice.
9. Choose additional fonts and borders to enhance the appearance of Nicole's invoice. Explain why you selected these characteristics. Delete the data for Rachel's order, then save the workbook as SC1IDS2.XLS. Test the operation of the worksheet using realistic data values. Print your enhanced worksheet, then close it without saving.

10. Open the SC1IDS1.XLS workbook and turn off the protection mode in preparation for modifying the workbook. Insert a new sheet between the Invoice and Macro sheets. Name the new sheet "Product." Create a product table that contains the product information shown in Figure 4. Excluding the column headings, name this table "Products." Print a copy of this sheet.

E 11. Nicole wants Excel to automatically look up the description and unit price in the product table when an item number is entered in the worksheet. If fewer than eight items are entered in the worksheet, the Item # in the unused lines is left blank. This causes the Description, Unit Price, and Extended Price columns in that row to also remain blank. This is accomplished by combining the IF function and the VLOOKUP function. The IF function tests for an empty cell in Item #. If a cell is empty, the Description, Unit Price, and Extended Price cells are left blank. The test for an empty cell uses two successive quotation marks (" "). A null, or empty, value is displayed in a cell using the same set of quotation marks. The VLOOKUP function uses the item number to obtain the appropriate description and unit price from the product table. Place appropriate formulas in the Description, Unit Price, and Extended Price cells. Test the worksheet with at least two orders; use a different number of items each time. Save the workbook as SC1IDS3.XLS. Use the print macro to print these invoices.

E 12. Protect the Description and Unit Price cells. Activate the worksheet protection mode. Test the worksheet with realistic data. Explain how you tested the protection for the Description, Unit Price, and Extended Price cells. Save the workbook as SC1IDS4.XLS.

13. Write instructions for operating Nicole's sales invoice worksheet.

14. What other changes or enhancements could Nicole make to improve her sales invoice worksheet?

E 15. Nicole wants to include an order form, which a customer can complete and return to Island Dreamz, with her catalog. Design this catalog order form. For ideas, you might want to research order forms in catalogs you have received. Create the form using Excel. Save the workbook as SC1IDS5.XLS, then print a copy of the blank order form.

16. Arrange and clearly identify the printouts and answers for all the problems in this case as your documentation for the case.

ADDITIONAL CASES

Additional Case 2

Performance Reporting for Boston Scientific

OBJECTIVES

In this case you will:
- Create and use a multiple sheet workbook
- Enhance worksheets with formatting
- Consolidate worksheet files
- Link worksheets
- Create a macro for combining files
- Create charts from summary data
- Create a print macro
- Add user-defined menu commands for macros
- Use Write as a client application

Boston Scientific* Boston Scientific is on the cutting edge of medical cost reduction. The company develops and manufactures catheters and other products that are used as alternatives to traditional surgery. As described by CEO Peter Nicholas: "We were one of the first companies to articulate the concept of less invasive procedures." Less invasive procedures are possible because current medical imaging techniques allow physicians to see inside the body and manipulate instruments through a natural opening or a tiny incision. Boston Scientific aggressively markets its products for these medical procedures. For example, a traditional coronary bypass operation often costs $50,000 to $70,000, including the hospital stay and weeks of recovery time. By contrast, clearing a clogged artery with one of Boston Scientific's catheters, which is inserted under the skin of a patient's arm, takes just a few hours and costs around $12,000.

*Adapted from: *Fortune*, "Boston Scientific," April 5, 1993, p. 97.

Although many of Boston Scientific's products are expensive relative to the cost of a scalpel, they enable a patient to leave the hospital much sooner and avoid huge hospital bills. For this reason, Boston Scientific's products are popular and sales continue to increase rapidly. Another important element in their growth is the company's ability to leverage technology across its four largely autonomous divisions: Medi-Tech (radiology), Mansfield (cardiology), Microvasive Endoscopy (gastroenterology), and Microvasive Urology.

Willow Shire joined Boston Scientific last year as a junior accountant. Her responsibilities include preparing the quarterly performance report that consolidates the financial results of the four divisions. Willow created a template worksheet for reporting quarterly financial results, a copy of which was sent to and completed by the controller at each division. Willow just received the workbook files from the four divisions. She now needs to prepare the consolidated statement of operation summarizing the division results.

You will prepare this statement by completing the following:

1. Read all the problems for this case and develop a planning analysis sheet to plan the consolidation worksheet for Boston Scientific. Use your planning analysis sheet to develop your Excel solution.
2. Open and review the workbook for each division: XC2BOSMT.XLS (Medi-Tech), XC2BOSMF.XLS (Mansfield), XC2BOSME.XLS (Microvasive Endoscopy), and XC2BOSMU.XLS (Microvasive Urology).
3. Create a multiple sheet workbook that contains a documentation sheet, a consolidation sheet, and a sheet for each division. Name the consolidation sheet "Consolidated Statement of Operations." Place the results for each division in its own sheet in the workbook. Assign appropriate names to the other worksheets. Include formulas in the consolidation sheet that add the division results to determine the corporate total. Apply appropriate formatting to enhance the title of each sheet. Save the workbook as SC2BOS1.XLS. Print the Consolidated Statement of Operations sheet.
4. Create a macro that lets Willow replace the consolidation data in the division worksheets with the data from the individual division workbook files and then prints all five statements of operation. Place the macro in a sheet named "Consol." Add a "Do Consol" command to the Tools menu to run the macro. Save the workbook as SC2BOS2.XLS. Run the macro. Print the sheet that contains the macro commands.

5. Create a stacked column chart that compares the operating earnings for each division by quarter. Place this chart on a separate worksheet. Save the workbook. Print the chart. Write a description of the information shown in this chart.

6. Create a pie chart that compares the operating earnings for the year (the earnings in the total column) for the four divisions. Place this chart on the sheet that contains the stacked column chart. Save the workbook, then print the charts.
7. Create a macro that prints the two charts. Place the macro on a separate sheet. Add a "Print Charts" command to the Tools menu to run the macro. Test the macro. Save the workbook. Print the macro.
8. Add user-defined commands to the Tools menu that run macros that let Willow replace or update the data for a selected division, or that let her redo the entire consolidation for all four divisions without printing the reports. Place these macros on a separate sheet named "Menu." Test the commands that run your macros. Save the workbook as SC2BOS3.XLS. Print the sheet that contains your macros for user-defined menu items.
9. Launch Write and create a memo to Mr. Nicholas that includes the chart from Problem 5. This memo should include your summary of the results displayed in the chart. Use object linking to include the chart in the memo. Save the document as SC2BOS2.WRI. Print the document with the chart.

10. Willow needs a summary report that contains the product sales and operating earnings data for all quarters and the annual total. She wants the report to list the product sales and operating earnings by division with a corporate total. Prepare a sketch of this report. Create the report as a separate workbook file. Use appropriate fonts and borders to enhance your report title. Use file linking to obtain the necessary data values from each of the individual division workbook files. Include a documentation sheet. Save the workbook as SC2BOS4.XLS, then print the summary report.
11. Revise your memo from Problem 9 by adding the summary report from Problem 10 as a table. The memo should now include both the chart from Problem 5 and the summary table from Problem 10. Save the document as SC2BOS4.WRI, then print the document. Did you use linking or embedding to place the summary table in the memo? Why or why not?
12. Revise the documentation sheet to reflect any changes you made to the workbook.
13. What else could Willow include in the consolidation workbook to make it more useful? Explain your answer.
14. Write instructions on how to work with the consolidation workbook. Assume the user knows how to launch and run Excel, but not how to do a consolidation.
15. Arrange and clearly identify the printouts and answers for all the problems in this case as your documentation for the case.

ADDITIONAL CASES

Additional Case 3

Negotiating Salaries for the National Basketball Association

OBJECTIVES

In this case you will:
- Create a database
- Combine worksheet files
- Create database filter lists
- Create a macro to print a database report
- Create a macro to prompt for data entry
- Use a data form to update a database
- Create a chart from summaries of filter lists
- Create a PivotTable summary
- Add user-defined menu commands

CASE

National Basketball Association When Dr. James Naismith nailed a peach basket to a pole, he could not possibly have envisioned the popularity of the sport that he founded. Since those early days of peach baskets and volleyballs, basketball has become one of the most popular sports in the world—especially in America.

The National Basketball Association (NBA) has become home to some of the greatest athletes in the world. The popularity of the NBA has soared over the last decade thanks to players like Michael Jordan, Julius Erving, "Magic" Johnson, and Larry Bird. This popularity has resulted in larger attendance at games, larger television viewing audiences, and an increase in advertising sponsorships that, in turn, has led to increased player salaries.

While growing up, Troy Jackson wanted to be a professional basketball player. However, during his senior year of college, Troy had reconstructive knee surgery, ending his changes to ever play competitive basketball. Troy was still determined to make it into the NBA one way or another. Upon graduation, Troy was offered a job in the NBA head offices in New York where he works on Commissioner David Stern's staff.

Commissioner Stern and his staff have become concerned with the large number of player salaries being decided through arbitration. Salary arbitration is the process of negotiating a contract when both sides cannot agree to a specific dollar amount. The arbitration process is conducted through an independent third party who listens to arguments from both sides and then makes a final determination about the terms of the contract. During the past several years, the number of contracts decided through arbitration has more than tripled.

To help the NBA head office keep track of these arbitration cases, Troy suggests developing an Excel database that lists the information show in Figure 5.

Figure 5
Data definition for a salary arbitration database

Field Name	Description
Player	Name of player involved in arbitration
Position	Position player plays (guard, center, forward)
Team	Name of team that is involved in arbitration
Player Bid	Amount that player is asking for
Team Bid	Amount that team is willing to pay
Settle	Amount that arbitrator feels is "fair"

The commissioner agrees that a database like this would be useful in maintaining a watchful eye over salaries being decided through arbitration. Commissioner Stern asks Troy to build the database and include a listing of all players that have gone through arbitration during the past three years.

You'll build the salary arbitration database by completing the following:

1. Read all the problems for this case and develop a planning analysis sheet in preparation for creating, modifying, and manipulating the database. Use your planning analysis sheet to develop your Excel solution.
2. Create the salary arbitration database using the data definition in Figure 5. List the field names in the same order as specified in the data definition. Include an appropriate title centered at the top of your worksheet. Select a typeface and point size for the title. Bold and underline the field names. Include a documentation sheet.
3. Add the records in Figure 6 to the salary arbitration database. Save the workbook as SC3NBA1.XLS.

Figure 6
Records for the salary arbitration database

Player	Position	Team	Player Bid	Team Bid	Settle
Miller, Reggie	Guard	Indiana	4450000	3850000	4270000
Smith, Charles	Forward	New York	2350000	1580000	2200000
Perkins, Sam	Center	Seattle	2450000	2100000	2390000
Gamble, Kevin	Forward	Boston	2650000	1950000	1960000

4. Open the file XC3NBA2.XLS and view its contents. This workbook contains a current list of players and teams who have entered into arbitration during the past three years. Make SC3NBA1.XLS your active workbook. Combine the contents of the XC3NBA2.XLS workbook with the salary arbitration database. Save the combined workbook as SC3NBA3.XLS. Preview and print the workbook.
5. Assign a name to the database range and other appropriate ranges for use with this database. Which ranges did you name? Why?
6. Add a row that contains the averages for the three salary fields between the database field names and the worksheet title. Use functions and range names to calculate these averages. Save the workbook as SC3NBA4.XLS. Preview and print the salary arbitration database.

7. Create three filtered lists: one each for the guards, forwards, and centers. Arrange each list in alphabetical order by player on a separate sheet. Name each sheet for the appropriate player position. Place an appropriate title above the list. Below each list, add formulas that average the salary fields for that list. Save the workbook as SC3NBA5.XLS. Preview and print each list separately.

E 8. Create a column chart on a separate sheet that summarizes the averages for each position. This chart should compare the player bid, team bid, and settle contract prices for each position (guard, forward, and center). Include the appropriate headings, labels, and legends. Name the sheet "Column Chart."

E 9. Create three print macros. One macro should sort the entire database by player and then print it. A second macro should sort each of the three lists by team and player and then print these reports. The final macro should print the column chart. Save the workbook as SC3NBA6.XLS. Run the macro that prints the column chart. Print the sheet that contains the macros.

E 10. Troy wants to update the player records in the database. Use a data form to change the data for Otis Thorpe to the following values:
    Player Bid   2250000
    Team Bid   1710000
    Settle   1990000
    Save the workbook as SC3NBA7.XLS. Print the database using the print macro. Were all the averages updated? Was the forwards list revised? If not, update this list.

E 11. Troy needs to add a new player record to the database. Use a data form to enter the following data:
    Player   Chapman, Rex
    Position   Guard
    Team   Washington
    Player Bid   1550000
    Team Bid   1200000
    Settle   1310000
    Save the workbook as SC3NBA8.XLS. Print the database using the print macro. Were all the averages updated? If not, which one were not updated? If necessary, make the required revisions to these average calculations.

12. Create a PivotTable of positions versus the averages for the player bid, team bid, and settle amounts. Place the PivotTable on a blank sheet after the column chart sheet. Save the workbook as SC3NBA8.XLS.

13. To make the salary arbitration database easier to use, add user-defined commands, which run the macros you have created, to the Tools menu. Test the menu items. Save the workbook as SC3NBA8.XLS.

E 14. Formulate a fourth filter list from the database. Explain why you selected this filter. Create the list for this filter on a separate sheet. Use an appropriate title for this list report. Save the workbook as SC3NBA9.XLS. Preview and print the list report.

15. Revise the documentation sheet if necessary.

16. What else could be included in the database to make it more useful? Explain your answer. Are there other macros or charts that would be helpful to include in the database? Describe how they would benefit the users of the database.

17. Write instructions for using this workbook. Assume the user knows how to launch and run Excel, but not how to use the salary arbitration database.

18. Arrange and clearly identify the printouts and answers for all the problems in this case as your documentation for the case.

ADDITIONAL CASES

Additional Case 4

Managing Tours for Executive Travel Services

OBJECTIVES

In this case you will:
- Create macros to sort a database and print reports
- Ask what-if questions about a completed worksheet
- Link worksheets
- Use Goal Seek
- Implement an If...Then...Else decision
- Create scenarios
- Create a data table
- Include worksheet data in a Write document

CASE — **Executive Travel Services** Executive Travel Services (ETS) of San Diego is a travel agency that specializes in selling packaged tours to business executives from Fortune 500 companies. ETS was started in 1982 by Tom Williams, a retired executive from a Fortune 500 company. As an executive, Tom often wished he could socialize with other top executives in an informal setting for several days. Using the idea, Tom founded ETS. ETS books tours that last from one to three weeks. The tours are designed to let executives enjoy a variety of activities while becoming acquainted with other executives.

In the last several months, the number of tour requests by executives has nearly doubled. ETS accidentally overbooked several of its more popular tours, such as the Orient Express. Tom discussed the overbooking problem with Melissa Merron, a recently hired travel associate. They agreed that an Excel database could be used to develop a tour management system, which would provide them with information necessary to avoid future overbooking problems. Tom asked Melissa to analyze the requirements for the database. She worked with Tom and the other ETS associates to develop the data definition shown in Figure 7.

Figure 7
Data definition for the Tours database

Field Name	Description
Tour	Tour name
Month	Month tour is scheduled to start
Type	Type of tour: Fish, Golf, Photo, or Relax
Sold	Number of seats sold for tour
Open	Number of seats still open for sale
Price	Price of tour

Melissa has set up the database. Tom would like her to make several changes to improve the operation of the tour management system by completing the following:

1. Read all the problems for this case and develop a planning analysis sheet in preparation for creating, modifying, and operating the tour management system. Use your planning analysis sheet to develop your Excel solution.
2. Open the XC4ETS1.XLS workbook. Review the Tours database. Examine the named ranges. What is missing from the database?
3. Add the appropriate field names in the order they are listed in the data definition. Center and bold each field name. Include a documentation sheet.
4. Enhance the appearance of the report title and subtitle:
    a. bold both titles
    b. italicize the subtitle
    c. increase the point size of the title to 14
   Print the Tours database. Save the workbook as SC4ETS2.XLS.
5. Sort the database with the Type field as the first sort key and the Tour field as the second sort key. Save the workbook as SC4ETS2.XLS. Preview and print the database.
6. Create a macro on a separate sheet that will do the sort described in Problem 5. Add a command to the Tools menu that runs the macro. Test the macro.
7. Create a macro that will print the Tours database using a named range. Add a command to the Tools menu that runs the macro. Run the macro, print the sheet, and save the workbook as SC4ETS3.XLS.
8. Tom wants to know how much revenue the tours are producing. Add a Total Revenue field to the database and place it immediately to the right of the Price field. Total revenue for a tour is calculated as the number of seats sold for a tour multiplied by the price charged for the tour. Add a formula that uses a range name to sum the total revenue for all tours. Place the formula so that additional records can be added easily to the database. Save the workbook as SC4ETS4.XLS. Print the Tours database. Circle the total revenue on the printout.
9. Filter the Tours database list to produce a report of all golf tours with a price less than $1,000. Adjust the column widths as needed. Place a title describing the list's contents above the list. Sort the list in ascending order by price. Print the list, then save the workbook as SC4ETS5.XLS.
10. Open the XC4ETS6.XLS workbook. This is ETS's projected income statement. What is missing from the income statement? How can you solve this problem?
11. Using a linking formula, include the total revenue for all tours from the Tours database in ETS's projected income statement. Add a documentation sheet to this workbook.
12. Add a rent expense of $12,000 in a new row inserted immediately below administrative expense. What is the net income for ETS? Create a macro that will print the income statement. Save the workbook as SC4ETS6.XLS. Run the print macro to produce a copy of the income statement, then print the macro.
13. Based on the expected revenue from the Tours database and considering the added rent expense, what commission rate could ETS pay and still realize a net income of $15,000?

E 14. Develop high-cost and low-cost scenarios for expenses. Create at least two ranges for these scenarios. Select appropriate expense items and/or key assumptions to include in the scenarios. Print a report with each scenario and circle the values used for each. Save the workbook as SC4ETS7.XLS. Write a summary comparing the scenarios.

E 15. Formulate a Goal Seek question using the workbook from Problem 14. Why is this goal seeking? Perform the Goal Seek analysis and print a report of the solution. Save the workbook as SC4ETS8.XLS. Write a summary interpreting your results.

E 16. Formulate an If...Then...Else condition for use with the projected income statement. Describe the business situation represented by the If...Then...Else condition. Implement this If...Then...Else condition. Save the workbook as SC4ETS9.XLS. Preview and print the results.

E 17. Formulate a two-input data table by selecting the input cells and the range of values to be examined for each cell. Explain why you selected these inputs to explore using the two-input data table. Create the data table. Save the workbook as SC4ETS10.XLS. Preview and print the data table.

E 18. Produce a chart from the data in the table from Problem 17. Include appropriate titles and legends. Save the SC4ETS10.XLS workbook, then print the chart. Review the results from the data table and the chart. Write a summary that explains these results.

E 19. Launch Write and create a memo to Tom that includes tables you obtain from both the Tours database and the projected income statement. This memo should list only the tours that are still available and the net income of ETS. Use a filter to produce the list of available tours and save this workbook as SC4ETS11.XLS. Save the document as SC4ETS11.WRI. Print the document.

20. What other information could Melissa produce for either the Tours database or the projected income statement? How would these reports support the ETS management's decision making?

21. Arrange and clearly identify the printouts and answers for all the problems in this case as your documentation for the case.

References

1 **Commands**
2 **Buttons**
3 **Functions**
4 **Visual Basic**

REFERENCE 1

Commands

This section describes the Excel menu commands. To display on-screen Help for any command, click the Help button on the toolbar, then choose any menu command. Excel displays a Help window that contains information about the command.

File Commands

New Opens a new workbook.

Open Opens existing files (workbooks, text files, Lotus files, etc.).

Close Closes the active workbook, prompting you to save changes.

Save Saves the active workbook with the current name.

Save As Saves the active workbook with a specified name.

Save Workspace Saves the active workbook(s) as well as their placement in the workspace.

Find File Searches the system for file(s) that meet certain specifications.

Summary Info Opens the Summary Information dialog box for viewing or editing.

Page Setup Sets margins, page numbering, headers, footers, etc., for printing.

Print Preview Simulates the printed document on screen; allows page setup changes.

Print Prints the workbook or specified sheets.

Print Report Creates and prints reports (customized sections of a workbook).

[File Name] Opens the specified file, also displaying the four most recently opened files.

Exit Ends the Excel session, prompting you to save changes to any open files.

Edit Commands

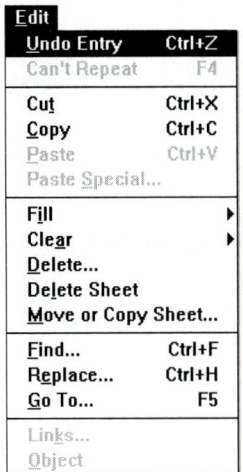

Undo [action] Reverses your most recent action (typing, cut, clear, etc.). If Undo is not possible, this command becomes 'Can't Undo.'

Redo [action] Restores the previous Undo.

Repeat [action] Repeats the previous action.

Cut Removes selected item(s) and places them on the Clipboard.

Copy Copies selected item(s) to the Clipboard, replacing previous Clipboard contents.

Paste Copies Clipboard contents to the current location.

Paste Special Pastes values, formats, formulas, or notes of cells copied onto the Clipboard; can be used to create links (not available for cut items).

Fill Copies values (or formulas) from one end of the selected range of cells to the entire range, in the direction specified in the submenu.

Clear Removes the selected cells' contents, formats, notes, or all three.

Delete Deletes the selected cells entirely. Adjacent cells might be shifted to fill the deleted cells.

Delete Sheet Removes the selected sheet(s), first prompting you for confirmation.

Move or Copy Sheet Moves or copies an entire sheet to a specified location in an open workbook or to a new workbook.

Find Searches the entire worksheet (or selected cells) for specified characters and selects the cell containing the first occurrence of those characters.

Replace Finds and replaces specified characters (text, numbers, or formulas) in an entire sheet or selected range.

Go To Selects specified cell(s) in the current worksheet or another worksheet.

Links Displays source documents for links to the workbook, changes links or their updating method (manual or automatic), and allows you to open source documents.

Object Allows you to edit an object from another application embedded in an Excel workbook.

View Commands

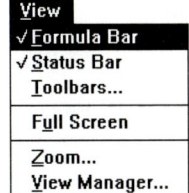

Formula Bar Displays or hides the formula bar.

Status Bar Displays or hides the status bar.

Toolbars Determines which toolbars are shown; creates customized toolbars.

Full Screen Removes the formula bar, status bar, and toolbars, allowing the menu bar and the worksheet to occupy the full screen.

Zoom   Changes the size of the cells in the worksheet.

View Manager   Creates different views of a worksheet and selects which view is shown.

Sized With Window   (Available only for chart sheet.) Makes chart sheet size dependent on window size.

Procedure Definition   (Available only for module.) Moves to the module and code that defines the selected procedure.

Object Browser   (Available only for module.) Shows methods and properties of objects.

Debug Window   (Available only for module.) Opens the debugging window, in which you can watch values as a procedure runs.

Insert Commands

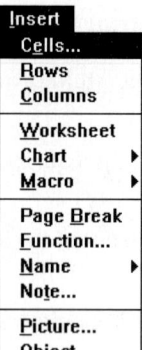

Cells   Inserts an individual cell by shifting others down or to the right.

Rows   Inserts an entire row of cells by shifting others down.

Columns   Inserts an entire column of cells by shifting others to the right.

Worksheet   Inserts a worksheet to the left of the sheet currently active.

Chart   Opens ChartWizard and inserts a chart on the active sheet or as a chart sheet.

Macro   Inserts a Visual Basic module, dialog sheet, or Excel 4.0 macro to the left of the sheet currently active.

Page Break   Inserts a page break. (Command becomes Remove Page Break if the active cell is above or to the left of the page break.)

Function   Opens Function Wizard, which creates a function in the formula bar and active cell.

Name - Define   Defines a name for a range, cell, formula, or value.

Name - Paste   Pastes a name into the formula bar.

Name - Create   Defines names for selected cells based on entries in top or bottom row, or right or left column, as indicated.

Name - Apply   Replaces range or cell references (in selected cells) with their names, if these exist.

Note   Inserts a note in the active cell; lists all notes in the sheet.

Picture   Inserts a picture (graphics file) from another application.

Object   Inserts an object from another application.

File   (Available only for module.) Inserts the previous text file in the sheet at the insertion point.

Insert Commands

Note: These Insert commands appear when you're working with a chart sheet or the active chart in a worksheet.

Titles   Add or edit titles to chart or its axes.

Data Labels   Adds labels to data point(s) in a chart.

Legend   Adds a legend to the right of the plot.

Axes   Shows or hides the axes of a chart.

Gridlines   Shows or hides vertical or horizontal gridlines on a chart.

Trendline   Inserts a regression line in a chart.

Error Bars   Attaches error bars to points in a chart.

New Data   Adds new data to a chart.

Worksheet, Chart, and **Macro** commands are unchanged from the worksheet Insert menu.

Run Commands

Note: These Run commands appear when you're working with modules.

Start   Runs a procedure from the beginning.

End   Stops a procedure that is running.

Reset   Stops a procedure that is running and resets all variables in the active workbook.

Step Into   Runs a procedure one step at a time, stepping into other procedures as called.

Step Over   Runs a procedure one step at a time, running other called procedures but not stepping into them.

Toggle Breakpoints   Sets or clears breakpoints in a procedure.

Clear All Breakpoints   Clears all breakpoints in all modules.

Format Commands

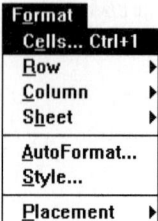

Cells   Changes the number formatting, alignment, font settings, borders, patterns, and protection status of selected cells.

Object   (Available only if an object is selected.) Changes font settings, text alignment, borders, etc., of the selected chart or object.

Row   Adjusts the height of selected rows; hides and unhides rows.

Column   Adjusts the width of selected columns; hides and unhides columns.

Sheet   Renames, hides, or unhides a sheet.

AutoFormat   Formats the selected range or table according to an "autoformat," a preset style for data.

Style   Defines a style based on number, font, alignment, border, patterns, and protection status.

Placement   Moves objects to the front of, or in back of, other objects; also allows grouping of several objects into one.

Format Commands

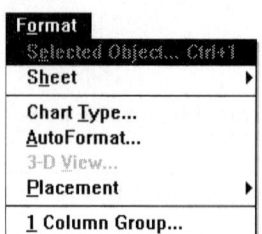

Note: These Format commands appear when you're working with a chart sheet or the active chart in a worksheet.

Selected Object   Opens the Formatting dialog box for the selected object. (This command changes depending on what type of object is selected.)

Sheet   Renames, hides, or unhides a sheet.

Chart Type   Changes the chart type.

AutoFormat   Applies a built-in or customized autoformat to a chart.

3-D View   Changes the viewing angle of a 3-D chart.

Placement   Moves objects to the front of, or in back of, other objects; also allows grouping of several objects into one.

[Name of Chart]   This command is the name of the active chart. Choosing it opens the Formatting dialog box for that chart type.

Tools Commands

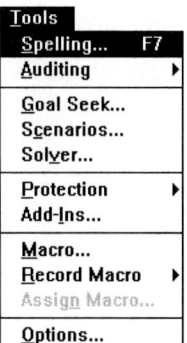

Spelling Checks spelling of all text in a sheet (including charts, text boxes, headers, footers, and notes).

Auditing Inserts arrows between cells related by formula reference.

AutoSave Automatically saves a workbook periodically (time interval specified). (Only available if you have installed the AutoSave add-in.)

Goal Seek Finds a solution to a formula by varying the value in a cell referred to by the formula.

Scenarios Creates and manipulates scenarios. (A scenario allows various cell values to be changed, which immediately affects their dependent cells.)

Solver Solves optimization problems with multiple constraints.

Protection Prevents changes to locked cells in worksheets, charts, objects, Visual Basic code, or dialog sheets. A password is established, allowing a sheet to be unprotected and modified in the future.

Add-Ins Selects the add-ins (additional commands and functions) available; these are automatically loaded when you start Excel.

Macro Runs, edits, or deletes macros.

Record Macro - Record New Macro Creates a macro (a sequence of Excel commands that can be repeated using a single key combination).

Record Macro - Use Relative References If selected, macros use relative cell references; if not, macros use absolute cell references.

Assign Macro Assigns a button, menu command, or graphic object to a macro, so that choosing the button or the command, or selecting the object, runs the macro.

Options Allows changes to the worksheet view, formula calculation method, edit settings, Lotus transition settings, chart settings, colors, and other options.

Data Analysis Opens the dialog box for the Analysis Toolpak, an Add-In consisting of statistical procedures and functions.

Tools Commands

Note: These Tools commands appear when you're working with modules.

Add Watch   Designates an expression to be watched in the Debug window, where its value is displayed as the macro runs.

Edit Watch   Edits or deletes expressions being watched.

Instant Watch   Gives the current value of the selected expression.

References   Adds or deletes objects available for use in a Visual Basic module.

Menu Editor   Makes changes to menus and menu bars for use in Visual Basic procedures and Add-Ins.

Attach Toolbars   Copies customized toolbars into a workbook.

Protection, Add-Ins, Make Add-In, Macro, Record Macro, and **Assign Macro** commands are unchanged from the worksheet Tools menu.

Data Commands

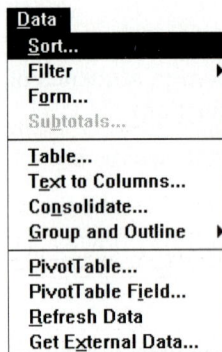

Sort   Sorts rows according to column contents.

Filter   Filters the worksheet by hiding rows that do not meet specified criteria.

Form   Performs operations on a list or database: searching, adding, and deleting records.

Subtotals   Inserts rows containing subtotals of values in one column. Excel subtotals the column for each new entry in another (specified) column.

Table   Creates a data table, the results of entering different values into one or more formulas.

Text to Columns   Converts one column of text to multiple columns based on specified separators.

Consolidate   Consolidates data from one or more source areas and displays it in table form in the destination area.

Group and Outline   Transforms selected data into outline form.

PivotTable   Starts the PivotTable Wizard. A PivotTable summarizes and totals data, grouped by row fields and column fields. The row and column fields can be interchanged, giving a different view of the data.

PivotTable Field   Used to change the summary functions for the data fields and for formatting numbers.

Refresh Data   Changes a PivotTable to reflect changes in the source data.

Get External Data   Starts MS Query, which allows you to retrieve information from lists and external data bases.

Window Commands

New Window Creates a duplicate of the active workbook, allowing you to view different parts of the workbook simultaneously. Changes in one window are reflected in all of its copies.

Arrange Arranges windows in the workbook: tiled (reduced and placed side by side), horizontal (evenly spaced from top to bottom), vertical (evenly spaced from left to right), or cascade (overlapping diagonally).

Hide Hides the active window.

Unhide Restores hidden windows.

Split Splits the active window into two or four panes, which then scroll simultaneously; command then becomes Remove Split.

Freeze Panes Freezes the cells above and to the left of the active cell; command then becomes Unfreeze Panes.

Help Commands

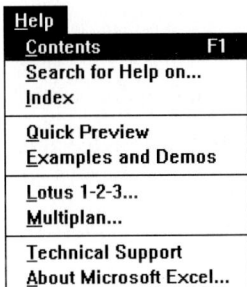

Contents Opens Help Contents.

Search for Help on Performs a search on Help topics, by specified key word(s).

Index Opens Help Index. Click letter buttons to go directly to items beginning with that letter.

Quick Preview Presents four on-line introductory lessons on Microsoft Excel.

Examples and Demos Provides instructional demonstrations covering a wide variety of topics.

Lotus 1-2-3 Provides instructions and demonstrations for the Excel equivalents of Lotus 1-2-3 commands.

Multiplan Provides instructions for the Excel equivalents of Microsoft Multiplan commands.

Technical Support Provides technical support information, including answers to commonly asked questions.

About Microsoft Excel Provides product ID and copyright information.

Shortcut Menu Commands

Note: These commands appear when you're working with shortcut menus.

Select All Sheets (Available only on the tab shortcut menu.) Selects all worksheets, chart sheets, dialog sheets, and modules in the open workbook.

Show Pages (Available only on the PivotTable shortcut menu.) Copies each page in a page field to a new worksheet.

Add Data Field (Available only on the PivotTable shortcut menu.) Adds the specified field to Data area. (All fields are listed in the submenu.)

R E F E R E N C E   2

Buttons

This section describes all the buttons found in Excel. To see the name of any button on the toolbar, position the pointer over the button and and its name will appear below the button.

File Buttons

Open Open the existing file

Save Save the active workbook

Print Print the active sheet

Print Preview Simulate the printed document on screen

Set Print Area Set the selected cells as the area to print

New Workbook Open a new workbook

Insert Worksheet Insert a new worksheet into the active workbook

Insert Chart Sheet Insert a chart sheet into the active workbook

Insert Module Insert a new module into the active workbook

Insert MS Excel 4.0 Macro Insert a new macro sheet into the active workbook

Find File Search the system for file(s) that meet certain specifications

Routing Slip Add or edit a routing slip, to send the workbook to multiple recipients on electronic mail

Send Mail Send the document as electronic mail

Update File Update the read-only file to the version last saved

Toggle File Status Change the file from read-only to read-write, or vice-versa

Insert Dialog Inserts a new dialog sheet before the selected sheet

Edit Buttons

Undo Undo the previous action

Repeat Repeat the previous action

Cut Remove selected item(s) and place them on the Clipboard

Copy Copy selected item(s) to the Clipboard

Paste Copy the Clipboard contents to the current location

Clear Contents Remove selected cells' contents

Clear Formats Remove formatting from selected cells or objects

Paste Formats Paste the formatting of copied cells to the selected cells

Paste Values Paste only the values of the copied cells to the selected cells

Format Painter Copy formats from current selection to next selection

Delete Delete cells entirely (adjacent cells shift to fill the space)

Delete Row Delete the selected row (rows below shift upward)

Delete Column Delete the selected column (columns to the right shift left)

Insert Insert cell(s) by shifting cell(s) down

Insert Row Insert row(s) above the selection point

Insert Column Insert column(s) to the left of the selection point

Fill Right Copy values or formulas from the left column of the selected range to the entire range

Fill Down Copy values or formulas from the top row of the selected range to the entire range

Formula Buttons

Equal Sign Insert an equal sign in the formula bar

Plus Sign Insert a plus sign in the formula bar

Minus Sign Insert a minus sign in the formula bar

Multiplication Sign Insert a multiplication sign in the formula bar

Division Sign Insert a division sign in the formula bar

Exponentiation Sign Insert an exponentiation sign in the formula bar

Left Parenthesis Insert a left parenthesis in the formula bar

Right Parenthesis Insert a right parenthesis in the formula bar

Colon Insert a colon in the formula bar

Comma Insert a comma in the formula bar

Percent Sign Insert a percent sign in the formula bar

Dollar Sign Insert a dollar sign in the formula bar

AutoSum Insert the Sum function, with the range above or to the left of the active cell, in the formula bar

Function Wizard Open the Function Wizard; create a function

Paste Names Paste worksheet names in the selected cells, using the Paste Names dialog box

Constrain Numeric (Available with Microsoft Windows for Pen Computing software.) Restrict writing recognition to numbers and punctuation

Formatting Buttons

Borders Choose a border type

Outline Border Add a border around the selected cell(s)

Left Border Add (or delete) a border to the left of cell(s)

Right Border Add (or delete) a border to the right of cell(s)

Top Border Add (or delete) a border above cell(s)

Bottom Border Add (or delete) a border below cell(s)

Bottom Double Border Add (or delete) a double border below cell(s)

Dark Shading Add dark shading to an object or cell(s)

Light Shading Add light shading to an object or cell(s)

AutoFormat AutoFormat according to the previous AutoFormat command

Currency Style Format selected cells to the current currency style

Percent Style Format selected cells to the current percent style

Comma Style Format selected cells to the current comma style

Increase Decimal Add one decimal place to the number(s) selected

Decrease Decimal Remove one decimal place from the number(s) selected

Text Formatting Buttons

Bold Type in boldface, or change the selection to boldface type

Italic Type in italics, or change the selection to italic type

Underline Type with underlining, or underline the selection

Strikethrough Draw a line through the selected text, cells, or objects

Font Color Choose a font color for selected text or cells from the color palette

Cycle Font Color Change the font color of selected text or cell(s)

Align Left Left-align text (in a chart or text box) or cell or button contents

Center Center text (in a chart or text box) or cell or button contents

Align Right Right-align text (in a chart or text box) or cell or button contents

Justify Align Adjust word-spacing to achieve full justification

Center Across Columns Center the text in one cell across the selected columns

Font Size Select a font size

Font Select a font

Style Select a style

Increase Font Size Enlarge the font to the next available size

Decrease Font Size Decrease the font to the next available size

Vertical Text Align the text vertically, with each character above the next

Rotate Text Up Rotate the text sideways, to be read from bottom to top

Rotate Text Down Rotate the text sideways, to be read from top to bottom

Double Underline Type with double underlining or underline the selection

Drawing Buttons

Line Draw a straight line

Arrow Draw an arrow

Freehand Draw a freehand line

Text Box Draw a box in which you can type text

Create Button Create a button for a macro or Visual Basic module

Selection Select graphic objects

Drawing Selection Select a graphic object; pointer changes to an arrow

Reshape Change the shape of a polygon

Rectangle Draw a rectangle or square (not filled)

Ellipse Draw an ellipse or circle (not filled)

Arc Draw an arc or circle segment (not filled)

Polygon Draw a polygon (not filled)

Freeform Draw shapes that are a combination of freehand and straight lines

Filled Rectangle Draw a rectangle or square (filled)

Filled Ellipse Draw an ellipse or circle (filled)

Filled Arc Draw an arc or circle segment (filled)

Filled Polygon Draw a polygon (filled)

Filled Freeform Draw shapes that are a combination of freehand and straight lines (filled)

Group Objects Group selected objects into one object

Ungroup Objects Separate previously grouped objects

Bring To Front Move an object(s) in front of other objects

Send To Back Move an object(s) behind other objects

Drop Shadow Add a shadow to the object or to selected cells

Drawing Display (or remove) the Drawing toolbar

Color Change the color of an object

Pattern Change the pattern and/or color of a filled object

Shape Select a drawing shape from the palette

Dark Shading Adds dark shading to an object

Light Shading Adds light shading to an object

Macro Buttons

Record Macro Create a new macro and begin recording actions

Stop Recording Stop recording actions, or stop a procedure that is running

Run Macro Run a macro; if a macro is being edited, run it from the insertion point

Step Macro Run an Excel 4.0 macro one step at a time; put Visual Basic procedures into break mode, and open the Debug window

Resume Macro Resume a paused macro

Insert Module Insert a new module into a workbook

Menu Editor Change menu bars and menu commands

Object Browser View and paste methods and properties

Toggle Breakpoint Set or clear a breakpoint

Instant Watch Display the value of the selected expression

Step Into Run a procedure one step at a time, stepping into other procedures as they are called

Step Over Run a procedure one step at a time, running other called procedures but not stepping into them

Function Wizard Display the Function Wizard to edit or insert a function

Paste Names Insert a name

Charting Buttons

Area Chart AutoFormat Create an area chart

Bar Chart AutoFormat Create a bar chart

Column Chart AutoFormat Create a column chart

Stacked Column Chart AutoFormat Create a stacked column chart

Line Chart AutoFormat Create a line chart with marks at each point

Pie Chart AutoFormat Create a pie chart with percentage labels

3-D Area Chart AutoFormat Create a 3-D area chart

3-D Bar Chart AutoFormat Create a 3-D bar chart

3-D Column Chart AutoFormat Create a 3-D column chart

3-D Perspective Column Chart AutoFormat Create a 3-D column chart with perspective

3-D Line Chart AutoFormat Create a 3-D line chart

3-D Pie Chart AutoFormat Create a 3-D pie chart with percentage labels

XY (Scatter) Chart AutoFormat Create an xy (scatter) chart with points marked (no lines)

3-D Surface Chart AutoFormat Create a 3-D surface chart

Radar Chart AutoFormat Create a radar chart with marks at each point

Line/Column Chart AutoFormat Create a column chart with the final series plotted as a line with points marked

Volume/High-Low-Close Chart AutoFormat Create a column chart combined with a line chart of three data series, namely, high, low, and closing stock prices

Doughnut Chart AutoFormat Create a doughnut chart

Default Chart Create a chart according to the defaults in the Chart tab of the Options dialog box

ChartWizard Open the ChartWizard and create or edit a chart

Vertical Gridlines Add or remove major gridlines for the category (horizontal) axis

Horizontal Gridlines Add or remove major gridlines for the value (vertical) axis

Legend Add or remove a legend

Chart Type Change the chart type

Utility Buttons

Camera Take a picture of the selected range

Calculate Now Calculate the formulas in all open files or in the formula bar

Spelling Check the spelling in the workbook or in the formula bar

Help Single-click: add a question mark to the pointer and click on a command, button, or any area of the screen to open that Help topic; Double-click: open Help Search

Show Outline Symbols Show (or hide) outline symbols for outlines in a worksheet

Select Visible Cells Select cells that are not hidden

Select Current Region Select cells outward from the active cell until blank cells are reached

Sort Ascending Sort a list according to the column containing the active cell, from lowest to highest

Sort Descending Sort a list according to the column containing the active cell, from highest to lowest

Lock Cell Prevent changes to a cell (document must be protected to activate the lock)

Freeze Panes Freeze panes above and to the left of the active cell

Zoom Control Reduce or enlarge the active worksheet

Zoom In Enlarge the active worksheet

Zoom Out Reduce the active worksheet

Scenario Show, add, or edit scenarios

Microsoft Word Start (or switch to) Microsoft Word

Microsoft PowerPoint Start (or switch to) Microsoft PowerPoint

Microsoft Access Start (or switch to) Microsoft Access

Microsoft FoxPro Start (or switch to) Microsoft FoxPro

Microsoft Project Start (or switch to) Microsoft Project

Microsoft Schedule+ Start (or switch to) Microsoft Schedule+

Microsoft Mail Start (or switch to) Microsoft Mail

Full Screen Remove the formula bar, status bar, and toolbars, allowing the menu bar and the worksheet to occupy the full screen

Data Buttons

PivotTable Wizard Start the PivotTable Wizard to create or edit a PivotTable

PivotTable Field Change the summary functions for the data fields, or the formatting of numbers

Refresh Data Update a PivotTable after a change in the source data

Ungroup Outline: remove grouping from selected rows or columns; PivotTable: separate grouped items, displaying all levels of data

Group Outline: group selected rows or columns; PivotTable: group several items into one

Show Pages Copy each page of a page field to a new worksheet

Show Detail Show all levels of detail in a PivotTable that has multiple row or column fields

Hide Detail Hide detail items and display only summary data in a PivotTable

AutoFilter Hide rows with a different value than the active cell, or perform AutoFilters using the down arrow buttons

TipWizard Buttons

TipWizard Display a tip in the TipWizard toolbar

Tip Help Open the Help topic pertaining to the current tip

TipWizard Box Suggest shortcuts for the current task

Auditing Buttons

Remove Dependent Arrows Remove arrows to cells containing formulas referring to the active cell

Trace Dependents Insert arrows from the active cell to cells with formulas referring to the active cell

Remove Precedent Arrows Remove arrows from cells referred to by a formula

Trace Precendents Insert arrows in cells referred to in the formula

Remove All Arrows Remove all auditing arrows

Trace Error Insert an arrow from the cell causing the error in the active cell

Attach Note Add a note to the selected cell

Show Info Window Display the Info window

Forms Buttons

Check Box Create a checkbox (drag into the sheet at the desired location)

Option Button Create an option button (drag into the sheet at the desired location)

Edit Box Create an edit box in a dialog sheet

Label Create a text label on a worksheet, chart, or dialog sheet

Group Box Create a group box

Scroll Bar Create a scroll bar

Spinner Create a spinner control

List Box Create a list box

Drop-Down Create a drop-down list

Combination List-Edit Create a combination list and edit box

Combination Drop-Down Edit Create a combination drop-down and edit box

Control Properties Change the properties of the selected control

Edit Code Switch to the module sheet to create or edit the code for the selected control

Toggle Grid Display or hide the dialog sheet grid

Tab Order Change the tab order of objects in the dialog sheet

Run Dialog Run the dialog box as its own window

Custom Buttons

Create a button to which you assign a macro

REFERENCE 3

Functions

This section lists Excel functions, which are the tools you use to perform calculations and actions automatically. Each description contains the syntax for that function and a brief description. To learn more about the details of each function, see Excel on-line Help.

ABS ABS(*number*) returns the absolute value of the number.

ACCRINT ACCRINT(*start, first_date, end, rate, par, frequency, basis*) returns the accrued interest on an investment paying periodic interest.

ACCRINTM ACCRINTM(*start, end, rate, par, basis*) returns the accrued interest on an investment paying interest at maturity.

ACOS ACOS(*number*) returns the arccosine (inverse cosine) of the number.

ACOSH ACOSH(*number*) returns the inverse hyperbolic cosine of the number.

ADDRESS ADDRESS(*row, column, abs_type, style, sheet*) returns a cell address as text.

AMORDEGRC AMORDEGRC(*cost, purchase, first, salvage, period, rate, basis*) returns the depreciation for each accounting period, for the French accounting system.

AMORLINC AMORLINC(*cost, purchase, first, salvage, period, rate, basis*) returns the depreciation for each accounting period, for the French accounting system.

AND AND(*argument1, argument2, . . .*) returns True if all arguments are true; otherwise returns False.

AREAS AREAS(*reference*) returns the number of areas (range of contiguous cells) in the reference.

ASIN ASIN(*number*) returns the arcsine (inverse sine) of the number.

ASINH ASINH(*number*) returns the inverse hyperbolic sine of the number.

ATAN ATAN(*number*) returns the arctangent (inverse tangent) of the number.

ATAN2 ATAN2(*x,y*) returns the arctangent (inverse tangent) of the angle from the positive x-axis to the point specified.

ATANH ATANH(*number*) returns the inverse hyperbolic tangent of the number.

AVEDEV AVEDEV(*number1, number2, . . .*) returns the average of the (positive) deviations of the points from their mean.

AVERAGE AVERAGE(*number1, number2, . . .*) returns the average of the numbers (up to 30).

BESSELI BESSELI(*x, n*) returns the Bessel function for purely imaginary arguments.

BESSELJ BESSELJ(*x, n*) returns the Bessel function.

BESSELK BESSELK(*x, n*) returns the modified Bessel function for purely imaginary arguments.

BESSELY BESSELY(*x, n*) returns the Bessel function.

BETADIST BETADIST(*x, alpha, beta, a, b*) returns the value of the cumulative beta probability density function.

BETAINV BETAINV(*p, alpha, beta, a, b*) returns the value of the inverse of the cumulative beta probability density function.

BIN2DEC BIN2DEC(*number*) returns the decimal equivalent of a binary number.

BIN2HEX BIN2HEX(*number*, *places*) returns the hexadecimal equivalent of a binary number, padded with leading zeros to the specified number of places (optional).

BIN2OCT BIN2OCT(*number*, *places*) returns the octal equivalent of a binary number, padded with leading zeros to the specified number of places (optional).

BINOMDIST BINOMDIST(*successes*, *trials*, *p*, *type*) returns the probability for the binomial distribution. (*type* is True for cumulative distribution function, False for probability mass function.)

CALL CALL calls a procedure in a dynamic link library or in a code resource.

CEILING CEILING(*number*, *significance*) returns the number rounded up to the nearest multiple of the significance value.

CELL CELL(*info_type*, *reference*) returns formatting, location, or contents of the upper-left cell in the reference.

CHAR CHAR(*number*) returns the character corresponding to the ANSI code number.

CHIDIST CHIDIST(*x*, *df*) returns the probability for the chi-squared distribution.

CHIINV CHIINV(*p*, *df*) returns the inverse of the chi-squared distribution.

CHITEST CHITEST(*actual_range*, *expected_range*) returns the value of the chi-squared distribution for the independence test statistic.

CHOOSE CHOOSE(*number*, *value1*, *value2*, . . .) returns a value from the list of values.

CLEAN CLEAN(*text*) removes nonprintable characters from text.

CODE CODE(*text*) returns the ANSI code value of the first character in the string.

COLUMN COLUMN(*reference*) returns the column number of the reference.

COLUMNS COLUMNS(*array*) returns the number of columns in a reference (or in an array).

COMBIN COMBIN(*x*, *n*) returns the number of combinations of *x* objects taken *n* at a time.

COMPLEX COMPLEX(*real*, *imag*, *suffix*) returns the complex number corresponding to the inputs.

CONCATENATE CONCATENATE(*text1*, *text2*, . . .) combines several strings into one (up to 30).

CONFIDENCE CONFIDENCE(*alpha*, *standard-dev*, *n*) returns a confidence interval for the mean.

CONVERT CONVERT(*number*, *from_unit*, *to_unit*) changes a measurement from one unit to another.

CORREL CORREL(*array1*, *array2*) returns the coefficient of correlation between *array1* and *array2*.

COS COS(*angle*) returns the cosine of *angle*.

COSH COSH(*number*) returns the hyperbolic cosine of the number.

COUNT COUNT(*value1*, *value2*, . . .) returns how many numbers are in the value(s).

COUNTA COUNTA(*value1*, *value2*, . . .) returns the count of non-blank values in the list of arguments.

COUNTBLANK COUNTBLANK(*range*) returns the count of blank cells in the range.

COUNTIF COUNTIF(*range*, *criteria*) returns the count of non-blank cells in the range that meet the criteria.

COUPDAYBS COUPDAYBS(*settlement*, *maturity*, *frequency*, *basis*) returns the number of days from the start of the coupon period until the date of settlement.

COUPDAYS COUPDAYS(*settlement*, *maturity*, *frequency*, *basis*) returns the number of days in the coupon period containing the date of settlement.

COUPDAYSNC COUPDAYSNC(*settlement*, *maturity*, *frequency*, *basis*) returns the number of days from the date of settlement until the next coupon date.

COUPNCD COUPNCD(*settlement*, *maturity*, *frequency*, *basis*) returns the coupon date following the date of settlement.

COUPNUM COUPNUM(*settlement*, *maturity*, *frequency*, *basis*) returns the number of coupon dates from the date of settlement to the maturity date.

COUPPCD COUPPCD(*settlement*, *maturity*, *frequency*, *basis*) returns the coupon date preceding the date of settlement.

COVAR COVAR(*array1*, *array2*) returns the covariance of *array1* and *array2*.

CRITBINOM CRITBINOM(*trials*, *p*, *alpha*) returns the smallest value so that the cumulative binomial distribution is less than or equal to the criterion value, *alpha*.

CUMIPMT CUMIPMT(*rate*, *periods*, *present_value*, *start_period*, *end_period*, *type*) returns the cumulative interest paid on a loan.

CUMPRINC CUMPRINC(*rate*, *periods*, *present_value*, *start_period*, *end_period*, *type*) returns the cumulative principal paid on a loan.

DATE DATE(*year*, *month*, *day*) returns the date in serial number form.

DATEVALUE DATEVALUE(*date_text*) returns the *date_text* in serial number form.

DAVERAGE DAVERAGE(*database*, *field*, *criteria*) returns the average of the records in the field that meet the criteria.

DAY DAY(*serial_number*) returns the day of the month in serial number form.

DAYS360 DAYS360(*start*, *end*, *method*) returns the total number of days between the starting and ending dates, based on a 360-day year.

DB DB(*cost*, *salvage*, *lifetime*, *period*, *month*) returns the depreciation of an item whose useful life is *lifetime* periods long, based on the fixed-declining balance method.

DCOUNT DCOUNT(*database*, *field*, *criteria*) returns the count of the records in the field that meet the criteria.

DCOUNTA DCOUNTA(*database*, *field*, *criteria*) returns the count of nonblank records in the field that meet the criteria.

DDB DDB(*cost*, *salvage*, *life*, *period*, *factor*) returns the depreciation of an item, based on the double-declining balance method, or by a method with a decline rate *factor*.

DEC2BIN DEC2BIN(*number*, *places*) returns the binary equivalent of a decimal number, padded with leading zeros to the specified number of places (optional).

DEC2HEX DEC2HEX(*number*, *places*) returns the hexadecimal equivalent of a decimal number, padded with leading zeros to the specified number of places (optional).

DEC2OCT DEC2OCT(*number*, *places*) returns the octal equivalent of a decimal number, padded with leading zeros to the specified number of places (optional).

DEGREES DEGREES(*angle*) returns the radian measurement in degrees.

DELTA DELTA(*number1*, *number2*) returns 1 if *number1* equals *number2*, and returns 0 if not.

DEVSQ DEVSQ(*number1*, *number2*, . . .) returns the sum of squared deviations from the mean of the numbers.

DGET DGET(*database*, *field*, *criteria*) returns a single value that meets the criteria, from the field.

DISC DISC(*settlement*, *maturity*, *price_per_$100*, *redemption_per_$100*, *basis*) returns the discount rate of a note with the specified values.

DMAX DMAX(*database*, *field*, *criteria*) returns the maximum value of the records in the field that meet the criteria.

DMIN DMIN(*database*, *field*, *criteria*) returns the minimum value of the records in the field that meet the criteria.

DOLLAR DOLLAR(*number*, *decimals*) returns the number formatted to currency style.

DOLLARDE DOLLARDE(*fractional_dollar*, *denominator*) returns the decimal equivalent of the dollar amount expressed as a fraction.

DOLLARFR DOLLARFR(*decimal_dollar*, *denominator*) returns a dollar amount expressed as a fraction.

DPRODUCT DPRODUCT(*database*, *field*, *criteria*) returns the product of the records in the field that meet the criteria.

DSTDEV DSTDEV(*database*, *field*, *criteria*) returns the sample standard deviation.

DSTDEVP DSTDEVP(*database*, *field criteria*) returns the population standard deviation.

DSUM DSUM(*database*, *field*, *criteria*) returns the sum of the field column of records that meet the criteria.

DURATION DURATION(*settlement_date*, *maturity_date*, *coupon_rate*, *yield*, *frequency*, *basis*) returns the annual duration of a note with periodic interest payments.

DVAR DVAR(*database*, *field*, *criteria*) returns the sample variance.

DVARP DVARP(*database*, *field*, *criteria*) returns the population variance.

EDATE EDATE(*date*, *months*) returns the serial number date of the day that is the specified number of *months* before (negative) or after (positive) *date*.

EFFECT EFFECT(*nominal_rate*, *periods*) returns the effective annual yield.

EOMONTH EOMONTH(*date*, *months*) returns the serial number date for the last day of the month that is *months* before or after *date*.

ERF ERF(*lower_limit*, *upper_limit*) calculates the integral of the error function from *lower_limit* to *upper_limit*.

ERFC ERFC(*x*) returns the complementary ERF function integrated from x to ∞.

ERROR.TYPE ERROR.TYPE(*error_val*) returns the number of the error value.

EVEN EVEN(*number*) returns the number rounded up to the nearest even integer.

EXACT EXACT(*text1*, *text2*) returns True if the two text strings are equal, and False if not.

EXP EXP(*number*) is the exponential function with base e.

EXPONDIST EXPONDIST(*x*, *lambda*, *type*) returns the probability for the exponential distribution. (*type* is True for cumulative distribution function, False for probability density function.)

FACT FACT(*number*) returns the factorial of *number*.

FACTDOUBLE FACTDOUBLE(*number*) returns the double factorial of *number*.

FALSE FALSE() returns the value False.

FDIST FDIST(*x*, *df1*, *df2*) returns the probability for the F distribution.

FIND FIND(*find_text*, *within_text*, *start*) searches *within_text* for *find_text*, returning the number of the character where it first occurs (optionally starting at character number *start*).

FINV FINV(*p*, *df1*, *df2*) returns the inverse of the F distribution.

FISHER FISHER(*x*) returns the value of the Fisher transformation evaluated at x.

FISHERINV FISHERINV(*y*) returns the value of the inverse Fisher transformation evaluated at y.

FIXED FIXED(*number*, *decimals*, *no_commas*) returns *number* as text, with *decimals* decimal points, and commas only if *no_commas* is false.

FLOOR FLOOR(*number*, *significance*) returns the number down to the nearest multiple of the significance value.

FORECAST FORECAST(*x*, *known_y's*, *known_x's*) returns a predicted (y) value for *x*, based on linear regression of the *known_y's* on the *known_x's*.

FREQUENCY FREQUENCY(*data_array*, *bins_array*) returns the frequency distribution of *data_array* as a vertical array, based on *bins_array*.

FTEST FTEST(*array1*, *array2*) returns the p-value of the one-tailed F statistic, based on the hypothesis that *array1* and *array2* are not significantly different (which is rejected for low p-values).

FV FV(*rate*, *periods*, *payment*, *present_value*, *type*) returns the future value of an investment with *periods* payments of size *payment*.

FVSCHEDULE FVSCHEDULE(*principal*, *schedule_array*) returns the future value of an investment with changing rates, stored in *schedule_array*.

GAMMADIST GAMMADIST(*x*, *alpha*, *beta*, *type*) returns the probability for the Gamma distribution with parameters *alpha* and *beta*. (*type* is True for cumulative distribution function, False for probability mass function.)

GAMMAINV GAMMAINV(*p*, *alpha*, *beta*) returns the inverse of the Gamma distribution.

GAMMALN GAMMALN(*x*) returns the natural log of the gamma function evaluated at *x*.

GCD GCD(*number1*, *number2*, . . .) returns the greatest common divisor of up to 29 numbers.

GEOMEAN GEOMEAN(*number1*, *number2*, . . .) returns the geometric mean of up to 30 numbers.

GESTEP GESTEP(*number*, *step*) returns 1 if *number* is greater than or equal to *step*, and 0 if not.

GROWTH GROWTH(*known_y's*, *known_x's*, *new_x's*, *constant*) returns the predicted (y) values for the *new_x's*, based on exponential regression of the *known_y's* on the *known_x's*.

HARMEAN HARMEAN(*number1*, *number2*, . . .) returns the harmonic mean of up to 30 numbers.

HEX2BIN HEX2BIN(*number*, *places*) returns the binary equivalent of a hexadecimal number, padded with leading zeros to the specified number of places (optional).

HEX2DEC HEX2DEC(*number*) returns the decimal equivalent of a hexadecimal number.

HEX2OCT HEX2OCT(*number*, *places*) returns the octal equivalent of a hexadecimal number, padded with leading zeros to the specified number of places (optional).

HLOOKUP HLOOKUP(*lookup_value*, *table_array*, *row*, *range_lookup*) searches the top row of *table_array* for *lookup_value*, and returns the value from the *row* that is in the same column as *lookup_value*. (*range_lookup* is True if, when an exact match is not found, the next highest value that is less than *lookup_value* is returned.)

HOUR HOUR(*serial_date_time*) returns the military hour corresponding to *serial_date_time*.

HYPGEOMDIST HYPGEOMDIST(*sample_successes*, *sample_size*, *population_successes*, *population_size*) returns the probability for the hypergeometric distribution.

IF IF(*test*, *true_value*, *false_value*) returns *true_value* if *test* is True, and *false_value* if *test* is False.

IMABS IMABS(*imnumber*) returns the modulus of a complex number.

IMAGINARY IMAGINARY(*imnumber*) returns the imaginary coefficient of a complex number.

IMARGUMENT IMARGUMENT(*imnumber*) returns the argument (angle from the positive x-axis) of a complex number.

IMCONJUGATE IMCONJUGATE(*imnumber*) returns the complex conjugate of a complex number.

IMCOS IMCOS(*imnumber*) returns the cosine of a complex number.

IMDIV IMDIV(*imnumber1*, *imnumber2*) returns the quotient of *imnumber1* and *imnumber2*.

IMEXP IMEXP(*imnumber*) is the exponential function for complex numbers.

IMLN IMLN(*imnumber*) returns the natural logarithm of a complex number.

IMLOG10 IMLOG10(*imnumber*) returns the common logarithm of a complex number.

IMLOG2 IMLOG2(*imnumber*) returns the base 2 logarithm of a complex number.

IMPOWER IMPOWER(*imnumber*, *power*) returns the complex number *imnumber* raised to the power *power*.

IMPRODUCT IMPRODUCT(*imnumber1*, *imnumber2*, . . .) returns the product of up to 29 complex numbers.

IMREAL IMREAL(*imnumber*) returns the real part of a complex number.

IMSIN IMSIN(*imnumber*) returns the sine of a complex number.

IMSQRT IMSQRT(*imnumber*) returns the square root of a complex number.

IMSUB IMSUB(*imnumber1*, *imnumber2*) returns the difference of *imnumber1* and *imnumber2*.

IMSUM IMSUM(*imnumber1*, *imnumber2*, . . .) returns the sum of up to 29 complex numbers.

INDEX INDEX(*reference*, *row*, *column*, *area*) returns the cell reference at the intersection of *row* and *column*; INDEX(*array*, *row*, *column*) returns the value of an element in an array.

INDIRECT INDIRECT(*reference_text*, *A1_style*) returns the evaluation of an A1-style reference, if *A1_style* is True, or an R1C1 reference if not.

INFO INFO(*type_text*) returns information regarding the operating environment.

INT INT(*number*) truncates a number to the units place.

INTERCEPT INTERCEPT(*known_y's*, *known_x's*) returns the y-intercept of the linear regression of *known_y's* on *known_x's*.

INTRATE INTRATE(*settlement_date*, *maturity_date*, *amount*, *redemption*, *basis*) returns the rate of interest for the investment.

IPMT IPMT(*rate*, *period*, *periods*, *present_value*, *future_value*, *type*) returns the interest for one period, where *type* is 0 if payments are due at the end of a period, and 1 if they are due at the beginning.

IRR IRR(*values*, *first_guess*) returns the internal return rate of incomes (losses) represented by *values*. Excel starts with *first_guess* (optional) and iterates toward the result.

ISBLANK ISBLANK(*value*) returns True if *value* is an empty cell, and False if not.

ISERR ISERR(*value*) returns True if *value* is any error except #N/A, and False if not.

ISERROR ISERROR(*value*) returns True if *value* is any error.

ISEVEN ISEVEN(*number*) returns True if *number* is even, and False if not.

ISLOGICAL ISLOGICAL(*value*) returns True if *value* is a logical value, and False if not.

ISNA ISNA(*value*) returns True if *value* is #N/A, and False if not.

ISNONTEXT ISNONTEXT(*value*) returns True if *value* is any non-text item, or blank, and returns False if not.

ISNUMBER ISNUMBER(*value*) returns True if *value* is a number, and False if not.

ISODD ISODD(*number*) returns True if the number is odd, and False if not.

ISREF ISREF(*value*) returns True if *value* is a reference, and False if not.

ISTEXT ISTEXT(*value*) returns True if *value* is text.

KURT KURT(*number1*, *number2*, . . .) returns the kurtosis of up to 30 numbers.

LARGE LARGE(*array*, *n*) returns the nth largest value in *array*.

LCM LCM(*number1*, *number2*, . . .) returns the least common multiple of up to 29 numbers.

LEFT LEFT(*text*, *number*) returns the leftmost *number* of characters in the string *text*.

LEN LEN(*text*) returns the length (number of characters) in the string *text*.

LINEST LINEST(*known_y's*, *known_x's*, *constant*, *stats*) returns coefficients on each x-value in linear regression of *known_y's* on *known_x's*. (*constant* is True if the intercept is forced to be 0, and *stats* is True if regression statistics are desired.)

LN LN(*number*) returns the natural logarithm of the number.

LOG LOG(*number*, *base*) returns the logarithm of the number, in the specified base. (Default is base 10.)

LOG10 LOG10(*number*) returns the common logarithm of a number.

LOGEST LOGEST(*known_y's*, *known_x's*, *constant*, *stats*) returns the bases of each x-value in exponential regression of *known_y's* on *known_x's*. (*constant* is True if the leading coefficient is forced to be 0, and *stats* is True if regression statistics are desired.)

LOGINV LOGINV(*p*, *mean*, *sd*) returns the inverse of the lognormal distribution, where the natural logarithm of the distribution is normally distributed with mean *mean* and standard deviation *sd*.

LOGNORMDIST LOGNORMDIST(*x*, *mean*, *sd*) returns the probability for the lognormal distribution, where the natural logarithm of the distribution is normally distributed with mean *mean* and standard deviation *sd*.

LOOKUP (for vectors) LOOKUP(*lookup_value*, *lookup_vector*, *result_vector*) returns the entry in *result_vector* corresponding to the *lookup_value* in the *lookup_vector*.

LOOKUP (for arrays) LOOKUP(*lookup_value*, *array*) is equivalent to HLOOKUP if *array* has more columns than rows, or an equal number. Otherwise, it is equivalent to VLOOKUP.

LOWER LOWER(*text*) returns the text in all lowercase letters.

MATCH MATCH(*lookup_value*, *lookup_array*, *match_type*) returns the position of *lookup_value* in *lookup_array*. (*match_type* specifies whether to accept exact matches only (0), to find the largest value less than or equal to *lookup_value* (1), or to find the smallest value greater than or equal to *lookup_value* (-1).)

MAX MAX(*number1*, *number2*, . . .) returns the largest of up to 30 numbers.

MDETERM MDETERM(*array*) returns the determinant of a matrix entered into an array.

MDURATION MDURATION(*settlement_date*, *maturity_date*, *coupon*, *yield*, *frequency*, *basis*) returns the modified Macauley duration of an investment with a par value of $100.

MEDIAN MEDIAN(*number1*, *number2*, . . .) returns the median of up to 30 numbers.

MID MID(*text*, *start*, *number*) returns *number* characters, starting with character number *start*.

MIN MIN(*number1*, *number2*, . . .) returns the smallest of up to 30 numbers.

MINUTE MINUTE(*serial_date_time*) returns the minute of the time given in serial number form, or as text.

MINVERSE MINVERSE(*array*) returns the inverse of an invertible matrix entered as an array.

MIRR MIRR(*values*, *finance_rate*, *reinvest_rate*) returns the modified internal rate of return, where *values* contains income or losses that earn at *reinvest_rate* (financed at *finance_rate*).

MMULT MMULT(*array1*, *array2*) returns the product of two matrices entered as arrays.

MOD MOD(*number*, *divisor*) returns the remainder of the division of *number* by *divisor*.

MODE MODE(*number1*, *number2*, . . .) returns the value most frequently occurring in up to 30 numbers, or in a specified array or reference.

MONTH MONTH(*serial_date*) returns the month in the date *serial_date*.

MROUND MROUND(*number*, *multiple*) returns the number rounded to the nearest specified multiple.

MULTINOMIAL MULTINOMIAL(*number1*, *number2*, . . .) returns the quotient of the factorial of the sum of numbers and the product of the factorials of the numbers.

N N(*value*) changes a value to a number.

NA NA( ) returns the error value #N/A.

NEGBINOMDIST NEGBINOMDIST(*failures*, *threshold_successes*, *probability*) returns the probability for the negative binomial distribution.

NETWORKDAYS NETWORKDAYS(*start_date*, *end_date*, *holidays*) returns the number of working days between the two dates, excluding holidays (optional).

NOMINAL NOMINAL(*yield*, *periods*) returns the nominal interest rate, given the effective yield and number of compounding periods.

NORMDIST NORMDIST(*x*, *mean*, *sd*, *type*) returns the probability for the normal distribution with mean *mean* and standard deviation *sd*. (*type* is True for the cumulative distribution function, and False for the probability mass function.)

NORMINV NORMINV(*p*, *mean*, *sd*) returns the inverse of the normal distribution with mean *mean* and standard deviation *sd*.

NORMSDIST NORMSDIST(*number*) returns the probability for the standard normal distribution.

NORMSINV NORMSINV(*probability*) returns the inverse of the standard normal distribution.

NOT NOT(*logical_value*) returns True if *logical_value* is false, and False if it is true.

NOW NOW( ) returns the current date and time in serial number form.

NPER NPER(*rate*, *payment*, *present_value*, *future_value*, *type*) returns the number of periods necessary for payment based on the given specifications. (*type* is 0 if payments are due at the beginning of each period, and 1 if they are due at the end.)

NPV NPV(*rate*, *value1*, *value2*, . . .) returns the present value of an investment with discount rate *rate*. The values represent payments and income, over equally spaced time periods.

OCT2BIN OCT2BIN(*number*, *places*) returns the binary equivalent of an octal number, padded with leading zeros to the specified number of places (optional).

OCT2DEC OCT2DEC(*number*) returns the decimal equivalent of an octal number.

OCT2HEX OCT2HEX(*number*, *places*) returns the hexadecimal equivalent of an octal number, padded with leading zeros to the specified number of places (optional).

ODD ODD(*number*) returns the number rounded up to the nearest odd integer.

ODDFPRICE ODDFPRICE(*settlement_date*, *maturity_date*, *issue_date*, *first_date*, *rate*, *yield*, *redemption*, *frequency*, *basis*) returns the price per $100 face value of an investment whose first period is long or short.

ODDFYIELD ODDFYIELD(*settlement_date*, *maturity_date*, *issue_date*, *first_date*, *rate*, *price*, *redemption*, *frequency*, *basis*) returns the yield of an investment whose first period is long or short.

ODDLPRICE ODDLPRICE(*settlement_date*, *maturity_date*, *last_date*, *rate*, *yield*, *redemption*, *frequency*, *basis*) returns the price per $100 face value of an investment whose last period is long or short.

ODDLYIELD ODDLYIELD(*settlement_date*, *maturity_date*, *last_date*, *rate*, *price*, *redemption*, *frequency*, *basis*) returns the yield of an investment whose last period is long or short.

OFFSET OFFSET(*reference*, *rows*, *columns*, *height*, *width*) returns a reference offset from another reference. *rows* and *columns* are integers specifying the offset, while *height* and *width* specify the size of the reference.

OR OR(*logical_value1*, *logical_value2*, . . .) returns True if any of its arguments are true, and False if not.

PEARSON PEARSON(*array1*, *array2*) returns the Pearson correlation coefficient between *array1* and *array2*.

PERCENTILE PERCENTILE(*array*, *n*) returns the nth percentile of the values in *array*.

PERCENTRANK PERCENTRANK(*array*, *value*, *significant_digits*) returns the percent rank of the value in the array, with the specified number or significant digits (optional).

PERMUT PERMUT(*x*, *n*) returns the number of permutations of *x* items taken *n* at a time.

PI PI( ) returns pi accurate to 15 digits.

PMT PMT(*rate*, *periods*, *present_value*, *future_value*, *type*) returns the size of payments for the specified note. (*type* is 0 if payments are due at the end of each period, and 1 if at the beginning.)

POISSON POISSON(*x*, *mean*, *type*) returns the probability for the Poisson distribution. (*type* is True for the cumulative distribution, and False for probability mass function.)

POWER POWER(*number*, *power*) returns *number* raised to *power*.

PPMT PPMT(*rate*, *period*, *periods*, *present_value*, *future_value*, *type*) returns the payment for the specified period. (*type* is 0 if payments are due at the end of the period, and 1 if at the beginning.)

PRICE PRICE(*settlement_date*, *maturity_date*, *rate*, *yield*, *redemption*, *frequency*, *basis*) returns the price per $100 face value of a note with the given specifications.

PRICEDISC PRICEDISC(*settlement_date*, *maturity_date*, *discount_rate*, *redemption*, *basis*) returns the price per $100 face value of a note that has been discounted.

PRICEMAT PRICEMAT(*settlement_date*, *maturity_date*, *issue*, *rate*, *yield*, *basis*) returns the price per $100 face value of a note that pays interest at maturity.

PROB PROB(*x_values*, *probabilities*, *value*) returns the probability associated with *value*, given the probabilities of a range of values.

PROB PROB(*x_values*, *probabilities*, *lower_limit*, *upper_limit*) returns the probability associated with values between *lower_limit* and *upper_limit*.

PRODUCT PRODUCT(*number1*, *number2*, . . .) returns the product of up to 30 numbers.

PROPER PROPER(*text*) returns the text with the first letters of words capitalized.

PV PV(*rate*, *periods*, *payment*, *future_value*, *type*) returns the present value of the investment with the given specifications. (*type* is 0 if payments are due at the start of each period, 1 if at the end.)

QUARTILE QUARTILE(*array*, *quartile_number*) returns the first, second, or third quartile, or the minimum value (*quartile_number* = 1), or the maximum value (*quartile_number* = 4).

QUOTIENT QUOTIENT(*dividend*, *divisor*) returns the quotient of the numbers, truncated to integers.

RADIANS RADIANS(*angle*) returns the radian measure of an angle, given in degrees.

RAND RAND() returns a randomly chosen number from 0 to but not including 1.

RANK RANK(*number*, *list*, *order*) returns the rank of the number in the list, counted from the largest, or from the smallest if *order* is unequal to 0.

RATE RATE(*periods*, *payment*, *present_value*, *type*, *first_try*) returns the rate per period of an investment with the specified values. (*type* is 0 if payments are due at the start of each period, 1 if at the end; *first_try* (optional) is a guess at the rate, which the function tries first.)

RECEIVED RECEIVED(*settlement_date*, *maturity_date*, *amount_invested*, *discount_rate*, *basis*) returns the maturity value of the investment.

REGISTER.ID REGISTER.ID(*module*, *procedure*, *function_return_type*) returns the register ID of a previously registered dynamic link library, or registers it if it is not registered.

REPLACE REPLACE(*text*, *start*, *number*, *replace_text*) replaces *number* characters of *text* with *replace_text*, starting with character number *start*.

REPT REPT(*text*, *number*) repeats *text* the specified number of times.

RIGHT RIGHT(*text*, *number*) returns the rightmost *number* of characters of *text*.

ROMAN ROMAN(*number*, *type*) returns the Roman numeral equivalent of a decimal number. (*type* is an optional value from 0 to 4, determining the concision of the Roman form.)

ROUND ROUND(*number*, *places*) rounds *number* to a certain number of decimal places (if *places* is positive), or to an integer (if *places* is 0), or to the left of the decimal point (if *places* is negative).

ROUNDDOWN ROUNDDOWN(*number*, *places*) rounds like ROUND, except always toward 0.

ROUNDUP ROUNDUP(*number*, *places*) rounds like ROUND, except always away from 0.

ROW ROW(*reference*) returns the row number of *reference*.

ROWS ROWS(*array*) returns the number or rows in *array* (an array or reference).

RSQ RSQ(*known_y's*, *known_x's*) returns the square of Pearson's product moment correlation coefficient.

SEARCH SEARCH(*find_text*, *search_text*, *start*) searches *search_text* for *find_text* (optionally starting *start* characters from the left of *search_text*) and returns the number of the character within *search_text* where *find_text* is first found.

SECOND SECOND(*serial_date*) returns the seconds in *serial_date*.

SERIESSUM SERIESSUM(*x*, *n*, *m*, *coefficients*) returns the sum of the power series $a_1 x^n + a_2 x^{n+m} + \ldots + a_i x^{n+(i-1)m}$, where $a_1, a_2, \ldots a_i$ are the *coeffiecients*.

SIGN SIGN(*number*) returns 0, 1, or −1, the sign of *number*.

SIN SIN(*angle*) returns the sine of *angle*.

SINH SINH(*number*) returns the hyperbolic sine of *number*.

SKEW SKEW(*number1*, *number2*, . . .) returns the skewness of up to 30 numbers (or a reference to numbers).

SLN SLN(*cost*, *salvage_value*, *useful_life*) returns the depreciation per year of an asset.

SLOPE SLOPE(*known_y's*, *known_x's*) returns the slope of a linear regression line.

SMALL SMALL(*array*, *n*) returns the *n*th smallest number in *array*.

SQLREQUEST SQLREQUEST(*connection_string*, *output_location*, *driver_prompt*, *query_text*, *column_names*) queries an external data source directly from a worksheet.

SQRT SQRT(*number*) returns the square root of *number*.

SQRTPI SQRTPI(*number*) returns the square root of *number**π.

STANDARDIZE STANDARDIZE(*x*, *mean*, *standard_deviation*) normalizes a distribution and returns the z-score of *x*.

STDEV STDEV(*number1*, *number2*, . . .) returns the sample standard deviation of up to 30 numbers, or of an array of numbers.

STDEVP STDEVP(*number1*, *number2*, . . .) returns the population deviation of up to 30 numbers, or of an array of numbers.

STEYX STEYX(*known_y's*, *known_x's*) returns the standard error of the linear regression.

SUBSTITUTE SUBSTITUTE(*text*, *replace_text*, *replace_with*, *number*) replaces every instance of *replace_text* with *replace_with* (optionally, it replaces the specified *number* of occurrences of *replace_text*).

SUBTOTAL SUBTOTAL(*function*, *reference*) subtotals the numbers in *reference* using a specified *function* (a number from 1 to 11, for AVERAGE, COUNT, COUNTA, MAX, MIN, PRODUCT, STDEV, STDEVP, SUM, VAR, and VARP).

SUM SUM(*number1*, *number2*, . . .) returns the sum of up to 30 numbers, or of an array of numbers.

SUMIF SUMIF(*range*, *criteria*, *sum_range*) returns the sum of the numbers in *range* (optionally in *sum_range*) according to *criteria*.

SUMPRODUCT SUMPRODUCT(*array1*, *array2*, . . .) returns the sum of the products of corresponding entries in up to 30 arrays.

SUMSQ SUMSQ(*number1*, *number2*, . . .) returns the sum of the squares of up to 30 numbers, or of an array of numbers.

SUMX2MY2 SUMX2MY2(*array1*, *array2*) returns the sum of the differences of squares of corresponding entries in two arrays.

SUMX2PY2 SUMX2PY2(*array1*, *array2*) returns the sum of the sums of squares of corresponding entries in two arrays.

SUMXMY2 SUMXMY2(*array1*, *array2*) returns the sum of the squares of differences of corresponding entries in two arrays.

SYD SYD(*cost*, *salvage_value*, *useful_life*, *period*) returns the sum-of-years digits depreciation of an asset.

T T(*value*) returns the text referred to by *value*.

TAN TAN(*angle*) returns the tangent of *angle*.

TANH TANH(*number*) returns the hyperbolic tangent of *number*.

TBILLEQ TBILLEQ(*settlement_date*, *maturity_date*, *discount_rate*) returns the bond equivalent yield of a Treasury bill.

TBILLPRICE TBILLPRICE(*settlement_date*, *maturity_date*, *discount_rate*) returns the price per $100 face value of a Treasury bill.

TBILLYIELD TBILLYIELD(*settlement_date*, *maturity_date*, *price_per_$100*) returns the yield of a Treasury bill.

TDIST TDIST(*x*, *df*, *number_of_tails*) returns the probability for the T distribution.

TEXT TEXT(*value*, *text_format*) returns a value as text, in a specified format.

TIME TIME(*hour*, *minute*, *second*) returns the time as a serial number.

TIMEVALUE TIMEVALUE(*time*) returns the time as a serial number, from any text_string time format.

TINV TINV(*p*, *df*) returns the inverse of the T distribution.

TODAY TODAY( ) returns the current date as a serial number date.

TRANSPOSE TRANSPOSE(*array*) returns the transpose of *array*.

TREND TREND(*known_y's*, *known_x's*, *new_x's*, *constant_not_zero*) returns the y-values of given input values (*new_x's*) based on regression of *known_y's* on *known_x's*.

TRIM TRIM(*text*) returns *text* with spaces removed, except for single spaces between words.

TRIMMEAN TRIMMEAN(*array*, *percent*) returns the mean of a set of values, excluding *percent* of the values, half from the top and half from the bottom.

TRUE TRUE( ) returns the value True.

TRUNC TRUNC(*number*, *digits*) truncates *number* to an integer (optionally, to a number of digits).

TTEST TTEST(*array1*, *array2*, *number_of_tails*, *type*) returns the p-value of a *t*-test, of *type* paired (1), two-sample equal variance (2), or two-sample unequal variance (3).

TYPE TYPE(*value*) returns the type of *value* (1 for numbers, 2 for text, 4 for logical value, 8 for formula, 16 for error value, and 64 for array).

UPPER UPPER(*text*) returns *text* in all uppercase letters.

VALUE VALUE(*text*) returns *text* as a number, and #VALUE if *text* is not a convertible value.

VAR VAR(*number1*, *number2*, . . .) returns the sample variance of up to 30 numbers (or an array or reference).

VARP VARP(*number1*, *number2*, . . .) returns the population variance of up to 30 numbers (or an array or reference).

VDB VDB(*cost*, *salvage_value*, *life*, *start*, *end*, *factor*, *do_not_switch*) returns the depreciation of an item for the period of time from the *start* period to the *end* period, using the double-declining balance method, or (optionally) the specified *factor* rate of decline.

VLOOKUP VLOOKUP(*lookup_value*, *table_array*, *column*, *range_lookup*) searches the left column of *table_array* for *lookup_value*, and returns the value from the *column* that is in the same row as *lookup_value*. (*range_lookup* is True if, when an exact match is not found, the next highest value that is less than *lookup_value* is returned.)

WEEKDAY WEEKDAY(*serial_date*, *type*) returns the day of the week of *serial_date*. Sunday is 1 if *type* is 1; Monday is 1 if *type* is 2, and Monday is 0 if *type* is 3.

WEEKNUM WEEKNUM(*date*, *type*) returns the number of the week of the year.

WEIBULL WEIBULL(*x*, *alpha*, *beta*, *type*) returns the probability for the Weibull distribution. (*type* is True for cumulative distribution function, False for probability mass function).

WORKDAY WORKDAY(*starting_date*, *working_days*, *holidays*) returns a serial date that is *working_days* after (or before if negative) *starting_date*.

XIRR XIRR(*values*, *payment_dates*, *first_guess*) returns the internal return rate of incomes (or losses) represented by *values*, when the payment dates are not necessarily periodic. Excel starts with *first_guess* and iterates toward the result.

XNPV XNPV(*discount_rate*, *values*, *payment_dates*) returns the net present value of a schedule of incomes (or losses) represented by *values*, when the payment dates are not necessarily periodic.

YEAR YEAR(*serial_date*) returns the year of *serial_date*.

YEARFRAC YEARFRAC(*starting_date*, *ending_date*, *basis*) returns the fraction of the year between two dates.

YIELD YIELD(*settlement_date*, *maturity_date*, *rate*, *price_per_$100*, *redemption_per_$100*, *frequency*, *basis*) returns the yield of a security paying periodic interest.

YIELDDISC YIELDDISC(*settlement_date*, *maturity_date*, *price_per_$100*, *redemption_per_$100*, *basis*) returns the yield of a discounted security.

YIELDMAT YIELDMAT(*settlement_date*, *maturity_date*, *issue_date*, *rate*, *price_per_$100*, *basis*) returns the yield of a security paying interest at maturity.

ZTEST ZTEST(*array*, *x*, *sigma*) returns the p-value of a two-tailed z-test.

> # REFERENCE 4

Visual Basic

This section describes selected Visual Basic objects and statements, as well as properties and methods you can apply to Application, Chart, Range, Workbook, and Worksheet objects. Italicized words represent information you supply, and boldface type indicates the exact word returned by Excel. Items in brackets are optional. For more information, see the Excel on-line Help.

Objects

AddIn   is an add-in, either installed or not.
AddIns   is a collection of AddIn objects.
Application   is a Windows application.
Arc   is an arc graphic object, on a chart or worksheet.
Arcs   is a collection of Arc objects.
Areas   is a collection of areas in a range.
Axes   is a collection of Axis objects.
Axis   is an axis on a chart.
AxisTitle   is the title of an axis on a chart.
Border   is the border of a cell or graphic object.
Borders   is a collection of Border objects.
Button   is a custom button on a chart or worksheet, not to be confused with a ToolbarButton.
Buttons   is a collection of Button objects.
Characters   is a collection of characters in a cell, text box, or custom button.
Chart   is a chart in a workbook.
ChartGroup   is a chart group on a chart.
ChartGroups   is a collection of ChartGroup objects.
ChartObject   is a chart embedded on a sheet.
ChartObjects   is a collection of ChartObject objects.
Charts   is a collection of chart objects in a workbook.
ChartTitle   is the title of a chart.
CheckBox   is a checkbox control on a dialog sheet or worksheet.
CheckBoxes   is a collection of CheckBox objects.
Corners   are the corners on a 3-D chart.
DataLabel   is a data label on a chart data series, or on a point of a data series.
DataLabels   is a collection of DataLabel objects.

Dialog   is an Excel dialog box.
DialogFrame   is the background box of a Dialog.
Dialogs   is a collection of Dialog objects.
DialogSheet   is a dialog sheet in a workbook, and contains exactly one Dialog.
DialogSheets   is a collection of DialogSheet objects.
DownBars   is a down bar on a chart.
Drawing   is a graphic object created by Freehand, Freeform, or Filled Freeform.
DrawingObjects   is the collection of all graphic objects on a sheet.
Drawings   is a collection of Drawing objects.
DropDown   is a drop-down list box.
DropDowns   is a collection of DropDown objects.
EditBox   is a box in a dialog that allows text input.
EditBoxes   is a collection of EditBox objects.
Font   is a font description.
Gridlines   are the major or minor gridlines on a chart.
GroupBox   is a static frame that labels and groups OptionButton objects.
GroupBoxes   is a collection of GroupBox objects.
GroupObject   is a group of graphic objects.
GroupObjects   is a collection of GroupObject objects.
Interior   is the interior of a cell or graphic object.
Label   is a (static) text object on a dialog sheet.
Labels   is a collection of Label objects.
Legend   is the legend of a chart.
LegendEntries   is a collection of LegendEntry objects.

LegendEntry is the text and data marker within a legend.
LegendKey contains the formatting properties for the associated legend entry.
Line is a line on a chart or worksheet, and is a graphic object.
Lines is a collection of Line objects.
ListBox is a list of items, any one of which can be selected.
ListBoxes is a collection of ListBox objects.
Menu is a drop-down, shortcut, or cascading menu.
MenuBar is a built-in or customized menu bar.
MenuBars is a collection of MenuBar objects.
MenuItem is an item on a menu, either a command or a separator bar.
MenuItems is a collection of MenuItem objects.
Menus is a collection of Menu objects.
Module is a Visual Basic module in a workbook.
Modules is a collection of Module objects.
Name is a defined name, built-in or customized.
Names is a collection of Name objects.
OLEObject is a linked or embedded OLE object, or a chart embedded on a worksheet.
OLEObjects is a collection of OLEObject objects.
OptionButton is a button that allows one of a list of options to be selected.
OptionButtons is a collection of OptionButton objects.
PageSetup is a page setup description.
Pane is the pane of a window.
Panes is a collection of Pane objects.
Picture is a graphic object made by the Camera button, or a bitmap or metafile.
PivotField is a pivot field, inside a PivotTable.
PivotFields is a collection of PivotField objects.
PivotItem is a pivot item, in a pivot field.
PivotItems is a collection of PivotItem objects.
PivotTable is a PivotTable on a sheet.
PivotTables is a collection of PivotTable objects.
PlotArea is the plot area of a chart.
Point is one point in a data series.
Points is a collection of Point objects.
Range is a cell or group of cells.
Rectangle is a rectangle graphic object on a chart or worksheet.
Rectangles is a collection of Rectangle objects.
Scenario is a scenario (one possible set of values of several variables) on a worksheet.
Scenarios is a collection of Scenario objects.
ScrollBar is a scroll bar in a window or list box.
ScrollBars is a collection of ScrollBar objects.

Series is a data series on a chart.
SeriesCollection is a collection of Series objects.
SeriesLines are the series lines on a bar chart or column chart.
Sheets is a collection of sheets in a workbook.
Style is a style description.
Styles is a collection of Style objects.
TextBox is a text box on a chart or worksheet, and is a graphic object.
TextBoxes is a collection of TextBox objects.
TickLabels is the text associated with tick marks on the axis of a chart.
Toolbar is a built-in or customized toolbar.
ToolbarButton is a button on a toolbar, not to be confused with a Button.
ToolbarButtons is a collection of ToolbarButton objects.
Toolbars is a collection of Toolbar objects.
Window is a window in Excel.
Windows is a collection of Window objects.
Workbook is an Excel workbook.
Workbooks is a collection of Workbook objects.
Worksheet is an Excel worksheet.
Worksheets is a collection of Worksheet objects.

Statements

AppActivate AppActivate *title* [,*wait*] activates the specified application window.
Beep Sounds the computer's beep tone.
ChDir ChDir *path* changes the current directory.
ChDrive ChDrive *drive* changes the current drive.
Close Close [*filenumberlist*] closes files.
Date Date = *date* sets the system date.
Do…Loop Do [{While or Until} *condition*] [*statements*] [Exit Do] [*statements*] Loop or Do [*statements*] [Exit Do] [*statements*] Loop [{While or Until} *condition*] repeats a loop of statements while (or until) *condition* is True, or an Exit Do statement is reached.
End End *procedure* ends a procedure (Function, If, Property, Select, Sub, Type, or With).
Erase Erase *arraylist* reinitializes all elements of a fixed-size array and deallocates memory space reserved for a dynamic array.
Exit Exit *procedure* exits the procedure (Do, For, Function, Property, Sub).
FileCopy FileCopy *source*, *destination* copies the *source* file to the *destination* file.

Function [Public or Private][Static] Function *name* [(*arglist*)][As *type*] [*statements*][Exit Function] [*statements*][*name* = *expression*] End Function defines a Function procedure.
Get Get[#]*filenumber*,[*recnumber*],*varname* reads from a disk file to a variable.
GoSub...Return GoSub *line* . . . *line* . . . Return goes to a subroutine in a procedure and returns when Return is reached.
GoTo GoTo *line* goes to the specified line in a procedure.
If...Then...Else If *condition* Then *statements* [Else *elsestatements*] executes *statements* if *condition* is True, and *elsestatements* (if present) if *condition* is False.
Input # Input #*filenumber*,*varlist* reads data from a sequential file to variables.
Let [Let] *varname* = *expression* sets *varname* equal to *expression*.
Line Input # Line Input #*filenumber*,*varname* reads an entire line from a sequential file to a string variable.
Lock...Unlock Lock [#]*filenumber*[,*recordrange*] . . . Unlock [#]*filenumber*[,*recordrange*] prevents access by other processes to a part of a file, or the entire file.
LSet LSet *stringvar* = *string* left-aligns *string* within *stringvar*. LSet *varname1* = *varname2* copies *varname2* of one user-defined type to *varname1* of a different user-defined type.
Mid Mid(*stringvar*,*start*[,*length*])=*string* replaces characters within *stringvar* with *string*.
MkDir MkDir *path* creates a new directory.
Name Name *oldpathname* As *newpathname* renames a file or directory.
On Error On Error GoTo *line* goes to *line* at the time of an error. On Error Resume Next continues execution at the time of an error. On Error GoTo 0 disables an error-handling routine.
On...GoSub On *expression* GoSub *destinationlist* goes to the destination determined by *expression*.
On...GoTo On *expression* GoTo *destinationlist* goes to the destination determined by *expression*.
Print # Print#*filenumber*,[*outputlist*] writes display-formatted data to the specified sequential file.
Put Put [#]*filenumber*,[*recnumber*],*varname* writes from a variable to a file.
Reset Closes all disk files that were opened with the Open statement.
Seek Seek [#]*filenumber*,*position* sets the read-write position within a file.

Select Case Select Case *textexpression* [Case *expressionlist_n* [*statements_n*]] . . .[Case Else [*elsestatements*]] End Select executes one group of statements, depending on expression values.
SendKeys SendKeys *string*[,*wait*] sends keystokes to the active window, waiting for them to be processed if *wait* is True.
Set Set *objectvar* = {*objectexpression* or Nothing} gives an object reference to a variable or property.
Stop Suspends execution in a procedure.
Sub [Public or Private][Static] Sub *name* [(*arglist*)] [*statements*] [Exit Sub] [*statements*] End Sub creates a Sub procedure.
Time Time = *time* sets the system time.
Type [Public or Private] Type *varname* *elementname* [([*subscripts*])] As *type* [*elementname* [([*subscripts*])] As *type*] defines a user-defined data type.
While...Wend While *condition* [*statements*] Wend executes a loop of statements as long as *condition* is True.
Width # Width#*filenumber*,*width* specifies the output-line width of a file.
With With *object* [*statements*] End With executes statements on a single object.

Properties

Note: All properties are preceded by the object to which they apply.
ActiveCell returns the active cell of the active worksheet. Applies to Application, Window.
ActiveChart returns the active chart, or Nothing if none are active. Applies to Application, Window, Workbook.
ActiveDialog returns the active dialog sheet, or Nothing if none are active. Applies to Application.
ActiveMenuBar returns or sets the active menu bar. Applies to Application.
ActivePrinter returns or sets the active printer. Applies to Application.
ActiveSheet returns the active sheet, or Nothing if none are active. Applies to Application, Window, Workbook.
ActiveWindow returns the active window, or Nothing if none are open. Applies to Application.
ActiveWorkbook returns the active workbook, or Nothing if none are active, or if the Info or Clipboard window is the active window. Applies to Application.

AlertBeforeOverwriting returns True if Excel displays a message before overwriting non-blank cells while dragging and dropping, and False if not. Can be set to True or False. Applies to Application.

Application returns the application that created the object. Applies to all objects.

AskToUpdateLinks returns True if Excel prompts the user to update links when files with links are opened, and False if such links are updated automatically. Can be set to True or False. Applies to Application.

Author returns the author of an object. Can be set for a workbook. Applies to AddIn, Workbook.

Bar3DGroup returns the bar ChartGroup on the specified 3-D chart. Applies to Chart.

CalculateBeforeSave returns True if workbooks are to be calculated before saving, and False if not. Can be set to True or False. Applies to Application.

Calculation returns or sets the calculation mode (xlAutomatic, xlManual, or xlSemiautomatic). Applies to Application, PivotField.

Caption returns the name of the title bar of the main Excel window, or empty if a name is not set. Applies to Application, AxisTitle, Button, Buttons, Characters, ChartTitle, CheckBox, CheckBoxes, DataLabel, DataLabels, DialogFrame, DrawingObjects, DropDown, DropDowns, EditBox, EditBoxes, GroupBox, GroupBoxes, Label, Labels, Menu, MenuBar, MenuItem, OptionButton, OptionButtons, TextBox, TextBoxes, Window.

CellDragAndDrop returns True if cell dragging and dropping is enabled, and False if not. Can be set to True or False. Applies to Application.

ChartArea returns the ChartArea of the chart. Applies to Chart.

ChartTitle returns the title of the specified chart. Applies to Chart.

CircularReference returns the range that contains the first circular reference on a sheet, or Nothing if there is none. Applies to Worksheet.

Colors returns or sets an array of colors in the workbook palette. Applies to Workbook.

Column returns the number of the first column of the first area in the range. Applies to Range.

ColumnWidth returns or sets the column width of all columns in the range. Applies to Range.

Column3DGroup returns the column ChartGroup on the specified 3-D group. Applies to Chart.

CommandUnderlines returns or sets command underlines, but in Excel for Windows this property always returns xlOn and produces an error if set to anything else. Applies to Application.

ConsolidationFunction returns the function code for the current consolidation mode. Applies to Worksheet.

ConsolidationOptions returns a three-dimensional array of logical values, referring to labels in top row, labels in left column, and create links for data. Applies to Worksheet.

ConsolidationSources returns an array of source sheet names for the current consolidation, or returns empty if there are none. Applies to Worksheet.

ConstrainNumeric returns True if handwriting recognition is limited to numbers and punctuation, and False if not. May be set to True or False. Used for Microsoft Windows for Pen Computing. Applies to Application.

CopyObjectsWithCells returns True if drawing objects are cut and copied with cells, and False if not. Can be set to True or False. Applies to Application.

Corners returns the corners of the specified 3-D chart. Applies to Chart.

Count returns the number of items in the specified collection. Applies to all collections.

CreateBackup returns True if a backup is created when the file is saved. Applies to Workbook.

Creator returns the application that created the specified object, as a 32-bit integer. Applies to all objects.

CurrentArray returns the range of an entire array if the cell is part of an array. Applies to Range.

CurrentRegion returns a range of the current region. Applies to Range.

CustomListCount returns the number of custom lists, including those that have been built in. Applies to Application.

CutCopyMode returns the Cut and/or Copy mode. In Cut mode, xlCut is returned; in Copy mode, xlCopy is returned; if not in either mode, False is returned. Applies to Application.

DataEntryMode returns or sets the Data Entry mode, in which you can enter data only in the unlocked cells of the selected range. The value is either xlOn, xlOff, or xlStrict, so that ESC will not exit Data Entry mode. Applies to Application.

DefaultFilePath returns or sets the default file path used when opening files. Applies to Application.

Dependents returns a range containing all dependents of a specified cell. Applies to Range.

DepthPercent returns or sets the depth percentage of a 3-D chart, as a portion of the chart width. Applies to Chart.

DirectPrecedents returns a range containing all direct precedents of a cell. Applies to Range.

DisplayAlerts returns True if alerts and messages are displayed when a macro is running, and False if not. Can be set to True or False. Applies to Application.

DisplayAutomaticPageBreaks returns True if automatic page breaks are displayed. Can be set to True or False. Applies to DialogSheet, Worksheet.

DisplayBlanksAs returns or sets the manner in which blank cells are plotted on a chart (either xlNotPlotted, xlInterpolated, or xlZero). Applies to Chart.

DisplayDrawingObjects returns or sets how drawing objects are displayed (either xlAll, xlPlaceholders, or xlHide). Applies to Workbook.

DisplayFormulaBar returns True if the formula bar is displayed, and False if not. Can be set to True or False. Applies to Application.

DisplayFullScreen returns True if Excel is in full-screen mode, and False if not. Can be set to True or False. Applies to Application.

DisplayInfoWindow returns True if the Info window is displayed, and False if not. Can be set to True or False. Applies to Application.

DisplayNoteIndicator returns True if cells with notes contain note indicators, and False if not. Can be set to True or False. Applies to Application.

DisplayRecentFiles returns True if the files most recently used are displayed in the File menu, and False if not. Can be set to True or False. Applies to Application.

DisplayScrollBars returns True if scroll bars are displayed, and False if not. Can be set to True or False. Applies to Application.

DisplayStatusBar returns True if the status bar is displayed, and False if not. Can be set to True or False. Applies to Application.

EditDirectlyInCell returns True if editing in cells is allowed, and False if not. Can be set to True or False. Applies to Application.

EnableTipWizard returns True if the TipWizard is enabled, and False if not. Can be set to True or False. Applies to Application.

EntireColumn returns the entire column(s) containing the specified range. Applies to Range.

EntireRow returns the entire row(s) containing the specified range. Applies to Range.

FileConverters returns a text array containing a list of installed file converters, each row corresponding to one file converter, or Null if none is installed. Applies to Application.

FileFormat returns the file format of the workbook. Applies to Workbook.

FilterMode returns True if the worksheet is in filter mode, and False if not. Applies to Worksheet.

FixedDecimal returns True if data are formatted with the number of FixedDecimalPlaces, and False if not. Can be set to True or False. Applies to Application.

FixedDecimalPlaces returns or sets the number of fixed decimal places. Applies to Application.

Font returns or sets the font of the specified object. Applies to AxisTitle, Button, Buttons, Characters, ChartArea, ChartTitle, DataLabel, DataLabels, DrawingObjects, GroupObject, GroupObjects, Legend, LegendEntry, PlotArea, Range, Style, TextBox, TextBoxes, TickLabels.

Formula returns or sets the formula of the specified object (in the language of the macro, A1 style). Applies to Button, Buttons, Picture, Pictures, Range, Series, TextBox, TextBoxes.

FormulaArray returns or sets the formula of a range. Applies to Range.

FormulaHidden returns True if the formula is hidden when the worksheet is protected. Can be set to True or False. Applies to Range, Style.

FormulaLocal returns or sets the formula of the specified object (in the user's language, A1 style). Applies to Range, Series.

FormulaR1C1 returns or sets the formula of the specified object (in the language of the macro, R1C1 style). Applies to Range, Series.

FormulaR1C1Local returns or sets the formula of the specified object (in the user's language, R1C1 style). Applies to Range, Series.

FullName returns the name of the specified object, with the disk path. Applies to AddIn, Workbook.

HasArray returns True if the cell is part of an array, and False if not. Applies to Range.

HasAxis returns a two-dimensional array indicating which axes are included on the specified chart. Applies to Chart.

HasFormula returns True if all of the specified cells contain formulas, False if none does, and Null otherwise. Applies to Range.

HasLegend returns True if the specified chart has a legend. Can be set to True or False. Applies to Chart.

HasPassword returns True if the specified workbook has a password, and False if not. Applies to Workbook.

HasRoutingSlip returns True if the specified workbook has a routing slip. Can be set to True or False. Applies to Workbook.

HasTitle returns True if the specified chart has a (non-hidden) title. Can be set to True or False. Applies to Axis, Chart.

Hidden returns True if the specified range is hidden. Can be set to True or False. Applies to Range, Scenario.

Iteration returns True if Excel uses iteration to resolve circular references, and False if not. Can be set to True or False. Applies to Application.

Keywords returns or sets the specified object's keywords. Applies to AddIn, Workbook.

Legend returns the chart's legend. Applies to Chart.

LibraryPath returns the Library directory path, not including the final separator. Applies to Application.

Line3DGroup returns the line ChartGroup of the specified 3-D chart. Applies to Chart.

LocationInTable returns the location of the upper-left corner of the specified range (xlRowHeader, xlColumnHeader, xlPageHeader, xlDataHeader, xlRowItem, xlColumnItem, xlPageItem, xlDataItem, or xlTableBody). Applies to Range.

Locked returns True if the specified range is locked. Can be set to True or False. Applies to Arc, Arcs, Button, Buttons, ChartObject, ChartObjects, Checkbox, CheckBoxes, DialogFrame, Drawing, DrawingObjects, Drawings, DropDown, DropDowns, EditBox, EditBoxes, GroupBox, GroupBoxes, GroupObject, GroupObjects, Label, Labels, Line, Lines, ListBox, ListBoxes, OLEObject, OLEObjects, OptionButton, OptionButtons, Oval, Ovals, Picture, Pictures, Range, Rectangle, Rectangles, Scenario, ScrollBar, ScrollBars, Spinner, Spinners, Style, TextBox, TextBoxes.

MathCoprocessorAvailable returns True if a math coprocessor is available, and False if not. Applies to Application.

MaxChange returns or sets the maximum change used per iteration when Excel is resolving circular references. Applies to Application.

MaxIterations returns or sets the maximum number of iterations allowed when Excel is resolving circular references. Applies to Application.

MemoryFree returns the unused memory available to Excel, in bytes. Applies to Application.

MemoryTotal returns the total memory available to Excel, in bytes. Applies to Application.

MemoryUsed returns the memory currently used by Excel, in bytes. Applies to Application.

MouseAvailable returns True if a mouse is available, and False if not. Applies to Application.

MoveAfterReturn returns True if the selection is moved when ENTER is pressed, and False if not. Can be set to True or False. Applies to Application.

Name returns the name of the application. Applies to AddIn, Application, Arc, AxisTitle, Button, Chart, ChartArea, ChartObject, ChartTitle, CheckBox, Corners, DataLabel, DataLabels, DialogFrame, DialogSheet, DownBars, Drawing, DropDown, DropLines, EditBox, ErrorBars, Floor, Font, Gridlines, GroupBox, GroupObject, HiLoLines, Label, Legend, Line, ListBox, Module, Name, OLEObject, OptionButton, Oval, Picture, PivotField, PivotItem, PivotTable, PlotArea, Range, Rectangle, Scenario, ScrollBar, Series, SeriesLines, Spinner, Style, TextBox, TickLabels, Toolbar, ToolbarButton, Trendline, UpBars, Walls, Workbook, Worksheet.

Next returns the next sheet, chart, or cell. Applies to Chart, DialogSheet, Module, Range, Worksheet.

NumberFormat returns or sets the format code of the specified object. Applies to DataLabel, DataLabels, PivotField, Range, Style, TickLabels.

OnCalculate returns or sets the name of the macro to be run when the worksheet is recalculated. Applies to Application, Worksheet.

OnData returns the procedure to be run when DDE- or OLE-linked data arrives in Excel from another application. Applies to Application, Worksheet.

OnDoubleClick returns or sets the macro to be run when the mouse is double-clicked. Applies to Application, Chart, DialogSheet, Module, Worksheet.

OnEntry returns or sets the procedure to be run when you enter data in the formula bar or in a cell. Applies to Application, Worksheet.

OnSheetActivate returns or sets the macro to be run when any sheet in any open workbook is activated. Applies to Application, Chart, DialogSheet, Module, Workbook, Worksheet.

OnSheetDeactivate returns or sets the macro to be run when any sheet in any open workbook is deactivated. Applies to Application, Chart, DialogSheet, Module, Workbook, Worksheet.

OnWindow returns or sets the procedure to be run when you switch to a window. Applies to Application, Window.

OperatingSystem returns the name and number of the current operating system. Applies to Application.

OrganizationName returns the registered organization name, as a string. Applies to Application.

Orientation returns an object's orientation. Applies to AxisTitle, Button, Buttons, ChartTitle, DataLabel, DataLabels, DrawingObjects, GroupObject, GroupObjects, PageSetup, PivotField, Range, Style, TextBox, TextBoxes, TickLabels.

PageBreak returns or sets page breaks (xlNone, xlManual, or xlAutomatic). Applies to Range.

PageSetup returns an object containing the page setup settings for the specified object. Applies to Chart, DialogSheet, Module, Window, Worksheet.

Parent returns the parent object for the object specified. Applies to all objects.

Path returns the path of the object, as a string, without the final separator and name of the object. Applies to AddIn, Application, Workbook.

PathSeparator returns the character "\". Applies to Application.

Perspective returns or sets the perspective (a number from 0 to 100) for the specified 3-D chart. Applies to Chart.

Pie3DGroup returns the pie ChartGroup for the specified 3-D chart. Applies to Chart.

PivotField returns the PivotField that contains the upper-left corner of the specified range. Applies to Range.

PivotItem returns the PivotItem that contains the upper-left corner of the specified range. Applies to Range.

PivotTable returns the PivotTable that contains the upper-left corner of the specified range. Applies to Range.

PlotArea returns the PlotArea of the specified chart. Applies to Chart.

PlotVisibleOnly returns True if visible cells are plotted and hidden cells are not. Can be set to True or False. Applies to Chart.

PrefixCharacter returns the prefix character of the specified cell. Applies to Range.

Previous returns the previous sheet (if applied to a worksheet object) or the previous cell (if applied to a range object). Applies to Chart, DialogSheet, Module, Range, Worksheet.

PreviousSelections returns the four previous ranges or names selected, as an array. Applies to Application.

PromptForSummaryInfo returns True if Excel prompts the user for summary information when new files are saved, and False if not. Can be set to True or False. Applies to Application.

ReadOnly returns True if the workbook was opened as a read-only file, and False if not. Applies to Workbook.

RecordRelative returns True if macros record with relative references, and False if absolute references are used. Can be set to True or False. Applies to Application.

ReferenceStyle returns or sets the reference style (A1 or R1C1) used by Excel. Applies to Application.

RoutingSlip returns the workbook's RoutingSlip. Applies to Workbook.

Row returns the first row number of the specified range. Applies to Range.

RowHeight returns or sets the row height of the specified range, in points. Applies to Range.

Saved returns False if changes have been made to the specified workbook since it was last saved. If set to True, the workbook can be closed without the save changes prompt. Applies to Workbook.

SaveLinkValues returns True if the workbook is saved with external link values. Can be set to True or False. Applies to Workbook.

ScreenUpdating returns True if screen updating is on, and False if not. Can be set to True or False. Applies to Application.

Selection returns the currently selected object in the active window. Applies to Application, Window.

SheetsInNewWorkbook returns or sets the number of sheets in new workbooks. Applies to Application.

ShowDetail returns True if the row or column detail is visible (the outline is expanded). Can be set to True or False. Applies to PivotItem, Range.

ShowToolTips returns True if ToolTips are shown, and False if not. Can be set to True or False. Applies to Application.

SizeWithWindow returns True if the specified chart resizes with the chart sheet window. Applies to Chart.

StandardFont returns or sets the standard font, as a string. Applies to Application.

StandardFontSize returns or sets the standard font size, in points. Applies to Application.

StartupPath returns the startup directory path, not including the final separator. Applies to Application.

StatusBar returns or sets the status bar text. Applies to Application.

Style returns or sets the style of the specified range. Applies to Range.

Summary returns True if the row or column is an outlining summary row or column. Applies to Range.

Text returns the text appearing in the specified cell, as a string. Applies to AxisTitle, Button, Buttons, Characters, ChartTitle, CheckBox, CheckBoxes, DataLabel, DataLabels, DialogFrame, DrawingObjects, DropDown, DropDowns, EditBox, EditBoxes, GroupBox, GroupBoxes, Label, Labels, OptionButton, OptionButtons, Range, TextBox, TextBoxes.
ThisWorkbook returns the workbook where the current code is running. Applies to Application.
Title returns or sets the title for the workbook. Applies to AddIn, Workbook.
Type returns the chart or worksheet type. Applies to Axis, Chart, ChartGroup, DataLabel, DataLabels, Series, Trendline, Window, Worksheet.
UpdateRemoteReferences returns True if the workbook's remote references will be updated. Can be set to True or False. Applies to Workbook.
UsableHeight returns the height of the space that a window can occupy in the application window. Applies to Application, Window.
UsableWidth returns the width of the space that a window can occupy in the application window. Applies to Application, Window.
UsedRange returns the range in the workbook that is currently used. Applies to Worksheet.
UserName returns or sets the current user name. Applies to Application.
UseStandardHeight returns True if the row height of the specified range is the same as the standard height for the whole sheet. Can be set to True. Applies to Range.
UseStandardWidth returns True if the column width of the specified range is the same as the standard width for the whole sheet. Can be set to True. Applies to Range.
Version returns the version of Excel. Applies to Application.
VerticalAlignment returns or sets the specified object's vertical alignment (xlBottom, xlCenter, xlDistributed, xlJustify, or xlTop). Applies to AxisTitle, Button, Buttons, ChartTitle, DataLabel, DataLabels, DrawingObjects, GroupObject, GroupObjects, Range, Style, TextBox, TextBoxes.
Walls returns the walls of the specified 3-D chart. Applies to Chart.
WallsAndGridlines2D returns True if the gridlines of the specified 3-D chart are drawn in 2-D. Applies to Chart.
WindowState returns or sets the window state (xlNormal, xlMaximized, or xlMinimized). Applies to Application, Window.
Worksheet returns the worksheet that contains the specifed range. Applies to Range.
WrapText returns True if Excel wraps text in the specified range. Can be set to True or False. Applies to Range, Style.

Methods

Activate Activates the specified object. Applies to Chart, ChartObject, DialogSheet, MenuBar, Module, OLEObject, Pane, Range, Window, Workbook, Worksheet.
ActivateMicrosoftApp ActivateMicrosoftApp(*index*) activates or starts the specified application. Applies to Application.
AddChartAutoFormat AddChartAutoFormat (*chart*, *name*, *description*) adds a customized chart autoformat with the specifications of *chart*. Applies to Application.
AddIns AddIns(*index*) returns all the add-ins in the Add-Ins dialog box, or the one specified by the optional *index*. Applies to Application.
Address Address(*rowAbsolute*, *columnAbsolute*, *referenceStyle*, *external*, *relativeTo*) returns the range referred to as a string (in the macro language). Applies to Range.
AdvancedFilter AdvancedFilter(*action*, *criteriaRange*, *copyToRange*, *unique*) performs a filter *action* (either xlFilterInPlace or xlFilterCopy) according to *criteriaRange*. Applies to Range.
ApplyDataLabels ApplyDataLabels(*type*, *legendKey*) adds data labels to the specified point or series, with the legend key next to the points if *legendKey* is True. Applies to Chart, Point, Series.
ApplyNames ApplyNames(*names*, *ignoreRelativeAbsolute*, *useRowColumnNames*, *omitColumn*, *omitRow*, *order*, *appendLast*) adds names to cells in the specified range. Applies to Range.
ApplyOutlineStyles Applies outlining styles to the specified range. Applies to Range.
AreaGroups AreaGroups(*index*) returns an area chart group specified by *index*, or all area chart groups if *index* is omitted. Applies to Chart.
AutoFill AutoFill(*destination*, *type*) fills the destination cells with the source range. Applies to Range.
AutoFilter AutoFilter without arguments displays or hides the AutoFilter down arrow buttons. AutoFilter(*field*, *criteria1*, *operator*, *criteria2*) filters the list according to the criteria and the *operator* (xlAnd or xlOr). Applies to Range.

AutoFit Resizes the width of the columns (or the height of the rows) in the specified range. Applies to Range.

AutoFormat AutoFormat(*gallery*, *format*) applies an autoformat to the specified chart. Applies to Chart.

AutoFormat AutoFormat(*format*, *number*, *font*, *alignment*, *border*, *pattern*, *width*) applies an autoformat to the specified range. (The final six arguments correspond to checkboxes in the AutoFormat dialog box.) Applies to Range.

AutoOutline Creates an outline for the specified range, or for the entire sheet if the range is one cell. Applies to Range.

Axes Axes(*type*, *axisGroup*) returns the specified axis, or all axes on the chart if the arguments are omitted. Applies to Chart.

BarGroups BarGroups(*index*) returns the index specified by *index*, or all bar chart groups in the chart if *index* is omitted. Applies to Chart.

BorderAround BorderAround(*lineStyle*, *weight*, *colorIndex*, *color*) creates a border around the range. Applies to Range.

Borders Borders(*index*) returns the border specified by *index*, or all borders in the range if *index* is omitted. Applies to Range, Style.

Buttons Buttons(*index*) returns the button specified by *index*, or all buttons in the chart or worksheet if *index* is omitted. Applies to Chart, DialogSheet, Worksheet.

Calculate Calculates all open workbooks. Applies to Application, Range, Worksheet.

Cells Cells(*rowIndex*, *columnIndex*) returns a collection of cells as a range, or the (optional) cell in *rowIndex*, *columnIndex*. Applies to Application, Range, Worksheet.

ChangeFileAccess ChangeFileAccess(*mode*, *writePassword*, *notify*) changes the access mode (xlReadWrite or xlReadOnly), write password, and whether or not there is notification when a file cannot be accessed immediately. Applies to Workbook.

ChangeLink ChangeLink(*name*, *newName*, *type*) changes a link (of type xlExcelLinks or xlOLELinks) from one document to another. Applies to Workbook.

Characters Characters(*start*, *length*) returns a number of characters from the specified range. Applies to AxisTitle, Button, Buttons, ChartTitle, CheckBox, CheckBoxes, DataLabel, DialogFrame, DrawingObjects, DropDown, DropDowns, EditBox, EditBoxes, GroupBox, GroupBoxes, Label, Labels, OptionButton, OptionButtons, Range, TextBox, TextBoxes.

ChartGroups ChartGroups(*index*) returns the chart group specified by *index*, or all chart groups in the chart if *index* is omitted. Applies to Chart.

ChartObjects ChartObjects(*index*) returns the chart specified by *index*, or all charts if *index* is omitted. Applies to Chart, DialogSheet, Worksheet.

Charts Charts(*index*) returns the chart specified by *index*, or all charts if *index* is omitted. Applies to Application, Worksheet.

ChartWizard ChartWizard(*source*, *gallery*, *format*, *plotBy*, *categoryLabels*, *seriesLabels*, *hasLegend*, *title*, *categoryTitle*, *valueTitle*, *extraTitle*) changes desired properties of the chart object (all arguments optional). Applies to Chart.

CheckBoxes CheckBoxes(*index*) returns the checkbox specified by *index*, or all checkboxes in the chart or worksheet if *index* is omitted. Applies to Chart, DialogSheet, Worksheet.

CheckSpelling CheckSpelling(*customDictionary*, *ignoreUppercase*, *alwaysSuggest*) checks the spelling of the specified object. CheckSpelling(*word*, *customDictionary*, *ignoreUppercase*) checks the spelling of the specified word. Applies to Application, Button, Buttons, Chart, CheckBox, CheckBoxes, DialogFrame, DialogSheet, DrawingObjects, GroupBox, GroupBoxes, GroupObject, GroupObjects, Label, Labels, OptionButton, OptionButtons, Range, TextBox, TextBoxes, Worksheet.

Clear Clears the entire specified range. Applies to ChartArea, Range.

ClearArrows Removes all auditing arrows from the worksheet. Applies to Worksheet.

ClearContents Clears the formulas from the range, or the data from the chart. Applies to ChartArea, Range.

ClearFormats Clears the formatting from the range. Applies to ChartArea, Floor, LegendKey, PlotArea, Point, Range, Series, Trendline, Walls.

ClearNotes Clears text notes and sound notes from the range. Applies to Range.

ClearOutline Clears the outline from the range. Applies to Range.

Close Close(*saveChanges*, *fileName*, *routeWorkbook*) closes the workbook, taking the specified actions. Applies to Window, Workbook, Workbooks.

ColumnDifferences ColumnDifferences(*comparison*) returns the range of cells whose contents differ from the cell in the same column as *comparison*. Applies to Range.

ColumnGroups ColumnGroups(*index*) returns the column chart group specified by *index*, or all the column chart groups if *index* is omitted. Applies to Chart.

Columns Columns(*index*) returns the column specified by *index*, or all the columns if *index* is omitted. Applies to Application, Range, Worksheet.

Consolidate Consolidate(*sources*, *function*, *topRow*, *leftColumn*, *createLinks*) consolidates data from multiple sources to one range on one worksheet. Applies to Range.

ConvertFormula ConvertFormula(*formula*, *fromReferenceStyle*, *toReferenceStyle*, *toAbsolute*, *relativeTo*) changes a formula's cell reference style (xlA1 or xlR1C1) and reference type (xlAbsolute, xlAbsRowRelColumn, xlRelRowAbsColumn, or xlRelative). Applies to Application.

Copy Copy(*destination*) copies the specified range to *destination*. Copy(*before*, *after*) copies the specified sheet before or after another sheet. Applies to Arc, Arcs, Button, Buttons, Chart, ChartArea, ChartObject, ChartObjects, Charts, CheckBox, CheckBoxes, DialogSheet, DialogSheets, Drawing, DrawingObjects, Drawings, DropDown, DropDowns, EditBox, EditBoxes, GroupBox, GroupBoxes, GroupObject, GroupObjects, Label, Labels, Line, Lines, ListBox, ListBoxes, Module, Modules, OLEObject, OLEObjects, OptionButton, OptionButtons, Oval, Ovals, Picture, Pictures, Point, Range, Rectangle, Rectangles, ScrollBar, ScrollBars, Series, Sheets, Spinner, Spinners, TextBox, TextBoxes, ToolbarButton, Worksheet, Worksheets.

CreateNames CreateNames(*top*, *left*, *bottom*, *right*) creates names for the specified range based on the top or bottom row or the left or right column. Applies to Range.

Cut Cut(*destination*) cuts the specified range to the Clipboard, or to *destination*, if included. Applies to Arc, Arcs, Button, Buttons, ChartObject, ChartObjects, CheckBox, CheckBoxes, Drawing, DrawingObjects, Drawings, DropDown, DropDowns, EditBox, EditBoxes, GroupBox, GroupBoxes, GroupObject, GroupObjects, Label, Labels, Line, Lines, ListBox, ListBoxes, OLEObject, OLEObjects, OptionButton, OptionButtons, Oval, Ovals, Picture, Pictures, Range, Rectangle, Rectangles, ScrollBar, ScrollBars, Spinner, Spinners, TextBox, TextBoxes.

DataSeries DataSeries(*rowcol*, *type*, *date*, *step*, *stop*, *trend*) creates a data series in the specified range. Applies to Range.

Delete Delete(*shift*) deletes the specified object; if in a range object, *shift* specifies how to replace the deleted cells (xlToLeft or xlUp). Applies to Arc, Arcs, Axis, AxisTitle, Button, Buttons, Characters, Chart, ChartObject, ChartObjects, Charts, ChartTitle, CheckBox, CheckBoxes, DataLabel, DataLabaels, DialogSheet, DialogSheets, DownBars, Drawing, DrawingObjects, Drawings, DropDown, DropDowns, DropLines, EditBox, EditBoxes, ErrorBars, Gridlines, GroupBox, GroupBoxes, GroupObject, GroupObjects, HiLoLines, Label, Labels, Legend, LegendEntry, LegendKey, Line, Lines, ListBox, ListBoxes, Menu, MenuBar, MenuItem, Module, Modules, Name, OLEObject, OLEObjects, OptionButton, OptionButtons, Oval, Ovals, Picture, Pictures, Point, Range, Rectangle, Rectangles, Scenario, ScrollBar, ScrollBars, Series, SeriesLine, Sheets, SoundNotes, Spinner, Spinners, Style, TextBox, TextBoxes, TickLabels, Toolbar, ToolbarButton, Trendline, UpBars, Worksheet, Worksheets.

DeleteChartAutoFormat DeleteChartAutoFormat (*name*) deletes the chart autoformat *name*. Applies to Application.

DeleteCustomList DeleteCustomList(*listNum*) deletes the custom list. Applies to Application.

DeleteNumberFormat DeleteNumberFormat (*numberFormat*) deletes the custom number format. Applies to Workbook.

Deselect Deselects the selection of the specified chart. Applies to Chart.

DialogBox Displays a dialog box from an Excel 4.0 macro sheet and returns the number of the control chosen (or False if Cancel is chosen). Applies to Range.

Dialogs Dialogs(*index*) returns the dialog specified by *index*, or all dialogs if *index* is omitted. Applies to Application.

DialogSheets DialogSheets(*index*) returns the dialog sheet specified by *index*, or all dialog sheets if *index* is omitted. Applies to Application, Workbook.

DoubleClick Equivalent to double-clicking the active cell, active object, or selected object. Applies to Application.

DrawingObjects DrawingObjects(*index*) returns the drawing object specified by *index*, or all drawing objects on the chart or worksheet if *index* is omitted. Applies to Chart, DialogSheet, Worksheet.

Drawings Drawings(*index*) returns the drawing specified by *index*, or all drawings on the chart or worksheet if *index* is omitted. Applies to Chart, DialogSheet, Worksheet.

DropDowns DropDowns(*index*) returns the drop-down list box control specified by *index*, or all drop-down list box controls on the chart or worksheet if *index* is omitted. Applies to Chart, DialogSheet, Worksheet.

End End(*direction*) returns the cell at the end of the region containing the specified range, in the *direction* xlToLeft, xlToRight, xlUp, or xlDown. Applies to Range.

FillDown Fills the range from the top cell(s) down, copying contents and formats. Applies to Range.

FillLeft Fills the range from the rightmost cell(s) to the left, copying contents and formats. Applies to Range.

FillRight Fills the range from the leftmost cell(s) to the right, copying contents and formats. Applies to Range.

FillUp Fills the range from the bottom cell(s) up, copying contents and formats. Applies to Range.

Find Find(*what, after, lookIn, lookAt, searchOrder, searchDirection, matchCase*) searches the range for *what*, starting (optionally) after the cell *after*. (*searchOrder* is xlByRows or xlByColumns; *searchDirection* is xlNext or xlPrevious.) Applies to Range.

FindFile Displays the Find File dialog box. Applies to Application.

FindNext FindNext(*after*) continues the search started with Find, optionally starting after the cell *after*. Applies to Range.

FindPrevious FindPrevious(*after*) continues the search started with Find, optionally starting after the cell *after*. Applies to Range.

FunctionWizard Starts the Function Wizard. The function is placed in the upper-left cell of the range. Applies to Range.

GetOpenFilename GetOpenFilename(*fileFilter, filterIndex, title*) displays the Open dialog box, and allows the user to choose a filename (which is returned) without opening the file. Applies to Application.

GetSaveAsFilename GetSaveAsFilename(*initialFilename, fileFilter, filterIndex, title*) displays the Save As dialog box and allows you to choose a filename (which is returned) without saving the file. Applies to Application.

Goto Goto(*reference, scroll*) selects the range (or a Visual Basic procedure) specified by *reference*, scrolling to show the range in the upper-left corner if desired. Applies to Application.

GroupBoxes GroupBoxes(*index*) returns the group box control specified by *index*, or all the group box controls on the chart or worksheet if *index* is omitted. Applies to Chart, DialogSheet, Worksheet.

GroupObjects GroupObjects(*index*) returns the group specified by *index*, or all groups on the chart or worksheet if *index* is omitted. Applies to Chart, DialogSheet, Worksheet.

Help Help(*helpFile, helpContextID*) displays the Help topic *helpContextID* (or Help contents if omitted). Applies to Application.

InchesToPoints InchesToPoints(*inches*) returns the points equivalent to *inches*. Applies to Application.

InputBox InputBox(*prompt, title, default, left, top, helpFile, helpContextID, type*) displays a dialog box and returns the information entered. Applies to Application.

Insert Insert(*shift*) inserts cells into the range. Applies to Characters, Pictures, Range.

Intersect Intersect(*arg1, arg2, . . .*) returns the rectangular intersection of the specified ranges. Applies to Application.

Item Item(*index*) returns part of a collection of objects. Applies to all collections.

Justify Justifies the text in the specified range to fill the range evenly. Applies to Range.

Labels Labels(*index*) returns the label specified by *index*, or all labels on the chart or worksheet if *index* is omitted. Applies to Chart, DialogSheet, Worksheet.

LinkInfo LinkInfo(*name, linkInfo, type, editionRef*) returns information about the specified link, of information *type* xlUpdateState or xlEditionDate. Applies to Workbook.

LinkSources LinkSources(*type*) returns an array of all the links in the workbook. Applies to Workbook.

ListBoxes ListBoxes(*index*) returns the list box control specified by *index*, or all list box controls on the chart or worksheet, if *index* is omitted. Applies to Chart, DialogSheet, Worksheet.

ListNames Pastes all (non-hidden) names in the worksheet, starting with the first cell of the specified range. Applies to Range.

MenuBars MenuBars(*index*) returns the menu bar specified by *index*, or all top-level menu bars if *index* is omitted. Applies to Application.

Modules Modules(*index*) returns the module specified by *index*, or all modules in the application or workbook if *index* is omitted. Applies to Application, Workbook.

Move Move(*before*, *after*) moves the specified sheet before or after another sheet. Applies to Chart, Charts, DialogSheet, DialogSheets, Module, Modules, Sheets, ToolbarButton, Worksheet, Worksheets.

Names Names(*index*, *indexLocal*, *refersTo*) returns the name specified by one of *index*, *indexLocal* (in the user's language), or *refersTo* (what the name refers to) or all names if no argument is given. Applies to Application, Workbook.

NavigateArrow NavigateArrow(*towardPrecedent*, *arrowNumber*, *linkNumber*) selects and returns the precedent, dependent, or error-causing cell(s). Applies to Range.

NewWindow Creates a new window in the workbook. Applies to Window, Workbook.

NoteText NoteText(*text*, *start*, *length*) creates or modifies the cell note of the upper-left cell in the range. Applies to Range.

Offset Offset(*rowOffset*, *columnOffset*) returns a range offset from the range object. Applies to Range.

OLEObjects OLEObjects(*index*) returns the OLE object specified by *index*, or all OLE objects if *index* is omitted. Applies to Chart, DialogSheet, Worksheet.

OnKey OnKey(*key*, *procedure*) sets the *procedure* to take place when a certain *key* is pressed. Applies to Application.

OnRepeat OnRepeat(*text*, *procedure*) sets the *procedure* to take place when Edit > Repeat is chosen. Applies to Application.

OnTime OnTime(*earliestTime*, *procedure*, *latestTime*, *schedule*) runs *procedure* within *earliestTime* and *latestTime*. Applies to Application.

OnUndo OnUndo(*text*, *procedure*) runs *procedure* when Edit > Undo is chosen. Applies to Application.

OpenLinks OpenLinks(*linkName*, *readOnly*, *link_type*) opens the documents referred to by *linkName*. Applies to Workbook.

OptionButtons OptionButtons(*index*) returns the option button control specified by *index*, or all option button controls on the chart or worksheet if *index* is omitted. Applies to Chart, DialogSheet, Worksheet.

Paste Paste(*type*) pastes chart data from the Clipboard to the specified chart, of *type* xlFormats, xlFormulas, or xlAll. Paste(*destination*, *link*) pastes the Clipboard contents to the specified worksheet. Applies to Chart, Pictures, Point or Series, SeriesCollection, DialogSheet, Worksheet.

PasteSpecial PasteSpecial(*format*, *link*, *displayAsIcon*, *iconFileName*, *iconIndex*, *iconLabel*) pastes the Clipboard contents onto the specified worksheet, using a specific format. PasteSpecial(*paste*, *operation*, *skipBlanks*, *transpose*) pastes a Clipboard range to the specified range, using the given characteristics. Applies to Range, DialogSheet, Worksheet.

Pictures Pictures(*index*) returns the picture specified by *index*, or all pictures in the chart or worksheet if *index* is omitted. Applies to Chart, DialogSheet, Worksheet.

PivotTables PivotTables(*index*) returns the PivotTable specified by *index*, or all PivotTables on the worksheet, if *index* is omitted. Applies to Worksheet.

PivotTableWizard PivotTableWizard(*sourceType*, *sourceData*, *tableDestination*, *tableName*, *rowGrand*, *columnGrand*, *saveData*, *hasAutoFormat*, *autoPage*) creates a PivotTable without displaying the PivotTable Wizard. Applies to Worksheet.

PrintOut PrintOut(*from*, *to*, *copies*, *preview*) prints the specified object. Applies to Chart, Charts, DialogSheet, DialogSheets, Module, Modules, Range, Sheets, Window, Workbook, Worksheet, Worksheets.

PrintPreview Displays the object as it will be printed. Applies to Chart, Charts, DialogSheet, DialogSheets, Range, Sheets, Window, Workbook, Worksheet, Worksheets.

Protect Protect(*password*, *drawingObjects*, *contents*, *scenarios*) protects a chart or worksheet. Applies to Chart, DialogSheet, Module, Workbook, Worksheet.

Protect(*password*, *structure*, *windows*) protects a workbook. Applies to Chart, DialogSheet, Module, Workbook, Worksheet.

Quit Exits Excel, prompting you to save changed workbooks unless DisplayAlerts is False. Applies to Application.

RadarGroups RadarGroups(*index*) returns the radar chart group specified by *index*, or all radar chart groups in the chart if *index* is omitted. Applies to Chart.

Range Range(*cell1*) or Range(*cell1*, *cell2*) returns a cell or a range of cells. Applies to Application, Range, Worksheet.

RecordMacro RecordMacro(*basicCode*, *xlmCode*) records *basicCode* if the recorder is recording into a Visual Basic module, or *xlmCode* if the recorder is recording into an Excel 4.0 macro sheet. Applies to Application.

Rectangles Rectangles(*index*) returns the rectangle specified by *index*, or all rectangles in the chart or worksheet if *index* is not specified. Applies to Chart, DialogSheet, Worksheet.

RemoveSubtotal Removes subtotals from the list in the range. Applies to Range.

Repeat Repeats your previous action. Applies to Application.

Replace Replace(*what*, *replacement*, *lookAt*, *searchOrder*, *matchCase*) replaces *what* with *replacement*, wherever it is found within the range. Applies to Range.

Resize Resize(*rowSize*, *columnSize*) resizes the specified range. Applies to Range.

RowDifferences RowDifferences(*comparison*) returns the range of cells whose contents differ from the cell in the same row as *comparison*. Applies to Range.

Rows Rows(*index*) returns the row specified by *index*, or all the rows in the range or worksheet if *index* is omitted. Applies to Application, Range, Worksheet.

Run Run(*macro*, *arg1*, arg2, . . .) runs a macro in any language. Run(arg1, arg2, . . .) runs an Excel 4.0 macro at the specified range (must be on a macro sheet). Applies to Application, Range.

RunAutoMacros RunAutoMacros(*which*) runs auto macros specified by *which* (xlAutoOpen, xlAutoClose, xlAutoActivate, xlAutoDeactivate). Applies to Workbook.

Save Saves changes to the current workbook. Save(*filename*) saves the workspace. Applies to Application, Workbook.

SaveAs SaveAs(*filename*, *fileFormat*, *password*, *writeResPassword*, *readOnlyRecommended*, *createBackup*) saves the sheet or workbook under a different name. Applies to Chart, DialogSheet, Module, Workbook, Worksheet.

SaveCopyAs SaveCopyAs(*filename*) saves the workbook to filename without changing the open workbook in memory. Applies to Workbook.

Scenarios Scenarios(*index*) returns the scenario specified by *index*, or all scenarios on the worksheet if *index* is omitted. Applies to Worksheet.

ScrollBars ScrollBars(*index*) returns the scroll bar control specified by *index*, or all scroll bar controls on the chart or worksheet if *index* is omitted. Applies to Chart, DialogSheet, Worksheet.

Select Selects the specified object. Select(*replace*) selects a sheet, replacing the previous selection if *replace* is True, and adding it to the selection if *replace* is False. Applies to Arc, Arcs, Axis, AxisTitle, Button, Buttons, Chart, ChartArea, ChartObject, ChartObjects, Charts, ChartTitle, CheckBox, CheckBoxes, Corners, DataLabel, DataLabaels, DialogFrame, DialogSheet, DialogSheets, DownBars, Drawing, DrawingObjects, Drawings, DropDown, DropDowns, DropLines, EditBox, EditBoxes, ErrorBars, Floor, Gridlines, GroupBox, GroupBoxes, GroupObject, GroupObjects, HiLoLines, Label, Labels, Legend, LegendEntry, LegendKey, Line, Lines, ListBox, ListBoxes, Module, Modules, OLEObject, OLEObjects, OptionButton, OptionButtons, Oval, Ovals, Picture, Pictures, PlotArea, Point, Range, Rectangle, Rectangles, ScrollBar, ScrollBars, Series, SeriesLine, Sheets, Spinner, Spinners, TextBox, TextBoxes, TickLabels, Trendline, UpBars, Walls, Worksheet, Worksheets.

SendKeys SendKeys(*keys*, *wait*) sends keystrokes into the key buffer of the specified application. Applies to Application.

SetDefaultChart SetDefaultChart(*formatName*) sets the chart template to the custom autoformat *formatName*. Applies to Application.

Sheets Sheets(*index*) returns the sheet specified by *index*, or all sheets if *index* is omitted. Applies to Application, Workbook.

ShortcutMenus ShortcutMenus(*index*) returns the shortcut menu specified by *index*. Applies to Application.

Show Scrolls the active window until the specified range is in view. Applies to Dialog, DialogSheet, Range, Scenario.

ShowAllData Makes all rows visible, in a filtered list. Applies to Worksheet.

ShowDataForm Shows the data form associated with the specified worksheet. Applies to Worksheet.

ShowDependents ShowDependents(*remove*) draws arrows to direct dependents of the specified range. If *remove* is True, one level of arrows is removed; if False or omitted, one level is added. Applies to Range.

ShowErrors Draws arrows to the error-causing cell. Applies to Range.

Sort Sort(*key1*, *order1*, *key2*, *type*, *order2*, *key3*, *order3*, *header*, *orderCustom*, *matchCase*, *orientation*) performs a sort on the range. Sort(*key1*, *order1*, *type*, *orderCustom*, *orientation*) performs a sort on a PivotTable. Applies to Range.

Styles Styles(*index*) returns the style specified by *index*, or all styles in a workbook if *index* is omitted. Applies to Workbook.

Subtotal Subtotal(*groupBy*, *function*, *totalList*, *replace*, *pageBreaks*, *summaryBelowData*) creates subtotals for the specified range. Applies to Range.

Table Table(*rowInput*, *columnInput*) creates a data table, optionally using row input or column input. Applies to Range.

TextBoxes TextBoxes(*index*) returns the text box specified by *index*, or all text boxes in the chart or worksheet if *index* is omitted. Applies to Chart, DialogSheet, Worksheet.

TextToColumns TextToColumns(*destination*, *dataType*, *textQualifier*, *consecutiveDelimiter*, *tab*, *semicolon*, *comma*, *space*, *other*, *otherChar*, *fieldInfo*) parses text in one column into the *destination* columns. Applies to Range.

Toolbars Toolbars(*index*) returns the toolbar specified by *index*, or all toolbars in the application if *index* is omitted. Applies to Application.

Undo Cancels your previous action. Applies to Application.

Ungroup Decreases the outline level of the specified range. Applies to DrawingObjects, GroupObject, GroupObjects, Range.

Unprotect Unprotect(*password*) removes protection from the specified chart, worksheet, or workbook. Applies to Chart, DialogSheet, Module, Workbook, Worksheet.

UpdateFromFile Updates a workbook with read-only status if the disk version is more recent than the workbook in memory. Applies to Workbook.

UpdateLink UpdateLink(*name*, *type*) updates the link *name*. Applies to Workbook.

Wait Wait(*time*) pauses macros until *time*. Applies to Application.

Windows Windows(*index*) returns the window specified by *index*, or all the windows in the application or workbook if *index* is omitted. Applies to Application, Workbook.

Workbooks Workbooks(*index*) returns the workbook specified by *index*, or all the open workbooks in the application if *index* is omitted. Applies to Application.

Worksheets Worksheets(*index*) returns the worksheet specified by *index*, or all the worksheets in the application or workbook if *index* is omitted. Applies to Application, Workbook.

Index

Special Characters

\> (greater than sign), EX 55, EX 141
< (less than sign), EX 55, EX 141
( ) (parentheses), EX 55, EX 145
<> (not equal to sign), EX 55, EX 141
! (exclamation point), EX 243
" " (quotation marks), EX 142
(number sign), EX 70-72
$ (dollar sign), EX 58
% (percentage operator), EX 55
& (ampersand), EX 55
* (asterisk), EX 31, EX 244
* (multiplication operator), EX 55
+ (addition operator), EX 55
= (equal sign), EX 31, EX 54, EX 55, EX 141
\>= (greater than or equal to sign), EX 55, EX 141
<= (less than or equal to sign), EX 55, EX 141
? (question mark), EX 243
^ (exponentiation operator), EX 55
' (apostrophe), EX 394
' ' (single quotation marks), EX 142
- (subtraction operator), EX 55
/ (division operator), EX 55
/ (slash), EX 31

A

About Microsoft Excel command, Help menu, EX 449
absolute references, EX 58, EX 148-150
activating
 charts, EX 168-169
 Microsoft Query add-in, EX 262-263
 Solver, EX 221
 toolbars, EX 103-104
active cell, EX 10, EX 11, EX 413, EX 414
active sheet, EX 10
Add Constraint dialog box, EX 218
Add Data Field command, Shortcut menu, EX 449
Add-Ins command, Tools menu, EX 447, EX 448
Add Watch command, Tools menu, EX 448
adding. *See* entering
addition operator (+), EX 55
Advanced Filter, EX 247
Align Left button, EX 452
Align Right button, EX 452
aligning cell contents, EX 92-93
alignment buttons, EX 90, EX 93
answer report, EX 224-228
 displaying, EX 225
 printing, EX 226
 sections, EX 225-226
apostrophe ('), starting comments, EX 394
apparent rounding errors, EX 299-303

application development. *See* macro(s); Visual Basic
Arc button, EX 452
Area Chart AutoFormat button, EX 453
area charts, EX 161
 predefined formats, EX 162
arguments
 functions, EX 131
 methods, EX 399
arithmetic mean, EX 134-136
Arrange command, Window menu, EX 449
Arrow button, EX 452
arrows, adding and positioning, EX 108
ASCII file, EX 262
Assign Macro command, Tools menu, EX 447, EX 448
asterisk (*)
 mathematical operator, EX 31
 wildcard, EX 244
Attach Note button, EX 455
Attach Toolbars command, Tools menu, EX 448
attached text, charts, EX 179
Auditing command, Tools menu, EX 447
Auditing menu buttons, EX 455
Auto Query button, MS Query, EX 353, EX 364
AutoFill feature, EX 50-52
AutoFilter, EX 247-252
AutoFilter button, EX 454
AutoFormat button, EX 451
AutoFormat command, Format menu, EX 65-67, EX 70-71, EX 446

automatic calculations
    PivotTables, EX 253-261
    recalculations, EX 33-34. *See also* Solver; what-if analysis
    recalculations in data tables, EX 325-326
Automatic Except Tables calculation, EX 325
automatic filling, EX 50-52
automatic formatting, EX 65-67, EX 70-71, EX 89
automatic headers and footers, EX 111-112
automatic performance of commands. *See* macro(s); modules
automating worksheet updates, EX 409-419
AutoSave command, Tools menu, EX 447
AutoSum button, EX 68-69, EX 451
AVERAGE function, EX 134-136, EX 456
axes, charts, EX 162, EX 407
Axes command, Insert menu, EX 445

B

Backspace key, correcting mistakes, EX 17, EX 18
Bar Chart AutoFormat button, EX 453
bar charts, EX 161. *See also* column charts
Binding constraints, EX 226
blank cells, AVERAGE function, EX 135
blank worksheets, renaming, EX 163
Bold button, EX 90, EX 452

boldfacing, EX 90-91, EX 146, EX 180
book-level name, EX 294
Book1 window, EX 8
Boolean variable, EX 412
border(s), EX 98-101
    adding to charts, EX 193
    adding to worksheets, EX 99, EX 100-101
    changing, EX 107-108
    deleting, EX 99-100
Border dialog box, EX 99-100
Border tab, EX 99, EX 100-101
Borders button, EX 90, EX 99, EX 451
Bottom Border button, EX 451
Bottom Double Border button, EX 451
Bring To Front button, EX 452
budget, consolidated, EX 273
building worksheets, EX 43, EX 47-50
button(s)
    alignment, EX 90, EX 93
    AutoSum, EX 68-69
    Bold, EX 90
    Borders, EX 99
    Close, EX 111
    Color, EX 90
    Currency Style, EX 324
    Decrease Decimal, EX 324
    Delete, EX 244-245
    font style, EX 90
    Format Painter, EX 96
    Function Wizard, EX 132
    Help, EX 34-35
    Increase Decimal, EX 323
    Italics, EX 90
    Margins, EX 111
    Microsoft Query toolbar buttons, EX 352-353
    New, EX 245-246
    Percent Style, EX 90
    Print, EX 110

    Run Macro, EX 401
    scroll arrow, EX 14
    Setup, EX 110-111, EX 111
    Spelling, EX 76-77
    Stop Macro, EX 392
    Summary, EX 330
    Underline, EX 90
    Undo, EX 18
button reference
    auditing, EX 455
    charting, EX 453-454
    data, EX 454
    drawing, EX 452-453
    edit, EX 450-451
    file, EX 450
    formatting, EX 451
    forms, EX 455
    formula, EX 451
    macro, EX 453
    text formatting, EX 452
    TipWizard, EX 455
    utility, EX 454

C

Calculate Now button, EX 454
calculations. *See also* automatic calculations; formula(s); functions
    center line of control charts, EX 389-390, EX 401-402
    control limits of control charts, EX 389-390, EX 405-409
    methods for PivotTables, EX 256-257
Camera button, EX 454
canceling changes, EX 18, EX 235
case sensitivity, EX 240
cash flow budget, EX 273
category (x) axis, EX 162

Index **EX 483**

category (x) axis title, EX 162
category labels, EX 162
cell(s), EX 11
   active, EX 10, EX 11, EX 413, EX 414
   adding text notes, EX 75-76
   blank, AVERAGE function, EX 135
   changing, EX 216, EX 217-218, EX 226
   clearing, EX 69-70
   contents. *See* cell contents
   copying formats with Format Painter button, EX 96
   copying using Visual Basic methods, EX 418-419
   defining cell or range names, EX 293-295
   deleting, EX 69-70
   displaying contents, EX 31
   formatting using Visual Basic properties, EX 418
   hidden, EX 317
   locked, EX 77-80
   moving to named cell, EX 295-296
   protecting, EX 77-80
   ranges. *See* ranges
   referencing in other worksheets, EX 282-283
   target, EX 216, EX 217-218, EX 225
   typing functions directly into, EX 132
   unlocking, EX 78-79
   values exceeding cell width, EX 70-72
cell contents
   aligning, EX 92-93
   changing, EX 16-17, EX 33-34
   copying, EX 56-57
   displaying, EX 153
   erasing, EX 69-70

cell references, EX 11
   absolute, EX 58, EX 148-150
   editing, EX 148-149
   formulas, EX 31, EX 54, EX 55
   relative, EX 57-58
   selecting with mouse, EX 59-60
   3-D references, EX 282
Cells command
   Format menu, EX 446
   Insert menu, EX 444
Center Across Columns button, EX 452
Center button, EX 452
centering
   column titles, EX 93
   printout, EX 113-114
   text across columns, EX 93
changing. *See also* editing; updating
   borders, EX 107-108
   cell contents, EX 16-17
   column width, EX 48-50, EX 71-72, EX 98
   data series in charts, EX 177-178
   font sizes, EX 91-92
   font styles, EX 90-91
   fonts, EX 91-92
   headers, EX 112-113
   patterns in charts, EX 171-173
   undoing changes, EX 18, EX 235
changing cells, EX 216
   answer report, EX 226
   Scenario Manager, EX 326
   setting up, EX 217-218
chart(s), EX 159-196. *See also* control charts
   activating, EX 168-169
   applying borders, EX 193

   boldfacing legends and axis labels, EX 180
   changing patterns, EX 171-173
   creating 3-D pie charts, EX 164-173
   creating column charts, EX 182-193
   creating line charts, EX 173-182
   creating with ChartWizard. *See* ChartWizard
   displaying, EX 14
   elements, EX 162-163
   embedded, EX 168
   highlighting data for, EX 26
   moving, EX 169-170
   positioning, EX 27
   predefined formats, EX 161-162
   previewing, EX 194
   printing, EX 23-25, EX 28-29, EX 194-195
   resizing, EX 169-170
   selecting, EX 168
   tips for creating, EX 196
   titles, EX 162, EX 179, EX 187-188
   types, EX 161
Chart command, Insert menu, EX 444, EX 445
chart line, EX 162
   calculating center line of control chart, EX 389-390, EX 401-402
chart sheet, EX 275
   inserting, EX 290-291
chart title, EX 162
Chart toolbar, EX 103
Chart Type button, EX 454
Chart Type command, Format menu, EX 446
Charting menu buttons, EX 453-454

ChartWizard, EX 27
   creating chart sheet, EX 290-291
   creating charts, EX 25-28
   creating column chart, EX 183
   creating line charts, EX 174-176
   creating 3-D column charts, EX 191
   creating 3-D pie charts, EX 166-167
   creating X-Bar control chart, EX 406-409
   revising data series, EX 177-178
ChartWizard button, EX 454
Check Box button, EX 455
choosing. *See* selecting
Clear All Breakpoints command, Run menu, EX 445
Clear command, Edit menu, EX 443
Clear Contents button, EX 450
Clear dialog box, EX 69
clearing. *See also* deleting; removing
   cells, EX 69-70
   test values, EX 74
Clipboard, adding pictures to column charts, EX 184-186
Close button, EX 111
Close command, File menu, EX 442
closing worksheets, EX 36
codes, formatting, headers and footers, EX 112
Colon button, EX 451
color(s)
   charts, EX 187
      selecting for lines in charts, EX 407-408
   worksheets, EX 101-103
Color button, EX 90, EX 453

column(s)
   centering text across columns, EX 93
   changing width, EX 48-50, EX 71-72, EX 98
   inserting, EX 63-65
   sorting data, EX 236-239
   titles, EX 67, EX 93
Column Chart AutoFormat button, EX 453
column charts, EX 161, EX 182-193
   adding pictures, EX 184-186
   displaying titles in colored boxes with shadows, EX 187-188
   stretching and stacking pictures, EX 186
   2-D, EX 189-190
   3-D, EX 188-193
Column command, Format menu, EX 446
column headings, EX 10, EX 113-114
column labels, PivotTables, EX 255-256
Column Width command, EX 71-72
Columns command, Insert menu, EX 444
combination charts, EX 161
Combination Drop-Down button, EX 455
Combination List-Edit button, EX 455
combined cash flow budget. *See* multiple worksheets
comma(s), number formats, EX 96-97
Comma button, EX 451
Comma format, EX 97
Comma Style button, EX 90, EX 451

command, user-defined, adding to Tools Menu, EX 419-421
command reference
   Data menu, EX 448
   Edit menu, EX 443
   File menu, EX 442
   Format menu, EX 446
   Help menu, EX 449
   Insert menu, EX 444-445
   Run menu, EX 445
   Shortcut menu, EX 449
   Tools menu, EX 447-448
   View menu, EX 443-444
   Window menu, EX 449
comments
   adding to worksheet, EX 105-109
   user-defined functions, EX 402-403
   Visual Basic, EX 394-395
compare values, EX 283
comparison operators, EX 141
complex problem solving, EX 212-228. *See also* Solver
   formulating problems, EX 214-215
   trial and error strategy, EX 215-216
computerized spreadsheets, EX 9
Consolidate command, Data menu, EX 448
consolidated cash flow budget, EX 273
consolidated worksheets. *See* multiple worksheets
Constrain Numeric button, EX 451
constraints, EX 216, EX 218-219
   adding, EX 220-221
   answer report, EX 226
   Binding and Not Binding, EX 226
   integer, EX 222-223
   slack, EX 226

Contents command, Help menu, EX 449
control, production process, EX 385-386. *See also* quality control
control charts
   calculating center line, EX 389-390, EX 401-402
   calculating control limits, EX 389-390, EX 405-409
   center line, EX 387
   control limits, EX 387
   creating X-Bar control chart, EX 406-409
   example, EX 386
   formatting, EX 407-408
   types, EX 387
Control Properties button, EX 455
control structures, Visual Basic, EX 415-417
Copy button, EX 450
Copy command, Edit menu, EX 443
copying
   cells, using Visual Basic methods, EX 418-419
   data from worksheet to Write report, EX 370-371
   formats with Format Painter button, EX 96
   formulas, EX 56-57, EX 59, EX 60, EX 139-140, EX 144-145, EX 147, EX 148-150
   modules, EX 119
   pictures to Clipboard, EX 184-185
   rows, EX 148-150
   test values, EX 61-63
   user-defined functions, EX 404
   worksheets, EX 292-293
correcting mistakes, EX 17-18, EX 76-77
Create Button button, EX 452
criteria, database queries, EX 355
Criteria pane, Microsoft Query, EX 355, EX 358-359
CTI WinApps group icon, EX 5, EX 6
CTI WinApps group window, EX 6
currency exchange rate, EX 293, EX 296-298
currency formats, EX 94-95, EX 283, EX 320, EX 324
Currency Style button, EX 90, EX 324, EX 451
currency variable type, Visual Basic, EX 412
Cut button, EX 450
Cut command, Edit menu, EX 443
Cycle Font Color button, EX 452

D

Dark Shading button, EX 451, EX 453
data. *See* cell contents; text; value(s)
data, transferring and sharing. *See* transferring and sharing data
Data Analysis command, Tools menu, EX 447
data forms, EX 239-244
   adding records, EX 245-246
   criteria search, EX 241-243
   deleting records, EX 244-245
   searching manually, EX 240
   wildcards, EX 243-244
Data Labels command, Insert menu, EX 445
data lists, EX 233-269. *See also* records
   card file representation, EX 234
   filtering, EX 247-252
   maintaining with data forms, EX 239-244
   PivotTables, EX 253-261, EX 262-269
   searching, EX 240-244
   sorting, EX 235-239
   updating, EX 244-247
data management, EX 233. *See also* data lists; database(s); records
data markers, EX 162
   selecting patterns, EX 185
Data menu
   button reference, EX 454
   command reference, EX 448
Data pane, Microsoft Query, EX 355
data point, EX 162
data series in charts, EX 162, EX 177-178
   formatting, EX 407-408
data tables, EX 316
   controlling worksheet recalculation, EX 325-326
   one-input, EX 317-321
   two-input, EX 321-325
database(s). *See also* data lists; records
   common fields linking relational databases, EX 349
   components, EX 347
   external, EX 262-269
   internal, EX 262
   querying. *See* Microsoft Query
   structure, EX 347-349
   tables and table names, EX 347
database functions, EX 131

date(s). *See also* value(s)
    displaying and formatting,
        EX 145–147
date functions, EX 131,
    EX 145–147
Date tool, EX 112
date variable type, Visual Basic,
    EX 412
dBASE file, EX 262
Debug Window command,
    View menu, EX 444
decimal places
    currency formats, EX 94–95,
        EX 320
    number formats, EX 96–97
    percentage formats,
        EX 97–98
decision-support worksheets,
    EX 15–17
decisions. *See also* Solver; what-
    if analysis
    making and documenting,
        EX 20
Decrease Decimal button,
    EX 324, EX 451
Decrease Font Size button,
    EX 452
Default Chart button, EX 453
Delete button, EX 244–245,
    EX 450
Delete Column button, EX 450
Delete command, Edit menu,
    EX 443
Delete key, clearing cells,
    EX 69–70
Delete Row button, EX 450
Delete Sheet command, Edit
    menu, EX 443
deleting. *See also* clearing;
    removing
    borders, EX 99–100
    cell contents, EX 69–70
    cells, EX 69–70

column and row headings,
    EX 113–114
gridlines, EX 113–114
headers, EX 112
records, EX 244–245
toolbars, EX 103, EX 109
worksheets, EX 288–289
dialog sheet, EX 390
Dim statement, Visual Basic,
    EX 413
disk drives, selecting, EX 6
displaying
    answer report, EX 225
    cell contents, EX 31, EX 153
    charts, EX 14
    dates, EX 145–147
    documentation, EX 275
    formulas, EX 32, EX 55,
        EX 116–117
    functions, EX 33
    macros, EX 393
    records in databases, EX 239,
        EX 265–266
    values, EX 70–72
#DIV/0! message, EX 258
dividing line, changing column
    width, EX 49–50
division operator (/), EX 31,
    EX 55
Division Sign button, EX 451
Do Until...Loop statement,
    Visual Basic, EX 416
Do While...Loop statement,
    Visual Basic, EX 416
document(s). *See* workbooks
documenting. *See also*
    comments
    decisions, EX 20
    headers and footers,
        EX 111–113
    workbooks, EX 274–276
    worksheets, EX 43,
        EX 74–76, EX 287–288

dollar sign ($), absolute
    references, EX 58
Dollar Sign button, EX 451
Do...Loop statement, Visual
    Basic, EX 416
double-precision floating point
    type, Visual Basic, EX 412
Double Underline button,
    EX 452
Doughnut Chart AutoFormat
    button, EX 453
doughnut charts, EX 161
Drawing button, EX 453
Drawing menu buttons,
    EX 452–453
Drawing Selection button,
    EX 452
Drawing toolbar, EX 103,
    EX 104
drives, selecting, EX 6
Drop-Down button, EX 455
Drop Shadow button, EX 452
drop shadows, EX 107
Dynamic Data Exchange (DDE)
    keeping linked files together,
        EX 377
    updating linked data, EX 360,
        EX 368

E

Edit Box button, EX 455
Edit Code button, EX 455
Edit menu
    button reference,
        EX 450–451
    command reference, EX 443
Edit mode, correcting mistakes,
    EX 17–18
Edit Watch command, Tools
    menu, EX 448

editing. *See also* changing; updating
  cell reference types, EX 148-149
  correcting mistakes, EX 17-18, EX 76-77
  embedded objects, EX 344-347
  text in charts, EX 178-179
electronic spreadsheets, EX 9
Ellipse button, EX 452
embedded charts, EX 168
embedded objects
  double-clicking to open source application, EX 340
  editing, EX 344-347
embedding data, EX 339-340. *See also* linking data
End command, Run menu, EX 445
End statement, Visual Basic, EX 395, EX 412
engineering functions, EX 131
entering
  arrows, EX 108
  borders in charts, EX 193
  borders in worksheets, EX 99, EX 100-101
  comments in worksheet, EX 105-109
  formulas, EX 54-56, EX 56
  gridlines in charts, EX 180
  labels, EX 47-48
  pictures in column charts, EX 184-186
  records, EX 245-246
  row and column labels in PivotTables, EX 255-256
  rows and columns, EX 63-65
  SUM function, EX 58
  test values, EX 61-63
  text in charts, EX 178-179
  text notes, EX 75-76
  titles in PivotTables, EX 267
equal sign (=), formulas, EX 31, EX 54, EX 55
Equal Sign button, EX 451
equal to operator (=), EX 141
erasing. *See* clearing; deleting; removing
Error Bars command, Insert menu, EX 445
error correction, EX 17-18, EX 76-77
errors
  apparent rounding errors, EX 299-303
  checking for possible errors, EX 298-299
Examples and Demos Preview command, Help menu, EX 449
Excel. *See* Microsoft Excel
exchange rate, EX 293, EX 296-298
exclamation point (!), for referencing worksheets, EX 282
Exit command, File menu, EX 442
exiting
  Excel, EX 36
  Windows, EX 36
exponentiation operator (^), EX 55
Exponentiation Sign button, EX 451
external databases
  accessing data, EX 263-266
  creating PivotTables from, EX 262-269

F

factors, EX 388
field(s), EX 233, EX 234
  common fields in relational databases, EX 349
  PivotTables, EX 253-261
  values in databases, EX 347
field names, EX 233, EX 234
  databases, EX 347
file(s). *See also* workbooks
  ASCII, EX 262
  dBASE, EX 262
File command, Insert menu, EX 444
File menu
  button reference, EX 450
  command reference, EX 442
[File Name] command, File menu, EX 442
Filename tool, EX 112
filenames, EX 53
  extensions, EX 22, EX 53, EX 80
  file naming scheme, EX 53
  Save As command, EX 21, EX 22-23, EX 53-54
Fill command, Edit menu, EX 443
Fill Down button, EX 451
Fill Down command, EX 148-149
fill handle, EX 51, EX 56-57
Fill Right button, EX 451
Filled Arc button, EX 452
Filled Ellipse button, EX 452
Filled Freeform button, EX 452
Filled Polygon button, EX 452
Filled Rectangle button, EX 452

filling worksheets automatically, EX 50-52
Filter command, Data menu, EX 448
filtering lists, EX 247-252
financial functions, EX 131, EX 137-140
Find command, Edit menu, EX 443
Find File button, EX 450
Find File command, File menu, EX 442
font(s), EX 90, EX 91-92
   sizes, EX 90, EX 91-92
   styles, EX 90-92
Font button, EX 452
Font Color button, EX 90, EX 452
font size box, EX 90
Font Size button, EX 452
font style buttons, EX 90, EX 452
Font tool, EX 112
footers, EX 111-113
Form command, EX 239, EX 448
format(s). *See also* formatting
   charts, predefined, EX 161-162, EX 189
   clearing, EX 69
Format Cells dialog box, EX 92, EX 99, EX 100-101
Format Chart Area dialog box, EX 169
Format Data Point dialog box, EX 185
Format menu, EX 49, EX 89, EX 98
   command reference, EX 446
Format Painter button, EX 96, EX 450

formatting, EX 87-109. *See also* format(s)
   activating toolbars, EX 103-104
   adding comments to worksheet, EX 105-109
   aligning cell contents, EX 92-93
   automatic, EX 65-67, EX 70-71, EX 89
   borders, EX 98-101
   cells, using Visual Basic properties, EX 418
   centering text across columns, EX 93
   chart lines, EX 181
   currency formats, EX 94-95, EX 283, EX 320, EX 324
   data series in charts, EX 407-408
   dates, EX 145-147
   fonts, font styles, and font sizes, EX 90-92
   Format Painter button, EX 96
   hidden cells, EX 317
   number formats, EX 96-97
   patterns and colors, EX 101-103
   percentage formats, EX 97-98
   PivotTables, EX 267-268
   planning formats, EX 87
   X-Bar control chart, EX 407-408
formatting codes, headers and footers, EX 112
Formatting menu buttons, EX 451
formatting toolbar, EX 89-90, EX 90, EX 103
Forms menu buttons, EX 455

formula(s), EX 31-32
   adding to combined worksheets, EX 304-306
   AutoSum button, EX 68-69
   copying, EX 56-57, EX 59, EX 60, EX 139-140, EX 144-145, EX 147, EX 148-150
   displaying, EX 32, EX 55, EX 116-117
   entering, EX 54-56, EX 56
   order of operations, EX 55-56
   prewritten. *See* functions; user-defined functions
   printing using modules, EX 117-121
   updating, EX 153-154
formula bar, EX 10, EX 55
Formula Bar command, View menu, EX 443
Formula menu buttons, EX 451
Freeform button, EX 452
Freehand button, EX 452
Freeze Panes button, EX 454
Freeze Panes command, Window menu, EX 276, EX 278, EX 449
Full Screen button, EX 454
Full Screen command, View menu, EX 443
Function command, Insert menu, EX 444
Function Wizard button, EX 132, EX 451, EX 453
functions, EX 32-33, EX 130-147
   alphabetical reference list, EX 456-466
   AVERAGE, EX 134-136, EX 456
   categories, EX 131
   displaying, EX 33

Function Wizard button, EX 132
IF, EX 141-145, EX 460
MAX, EX 132-133, EX 462
MIN, EX 134, EX 462
nesting, EX 300
PMT, EX 137-140, EX 463
ROUND, EX 300-303, EX 464
SUM, EX 32-33, EX 58-59, EX 68-69, EX 465
syntax, EX 131
TODAY, EX 145-147, EX 465
typing directly in cells, EX 132
user-defined. *See* user-defined functions
VLOOKUP, EX 283-286, EX 466

G

General format, EX 89
Get External Data button, PivotTable, EX 366
Get External Data command, Data menu, EX 448
Go To command, Edit menu, EX 295-296, EX 443
Goal Seek command, EX 208-212, EX 447
graph(s). *See* chart(s)
graphical objects
    adding to column charts, EX 184-186
    adding to workbook, EX 372-375
    stretching and stacking in column charts, EX 186
greater than operator (>), EX 141

greater than or equal to operator (>=), EX 141
greater than or equal to sign (>=), EX 55
greater than sign (>), EX 55
gridlines
    adding to charts, EX 180
    removing, EX 113-114
Gridlines command, Insert menu, EX 445
Group and Outline command, Data menu, EX 448
Group Box button, EX 455
Group button, PivotTable, EX 366, EX 367, EX 454
Group Objects button, EX 452
grouping
    PivotTable data, EX 366-368
    worksheets, EX 306-308

H

handles
    embedded charts, EX 168
    fill, EX 51
headers, EX 111-113
    answer report, EX 226
    changing, EX 112-113
    deleting, EX 112
headings
    columns, EX 10, EX 113-114
    rows, EX 10, EX 113-114
Help button, EX 34-35, EX 454
    MS Query, EX 353
Help menu, EX 35
    command reference, EX 449
Help mode, EX 34-35
hidden cells, EX 317
Hide command, Window menu, EX 449
Hide Detail button, EX 454

highlighting ranges, EX 26
Horizontal Gridlines button, EX 454
horizontal lines, EX 99
horizontal scroll bar, EX 10, EX 11, EX 14

I

icons
    CTI WinApps group, EX 5, EX 6
    Make Excel 5.0 Student Disks, EX 6
    Microsoft Office group, EX 7
IF function, EX 141-145, EX 460
If...Then...Else statement, Visual Basic, EX 415
importance weights, EX 15, EX 16-17
in control, production process, EX 385-386
Increase Decimal button, EX 323, EX 451
Increase Font Size button, EX 452
Index command, Help menu, EX 449
input
    planning worksheets, EX 45
    prompting for user input, EX 413-415
input values
    displaying separately, EX 279
    one-input data table, EX 318
    two-input data table, EX 322-323
InputBox dialog box, EX 414
InputBox method, Visual Basic, EX 413-414
Insert button, EX 450

Insert Chart Sheet button, EX 450
Insert Column button, EX 451
Insert command, EX 63-65
Insert Dialog button, EX 450
Insert menu commands, EX 444-445
Insert Module button, EX 450, EX 453
Insert MS Excel 4.0 Macro button, EX 450
Insert Row button, EX 451
Insert Workbook button, EX 450
inserting
    chart sheet, EX 290-291
    new worksheets, EX 288-290
Instant Watch button, EX 453
Instant Watch command, Tools menu, EX 448
integer constraint, EX 222-223
integer variable type, Visual Basic, EX 412, EX 413
integrating data between applications. *See* embedding data; linking data
interest rates
    displaying in chart sheet, EX 290-291
    displaying in data tables, EX 316-325
    prime rate, EX 316
internal databases, EX 262
Italic button, EX 90, EX 452
italicizing, EX 90, EX 91, EX 106-107

J

Justify Align button, EX 452

K

keyboard
    clearing cells, EX 69-70
    correcting mistakes, EX 17, EX 18
keywords, Visual Basic, EX 394

L

Label button, EX 455
label text, charts, EX 178
labels
    charts, EX 162, EX 180
    columns, PivotTables, EX 255-256
    entering, EX 47-48
    entering automatically, EX 51-52
    freezing in place, EX 276, EX 278
    PivotTables, EX 255-256
    rows, PivotTables, EX 255-256
landscape orientation, EX 111
largest number, finding, EX 132-133
launching Excel, EX 7-8
Left Border button, EX 451
Left Parenthesis button, EX 451
Legend button, EX 454
Legend command, Insert menu, EX 445
legends, charts, EX 162, EX 163, EX 180
less than operator (<), EX 141
less than or equal to operator (<=), EX 141
less than or equal to sign (<=), EX 55
less than sign (<), EX 55

Light Shading button, EX 451, EX 453
line(s). *See also* border(s)
    calculating center line of control charts, EX 389-390, EX 401-402
    formatting chart lines, EX 181
Line button, EX 452
Line Chart AutoFormat button, EX 453
line charts, EX 161, EX 173-182
    adding and editing text, EX 178-179
    adding horizontal gridlines, EX 180
    boldfacing legends and axis labels, EX 180
    formatting lines, EX 181
    revising data series, EX 177-178
Line/Column Chart AutoFormat button, EX 453
linking data, EX 340-344. *See also* embedding data
    Excel as OLE client with Paintbrush as OLE server, EX 372-375
    Excel as OLE server for Write document, EX 369-372
    keeping linked files together, EX 377
    using Dynamic Data Exchange (DDE), EX 360, EX 368
Links command, Edit menu, EX 443
List Box button, EX 455
lists. *See* data lists
loan payments, EX 137-140
Lock Cell button, EX 454
locked cells, EX 77-80

Index   EX 491

logical functions, EX 131, EX 141-145
logical test argument, IF function, EX 141-142
long integer variable type, Visual Basic, EX 412
lookup functions, EX 131, EX 283. *See also* VLOOKUP function
lookup table, EX 283, EX 285
lookup value, EX 283, EX 285
Lotus 1-2-3 command, Help menu, EX 449

M

macro(s). *See also* modules; Visual Basic
   add-in, EX 262. *See also* Microsoft Query
   adding command to Tools Menu for running, EX 419-421
   comments, EX 395
   compared with procedures and modules, EX 390-391
   recording, EX 391-394
   running, EX 400-401
   spaces not allowed in names, EX 392
   types of macro sheets, EX 390-391
   viewing, EX 393
Macro command, EX 118-119
   Insert menu, EX 444, EX 445
   Tools menu, EX 447, EX 448
Macro menu buttons, EX 453
Macro Options dialog box, EX 420
main procedure, EX 395
Make Add-In command, Tools menu, EX 448

Make Excel 5 Comprehensive Student Disks icon, EX 6
Manual calculation, EX 325
Margins button, EX 111
math functions, EX 131
mathematical operators, EX 31
MAX function, EX 132-133, EX 462
mean, EX 134-136
memory, random access (RAM), EX 12
menu(s)
   command reference, EX 442-449
   Format, EX 49, EX 89
   Help, EX 35
   Shortcut, EX 89
menu bar, EX 10
Menu Editor button, EX 453
Menu Editor command, Tools menu, EX 448
methods, Visual Basic
   Copy, EX 418-419
   example, EX 399
   InputBox, EX 413-414
   reference list, EX 474-480
   syntax, EX 399
   types, EX 398
   Value, EX 417
Microsoft Access, EX 353-354
Microsoft Access button, EX 454
Microsoft Excel 4.0 macro sheets, EX 390
Microsoft Excel 5.0 for Windows
   description, EX 9
   exiting, EX 36
   integrating with other Windows applications, EX 337-377
   launching, EX 7-8
Microsoft Excel Help window, EX 35
Microsoft Excel Student Disks, EX 4-6

Microsoft Excel window, EX 8, EX 9-11
Microsoft FoxPro button, EX 454
Microsoft Mail button, EX 454
Microsoft Office group icon, EX 7
Microsoft Paintbrush
   adding pictures to column charts, EX 184-186
   editing existing drawing, EX 342-344
   Excel as OLE client with Paintbrush as OLE server, EX 372-375
Microsoft PowerPoint button, EX 454
Microsoft Project button, EX 454
Microsoft Query
   accessing data in external databases, EX 263-266
   activating MS Query add-in, EX 262-263
   Criteria Pane, EX 358-359
   launching, EX 350
   linking tables for combined data, EX 361-362
   querying more than one table, EX 361-366
   querying only one table, EX 356-358
   selecting data source, EX 353-355
   toolbar, EX 352-353
Microsoft Query application window, EX 264
Microsoft Query Cue Cards, EX 350-352
Microsoft Schedule+ button, EX 454
Microsoft Windows, exiting, EX 36
Microsoft Word button, EX 454

Microsoft Write
    embedding graphics from
        Paintbrush, EX 342-344
    launching, EX 340-341
    linking report to Excel data,
        EX 369-372
MIN function, EX 134, EX 462
Minus Sign button, EX 451
mistakes. *See* error correction
modules, EX 117-121
    compared with macros and
        procedures, EX 390-391
    copying, EX 119
    editing, EX 390
    opening, EX 117-118
    running, EX 118-119
    tips for using, EX 121
mouse, selecting cell
    references, EX 59-60
Move or Copy Sheet command,
    Edit menu, EX 443
moving. *See also* positioning
    worksheets, EX 291-292
MS Query. *See* Microsoft Query
Multiplan command, Help
    menu, EX 449
multiple worksheets,
    EX 273-308
    checking for errors,
        EX 298-299
    creating consolidation
        worksheet, EX 303-304
    documenting, EX 275-276,
        EX 287-288
    entering formulas,
        EX 304-306
    grouping and ungrouping,
        EX 306-308
    referencing cells and ranges
        in other worksheets,
        EX 282-283
    using LOOKUP functions,
        EX 283-287

multiplication operator (*),
    EX 31, EX 55
Multiplication Sign button,
    EX 451

N

Name - Apply command, Insert
    menu, EX 444
Name - Create command, Insert
    menu, EX 444
Name - Define command,
    Insert menu, EX 294, EX 444
Name - Paste command, Insert
    menu, EX 444
[Name of Chart] command,
    Format menu, EX 446
names
    book-level, EX 294
    defining cell and range
        names, EX 293-295
    moving to named cells,
        EX 295-296
    rules for referencing cells
        and ranges in other
        worksheets, EX 282-283
    sheet-level, EX 294
naming. *See also* renaming
    fields, EX 233, EX 234
    rules for defining names,
        EX 294
    worksheets, EX 52. *See also*
        filenames
negative numbers
    currency formats, EX 94,
        EX 283
    payment amounts, EX 138
nesting functions, EX 300
New button, EX 245-246
New command, File menu,
    EX 442

New Data command, Insert
    menu, EX 445
New Window command,
    Window menu, EX 449
New Workbook button, EX 450
non-adjacent ranges, selecting,
    EX 165-167
Not Binding constraints, EX 226
not equal to operator (<>),
    EX 141
not equal to sign (<>), EX 55
notation, currency formats,
    EX 94-95
Note command, Insert menu,
    EX 444
nper argument, PMT function,
    EX 137
number(s). *See* negative
    numbers; positive numbers;
    value(s)
number formats, EX 96-97
number sign (#), replacement,
    EX 70-72
NumberFormat property, Visual
    Basic, EX 418

O

Object Browser button, EX 453
Object Browser command,
    View menu, EX 444
Object command
    Edit menu, EX 443
    Format menu, EX 446
    Insert menu, EX 444
Object Linking and Embedding
    (OLE), EX 369-377
    embedding data, EX 339-340
    keeping linked files together,
        EX 377

Index **EX 493**

linking Excel worksheet to Write report, EX 369-372
using Excel as OLE client and Paintbrush as OLE server, EX 372-375
objects, EX 105-109. *See also* chart(s); graphical objects
objects, Visual Basic, EX 396-398
reference list, EX 467-468
observations, EX 385
ODBC Data Sources dialog box, EX 264
on-line Help, EX 34-35
one-input data table, EX 317-321
Open button, EX 450
Open command, File menu, EX 442
opening
modules, EX 117-118
workbooks, EX 12-14
operations, order, EX 55-56
operators
comparison, EX 141
formulas, EX 54, EX 55
mathematical, EX 31
Option button, EX 455
Options command, Tools menu, EX 447
order of operations, EX 55-56
out of control, production process, EX 386
Outline Border button, EX 451
output, planning worksheets, EX 45
output area, two-input data table, EX 321-322
output values
one-input data table, EX 318, EX 320
two-input data table, EX 324

P

p control chart, EX 387
page(s), printing specific pages, EX 28-29
Page Break command, Insert menu, EX 444
Page Number tool, EX 112
Page Setup command, EX 111, EX 194-195, EX 442
Paintbrush. *See* Microsoft Paintbrush
parameters, Solver, EX 216
parentheses ( )
order of operations, EX 55
surrounding negative currency values, EX 283
TODAY function, EX 145
passwords, EX 78
Paste button, EX 450
Paste command, Edit menu, EX 443
Paste Formats button, EX 450
Paste Names button, EX 451, EX 453
Paste Special command, Edit menu, EX 443
Paste Values button, EX 450
pasting data, EX 338-339
Pattern button, EX 453
patterns
charts, EX 171-173
worksheets, EX 101-103
payments, EX 137-140
Percent Sign button, EX 451
Percent Style button, EX 90, EX 451
percentage formats, EX 97-98
percentage operator (%), EX 55
Picture command, Insert menu, EX 444
pictures. *See* graphical objects

Pie Chart AutoFormat button, EX 453
pie charts, EX 161. *See also* 3-D pie charts
PivotTable command, Data menu, EX 448
PivotTable Field button, EX 454
PivotTable Field command, Data menu, EX 448
PivotTable Wizard button, EX 454
PivotTables, EX 253-261
adding row and column labels, EX 255-256
adding titles, EX 267
completing, EX 258-261
creating from external databases, EX 262-269, EX 362, EX 365-366
formatting, EX 267-268
generating, EX 253-255
grouping data, EX 366-368
linking to Write report, EX 371-372
MS Query add-in, EX 262-269
Query and Pivot toolbar, EX 366
selecting calculation methods, EX 256-257
selecting data fields, EX 256
Placement command, Format menu, EX 446
planning
format, EX 87
worksheets, EX 43-46, EX 127-129, EX 201-202
Plus Sign button, EX 451
PMT function, EX 137-140, EX 463
pointer, EX 11, EX 34
Polygon button, EX 452
portrait orientation, EX 111

positioning
    arrows, EX 109
    charts, EX 27, EX 169-170
    toolbars, EX 104
    wedges, EX 171
positive numbers
    currency formats, EX 94
    payment amounts, EX 138, EX 139
previewing
    charts, EX 194
    worksheets, EX 110-111
primary key, relational databases, EX 347
Print button, EX 110, EX 450
Print command, EX 23-25, EX 28-29, EX 442
Print Preview command, File menu, EX 442
Print Report command, File menu, EX 442
printing, EX 110-115
    answer report, EX 226
    centering printout, EX 113-114
    charts, EX 23-25, EX 28-29, EX 194-195
    formulas, using modules, EX 117-121
    headers and footers, EX 111-113
    landscape orientation, EX 111
    portrait orientation, EX 111
    previewing charts, EX 194
    previewing worksheets, EX 110-111
    recording macro for printing worksheet, EX 391-394
    removing cell gridlines and row/column headings, EX 113-114
    sales analysis report, EX 375-376

specific pages, EX 28-29
    worksheets, EX 23-25, EX 28-29, EX 194-195
problem solving. See Scenario Manager; Solver; what-if analysis
Procedure Definition command, View menu, EX 444
procedures, Visual Basic
    automating worksheet updates, EX 409-419
    compared with macros and modules, EX 390-391
    writing, EX 411-419
production process. See also quality control
    definition, EX 384
    in control, EX 386
    out of control, EX 387
prompting for user input, EX 413-415
properties, Visual Basic
    definition, EX 396
    NumberFormat, EX 418
    reference list, EX 469-474
    returning values, EX 397-398
    setting, EX 397
    types, EX 397
Protect Document command, EX 78
protecting cells, EX 77-80
Protection command, Tools menu, EX 447, EX 448
pv function, PMT function, EX 137

Q

quality control. See also control charts
    in control, EX 385-386
    out of control, EX 386

production process, EX 384-386
    reasonable variations, EX 385
    sample range (R), EX 386
    variations, EX 384
queries, EX 241-243, EX 347
Query and Pivot toolbar, EX 366
Query Now button, MS Query, EX 353
querying databases. See Microsoft Query
question mark (?), wildcard, EX 243
Quick Preview command, Help menu, EX 449
quotation marks
    double (""), IF function, EX 142
    single (') for referencing worksheets, EX 282

R

R control chart, EX 387
Radar Chart AutoFormat button, EX 453
radar charts, EX 161
random access memory (RAM), EX 12
range (R), sample, EX 386
ranges, EX 26
    average of numbers, EX 134-136
    copying formats with Format Painter button, EX 96
    defining cell or range names, EX 293-295
    largest number, EX 132-133
    moving to named range, EX 295-296
    non-adjacent, selecting, EX 165-167

referencing in other worksheets, EX 282-283
selecting, EX 26
sheet range, EX 282, EX 306
smallest number, EX 134
rate argument, PMT function, EX 137
raw scores, EX 15, EX 16
reasonable variations, quality control, EX 385
recalculation
    automatic, EX 33-34. *See also* Solver; what-if analysis
    Automatic Except Tables, EX 325
    controlling in data tables, EX 325-326
    Manual, EX 325
Record Macro - Record New Macro command, Tools menu, EX 447
Record Macro - Use Relative References command, Tools menu, EX 447
Record Macro button, EX 448, EX 453
Record New Macro dialog box, EX 392
records. *See also* data lists; row(s)
    adding, EX 245-246
    definition, EX 233
    deleting, EX 244-245
    displaying, EX 265-266
    examples, EX 234
    relational databases, EX 347
    searching for. *See* searching data lists
    single, displaying, EX 239
Rectangle button, EX 452
Redo command, Edit menu, EX 443

#REF! error value, EX 284
reference functions, EX 131
references. *See* cell references
References command, Tools menu, EX 448
referencing cells in other worksheets, EX 282-283
reformatting, EX 70-71
Refresh Data button, PivotTable, EX 366, EX 454
Refresh Data command, Data menu, EX 448
relational databases. *See* database(s)
relative references, EX 57-58
Remove All Arrows button, EX 455
Remove Dependent Arrows button, EX 455
Remove Precedent Arrows button, EX 455
removing. *See also* clearing; deleting
    split window, EX 20-21
Rename Sheet dialog box, EX 52
renaming
    blank worksheets, EX 163
    worksheets, EX 52
Repeat button, EX 450
Repeat command, Edit menu, EX 443
Replace command, Edit menu, EX 443
reports, Solver, EX 224-228
Reset command, Run menu, EX 445
Reshape button, EX 452
resizing. *See* sizing
result cells, Scenario Manager, EX 326
result set
    Microsoft Query, EX 355
    updating, EX 360

Resume Macro button, EX 453
Return Data button, MS Query, EX 353
returning property values, EX 397-398
revising. *See* changing; editing; updating
Right Border button, EX 451
Right Parenthesis button, EX 451
Rotate Text Down button, EX 452
Rotate Text Up button, EX 452
rotating 3-D column charts, EX 192-193
ROUND function, EX 300-303, EX 464
rounding errors, apparent, EX 299-303
Routing Slip button, EX 450
row(s). *See also* records
    copying, EX 148-150
    in data lists, sorting, EX 236
    inserting, EX 63-65
Row command, Format menu, EX 446
row headings, EX 10, EX 113-114
row labels, PivotTables, EX 255-256
Rows command, Insert menu, EX 444
Run Dialog button, EX 455
Run Macro button, EX 401, EX 453
Run menu commands, EX 445
running
    macros, EX 400-401
    modules, EX 118-119

S

sample range (R), quality control, EX 386
Save As command, EX 21, EX 22-23, EX 53-54, EX 442
Save button, EX 450
Save command, EX 21, EX 22, EX 442
Save Workspace command, File menu, EX 442
saving
    workbooks, EX 21-23, EX 53-54
    worksheets as templates, EX 80-81
Scenario button, EX 454
Scenario Manager, EX 326-329
    creating scenarios, EX 327-328
    setting up summary values area, EX 326-327
    viewing results, EX 329
scenario summary report
    creating, EX 330-331
    summary cell requirements, EX 326, EX 330
Scenarios command, Tools menu, EX 447
scores
    raw, EX 15, EX 16
    weighted, EX 15
scroll arrow buttons, EX 14
Scroll Bar button, EX 455
scroll bars, EX 10, EX 11, EX 14
scroll box, EX 14
scrolling
    freezing column labels in place, EX 276, EX 278
    manually, through data lists, EX 240-241
    worksheets, EX 14

Search for Help on command, EX 449
searching data lists
    criteria search, EX 241-243
    manually, EX 240
    wildcards, EX 243-244
Select All Sheets command, Shortcut menu, EX 449
Select Current Region button, EX 454
Select Visible Cells button, EX 454
Selected Object command, Format menu, EX 446
selecting
    calculation method for PivotTables, EX 256-257
    cell references, EX 59-60
    charts, EX 168
    currency formats, EX 95
    non-adjacent ranges, EX 165-167
    objects, EX 105
    patterns for data markers, EX 185
    ranges, EX 26
    wedges, EX 171
Selection button, EX 452
Send Mail button, EX 450
Send To Back button, EX 452
series
    data, in charts. *See* data series in charts
    filling worksheets automatically, EX 50-52
Set Print Area button, EX 450
setting Visual Basic properties, EX 397
Setup button, EX 110-111, EX 111
shadow, charts, EX 187-188
Shape button, EX 453
sharing data. *See* transferring and sharing data

Sheet command, Format menu, EX 446
sheet-level name, EX 294
sheet range, EX 282, EX 306
sheet tabs, EX 10, EX 11
    dragging, EX 291
sheets. *See* worksheets
Shortcut menu, EX 89
    command reference, EX 449
Show Detail button, EX 454
Show/Hide Criteria button, MS Query, EX 353
Show Info Window button, EX 455
Show Outline Symbols button, EX 454
Show Pages button, EX 454
Show Pages command, Shortcut menu, EX 449
single-precision floating point type, Visual Basic, EX 412, EX 413
single quotation marks (' ') in worksheet references, EX 282
Sized With Window command, View menu, EX 444
sizing
    charts, EX 169-170
    fonts, EX 91-92
    text boxes, EX 107
slack, constraints, EX 226
slash (/), mathematical operator, EX 31
Solver, EX 216-228
    activating, EX 221
    adding constraints, EX 220-221
    entering constraints, EX 218-219
    generating answer reports, EX 224-228
    generating solutions, EX 219-220

Index **EX 497**

integer constraints, EX 222-223
setting up target cells and changing cells, EX 217-218
Solver command, Tools menu, EX 447
Solver Parameters dialog box, EX 216, EX 218
Sort Ascending button, EX 454
Sort command, EX 235, EX 448
Sort Descending button, EX 454
sorting data, EX 235-239
    by one column, EX 236-237
    by two columns, EX 238-239
spaces
    not allowed in macro names, EX 392
    worksheet names, rules for referencing, EX 282
Spelling button, EX 76-77, EX 454
Spelling command, Tools menu, EX 447
Spinner button, EX 455
split bar, dragging, EX 20-21
Split command, Window menu, EX 20, EX 449
splitting worksheet windows, EX 19-20
spreadsheets, EX 9
Stacked Column Chart AutoFormat button, EX 453
stacking pictures, EX 186
Standard toolbar, EX 103
Start command, Run menu, EX 445
statements, Visual Basic, EX 400
    reference list, EX 468-469
statistical functions, EX 131
    AVERAGE, EX 134-136, EX 456
    MAX, EX 132-133, EX 462
    MIN, EX 134, EX 462

statistical process control (SPC)
    control charts, EX 386-390
    definition, EX 383
    quality control techniques, EX 384-386
status bar, EX 10, EX 11
Status Bar command, View menu, EX 443
Step Into button, EX 453
Step Into command, Run menu, EX 445
Step Macro button, EX 453
Step Over button, EX 453
Step Over command, Run menu, EX 445
Stop Macro button, EX 392
Stop Recording button, EX 453
stretching pictures, EX 186
Strikethrough button, EX 452
string variable type, Visual Basic, EX 412
Student Disks, EX 4-6
style box, EX 90
Style command, Format menu, EX 446
sub procedures, Visual Basic, EX 395
Sub statements, Visual Basic
    requirements, EX 395, EX 412
    structure, EX 395
Subtotals command, Data menu, EX 448
subtraction operator (-), EX 55
SUM function, EX 32-33, EX 58-59, EX 465
    AutoSum button, EX 68-69
    entering, EX 58
Summary button, EX 330
Summary Info command, File menu, EX 442
syntax
    Do...Loop statements, EX 416
    functions, EX 131

    If...Then...Else statement, EX 415
    user-defined functions, EX 402
    Visual Basic, EX 394

T

Tab Order button, EX 455
Table command
    Data menu, EX 448
    data tables, EX 317, EX 320, EX 324
Table pane, Microsoft Query, EX 355
tables. *See* data lists; data tables; database(s)
Tabname tool, EX 112
target cells, EX 216
    answer report, EX 225
    setting up, EX 217-218
Technical Support command, Help menu, EX 449
templates, EX 43, EX 80-81
test values, EX 61-63, EX 73-74
testing
    worksheet protection, EX 80
    worksheets, EX 61-63, EX 73-74
text, EX 31. *See also* labels; legends; title(s)
    adding and editing in charts, EX 178-179
    boldfacing, EX 90-91, EX 146, EX 180
    centering across columns, EX 93
    filling worksheets automatically, EX 50-52
    italicizing, EX 90, EX 91, EX 106-107
Text Box button, EX 452

Text Box tools, EX 105, EX 106
text boxes, EX 105–109
 sizing, EX 107
Text Formatting menu buttons, EX 452
text functions, EX 131
text notes, EX 75–76
Text to Columns command, Data menu, EX 448
3-D Area Chart AutoFormat button, EX 453
3-D area charts, EX 161
3-D Bar Chart AutoFormat button, EX 453
3-D bar charts, EX 161
3-D Column Chart AutoFormat button, EX 453
3-D column charts, EX 161, EX 188–193
 predefined formats, EX 189
 rotating, EX 192–193
3-D Line Chart AutoFormat button, EX 453
3-D Perspective Column Chart AutoFormat button, EX 453
3-D Pie Chart AutoFormat button, EX 453
3-D pie charts, EX 161, EX 164–173
 changing patterns, EX 171–173
 moving, EX 169–170
 pulling out wedges, EX 170–171
 resizing, EX 169–170
 selecting and activating, EX 168–169
 selecting non-adjacent ranges, EX 165–167
3-D references, EX 282
3-D Surface Chart AutoFormat button, EX 453
3-D surface charts, EX 161

3-D View command, Format menu, EX 446
tick mark label, EX 162
time(s). *See* value(s)
time functions, EX 131
Time tool, EX 112
Tip Help button, EX 455
TipWizard Box button, EX 455
TipWizard button, EX 455
TipWizard buttons, EX 455
title(s)
 adding to PivotTables, EX 267
 answer report, EX 225
 category (x) axis, EX 162
 centering, EX 93
 charts, EX 162, EX 179, EX 187–188
 columns, EX 67, EX 93
 value (y) axis, EX 162
 worksheet, EX 47, EX 67, EX 93
title bar, EX 10
Titles command, Insert menu, EX 445
TODAY function, EX 145–147, EX 465
Toggle Breakpoint button, EX 453
Toggle Breakpoints command, Run menu, EX 445
Toggle File Status button, EX 450
Toggle Grid button, EX 455
toolbars, EX 10
 activating, EX 103–104
 deleting, EX 103
 formatting, EX 89–90, EX 93
 positioning, EX 104
 removing, EX 109
 Visual Basic, EX 394
Toolbars command, View menu, EX 443

Tools menu
 adding user-defined command, EX 419–421
 command reference, EX 447–448
Top Border button, EX 451
Total Pages tool, EX 112
Trace Dependents button, EX 455
Trace Error button, EX 455
Trace Precedents button, EX 455
transferring and sharing data
 Dynamic Data Exchange (DDE), EX 360
 embedding data, EX 339–340
 keeping linked files together, EX 377
 linking data, EX 340–344
 Object Linking and Embedding (OLE), EX 369–377
 pasting data, EX 338–339
Trendline command, Insert menu, EX 445
trial and error strategy, EX 207–208, EX 215–216
trig functions, EX 131
TROUBLE? paragraphs, EX 4
tutorials, using effectively, EX 4
two-input data table, EX 321–325
2-D column charts, EX 189–190

U

unattached text, charts, EX 179
Underline button, EX 90, EX 452
Undo button, EX 18, EX 450
Undo command, EX 18, EX 235, EX 288, EX 443
Ungroup button, PivotTable, EX 366, EX 454

Ungroup Objects button, EX 452
ungrouping worksheets, EX 306-308
Unhide command, Window menu, EX 449
unlocking cells, EX 78-79
Update File button, EX 450
updating. *See also* changing; editing
   automating worksheet updates, EX 409-419
   data lists, EX 244-247
   data series in charts, EX 177-178
   formulas, EX 153-154
   result set, EX 360
user-defined functions
   calculating center line for control chart, EX 389-390, EX 401-402
   calculating control limits for control chart, EX 389-390, EX 405-409
   comments, EX 402-403
   copying and editing, EX 404
   creating in Visual Basic, EX 402-404
   structure, EX 402
user input, prompting for, EX 413-415
Utility menu buttons, EX 454

V

value(s), EX 30. *See also* negative numbers; positive numbers
   changing, EX 33-34
   currency formats, EX 94-95
   displaying, EX 70-72
   exceeding width of cell, EX 70-72

filling worksheets automatically, EX 50-52
formulas, EX 31, EX 54, EX 55
integer constraint, EX 222-223
largest, finding, EX 132-133
smallest, finding, EX 134
test, EX 61-63, EX 73-74
Visual Basic procedure for entering, EX 417
value (y) axis, EX 162
#VALUE! error value, EX 284
value if false argument, IF function, EX 142
value if true argument, IF function, EX 142
Value method, Visual Basic, EX 417
variables, Visual Basic
   Boolean, EX 412
   declaring, EX 413
   types, EX 412
   variant, EX 412-413
variations, quality control, EX 384
Vertical Gridlines button, EX 454
vertical lines, EX 99
vertical scroll bar, EX 10, EX 11, EX 14
View Manager command, EX 444
View menu commands, EX 443-444
viewing. *See* displaying
Visual Basic, EX 394-400
   comments, EX 394-395
   control structures, EX 415-417
   Do Until...Loop statement, EX 416
   Do While...Loop statement, EX 416
   Do...Loop statement, EX 416
   If...Then...Else statement, EX 415

   keywords, EX 394
   methods, EX 398-399
   objects, EX 396-398
   prompting for user input, EX 413-415
   properties, EX 396-398
   statements, EX 400
   sub procedures, EX 395
   toolbar, EX 394
   user-defined functions, EX 402-404
   variable types, EX 412-413
   writing procedures, EX 411-419
Visual Basic reference
   methods, EX 474-480
   objects, EX 467-468
   properties, EX 469-474
   statements, EX 468-469
VLOOKUP function, EX 283-286, EX 466
Volume/High-Low-Close Chart AutoFormat button, EX 453

W

wedges, pulling out of pie charts, EX 170-171
weighted scores, EX 15
what-if analysis, EX 152-154, EX 206-228. *See also* data tables; Scenario Manager; Solver
   complex problems, EX 212-216
   Goal Seek command, EX 208-212
   trial and error method, EX 207-208, EX 215-216
   using Scenario Manager, EX 326-329

whole numbers, integer
   constraint, EX 222-223
wildcards, searching data lists,
   EX 243-244
window(s)
   Book1, EX 8
   CTI WinApps group, EX 6
   Excel, EX 9-11
   Microsoft Excel, EX 8
   Microsoft Excel Help, EX 35
   worksheet. *See* worksheet
      window
Window menu commands,
   EX 449
window panes, EX 19-20
workbooks, EX 9
   documenting, EX 274-276
   opening, EX 12-14
   organizing effectively,
      EX 274-282
   saving, EX 21-23, EX 53-54
   types of sheets, EX 390-391
Worksheet command, Insert
   menu, EX 444, EX 445
worksheet window, EX 10-11
   attaching toolbars, EX 104
   removing splits, EX 20-21
   splitting, EX 19-20
worksheets, EX 9. *See also*
   cell(s); multiple worksheets;
   ranges
   active, EX 10
   adding comments,
      EX 105-109
   automating worksheet
      updates, EX 409-419
   blank, renaming, EX 163
   building, EX 47-50
   changing column width,
      EX 48-50
   checking for errors,
      EX 298-299
   closing, EX 36
   copying, EX 292-293

decision-support, EX 15-17
deleting, EX 288-289
documenting, EX 43,
   EX 74-76, EX 275-276,
   EX 287-288
entering labels, EX 47-48,
   EX 51-52
filling automatically,
   EX 50-52
formatting. *See* formatting
formulas, EX 31-32
functions, EX 32-33
inserting, EX 288-290
modifying documentation
   worksheet, EX 287-288
moving, EX 291-292
planning, EX 43-46,
   EX 127-129, EX 201-202
print preview, EX 110-111
printing, EX 23-25,
   EX 194-195
printing formulas using
   modules, EX 117-121
printing specific pages,
   EX 28-29
protecting cells, EX 77-80
referencing cells and ranges
   in other worksheets,
   EX 282-283
renaming, EX 52
saving as templates, EX 80-81
scrolling, EX 14
selecting with Visual Basic
   procedure, EX 413
testing, EX 61-63, EX 73
text, EX 31
title, EX 47
titles, EX 93
types of workbook sheets,
   EX 390-391
values, EX 30
zones, EX 98-99
Write. *See* Microsoft Write

X

x (category) axis, EX 162
x (category) axis title, EX 162
X-Bar average, statistical process
   control (SPC), EX 385
X-Bar control chart, EX 387. *See
   also* control charts
   creating, EX 406-409
   formatting, EX 407-408
.XLS filename extension, EX 22,
   EX 53
.XLT filename extension, EX 80
XY (Scatter) Chart AutoFormat
   button, EX 453
XY charts, EX 161

Y

y (value) axis, EX 162
   title, EX 162
   X-Bar chart, formatting,
      EX 407

Z

zeros, AVERAGE function,
   EX 135
zones, EX 98-99
Zoom command, View menu,
   EX 444
Zoom Control button, EX 454
Zoom In button, EX 454
Zoom Out button, EX 454

TASK REFERENCE
MICROSOFT EXCEL 5.0 FOR WINDOWS

*Italicized page numbers indicate the first discussion of each task. An * in the Mouse or Keyboard column indicates that instructions continue from the * in the Menu column.*

TASK	MOUSE	MENU	KEYBOARD
AutoFill a range of cells EX 50	Drag fill handle to highlight the cells to be filled.		
AutoFilter, activating EX 247		Click any cell in the list you want to filter. Click Data, click Filter, then click AutoFilter.	Click any cell in the list you want to filter. Press [Alt][D], press [F], then press [F].
AutoFormat a range of cells EX 65	See Reference Window "Using AutoFormat."		
AutoSum button, activate EX 68	Click the cell where you want the sum to appear. Click [Σ]. Make sure the range address in the formula is the same as the range you want to sum.		Click the cell where you want the sum to appear. Press [Alt][=]. Make sure the range address in the formula is the same as the range you want to sum.
Bold cell contents EX 90	Highlight the cell or range you want to format. Click [B].	Highlight the cell or range you want to format. Click Format, click Cells..., click the Font tab, then click Bold in the Font Style list box.	Highlight the cell or range you want to format. Press [Ctrl][B].
Border, add EX 98	See Reference Window "Adding a Border."		
Border, remove EX 98	See Reference Window "Removing a Border."		
Cancel action			Press [Esc].
Cell references, edit EX 148	See Reference Window "Editing Cell Reference Types."		
Cell references, in other worksheets EX 282	See Reference Window "Referencing Cells and Ranges in Other Worksheets."		
Center cell contents EX 92	Highlight the cell or range you want to format. Click [■].	Highlight the cell or range you want to format. Click Format, click Cells.... *Click the Alignment tab, then click the Center option button in the Horizontal box.	Highlight the cell or range you want to format. Press [Alt][O], then press [E].*
Center text across columns EX 93	Highlight a range—include the text you want to center and at least one cell in each of the columns across which you want to center the text. Click [■].	Highlight a range—include the text you want to center and at least one cell in each of the columns across which you want to center the text. Click Format, then click Cells.... *Click the Alignment tab, then click the Center across selection option button in the Horizontal box.	Highlight a range—include the text you want to center and at least one cell in each of the columns across which you want to center the text. Press [Alt][O], then press [E].*

TASK REFERENCE
MICROSOFT EXCEL 5.0 FOR WINDOWS

Italicized page numbers indicate the first discussion of each task. An * in the Mouse or Keyboard column indicates that instructions continue from the * in the Menu column.

TASK	MOUSE	MENU	KEYBOARD
Center the printout EX 113		Click File, click Page Setup...., click the Margins tab, then click Horizontally and/or Vertically.	Press [Alt][F], press [U], press [M], then press [Alt][Z] and/or [Alt][V].
Chart, activate EX 168	Double-click anywhere within the chart border.		
Chart, add or remove gridlines EX 180	Select the chart. Click 📊 on the Chart toolbar.		
Chart, adjust size EX 169	Select the chart and drag handles.		
Chart, applying a pattern to a data marker EX 171	See Reference Window "Selecting a Pattern for a Data Marker."		
Chart border EX 193	See "Applying a Border Around a Chart" in Tutorial 5.		
Chart, creating picture chart EX 184	See Reference Window "Creating a Picture Chart."		
Chart, delete		Select the chart. Click Edit, then click Cut.	Select the chart. Press [Del].
Chart, move EX 169	Select the chart and drag it to a new location.		
Chart, revising using the ChartWizard EX 177	See Reference Window "Revising the Chart Data Series Using the ChartWizard."		
Chart, rotating a 3-D chart EX 192	Activate a 3-D chart. Click the intersection of any two axes to select the corners of the chart. Drag any corner to adjust the elevation and rotation of the chart.	Activate a 3-D chart. Click Format, then click 3-D View.... *Type the values you want in the elevation and rotation boxes.	Activate a 3-D chart. Press [Alt][O], then press [V].*
Chart, select EX 168	Click anywhere within the chart border.		
Chart title, add EX 176		Activate the chart. Click Insert, click Titles..., click the chart title box to display an ×, then click the OK button. *Highlight the word "Title" in the chart title, press [Del], then type the desired title.	Activate the chart. Press [Alt][I], press [T], press [T], then press [Enter].*
ChartWizard, activate EX 25	See Reference Window "Creating a Chart with ChartWizard."		

TASK REFERENCE
MICROSOFT EXCEL 5.0 FOR WINDOWS

*Italicized page numbers indicate the first discussion of each task. An * in the Mouse or Keyboard column indicates that instructions continue from the * in the Menu column.*

TASK	MOUSE	MENU	KEYBOARD
Clear cell contents *EX 69*	See Reference Window "Clearing Cells."		
Close the worksheet *EX 36*	Double-click the worksheet Control menu box ▭.	Click File, then click Close.	Press [Alt][F], then press [C].
Colors, applying to a range of cells *EX 101*	See Reference Window "Applying Patterns and Color."		
Column width, adjust *EX 48*	See Reference Window "Changing Column Width."		
Copying a sheet *EX 292*	Press and hold down [Ctrl] while dragging the sheet tab to the desired location.	Click Edit, then click Move or Copy Sheet…. *Click the Create a Copy checkbox, select the new location in the Before Sheet list, then click the OK button.	Press [Alt][E], then press [M].*
Copy cell contents using the Copy command	Highlight the cell or range you want to copy, then click 📋.	Highlight the cell or range you want to copy, click Edit, then click Copy.	Highlight the cell or range you want to copy, press [Alt][E], then press [C].
Copy cell contents using the fill handle *EX 56*	See Reference Window "Copying Cell Contents with the Fill Handle."		
Data Form, adding a record *EX 245*	See Reference Window "Adding a Record Using the Data Form."		
Data Form, deleting a record *EX 244*	See Reference Window "Deleting a Record Using the Data Form."		
Data Form, searching for a record *EX 241*	See Reference Window "Searching for a Record Using the Data Form."		
Data List, sorting rows *EX 235*	See Reference Window "Sorting Rows in a Data List."		
Data list, retrieving external data		Select the sheet where you want the new data to appear. Click Data, then click Get External Data to activate MS Query. *Select the desired data source in the Select Data Source dialog box. (If necessary, click Other… to display a list of possible data sources.) Select the desired data file in the Add Tables dialog box. Double-click the asterisk in the list of field names to display all the records. Click File, then click Return Data to Microsoft Excel.	Select the sheet where you want the new data to appear. Press [Alt][D], then press [X] to activate MS Query.*

TASK REFERENCE
MICROSOFT EXCEL 5.0 FOR WINDOWS

Italicized page numbers indicate the first discussion of each task. An * in the Mouse or Keyboard column indicates that instructions continue from the * in the Menu column.

TASK	MOUSE	MENU	KEYBOARD
Data Table, creating a one-input *EX 317*		Highlight the table range, click Data, then click Table…. *Enter the column input cell, then click the OK button.	Highlight the table range, press [Alt] [D], then press [T].*
Data Table, creating a two-input *EX 321*		Highlight the table range, click Data, then click Table…. *Enter the row input cell, enter the column input cell, then click the OK button.	Highlight the table range, press [Alt] [D], then press [T].*
Delete a row or column		Click the heading(s) of the row(s) or column(s) you want to delete, click Edit, then click Delete….	Click the heading(s) of the row(s) or column(s) you want to delete, press [Alt] [E], then press [D].
Delete a worksheet *EX 288*	See Reference Window "Deleting a Sheet."		
Display formulas *EX 116*		Click Tools, then click Options…. *Click View tab, then click the Formulas box in the Windows Options box to display an ×.	Press [Alt] [T], then press [O].*
Embedded Objects, editing *EX 344*	See Reference Window "Editing an Embedded Object Using OLE."		
Enter a formula *EX 54*	See Reference Window "Entering a Formula."		
Exit Excel *EX 36*	Double-click the Excel Control menu box ▭.	Click File, then click Exit.	Press [Alt] [F], then press [X].
Filtering a list *EX 247*	See Reference Window "Filtering a List with AutoFilter."		
Font, select *EX 90*	Highlight the cell or range you want to format. Click the Font down arrow button in the toolbar, then click the desired font.	Highlight the cell or range you want to format. Click Format, then click Cells…. *Click the Font tab, then click the desired font in the Font box.	Highlight the cell or range you want to format. Press [Alt] [O], then press [E].*
Font, size *EX 90*	Highlight the cell or range you want to format. Click the Font Size down arrow button in the toolbar, then click the desired font size.	Highlight the cell or range you want to format. Click Format, then click Cells…. *Click the Font tab then click the desired font size in the Size box.	Highlight the cell or range you want to format. Press [Alt] [O], then press [O].*

TASK REFERENCE
MICROSOFT EXCEL 5.0 FOR WINDOWS

Italicized page numbers indicate the first discussion of each task. An * in the Mouse or Keyboard column indicates that instructions continue from the * in the Menu column.

TASK	MOUSE	MENU	KEYBOARD
Footer, edit *EX 111*	Click the Setup button in the Print Preview window.*	Click File, then click Page Setup.... *Click the Header/Footer tab in the Page Setup dialog box. Click the Footer down arrow button to choose a preset footer, or click the Custom Footer button and edit the existing footer in the Footer dialog box.	Press [Alt][F], then press [U].*
Format currency *EX 94*	Select the cell or range of cells you want to format. Click [$].	Select the cell or range of cells you want to format. Click Format, then click Cells.... *Click the Number tab, click Currency in the Category box, then click the desired format code.	Select the cell or range of cells you want to format. Press [Alt][O], then press [E].*
Format date *EX 145*		Select the cell or range of cells you want to format. Click Format, then click Cells.... *Click the Number tab, click Date in the Category box, then click the desired format code.	Select the cell or range of cells you want to format. Press [Alt][O], then press [E].*
Format Painter button, activate *EX 96*	Select the cell or range of cells with the format you want to copy. Click [icon], then select the cell or range of cells you want to format.		
Format percentage *EX 97*	Select the cell or range of cells you want to format. Click [%].	Select the cell or range of cells you want to format. Click Format, then click Cells.... *Click the Number tab, click Percentage in the Category box, then click the desired format code.	Select the cell or range of cells you want to format. Press [Alt][O], then press [E].*
Function, AVERAGE *EX 134*	See Reference Window "Using AVERAGE to Calculate the Average of the Numbers in a Range of Cells."		
Function, enter *EX 130*	See Reference Window "Typing Functions Directly in a Cell."		
Function, IF *EX 141*	See Reference Window "Using the IF Function to Specify the Conditions."		
Function, MAX *EX 132*	See Reference Window "Using MAX to Display the Largest Number in a Range of Cells."		
Function, MIN *EX 134*	See Reference Window "Using MIN to Display the Smallest Number in a Range of Cells."		
Function, PMT *EX 137*	See Reference Window "Using PMT to Calculate a Monthly Payment."		

TASK REFERENCE
MICROSOFT EXCEL 5.0 FOR WINDOWS

Italicized page numbers indicate the first discussion of each task. An * in the Mouse or Keyboard column indicates that instructions continue from the * in the Menu column.

TASK	MOUSE	MENU	KEYBOARD
Function, ROUND EX 300	See Reference Window "Using ROUND to Round the Stored Results of a Formula to the Desired Number of Decimals."		
Function, SUM EX 58	See Reference Window "Entering the SUM Function."		
Function, VLOOKUP EX 283	See Reference Window "Using VLOOKUP to Display Values Found in a Lookup Table."		
Function Wizard, activate EX 132	See Reference Window "Using the Function Wizard."		
Goal Seek, activate EX 208	See Reference Window "Using Goal Seek."		
Go To command EX 295	See Reference Window "Using the Go To Command."		
Gridlines, add or remove from printout EX 113	Click the Setup button in the Print Preview window.*	Click File, then click Page Setup. *Click the Sheet tab in the Page Setup dialog box. In the Print box, insert an × in the Gridlines box to add gridlines, delete the × to remove gridlines.	Press [Alt][F], then press [U].*
Grouping worksheets EX 306	See Reference Window "Grouping and Ungrouping Worksheets."		
Header, edit EX 111	Click the Setup button in the Print Preview window.*	Click File, then click Page Setup. *Click the Header/Footer tab in the Page Setup dialog box. Click the Header down arrow button to select a preset header, or click the Custom Header button to edit the existing header in the Header dialog box.	Press [Alt][F], then press [U].*
Help button, activate EX 34	See Reference Window "Using the Help Button."		
Highlight a range EX 26	Position pointer on the first cell of the range. Press and hold the mouse button and drag the mouse through the cells you want, then release the mouse button.		Select the first cell of the range. Press and hold down [Shift] and use the arrow keys to select the cells you want, then release [Shift].
Insert a chart sheet EX 290	See Reference Window "Inserting a Chart Sheet."		
Insert a row or column EX 63	See Reference Window "Inserting a Row or Column."		
Insert a worksheet EX 288	See Reference Window "Inserting a Worksheet."		
Italicize cell contents EX 90	Highlight the cell or range you want to format. Click [I].	Highlight the cell or range you want to format. Click Format, click Cells..., click the Font tab, then click Italic in the Font Style list box.	Highlight the cell or range you want to format. Press [Ctrl][I].

TASK REFERENCE
MICROSOFT EXCEL 5.0 FOR WINDOWS

Italicized page numbers indicate the first discussion of each task. An * in the Mouse or Keyboard column indicates that instructions continue from the * in the Menu column.

TASK	MOUSE	MENU	KEYBOARD
PivotTable, grouping data in EX 366	See Reference Window "Grouping Data in a PivotTable."		
Portrait (normal) printing EX 111	Click the Setup button in the Print Preview window.*	Click File, then click Page Setup. *Click the Page tab in the Page Setup dialog box, then click the Portrait option button in the Orientation box.	Press [Alt][F], then press [V].*
Print a worksheet EX 23	See Reference Window "Printing a Worksheet."		
Print Formulas module EX 117	See "Tips for Using the Print Formulas Module" in Tutorial 3.		
Print Preview EX 110	Click [icon].	Click File, then click Print Preview.	Press [Alt][F], then press [V].
Protecting cells EX 77	See Reference Window "Protecting Cells."		
Remove split worksheet window EX 20	Double-click any part of the split bar.	Click Window, then click Remove Split.	Press [Alt][W], then press [S].
Right-align cell contents EX 92	Highlight the cell or range you want to format. Click [icon].	Highlight the cell or range you want to format. Click Format, click Cells.... *Click the Alignment tab, then click the Right option button in the Horizontal box.	Highlight the cell or range you want to format. Press [Alt][O], then press [E].*
Save workbook as a template EX 80		Create a workbook, click File, then click Save As. *Type the name you want for the template, select the drive and directory in the File Name box. Click Template in the File Save As Type box.	Create a workbook, press [Alt][F], then press [A].*
Save workbook with a new filename EX 21	See Reference Window "Saving a Workbook with a New Filename."		
Save workbook with the same filename EX 21	Click [icon].	Click File, then click Save.	Press [Ctrl][S].
Scenarios, adding EX 327		Click Tools, click Scenarios..., click the Add... button, enter scenario name, changing cells, and comments, then click the OK button.	Press [Alt][T], press [C], press [Alt][A], enter scenario name, changing cells, and comments, then press [Enter].
Scenarios, viewing EX 329		Click Tools, click Scenarios..., click the scenario name, then click the Show button.	Press [Alt][T], press [C], select the scenario name using arrow keys, then press [Alt][S].

TASK REFERENCE
MICROSOFT EXCEL 5.0 FOR WINDOWS

*Italicized page numbers indicate the first discussion of each task. An * in the Mouse or Keyboard column indicates that instructions continue from the * in the Menu column.*

TASK	MOUSE	MENU	KEYBOARD
Scenario Summary, creating EX 330		Click Tools, click Scenarios..., click the Summary button, enter the result cells, then click the OK button.	Press [Alt][T], press [C], press [Alt][U], enter the result cells, then press [Enter].
Select entire column	Click column heading.		
Select entire row	Click row heading.		
Select entire worksheet	Click the Select All button.		
Select range EX 26	See Highlight a range.		
Sheet, activating	Click the sheet tab for the desired sheet.		
Sheet, move or copy		Click Edit, then click Move or Copy Sheet.... *Select the workbook you want to move or copy the sheet to in the To Book box. Indicate where you want the sheet to appear in the workbook in the Before box. Click Create a Copy if you want to Copy the sheet instead of removing it from its original location.	Press [Alt][E], then press [M].*
Sheet tab, rename EX 52	Double-click the sheet tab.*	Select the sheet, click Format, click Sheet, then click Rename. *Type the new sheet name in the Rename Sheet dialog box.	Select the sheet, press [Alt][O], press [H], then press [R].*
Shortcut menu, activate EX 89	Select the cells or objects to which you want to apply the command, click the right mouse button, then select the command you want.		Select the cells or objects to which you want to apply the command, press [Shift][F10], then select the command you want.
Solver, activate EX 216	See Reference Window "Using Solver."		
Spelling button, activate EX 76	See Reference Window "Using the Spelling Button."		
Split the worksheet window EX 19	Drag the horizontal or vertical split box to the desired position.	For vertical pages, select a column, click Window, then click Split. For horizontal pages, select a row, click Window, then click Split.	For vertical pages, select a column, press [Alt][W], then press [S]. For horizontal pages, select a row, press [Alt][W], then press [S].
Split window, move to	Click the window.		

TASK REFERENCE
MICROSOFT EXCEL 5.0 FOR WINDOWS

Italicized page numbers indicate the first discussion of each task. An * in the Mouse or Keyboard column indicates that instructions continue from the * in the Menu column.

TASK	MOUSE	MENU	KEYBOARD
Text box, add *EX 105*	See Reference Window "Adding a Text Box and Comment."		
Text note, add *EX 75*	See Reference Window "Adding a Text Note."		
Text note, read or edit	Double-click the cell containing the text note.		
Toolbar, add or remove *EX 103*	See Reference Window "Activating and Removing Toolbars."		
Underline cell contents *EX 90*	Highlight the cell or range you want to format. Click [U].	Highlight the cell or range you want to format. Click Format, click Cells..., then click the Font tab. Click the Underline down arrow button, then select the desired type of underline.	Highlight the cell or range you want to format. Press [Ctrl][U].
Undo the previous action *EX 18*	Click [↶].	Click Edit, then click Undo.	Press [Alt][E], then press [U].
Ungrouping worksheets *EX 306*	See Reference Window "Grouping and Ungrouping Worksheets."		
Unprotecting worksheets *EX 79*		Click Tools, click Protection, then click Unprotect Sheet.... *If you previously entered a password, enter the password in the Unprotect Sheet dialog box.	Press [Alt][T], then press [P].*
Updating an MS Query result set *EX 360*	See Reference Window "Updating a Result Set in Excel."		
Worksheet calculation, controlling *EX 325*		Click Tools, then click Options.... *Click the Calculation tab, select the calculation option, then click the OK button.	Press [Alt][T], then press [O].*